CONSUMER BEHAVIOR

CONSUMER BEHAVIOR THIRD EDITION

James F. Engel Director of Communications Program, Graduate School, Wheaton College, Illinois

Roger D. Blackwell Professor of Consumer Behavior, The Ohio State University

David T. Kollat Vice-President, The Limited Stores, Inc., Columbus, Ohio

THE DRYDEN PRESS
HINSDALE, ILLINOIS

EDITORS' FOREWORD

The Advisory Editors are especially pleased to introduce the Third Edition of CONSUMER BEHAVIOR by Professors Engel, Blackwell, and Kollat. Since 1968 this book has set the standard for texts in this area. And a high standard it is, with its insightful blend of theory, methodology, and empirical findings.

The Third Edition maintains this useful balance of materials, while updating all of its components. Particularly relevant to the marketing student and practitioner are the connections that the authors make between consumer behavior theory and managerial strategy. This is a book that will appeal both to those interested in consumer behavior as an intellectual discipline and those who wish to apply its principles to marketing decision making.

All in all, the authors' Third Edition is a solid contribution to the literature of marketing and the behavioral sciences. CONSUMER BEHAVIOR will continue to set the pace in this field for years to come.

Paul E. Green and
Phillip T. Kotler

Preface

One of the most remarkable developments of the last two decades is the dynamic emphasis on the consumer as the focal point of the economic system. Today's emphasis on consumerism is just one manifestation of the changes that have taken place. At one time, for example, the subject of consumer behavior received only incidental emphasis in marketing courses in schools of business. Today, however, it has come into its own as a distinct area for scholarly investigation, as is attested by a burgeoning increase in published literature.

In part the awakened interest in the consumer is the result of a dramatic shift in demand-supply relationships, a change that has, in effect, placed the consumer in the fortunate position of being free to choose from many options. Thus business firms now are compelled to design and sell products that conform to the consumer's desires. "Consumer orientation" by the business firm, in turn, requires a solid basis of fact. It is not surprising, then, that analysis of the consumer has assumed a new importance.

Consumer welfare also has become a topic of great political significance because of growing signs that the economic system does not always function to serve the consumer's interests to a desirable extent. Hence, new legislation and regulatory activity have been proposed and implemented, but all too frequently these steps have been taken without a full understanding of the implications from the consumers' point of view.

A parallel development is a widespread recognition that consumer education is both necessary and desirable. As Toffler points out in *Future Shock*, the range of choice alternatives is beyond the grasp of any individual, and the rate of environmental change can have real pathological implications.[1] Therefore, consumer education programs play an increasingly vital role, and these programs, in turn, must be based on a sophisticated understanding of consumer behavior from a variety of perspectives.

Finally, it is noteworthy that scholars from many fields are focusing attention on the consumer. It is recognized that this can be a useful testing ground for theories and methods of various types, and there is less current disdain in the social and behavioral sciences for research in the "real world." The authors look back with amusement at the changes in response of one social psychologist who, in the middle 1960s, was contemptuous of our work and that of our students as being tainted and not pure. Not long thereafter he approached one of us, undoubtedly using a disguise and the rear entrance, to inquire about consulting opportunities. Then, just a few years later, he came in through the front door, so to speak, and began to view consumer behavior as a legitimate discipline in its own right and a worthy subject for some of his own research.

The purposes of this book have remained essentially unchanged from those stated in both the 1968 and 1973 editions. It is written to meet the needs of practitioners from varying perspectives, as well as those who have a more theoretical interest in the subject. More specifically, its objectives are: (1) to explore and evaluate an extensive body of both published and unpublished research evidence; (2) to advance generalizations and propositions from this evidence whenever possible; (3) to assess the practical implications of the various processes and facets of consumer motivation and behavior; and (4) to pinpoint areas where research is lacking. Because of the backgrounds and interests of the authors, the perspective is primarily that of the field of marketing. This also is true of the great majority of published literature in the field, by the way, but those with differing perspectives will also find much of value here. Increasingly we have attempted to assume a broader perspective wherever possible.

The reader who is looking for mere description should turn elsewhere. While no particular background in the behavioral sciences is assumed, the authors share the philosophy that more harm than good is done by ignoring questions of methodology and theoretical substance. As a result, findings frequently are critically assessed in an attempt to determine the extent to which valid generalizations can be advanced.

The basic method of exposition is a conceptual model of consumer behavior that has been revised in some important aspects since the 1973

1 Alvin Toffler, *Future Shock* (New York: Random House, 1970).

edition. The present version bears only a scant family resemblence to its 1967 forefather, reflecting the dramatic growth in knowledge since that time. The revised model highlights the consumer decision process more sharply and represents, we feel, a step forward in specification of the linkages between variables. We have also been more cognizant of the need for more precise definitions, formalization of variables and their hypothesized linkages, and clarification of the problems of operationalization and testing. Following the lead of Howard and others, we have now stated this model in precise quantifiable terms so that it can be tested in a more definitive manner. Many readers with a pragmatic perspective will be uninterested in this development, but others will find Chapter 20 to be quite a departure from the discussion in preceding editions.

We have also endeavored to stress the practical implications of subject matter more in this edition. In that sense, the writing style is a bit "lighter" and hopefully more readable. We have tried to avoid introducing unnecessary complexity, because we feel that some contemporary writing in this subject area is guilty of the same charge leveled by an eminent theologian against certain colleagues in his field: "Part of the shame of the theology of the recent past is that sometimes it has been made deliberately foggy, under the fatuous assumption that what cannot be understood is somehow more profound."[2]

Both the quantity and the sophistication of relevant published research findings have increased sharply since the second edition. Therefore, we have had to be even more selective in isolating those that are cited. While our objective has been to be comprehensive in each subject area, there undoubtedly are gaps in coverage. We genuinely hope that no colleague will take offense if his or her work is not adequately recognized.

We gratefully acknowledge the many comments and suggestions provided by users of the first two editions. We are particularly grateful to Professor Robert Woodruff of the University of Tennessee who painstakingly evaluated the entire second edition and offered a number of really useful suggestions. This served to confirm much of what we have been trying to accomplish but also pointed out some real shortcomings that hopefully have been remedied in this edition. A similar review by Professor Harold Kassarjian of UCLA also proved to be quite helpful. His was more fun to use, by the way, because, in typical Kassarjian manner, he rarely "deleted the expletives."

A number of people also reviewed the current manuscript, and special thanks must be given to Bob Woodruff, Professor David Gardner of the University of Illinois at Champaign-Urbana, and Professor W. Wayne Talarzyk of The Ohio State University. Once again Professor Paul Green of the University of Pennsylvania also critically evaluated the manuscript. His scrutiny is an exacting one indeed. All of these colleagues and friends continued to contribute much to whatever success this book has achieved.

The reader will notice a change in the order of the authors' names on

---

2 D. Elton Trueblood, *A Place to Stand* (New York: Harper & Row, 1969), p. 8.

this edition. This reflects the unavoidable fact that David Kollat could not take as active a role as was true formerly, because the demands of a new job did not square with publication deadlines. Yet, he continues as a full member of the team, and the three of us look forward to many years of continued friendship and fruitful collaboration, even though our respective careers certainly have taken on some new directions since about 1972.

The senior author is especially grateful to his wife and three daughters who permitted him to escape for a number of days to Lost Grove, the Engel family retreat in southwest Wisconsin, for periods of undisturbed writing amidst the beauty of nature. As is always the case, those who are closest to us are the ones who pay the greatest price as book deadlines approach. Once again we dedicate this book to these unsung heroes.

Wheaton, Illinois   James F. Engel
Columbus, Ohio   Roger D. Blackwell
Columbus, Ohio   David T. Kollat

TABLE OF CONTENTS

CONSUMER BEHAVIOR

PART 1

INTRODUCTION & OVERVIEW

What is consumer behavior all about? Is it a legitimate subject of inquiry? Why should it receive emphasis as a separate area of study within the general field of marketing? These and many other questions are considered in this introduction, which serves as a framework of concepts around which subsequent parts of the text are built.

Of particular significance is Chapter 2, which presents a diagrammatic model of consumer motivation and behavior. A model of this type is indispensable for showing how various elements fit together to shape behavior. It begins with inputs of various types from the environment and ends with the consequences of a terminal act such as a purchase. All intervening steps and processes are clearly designated so that the relation of each to the whole becomes apparent. It is important that the chapter be given considerable critical emphasis, since the model presented here is followed step by step in subsequent chapters of the book.

CHAPTER 1

Understanding the consumer

If by some strange chance a modern day Rip Van Winkle were to awake after sleeping for a couple of decades, what would he most likely notice first in the contemporary fast moving world? Certainly he would soon become aware that striving for material gain is a way of life. He would observe the incredible variety of consumer products offered for sale everywhere he looks, many of which were introduced on the market only within the past few months. His senses would be bombarded with incessant advertising, much of which seems to feature the words "new," "white," "cool," "power," "refreshing," "relief." Rip would be amazed to discover that over $20 billion is spent annually on advertising in the United States alone. In short, he would come to the early conclusion that selling, buying, and consuming lie at the very core of life in most of the developed countries of the world.

The target of all this activity ultimately is a person known as a consumer, who must somehow wade through the flood of competing products and the myriad of frequently contradictory advertising and selling claims. What kind of person is this consumer? What determines motivation and behavior in the marketplace? These questions and others define the subject matter of consumer behavior—*those acts of individuals directly involved in obtaining and using economic goods and services, including the decision processes that precede and determine these acts.*

What makes the consumer tick?

It is sometimes mistakenly assumed that marketers have some magic power whereby they can induce the consumer to behave exactly as they

3

wish. There is an element of truth in this generalization, but it overlooks the fact that about 90 percent of all new products introduced each year either fail totally or fall short of expectations. Why does this take place? Are businesses manipulating consumers, or is the reverse taking place? Examination of some case histories will quickly provide the answer and the basis for some important generalizations about consumer behavior, which will serve as the foundation for the remainder of this book.

The new products that do not make it

Mennen E was one of the many new products introduced during the early 1970s. It was launched with a $12 million advertising expenditure on the assumption that it would become a leading contender in the $475 million deodorant category.[1] The selling appeal was that the use of vitamin E enabled the elimination of harsh germicides. It was lauded as the first deodorant breakthrough in 25 years, but it failed miserably in the market. The reason: the inclusion of vitamin E was perceived by consumers as being totally unimportant.

During that same period of time, the Scott Paper Company introduced Raggedy Ann/Andy as a new concept in throw away diapers.[2] One was packaged in pink for girls, and its counterpart for boys appeared in blue. The product was withdrawn from the market at a loss of nearly $13 million for the reason that it did not offer a benefit the consumer really wanted. Marketing efforts stressed features that were disregarded by the consumer as irrelevant in the contemporary culture.

Finally, the "ultimate in cake mixes" was introduced some years ago.[3] All the consumer had to do was add water and achieve the perfect cake. But the product went nowhere. Finally it was discovered that the purchaser (usually a housewife) felt cheated if she did nothing physical in the making of the cake. In effect, it rubbed against her self image as a homemaker and cook. Later the product was successfully reintroduced with one change: the consumer had to add an egg.

A few of the winners

The above examples illustrated products which went against the grain of consumer demand, but notice the difference in these case histories.

Vitalis, made by Bristol-Myers, dominated the men's haircare market for many years. This rapidly changed after introduction of Dry Look aerosol hair groom by Gillette.[4] Gillette research discovered that men had no desire to plaster their hair down so that it looked greasy, and this was especially important with the longer hair styles. Advertisements proclaimed, "The wethead is dead. Long Live the Dry Look from Gillette." The product succeeded because it solved a problem faced by many men.

The mouth care market historically has been difficult to penetrate, and it has long been dominated by Crest, Colgate, and Gleem. Yet, research

1 Theodore G. N. Chin, "New Product Success and Failures—How to Detect Them in Advance," *Advertising Age* (September 24, 1973), p. 61.

2 *Ibid.*, p. 62.

3 Jerry Della Femina, *From Those Wonderful Folks Who Gave You Pearl Harbor* (New York: Simon and Schuster, 1970), p. 37.

4 Chin, "New Product," p. 61.

indicated that not everyone was satisfied with these alternatives and that a niche could be gained by a new product that offered better taste for children, a gel formula for fast spreading on the brush, bright color, and stannous fluoride.[5] Aim toothpaste was designed to meet these desires, and it has gained a profitable share of the market with its promise, "Take Aim against cavities."

Finally, a product that goes from nothing to $70 million in sales in one year is doing something right. General Mills found that its new product Hamburger Helper was perceived as a real timesaving boon by the busy housewife. Here are the benefits that generated such a response: "Help for five. One pan, one pound of hamburger, and one package of Hamburger Helper change hamburger into a real dinner dish for a family of five."[6]

Each of the six products discussed here offered a distinction of some type. The difference lies in the way in which these product attributes were perceived and responded to by the consumer. Those products having attributes perceived as being pertinent to a real problem and to a definite felt need quickly became profitable, whereas others failed in spite of all of the manufacturer's marketing muscle. In the final analysis the consumer is the arbiter of market success.

What is the key to success?

The case examples are helpful in isolating some of the foundational principles of consumer behavior. Each of the five stated here will, of course, be elaborated and defined more extensively later. They are of sufficient importance, however, to warrant separate mention now.

Basic generalizations about consumer behavior

Consumer behavior is purposeful. Purchasing and consumption behavior can appear to be completely illogical to the outside observer. Unfortunately, such a judgment usually can only be based on the assumption that the observer's standards and behaviors are the only correct ones. This is especially dangerous when these opinions become the basis for governmental action or judicial decree. Snygg and Combs' warning is worthy of careful consideration:

> Laying aside, for the moment, the objective facts about behavior that some of us have learned, let each of us look at his own behavior as we actually see it while we are behaving. We find lawfulness and determinism at once. From the point of view of the behaver himself, behavior is caused. It is purposeful. It always has a reason. . . . When we look at other people from an external, objective point of view their behavior may seem irrational because we do not experience the [psychological] field as they do. . . . But at the instant of behaving the actions of each person seem to him to be the best and most effective acts he can perform under the circumstances. If, at that instant, he knew how to behave more effectively, he would do so.[7]

5 Kenneth Roman and Jane Maas, *How to Advertise* (New York: St. Martin's Press, 1976), p. 7.
6 Chin, "New Product," p. 62.
7 Donald Snygg and Arthur W. Combs, *Individual Behavior* (New York: Harper & Row, 1949), p. 12.

The consumer is sovereign. Each individual has full ability to "see and hear what he or she wants to see and hear." Information from advertising and selling is processed *selectively*, and that which is not felt to be pertinent is either ignored, disregarded, or forgotten. The fact that the consumer is not an unthinking robot is conclusively demonstrated by evidence generalized from two decades of research into television advertising. Only about one-third of those commercials a person is exposed to make any active impression in memory. Of those which are attended to, only about half are correctly comprehended, and fewer than five percent are actively recalled for as long as 24 hours. Incoming information thus is disregarded if it is seen to be irrelevant.

Consumer motivation and behavior can be understood through research. Consumer behavior is a process, of which the purchase is only one stage. There are many underlying influences, both internal and external from the social environment. The combination of these inputs and internal factors can be complex indeed. Yet, the tools of marketing research can assess motivation and behavior with considerable accuracy. Perfect prediction of behavior never is possible, but properly designed research efforts can significantly lower the risks of the types of product failure cited above.

Consumer motivation and behavior can be influenced. While the consumer cannot knowingly be induced to act in a way contradictory to his or her own goals or purposes, motivation and behavior can be influenced by outside sources. This influence is not successful, however, unless motivational factors are understood through research and correctly adapted to through the product offered, price, distribution, and promotion. In other words, the total marketing offering must be designed so that the consumer perceives its features as providing an answer to a perceived problem and felt needs. The three product successes cited above are good illustrations of the real meaning of creative adaptation to a rapidly changing consumer environment, whereas the failures demonstrate what can happen when this principle is disregarded for one reason or another.

Consumer influence and persuasion in the context discussed here is a socially legitimate activity. Note that the consumer, in effect, sets the agenda for the whole process. The influence process becomes unethical, however, if anything is done to interfere with free choice through intentional deception or distortion or through the exercise of monopoly power. Unfortunately, abuses are sufficiently common and flagrant that consumer protection legislation and education play an increasingly significant role. Much more is said on this point throughout the book.

There is a need for consumer education. The consumer can be both purposeful and sovereign but still behave unwisely in the sense of not making the "best buy." Outcomes might be quite different if the individual had more insight on ways to evaluate products and their selling claims.

There is a famous case history that illustrates this point. A manufacturer put out a new ceiling tile without holes or perforations of any kind, and it could be demonstrated that sound absorption capability was markedly improved. Yet, consumers rejected the product on the basis that an effective ceiling tile must have holes. After a period of unsuccessfully fighting this misbelief through advertising, the manufacturer inserted the holes and thereby reduced the performance of the product. Sales then responded positively. A more knowledgeable consumer would have reacted quite differently to this manufacturer's initial efforts.

The seller is placed in a dilemma in this kind of circumstance. Efforts at reeducation often are disregarded totally. Fortunately, consumer education is now becoming common in secondary schools and through community organizations of various types. In so doing, the consumer is taught to evaluate product offerings and appeals in a much more sophisticated manner. The sensitive marketer, in turn, has nothing to fear if product claims are truthful.

The economic and social role for consumer research

Why should consumer behavior be singled out as a topic for intensive study? One answer might simply be to provide understanding about an important aspect of general human behavior. More direct reasons exist, however. Of greatest importance, the applied discipline of consumer behavior is useful in development of more efficient use of marketing resources and in arriving at solutions to the problems of marketing management. In addition, growing attention is now being paid to the important subject of consumer protection. This is the essential motivation for increased governmental regulation and for burgeoning interest in consumer education. Finally, consumer research serves as essential input for public policy in general.

Consumer behavior and marketing management

Individuals responsible for managing business enterprises and other organizations need to understand consumer behavior in order to adapt the products and distributive resources of the organization to the demands of consumers. A few of the ways consumer research and analysis assist in attaining organizational objectives are described below.

Evaluating new market opportunities

An important reason for studying consumer behavior is evaluation of consumer groups with unsatisfied needs or desires. Requirements for success of any organization include not only the ability to *recognize unmet needs* but also to understand whether those needs will be expressed as *economically feasible markets* and what *organizational response is required for success in selling to those needs*.[8] Firms that organize their resources capably and flexibly toward unmet needs are sometimes

8 Theodore Levitt, "The New Markets—Think before You Leap," *Harvard Business Rev.* (May-June 1969), pp. 53–67.

described as consumer oriented or operating under the "marketing concept."[9]

Evaluation of new markets varies in difficulty according to the affluence and sophistication of a country's economy. In the case of an emerging nation, evaluating new markets may be simply a process of determining how much economic power can be generated and how quantities of basic needs—food, housing, medical care, and so on—can be supplied. When most of the citizens do not have enough basic food to eat, it is not difficult to locate new market opportunities. The best market opportunity is simply more food, probably of the same types already being consumed. Until a society reaches a point where a significant number of its members are above a subsistence level, the determination of new market opportunities is fairly obvious.

In an affluent, industrialized society new market opportunities do not arise by simply providing more of what is already being consumed (except, perhaps, for disadvantaged minorities within the society). New market opportunities arise because of other reasons, and these reasons make prediction of consumer response somewhat more difficult.

Geographic mobility is one reason why new market opportunities arise. People live where they did not live before and thus create new markets. They abandon old purchase loyalties and perhaps old product preferences. They seek consumption information from new sources. Aggressive business enterprises recognize the new markets created by geographic mobility and build new supermarkets, new discount stores, and new shopping centers. They use new media and new campaign themes to exploit the new market opportunities of suburbia and interurbia.

Social mobility provides another source of new market opportunities. As people become more educated and acquire a more sophisticated social milieu, their interests change and they participate in increased social interaction. They become aware of new types of leisure, requiring new types of products. With increased socialization, awareness of innovations such as health spas, stereo multiplexing systems, gourmet foods, and day-care centers is diffused rapidly. Thus mass markets for such items become feasible. Social positions change for *groups of individuals* as well as for *individuals within groups*, opening up markets previously confined to other consumer groups.

Psychic mobility in an affluent society results in new market opportunities for discerning firms. Along with physical and social mobility, people frequently express themselves more fully or change their conception of themselves and their environment. In this new conception, a man's inner self is no longer fixed and immutable. Personality is free to deviate from rigidly prescribed social norms, and people can express their desires

---

9 Much has been written about the marketing concept. A classic statement is Robert L. King, "An Interpretation of the Marketing Concept," paper presented at the 31st Annual Conf. of the Southern Economic Association, Memphis, Tenn. (Nov. 10, 1961); reprinted in Steven J. Shaw and C. McFerron Gittlinger (eds.), *Marketing in Business Management* (New York: Crowell-Collier-Macmillan, 1963), pp. 35–39.

(perhaps previously dormant) in many new ways. Apparel becomes not just a covering but an expression of one's feelings and perhaps a badge of his approval of others. Home furnishings express a family's new ability to deviate from rigid prescriptions. The same is true for many other products. This occurs mostly, of course, in an economy where substantial portions of the population have discretionary income to purchase more than just more of the same. Understanding this phenomenon is a key to success for firms seeking growth by expansion in new market opportunities.

Choosing market segments

No two people are exactly alike. That statement is readily accepted when thinking of the physical aspects of a human being. It is also true, however, in other aspects of human behavior which eventually are manifested in individual preferences for consumption. Traditional economic and marketing thought contained the implicit assumption that people demanded products alike. On the contrary, however, personal preferences for many products are no more all alike than are fingerprints!

The challenge of market segmentation is to determine groups of people whose preferences are sufficiently similar to each other, yet different from other groups, to justify modification of a product to the preferences of that specific group. Concurrently, a challenge exists for marketing organizations to develop the product and distribution offered in such a way as to make differenees from competitors discernible to consumers. The implications of this search for market segmentation and product differentiation will be analyzed in later chapters.

Increasing efficiency of strategy and tactics

Competition in a marketing economy is a precarious activity, always subject to encroachment or outright assault by competitors. Effectiveness requires continual improvement in the efficiency of the strategy and tactics employed by firms that are successful marketers. Reliable analysis of consumer behavior is an essential input to the development of effective marketing strategy.[10]

Consumer analysis focuses on the *causes* rather than the results of effective marketing strategy. Analysis of sales trends, for example, would be an analysis of results. Consumer analysis seeks to determine the underlying conditions that are true about consumers, and which cause an obvious result of increasing the efficiency of existing strategies and tactics.

Many questions about marketing strategy and tactics involving the analysis of consumer behavior need to be answered. It would be impossible to prepare a complete list of such questions, but some idea of the comprehensiveness of topics in marketing that can be improved by consumer analysis is suggested in the following list of questions, which represent only a small subset of those considered in this book:

10 For background material on marketing strategy, see David T. Kollat, Rogert D. Blackwell, and James Robeson, *Strategic Marketing* (New York: Holt, Rinehart and Winston, 1972).

1. Do consumers pass through a hierarchy of response stages in evaluating products?

2. How are models of consumer behavior useful in the development of marketing strategy?

3. What is the significance of motives in arousal of buying behavior?

4. How is sensation translated into meaning about brands or products?

5. What types of advertising appeals are the most effective in different product categories?

6. How can the "boredom barrier" of advertising be broken?

7. Is "subliminal" advertising effective?

8. How do buyers learn about new brands and products?

9. How do buyers form likes and dislikes toward salesmen and stores?

10. How do new residents learn about stores and brands?

11. How persuasible are prospective buyers?

12. Do personality differences correlate highly with brand choice?

13. Does advertising really bring about much attitude change?

14. Does the development of favorable attitudes toward a brand lead automatically to more sales?

15. What is a persuasive communication?

16. How many times should an ad run?

17. How important is the "youth culture" in the development of marketing strategy?

18. Is it better to have one brand that appeals to all social classes or several brands designed for specific social classes?

19. Do black consumers respond to marketing strategies differently than nonblack consumers?

20. To what degree can marketing strategy that is effective in the United States also be effective in other countries?

21. Can marketing efforts effectively increase informal conversations about a particular product enough to result in additional sales?

22. What life styles will create markets for new products in the future?

23. To what member of the family should promotion be directed?

24. Can buyers be stimulated to buy products for which they do not recognize a need?

25. How and when do buyers seek information about a product?

26. What are the most influential information sources about a product?

27. How does the importance of information source vary among market segments?

28. To what extent can consumers be influenced while they are in retail stores?

29. How do buyers evaluate alternative brands and suppliers?

30. Which product attributes are evaluated by consumers?

31. How do consumers choose retail stores?

32. How important is the image of a firm?

33. How do buyers react when preferred brands are unavailable?

34. What types of consumers are "deal prone"?

35. Should salesmen be recruited to have personalities similar to those of their customers or personalities different from customers?

36. How effectively can "impulse" purchasing be stimulated?

37. Under what circumstances does a marketing program have follow-up or "sleeper" effects?

38. What is the optimum number and type of retail outlets?

39. Are some customers more "loyal" to a brand than others? How does this influence marketing strategy?

40. Do some persons consistently buy new products before other segments of the population?

Improving retail performance

A revolution in retailing institutions and performances appears to be underway in North America, much of Europe, Japan, Scandinavia, and certain other areas. Consumer analysis is an essential input to the understanding of the cause of this revolution and in predicting the future changes that will be required to improve the efficiency of retailing performance.

Retailing is the final link in the process of moving goods from producer to consumer. It is for this reason that retailing places such heavy reliance on correct analysis of consumer behavior and is emphasized as a reason for consumer analysis. Regardless of how much value the manufacturer has built into the product, how well this value is communicated to the consumer, and how smoothly the production and physical distribution system may be functioning, it is the retailer who either consummates or obstructs the sale.

There has been much progress in recent years in improvement of what might be called the cost-revenue approach to improved retailing performance, but there were limited advances in what might be called the demand-analysis approach. Significant advances have been made in accounting control, computerized inventory systems, merchandise planning, location selection, physical layout, warehousing, and other operational aspects of retailing management. These technologies have been diffused so widely, however, that their potential for differentiating one retailing firm from another is approaching diminishing returns. The alternative is to increase the ability to understand, predict, and stimulate consumer response to a retailing firm's offering. Improved strategies to produce a more appealing offering provide an increasing potential as a basis for differentiating one retailing firm from another in profitability and consumer satisfaction.

Retailing performance is of critical concern in consumer behavior for another reason. The additional reason is the essential role retailing institutions play in total urban planning. The type of retailing institutions that will exist in cities of the next decade influence the kind of transportation cities will need, the kind of communication system (that is, the rise of telecommunications systems for transactions), the location and form of leisure activities, and the kind of integration with other time-consuming activities required for "new towns" and revitalization of existing cities. Thus the strategies of many types of business firms will be affected profoundly by the *form* and *place* of retailing transactions.

Consumer protection

The cornerstone of a free enterprise economy is the right of the consumer to make an informed choice from an array of product alternatives, which is not restricted by exercise of monopoly power. The consumer cannot make a knowledgeable choice, of course, if inaccurate or incomplete information is provided through a deliberate effort to mislead and manipulate. Moreover, restricted choice is the inevitable consequence of monopoly power, in which case profit results from this fact alone and not from service to the consumer.

Outright deception is regulated by governmental agencies and by voluntary business organizations such as the Advertising Review Board. Nevertheless, every consumer can point to examples where he or she has been deceived by less than full disclosure. Unfortunately the incidence of this type of abuse does not seem to be declining. Monopoly power also is regulated to a degree by antitrust legislation, and some of its more blatant forms are not observed today. Monopoly gain can result, however, when an economy shifts from one of abundance to one characterized by scarcity. This was certainly the case in many industries during the energy crisis of the middle 1970s in the United States. The producer now was in a position to shift limited resources to the most profitable products, regardless of consumer desires. The consumer really had no option whatsoever, and short run financial considerations frequently took the place of service to the consumer. Finally this situation was reversed by the recession that followed, but it does illustrate the degree to which consumer orientation can disintegrate into a mere platitude rather than a central aspect of business life.

In a market economy governmental regulation always will be required to curb these abuses, and consumer protection legislation has expanded remarkably at all levels of government. All too frequently such legislation is based on the opinions of a small group of people rather than on consumer research focusing on the consequences of these abuses of consumer behavior. The outcome tends to be ineffective and, in some instances, counterproductive consumer legislation. There now is a growing awareness that greater reliance must be placed on research if consumer protection is to function as intended.

Consumer education is the most productive long range strategy. The consumer can be taught how to detect the presence of deception and other abuses and made aware of the remedies that exist and the opportunities for redress. Also, everyone can benefit from insight into money-saving buying strategies. These programs also must be based on research into consumer motivation and behavior. Otherwise, educational programs can be totally irrelevant for the real world of consumer life.

Essential input for public policy

The principle of individual choice permeates the economic theories and practices of many societies in the world. No disciplined determination of public policy can exist, therefore, without assumptions—correct or incorrect—about how consumers as individuals will choose to spend their money, time, energy, and votes. To design public policy that will be accepted by consumers and will be efficient as a solution to societal problems requires thorough understanding of the needs, desires, and aversions of the consumers for whom the policies are developed.

Kotler and Zaltman have commented that even products with obvious value to a society, such as free medical care, pollution control, or public transportation, must be presented with understanding of consumer behavior and sophistication in marketing programs if the products are to be accepted by the society's consumers.[11] A good example of the need for consumer analysis as an input in public policy might be in the area of urban transportation. It is apparent from the failures of many United States urban transportation systems that there is an enormous need to design urban transit systems to appeal to individual consumers' tastes if high usage is to be attained. In an industrialized society, the practical alternative to designing public policy with analysis of consumer behavior is forceful coercion to gain acceptance.

In the communal society that is becoming common worldwide, more and more *individual* consumption decisions impact other individuals, especially in the tightly interwoven fabric of consumption.[12] The individual choices of consumers concerning automobiles, for example, affect immensely the air breathed by all other consumers. The choices of consumers about detergents, in another example, affect the water quality for many other consumers. When public policy is enacted without

---

11 Philip Kotler and Gerald Zaltman, "Social Marketing: An Approach to Planned Social Change," *J. Marketing,* vol. 35 (July 1971), pp. 3–12.

12 Daniel Bell, "The Post-Industrial Society: A Speculative View," in Edward and Elizabeth Hutchings (eds.), *Scientific Progress and Human Values* (New York: Elsevier, 1967), pp. 154–170.

adequate understanding of why and how consumers are going to make their individual decisions, chaos in public policy may ensue to the detriment of those whom policy makers had hoped to help. It is increasingly difficult to consider consumer decisions "private" because of their impact on many "public" areas. This interlocking of interests is described by Laurence Feldman:

> . . . there are signs that the marketing system's ability to promote consumption and to provide consumers with a growing range of choice is increasingly inconsistent with the needs of the larger society. One reason for this is that marketing decisions have been made which expanded the range of consumer product choice but disregarded their environmental impact. There has been a failure to recognize that these products, which are marketing outputs designed for individual satisfaction, are simultaneously inputs to a larger environmental system and as such the well-being of society.[13]

As an emerging academic discipline

For most of this century, economists and marketers were the only ones who worried much about consumer behavior. Many theories were developed, usually reflecting little more than armchair analysis. There was no concentrated study of the consumer undertaken with the intent of building a consistent field of knowledge.

Matters began to change after World War II when marketers suddenly discovered that they possessed vastly more productive capacity than the market could absorb. The interests of firms shifted from production to marketing—to adaptation of output to the needs and desires of the consumer. This, in turn, gave rise to a strong demand for greater knowledge about consumer behavior.

Trained psychologists found their way into the business world and launched an era of inquiry known as "motivation research." While the outcome of this invasion was not especially notable (it generated more heat than light), it did serve to stimulate awareness that the behavioral sciences have much to contribute both to marketing and to consumer education.

Consumer behavior emerged as a legitimate field of academic study during the 1960s as marketers and economists began to develop expertise in the behavioral sciences. Suddenly, the behavioral sciences became the "in" thing. Marketers, in particular, borrowed rather indiscriminately from social psychology, sociology, anthropology, or any other field of study that might tangent with consumer behavior in some way, no matter how remote. Yet, in retrospect, this sense of indirection characterizes any field in its immaturity. Soon this unfocused inquiry began to assume maturity.

While a more definitive historical overview is provided in Part 6, it should be noted that a major step forward occurred after the publication

---

13 Laurence P. Feldman, "Societal Adaptation: A New Challenge for Marketing," *J. Marketing,* vol. 35 (July 1971), pp. 54–60. Reprinted by permission of the publisher.

of three pioneering books in the middle 1960s.[14] These books defined important variables, specified functional relationships between them, and clarified the practical implications for marketers and, to a much lesser degree, for consumer education., Soon courses on consumer behavior became commonplace, and scientists from various behavioral sciences began to view the consumer as a legitimate focus of inquiry. Researchers from these diverse backgrounds were united through the formation of the Association for Consumer Research following a conference sponsored by the authors at Ohio State University in 1969. As of this writing, membership is nearing 750.

The outcome is that consumer behavior is now an important field of study in its own right. The literature has grown sharply,[15] and the *Journal of Consumer Research* was first published in 1975. Research contributions also are increasingly appearing in the literature of related behavioral sciences. In other words, research in consumer behavior is now making important contributions to knowledge of human behavior in general. The field has grown from infancy to a healthy state of adolescence.

Summary

Consumer behavior is defined as the acts of individuals directly involved in obtaining and using economic goods and services, including the decision processes that precede and determine these acts. Many of the principles that explain consumer behavior overlap with industrial behavior, although it is only the former that is emphasized in this text.

A useful method of analysis of consumer behavior is the decision-process approach, which examines the events that precede and follow a purchase. Consumer behavior as a field of study is an interdisciplinary and applied approach based upon an analytical framework rather than merely a description of behavior.

The rationale for studying consumer behavior involves two primary emphases. One emphasis is upon macromarketing problems, or how a society meets the economic needs of its people. The other emphasis is upon micromarketing problems, or the administration of specific elements of an economy. Analysis of consumer behavior is increasingly an essential input in formulating public policies, in understanding the role of marketing in society, and in understanding the nature of planning in a society that permits individual choices. From a managerial perspective, consumer analysis is essential for evaluating new market opportunities, choosing market seg-

14 See Francesco M. Nicosia, *Consumer Decision Processes: Marketing and Advertising Implications* (Englewood Cliffs, N.J.: Prentice-Hall, 1966); John A. Howard and Jagdish N. Sheth, *The Theory of Buyer Behavior* (New York: John A. Wiley & Sons, 1969); and James F. Engel, David T. Kollat, and Roger D. Blackwell, *Consumer Behavior,* first edition (New York: Holt, Rinehart and Winston, 1968).

15 There now are a number of source books and texts in this field. Some of the more widely-used sources are Fred D. Reynolds and William D. Wells, *Consumer Behavior* (New York: McGraw-Hill, 1977); Carl E. Block and Kenneth J. Roering, *Essentials of Consumer Behavior* (Hinsdale, Ill.: Dryden, 1976); Joe Kent Kerby, *Consumer Behavior Conceptual Foundations* (New York: Dun-Donnelley, 1975); Arch G. Woodside, Peter D. Bennett, and Jagdish N. Sheth (eds.), *Consumer and Industrial Buyer Behavior* (New York: Elsiver North Holland, 1976); Flemming Hansen, *Consumer Choice Behavior* (New York: The Free Press, 1971); and Rom J. Markin, *Consumer Behavior: A Cognitive Orientation* (New York: Macmillan, 1974).

ments, increasing efficiency of marketing strategy and tactics, and improving retailing performance. This book emphasizes the relationships between decisions of both types with an awareness of the increasing impact individual consumer decisions have upon the well-being of the economic system.

Review and discussion questions

1. Which of the following decisions should be considered legitimate topics of concern in the study of consumer behavior? (a) selection of a college by a student, (b) purchase of a life insurance policy, (c) smoking a cigarette, (d) selecting a church to join, (e) selecting a dentist, (f) visiting an auto showroom to see new models, and (g) purchasing a college textbook.

2. Examine current advertisements for consumer products and select one for a new product. Will this product succeed in the long run in the consumer market place? What factors determine success?

3. A family has just come into the local office of a lending agency asking for a bill consolidation loan. Payments for a new car, television, stereo, bedroom set, and central air conditioning have become excessive. The head of the family does not have a steady source of income, and real help is now needed. Is this an example of purposeful consumer behavior, or has this family been manipulated into making unwise purchases?

4. If it is true that motivations and behavior can be understood through research, is it also true that the marketer now has greater ability to influence the consumer adversely than would have been true in an earlier era?

5. It is obvious that new markets have been created in the last few decades by such trends as the exodus to the suburbs. What new markets appear to be likely in the new decades due to geographic mobility?

6. Describe some products that appear to have arisen in recent years because of psychic mobility.

7. What contributions does the analysis of consumer behavior make to the field of finance? of production? of real estate? of insurance? of top management administration?

8. Would it be equally necessary to understand consumer behavior if the economic system were not one of free enterprise? In other words, is the subject matter of this book only of interest to those in capitalistic systems, or does it also have relevance for socialism and communism?

9. What differences in perspective on consumer behavior would you expect to find among the following types of researchers? (a) experimental psychologist, (b) social psychologist, (c) clinical psychologist, (d) anthropologist, (e) sociologist, and (f) economist?

10. Consumer protection is an important issue. What areas of consumer behavior appear to be most in need of increased regulation and/or consumer education?

CHAPTER 2

Consumer decision processes:
An overview

The reasons for studying and analyzing consumer motivation and behavior were considered in Chapter 1. Behavior, not surprisingly, can be the result of a myriad of influences. It is the purpose of the present chapter to provide an overview of consumer decision processes in order to lay the conceptual framework for the remainder of the book. The chapter begins with a discussion of basic factors in the study of human behavior in general and then shifts to consideration of consumer decision processes and research strategies appropriate to the understanding of these phenomena. Then a comprehensive model of consumer motivation and behavior is presented, followed by examples provided for the purpose of illustration. Most of the following chapters illuminate one aspect of this broader model, and it may prove useful from time to time to refer back to this chapter in order to retain a grasp of the overall structure.

The study of human behavior

A person is influenced by many forces, the sum total of which is designated as the *psychological field.* First, each person is motivated by internal basic needs. These are activated in the present time period without particular influence from the past or anticipation of the future. In this sense, man does not differ greatly from lower forms of animal life. The human being is not time bound, however, and is fully capable of recalling and being influenced by the past as well as anticipating future consequences of behavior. The past may function through learned patterns of behavior and ways of thinking, many of which are largely unconscious. In addition, a person is profoundly influenced by the surrounding environment, especially the social role of others. All of these factors are significant, and any realistic theory of consumer behavior must comprehend each in a consistent and realistic manner.

The role of the social environment requires further clarification. In one sense, other people serve a supportive function both in the goods they make and share and in the opportunity offered to give love and affection. Another role is a constraining one, for a person is seldom free to act as would be the case if urges were permitted free expression. Social mores and guides become established and limit freedom of action. Some of these constraints are necessary for maintenance of order and become codified as laws. Others are required for the effective functioning of groups and emerge as norms or accepted patterns of social behavior.

By taking the perspective that a person is subject to compound and sometimes conflicting motivational determinants, it is possible to grasp the complexity of forces underlying behavior. Each individual must adapt to his or her own psychological field, and this field is reality to that person. Patterns of behavior become established to permit workable and meaningful patterns of adaptation.

Explaining human behavior

The complexity of the psychological field is not the only difficulty faced by the analyst of human action because mental processes cannot be observed directly. The result is that explanations of what transpires can be only an inference as to what must have taken place to cause the individual to act as he or she did. Figure 2.1 clarifies the nature of this dilemma.

Figure 2.1 Basic model for study of human behavior

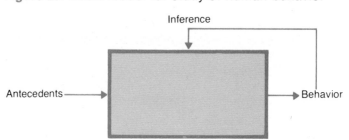

Antecedents are the inputs or stimuli that trigger action, and behavior is the output or result. The individual's mental processes stand between inputs and outputs and are forever hidden from view. For this reason they are sometimes described as being located within an inpenetrable *black box*. Any explanation of what took place within the black box as a result of the input can be only an inference made by the analyst.

To take an example, assume that a person reacts negatively and perhaps violently when he answers his telephone and hears a voice say, "Good evening; we are pleased to tell you that you are one of the very few in this city who will be permitted to purchase *Blab* magazine at half price." He may slam the receiver in the salesperson's ear. A relationship is thereby established between the antecedent (the call) and the behavior (slamming the receiver). This relationship is affected by something within the black box, but this "something," whatever it might be, cannot be observed directly from this sequence. Perhaps the analyst will conclude that the person has a strong attitude against telephone solicitation. Yet what is an attitude? It is only an inference that is made concerning some variable which intervened between the stimulus and the response.

The concept of *intervening variable* is an important one and is defined by one authority as follows:

> The qualifying adjective "intervening" is used to convey the notion that postulated states, conditions, or processes intervene between the behavior and its observable correlates or antecedents. These variables cannot be observed directly.[1]

The inference problem

It should be apparent from this brief discussion that many of the more common explanatory terms are nothing more than inferred intervening variables. For this reason, many schools of thought have arisen, each of which views the same phenomenon and postulates different intervening variables. In part, these differences arise because analysts have varying purposes. The result, of course, is that there can be real disagreement on the meaning of such familiar terms as "need," "motive," and "attitude." Indeed, it is difficult to find definitions acceptable to all; therefore, it is necessary to specify the meanings of terms with as much precision as possible.

Models of consumer behavior

With the emergence of consumer behavior as a subject for intensive study in its own right, there was understandable confusion with respect to important explanatory variables. A great step forward occurred with the publication of three models of consumer behavior in the 1960s,[2] two of which have proved to be especially influential and have undergone substantial revision over the years.[3] These models are discussed in detail in Chapter 20.

A model is nothing more than a replica of the phenomena it is intended to designate. In effect, it specifies the elements within the black box,

1 Judson S. Brown, *The Motivation of Behavior* (New York: McGraw-Hill, 1961), p. 28. Reprinted by permission of the publisher.

2 See Francesco M. Nicosia, *Consumer Decision Processes: Marketing and Advertising Implications* (Englewood Cliffs, N.J.: Prentice-Hall, 1966); John A. Howard and Jagdish N. Sheth, *The Theory of Buyer Behavior* (New York: Wiley, 1969); and the first edition of this text published in 1968 by Holt, Rinehart & Winston, Inc.

3 The Howard and Sheth model was revised in John U. Farley, John A. Howard and L. Winston Ring, *Consumer Behavior Theory and Application* (Boston: Allyn & Bacon, Inc., 1974). The Engel, Kollat, and Blackwell model was revised in the second edition of this text published in 1973.

represents the nature of relationships between them, and clarifies the manner in which behavior is affected.

Models of consumer behavior usually are elaborate flow charts of the behavioral process being depicted. Relationships between some elements can only be hypothesized at this time because of the paucity of needed research. While there is much yet to be learned, a model of consumer behavior offers significant advantages, first of all, to the student and the researcher:

1. *A frame of reference is provided for research.* Through description of elements and relationships, gaps in information and potential areas for fruitful inquiry are identified with a clarity not otherwise possible.

2. *Research findings can be integrated into a meaningful whole.* When a model is available of the entire process of consumer behavior, it becomes feasible to utilize research findings from a variety of behavioral sciences with greater sophistication and precision. In other words, an understanding of underlying relations provides a perspective for assessing the significance of new research data.

3. *Models become useful in theory construction.* Researchable hypotheses flow readily from a carefully designed model, and a basis is thus provided for extending knowledge.

4. *Explanations are provided for performance of the system.* A mere description of the motivational determinants of buyer action is of little use; it is necessary, rather, to explain relations and thereby gain in ability to predict outcomes under varying sets of circumstances. This process is virtually impossible without a model of some type, no matter how crude.

5. *The student of consumer behavior is assisted in grasping the nature of variables and their linkages.* A model thus can provide real pedagogical advantages, and this fact, in itself, justifies their development and use.

Models also are of real help in marketing research. Every decision maker possesses a model of consumer behavior. That is to say, each person has at least some idea of the things that should be studied. The problem enters, however, when the model used is incomplete or inadequate. To take just one example, it is common to think of advertising only in terms of its influence on sales. Therefore, all measures of success will be monetary in nature, consistent with this point of view. But this completely overlooks the fact that behavior is a process with a number of stages prior to a buying action, as the following pages will reveal. Advertising might have led to a change in attitude that will be manifested in a purchase at a later time. In this instance, the advertising effort could easily be judged a failure when, in fact, the intended purpose was accomplished.

The point, then, is that the decision maker also must have an *accurate* and *comprehensive* model both to guide the information utilized in formation of strategy and that used to assess effectiveness. This becomes especially serious when it is realized that a naive or overly simplistic model can lead to completely erroneous actions without the decision maker even being aware of this fact.

The nature of consumer decision processes

Almost 70 years ago, John Dewey itemized what he termed the steps in problem solving to explain the process an individual goes through in arriving at a decision.[4] Since that time many conceptualizations of the phases in problem solving have been advanced.[5] The advantage of this perspective is that it views behavior as a *process* rather than as a discrete act and is as concerned with how a decision is reached as it is with the decision itself.

There are five important phases of consumer decision making behavior which should be understood by all in the study of consumer behavior:

1. *Problem recognition.* What happens to initiate the process?

2. *Search.* What sources of information are used to arrive at a decision, and what is the relative influence of each?

3. *Alternative evaluation.* What criteria and other factors are used by the consumer to assess alternatives? Which are most influential in motivating a purchase intention?

4. *Choice.* What selection is made from the available alternatives?

5. *Outcomes.* Is choice followed by satisfaction or by doubt that a correct decision was made?

The decision process perspective provides important information for marketing decision making. Knowledge about such things as the relative importance of various information sources, the criteria used to evaluate alternative brands, and so on, is useful in designing product, price, channel, and selling strategies.

For example, a manufacturer of color television sets has discovered that buyers are technically unable to evaluate the performance of competing brands. Yet they desire a set that is technologically sophisticated. As a consequence, advertising points out that component parts also are utilized in the space program and elsewhere where technological sophistication and dependability are important. Presumably the campaign will create enough confidence in the company that consumers will be satisfied with their choice.

4 John Dewey, *How We Think* (New York: Heath, 1910), p. 72.

5 See, for example, Orville Brim, David C. Glass, David E. Lavin, and Norman Goodman, *Personality and Decision Processes* (Stanford, Calif.: Stanford University Press, 1962), p. 9; Robert M. Gagné, "Problem Solving and Thinking," in P. R. Farnsworth and Q. McNemar (eds.), *Annual Review of Psychology* (Palo Alto, Calif.: Annual Reviews, 1959), pp. 147–72.

A model of the decision process

The model of consumer behavior used in this book is designed to explain each phase of the decision process (see Figure 2.2). Fundamentally, it is

Figure 2.2 The stages in the consumer decision process

an elaboration of the black box model, specifying inputs, variables within the black box itself, social and environmental influences, and outcomes. This is the third version of what has become known as the Engel, Kollat, and Blackwell model. Each revision reflects advances in knowledge. Modifications are undertaken first to provide a better description of the process and secondly to clarify relationships between variables so that more precise guidance is given for research applications.

Each of the remaining sections of the book explains a phase of the decision process through use of this model, beginning with problem recognition. In other words, a model of consumer behavior is never an end in itself but is designed to illuminate the decision process.

In this introductory chapter only anecdotal support is given for the model through use of two different research examples. The more rigorous theoretical and empirical foundations are elaborated throughout the book. Chapter 20 then contains a formal theoretical statement of this model, and it is compared with other models of the same process. The discussion below only gives a very brief overview of the decision process and the model itself.

Problem recognition occurs when an individual perceives a difference between an ideal state of affairs and the actual state at any given moment. Figure 2.3 contains the first simplified depiction of the model of consumer

Figure 2.3 Problem recognition

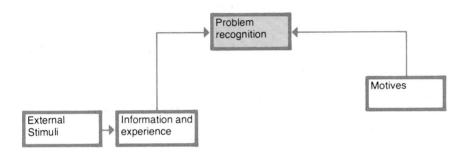

behavior, showing only how problem recognition occurs. There are two basic sources: (1) an external stimulus of some sort and (2) motive activation. The black box is now relabeled as the *central processing unit* to highlight its important role in the processing and storage of incoming information.

First, problem recognition, or *arousal* as it is sometimes termed, can be activated solely by motive without any type of external stimulation. Motives are enduring predispositions to strive to attain specified goals, and they contain both an arousing and a directing dimension. An activated motive stimulates a state of drive that is consciously felt. Then motive-satisfying behavior is initiated. A good example is the onset of thirst. The drive to reduce thirst is not ignored for long, because it signals a real difference between the present state of affairs and the desired state (absence of thirst).

External stimuli are the other primary means of bringing about problem recognition. Technically, the model should show that the new information or experience triggers motive, which, in turn, leads to problem recognition. It will become apparent later, however, that a model of this type gets unduly complex with arrows going in every direction if some necessary simplifications are not made. Thus, it is shown here by a direct arrow to problem recognition merely for simplification and clarity.

New information works this way. Assume that an individual is thumbing through a magazine and sees an advertisement for a German chocolate cake mix. The picture of the cake, an external stimulus, enters the individual's conscious (referred to in this book as the *central processing unit*) and highlights the ideal state, thereby triggering a feeling of hunger.

Not every perceived discrepancy between ideal and actual will result in problem recognition. There is a minimum level of perceived difference which must be surpassed before behavior is activated. This threshold is learned and will vary with circumstances.

Search

Once a problem is recognized, the consumer must then assess the available alternatives for action. The initial step is an internal search within the central processing unit to determine whether or not sufficient information is available. Often one brand is strongly preferred over others, and a decision is made on the spot to make a purchase during the next trip to a shopping center. This provides an example of *routinized buyer behavior*, which is discussed in more detail later. If the internal search does not prove to be sufficient, however, external search is activated. This process is illustrated in Figure 2.4.

Figure 2.4 The search process

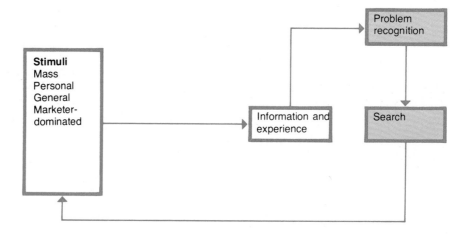

Once again the model is depicted only in very simplified form showing one internal variable—stored information and experience. Others, such as attitudes, beliefs, and personality, are introduced later. The primary purpose now is to illustrate what happens to incoming information as it is processed and evaluated.

Internal search for information occurs instantaneously and largely unconsciously. If feedback shows that there is sufficient information already stored, it is probable, all other things being equal, that there will be no external search. Often information is insufficient. A husband and wife, for instance, have little or no awareness of the advantages and limitations of the competing makes of color television. They may not, in addition, know the appropriate criteria to use in evaluating these alternatives. Hence, they might consult friends or relatives or turn to one of the published sources that rates products on technical performance. These are examples of interpersonal and mass communication that are *general* in nature and are not controlled by the marketer. They also no doubt will be influenced by advertisements and personal selling undertaken by the marketer for the express purpose of consumer influence. Search continues until enough information is gathered to permit an enlightened evaluation.

There are individual differences in willingness to engage in search. First, some people are known to be cautious and unwilling to act even when alternatives are known because of perceived risk of making a wrong decision. Hence, further information is sought as additional justification. Others are willing to act largely on hunch and intuition. The extent of search always is determined by the balance between expected gains and the costs of time, energy, and financial outlay that are necessitated.

Before moving on to alternative evaluation, the next stage in the decision sequence, it is necessary to clarify how people "make sense" of incoming information. This is now commonly referred to as *information processing*, and the stages are illustrated in Figure 2.5.

Information processing

Figure 2.5 Information processing

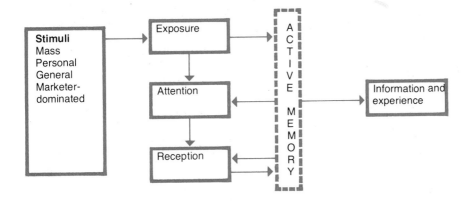

It was stressed in Chapter 1 that each one of us is highly selective in the use of incoming information. In fact, there often is quite a variation between the actual content of a message and the content as it is perceived and retained by the consumer. Information loss and distortion occur as new information is passed through *active memory*. As we will show later, there are a number of items stored in memory—attitudes, motives, personality traits, and so on. Not all of this memory is instantly accessible. That portion used in the processing and interpretation of incoming information is what we have designated here as the *active* memory. In a sense, it serves as a type of filter through which everything is passed. Some things are lost, others are made more clear, others are changed. Active memory is depicted with a dotted outline in Figure 2.5, by the way, to designate the fact that its existence and functions can only be inferred and not directly observed or measured as can most of the other variables in the model.

Now, how does information processing take place? A housewife is in a supermarket with an extensive shopping list. Yet, she has not written everything down and frequently will use the items on the shelves as a reminder of what she and her family need. As she walks she scans the shelves and thus is *exposed* to a variety of stimuli. Information processing, then, begins with exposure, at which time the individual is in physical proximity to an informational stimulus such that there is opportunity for one or more of the senses to be activated. This makes the obvious point that the marketer's first task is to get the intended message to the right person at the right point in time.

As she progresses down the aisle, her eye stops at a display of canned tomato soup. Now it can be said that *attention* has been attracted. Attention is defined as the active processing of an exposed stimulus such that a conscious impression is made within the active memory. Attention is highly selective, however, and many stimuli are completely filtered out. The key fact is whether or not the stimulus has *pertinence* for that individual in terms of attitudes, beliefs, and life style. Those which do not simply never pass from active memory into permanent or long term memory.

It is well known that an aroused motive activates an "on-off" mechanism in information processing. We are especially alert to those stimuli seen to be relevant in satisfying the aroused drive and vice versa. Perhaps our housewife has come to the store with an active recall of her husband's request to serve some tomato soup again soon. A desire to serve pleasing meals thus could cause the soup display to stand out, whereas it might be largely ignored under other conditions.

Attention is a necessary but not sufficient precondition for message *reception*—the accurate comprehension of the meaning of the stimulus and storage of that information in long term memory. The filtering effect of active memory can serve to distort meaning in such a way that some things are amplified whereas others are diminished or ignored. It is common for a prospect to miss the point of a commercial completely and attribute a meaning that never was intended. Sometimes this distortion occurs to make the perceived meaning more consonant with the individual's own beliefs and preferences. For example, a consumer with a preference for a particular brand of coffee brewed using traditional methods may completely misinterpret taste test results alleging that freeze dried coffee tastes as good as home brewed.

Not every correctly comprehended message enters into permanent memory, because there also is a tendency to retain only those compatible with our present beliefs. Even if the taste test results for freeze dried coffee were properly understood, the "filter" still can function to block the entry of this new information and thus preserve the existing preference for the "home brew."

The final stage of information processing, shown in Figure 2.5, is new information or experience that enters into permanent storage. Obviously it can affect all other things stored within memory and bring about changes. In the content of consumer behavior, however, the greatest changes will be in product beliefs and attitudes, intentions to purchase, and, hopefully, in actual purchase behavior. More is said about this later.

It should not be inferred from this brief discussion that all attempts at consumer influence will be futile because of selective information processing. If this were the case, $20 billion would not be spent annually on advertising in the United States. Selective screening occurs most frequently when the individual is not in a state of active problem recognition and is not engaged in a voluntary search for information. Many advertisements are designed to trigger problem recognition, and these are most readily ignored. The person engaged in voluntary search, however, will be far more open and receptive.

Once information has been received, the consumer then must evaluate the alternatives and arrive at a purchase decision. This process involves the interaction of several different types of variables.

Alternative evaluation

Response to incoming information. New information enters into memory initially in the form of information and experience. From there, it can exert an effect on two key variables within the central processing unit: (1) *evaluative criteria* and (2) *beliefs*. A change in belief, in turn, leads to a change in *attitude* which, all things being equal, will result in establishment of a *purchase intention* or change in existing intentions. Intentions also are affected by other considerations as later discussion will reveal. All of this is shown in Figure 2.6.

Evaluative criteria are the specifications and standards used by consumers to evaluate products and brands. Low price and durable performance are examples. In other words, these are the desired outcomes from choice and use expressed in the form of the specifications used in the comparison and analysis process. The direct arrow in Figure 2.6 from *motives* indicates that evaluative criteria, to a large extent, are a concrete product-specific manifestation of underlying personal goals. As a result, they can be very resistant to marketer influence. Nevertheless, new information can bring about change, especially if it is perceived as being general (nonmarketer-dominated) and educational in nature.

Beliefs, on the other hand, represent information that links a given product or brand to evaluative criteria. These can be readily influenced by the marketer. For instance, the consumer might specify that decay prevention is the most important desired attribute in toothpaste. Through exposure to promotional appeals, one might then arrive at the belief that one particular brand is most efficient in terms of decay prevention. In all likelihood this belief will result in product trial. Belief formation and change is a primary goal of marketing strategy.

Once beliefs have been formed or changed, *attitudes* also will be affected. An attitude is defined as a learned predisposition to respond consistently in a favorable or unfavorable manner with respect to a given

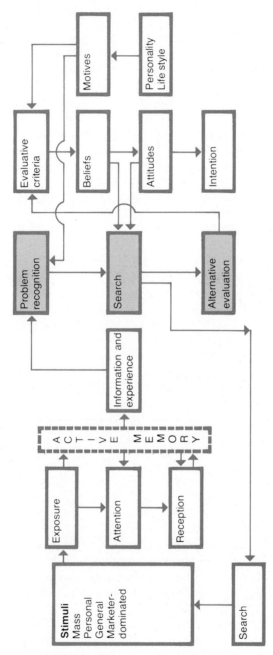

Figure 2.6 Alternative evaluation

alternative. An attitude, then, is a positive or negative evaluation of the consequences of using a particular product or brand. To the extent that an attitude reflects important basic goals, it becomes resistant to change.

Attitudes undoubtedly stand as one of the most analyzed phenomena in general human behavior. Many organizations spend considerable sums in trying to change consumer attitudes. Yet, some have questioned the value of even trying to change attitude for the reason that attitude change does not necessarily lead to desired changes in behavior. Recently it has become recognized that yet another variable intervenes between attitudes and behavior—*intentions*. An intention represents the subjective probability that a specified action will be undertaken, in this case the choice of a particular brand. It now can be concluded that a change in attitude leads to a change in intentions. A changed intention, in turn, is followed by changed behavior if one takes account of certain environmental factors discussed in the next section. Therefore, attitude change *is* a valid marketing goal, and the key to strategy is to change the belief structure on which the attitude is based.

Environmental influence. Figure 2.7 introduces two factors from the external environment that also affect intentions along with attitude: (1) *normative compliance* (the existence of perceived social influence on choice plus motivation to comply with those pressures) and (2) *anticipated circumstances* (the state of present income, economic conditions, and other factors). These are treated as *internalized* environmental influences and thus may be viewed as stored information and experience.

Normative compliance requires more than just the existence of influence on choice from friends, relatives, and others. The individual also must be motivated to comply, and this sensitivity to influence is a factor in one's personality makeup. Some are more likely to respond than others.

Anticipated circumstances can obviously represent a host of factors. The most important consideration usually will be personal income. If sufficient funds are not available, purchase intentions may not be acted upon for a considerable period of time.

To sum up, Figure 2.7 indicates that buying intentions are the outcome of attitudes, normative compliance, and anticipated circumstances. If one knows the general status of these influences, behavior can be predicted with fair accuracy. Attempts to change behavior, in turn, focus on changes in the structure of beliefs. Changed beliefs usually will lead to changed attitudes.

The function of personality and life style. Personality has been mentioned several times as an important underlying variable. The term life style is used interchangeably here. It is defined as the pattern of enduring traits, activities, interests, and opinions that determine general behavior and thereby make one individual distinctive in comparison with another. It is the product of initial genetic makeup and a lifetime of experience. But, in addition, it is strongly conditioned by internalized *cultural norms and values*. If one has a good understanding of cultural determinants of

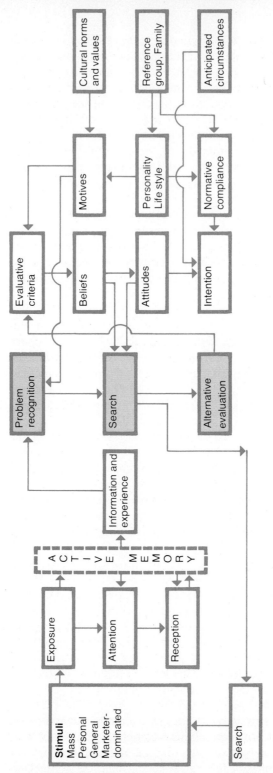

Figure 2.7 Perceived environmental influences on intentions and life style

thinking and behavior, it is possible to predict some types of consumer behavior without marketing research. This has long been the contribution of cultural anthropology.

The measurement of life style has assumed an important role in marketing research in recent years. This type of analysis is referred to as psychographic research, and it is the subject of Chapter 7. The goal is to understand the consumer in as rich detail as possible. Advertising artists and writers are especially helped in the use of illustrations and appeals most appropriate for those in the target audience. There are numerous other applications as well.

Choice and its outcomes

Figure 2.8 completes the model of consumer behavior in two ways. First, it shows the three determinants of search behavior by arrows stemming from problem recognition, beliefs, and attitudes. This restates more formally what was said earlier and also labels the various sections of the model. Furthermore, it depicts *choice* and *outcomes*, the last two stages of the decision-making process.

Choice generally will follow the formation of a purchase intention, but perceived *unanticipated circumstances* can serve as a barrier. These can take a variety of forms: change in income, change in family circumstances, nonavailability of alternatives, and so on. In such instances, intentions either remain in existence until a later time or the decision making process begins anew.

Choice often is accompanied by the necessity to select the best retail outlet and to engage in negotiation before the purchase is made. These actions are of real significance in retailing strategy and are the subject of Chapter 19.

Figure 2.8 illustrates the two outcomes of choice. First and most important is *satisfaction*. The satisfied customer arrives at the evaluation that the chosen alternative is consistent with prior beliefs and attitudes. The dotted feedback arrow to information and experience indicates that this information then becomes stored in memory for use in future purchase decisions. It is likely to have an especially strong effect on beliefs and consequently upon attitudes.

Another possible outcome is *post-decision dissonance*. This is a state of post-decision doubt motivated by awareness that one alternative was chosen and beliefs that unchosen alternatives also have desirable attributes. Dissonance is especially likely if the purchase is financially burdensome and several attractive alternatives were rejected. The purchaser now might be sensitive to information that confirms the choice and thereby relieves doubt. Therefore, post-decision search for information is not unusual in such circumstances.

Variations in decision processes

Thus far discussion has focused on the most comprehensive type of decision making—extended problem solving—complete with search and alternative evaluation. Most buying decisions do not require such an extensive process, however. At the opposite extreme is habitual or routine decision-process behavior. Obviously this will be the most com-

Figure 2.8 A complete model of consumer behavior

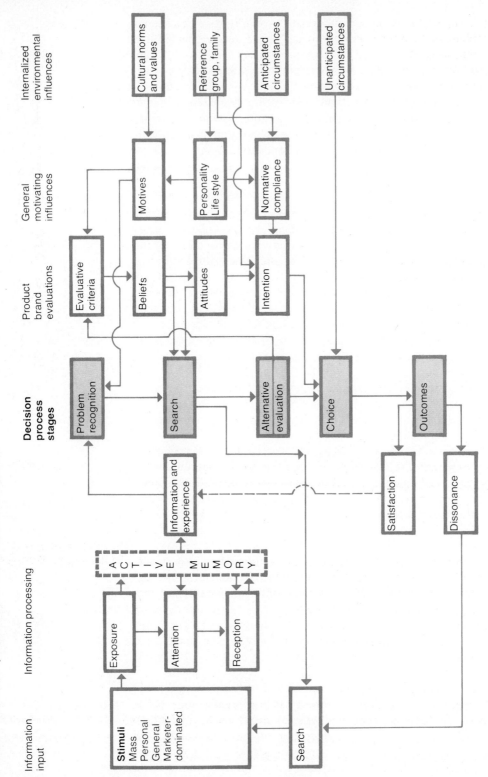

Information input | Information processing | | | | Product brand evaluations | General motivating influences | Internalized environmental influences

mon in that it seems to be human nature to form habits as quickly as possible. Problem recognition will lead directly to a purchase intention and then to a purchase. Beliefs and attitudes are fixed in the form of brand loyalty. Brand loyalty is of great concern to marketers, and it is discussed in more detail in Chapter 17.

In a sense, extended problem solving and routine behavior lie at the two ends of a continuum. In between is limited decision-process behavior, which occurs when there is good information about the domain of feasible alternatives but insufficient information about each to permit a sound decision. Thus, there is likely to be a certain amount of search and alternative evaluation.

Obviously the difference between these types of decision making is more one of degree than of kind. One possible determinant is the presence or absence of perceived risk. Risk may be financial, physical, or social. The consumer is aware that a wrong decision will have undesirable consequences, and extended problem solving often is resorted to in the hopes of reducing risk to tolerable levels. Many factors, then, are likely to evoke extended decision-process behavior. The extent of decision making varies greatly depending upon the individual, the social environment, and certain product and situation characteristics to be detailed later.

Using the model to explain consumer behavior

The discussion of the model and its components has, by necessity, been brief, and it is useful to trace two distinctly different buying situations: (1) the purchase of a small automobile and (2) the purchase of a laundry detergent.

While the discussion thus far has largely centered on an individual consumer, it is clear that social influences are important. The outcomes from one person's actions can serve as inputs for others. The model, therefore, can easily be utilized to explain the buying process of a family as well as that of an individual.

Purchase of the Volkswagen Dasher[6]

For most people the purchase of a new and previously unknown make of automobile will require extended problem-solving behavior. Experience with the Dasher introduced to the American public in January 1974 (see the introductory ad in Figure 2.9) was limited only to awareness of the Volkswagen name. Also the financial commitment was considerable, and the psychological stakes in selecting the right alternative were high. Almost 300 people who bought Dashers in April 1974 were interviewed, and some of the key findings are presented below.

Characteristics of purchasers. Dasher buyers tend to concentrate in the following demographic categories: married (74.8 percent); male (77.1 percent); under 35 (42.3 percent); college educated or beyond (77.2

6 Adapted from Roger D. Blackwell, James F. Engel, and W. Wayne Talarzyk, *Contemporary Cases in Consumer Behavior* (Hinsdale, Ill.: The Dryden Press, 1977), pp. 360–74.

Figure 2.9 Example of introductory print advertisement

Source: Reprinted by permission of Volkswagen of America.

percent); professional occupation (40.1 percent); higher income (nearly two-thirds beyond $15,000).

Problem recognition. Problem recognition usually occurs from factors beyond the marketer's control. In the purchase of a new automobile, for example, a problem becomes recognized most frequently when the currently owned vehicle becomes unsatisfactory for a variety of reasons. This may be generated by mechanical wear.

It is interesting to note, by the way, that 34.8 percent disposed of a Volkswagen when they acquired a Dasher. An additional 20 percent disposed of a smaller import or compact American car, thus indicating the presence of a desire to "move up" to a make that offered the advantages of small size along with better performance and the addition of luxury features.

Search. The data in Figure 2.10 indicate that television commercials were the major source of initial awareness of the Dasher. Magazine and

Figure 2.10 Sources of initial awareness of the Dasher

TV commercial	36.7%
Articles (magazines/newspapers)	16.4
At dealership (showroom/salesmen)	15.7
Advice of friends/relatives	6.8
Through Fox/Passat	5.3
Newspaper ads	4.7
Advertising (general)	4.6
Magazine ads	4.2
Other	5.6
Total	100.0%

newspaper articles were second in importance. The advice of friends and relatives ranked far down the list, undoubtedly because of the newness of this make. Results often are quite different with a more established make.

Alternative evaluation. The evaluative criteria utilized by Dasher buyers are itemized in Figure 2.11. Of these ten, gas mileage proved to be the dominant consideration. Manufacturer's reputation was next in order, as might be expected from the large number who traded in a Volkswagen Beetle. Apparently previous experience with this company had been satisfactory. Quality of workmanship and warranty coverage were the only additional criteria receiving frequent mention.

It is highly revealing to compare the customer's specifications with the sales points mentioned in the dealer's showroom. These appear in Figure 2.12. There should be a close match between them, but that apparently did not prove to be the case. Gas mileage did receive the most frequent mention, but there was a large discrepancy from then on. For example,

Figure 2.11 Evaluative criteria mentioned at least once as reason for purchase of the Dasher

Gas mileage	79.7%
Manufacturer's reputation	28.9
Quality of workmanship	22.8
Previous experience with make	21.3
Warranty coverage	18.2
Resale value	18.0
Handling ease	13.4
Interior room	13.0
Value for money	6.6
Exterior styling	6.5

Figure 2.12 Sales points mentioned at time of purchase

Gas mileage/economy	28.8%
Roominess	17.0
Front-wheel drive	16.2
None (poor salesmanship)	14.8
Handling/ease of driving	14.4
Economy of operation	12.9
Owner's Security Blanket/computer analysis	8.5
No sales points necessary (presold; knew more than salesman)	8.1
Engine, water-cooled/front-mounted	8.1
Performance	5.9
Design/style	5.5
Features (standard on Dasher but options/accessories on other makes)	5.5
Service	5.5
Quality of workmanship/construction	4.4
Safety	4.4
Engineering	4.4
Other	45.1

quality of workmanship rarely was stressed. Little attempt was made to capitalize upon reputation of manufacturer and previous positive experience with Volkswagens. The salesman tended either to do little or no real selling or to stress performance characteristics that were of less importance to the buyer. It should come as no surprise that initial sales results of the Dasher were far below expectations. The problem may lie at the level of dealership.

The Dasher carried a higher price tag than the traditional Beetle. Only 15.9 percent of those interviewed said that the price was about what was expected. Nearly half said that it was a little more than expected, and more than a third said it was a lot more than expected. The justifications given by salesmen for the price are in Figure 2.13. Quality of workmanship was stressed most frequently along with general inflation. Quality as an explanation should have been well received given the importance of this factor in the purchase decision.

Figure 2.13 Salesmens' justification for greater-than-expected price for the Dasher

Quality/workmanship	17.7%
General inflation	17.1
Didn't (salesman did not attempt to justify)	12.5
Dollar devaluation	11.8
Features (standard on Dasher; extra on other makes)	9.2
No reductions from list price	7.8
Unique car (superior/new)	6.5
Couldn't (salesman tried to justify but, according to customer, failed)	6.5
Increased value of trade-in	5.9
Low operating cost	5.2
Value for the money	3.9
Owner's Security Blanket	3.9
Performance	3.9
Increased production costs	3.9
Gas mileage	3.2

Choice. Part of the choice process is selection of the dealer. The data in Figure 2.14 indicate that physical proximity was the dominant consideration, with previous experience a distant second. Other factors were of less importance.

Figure 2.14 Primary reason for dealership selection

Closeness to dealer	40.9%
Previous experience	10.6
Service	8.2
Dealership personnel	7.8
Dealer reputation	7.2
Only one	6.2
Trade-in	5.8
Advice of friends	4.0
Other	9.3
Total	100.0%

Outcomes. Ownership satisfaction is of critical importance in continued loyalty to a given company. In the case of the Dasher, satisfaction was related to reaction to price. If the price was about as expected, the buyer tended to be quite satisfied, whereas satisfaction was much lower when the price was more than expected (see Figure 2.15).

Implications. Sales of the Dasher fell below expectations. Price appeared to be a major factor, and the relationship of reaction to price and buyer satisfaction is a real danger sign. The dissatisfied owner rarely keeps these reactions to himself, and future sales are bound to be affected. Furthermore, the quality of salesmanship at the dealer level reflected a poor grasp

Figure 2.15 Satisfaction versus initial reaction to price

	Dasher price was	
	About what expected	A little/lot more than expected
Completely/very satisfied	70.7%	50.7%
Fairly well satisfied	19.5	26.9
Somewhat dissatisfied	4.9	19.2
Very dissatisfied	4.9	3.2
	100.0%	100.0%

of buyer expectations. A reversal of the negative trend will depend in large part on remedial action taken in the marketing program.

The purchase of a laundry detergent[7]

Laundry detergents generally are purchased on the basis of habit rather than extended problem solving. A problem is recognized when the housewife runs out of detergent, and her decision usually calls for purchase of a preferred brand on her next visit to the grocery store. There is no need to engage in conscious weighing of alternatives or external search for information. The situation changes, of course, when a significant new product comes on the market, but innovations of that magnitude are a rarity in this industry.

Survey results showed that women evaluate a detergent on the following bases: (1) cleaning ability (96 percent), (2) low suds (54 percent), (3) safety to colors (48 percent), (4) whitening and brightening ability (44 percent), (5) price (31 percent), and (6) fresh smell (20 percent). In addition to these evaluative criteria, 86 percent favored a powdered form, and 60 percent prefer to use warm water.

Several major brands were found to rate highest on these criteria, with Tide being the dominant favorite. These ratings of brand attitude closely paralleled market shares. The result is strong loyalty toward one or two preferred brands and only relatively small incidence of permanent brand switching. If the housewife does switch it tends to be a temporary action to take advantage of a price reduction.

Those who were interviewed, for the most part, evidenced satisfaction with their present alternative. Post-decision evaluation, therefore, seldom takes place.

It becomes difficult under this type of decision making based on strong brand loyalty to induce a brand switch through marketing efforts. Thus, the objectives for the leading manufacturers usually call for maintenance of the present market share through continual product improvement to prevent competitive inroads and a high level of advertising to retain present levels of awareness and preference. Also it is important to feature

7 This section is based on a study undertaken at Ohio State University in cooperation with the Procter and Gamble Company.

price reductions through coupons and other means both to stimulate consumer purchase and to generate interest by retailers in stocking and displaying the product.

Summary

This chapter provided the conceptual framework for the remainder of the book. Its primary purpose has been to clarify the importance of the decision process perspective. It was pointed out that the consumer decision process has five distinct steps: (1) problem recognition; (2) search for information; (3) alternative evaluation; (4) choice; and (5) outcomes of choice (satisfaction and dissonance). The extent to which each step is undertaken depends upon whether or not the purchase is of sufficient importance to warrant extended problem solving. Most decisions are based on habit, in which case problem recognition is followed by choice without search and analysis.

Many variables affect the decision process. A model of consumer behavior was introduced briefly to delineate these significant variables and to illustrate how they affect the behavioral process. Each is discussed at length elsewhere in the book. The chapter concluded with two examples of consumer studies where this model was utilized to gain insights into the decision processes and to reveal marketing strategies.

The remainder of the book is organized around the stages of the decision process. Part 2 probes into the social and cultural environment and the role it has on behavior. This is an important factor in understanding behavior, and this background must be established at the outset. The next three parts then focus on problem recognition, search, alternative evaluation, and choice and its outcomes. Part 6 presents an integrated perspective on consumer behavior and delves more deeply into the subject of models of consumer behavior and the research implications. The concluding section raises the important issues of consumer protection and the ethics of consumer influence.

Review and discussion questions

1. One authority says that an attitude is a "set to respond." Another says it is a "tendency to evaluate people and things along a continuum of positive to negative." Still another says it is a "predisposition to think and act in a certain way." Why should there be such variation in definition of a common term?

2. What is a model? What role does a model play in understanding consumer behavior?

3. What arguments can be advanced to defend the widespread tendency for many people in marketing, especially those who have been trained since 1960, to specialize in one or more of the related behavioral sciences? What possible dangers exist?

4. In speaking of the problems that might result from psychological analysis of consumer behavior, Vance Packard stated, "Much of it seems to represent regress rather than progress for man in his struggle to become a rational and

self-guiding being" (*Hidden Persuaders*, New York: McKay, 1957, p. 6). The main point is that marketing persuaders now have new tools that enable them to manipulate the consumer and circumvent processes of reasoning. Comment.

5. How might a large manufacturer of automatic washers and dryers use a decision-process approach to better understand how consumers purchase his product?

6. Mrs. Jones is ironing and watching her favorite afternoon soap opera, which is on the air from 2:30 to 3:00 P.M. There are seven commercials in 30 minutes, and she does not leave the room. Yet she cannot recall a single commercial after the show has ended, whereas she can recount the plot of the story in detail. What explanations can be given?

7. Much buying supposedly occurs on impulse; that is, a person sees a display or other stimulus and buys with little or no forethought. Can impulse behavior be accounted for in the model? How?

8. In analyzing the entire model, is it complete in the sense of encompassing all the major elements in the psychological field? What changes, if any, might be made?

9. Latin American culture differs in major ways from the North American culture. For example, people tend to be more important than things. Materialism, while significant, does not dominate this concern with the feelings of others. Time tends to be of little consequence. "If it doesn't get done today, there is always tomorrow" is not an unusual sentiment. Finally, "machismo" or assertion of manly superiority is a powerful male motivation in all phases of life. While there is much more to be said about the Latin culture, how would these three factors affect consumer behavior in that setting as compared with the North American environment?

10. Compare and contrast the decision processes that might be involved in the purchase of a sport coat if the purchase is represented as (a) extended decision-process behavior, (b) limited decision-process behavior, (c) habitual decision-process behavior. Which type of decision making would be most likely? Why?

11. Indicate which type of decision making would be most likely in each of the following situations (assume all things are equal): (a) past experience with the product has been unsatisfactory, (b) the product is purchased each week, (c) a new home has been purchased, (d) the consumer earns less than $3,000 per year, (e) the product is needed immediately.

12. What is meant by perceived risk? What is the relevance of this concept?

13. "Charles Terwilliger is a high school senior and faces the dilemma of choosing a college. He is a good student and has made all-state mention as defensive end in football. His father is a graduate of a well-known eastern school and would like to see Charles go there. Two schools in his home state have offered him football scholarships, and one has twice been national champion in the past five years. Charles's three best friends, however, are going to live at home and go to the local university, whereas the girl he has dated for three years will be attending a university on the West Coast, 2,000 miles away. He has applied to all of these schools and has been accepted. He

needs financial aid and plans to become a consulting engineer. Finally he accepts the football tender at the school in his state, which has been national champion; in addition, this university has a good engineering curriculum. The problem, though, is that he has no friends there and has no real desire to join a fraternity, the apparent key to popularity." To test your grasp of the model presented in this chapter, explain what must have happened during and after this decision. Make any assumptions that are necessary.

PART 2

THE SOCIAL & CULTURAL ENVIRONMENT

The preceding two chapters have presented an overview of the decision process of consumers. Now the task is to begin to examine the determinants of behavior in more detail.

The question can be asked: Where should one begin in the effort to understand why people do the things they do and make the choices they make? Although a variety of beginnings are possible, one logical starting place is with the broad environmental variables that shape and constrain consumer choices.

Environmental influences such as cultural, economic, and demographic realities are lifetime experiences. That is, they not only influence specific consumer choices but they are operative from birth to determine and shape the nature of a person in ways that influence all decisions of the person. Because of the generic nature of environmental influences, they become especially important when large segments of the population experience the same environmental influences. When social and cultural influences are operative for a large group of persons, that group may be identified as a market segment for which specific communication or marketing strategies are appropriate.

Four chapters are presented in this part of the textbook, analyzing environmental influences on consumer behavior. They present some of the most important and most interesting, yet often neglected and misunderstood, aspects of the study of consumer behavior.

Chapter 3 analyzes the broadest category of environmental influences, the economic structure variables that provide the economic context of consumer behavior. The economic and demographic structures of markets in the United States are described, but many of the trends discussed here are also occurring in other industrially advanced countries.

The topic of cultural norms and values is introduced in Chapter 4. In this chapter, the emphasis is upon values in a cross-cultural setting, both in various nations and in various subcultures such as ethnic, racial and religious groups. A subsection of the chapter discusses black consumer behavior as compared with white consumer behavior. This chapter also contains a description of formal methods of studying cultural norms and values, especially from a cross-cultural approach.

Is social class becoming more or less important as a phenomenon in the American culture? Chapter 5 analyzes this issue and the process of stratification. This chapter describes the factors that determine a person's social class, some methods of measuring social class, and some of the empirical research which indicates differential consumer behavior between social classes.

Chapter 6 describes reference group and family influences on consumer decisions. Reference groups play an important role in determining individual decisions and function in society as conformity-enforcing devices. Family influences are of great importance in consumer behavior as reference group influences on individual decisions. In addition, there is much to be learned from studying the decisions of families considered as buying units. This chapter describes the basic terminology involved in analysis of family buying, as well as the empirical research that is emerging concerning family structure and decision-making.

The final chapter in the part concerns life styles and their role in developing marketing strategy. In many ways, this chapter is built upon the previous four chapters because life styles encompass all of the other economic and sociopsychological chapters described in this part, in a manner that is particularly useful in the development of marketing strategy.

CHAPTER 3

Economic and demographic influences on consumption

After studying consumer behavior, a young consumer was heard to comment that he needed to buy a new car and wanted to buy a car that was closely matched to his "life style." He studied marketing offerings carefully and concluded that there existed a car that was precisely matched to the life style preferences of his market segment. The car was a Porsche Turbo Carerra! When checking the price of the car, however, he sadly concluded that the car did not meet his economic circumstances even though it satisfied his attitude and belief structure quite well.

Effects of the internalized environment on intentions and choices

The incident with the Porsche described above demonstrates the influence that demographic and economic variables may have on intentions and choices of a product. *Anticipated* circumstances are internalized into the mind of the consumer and become part of the consumer's decision making process, resulting in intentions to purchase a particular product or brand. These anticipated circumstances include economic, demographic and other variables and may operate either as a positive (inducing) constraint or as a negative (inhibiting) constraint. In the Porsche example, the consumer may be thinking of the intended use of the car, may be reflecting his age, employment, or residence location, and other circumstances that have been *internalized from the environment* of the consumer and that are consciously or unconsciously considered in forming preferences or intentions.

Even though a consumer intends to make a purchase, the actual choice process may be modified by *unanticipated circumstances.* Those unanticipated circumstances may include sudden changes in income (such as those caused by unemployment), changes in residence or physical circumstances (such as low temperatures in a home caused by an energy crisis) or other variables which become internalized in the consumer's mind and affect the choice process. Other unanticipated variables may include marketing-dominated variables such as price deals, coupons, stock-outs, salesperson influences and so forth. This latter type of influence will be discussed in some depth in Chapters 9 and 10 and in 18. The process of influence on intentions and choices by internalized environmental variables is shown in Figure 3.1.

Figure 3.1 Influences of anticipated and unanticipated circumstances on intention and choice

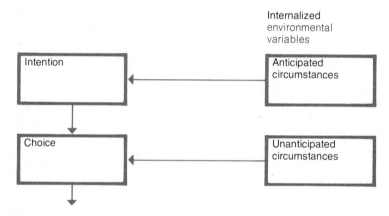

The market potential for any product is created by people with economic resources with which to satisfy their needs and desires. The logical starting point for a consumer analyst, therefore, is the determination of the numbers of people that exist (demographics) and the amount of economic resources those people have (income, employment, and so forth). More detailed analysis of population demographics (by age, family status, mobility, and so forth) may provide information not only about ability to buy but often may be helpful in understanding their predisposition to buy a product. In other words, the needs and desires of consumers may be closely associated with their age, family condition, geographic location, mobility, and so forth.

In the preparation of a marketing research report for business or other organizations, the starting place is usually a demographic and economic analysis. A structural analysis of consumption is necessary to establish the parameters of demand for a product. Additionally, a preliminary analysis of demographic and economic factors is usually necessary before beginning more in-depth studies of behavioral variables. The sampling plan for determining which customers are to be studied, for example, usually requires detailed compilation of information about age structure, geographic characteristics, or other demographic variables.

Most marketing research reports will include information about some or all of the following circumstances of consumers: age, income, education, geographic characteristics, sex and/or marital characteristics.

In the following pages, some of the important demographic and economic trends are described as they are occurring in the United States and, generally, in other industrial countries. Following the description of these trends, two examples are provided that demonstrate how these characteristics may influence consumer intentions and choices and how one successful firm, Steak and Ale, adapts to changes in demographic trends. At the end of the chapter, an additional circumstance of choice, consumer time budgets, is also analyzed.

Sources of demographic and economic data

The purpose of this chapter is to describe the kinds of variables a consumer analyst might consider as a starting place in understanding the purchase and consumption of products. When considering broad situational variables of demographic and economic influence, it is a safe assumption to believe that the needed data probably exist if only they can be found. A diligent analyst of consumer behavior can find much useful information from secondary sources in a good research library. This section describes some of the most useful and basic of these sources.

Census data

The first nationwide population census in the United States was conducted in 1770. It took 18 months to complete and was an enumeration of "free and slave" persons in each state. In 1820, questions on citizenship and industry were added and in 1850 questions were added pertaining to marital status, place of birth, occupation, and value of real estate. In 1950, the Census Bureau introduced several sampling techniques as alternative methods to collecting census required information and today many questions that are described as "census data" are really sampling data based on interviews of 5 to 20 percent of the population. Only a few basic questions (head of household, race, age, sex, marital status) are asked of 100 percent of the population queried.

The most important source of demographic data in the United States is probably the Bureau of Census of the U.S. Department of Commerce. The nature of the data collected and reported by the Census is described in Figure 3.2. The Bureau of Economic Analysis of the Department of Commerce provides additional information of great value including demographic projections of midyear population, per capita income, total employment and total personal earnings, cross-tabulated by various classifications. Their projections extend through 1990.

Several nongovernment sources of demographic and market data are important to consumer researchers. One of these is the American Research Bureau, which compiles data on the basis of area of dominant

Figure 3.2 Summary census reports by subject

Subject
Number of inhabitants
Summary characteristics

General and social characteristics
Age:
　Single years of age
　Age groups
Race
Nativity and parentage
Place of birth
Country of birth or country of origin
Mother tongue
Citizenship
Year of immigration
Residence in 1965
　By selected classes of migrants
Year moved into present house
School enrollment
Years of school completed
　Persons 16 to 24 years old
　Family heads
　By age
　By occupation
　By income
　By poverty status
　Percent by level of school completed
Vocational training
Work disability
Veteran status
Marital status
Marital history
Fertility:
　Children ever born
　Own children under 5 years old
Households and household relationship
Group quarters
Inmates of institutions

Families:
　By presence or number of own
　　children under 18 years old
By type and composition
By characteristics of head and
　wife
By earnings or income
By poverty status
Subfamilies
Unrelated individuals
　By age
　By marital status
　By income
　By poverty status

Economic characteristics
Labor force status
Employment status
　By age
　By school enrollment
　For males 16–21 not attending
　　school
　By earnings or income
　By poverty status
Hours worked
Weeks worked in 1969
　By occupation or industry
　By earnings or poverty status
Work experience in 1969
Year last worked

Subject
Occupation:
　By detailed classification
　By age
　By years of school completed
　By employment characteristics
　By industry
　By class of worker

By earnings or income
By poverty status
By occupation 5 years ago
Of experienced unemployed
Industry:
　By detailed classification
　By age
　By employment characteristics
　By occupation
　By class of worker
　By earnings or income
Class of worker
Activity 5 years ago
　Place of work
　Means of transportation to work
Income in 1969:
　Persons
　　By family status
　　By years of school completed
　　By employment characteristics
　　By type of income
　Unrelated individuals
　Households
Earnings in 1969:
　By occupation
　By industry
　By place of work
　By weeks worked

Subject
Poverty status in 1969:
　Persons
　Families
　　By characteristics of head
　　By presence or number of
　　　children under 18
　　By type of income
　Unrelated individuals
　Households

Note: Only the major subjects are listed above; many cross-tabulations exist, and data are also provided for various geographical areas.
Source: U.S. Bureau of the Census, Census of Population: *1970 Vol. 1, Characteristics of the Population* Part 1 United States Summary—Section I and II.

influence or ADI, a geographical market area comprised of contiguous counties defined on the basis of measurable television viewing patterns. For each ADI, information is available concerning the estimated number of television households by county, number of adult women and number of adult men in ADI, number of teenagers in ADI, and number of children between two and 12 years old.

"Survey of Buying Power"

Another widely used source of demographic and economic data is *Sales Management's* "Survey of Buying Power" (SBP). Published in July each year, the SBP contains data on population, effective buying income, and retail sales data for all standard metropolitan statistical areas, states, counties and cities in the United States and for most metropolitan areas, provinces, counties, and cities in Canada.

Realizing the need to make the mountains of demographic data accumulated by the Bureau of the Census more usable and actionable by marketing researchers, a firm was formed called the Claritas Corporation. (Claritas is the Latin Word for "clarity" or "intelligibility.") By drawing upon many agencies of the federal government and the U.S. Postal Service for data, the Claritas Corporation was able to detail the demographic and economic characteristics for each residential ZIP code area in the United States. The result of their work is published in the *National Zip Code Encyclopedia,* which gives detailed population and housing data for all of the over 38,000 residential ZIP areas throughout the United States. In addition to these sources, the National Planning Association and many other organizations publish data helpful in describing the demographic characteristics of consumer demand.

The total population of the United States is still expanding and is projected to reach 234.1 million in 1985. In Canada, the projected population will be between 26 and 28 million people by that date.[1] In these and other highly industrialized countries population growth is slowing, and at some point in the future it will hit ZPG—zero population growth. This will dramatically affect marketing strategies that have historically been built upon the assumption of increasing *quantities* of consumers and must shift to emphasis upon development in the *quality* of consumption rather than quantity.

Although markets in the United States are still increasing, the increases are not uniform by age group. Figure 3.3 describes the changes in the population by age group and shows a dramatic rise in the 25–34 age group in the years prior to 1980. This is of particular significance in explaining intentions to buy because of the increase in new households that accompanies such a population trend and the attendant demand for equipping those households. Such a trend results in the purchase of new homes or apartment units, furniture and home furnishings, major and minor appliances, and changed clothing requirements. Correlated with the purchase of those products is a rise in services such as financial services, home care services (or the substitute—do-it-yourself products), and many other services.

Significant changes in consumer demand of another type will occur in the time period of 1980 to 1985, however. Particularly important is the declining rate of growth of the 25–34 age market as these people become older and move into the 35–44 category. During this time period, there will simultaneously be a reduction in the rate of growth of first-time and replacement purchasers of many types of household goods. Marketing

---

1 Additional details of the demography of Canadian markets may be found in Edward B. Harvey, "Demographics and Future Marketing Implications in Canada," *The Business Quarterly*, vol. 41 (Summer 1976), pp. 61–65.

Figure 3.3 Estimates and projections of the total population by age group, United States 1974–1985 (selected years)

Age group	1974		1980		1985		Change: 1974–1980		Change: 1980–1985	
	Number	Percent	Number	Percent	Number	Percent	Number	Percent	Number	Percent
0–4	16.3	7.7%	17.3	7.8%	19.8	8.4%	1.0	6.1%	2.5	14.5%
5–9	17.6	8.3	16.1	7.2	17.5	7.5	(1.5)	(8.5)	1.4	8.7
10–14	20.7	9.8	17.8	8.0	16.6	7.1	(2.9)	(14.0)	(1.2)	(6.7)
15–19	20.8	9.8	20.6	9.2	18.0	7.7	(.2)	(1.0)	(2.6)	(12.6)
20–24	18.7	8.8	20.9	9.4	20.5	8.7	2.2	11.8	(.4)	(1.9)
25–34	29.7	14.0	36.1	16.2	39.9	17.0	6.4	21.6	3.8	10.5
35–44	22.8	10.8	25.7	11.6	31.3	13.4	2.9	12.7	5.6	21.8
45–54	23.9	11.3	22.6	10.2	22.4	9.6	(1.3)	(5.4)	(.2)	(.9)
55–64	19.5	9.2	21.0	9.4	21.5	9.2	1.5	7.7	.5	2.4
65 and over	21.8	10.3	24.5	11.0	26.6	11.4	2.7	12.4	2.1	8.6
Total	211.8	100.0%	222.6	100.0%	234.1	100.0%	10.8	5.1%	11.5	5.2%

Source: U.S. Department of Commerce and authors' calculations.

organizations that relied on new households coming into the market will have to shift to other means—such as broadened product lines or diversification, rather than natural growth of the population—in order to achieve significant growth.

A significant by-product of the changing age composition is its effect on mobility of the population. During a recent year, Department of Commerce statistics revealed the following percent of population moving in each age group:

Age:	Percentage of population moving
3–13	36.4
14–17	23.0
18–24	23.9
25–34	51.5
35–44	27.5
45–64	17.7

Understanding the differential mobility rates leads to important marketing adaptation. Less brand loyalty in geographically specific market offerings—such as banks, grocery stores, services, and so forth—could be expected in the younger (especially 25–34 age group) market segments. This requires more aggressive advertising and communication strategies. At the same time, this mobility may provide greater loyalty among high mobility segments to establishments that have a recognized level of quality in all geographic areas. Firms like McDonald's, Steak and Ale, and T.G.I. Friday may benefit from a recognizable name compared to local firms.

Figure 3.3 also reveals the continuing and expanding importance of the "seniors" or "mature" markets—those in the age group over 65. This group may have restricted money budgets and limited needs for new or replacement durable goods but expanded time budgets and greater needs for services.

Increasing education of consumers

Consumers in much of the world are becoming more educated. In 1960, there were only 8.2 million college graduates in the United States, but by 1980, college graduates are projected to number more than 19 million. Figure 3.4 displays the number of consumers estimated to be at each level

Figure 3.4 Estimates and projections of persons by highest level of educational achievement, United States 1975–1985 (selected years)

| Educational level | Persons 25 years and over (in millions of persons) | | | | | | Change: 1975–1980 | | Change: 1980–1985 | |
| | 1975 | | 1980 | | 1985 | | | | | |
	Number	Percent	Number	Percent	Number	Percent	Number	Percent	Number	Percent
Elementary school or less	27.0	22.8%	23.5	18.3%	20.1	14.4%	(3.5)	(13.0%)	(3.4)	(14.5%)
Some high school	19.9	16.8	20.9	16.3	21.6	15.4	1.0	5.0	.7	3.3
High school graduate	42.8	36.3	48.7	37.9	54.4	39.0	5.9	13.8	5.7	11.7
Some college	13.3	11.3	16.1	12.5	19.2	13.7	2.8	21.1	3.1	19.3
College graduate or more	15.1	12.8	19.3	15.0	24.5	17.5	4.2	27.8	5.2	26.9
Total	118.2	100.0%	128.5	100.0%	139.9	100.0%	10.3	8.7%	11.4	8.9%

Source: U.S. Department of Commerce and authors' calculations.

of educational achievement and projects that by 1985 less than 15 percent of adults over 25 will have only an elementary school or less education.

The effect of higher education is likely to be greater sophistication in consumer decisions. As such, consumers are likely to be more demanding in the areas of product quality, warranties, sales assistance and a variety of marketing policies. Moreover, they will be supported in their demands by the multitude of consumer protection agencies which have evolved in recent years and which proliferate with increasing levels of education. Education affects many areas of consumer behavior, including media preferences, time and leisure preferences and even the types of messages that are most likely to be effective.

Increasing employment of women

Women have generally been recognized as the primary purchasers for many consumer products. It is of special importance, therefore, when the proportion of women who are employed outside the home is also increasing. Excluding women 65 years of age and over and those with children under 6 years of age, more than 40 percent of all women are employed outside the household. Figure 3.5 shows that the percentage varies depending upon age and marital status.

Figure 3.5 Estimates and projections of characteristics of women in the labor force, United States 1950–1985 (selected years)

Characteristics of women	1950	1960	1970	1973	1980	1985
General characteristics						
Percent of women in labor force	33.3%	37.1%	42.8%	44.2%	45.0%	45.6%
Percent of married women in labor force	23.8	30.5	40.8	42.2		
Labor force participation rates—all women						
16–19	80.3%	79.6%	88.0%	94.9%	90.8%	92.4%
20–24	45.5	46.1	57.5	61.6	63.4	64.9
25–34	33.5	35.8	44.8	49.9	50.2	50.9
35–44	38.1	43.1	50.9	52.8	53.2	54.4
45–54	38.1	49.3	54.0	53.2	56.2	57.4
55–64	27.5	36.7	42.5	41.1	44.7	45.4
65 and over	8.9	10.5	9.2	8.4	8.6	8.5
Labor force participation rates—married women						
16–19	24.0%	25.3%	36.0%	42.2%		
20–24	28.5	30.0	47.4	52.9		
25–34	23.8	27.7	39.3	44.1		
35–44	28.5	36.2	47.2	49.3		
45–64	21.8	34.2	44.1	42.9		
65 and over	6.4	5.9	7.9	6.5		
Stage in family life cycle						
No children under 18 present	30.3%	34.7%	42.2%	42.8%		
Children 6 to 17 years only	28.3	39.0	49.2	50.1		
Children under 6 years	11.9	18.6	30.3	32.7		

Source: U.S. Department of Labor and authors' calculations.

The emergence of more and more women working outside the home suggests circumstances creating new opportunities for sales of numerous products and services, including cosmetics, apparel, day-care centers, and convenience foods. In addition, they are more receptive to time and labor-saving products and services, cleaning and home maintenance services and so on. Furniture and home furnishings products that are aesthetically acceptable and require mimimum maintenance and upkeep are particularly well-positioned to capitalize on the anticipated circumstances of many consumers.

Increasing employment of women may also force reevaluation of store hours and delivery schedules. Perhaps a noon to 10:00 P.M. configuration may be more appropriate than a conventional schedule of store hours. Media that require a minimum of time or permit dual usage (such as listening to radio while performing household tasks) may become more valuable.

At the same time that direct effects of women working are considered, indirect effects may also result. Males may become more involved in household care as a result of shared responsibilities with females and consequently become more aware of the marketing of household products. Similarly, grocery stores are discovering that grocery shopping is increasingly done by males or in shared shopping modes. Additional effects on family decisions resulting from women working are considered in Chapter 6 (Family and reference group influences).

The proliferation of affluence

For several decades, millions of Americans have enjoyed steadily increasing earnings. Although there have been setbacks in individual years, this improvement resulted in the shift of millions of families from lower earning levels to the middle income brackets. There are significant economic problems—such as inflation, shortages of energy and unemployment—but assuming methods of coping with these problems can be achieved, the time frame of 1975 to 1985 should be one in which several million families will also move into upper income categories. These projections are shown in Figure 3.6.

Figure 3.6 Estimates and projections of households by income class, United States 1972–1985

Income class (in constant 1972 dollars)	Households (in millions)						Change: 1972–1980		Change: 1980–1985	
	1972		1980		1985					
	Number	Percent	Number	Percent	Number	Percent	Number	Percent	Number	Percent
Under $3,000	9.6	14.0%	9.3	12.0%	9.3	11.0%	(.3)	(3.1%)	-0-	-0-%
$3,000–5,000	7.5	11.0	8.1	10.5	8.4	10.0	.6	8.0	.3	3.7
$5,000–7,000	7.2	10.5	7.7	10.0	7.6	9.0	.5	6.9	(.1)	(1.3)
$7,000–10,000	10.9	16.0	11.2	14.5	11.8	14.0	.3	2.8	.6	5.4
$10,000–15,000	15.7	23.0	17.8	23.0	18.5	22.0	2.1	13.4	.7	3.9
$15,000–25,000	13.3	19.5	17.0	22.0	21.0	25.0	3.7	27.8	4.0	23.5
$25,000 and over	4.1	6.0	6.2	8.0	7.6	9.0	2.1	51.2	1.4	22.6
Total	68.3	100.0%	77.3	100.0%	84.2	100.0%	9.0	13.2%	6.9	8.9%

Source: U.S. Department of Commerce, Conference Board, and authors' calculations. Reprinted by permission of The Conference Board.

There are several reasons for the proliferation of affluence, but one of the most important is the rising number of multiple-earner households, chiefly the phenomenon or working wives described earlier. For families earning $15,000 and over in the mid-'70s about 75 percent were characterized as multiple wage-earner families.

Several implications may be drawn from the projections of income in Figure 3.6. One pertains to the social problem created by pockets of poverty in the midst of affluence. Many observers would argue that the frustration of the outnumbered poor is accentuated by the realization that most others in a society are affluent and can buy the "good things" offered in a market economy. Thus, an advertisement on television describing an attractive auto or appliance is viewed by poor families just as often as affluent families with positive effects on beliefs and attitudes toward the product but always accompanied by the frustrating realization that economic circumstances do not permit the poor family to choose what the rest of the society can buy.

A more positive effect of the proliferation of affluence is the rise in discretionary choices made possible by the majority of a society rising above the economic level of subsistence. Something more than basic food, clothing and shelter is possible for the majority of the society, permitting the satisfaction of a wide range of self-desires for what has been described as the "me" generation. The discretionary society has even been described as the "indiscretionary society" since it includes the freedom to be indiscreet or indulge in one's most personal preferences. One consumer may form intentions that result in spending discretionary income on stereo components, another on clothing, another on autos, another on travel and so forth.

What one consumer chooses to buy with his or her economic resources may seem imprudent to another. That simply verifies that a truly discretionary economy is operating in which individuals express their personal tastes and preferences rather than having no discretion in their purchases (as in an impoverished economy) or having the tastes and preferences of some other person imposed on them (as in a controlled economy).

In an affluent society, the majority of consumers can *buy most anything they want, but they cannot buy everything they want!* Life, to a much greater extent than where affluence is not widespread, is a continual process of choices between a huge array of goods and services from which some or even many but almost never all can be chosen. It is the great increase in choice possibilities and the complexity of decision influences that has in part stimulated consumer research and given rise to so many courses in the discipline of consumer behavior.

Discretionary income is a concept that applies to a broad range of American consumers, but recently marketing organizations are focusing more attention on families with *supernumerary income*, or those families who are relatively rich. In 1974, for example, 22 percent of the families in the United States had incomes of over $20,000 with an average income in that bracket of $29,200.[2] This set of economic circumstances has account-

2 An excellent discussion of this and other trends in affluence is available in Fabian Linden, *Consumers and Markets* (New York: National Industrial Conference Board, 1976). Also see George H. Brown, "Census Projections: 1970 to 1985," *Management Accounting* (January 1973), pp. 11–14; George H. Brown, "America's New Demographic Profile," The Conference Board *Record* (October 1975), pp. 53–56. For a discussion of some of the threats to affluence see Edmund Faltermayer, "Ever Increasing Affluence Is Less of a Sure Thing," *Fortune* (April 1975), pp. 92–97 ff.

ed for spectacular growth in the demand for many goods and services such as winter vacations, imported wines, gourmet cooking supplies, personal development services and a wide range of other items. The purchases of this segment account for a much greater concentration of the total sales of some companies than the proportion of the population represented in this segment.

The geography of demand

Geography is an important discipline in the study of spatial aspects of market. Geographical circumstances most profoundly affect the location of retailing facilities but may also be important in media exposure and in certain types of product preferences. Two of the most important geographic influences include the rising importance of metropolitan areas and the uneven growth of regions.

A long-term population concentration is occurring in metropolitan areas. Figure 3.7 shows that the population of the United States is projected to be 73 percent metropolitan by 1980 and to be 76 percent by 1990. Income distribution, or purchasing power, is even more concentrated in metropolitan areas.

Rising importance of metropolitan areas

Figure 3.7 Population and income distribution in metropolitan areas

	Population density people/sq.mi.		Population distribution			Income distribution		
	Non-metro	Metro	Non-metro	Central cities	Other metro	Non-metro	Central cities	Other metro
1950	20.0	410	44%	35%	21%	38%	35%	27%
1960	20.5	365	37	33	30	32	33	35
1970	20.3	325	31	32	37	27	32	41
1980	20.3	300	27	28	45	23	28	49
1990	20.3	290	24	25	51	21	25	54

Source: U.S. Bureau of the Census and authors' calculations.

Suburbs are the real winners in population growth. Since World War II, the population of the suburbs has been increasing more than twice as fast as the total population and over five times as fast as the central cities. With growing urban problems, the growth in the number of young families, and with rising affluence, the United States will become even more of a suburban society during the next few years. Mass transportation experts, financial officials and city planners are trying to stop the exodus to the suburbs, but consumers show no signs of reversing the life style preferences that seem most compatible with suburban residences.

An interesting result of these two trends—moving from rural areas to cities and from central cities to suburbs—is the decrease in population density of metropolitan areas, revealed in Exhibit 3.7. This trend has been amplified by the rising prices of adjacent farm land frequently making retention of the land for farm purposes not viable. The net result for marketing facilities has been the rise of the supersize, regional shopping center requiring large amounts of acreage on freeways outside of the densely populated suburbs—which, in turn, contributes to even more growth away from the downtown or central city.

Uneven regional growth

Within the United States and Canada, wide differences exist in the growth rates of states or provinces, requiring marketing organizations to adapt continuously to these migrations. Areas that are enjoying above average growth rates tend to have certain distinguishing characteristics. For the most part, they tend to be located near the water, and/or in warmer climates, and/or in areas noted for winter sports activities, and/or in areas where energy is relatively plentiful and inexpensive. These trends are of great importance to marketing locations in planning distribution centers and store networks as well as having important effects upon product preferences for many types of goods.

Geography and marketing

Increasingly, the study of consumer behavior involves the use of geography, and it is therefore natural that the tools of geography be adapted to consumer research. One kind of statistical-geographic research that is proving to be useful is the plotting of population centers of the United States. Another tool from the discipline of geography is one where *combinations of demographic attributes* are reproduced in map form. An organization that has discovered that both income and education, for example, are important circumstances affecting consumer intentions and choices could use this technique to prepare a map that instantly discloses the geographic regions that are appropriate markets.

Demographic analysis and marketing strategy

A demographic and economic analysis of the circumstances affecting consumer intentions and choices is capable of yielding direct applications to marketing strategy. One example of such an application is shown in Figure 3.8, in which Management Horizons, a consulting organization, has prepared a systematic analysis of demographic trends for retailing organizations. In that exhibit, it may be seen that 14 demographic trends have been identified. Each of these trends has been analyzed in terms of probable positive or negative effects on sales of products by merchandise line, and the results are shown in the matrix on Figure 3.8.

Case example— Steak and Ale, Inc.

A further example of how demographic analysis is useful in understanding the success or failure of marketing offerings is provided by a case example—Steak and Ale, Inc.

Steak and Ale opened 27 new restaurants in 1977 to add to their 100 existing restaurants at the beginning of the year. With sales of over $150 million and over 10,000 employees, this was a long way from the one 96-seat restaurant opened in Dallas in 1965. It ranks as one of the most

Figure 3.8 Demographic impact on marketing strategy

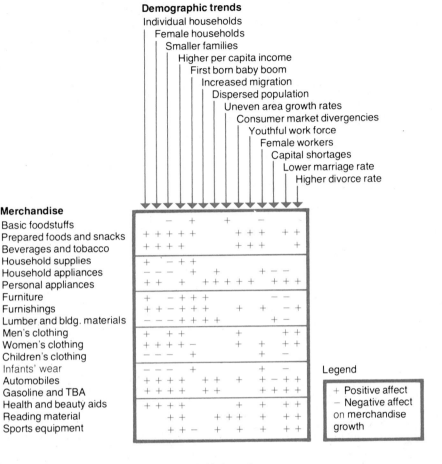

Demographic trends
Individual households
Female households
Smaller families
Higher per capita income
First born baby boom
Increased migration
Dispersed population
Uneven area growth rates
Consumer market divergencies
Youthful work force
Female workers
Capital shortages
Lower marriage rate
Higher divorce rate

Merchandise
Basic foodstuffs
Prepared foods and snacks
Beverages and tobacco
Household supplies
Household appliances
Personal appliances
Furniture
Furnishings
Lumber and bldg. materials
Men's clothing
Women's clothing
Children's clothing
Infants' wear
Automobiles
Gasoline and TBA
Health and beauty aids
Reading material
Sports equipment

Legend
+ Positive affect
− Negative affect
on merchandise
growth

Source: Reprinted by permission of Management Horizons, Inc.

dramatic success stories of the past decade. The chain emphasizes a rational, limited lunch and dinner steak menu in an informal Old English atmosphere. The restaurants are opened under the name "Jolly Ox" where legislation prohibits use of an alcoholic beverage in a name and as "Three Crowns" in Canada.

Steak and Ale's primary market is the young, married, affluent family. Prices for a dinner or lunch meet or beat local competition for a comparable meal. The labor content is kept low by offering a limited menu and a self-service salad bar and by employing part-time college students.

Many interrelated demographic factors have contributed to the success of the Steak and Ale chain, but perhaps the most important is the increased number of working wives who in turn increase their food-away-from-home expenditures. The trends place a premium on convenience at a reasonable price—and Steak and Ale meets those requirements. They are positioned with an upscale thematic restaurant concept to serve a rapidly expanding "young married" market.

The importance of demographic analysis in marketing strategy is explained by the management of Steak and Ale:

> We are participants in an industry offering a service for which there is a large consumer demand. The demand can be expected to increase due to such economic, demographic and sociological factors as increasing personal disposable income, increasing number of young adults, increasing number of working wives and increasing leisure time. Our challenge continues to be one of satisfying this demand in a steady orderly manner.[3]

Consumer time budgets

The rising affluence of recent decades has led to a growing recognition that consumer resources consist of two budget constraints—a *money budget* and a *time budget*. Although rising incomes mean that consumers conceivably can *buy* more of everything, they cannot conceivably *do* more of everything. Doing more things, as opposed to buying more things, requires an additional resource—time. Understanding the circumstances that affect consumer intentions must include, therefore, time budgets.[4]

The value of time increases relative to money as money budgets increase. Whereas money budgets have no theoretical expansion limits, time has an ultimate restraint. It can readily be seen that as discretionary income continues to increase in a society, markets for time-related goods or services become more important. The consumer implications are described by Garretson and Mauser:

> The affluent citizen . . . will be oriented to *buying time rather than product*. His chief concern will be to provide himself with free time in which he can conveniently use products that function to conserve time for leisure and pleasure. It is scarcity which creates value. Hence, as scarcity of product disappears, the scarcity of time ascends the value scale.[5]

For the consumer, time must be consumed both in learning about consumption choices and in consuming products and services.[6] Traditionally, however, these activities were not treated in a framework that recognized their costs from the consumer's time budget. Frequently, the 24 hour budget of consumers was naively regarded as a two-component

3 Steak and Ale Restaurants of America, Inc., *Annual Report,* 1974.

4 This section is developed from Justin L. Voss and Roger D. Blackwell, "Markets for Leisure Time," in Mary Jane Slinger (ed.), *Advances in Consumer Research* (Chicago: Association for Consumer Research, 1975), pp. 837–45.

5 Robert C. Garretson and Ferdinand F. Mauser, "The Future Challenges Marketing," *Harvard Business Review,* vol. 41 (November–December 1963), pp. 168 ff.

6 Philip B. Schary, "Consumption and the Problem of Time," *Journal of Marketing,* vol. 35 (April 1971), pp. 50–55.

budget, work and leisure. This conceptualization is shown in the upper portion of Figure 3.9.

Figure 3.9 Conceptualizations of consumer time budgets and leisure

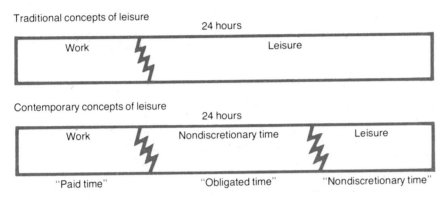

Traditional concepts of leisure

24 hours

| Work | Leisure |

Contemporary concepts of leisure

24 hours

| Work | Nondiscretionary time | Leisure |

"Paid time"   "Obligated time"   "Nondiscretionary time"

A contemporary conceptualization of consumer time budgets is shown in the lower portion of Figure 3.9, in which consumer time budgets are divided into three blocks of time—work (paid time), nondiscretionary time and discretionary time.[7] It is only this latter block of time that can be truly regarded as leisure time, Voss concludes:

> Leisure . . . may be defined as follows: Leisure is a period of time referred to as discretionary time. It is that period of time when an individual feels no sense of economic, legal, moral, or social compulsion or obligation, nor of physiological necessity. The choice of how to utilize this time period is solely his.[8]

Time goods

A contemporary conceptualization of consumer time budgets leads to the recognition that goods and services have important time properties. Products and services classified by their time properties may be called *time goods* and the time properties of goods have important marketing implications.

Time-using goods. One category of products and services is that which requires the use of time with the product. Examples would be watching television, skiing, fishing, golfing, tennis and many other activities usually classified as leisure time activities. They would normally fall in the portion of time called discretionary time or leisure in Figure 3.9.

7 Voss and Blackwell, "Markets."

8 Justin Voss, "The Definition of Leisure," *Journal of Economic Issues*, vol. 1 (June 1967), pp. 91–106. Voss analyzes conceptions of leisure for analytical purposes. For other conceptions of leisure, see Max Kaplan, "Leisure: Issues for American Business," paper presented to National Association of Business Economists (October 26, 1970), pp. 7–8.

To understand the nature of time-using goods of the discretionary type that would be purchased, it is necessary to understand what is happening to the other categories of time usage in a typical 24-hour day. Contrary, perhaps, to popular opinion there has been no significant decline in the workweek since the end of World War II.[9] The only increases in leisure time, from reduced paid time, have been associated with an increased number of holidays, length of vacations and earlier retirement. Nondiscretionary time, or obligated time, includes physical obligations (sleeping, commuting, personal care, and so forth), social obligations (which seem to increase with urbanization and the rising proportion of professional and white collar occupations) and moral obligations. It appears that nondiscretionary activities also are not declining and, at least in consumer perceptions, are increasing. Thus, the net effect of trends in time usage leads to a feeling by many consumers of *less leisure rather than more*. When the effect of increased money budgets is considered, the conclusion must be that consumers will be willing to pay more money to enjoy their limited leisure time. In such an economy, it would be predicted that consumers would be willing to pay more and more dollars to enjoy their leisure time (such as is required in travel, skiing, expensive sports equipment, and so forth) and would be likely to switch from less intense leisure activities such as golf to more intense leisure activities such as tennis. This hypothesis was supported in a study of leisure-time satisfactions in which highly educated and high income men (presumably busier) were much more likely to derive satisfaction from tennis than from golf.[10]

Time-saving goods. One way for consumers to obtain increased discretionary time (leisure), is to decrease nondiscretionary time. That frequently may be achieved through the purchase of goods and services.

Services represent the obvious marketing offering that provides additional discretionary time. The purchase of lawn mowing or lawn fertilizing service (such as Chem-lawn) may free the consumer for true leisure activities. Similarly, much of the restaurant and frozen food industry can be considered to be selling time. Convenience goods and disposable products of many types are ways in which the consumer can "buy time." Jet airplanes may cost more money but whisk a consumer away to Florida in order to have more leisure compared to driving in an auto. Finally, many so-called "labor saving" devices or consumer durable goods are actually "time-saving" products.

There is an increasing recognition by marketing organizations that the desire to save time is an important marketing element. This may lead to

9 Geoffrey H. Moore, "Measuring Leisure Time," The Conference Board *Record* (July 1971), pp. 53–54. Belief in a reduced workweek may be due to confusion in statistics, which as typically reported are usually based upon manufacturers' payrolls. As such, they usually include both full-time and part-time workers, which distorts the averages for all workers in decades of increasing proportions of part-time workers. Also, manufacturers' payroll records do not include second jobs, which are part of the workweek from the consumer's perspective. It is also misleading to consider only manufacturing statistics in an era when a rising proportion of workers are technical, professional and managerial— and may have longer workweeks than manufacturing employees.

10 Douglass K. Hawes, W. Wayne Talarzyk, and Roger D. Blackwell, "Consumer Satisfactions from Leisure Time Pursuits," in Mary J. Slinger, *Advances*, pp. 817–36, at p. 822.

the introduction of new products (microwave ovens, dishwashers, and so forth) or may lead to "positioning" strategies in which time properties are featured in communications about the product, along with other benefits of the product. Examples of such products are the Mod 4 home appliances, marketed by Black and Decker, which are featured as saving time as well as money and energy.

The technology necessary to measure time expenditures is embryonic although the important steps of dimensioning the problem have been advanced by Jacoby in a paper, which also serves as the most complete literature review available on the role of time in consumer behavior.[11] A relatively simple approach to measuring consumer time budgets is a questionnaire in which consumers are asked to recall the amounts of time spent in various activities. A diary is sometimes more accurate, but the additional complexity and nonresponse bias may offset this accuracy.[12] Using such a recall questionnaire, Hawes asked a nationwide sample of men and women to recall their major activities and found the results shown in Figure 3.10.

Measuring consumer time expenditures

In recent years, a sizable amount of research and analysis has been undertaken on the topic of time budgets and their relationship to economic or consumer behavior.[13] It is clear that products are not limited to their physical attributes but acquire their costs and achieve their satisfaction in a way that requires the human input of time.[14]

Figure 3.10 Time budgets of U.S. families

Activity	Average hours spent each week	
	Females	Males
Sleeping, napping	51.4	51.1
Eating meals (breakfast, lunch, dinner)	11.7	11.5
Personal care	8.2	6.7
Working at your job (including *all* paid employment)	15.6	41.0
Commuting to and from work	1.9	4.6
Other work-related activity (meetings, reading, study, "homework")	2.7	3.3
Housework, necessary home maintenance and lawn care	22.8	5.7

11 J. Jacoby, G. J. Szybillo, and C. K. Berning, "Time and Consumer Behavior: An Interdisciplinary Overview," *The Journal of Consumer Research*, 2 (March 1976), pp. 320–39.

12 Doyle Bishop, Claudine Jeanrenaud, and Kenneth Lawson, "Comparison of a Time Diary and Recall Questionnaire for Surveying Leisure Activities," *Journal of Leisure Research*, vol. 7 (1975), pp. 73–80.

13 B. Linder, *The Harried Leisure Class* (New York: Columbia University Press, 1970); J. F. Murphy, *Concepts of Leisure* (Englewood Cliffs: Prentice-Hall, 1974); J. Neulinger, *The Psychology of Leisure* (Springfield, Illinois: Charles C. Thomas, 1974); M. Kaplan, *Leisure: Theory and Policy* (New York: John Wiley and Sons, Inc., 1975).

14 These concepts are expanded in a formal statement in Douglass K. Hawes, et al., "Measuring Consumer Satisfactions for a Household Production Function Model of Leisure-Time Activities," *WPS* 76–17 (Columbus, Ohio: The Ohio State University, 1976).

Figure 3.10 Time budgets of U.S. families (continued)

Activity	Average hours spent each week	
	Females	Males
Shopping	4.2	1.9
Playing with or helping your children	10.2	5.0
Reading newspapers and magazines	5.1	5.1
Watching television	15.7	14.3
Hobbies, games, crafts, etc.	5.6	4.1
Visiting with friends or relatives	6.0	4.7
Participating in sports or athletics	1.3	1.9
Attending sporting events as a spectator	.7	.9
Entertainment outside the home (*other than* sporting events)	3.2	3.2
Other major activities	2.2	2.2
	168.5	167.2

Source: Douglass Hawes, "Time Budgets and Consumer Leisure-Time Behavior." Paper presented to Association for Consumer Research (Atlanta, 1976). Reprinted by permission.

Summary

A good starting place in the analysis of consumer behavior is the economic and demographic context of consumption. These variables become internalized within the consumer and influence intentions and choices of the consumer. Economic, demographic and other variables may affect consumer decisions either as *anticipated* or *unanticipated* circumstances.

Some key economic and demographic trends in the American economy include a changing age composition of the population, increased educational sophistication, changing employment of women, a proliferation of affluence, and a changing geography of demand.

Consumer behavior is affected by *time budgets* as well as money budgets. Products may therefore be analyzed in terms of their *time-using* properties as well as their *time-saving* properties. A useful method of analyzing such properties is by classifying consumer time expenditures into work (paid time), nondiscretionary time activities, and leisure (discretionary time activities).

Review and discussion questions

1. Why is the consideration of economic and demographic variables important in the study of consumer behavior?

2. Analyze the kinds of scenarios that might develop that would prevent the proliferation of affluence from continuing in the future.

3. Assume that you are a market official for a large furniture retailer. Prepare

a marketing program that would be successful in reaching consumers in the 25–34 age group.

4. Assume that you are the marketing official of a supermarket. Prepare a marketing program that would be successful in reaching consumers in the over-65 age group.

5. Describe the relationship that flexi-time or the four-day workweek has on consumption, using the analysis of time budgets presented in this chapter.

CHAPTER 4

Cross-cultural and sub-cultural influences

The role of cultural influences in providing norms of behavior—which an individual may accept or from which an individual may deviate—is illustrated in the following quotation by Slotkin. The dialogue occurs with a person taken to a mental hospital during a hot summer spell, whose responses appeared normal until the following dialogue:

Q. How did you happen to come here?
A. I don't know. I was just minding my own business.
Q. Who brought you here?
A. The police.
Q. What had you been doing?
A. Nothing. Just minding my own business.
Q. What were you doing at the time?
A. Just walking along the street.
Q. What street?
A. (He gave the name of one of the busiest streets in the city.)
Q. What had you done just before that?
A. It was hot, so I took my clothes off.
Q. All your clothes?
A. No. Not my shoes and stockings.
Q. Why not those too?
A. The sidewalk was too hot.[1]

This man probably viewed his behavior as acceptable to himself but,

1 James S. Slotkin, *Social Anthropology* (New York: Macmillan, 1950), pp. 70–71.

judged by the norms of his society, his behavior was unacceptable and must therefore be modified. While this individual *deviated* from norms, most individuals *conform to the norms of groups.*

This chapter describes the role of cultures and subcultures in providing norms for behavior of consumers. In some instances, this involves the comparison of norms in one nation with those of another nation, as is required in the design of global marketing strategies. In other instances, it involves the examination of the norms of groups within the total society—called subcultures. The latter may include ethnic, religious, and racial groups as well as subcultures with less defined criteria for membership such as the "youth subculture." In this chapter, particular attention is focused upon the black subculture in the United States and upon the French subculture in Canada. The chapter concludes with an introduction to marketing research methods that are particularly appropriate in cross-cultural analysis.

Nature of culture

"Culture" is a term used in many varied ways; it is used in the analysis of consumer behavior to mean the *complex of values, ideas, attitudes, and other meaningful symbols created by people to shape human behavior and the artifacts of that behavior, transmitted from one generation to the next.* Culture does not refer to the instinctive response tendencies of people nor does it include the inventive innovations occurring within an individual's lifetime that take place as one-time solutions to unique problem situations.

Culture includes both abstract and material elements. Abstract elements include values, attitudes, ideas, personality types, and summary constructs such as religion. These are learned patterns of behavior, feeling, and reaction that are transmitted from one generation to succeeding ones. Material elements of the culture are very diverse and include items such as computers, drawings, tools, buildings, products, advertisements, and many of the other artifacts of a society.

Material aspects (such as products) are the results of consumer choices. It is more important to our understanding of consumer choices at this point, however, to focus analysis upon the abstract elements of culture. In the model of consumer behavior used in this book, it may be seen that *cultural values* and *norms are a key influence on motives*, or the underlying drives in consumer behavior. Thus, we need to understand how culture functions, both to understand how behavior is motivated and influenced toward conformity with other consumers.

The process of a consumer absorbing or learning the culture in which a person is raised is called *socialization.* The process of learning a new culture is called *acculturation.* Many groups of people contribute to the socialization or acculturation of an individual.

The most basic source of socialization is the family. This is true for a number of reasons, including the fact that the family is the primary screening agent of culture in the formative childhood years in many societies.

The influence of all other groups has traditionally been "filtered" by members of the family in the early years of the typical individual.

Reference groups such as work groups for adults and friendship groups for all ages are important transmitters of culture. They may also "filter" the values of the broader culture and shape the values of a consumer. Social classes, racial, and other ethnic groups are also important in defining and transmitting culture to the individual. Each of these groups is discussed in this and following chapters.

Sources of cultural norms

Norms are *quantitative statements or beliefs held by a concensus of a group concerning the behavior rules for individual members.* The source of a culture's norms of behavior is within the culture itself. Several assumptions about this process are generally accepted in anthropology.[2]

Culture is a set of *learned responses.* Humans are not born with their norms of behavior in the way that animals are born with instincts. Instead, norms and values must be learned from the environment through a process of reward and punishment by a society of its members who adhere to or deviate from the group's norms.

Cultural items learned early in life tend to resist changes more strongly than those learned late in life. This fact has important implications for marketing strategy, since those cultural elements learned early in life are likely to be highly resistant to promotional effort of marketers. When an advertiser is dealing with deeply ingrained, culturally defined behavior, it is usually easier to conform to the cultural values rather than attempt to change them through advertising. While advertisers usually cannot change cultural values for the benefit of specific products, it should be recognized that the content or themes of advertising may in themselves be transmitters and reinforcers of cultural values.[3]

Culture is *inculcated from one generation to another.* Primarily, culture is passed on from parents to children but institutions such as schools and religious groups are important also, as Chapter 7 describes. While the institutions of one generation are heavily involved in the inculcation process, individuals may accept all or some portion of these inculcated values depending upon the individual's own make-up, reference group influences, and movement between groups with differing norms of behavior.

Cultural values are *social phenomena* in that they refer to group habits or norms rather than an individual's way of behaving. This is of particular importance to marketing strategists since most marketing programs must be designed for groups of persons (market segments) rather than individual preferences or behavior.

People belong to many groups, however, and sometimes the various groups to which they belong will have norms or values that conflict with

---

2 This discussion is based upon G. P. Murdock, "Uniformities in Culture," *American Sociological Review,* vol. 5 (1940), pp. 361–69; Omark K. Moore and Donald Lewis, "Learning Theory and Culture," *Psychological Review,* vol. 59 (1952), pp. 380–88.

3 A particularly strong statement of this position is found in Jules Henry, *Culture Against Man* (New York: Random House, 1963); Jules Henry, *Pathways to Madness* (New York: Random House, 1971).

each other. A person may find the business organization has norms of behavior that conflict with his or her religious, racial, or other cultural norms. Even within the organization, norms of behavior exist for marketing people that are different from financial, personal, production, or research and development executives.[4]

Cultural norms *reward socially gratifying responses.* Culture develops and exists, almost as if it were an entity in itself, to meet the basic biological and secondary needs of a society. When norms are no longer gratifying to the existence of that society, they become extinguished because individual members are no longer rewarded for adhering to them.

An example of this can be observed in the development of individuals to fill occupations needed by a society to perpetuate itself. Physicians and scientists must engage in many years of difficult, relatively nonproductive labor before they are able to perform the services a society regards as essential for survival. To induce individuals to enter these strenuous positions, a society organizes itself in such a way that material and social rewards are given to people who enter these positions. In an era when national defense is a great need of the society, for example, esteem and other rewards are given to military strategists or defense-related scientists. As a society changes from strong national defense needs to a need for solution to ecological or energy problems, the society will evolve in such a way that greater rewards are provided to scientists working on these problems than to military leaders.

The principle of gratification in the perpetuation of cultural norms is of considerable significance to marketing organizations. This is because of the insight that can be gained into the types of products and marketing practices that will be permitted and rewarded in a society and those that will be unrewarded or eliminated. Only products and marketing practices that gratify the current needs of a society will, in the long-run, be permitted or retained by the society.

Finally, culture is *adaptive,* either through a dialectical or evolutionary process. Culture responds to the physical and social environment in which it operates and has contact. Dialectical or sharply discontinuous cultural change, associated with persons such as Hegel and Marx, occurs when the value system of a culture becomes associated with the gratification of only one class or group. In such instances, other classes of the society reject the logic of the value system and replace it (perhaps suddenly, in a revolution) with a new value system. In an evolutionary process, change occurs but is a process of modification rather than revolution.[5]

The adaptive nature of culture is important in developing an understanding of consumer behavior. In the past, cultural change was usually

4 Robert C. Shirley, "Values in Decision Making: Their Origin and Effects," *Managerial Planning* (January/February 1975), pp. 1–5.

5 A lucid discussion of the contrasting philosophies of dialectical and evolutionary change in the values of a society is provided by an economist who has influenced marketing thought considerably. See Kenneth Boulding, *A Primer on Social Dynamics* (New York: Free Press, 1970), esp. chap. 2, "Organizers of Social Evolution."

slow and gradual. It appears, however, that the vastly accelerated technological change that characterizes contemporary societies is also reflected in the values and ideas of the society. The effect of such changes, together with the rapid changes in institutions described in the preceding chapter, is creating an environment in which strategies based upon assumptions about values must be more closely monitored and evaluated than in the past.

A number of research projects are maintained by business organizations in an attempt to monitor changing values as they impact consumer choices. The most comprehensive of these is called "Monitor" and is maintained through annual surveys of 2,500 persons in a national study by Daniel Yankelovich, Inc. The nature of Monitor and its reasons for existence are described as follows:

> . . . Monitor is a business service designed to provide marketers of consumer goods and services with annual statistical information on the nature of social change in the United States, along with a picture of the way changing social values are affecting people's behavior as consumers. In recent years, marketers have become increasingly sensitized to the importance of changing *social values* as a major influence on consumer behavior. Monitor is a unique service which provides empirically-derived, statistical data on social change, with particular emphasis on how changing social values are impacting on consumer behavior.[6]

The process by which values of a subculture evolve can be described as a *trickle-up process*. In general, many of the values appear to be initiated by youth, especially upscale (high income and education) youth, and in several of the trends the initiating force is most often upscale young women. The group most resistant to these new values appears to be downscale older people, especially men. Researchers in this area have concluded that many of the new values are accepted first by young upscale persons and then are picked up by young downscale consumers. Older upscale people then move toward these new values well ahead of the downscale older groups. Thus, instead of social values moving from older groups in a society and trickling down to younger groups, it appears that social values now trickle up from young to old, with the upscale (in affluence and education) being the most receptive in both age groups.

Culture and communication strategy

Designing effective communication or marketing strategy requires consideration of the culture of the target audience. Members of a cultural group have similar ways of seeing, giving meaning to, and classifying objects—called cognitive structures. The basic lifetime experiences of the group members mold and shape their cognitive structures along similar

6 Daniel Yankelovich, *The Yankelovich Monitor* (New York: Daniel Yankelovich, Inc., 1974), p. 1.

lines resulting in similar perceptions of their social environment. The effects of cultural influences provide, therefore, basic differences in information processing between cultural groups.[7]

The failure to recognize differences in information processing between cultural groups can lead to many blunders in advertising and marketing programs where managers are dealing with a culture other than ones with which they are familiar. Colgate-Palmolive introduced Cue toothpaste in French-speaking countries, not knowing that "cue" was a pornographic word in French. General Mills attempted to enter the British cereal market with a package showing an "all-American" youngster. This did not appeal to a culture that possesses a more formal view of the role of children. Goodyear Tire and Rubber demonstrated the strength of its "3T" tire cord in the United States by showing a steel chain breaking. When this demonstration was to be included in German advertising, however, it was perceived as uncomplimentary to steel chain manufacturers and regarded as improper. In Quebec, a canned fish manufacturer attempted to market that product through an advertising program that showed a woman in shorts, golfing with her husband, and intending to serve canned fish for the evening meal. The program was a failure because, as studies by an anthropologist disclosed, all three of these activities violate the norms of that culture.[8]

Another example where lack of cultural awareness resulted in a marketing blunder is illustrated by the following case of a western-oriented tobacco company attempting to enter a new market:

> The managers of a joint-venture tobacco company in an Asian country were warned that their proposed new locally named (a token adaptation) and manufactured filtered cigarettes would fail. Filters had not yet been introduced there. Nevertheless, the resident Western managers, along with their local executives whose SRC (self-reference criterion) was dominantly Western because of their social class and education, puffed smugly on their own U.S. filtered cigarettes while the product flopped, leaving the company with idle equipment and uncovered setup and launch costs.
>
> The basic reason for the prediction of failure was a difference in fear of death—especially from cancer of the lungs. A life expectancy of 29 years in that Asian country does not place many people in the lung cancer age bracket. Moreover, for those in this age bracket, there is not the general cultural value of sanitation, the literacy rate, or a Reader's Digest type of magazine to motivate them to give up unfiltered cigarettes.[9]

7 Harry C. Triandis, "Subjective Culture and Economic Development," *International Journal of Psychology*, vol. 8 (1973), pp. 163–80. For further development of this, see Peter L. Wright, "Cultural Differences and Consumer Information Processing: A Critical Review," paper presented at the American Psychological Association National Conference, Montreal, August 1973. Also Michael Cole and Jerome Bruner, "Cultural Differences about Psychological Processes," *American Psychologist*, vol. 26 (October 1971), pp. 867–76.

8 These and other examples are contained in David A. Ricks, Jeffrey S. Arpan and Marilyn Y. Fu, *International Business Blunders* (Columbus: Grid Publishing, 1975).

9 Charles Winick, "Anthropology's Contributions to Marketing," *Journal of Marketing* (July 1961), p. 53.

Needed: cultural competence

Cultural awareness is necessary both for domestic communications programs and for global communications programs. Communications strategies may be ineffective with some markets because those who design them are not aware of the cognitive structure of subcultures within the market, such as often has been the case when white executives designed marketing programs to reach black markets in the United States. Similar phenomena have occurred when urban executives tried to reach rural France or Portugal without an awareness of the degree of provincialism that may be present.

The need for cultural understanding and research is particularly evident when a communications strategist attempts to deal with the cultures of other countries. An American executive may build a communications program without realizing that values common to the American culture, such as individualism, emphasis on youthfulness, informality, respect of hard work and so forth, may not be part of the cognitive structure of the host country.[10] For international executives to have "cultural competence," they must, among other things, have:

1. Sensitivity to cultural differences.

2. Cultural empathy, or the ability to "understand the inner logic and coherence of other ways of life, plus the restraint not to judge them as bad because they are different from one's own ways."

3. Ability to withstand the initial cultural shock, or "the sum of sudden jolts that awaits the unwary American abroad."

4. Ability to cope with and to adapt to foreign environment without "going native."[11]

Domestically or in other countries, cultural research is of importance to an organization both for describing current cultural values and in predicting changes that are likely to occur in cultural values. Different methodologies or types of information may be required for predicting future directions that describe current values, however. Future predictions require longitudinal (measures over time) methodologies or, if that is not feasible, measures of carefully defined segments, which may be "leading indicators" of the future values of others in the culture.

Methods of studying culture

There is an increasing recognition for the need to conduct research that yields understanding of the norms and values of a culture. Many of the

10 James A. Lee, "Cultural Analysis in Overseas Operations," *Harvard Business Review*, vol. 44 (March–April, 1966), pp. 106–14, at p. 107. Copyright © 1966 by the President and Fellows of Harvard College; all rights reserved. Theodore O. Wallin, "The International Executive's Baggage: Cultural Values of the American Frontier," *MSU Business Topics*, vol. 24 (Spring 1976), pp. 49–58.

11 Y. Hugh Furuhashi and Harry F. Evarts, "Educating Men for International Marketing," *Journal of Marketing*, vol. 31, pp. 51–53 (January 1967). The authors attribute some of these ideas to Harlan Cleveland, Gerald J. Mangone, and John Clark Adams, *The Overseas Americans* (New York: McGraw-Hill, 1960).

standard techniques of psychological research or marketing can be used or adapted to the problem of studying culture, but sometimes special techniques are needed. Often they are adapted from anthropology, linguistics, or sociology,[12] but more recently attempts have been made to adapt these techniques to the special problems of marketing and communications.[13]

Cultural research need not be highly quantitative to be useful. Becker analyzed sociological methodology and came to the conclusion that the major awards for outstanding contributions often have gone to studies centering on individual qualitative analysis. He observed:

> Methodologists particularly slight three methods used by prize winners. They seldom write on participant observation, the method that produced Skolnick's *Justice Without Trial* and Goffman's *Asylums*. They seldom write on historical analysis, the method that produced Erickson's *Wayward Puritans* and Bendix's *Work and Authority in Industry*. And they seldom write on what few of us even perceive as a method—the knitting together of diverse kinds of research and publicly available materials which produced Frazier's *Black Bourgeoisie*. All three methods allow human judgment to operate, unhampered by algorithmic procedures, though they all allow the full presentation of the bases of those judgments that satisfy scientific requirements.[14]

Some cultural research methodology is described in the following pages. Although separate methodologies are described, hybrid or combination methodologies are encountered and frequently utilize personal insight and logical synthesis. The methods described below include mass observations and participant observation, content analysis, cross-sectional studies and longitudinal studies. Cross-cultural methodology might be considered as a separate methodology or as a combination of some of the above, but this approach is presented in a separate section following this one.

Intensive field studies are common as a method of gathering cultural data. Field studies involve the placement of investigators into a culture for intensive collection of data through observation or the administration of tests. Two types of field studies are described below.

Intensive field studies

12 Introductions to methodology for cultural research and descriptions of specific technique can be found in B. K. Stravianis, "Research Methods in Cultural Anthropology," *Psychological Review*, vol. 57, pp. 334–44 (1950); Gardner Lindzey, *Projective Techniques and Cross-Cultural Research* (New York: Appleton, 1961); Charles E. Osgood and Thomas A. Sebeck, "Psycholinguistics: A Survey of Theory and Research Problems," a Morton Prince Memorial Supplement to *Journal of Abnormal and Social Psychology*, vol. 49 (1954); Francis L. K. Hsu, ed., *Psychological Anthropology: Approaches to Culture and Personality* (Homewood, Ill.: Dorsey Press, 1961); Bert Kaplan, ed., *Studying Personality Cross-Culturally* (New York: Harper & Row, 1961); R. L. Carneiro and S. F. Tobias, "The Application of Scale Analysis to the study of Cultural Evolution," transcript, New York Academy of Science, ser. 2, vol. 26, pp. 196–207 (1963); Allen D. Grimshaw, "Sociolinguistics," in I. de Sola Pool and Wilbur Schramm, eds., *Handbook of Communication* (Chicago: Rand McNally, 1973), pp. 47–92.

13 Peter Cooke, "Market Analysis Utilizing Cultural Anthropological Indicators," *European Journal of Marketing*, vol. 6 (1972), pp. 26–34; Yoram Wind and Susan Douglas, "Some Issues in International Consumer Research," *European Journal of Marketing*, vol. 8 (1974), pp. 204–17; Charles Lamb, "Domestic Applications of Comparative Marketing Analysis," *European Journal of Marketing*, vol. 9 (1975), pp. 167–72.

14 Howard S. Becker, *Sociological Work* (Chicago: Aldine, 1970), pp. 6–7.

Mass observations. The technique of mass observation refers to the process of researchers interacting with members of a culture who appear to understand the culture of the group, listening to conversations, and attempting to synthesize these experiences into conclusions about the culture. Because of the subjective nature of this type of research process, its primary value is only for the preliminary investigation of market potential and for developing hypotheses to be investigated in more systematic methodologies.

African culture and its effects on marketing provide an example of the type of study reported frequently in the marketing literature. Deeply ingrained cultural values against free enterprise and trade are reported by Albaum and Rutman to exist in Tanganyika.[15] The Bantu markets of South Africa have such a low cultural definition of women's status that all purchases must be approved by men, according to Omana.[16] Fragmentation of markets is substantial in South Africa because of the existence of a variety of subcultures, reports Thorelli.[17] He finds that there are even greater differences between the consumption preferences of young and old and between urban and rural than in western cultures.

In Nigeria, mass observation studies reveal the importance of curiosity as a cultural value in the acceptance of new products. Other cultural values in Nigeria are reported by Baker:

> A deep seated impression of recent colonial rules is one that permeates widely. Status consideration is another, though appropriate symbols can vary. Personalities are important but dissimilar: the Yoruba of the western region is a very out-going and friendly individual, while the Hausa of the northern region is rather quiet and reserved. Religious preferences are primarily Christian and Moslem, and each demands a certain awareness of its respective precepts. Colors may be important; for the Yoruba, blue is widely favored. Even the direction of hands and eyes is sometimes significant.[18]

Other field studies have reported cultural differences on marketing in Spain,[19] Peru,[20] Chile,[21] and various Latin American countries.[22] Some-

15 Gerald Albaum and Gilbert L. Rutman, "The Cooperative-Based Marketing System in Tanganyika," *Journal of Marketing*, vol. 31, pp. 54–58 (October 1967).

16 Charles J. Omana, "Marketing in Sub-Sahara Africa" in Peter D. Bennett, ed., *Marketing and Economic Development* (Chicago: American Marketing Association, 1965), pp. 128–39.

17 Hans B. Thorelli, "South Africa: Its Multi-Cultural Marketing System," *Journal of Marketing*, vol. 32, pp. 40–48 (April 1968).

18 Raymond W. Baker, "Marketing in Nigeria," *Journal of Marketing*, vol. 29, pp. 40–48, at pp. 46–47 (July 1965). Reprinted by permission of the publisher.

19 Edwin H. Lewis, "Marketing in Spain," *Journal of Marketing*, vol. 28, pp. 17–21 (October, 1964); Joseph R. Guerin, "Limitations of Supermarkets in Spain," *Journal of Marketing*, vol. 28, pp. 22–26 (October 1964).

20 Donald G. Halper, "The Environment for Marketing in Peru," *Journal of Marketing*, vol. 30, pp. 42–46 (July 1966).

21 Peter D. Bennett, "Retailing Evolution or Revolution in Chile," *Journal of Marketing*, vol. 30, pp. 38–41 (July 1966).

22 Charles C. Slater, "Marketing Processes in Developing Latin American Societies," *Journal of Marketing*, vol. 32, pp. 50–55 (July 1968); and Arieh Goldman, "Outreach of Consumers and the Modernization of Urban Food Retailing in Developing Countries," *Journal of Marketing*, vol. 38 (October 1974), pp. 8–16.

times such field studies report only economic and technical aspects of the culture, and sometimes the studies are a combination of economic structure data and personal interpretation based upon an on-site visit.

In recent years, considerable knowledge has been obtained from such studies concerning marketing in the cultures of socialist countries. In Poland, the rise in output of consumer goods (compared to industrial goods) has increased the need for research on consumers, and much of this research is behavioral in nature rather than limited to consumption statistics.[23] In other Eastern European countries, marketing research is focusing on lifestyles of families to determine their need for television sets, frying pans and so forth in order to determine production plans in a planned economy.[24] Other studies focus on the structural or bureaucratic processes necessary for marketing in communist countries.[25]

A major problem with mass-observation techniques is that they rely upon the observer's ability to be objective and comprehensive as well as the ability to select the proper people or activities to be included in the study. The problem with such studies, even though they are useful, is stated by Duijker and Frijda, ". . . there is no systematic sampling; the situations are not standardized; (and) much of the material gathered is irrelevant to the specific problem studied."[26]

Participant-observer studies. Field studies of a culture by an investigator or team of investigators living in intimate contact with a culture and making voluminous notes of what is observed are called participant-observer studies. They are only "one step up" in rigor of respondent selection than mass observations but may be quite rigorous in the depth of inquiry. The data collection may include records of what is observed, interviews with "key" informants, and structured methods, such as attitude scales, projective tests, and other forms.

The contemporary ethnographic researcher lives among the people he or she is observing and questioning, and attempts to become an accepted part of the cultural unit under study. A classic study using such a method is Whiting's *Becoming a Kwoma*,[27] in which the investigator spent nearly a year developing relationships with residents of the tiny village of Rumbima in New Zealand in order to collect data on the most basic values of the society. One authority has described the approach of the anthropologist in this manner:

23 Hart Walters, Jr., "Marketing in Poland in the 1970s: Significant Progress," *Journal of Marketing*, vol. 39 (October 1975), pp. 47–51.

24 Charles S. Mayer, "Marketing in Eastern European Socialist Countries," University of Michigan *Business Review*, vol. 28 (January 1976), pp. 16–21.

25 Jeffrey M. Hertzfeld, "Setting Up Shop in Moscow," *Harvard Business Review*, vol. 52 (September–October 1974), pp. 137–42; James A. Brunner and George Taoka, "Marketing Opportunities and Negotiating in the People's Republic of China," *Baylor Business Review*, no. 102 (1975), pp. 7–22; Berend H. Feddersen, "Markets behind the Iron Curtain," *Journal of Marketing*, vol. 31, pp. 1–5 (July 1967).

26 H.C.J. Duijker and N.H. Frijda, *National Character and National Stereotypes: Confluence*, vol. 1 (Amsterdam: North-Holland, 1960), p. 120.

27 John W.M. Whiting, *Becoming a Kwoma* (New Haven, Conn.: Yale University Press, 1941).

He studies his fellow men not solely as a dispassionate observer but also as a participant observer. He tries to feel with them, to see things as they see them, to experience some portion of their life with them. On the other hand, he tries to balance his identifications with detached objectivity.[28]

The participant-observer has been relatively unused in marketing studies as a formal technique, but it offers much potential. Informally, the technique is used all the time because the marketing researcher working with a common consumer product is already a "participant observer" in the culture absorbing the product the marketer sells. Eventually, however, consumer researchers may send observers into alien subcultures to conduct in-depth cultural studies. For example, a company might station an ethnographer in cultural subunits such as a black family, a retirement village, an apartment community of young noncollege-educated couples, or an area of the city composed of a different social class from that of the marketing executives and researchers. The ethnographer is trained to make careful observations of every element of behavior relevant to purchasing of the product as well as background material in the form of general cultural values. In addition to his or her own observations, the ethnographer relies upon interaction with informants for explanations, clarifications, and amplifications of the activities observed.

Observer-participant studies have two major weaknesses: (1) they usually do not have a systematic sampling plan[29] and (2) the presence of the observer as a particpant may introduce changes in the culture.[30] Thus the anthropological field study is sometimes criticized for its lack of objectivity and comprehensiveness. However, what the anthropologist sacrifices in methodological rigor in his participant-observer field he makes up for in an approach that is often richer in content, more ramified, and more pertinent to behavior in everyday life settings.

Participant-observer studies have been used very little in marketing although some studies have focused upon similar topics using in-depth interviews, panels and related techniques.[31] In the future, more communications strategists may see the value of understanding the deeply-ingrained, cultural meanings of a product or of messages about the product and use more often the true ethnographic field study. The relevance to a company could be much greater than it probably has been to date as companies grow in their understanding of the need for a

28 Clyde Kluckhohn, "Common Humanity and Diverse Cultures," in Daniel Lerner, ed., *The Human Meaning of the Social Sciences* (Cleveland, Ohio: World Publishing, 1959), pp. 251–52.

29 For a discussion of informant sampling problems in ethnographic research, see B. D. Paul, "Interview Techniques and Field Relationships," in A. L. Kroeber et al., eds., *Anthropology Today: An Encyclopedia* (Chicago: University of Chicago Press, 1953), pp. 430–51.

30 Methods to prevent reactivity in a wide variety of research problems, including participant observation, are presented in Eugene J. Webb et al., *Unobtrusive Measures: Nonreactive Research in the Social Sciences* (Chicago: Rand McNally, 1966).

31 Studies of culture using standard marketing research techniques can be found in most marketing and advertising journals. The most complete description of cultural values surrounding consumer products and decision processes in America based primarily on depth interviews is in Ernest Dichter, *Handbook of Consumer Motivations* (New York: McGraw-Hill, 1964).

complete understanding of consumer decisions in foreign cultures. A model of consumer behavior can be a very helpful tool in such situations as a guide to indicate what information should be collected for the analysis of consumer decisions.

Content analysis is a technique for determining the values, themes, role prescriptions, norms of behavior, and other elements of a culture from the verbal materials produced by the people of a culture in the ordinary course of events.[32] The main advantages of content analysis are that (1) it can be used where personal contact is difficult or impossible, and (2) it is unobtrusive; a culture can be studied without individuals within the culture being aware of the investigation. **Content analysis**

The breadth of topics that can be studied in a culture is large, as is the variety of materials that can be used as sources of information. In one classic study, the achievement motivations that characterize a society were studied by McClelland through a content analysis of children's stories.[33] More recently, values of societies have been studied with a variety of content analyses of newspapers, magazines, and other media.[34]

The use of content analysis in marketing studies has been limited. Most that has been done has focused upon values and roles expressed in advertisements. A comparison of advertising content in India and America was done, for example, by Singh and Huang.[35] In a meticulously designed and carefully executed study, Kassarjian analyzed occupational roles of Negroes in America, discovering some changes in occupational roles but the continuation of many stereotypes.[36] Other methodologies involving content analysis have focused upon the roles of women in advertisements revealing, with some changes in recent years, basically chauvinistic presentations of women as homemakers, in fashion settings and as sex objects.[37]

Cross-sectional studies of culture have been applied to marketing problems recently. They have the same goals as mass observations and **Cross-sectional studies**

32 For details of the method, see Bernard Berelson, *Content Analysis in Communication Research* (New York: Free Press, 1952). See also various readings in I. Pool, ed., *Trends in Content Analysis* (Urbana, Ill.: University of Illinois Press, 1959); R. C. North et al., *Content Analysis: A Handbook with Applications for the Study of International Crisis* (Evanston, Ill.: Northwestern University Press, 1963).

33 D.C. McClelland, *The Achieving Society* (Princeton, N.J.: Van Nostrand, 1961).

34 H.D. Lasswell, "The World Attention Survey," *Public Opinion Quarterly*, vol. 3 (1941), pp. 456–62; I. Pool, *The Prestige Papers: A Survey of Their Editorials* (Palo Alto, Calif.: Stanford University Press, 1952); I. Wayne, "American and Soviet Themes and Values: A Content Analysis of Pictures in Popular Magazines," *Public Opinion Quarterly*, vol. 20 (1956), pp. 315–20; R.C. Angell, "Social Values of Soviet and American Elites: Content Analysis of Elite Media" *Journal of Conflict Resolution*, vol. 8 (1964), pp. 424–85.

35 P.N. Singh and S.C. Huang, "Some Socio-Cultural and Psychological Dominants of Advertising in India: A Comparative Study," *Journal of Social Psychology*, vol. 57, pp. 113–21 (1962).

36 Harold H. Kassarjian, "The Negro and American Advertising, 1946–1965," *Journal of Marketing Research*, vol. 6, pp. 29–39 (February 1969).

37 Alice E. Courtney and Sarah W. Lockeretc, "A Woman's Place: An Analysis of the Roles Portrayed by Women In Magazine Advertisements," *Journal of Marketing Research*, vol. 8 (February 1971), pp. 92–95, and Louis C. Wagner and Janis B. Banos, "A Woman's Place: A Follow-up Analysis of the Roles Portrayed by Women in Magazine Advertisements," *Journal of Marketing Research*, vol. 10 (May 1973), pp. 213–14.

participant-observer studies but are based upon more systematic sampling procedures in an attempt to produce a representative cross section of the culture or subculture investigated. Questions are formulated that will reveal values or behavioral norms of a culture and are presented to a large sample, often using probability or quota selection procedures.

An important advantage of cross-sectional studies of cultural values is, with adequate sample sizes, the ability to describe values of subcultures as well as values of the entire culture. Such an analysis may lead to the conclusion that no "overall" value exists in a culture but rather that a society is composed of the values of many subcultures. In some countries, the diversity and intensity of such subcultural values may be so incompatible that political and social separatism is the result. The United States has often been called the "melting pot" because of the belief that so many subcultures have become blended together. Actually, the United States may not be so much of a "melting pot" as a pluralistic society in which tolerance of the values of different subcultures is high enough and so supported by constitutional provisions, that the nation can function satisfactorily with separation or fractionalization. Understanding these subcultures, however, is improved by the use of large-scale or cross-sectional studies, which permit measurement of the subcultures.

Cross-sectional studies employing large samples and quantitative measures also are useful in identifying values of subcultures that may be "forerunners" of the total culture. A good example of this is provided by the study reported in Figure 4.1. In this study, similar questions were

Figure 4.1 CBS cross-sectional study of youth and parents (selected questions and responses)

(1) The following statements represent some traditional American values. Which of them do you *personally believe in* and which do you *not believe in*?

		Youth			Parents	
						Parents non-college youth (%)
					Parents college youth (%)	
		Total youth (%)	College (%)	Non-college (%)	Total parents (%)	
(a)	Hard work will always pay off					
	Believe in	74	56	79	83	76	85
	Do not believe in	26	43	21	17	24	15
(b)	Everyone should save as much as he can regularly and not have to lean on family and friends the minute he runs into financial problems						
	Believe in	86	76	88	96	90	98
	Do not believe in	14	24	11	3	10	2

Figure 4.1 CBS cross-sectional study of youth and parents
(selected questions and responses) (*continued*)

	Youth			Parents		
	Total youth (%)	College (%)	Non-college (%)	Total parents (%)	Parents college youth (%)	Parents non-college youth (%)
(c) Depending on how much strength and character a person has, he can pretty well control what happens to him						
Believe in	74	62	77	74	71	75
Do not believe in	26	38	23	24	28	23
(d) Belonging to some organized religion is important in a person's life						
Believe in	66	42	71	89	81	91
Do not believe in	34	57	28	11	17	9

(2) Many people feel that we are undergoing a period of rapid social change in this country today, and that people's values are changing at the same time. Which of the following changes would you *welcome*, which would you *reject*, and which would *leave you indifferent?*

	Total youth (%)	College (%)	Non-college (%)	Total parents (%)		
(a) Less emphasis on money						
Would welcome	57	72	54	Not asked of		
Would reject	13	11	13	Parents		
Leave indifferent	30	17	33			
(b) Less emphasis on working hard						
Would welcome	30	24	32			
Would reject	46	48	45			
Leave indifferent	23	28	22			
(c) More emphasis on law and order						
Would welcome	76	57	81			
Would reject	10	23	7			
Leave indifferent	12	19	11			
(f) More sexual freedom						
Would welcome	27	43	22			
Would reject	39	24	43			
Leave indifferent	34	33	34			
(g) More vigorous protests by blacks and other minority groups						
Would welcome	12	23	9			
Would reject	73	56	77			
Leave indifferent	15	20	14			

(18) Which of the following considerations will have a relatively strong influence on your choice of career?

Figure 4.1 CBS cross-sectional study of youth and parents
(selected questions and responses) (*continued*)

	Youth			Parents		
	Total youth (%)	College (%)	Non-college (%)	Total parents (%)	Parents college youth (%)	Parents non-college youth (%)
Your family	35	31	36	Not asked of Parents		
The money that you can earn	47	41	49			
The prestige or status of the job	21	23	20			
The security of the job	45	42	46			
The ability to express yourself	47	66	43			
The challenge of the job	52	71	47			
The opportunity to make a meaningful contribution	60	76	56			

(24) For each of the following, please tell me whether you feel it needs no substantial change, needs moderate change, needs fundamental reform, or should be done away with.

Big business						
No substantial change	20	10	23	Not asked of Parents		
Moderate change	52	52	52			
Fundamental reform	24	34	21			
Done away with	3	3	3			
The military						
No substantial change	20	10	23			
Moderate change	43	29	46			
Fundamental reform	29	49	25			
Done away with	7	11	6			
The universities						
No substantial change	20	11	23			
Moderate change	50	56	49			
Fundamental reform	28	32	27			
Done away with	1	—	1			

Note: Question numbers and letters correspond to source.

Source: From the CBS News, "Generations Apart" survey published in *Public Opinion: Changing Attitudes on Contemporary Political and Social Issues* (New York: R. R. Bowker, 1972). © CBS Inc., 1972.

asked of youth and their parents and were compared. Additionally, the responses of college youth are tabulated separately from noncollege youth, revealing earlier acceptance of changed values in most instances among college youth than among noncollege youth.

There are subgroups within subcultures. This is demonstrated by looking at Figure 4.2 which, although it is based upon a different study, amplifies the information in Figure 4.1. In the youth-parent study, college youth were compared to noncollege youth. However, the culture found on one campus may be greatly different than on another campus. Figure 4.2 shows, for example, that 75 percent of Sarah Lawrence College students are definitely or somewhat in favor of socialization of basic industries compared to only 28 percent at the University of South

Figure 4.2 Cross-sectional study of values in representative campuses (selected questions and responses)

19-36. Indicate your views on the following twenty political proposals for the United States by writing in a number signifying the following:

(1) Definitely in favor
(2) Somewhat in favor
(3) Indifferent or no opinion
(4) Somewhat opposed
(5) Definitely opposed

19. Full socialization of all industries:

	SL %	Wms %	Yale %	Marq %	BU %	Ind %	SC %	Hwd %	Reed %	Dav %	Bran %	Stan %
(1)	11	2	8	2	9	4	—	10	11	4	7	3
(2)	34	13	17	9	29	14	8	26	27	11	30	17
(3)	9	7	11	11	11	9	11	18	16	8	8	7
(4)	21	28	25	21	20	20	18	16	14	25	26	23
(5)	24	49	40	56	29	51	61	25	29	51	23	48

20. Socialization of basic industries

	SL	Wms	Yale	Marq	BU	Ind	SC	Hwd	Reed	Dav	Bran	Stan
(1)	34	10	21	9	26	13	4	31	29	12	25	15
(2)	41	29	34	23	34	20	24	27	28	23	34	29
(3)	8	8	6	10	9	8	12	13	11	5	8	8
(4)	5	28	22	26	15	22	20	15	13	31	17	22
(5)	9	26	17	32	13	34	40	9	16	28	11	24

21. National Health Insurance

	SL	Wms	Yale	Marq	BU	Ind	SC	Hwd	Reed	Dav	Bran	Stan
(1)	63	39	54	28	56	30	31	54	58	27	61	32
(2)	18	35	28	35	27	28	34	25	18	46	22	38
(3)	14	14	13	15	11	20	15	14	10	11	9	15
(4)	3	6	3	13	3	10	12	3	8	9	1	7
(5)	—	5	2	8	1	8	7	—	3	5	2	4

30. Have you ever smoked marijuana?
(1) Yes   (2) No

	SL %	Wms %	Yale %	Marq %	BU %	Ind %	SC %	Hwd %	Reed %	Dav %	Bran %	Stan %
(1)	82	75	65	33	74	42	34	40	76	33	65	66
(2)	18	24	34	67	25	58	65	56	22	66	33	33

48. All things considered, do you think more lenient college administrations standards for black applicants should be adopted?
(1) Yes   (2) No   (3) Unsure or no opinion

	SL %	Wms %	Yale %	Marq %	BU %	Ind %	SC %	Hwd %	Reed %	Dav %	Bran %	Stan %
(1)	59	61	55	36	42	38	24	63	50	54	62	63
(2)	26	24	25	48	38	45	65	24	22	35	22	20
(3)	11	11	17	15	15	12	9	9	23	9	13	17

91. Would you say that at the present time
(1) I am in substantial agreement with the religious tradition in which I was raised?

Figure 4.2 Cross-sectional study of values in representative campuses (selected questions and responses) (*continued*)

(2) I partially agree with the religious tradition in which I was raised but have important reservations?

(3) I wholly reject the religious tradition in which I was raised?

	SL %	Wms %	Yale %	Marq %	BU %	Ind %	SC %	Hwd %	Reed %	Dav %	Bran %	Stan %
(1)	13	8	11	17	9	17	18	11	10	10	20	9
(2)	65	71	54	74	56	52	62	63	47	74	61	61
(3)	22	20	33	6	32	27	19	24	40	16	19	27

95. Below are several very brief, rough statements of various conceptions of the Deity. Check the one that most nearly approximates your views.
    (1) There is an immensely wise, omnipotent, three-person God Who created the universe and Who maintains an active concern for human affairs.
    (2) There is a God precisely as described in (1) except that He is absolutely One and in no sense possesses trinitarian nature.
    (3) I believe in a God about Whom nothing definite can be affirmed except that I sometimes sense Him as a mighty "spiritual presence" permeating all mankind and nature.
    (4) There is a vast, impersonal principle of order or natural uniformity working throughout the whole universe and which, though not conscious of mere human life, I choose to call "God."
    (5) Because of our ignorance in this matter, I see no adequate grounds for either affirming or denying the existence of God.
    (6) I reject all belief in anything that could reasonably be called "God" and regard every such notion as a fiction unworthy of worship.
    (7) Other

	SL %	Wms %	Yale %	Marq %	BU %	Ind %	SC %	Hwd %	Reed %	Dav %	Bran %	Stan %
(1)	3	5	14	45	9	24	39	21	5	23	2	15
(2)	3	3	2	3	2	4	1	3	2	1	3	1
(3)	22	28	26	29	30	29	25	23	8	35	20	25
(4)	22	21	20	6	22	16	10	21	17	13	28	24
(5)	22	18	16	4	18	13	11	16	29	11	23	15
(6)	9	4	8	2	6	4	3	4	16	6	8	9
(7)	11	17	7	8	6	6	5	6	16	8	9	7

Notes: Question numbers correspond to source.

The schools included were Sarah Lawrence College (SL), a small, private, nonsectarian women's school; Williams College (Wms), a small, private nonsectarian men's liberal arts college in New England; Yale University (Yale), a large, private nonsectarian school in Connecticut; Marquette University (Marq), a large, Milwaukee-based coeducational Catholic school; Boston University (BU), a large, private coeducational school with many commuter students; Indiana University, (Ind), a giant Midwestern land-grant institution dominating the small city of Bloomington; the University of South Carolina (SC), a recently integrated state-supported school of the South; Howard University (Hwd), a private, nondenominational, predominantly black university in Washington, D.C.; Reed College (Reed), a small, private coeducational school in Portland, Ore., noted for educational and political progressivism; Davisons College (Dav), a small, private Presbyterian men's school in rural North Carolina; Brandeis University (Bran), a medium-sized school in Boston with a predominantly Jewish student body and a reputation for political liberalism; and Stanford University (Stan), a large, private California university traditionally catering to the upper middle and upper classes.

Source: Philip P. Ardery, "Opinion on the Campus," *National Review*, vol. 23 (June 15, 1971), pp. 635–50. Reprinted with permission from *National Review Magazine*, 150 E. 35th St., New York, New York 10016.

Carolina. This figure also shows some of the dangers of describing a culture with "national" averages, which hide the diversity that may actually exist between subcultures.

Longitudinal research involves studies of specified phenomena running over an extended period of time. Longitudinal studies have been used in other areas of consumer research, but only recently has this method of research been applied much to the study of values. Longitudinal research is essential, however, for accurate monitoring of changes in values and preparing a data base useful for the prediction of future value systems. Two basic types of longitudinal studies exist: continuous panels and repeated representative samples.

Longitudinal studies of values

Continuous panels. A continuous panel is a group of consumers who agree to respond to requests for information on a repeated basis over an extended period of time.[38] The panel is often selected to correspond with demographic characteristics of the population. Panel members are asked the same questions in repeated time periods to measure changes in their attitudes, values, or behavior.

The panel as a source of information has the following weaknesses:

> First, there is the question of whether persons who are willing to join a panel and to continue participating over a period of time are ipso facto "different" from other persons. There is some evidence to suggest that panel members are different . . .
>
> A second inherent problem in panels is that membership in a panel may, in itself, affect the behavior of the members, or at least affect what they report.[39]

It has generally not been practical in the past to measure values by interviewing the same consumers because of the long time periods between interviews needed for analysis of value shifts, but such panel studies can be valuable by analyzing different segments of members (such as by age groups) and analyzing whether or not shifts seem to be occurring as consumers advance in age.

Repeated measures. A more practical method of measuring value shifts is through repeated studies of representative samples of the culture. The selection of respondents is generally done using probability samples to achieve projectability. In the United States, a number of organizations have collected data using such methods and trends are now being observed. Some of the more commonly used polls or surveys of such type include the Gallup Poll, the Harris Poll, the Yanklelovich "Monitor," and

---

38 For an introductory discussion of the characteristics of consumer panels, see Robert D. Buzzell, Donald F. Cox, and Rex V. Brown, *Marketing Research and Information Systems* (New York: McGraw-Hill, 1969), pp. 230–40; also Paul E. Green and Donald S. Tull, *Research for Marketing Decisions* (Englewood Cliffs, N.J.: Prentice-Hall, 1970), pp. 97–102.

39 Buzzell et al., *Marketing Research*, pp. 231–32.

repeated surveys by Opinion Research Corporation. Typical examples of such studies by two organizations, Harris and Gallup, are presented in Figure 4.3. It is desirable to compare topics surveyed by various polling

Figure 4.3 Repeated measures of consumer values

The growing disaffection of American consumers

Statement	Percent believing			Change 1966–1974
	1966	1972	1974	
Rich get richer	45%	68%	79%	75.6%
Leaders don't care about me	26	50	63	42.3
What I think doesn't count	37	53	60	62.2

Source: The Harris Poll, © by the *Chicago Tribune*. World rights reserved.

Growing frustration, distrust and alienation

Statement	Percent responding "yes"			Change 1963–1973
	1963	1969	1973	
Satisfied with:				
Your standard of living	77	—	71	(7.8%)
The work you do	85	87	89	(7.1)
Children's education	66	64	61	(7.8)
Honesty of people	34	—	22	(35.3)
Family's future	64	58	53	(17.2)

Source: Gallup Poll, various releases. Reprinted by permission of The Gallup Poll, Princeton, New Jersey 08540.

organizations, even though the questions involved may not be exactly the same. The results shown in Figure 4.3 agree with each other in the conclusion that the American consumer is increasingly alienated or frustrated. Such values may lead to a rise in distrust in advertising, changed voting preferences, militant consumerism or other changes.

Studies of a wide variety of cultural, economic and social changes over time are available to the marketing analyst even though they generally have not been prepared for marketing purposes.[40] One reason for monitoring such changes is to predict future directions in the marketing environment. Effective strategies in almost all types of organizations

40 Eleanor B. Sheldon and Wilbert E. Moore, eds., *Indicators of Social Change: Concepts and Measurements* (New York: Russell Sage Foundation, 1968). A basic source for many types of social and economic trend data is Bureau of the Census, *Historical Statistics of the United States: Colonial Times to 1970, Bicentennial Edition* (Washington: U.S. Government Printing Office, 1976).

increasingly require a future orientation and analysis of value systems as central to the methodology of futurology.[41]

Cross-cultural analysis of consumer behavior

Organizations of all types are increasingly global in nature. The research methodologies and analytical perspectives required to understand consumer behavior also need to be global in nature. One approach for accomplishing this is the set of methods and knowledge developed in the discipline of anthropology known as cross-cultural analysis.

Cross-cultural analysis is the systematic comparison of similarities and differences in the behavioral and material aspects of cultures. Cross-cultural analysis is appropriate in the investigation of domestic marketing problems (such as youth and middle-aged market segments, black and white markets, geographic markets, or rural and urban markets) and for the investigation of foreign markets.

Cross-cultural methods of analysis were developed in anthropology and are founded upon an interest in cataloguing similarities and contrasts among peoples of various cultures.[42] Among societies so remotely located that they could not possibly have come into contact with each other, remarkable similarities are found in the methods with which they handle common problems. Some of the similarities between cultures, defined as items prohibited or compelled by the culture, are described in Figure 4.4.

Cross-cultural analysis in anthropology

The methodology of cross-cultural studies in anthropology and in consumer behavior involves all of the methodologies described earlier in this chapter, but adapted to the special requirements of making systematic comparisons across cultures. Cultural methods require special techniques to handle differences in language, structural characteristics of the societies, and values of the investigator that differ from the culture under study. The details of these methods are beyond the scope of this book.[43] Scientific studies of cross-cultural problems can usually be conceptualized, however, into the following stages:

Cross-cultural research methodology

1. Statistical comparisons of societies involved in the study

2. Broad typological comparisons

41 For expansion of this perspective and a review of relevant research techniques, see David T. Kollat, "Environmental Forecasting and Strategic Planning: Perspectives on the Methodology of Futurology," paper presented at the American Marketing Association Fall Conference, Minneapolis, Minn. (September 1, 1971). Also, see current issues of *The Futurist*, published by the World Future Society, P.O. Box 30369, Bethesda Branch, Washington, D.C. 20014.

42 For a discussion of this premise, see Clyde Kluckhohn, "Universal Categories of Culture," in A. L. Kroeber, ed., *Anthropology Today* (Chicago: University of Chicago Press, 1953), pp. 507–23.

43 An introduction to cross-cultural methods is Frank W. Moore, ed., *Readings in Cross-Cultural Methodology* (New Haven, Conn.: Human Relations Area Files Press, 1961); Oscar Lewis, "Comparisons in Cultural Anthropology," in William L. Thomas, Jr., ed., *Current Anthropology: A Supplement to Anthropology Today* (Chicago: University of Chicago Press, 1956), pp. 259–92; R.W. Brislin, W.J. Lonner and R.M. Thorndike, *Cross-Cultural Research Methods* (New York: John Wiley and Sons, Inc., 1973).

Figure 4.4 Behaviors prohibited and compelled in 25 primitive cultures

(1) **Behavior items both prohibited and compelled in the 25 cultures**

Eating, drinking, vocalizing, talking, defecating, urinating, playing, marrying, working, harming others, harming self.

(2) **Behavior items prohibited**

Sucking, cannibalism, biting, crying, . . . incest, adultery, . . . murdering, stealing, assuming another's prerogatives, harming food, hindering manufacturing, hindering course of war, inviting bad luck, . . . being angry, . . . deceiving others, angering others, committing suicide, destroying goods, committing treason, being jealous, being irresponsible, hating, playing, being lazy.

(3) **Behavior items compelled**

Wailing, weeping, sleeping, giving, entering, being formal, . . . mourning, naming others, respecting others, cleansing self, protecting others, obeying others, purifying self, being secluded, helping others, learning, avoiding retaliation, . . . avenging, being hospitable, concealing parts of body, . . . expressing grief, fighting outgroup, pacifying others, being friendly, thanking others, being fertile, participating in food quest, . . . being brave, avoiding bad luck, ensuring good luck, aiding food quest, being generous, being kind, manufacturing, being industrious.

Source: From "Society, Culture, and the Human Organism," by C. S. Ford *Journal of General Psychology,* 1939, vol. 20, pp. 135–79; reprinted in Frank W. Moore, ed., *Readings in Cross-Cultural Methodology* (New Haven, Conn.: Human Relations Area Files Press, 1961), pp. 130–65, at p. 158. Reprinted by permission of Journal Press.

3. Descriptive, functional analyses of one or more aspects of culture

4. Descriptive and analytical comparisons of total culture

5. Restudies by the same investigator

6. Restudies by different investigators

Cross-cultural marketing strategies

Marketing on a global or international basis has increased in importance in recent years, causing a rising concern about the policy of developing strategies and programs that are appropriate across national boundaries. To accomplish such an objective requires much more attention to analysis of the culture, which provides the environment for the success or failure of such marketing strategies.

Standardization versus localization. There is considerable controversy in the practice of marketing concerning whether or not advertising and other elements of the marketing program can be standardized across a number of cultures or whether it must be localized for each culture. Erik Elinder initiated the position that consumer behavior is subject to cultural universals and that advertising can be standardized.[44] Fatt amplifies this position by stating that "even different peoples are *basically* the same, and that an international advertising campaign with a truly universal

44 Erik Elinder, "How International Can European Advertising Be?" *Journal of Marketing,* vol. 29, pp. 7–11 (April 1965).

appeal can be effective in any market."[45] He illustrates his position with these examples:

> The desire to be beautiful is universal. Such appeals as "mother and child," "freedom from pain," "glow of health," know no boundaries.
>
> In a sense, the young women in Tokyo and the young women in Berlin are sisters not only "under the skin," but on their skin and on their lips and fingernails, and even in their hair styles. If they could, the girls of Moscow would follow suit; and some of them do.[46]

There are many obstacles, but a trend does appear to be developing toward greater standardization.[47] In a study of 27 multinational companies operating in the United States and Europe, including companies such as General Foods, Nestlé, Coca-Cola, Procter & Gamble, Unilever, and Revlon, Sorenson and Wiechmann found that 63 percent of the total marketing programs were rated as "highly standardized."[48] The results of this study show that, as one would expect, the more similar are countries, the higher percentage of the marketing program that can be standardized. These authors concluded by describing the importance of cross-cultural (or "cross-border") analysis:

> . . . managements of multinationals should give high priority to developing their ability to conduct *systematic cross-border analysis*, if they are not already doing so. Such analysis can help management avoid the mistake of standardizing when markets are significantly different. At the same time, systematic cross-border analysis can help avoid the mistake of excessive custom-tailoring when markets are sufficiently similar to make standardized programs feasible.[49]

A realistic assessment of the standardization-localization controversy is that the management of a firm must be adaptive to some elements of the marketing program that are localized and others that are standardized. Marketing strategy that is not built upon an understanding of cultural realities will have unpredictable success patterns.[50] Yet, there is ample evidence to show that marketing strategies can be developed that are applicable worldwide.[51] One study shows that about two-thirds of interna-

45 Arthur C. Fatt, "The Danger of 'Local' International Advertising," *Journal of Marketing*, vol. 31, pp. 60–62 (January 1967).

46 Fatt, "Dangers," p. 61; also Arthur C. Fatt, "A Multi-National Approach to International Advertising," *International Executive*, vol. 7, pp. 5–6 (Winter 1965).

47 Robert D. Buzzell, "Can You Standardize Multinational Marketing?" *Harvard Business Review*, vol. 46, pp. 102–13 (November–December, 1968).

48 Ralph Z. Sorenson and Ulrich E. Wiechmann, "How Multinationals View Marketing Standardization," *Harvard Business Review*, vol. 53 (May–June, 1975), pp. 38–56.

49 *Ibid*, p. 48.

50 Montrose Sommers and Jerome Kernan, "Why Products Flourish Here, Fizzle There," *Columbia Journal of World Business*, vol. 2, pp. 89–97 (March–April, 1967).

51 Dean Peebles, "Goodyear's Worldwide Advertising," *The International Advertiser*, vol. 8, pp. 19–22 (January 1967) (both good and weak examples are cited in this article); Walter P. Margulies, "Why Global Marketing Requires a Global Focus on Product Design," *Business Abroad*, pp. 22–23 (August 22, 1966); Norman Heller, "How Pepsi-Cola Does It in 110 Countries," In John S. Wright and Jac L. Goldstrucker, eds., *New Ideas for Successful Marketing* (Chicago: American Marketing Association, 1966), pp. 700–15.

tional firms practice policies emphasizing a localized, decentralized policy.[52] There is a growing literature of research and analysis, however, indicating that the most effective results are achieved where home office executives are sensitive to global cultures while those at local (national) or decentralized levels are responsible and flexible.[53] A firm that is highly centralized in its global operations has been described by some researchers as having an ethnocentrism orientation while a decentralized firm is one having a regiocentric or geocentric orientation; the desirability of the particular orientation depends on several factors: the size of the firm, experience in a given market, the size of the potential market, and the type of product and its cultural dependency.[54]

Cross-cultural marketing research

Marketing researchers have begun to conduct cross-cultural studies in recent years, although the practice is still embryonic. The previous lack of cross-cultural studies is probably due to lack of familiarity with cross-cultural methods, the expense of such studies for academic researchers, and the tendency for United States multinational business firms to spend only a minimum amount on marketing research when entering foreign markets compared to their expenditures on domestic markets.[55]

British marketing researchers appear to have a longer history of cross-cultural research than United States researchers. Their findings have been tested for applicability to United States markets, and Ehrenberg and Goodhardt report that mathematical models of repeat-buying habits developed from data on British consumers yield useful results for United States purchasers.[56] This study is important because it lends credence to the belief that consumer models and theories are applicable on a worldwide basis. Other cross-cultural studies have been conducted by Dunn[57] using the case method of comparison and Lorimor and Dunn using the semantic differential and other measures of advertising effec-

52 James H. Donnelly, Jr., and John K. Ryans, Jr., "The Role of Culture in Organizing Overseas Operations: The Advertising Experience," University of Washington *Business Review*, vol. 30, pp. 35–41 (Autumn 1969). For additional details, see John K. Ryans, Jr., and James H. Donnelly, Jr., "Selected Practices of United States 'International' Advertising Agencies," University of Washington *Business Review*, vol. 3, pp. 43–55 (Autumn 1970). This study is also briefly reported in John K. Ryans, Jr., and James H. Donnelly, Jr., "Standardized Global Advertising, a Call as Yet Unanswered," *Journal of Marketing*, vol. 33, pp. 57–59 (April 1969).

53 Richard M. Bessom, "Corporate Image Strategy for Multinations," *Atlantic Economic Review*, (July–August, 1974), pp. 47–51; David Gestetner, "Strategy in Managing International Sales," *Harvard Business Review*, vol. 52 (September–October 1974), pp. 103–08; Howard V. Perlmutter and David A. Heenan, "How Multinational Should Your Top Managers Be?" *Harvard Business Review*, vol. 52 (November–December 1974), pp. 121–32; Harry L. Davis, Gary D. Eppen, and Lars-Gunner Mattson, "Critical Factors in Worldwide Purchasing," *Harvard Business Review*, vol. 52 (November–December 1974), pp. 81–90. For a theoretical framework to analyze markets and marketing, see Robert Bartels, "Are Domestic and International Marketing Dissimilar?" *Journal of Marketing*, vol. 32 (July 1968), pp. 56–61.

54 Yoram Wind, Susan P. Douglas, and Howard V. Perlmutter, "Guidelines for Developing International Marketing Strategies," *Journal of Marketing*, vol. 37 (April 1973), pp. 14–23.

55 Support for this statement is provided in a study by Richard H. Holton, "Marketing Policies in Multinational Corporations," *California Management Review*, vol. 13, pp. 57–67, at p. 62 (Summer 1971).

56 A.S.C. Ehrenberg and G.J. Goodhardt, "A Comparison of American and British Repeat-Buying Habits," *Journal of Marketing Research*, vol. 5, pp. 29–33 (February 1968).

57 S. Watson Dunn, "The Case Study Approach in Cross-Cultural Research," *Journal of Marketing Research*, vol. 3, pp. 26–31 (February 1966).

tiveness.[58] The semantic differential has also been used successfully in a study of Japanese and United States ratings of products from various countries.[59] The problems of attitude scaling have been investigated in the context of French-English differences among consumers in Quebec, Canada,[60] and a significant study of source and message effects on French and Anglo Canadians was recently conducted by Tamilia.[61] The use of traditional economic comparisons for cross-cultural analysis is illustrated by Goldman's study of Soviet and American consumers.[62]

A pioneering cross-cultural study was published by Sethi, which involved a cluster analysis of 86 countries on 12 environmental and societal factors. While this study did not involve values, it does provide provocative methodology that might be applied to additional dimensions. Using the BC TRY system of cluster analysis to group variables in such a way as to maximize within-group similarities and between-group differences, Sethi found clusters, which he labeled: (1) production and transportation, (2) personal consumption, (3) trade, and (4) health and education. After the variables were grouped, countries were classified into clusters according to their scores on the clustered variables. Seven clusters were formed from the 86 countries. For example, countries such as Nigeria, Sudan, Dahomey, Tanzania, and South Viet Nam were part of one cluster while Syria, Thailand, United Arab Republic, and the Philippines were part of the countries in another cluster. The United States could not be grouped with any of the other countries.[63] While this study is embryonic and does not yield data corresponding to consumer decisions or marketing strategy, it does provide the basis for much additional development potentially valuable in understanding ways of grouping markets together for common marketing programs.[64]

Overcoming language problems. It is sometimes difficult to overcome language problems in cross-cultural studies, and a number of techniques have been developed to achieve cross-cultural equivalency in language. A literal translation or a translation by someone who is not familiar with the culture of the language as well as its literal meaning may result in serious marketing mistakes. An example was a widely publicized situation in Canada in which Hunt-Wesson attempted to use the "Big John" family brand name by translating it into French as "Gros Jos," which is a

58 E.S. Lorimor and S. Watson Dunn, "Four Measures of Cross-Cultural Advertising Effectiveness," *Journal of Advertising Research*, vol. 8, pp. 11–13 (1968).

59 Akira Nagashima, "A Comparison of Japanese and U.S. Attitudes toward Foreign Products," *Journal of Marketing*, vol. 34, pp. 68–74 (January 1970).

60 Richard W. Crosby, "Attitude Measurement in a Bilingual Culture," *Journal of Marketing Research*, vol. 6, pp. 421–26 (November 1969).

61 Robert D. Tamilia, "A Cross-Cultural Analysis of Selected Source Effects on Information Processing: An Empirical Study of French and English Canadian Consumers," unpublished Ph.D. dissertation, Ohio State University, 1977.

62 Marshall I. Goldman, "A Cross-Cultural Comparison of the Soviet and American Consumer," in Moyer, *op. cit.,* pp. 195–99.

63 S. Prakash Sethi, "Comparative Cluster Analysis for World Markets," *Journal of Marketing Research*, vol. 8, pp. 348–54 (August 1971).

64 Also see Robert D. Schooler and Carl Ferguson, "A Model to Determine the Activated Potential of Foreign Markets," *Marquette Business Review* (Fall 1974), pp. 129–36.

colloquial French expression denoting a woman with big breasts. The incident caused *Playboy* magazine to award its annual "Booby Boo Boo Award" to the company.

When it is desired to use the same name throughout the world rather than translate a brand name, careful research and analysis may determine a brand name that can be used widely without translation. Walter Margulies suggests the following questions be researched or analyzed in the attempt to find an English name that can be used on a cross-cultural basis:

1. Does the English name of the product have another meaning, perhaps unfavorable in one or more of the countries where it is to be marketed?

2. Can the English name be pronounced everywhere? For example, Spanish and some other languages lack a *k* in their alphabets, an initial letter in many popular U.S. brand names.

3. Is the name close to that of a foreign brand or does it duplicate another product sold in English-speaking countries?

4. If the product name is distinctly American, will national pride and prejudice work against the acceptance of the product?[65]

The most useful and straightforward technique for overcoming language proglems is *back-translation*. In the back-translation procedure, a message (word or a series of words) is translated from its original language to the translated language and back to its original language by a number of translators. This process is repeated several times with the translated versions being interchanged with the original among the translators. The purpose of the iterations is an attempt to achieve conceptual equivalency in meaning by controlling the various translation biases of the translators.[66]

An example of a research instrument prepared in two languages is shown in Figure 4.5. This is a questionnaire given to passengers on Canadian Pacific Airlines, which serves both French and English speaking customers on a regular basis. Figure 4.5 displays the equivalent forms of the survey in each language.

Analyzing global markets

To conclude this section on cross-cultural marketing research, Figure 4.6 is presented. In some instances, marketing strategists are confronted with cultures quite similar and in others with cultures very different. In too many unfortunate cases, what has "worked" in the United States has been applied to a foreign market without understanding if the cultural

65 Walter P. Margulies, "Why Global Marketing Requires a Global Focus on Product Design," *Business Abroad*, vol. 94 (January 1969), p. 22.

66 Richard W. Brislin, "Back-Translation for Cross-Cultural Research," *Journal of Cross-Cultural Psychology*, vol. 1 (September 1970), pp. 185–216; and Osward Werner and Donald T. Campbell, "Translating, Working through Interpreters, and the Problems of Decentering," in Raoul Naroll and Ronald Cohen, eds., *A Handbook of Method in Cultural Anthropology* (Garden City, New York: The Natural History Press, 1970), pp. 398–420.

Figure 4.5 Would you like to help us help you?
Part of a Canadian Pacific Airlines questionnaire

Pouvons-nous Compter sur Votre Collaboration?

Pour pouvoir vous offrir un service aussi parfait que possible, nous aimerions connaître plus de détails sur vous-même, votre voyage et vos opinions.

Nous vous serions reconnaissants de bien vouloir remplir le questionnaire ci-joint durant ce voyage.

Au cas où vous voyagez en groupe, chaque participant de plus de onze ans est invité à remplir également ce questionnaire.

Vos réponses nous aideront à améliorer notre service à et rendre vos voyages subséquents encore plus agréables.

Nous vous remercions et vous souhaitons de passer un bon voyage.

Remarque: Les employés de la compagnie aérienne et leurs dépendants ne sont pas supposés remplir ce formulaire.

SONDAGE AUPRES DES PASSAGERS DES VOLS DOMESTIQUES

CP Air vous remercie de bien vouloir remplir ce questionnaire et apprécie votre collaboration à ce sujet. Vos réponses seront employées à des fins statistiques seulement et seront considérées strictement confidentielles.

No. de vol_____ Date _____ Mois Jour

1. a) Veuillez inscrire le nom de la compagnie aérienne qui a émis votre billet.

    b) Veuillez maintenant inscrire le numéro qui figure à l'angle droit supérieur de votre coupon de billet, même s'il n'a pas été émis par CP Air. (Les informations notées sur votre coupon-billet seront employées à des fins statistiques seulement et son strictement confidentielles.)

    Numéro du billet _____

2. Dans quelle ville êtes-vous monté(e) a bord de cet avion?
    Ville _____ Province

3. Où se trouve votre domicile actuel?
    Ville ____ Province/Etat ____ Pays

4. Quel est ou, si vous rentrez chez vous, quel a été le lieu de destination principal de votre voyage?
    Ville ____ Province/Etat ____ Pays

Would you like to help us help you?

In order to give you the best possible service, we need to know more about you, your journey and your opinions.

We would like you to complete, the following questionnaire at your convenience during this flight.

If you are travelling with a group, we would like each person over the age of 11 to complete a questionnaire.

The answers to these questions will be of great help to us in planning to meet your future travel requirements.

Thank you—and enjoy a pleasant journey.

Note: Airline employees and their dependents should not complete this questionnaire.

DOMESTIC

We at CP Air would like to thank you for your cooperation in answering this questionnaire. The information received will remain strictly confidential and will only be used for statistical purposes.

Flight No. _____ Date _____ Month Day

1. a) Will you please write in the name of the airline that issued your ticket?

    b) And now, will you please write in your ticket number (top right hand corner of your ticket coupon) even if it was not issued by CP Air. (The information provided on your ticket coupon will be used for statistical purposes only and will be treated in strict confidence.)

    Ticket Number_____

2. In which city did you board this particular flight?
    City _____ Province

3. In what city are you now living?
    City/Town ____ Province/Centre ____ Country

4. What is the main destination of your journey, or if you are now returning home, what was your main destination away from home?
    City/Town ____ Province/State ____ Country

Source: Reprinted by permission of the Marketing Planning Department, CP Air, Vancouver, Canada.

conditions were the same or not. A marketing strategist can improve the prediction of success by a careful analysis of the cultural conditions in the existing market, followed by another careful analysis of the cultural conditions in the market he or she contemplates entering. Where differences are observed, adjustment in the strategy employed can be undertaken. An outline for systematically analyzing the cultural determinants of success in each market is provided in Figure 4.6. This outline is designed to be used either with formal research methods (such as those described above) or, if research is not feasible, as an outline for critical thinking and analysis in the design of global strategy.[67]

67 For an introduction to sources of information about global markets, see David T. Kollat, Roger D. Blackwell and James F. Robeson, *Strategic Marketing* (New York: Holt, Rinehart and Winston, Inc., 1972), pp. 173–78. Also see Warren J. Keegan, "Multinational Scanning: A Study of the Information Sources Utilized by Headquarters' Executives in Multinational Companies," *Administrative Science Quarterly* (1975), pp. 411–421.

Figure 4.6 Outline of cross-cultural analysis of consumer behavior

1. **Determine relevant motivations in the culture:**

   What needs are fulfilled with this product in the minds of members of the culture? How are these needs presently fulfilled? Do members of this culture readily recognize these needs?

2. **Determine characteristic behavior patterns:**

   What patterns are characteristic of purchasing behavior? What forms of division of labor exist within the family structure? How frequently are products of this type purchased? What size packages are normally purchased? Do any of these characteristic behaviors conflict with behavior expected for this product? How strongly ingrained are the behavior patterns that conflict with those needed for distribution of this product?

3. **Determine what broad cultural values are relevant to this product:**

   Are there strong values about work, morality, religion, family relations, and so on, that relate to this product? Does this product connote attributes that are in conflict with these cultural values? Can conflicts with values be avoided by changing the product? Are there positive values in this culture with which the product might be identified?

4. **Determine characteristic forms of decision making:**

   Do members of the culture display a studied approach to decisions concerning innovations or an impulsive approach? What is the form of the decision process? Upon what information sources do members of the culture rely? Do members of the culture tend to be rigid or flexible in the acceptance of new ideas? What criteria do they use in evaluating alternatives?

5. **Evaluate promotion methods appropriate to the culture:**

   What role does advertising occupy in the culture? What themes, words, or illustrations are taboo? What language problems exist in present markets that cannot be translated into this culture? What types of salesmen are accepted by members of the culture? Are such salesmen available?

6. **Determine appropriate institutions for this product in the minds of consumers:**

   What types of retailers and intermediary institutions are available? What services do these institutions offer that are expected by the consumer? What alternatives are available for obtaining services needed for the product but not offered by existing institutions? How are various types of retailers regarded by consumers? Will changes in the distribution structure be readily accepted?

Subcultural influences on consumer behavior

Subcultural influences refer to the norms and values of subgroups within the larger or national culture. Individual consumers may be influenced only slightly by membership in specific subgroups or the subgroups may be the dominant force on the personality and life style of the consumer.

Four types of subcultures are described below. They are nationality groups, religious groups, geographic areas, and racial groups. The last type, because of its importance in contemporary American culture, is given a more extended analysis.

Nationality groups Many large cities contain relatively homogeneous groups within the city composed of nationality groups. These include Puerto Rican communities in New York, Cuban communities in Florida, and areas in many cities composed of first and second generation Scandinavians, Germans, Italians, Polish, Irish, Mexican-Americans, and so forth. Some of the persons in these communities become acculturated to the surrounding environment and lose much of their ethnic identity as a nationality group, but in other situations members retain their native language, live and move about in a restricted area of the city, interact primarily with other members of the nationality, and search for products similar to those in "the old country."

Areas of a city may become identified with members of a specific nationality. In such situations, retailers (and wholesalers) sell products appealing to the subculture and provide centers for cultural maintenance. Frequently newspapers and radio stations (and occasional television programs, such as Spanish programs in New York and Florida) are directed toward these markets. A dealer organization strong in ethnic markets may be essential in large cities. It is probably impossible to be successful with many products in New York City, for example, without knowledge of and adaptation to ethnic markets. General Motors is reported to be more successful than its competitors in New York City because of its strong penetration into ethnic markets through a dealer organization built upon subcultural norms and values. Funeral firms, physicians and dentists, and many other service organizations are heavily oriented toward the language and values of nationality groups.

Religious subcultures

Religious groups may provide important subcultures among groups in which members conform closely to group norms. Mormons, for example, may refrain from purchasing tobacco, liquor, and certain stimulants; Christian Scientists restrict their search for information and use of medicines; Seventh Day Adventists limit their purchase of meat and frequently purchase vegetable-based foods;[68] Jewish consumers may purchase kosher or other traditional foods; Christians from fundamental denominations may avoid ostentatious displays of jewelry or other wealth; the Amish avoid mechanized life styles and individualized personal appearance. Some Christians identified with the Jesus Movement may be creating a new subculture based upon basic, first century Christianity in contrast with contemporary conspicuous consumption.

Geographic areas

Geographic areas in a nation develop their own subculture. In the United States, the Southwest appears to have a characteristic style of life that emphasizes the casual form of dress, outdoor entertaining, and unique forms of recreation. Decision-making in the Southwest may also be less

---

68 An example of a marketing strategy originally designed for one subculture, Seventh Day Adventism, which has developed a much wider appeal, is found in the base, "Worthington Foods," in Wayne Talarzyk, *Contemporary Cases in Marketing* (Hinsdale, Illinois: Dryden Press, 1974), pp. 76–81.

rigid and perhaps more innovative than the conservative, inhibited attitudes toward new products and programs that supposedly characterize the Midwest. The climate, religious and nationality influences may be highly interrelated to geographic influences, however.[69]

French-Canadian markets. One of the largest and most distinct subcultures in North America is the French-Canadian area of Canada, mostly in Quebec. This might be considered either a nationality group or a geographic subculture. The Province of Quebec accounts for over 27 percent of the Canadian population and about 25 percent of income and retail sales.[70] There is a general belief by many observers that the distinct values of the French culture have been ignored by English-oriented advertisers, thereby creating a social problem as well as limiting the potential effectiveness of communications to the French market. To some extent, disadvantaged French Canadians may have been treated differently because of different social class groupings than English markets.[71]

A key question that faces marketing strategists who must deal with both the French Canadian (FC) and English Canadian (EC) consumer is the degree to which advertising and other elements of the marketing program are transferable between each subculture. From anecdotal evidence and experience, some observers have concluded that separate advertising material must be developed to be effective in the FC subculture.[72] Although some research has begun to emerge to define similarities and differences between FC and EC consumers,[73] it focuses mostly only limited aspects of consumer behavior and lacks a conceptual framework

69 Several empirical research projects have recently emerged of a cross-cultural nature that attempt to define bases for similarities and differences between markets. In addition to the citations in the preceding pages, consumer analysts interested in this subject should read studies such as the following: Susan P. Douglas, "Cross-National Comparisons and Consumer Stereotypes: A Case Study of Working and Non-Working Wives in the U.S. and France," *Journal of Consumer Research*, vol. 3 (June 1976), pp. 12–20; Robert T. Green and Erick Langeard, "A Cross-National Comparison of Consumer Habits and Innovator Characteristics," *Journal of Marketing*, vol. 39 (July 1975), pp. 34–41; Johan Arndt, "Temporal Lags in Comparative Retailing," *Journal of Marketing*, vol. 36 (October 1972), pp. 40–45; John J. Painter and Kent L. Granzin, "A Differential Study of Shopping Behavior in England, Mexico and the United States," Working Paper, College of Business, University of Utah, 1976.

70 Detailed estimates of market statistics for each province are available in "Canadian Survey of Buying Power," *Sales and Marketing Management* (July 26, 1976), Section D. Also see projections of Canadian markets in Edward B. Harvey, "Demographics and Future Marketing: Implications in Canada," *The Business Quarterly* (Summer 1976), pp. 61–65, which is based upon Statistics Canada, Population Projections for Canada and the Provinces, 1972–2001 (Catalogue No. 91–514).

71 Pierre C. Lefrancois and Gilles Chatel, "The French-Canadian Consumer: Fact and Fancy," in J.S. Wright and J.L. Goldstucker, eds., *New Ideas for Successful Marketing* (Chicago: American Marketing Association, 1966), pp. 705–17; Bernard Blishen, "Social Class and Opportunity in Canada," *Canadian Review of Sociology and Anthropology*, vol. 7 (May 1970), pp. 110–27.

72 R. Gelfand, "French-Canadian Is More Purposive to Ads than English Counterpart," *Advertising Age* (November 16, 1964), p. 124; R. Gelfand, "It's Much More than Language," *Marketing* (June 9, 1969), pp. 18 ff; R. Gelfand, "French Canada as a Minority Market," in Ronald C. Curhan, ed., *1974 Combined Proceedings* (Chicago: American Marketing Association, 1975), pp. 680–82; Maurice Watier, "Pris dans le Moule Americain," *Culture Vivante*, no. 16 (February 1970), pp. 8–12.

73 Lefrancois and Chatel, "The French Consumer"; Richard W. Crosby, "Attitude Measurement in a Bilingual Culture," *Journal of Marketing Research*, vol. 6 (November 1969), pp. 421–26; Doug Tigert, "Can a Separate Marketing Strategy for French Canada Be Justified: Profiling English-French Markets through Life Style Analysis," in D. Thompson and D. Leighton, eds., *Canadian Marketing: Problems and Prospects* (Toronto: John Wiley and Sons, Canada Ltd., 1973), pp. 113–42.

Figure 4.7 Example of a cross-cultural advertisement in Canada

Source: Reprinted by permission of DuPont of Canada Limited, Textile Division, Montreal, Quebec.

for evaluating cross-cultural communications.[74] Figure 4.7 presents an advertisement for DuPont of Canada which illustrates how advertising can be designed to be transferable to two cultures. The success of the ad includes reliance on graphics rather than copy for the majority of the message presentation.

Tamilia's research comparing communications with FC and EC consumers on a cross-cultural basis indicates the potential for increasing effectiveness in advertising communications by the use of a communications model that identifies the perceptual process of each subculture. Previous research comparing ethnic personality and communications led Tamilia to conclude that the French would evaluate objects more along concrete, objective, direct, and sensual or sensorial dimensions. Therefore, in communications that emphasized the source more than the message, the French would exhibit a greater affinity with the source of the communication and how the source is positioned in the consumer's effective-meaning system rather than the message, which presumes a more cognitive orientation. This is also compatible with some life style research by Tigert indicating that the French seem to be more responsive to people-oriented advertisements than message-oriented advertisements. Tamilia conducted his study in Montreal and Quebec City and concluded

74 Robert Tamilia, "Cross-Cultural Advertising Research: A Review and Suggested Framework," in Ronald C. Curhan, ed., *1974 Combined Proceedings*, "French Canada," pp. 131–34.

that French Canadians do react more to the source of the advertisements than do English Canadians who are more message-oriented.[75] This type of research, while only investigating part of the marketing program needed to reach a subculture effectively, indicates the potential for future advances. In addition to obtaining the objective of increased effectiveness of communication, the Quebec government has issued a statement, following a study by 17 *offices de la Langue Francaise*, encouraging advertisers to improve the quality of French advertising and linguistics.[76]

Because of the size of the French Canadian market, the world attention Quebec is receiving due to the separatism movement and the distinctiveness of the FC market, a great deal of interest is being generated in the cross-cultural aspects of FC and EC consumers. However, the research that occurs here is also of great interest in understanding many other, perhaps less visible, market situations of a similar nature such as Spanish-speaking Mexican-Americans in California, bilingual markets in Belgium and so forth, as well as black and white markets in the United States.

Black cultural influences on consumption

Racial influences provide another subculture affecting consumption. In the United States, the black subculture predominates among nonwhite groups, although Oriental groups are sometimes important in some mainland communities and in Hawaii.

Black culture does not mean the same as black skin color. The black culture arises out of a common heritage of slavery conditioned by income deprivation, a shared history of discrimination and suffering, confined housing opportunities, and denial of participation in many aspects of the majority culture. Some persons with black skin grew up with mostly white neighbors and friends, were relatively affluent, and were not exposed to the black culture (because it was generally not presented in white communications media or educational institutions). These individuals may not share black life styles, may have difficulty communicating in the black idiom and may prefer the music of Carole King to Aretha Franklin. Conversely, in contemporary society there are some white individuals who have chosen to assimilate black culture even though they retain white skin.

It should be understood that the "black market" must be considered as consisting of a core of values and economic realities with recognition of substantial variation just as there is among white markets. Within the black market, segmentation strategies are possible just as is true in dealing with white markets. The smaller size of black markets limits the

75 Tamilia, 1977, "Cross-Cultural Advertising."
76 Brian Heath, "The French Language Market," *Marketing* (June 5, 1972), pp. 19–46.

feasibility of segmentation strategies, however. Also, greater homogeneity in black markets than in white markets seems to be an accurate generalization. In addition, black consumers are adopting many of the consumption patterns of middle-class white majority society. The dilemma of black consumers, Bauer et al. report, is whether to accept consumption values of the white culture or whether to reject them. It appears that, in general, black consumers implicitly accept middle-class white values toward consumption but are at a disadvantage in obtaining them.[77]

Structural influences on black culture

Structural influences shape black subculture and simultaneously inhibit its manifestations. Four primary structural influences include poverty, inadequate educational institutions, differential family characteristics, and discrimination. These are briefly described.

Income deprivation

The black culture is frequently confused with the low-income culture. There is good reason why this confusion exists. Black consumers average much less income than do white consumers. Even Spanish-Americans (the "brown" subculture) earn more on the average than do black consumers, even though blacks have higher rates of education than browns.[78] Figure 4.8 shows the median family income of black families in

Figure 4.8 Median family income of black and white families, 1950 and 1975

	Median family income	
	1950	1975
White families	$3,445	$14,268
Black families	1,869	9,321

Source: U.S. Bureau of the Census, *Current Population Reports*, Series P-60, No. 108.

1975 to be $9,321 compared to $14,268 for white families. More dramatic perhaps is the proportion of black consumers who live below the poverty level as defined by the U.S. Department of Commerce. Figure 4.9 shows that 29.3 percent of all black families were below poverty level in 1975 compared to only 9.7 percent of white families. The differences in income are not attributable only to education differences, because in 1975, 39.3 percent of white families with four or more years of college were in the

77 Raymond A. Bauer, Scott M. Cunningham, and Lawrence H. Wortzel, "The Marketing Dilemma of Negros," *Journal of Marketing*, vol. 29, pp. 1–6 (July 1965). Also see Raymond A. Bauer and Scott M. Cunningham, "The Negro Market," *Journal of Advertising Research*, vol. 10, pp. 3–13 (April 1970).
78 "Brown Is Richer than Black," *Sales Management* (December 31, 1971), p. 2.

Figure 4.9 Persons below the poverty level (United States 1960–1975, selected years)

Race	1960		1965		1970		1975	
	Number below poverty level (millions)	Percent below poverty level	Number below poverty level (millions)	Percent below poverty level	Number below poverty level (millions)	Percent below poverty level	Number below poverty level (millions)	Percent below poverty level
White	28.3	18	22.5	13	17.5	9.9	17.8	9.7
Black and Other Races	11.5	56	10.7	47	7.9	32	8.1	29.3
Total	39.9	22	33.2	17	24.3	12.6	25.9	12.3

Source: U.S. Department of Commerce, *Current Population Reports,* Series P-20.
Note: The poverty threshold for a nonfarm family of four was $2,973 in 1959, $3,968 in 1970, and $5,500 in 1975.

over-$25,000 income category while only 29.4 percent of black families with four years of college were in that category.

The structural realities of income deprivation have two effects on studies of the black subculture. First, there is the direct effect on the culture—on the thinking about being poor by consumers. The second effect is one of methodological complexity in research on black consumption. The question in many marketing studies becomes one of separating out the effects on consumption due to lack of income versus the effects of being a part of the black subculture. Some of the studies reported in this chapter attempt to correct for this situation, but frequently marketing studies do not focus on this distinction.

It is important to note that although a predominant cultural fact is income deprivation, there are significant numbers of black consumers who are middle or upper income. Figure 4.10 shows the distribution of income for white and black families, revealing 16 percent of American black families with incomes over $15,000 (compared to 38 percent of white families).[79] In spite of increases during the 1960s, however, black families were hit harder by the recessions of the 1970s, and much progress was slowed because black families are more likely to be unemployed during recessions than are white families.[80]

Educational deprivation

The inadequacy of educational institutions to equip black consumers to compete in the marketplace is a significant structural characteristic that has forced black consumers to develop abilities without the advantage of formal education, in many instances. In spite of rising numbers of blacks enrolled in schools, the evidence is substantial that the institutions have been ineffective, because of inadequate resources or by design, at helping

79 "Black America; Still Waiting for Full Membership," *Fortune* (April 1975), pp. 162–72.
80 Curtis L. Gilroy, "Black and White Unemployment: The Dynamics of the Differential," *Monthly Labor Review* (February 1974), pp. 38–47. Also see Stanley H. Masters, *Black-White Income Differentials: Empirical Studies* (New York: Academic Press, 1975).

Figure 4.10 The changing pyramid of black family income

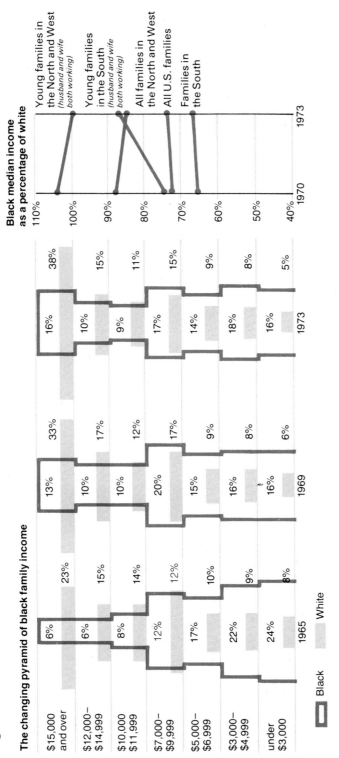

The changing pyramid of black family income

Black median income
as a percentage of white

□ Black

▨ White

Source: U.S. Department of Commerce, Bureau of the Census. Reprinted from "Black America: Still Waiting for Full Membership," *Fortune* (April 1975). p. 162.

black consumers master the educational skills needed for full participation.[81]

Differential family characteristics

The differential family characteristics of the black subculture are important influences on the black consumers. Alleged instability of black families influences other values. The high proportion of black families headed by females also accounts for some of the poverty of black families. A study by the U.S. Department of Labor concluded:

> At the heart of the deterioration of the fabric of Negro society is the deterioration of the Negro family . . .
>
> There is probably no single fact of Negro American life so little understood by whites. . . . It is more difficult, however, for whites to perceive the effect that three centuries of exploitation have had on the fabric of Negro society itself. Here the consequences of the historic injustices done to Negro Americans are silent and hidden from view. But here is where the true injury has occurred; unless this damage is repaired, all the effort to end discrimination and poverty and injustice will come to little.[82]

A very complete review of the literature by Farley and Hermalin shows major differences in family stability between blacks and whites using criteria such as proportion living with spouse, proportion of illegitimate births, premarital conceptions, and children living with both parents.[83] Duncan and Duncan found that family stability affects life chances on such variables as improvement in occupational success.[84]

A striking feature of the black population now and in the future is that

81 Thomas F. Pettigrew, "Racial Segregation and Negro Education," in Daniel P. Moynihan, ed., *Toward a National Urban Policy* (New York: Basic Books, 1970), pp. 167–77; also Howard M. Bahr and Jack P. Gibbs, "Racial Differentiation in American Metropolitan Areas," *Social Forces*, vol. 45, pp. 521–32, especially pp. 522–23 (June 1967). Differences in education and other structural variables are analyzed in Charles B. Nam and Mary G. Powers, "Variations in Socioeconomic Structure by Race, Residence, and the Life Cycle," *American Sociological Review*, vol. 30, pp. 97–103 (February 1965); Calvin F. Schmid and Charles E. Nobbe, "Socioeconomic Differentials among Nonwhite Races," *American Sociological Review*, vol. 30, pp. 909–22 (December 1965); and Michael Hout and William R. Morgan, "Race and Sex Variations in the Causes of the Expected Attainments of High School Seniors," *American Journal of Sociology*, vol. 81 (1975), pp. 364–93. For a discussion of integration and education, see Lawrence T. Cagle, "Social Characteristics and Educational Aspirations of Northern, Lower-Class, Predominantly Negro Parents Who Accepted and Declined a School Integration Opportunity," *Journal of Negro Education*, vol. 37, pp. 406–17 (Fall 1968). Some dissenting research has recently been published minimizing the effect of race in the educational system, such as: Jerold Heiss and Susan Owens, "Self-Evaluations of Blacks and Whites," *American Journal of Sociology*, vol. 78 (1973), pp. 360–69; Eleanor R. Hall, "Motivation and Achievement in Black and White Junior College Students," *Journal of Social Psychology*, vol. 97 (1975), pp. 107–13, and Ross M. Stolzenberg, "Education, Occupation, and Wage Differences between White and Black Men," *American Journal of Sociology*, vol. 81 (1975), pp. 298–321.

82 Office of Policy Planning and Research of U.S. Department of Labor, *The Negro Family: The Case for National Action* (Washington, D.C.: U.S. Government Printing Office, 1965), p. 5. This reference includes many statistical data on black families.

83 Reynolds Farley and Albert I. Hermalin, "Family Stability: A Comparison of Trends between Blacks and Whites," *American Sociological Review*, vol. 36, pp. 1–17 (February 1971). An interesting study comparing fertility among blacks and other minority groups shows that the higher fertility rates of blacks are associated with education and urbanization. When those two variables are controlled, blacks have lower fertility rates than whites. See Calvin Goldscheider and Peter R. Uhlenberg, "Minority Group Status and Fertility," *American Journal of Sociology*, vol. 74, pp. 361–72 (January 1969).

84 Beverly Duncan and Otis D. Duncan, "Family Stability and Occupational Success," *Social Problems*, vol. 16, pp. 286–301 (Winter 1969).

it is very young. In 1975 half of all black persons in the United States were under 23.4 years of age. The median age of the white population was 29.6 years. By 1985 the median age for blacks will be between 19 and 25 years as compared to a range of 27 to 30 years for the whites.

The effects of discrimination on the black subculture are so massive and enduring that they cannot be ignored in the analysis of consumer behavior, even though analysis of the topic is beyond the scope of the present discussion.[85] No analysis of expenditure patterns by black families is reasonable without examining the effects of forced housing conditions to which black families have been subjected. Black consumers wishing to move to middle- and upper-class areas of the city have often been prohibited from doing so. Even if some houses were available on an open basis, the black consumer's choices may have been limited by the unavailability of normal financing and social pressure from the potential neighbors.[86] The pressures may be so great that the black family is discouraged from moving into housing in which it can take pride in ownership. One possible alternative is to purchase status products other than housing.[87]

Discrimination

Evaluative criteria of black consumers may be considerably different when the effects are considered of their being eliminated from sources of power in the businesses that provide their goods, the government that is supposed to protect their interests as consumers,[88] or even the unions that are supposed to obtain jobs with which to buy goods.[89] One study concluded through a Markov model analysis that racial differences in occupation would decline sharply after only one generation in which discrimination was absent.[90] It seems reasonable to assume that the black subculture would provide feelings of skepticism toward claims of white-owned businesses that have contributed to keeping them locked in segregated residential patterns, limited employment opportunities, and supported invisibility in the media.[91] It is not surprising that advertisers should worry about the effect of their advertising upon black consumers

85 For an introduction to this topic, see *Report of the National Advisory Commission on Civil Disorders* (New York: Bantam, 1968); Michael Harrington, *The Other America* (New York: Macmillan, 1962); William H. Grier and Price M. Cobbs, *Black Rage* (New York: Basic Books, 1968); Stokeley Carmichael and Charles Hamilton, *Black Power: The Politics of Liberation* (New York: Random House, 1967).

86 James F. Engel and Roger D. Blackwell, "Attitudes of Affluent Suburbia toward the Negro Neighbor," *MSU Business Topics*, pp. 42–49 (Autumn 1969). Also see M.R. Straszheim, "Housing Market Discrimination and Black Housing Consumption," *Quarterly Journal of Economics* (February 1974), pp. 19–43, and Richard Muth, "Black Segregation and Urban Problems," *Journal of Contemporary Business*, vol. 3 (Spring 1974), pp. 15–28.

87 Bauer and Cunningham, *Studies*.

88 Richard F. America, Jr., "What Do You People Want," *Harvard Business Review*, pp. 103–12 (March–April 1969). America's solution to this problem is to transfer ownership of 10 percent of business to minority groups.

89 Richard L. Rowan, "Discrimination and Apprentice Regulation in the Building Trades," *Journal of Business*, (October 1967); Leonard A. Rapping, "Union-Induced Racial Entry Bar," *Journal of Human Resources*, vol. 4, pp. 447–74 (1971).

90 Stanley Lieberson and Glenn V. Fuguitt, "Negro-White Occupational Differences in the Absence of Discrimination," *American Journal of Sociology*, vol. 73, pp. 188–200 (September 1967).

91 The effects of segregation are clearly shown in Bonnie Bullough, "Alienation in the Ghetto," *American Journal of Sociology*, vol. 72, pp. 469–78 (March 1967).

when attitudes are held such as those of a 17-year-old black male involved in the Newark riots of 1967:

> I'm not out to get Whitey . . . I'm just out to get out . . . They talk about getting out . . . They carried signs about getting out . . . Now looks like you got to burn the place down and shoot your way out . . .[92]

Black consumption patterns

The black subculture results in significant and direct influence on the consumption patterns of black consumers. The similarities between black and white markets are much greater than the differences, but there are some significant differences.[93] The vice-president for special markets observes, however, that most of the so-called racial behavior of black consumers involves their reactions to the interracial situation.[94]

Many factors must be considered in developing a marketing strategy for black markets beside behavioral preferences.[95] A fast-food chain, for example, completed a market research project among black consumers and found significantly fewer per capita purchases of the chain's product than among whites. Some of the chain's stores located in black, inner-city areas had the highest volume of any stores in the nation. At first, executives were bewildered by the research findings that appeared to contradict their experience. The answer, of course, involved the population density ratios of the areas surrounding the store. While the average consumption per person was lower, so many more persons lived in the neighborhood that the store's total volume was high.

There has been considerable consumer research in the past decade concerning black consumer patterns. These have been reviewed by Bauer and Cunningham[96] and by Alexis and Smith;[97] thus only a few major examples are provided in this text. Environmental influences were described at the beginning of this section. The following pages describe search processes of black consumers, alternative evaluation and experience levels, and choice processes.

Search processes and interpersonal communications

Considerable research has focused on communications in black communities and search processes of black consumers. Major findings are reported below with attention given to mass-media influences and to interpersonal communications.

1. Black consumers appear to be reached more effectively by general

92 David Gottlieb, "Poor Youth: A Study in Forced Alienation," *Journal of Social Issues*, pp. 91–119 (1969).

93 The debate on this subject is discussed in Raymond O. Oladipupo, *How Distinct Is the Negro Market?* (New York: Ogilvy and Mather, 1970).

94 H. Naylor Fitzhugh, in "The Negro Market—Two Viewpoints," *Media Scope*, at p. 72 (November 1967).

95 D. Parke Gibson, *The $30 Billion Negro* (New York: Macmillan, 1969).

96 Raymond A. Bauer and Scott M. Cunningham, *Studies in the Negro Market* (Cambridge, Mass.: Marketing Science Institute, 1970). Also, a similar synthesis is available in Donald Sexton, "Black Buyer Behavior," *Journal of Marketing*, vol. 36 (October 1972), pp. 36–39.

97 Marcus Alexis and Clyde M. Smith, "Marketing and the Inner-City Consumer," *Journal of Contemporary Business*, vol. 2 (Autumn 1973), pp. 45–80.

media for advertisers appearing in both black and white media and by black-oriented media for products specifically directed to black consumers.[98]

2. The use of black models in advertising did not increase in the period of 1946 to 1965 (although the social status of blacks in ads had increased) but the proportion of blacks in ads did increase (from 4 percent to 13 percent) from 1967 to 1974.[99]

3. Black consumers react more favorably to advertisements with all black models or to integrated models than to advertisements with all white models.[100] Whites in these same studies appear to react to black models as favorably or more so than white models, although this varies by product category[101] and by amount of prejudice.[102] Black consumers under the age of 30 appear to react unfavorably to advertisements with integrated settings.[103]

4. Black consumers appear to respond (in recall and attitude shift) more positively to advertisements than do white consumers.[104]

5. Black consumers listen to radio more than whites, particularly in the evenings and on weekends, although blacks listen to FM radio less than whites.[105]

6. Black television viewers dislike programs emphasizing white orient- ed subjects such as families, organizations, and similar topics and

98 John V. Petrof, "Reaching the Negro Market: A Segregated vs. a General Newspaper," *Journal of Advertising Research*, vol. 8, pp. 40–43 (April 1968).

99 Harold H. Kassarjian, "The Negro and American Advertising, 1946–1965," *Journal of Marketing Research*, vol. 6, pp. 29–39 (February 1969); also William H. Boyenton, "The Negro Turns to Advertising," *Journalism Quarterly*, vol. 42, pp. 227–35 (Spring 1965). Motivations of advertisers for using black models are reported in Taylor W. Meloan, "Afro-American Advertising Policy and Strategy," in Bernard A. Morin, ed., *Marketing in a Changing World* (Chicago: American Marketing Association, 1969), pp. 20–23. More recent increases are reported in Ronald Bush, Paul Solomon, and J. F. Hair, Jr., "There Are More Blacks in Commercials," *Journal of Advertising Research*, vol. 17 (February 1977), pp. 21–30.

100 Arnold M. Barban, "The Dilemma of 'Integrated' Advertising," *Journal of Business*, vol. 42, pp. 477–96 (October 1969); B. Stuart Tolley and John J. Goett, "Reactions to Blacks in Newspapers," *Journal of Advertising Research*, vol. 11, pp. 11–17 (April 1971); John W. Gould, Normal B. Sigband, and Cyril E. Zoerner, Jr., "Black Consumer Reactions to 'Integrated' Advertising: An Exploratory Study," *Journal of Marketing*, vol. 34, pp. 20–26 (July 1970); Pravat K. Choudhury and Lawrence S. Schmid, "Black Models in Advertising to Blacks," *Journal of Advertising Research*, vol. 14 (June 1974), pp. 19–22.

101 William V. Muse, "Product-Related Response to Use of Black Models in Advertising," *Journal of Marketing Research*, vol. 8, pp. 107–09 (February 1971); James E. Stafford and Al E. Birdwell, "Verbal versus Non-Verbal Measures of Attitudes: The Pupilometer," paper presented at the Consumer Behavior Workshop, American Marketing Association, Columbus, Ohio (August 1969); Mary Jane Schlinger and Joseph T. Plummer, "Advertising in Black and White," *Journal of Marketing Research*, vol. 9 (May 1972), pp. 149–53; Ronald Bush, Robert Gwinner, and Paul Solomon, "White Consumer Sales Response to Black Models," *Journal of Marketing*, vol. 38 (April 1974), pp. 25–29.

102 James W. Cagley and Richard N. Cardozo, "Racial Prejudice and Integrated Advertising: An Experimental Study," in McDonald, *op. cit.*, pp. 52–56; Carl E. Black, "White Backlash to Negro Ads: Fact or Fantasy," *Journalism Quarterly*, vol. 49 (Summer 1972), pp. 258–62.

103 Gould et al., "Black Consumer," p. 25; Michael K. Chapko, "Black Ads Are Getting Blacker," *Journal of Communication* (Autumn 1976), pp. 175–78.

104 Tolley and Goett, "Reactions," pp. 13–14; Petrof, "Reaching the Negro Market," p. 42.

105 Gerald J. Glasser and Gale D. Metzger, "Radio Usage by Blacks," *Journal of Advertising Research*, vol. 15 (October 1975), pp. 39–45.

watch more on the weekends in contrast to whites' higher viewing through the week.[106]

7. Participation by blacks in social organizations is higher than by whites with comparable socioeconomic characteristics, especially in the lowest income groups. Blacks are more likely than whites to belong to church and political groups and equally likely to belong to civic groups.[107]

8. Black opinion leadership and community control appears currently to be in a period of conflict between "old line" upper-class black leaders who were acceptable to white power holders, and upwardly mobile, usually young, aggressive blacks willing to tap latent aggressions toward "uppity niggers," "Jew merchants," and "crackers."[108]

Alternative evaluation

The process of evaluating alternative offerings in the marketplace appears to be influenced by a number of experience and environmental variables, which, in turn, affect the beliefs, attitudes, and intentions of black consumers. A number of studies have disclosed some generalizations that may be true about black consumers, although considerable caution is necessary in interpreting such findings because of the danger of ignoring variations that occur between market segments within the black market. Barry and Harvey, after surveying many of the studies of black consumer behavior, concluded the heterogeneous elements of the black market consist of four distinct market subsections, which they describe as (1) "Negroes," (2) "blacks," (3) "Afro-Americans," and (4) "recent foreign black immigrants."[109] Although it would be incorrect to assume that segments do not exist within the black market, most research has not made such delineations. The following generalizations are typical of the research based upon the less refined classification of black-white consumer behavior.

1. Blacks save more out of a given income than do whites with the same incomes.[110] Blacks use fewer savings and insurance services, however, and end up with less total financial resources than white families of equivalent income and tend to use the less advantageous

106 James W. Carey, "Variations in Negro-White Television Preference," *Journal of Broadcasting*, vol. 10, pp. 199–211 (1966).

107 These findings are in contrast with previously held beliefs about black social interaction, but the evidence is reasonably convincing for the more recent conclusions. See Anthony M. Orum, "A Reappraisal of the Social and Political Participation of Negros," *American Journal of Sociology*, vol. 72, pp. 32–46 (July 1966); Marvin E. Olsen, "Social and Political Participation of Blacks," *American Sociological Review*, vol. 35, pp. 682–96 (1970).

108 These terms and research are from Seymour Leventman, "Class and Ethnic Tensions: Minority Group Leadership in Transition," *Sociology and Social Research,* vol. 50, pp. 371–76 (April 1966); also Frank A. Petroni, "Uncle Toms: White Stereotypes in the Black Movement," *Human Organization*, vol. 29, pp. 260–66 (Winter 1970).

109 Thomas E. Barry and Michael G. Harvey, "Marketing to Heterogeneous Black Consumers," *California Management Review*, vol. 17 (Winter 1974), pp. 50–57.

110 Marcus Alexis, "Some Negro-White Differences in Consumption," *American Journal of Economics and Sociology*, vol. 21 (January 1962).

types of financial services with the end result that the savings approach of blacks tends to widen the gap of well-being between black and white households.[111] The usage of checking accounts by blacks is almost half the rate among white families.[112]

2. Blacks spend more for clothing and nonautomobile transportation; less for food, housing, medical care, and automobile transportation; and equivalent amounts for recreation and leisure, home furnishings, and equipment than comparable levels of whites.[113]

3. Blacks tend to own more larger, and perhaps more luxury, cars and fewer foreign cars. Ownership of large cars may be required because of the larger size among black families and the need for more pooled transportation.[114]

4. Blacks appear to be more brand loyal than equivalent whites.[115]

5. Black families purchase more milk and soft drinks, less tea and coffee, and more liquor than white families. In 1962 blacks accounted for almost one half of all rum consumption in the United States, 41 percent of all gin, over 50 percent of all Scotch whiskies, and over 77 percent of the Canadian whiskies.[116]

6. Blacks spend more time in commuting to work, travel longer distances, and have lower per capita consumption of automobiles than whites.[117]

Choice processes of blacks and whites do not show dramatic differences except where circumstances (such as nonavailability of quality retail offerings) create or cause differences. Basically, the black consumer is a practical and economical shopper first and foremost and "black" second.[118] Some distinctives that have been disclosed in black choice processes, however, are reported in the following studies. **Choice processes**

111 S. Roxanne Hiltz, "Black and White in the Consumer Financial System," *American Journal of Sociology*, vol. 76, pp. 987–99 (1971). For changes, see Charles Van Jassel, "The Negro as a Consumer—What We Know and What We Ought to Know," in M.S. Moyer and R.E. Vosburgh, eds., *Marketing for Tomorrow . . . Today* (Chicago: American Marketing Association, 1967), pp. 166–68.

112 Edward B. Selby, Jr., and James T. Lindley, "Black Consumers—Hidden Market Potential," *The Bankers Magazine* vol. 156 (Summer 1973), pp. 84–87.

113 Alexis, "Some Negro-White Differences"; also James Stafford, Keith Cox, and James Higginbotham, "Some Consumption Pattern Differences between Urban Whites and Negroes," *Social Science Quarterly*, pp. 619–30 (December 1968).

114 Fred C. Akers, "Negro and White Automobile-Buying Behavior: New Evidence," *Journal of Marketing Research*, vol. 5, pp. 283–90 (August 1968); Carl M. Larson and Hugh G. Wales, "Brand Preferences of Chicago Blacks," *Journal of Advertising Research*, vol. 13 (August 1973), pp. 15–21.

115 Frank G. Davis, "Differential Factors in the Negro Market," (Chicago: National Association of Market Developers, 1959), p. 6; privately published report based upon data collected by *Ebony* magazine.

116 Data from Bernard Howard and Co., Inc., and *Ebony*, reported in Oladipupo, *How Distinct?*, pp. 30–34.

117 James O. Wheeler, "Transportation Problems in Negro Ghettos," *Sociology and Social Research*, vol. 53, pp. 171–79 (January 1969).

118 W. Leonard Evans, Jr., "Ghetto Marketing: What Now?" in Robert L. King, ed., *Marketing and the New Science of Planning* (Chicago: American Marketing Association, 1968), pp. 528–31.

1. Black consumers appear to have more awareness of both private and national brands than do white consumers and to be better informed about prices than white counterparts.[119]

2. Black consumers appear to respond as well to package design (for beer) designed for white consumers as for packages designed specifically for black consumers.[120]

3. Black consumers tend not to shop by phone or mail order as much as white consumers.[121]

4. Black grocery consumers tend to make frequent trips to neighborhood stores. This may be due to inadequate refrigeration and storage and lack of transportation that would allow carrying large amounts of groceries.[122]

5. Black consumers tend to shop at discount stores compared to department stores more than do comparable white consumers.[123]

6. Black consumers tend to be unhappier with supermarket facilities and functions than do white consumers (with complaints including poor prices, poor cleanliness, crowded conditions, poor displays, and unfriendly employees).[124]

7. Black consumers place more emphasis upon convenience, shopping location, price, quality, and service than upon the appeal of buying black, although younger segments of the black community place more appeal on buying from black-owned firms.[125]

8. Black consumers tend to "shop around" less than do white consumers.[126]

This section on choice processes in the retail environment can be concluded by raising an additional question concerning whether the sub-

119 Robert L. King and Earl Robert DeManche, "Comparative Acceptance of Selected Private-Branded Food Products by Low-Income Negro and White Families," in McDonald *op. cit.*, pp. 63–69. The sample size in this study is very small, however. Feldman and Starr also found that black consumers were more concerned with price than white consumers who were more concerned with value.

120 Herbert E. Krugman, "White and Negro Responses to Package Design," *Journal of Marketing Research*, vol. 3, pp. 199–200 (May 1966).

121 Laurence P. Feldman and Alvin D. Star, "Racial Factors in Shopping Behavior," Keith Cox and Ben Enis, eds., *A New Measure of Responsibility for Marketing* (Chicago: American Marketing Association 1968), pp. 216–26; Keith K. Cox, James B. Higginbotham, and James E. Stafford, "Negro Retail Shopping and Credit Behavior," *Journal of Retailing*, vol. 48 (Spring 1972), pp. 54–66.

122 Donald F. Dixon and Daniel J. McLaughlin, Jr., "Shopping Behavior, Expenditure Patterns, and Inner City Food Prices," *Journal of Marketing Research*, vol. 8, pp. 960–99 (February 1971); Feldman and Star present data to show that blacks do not shop more frequently than whites, however.

123 Feldman and Star, "Racial Factors"; similarity between blacks and whites was found, however, in Cox, et al., "Negro Retail Shopping," p. 60.

124 John V. Petrof, "Attitudes of the Urban Poor toward Their Neighborhood Supermarkets," *Journal of Retailing*, vol. 47, pp. 3–17 (Spring 1971).

125 Dennis H. Gensch and Richard Staelin, "The Appeal of Buying Black," *Journal of Marketing Research*, vol. 9 (May 1972), pp. 141–48; Dennis Gensch and Richard Staelin, "Making Black Retail Outlets Work," *California Management Review*, vol. 15 (Fall 1972), pp. 52–62.

126 Donald E. Sexton, Jr., "Differences in Food Shopping Habits by Area of Residence, Race, and Income," *Journal of Retailing*, vol. 50 (Spring 1974), pp. 37–48.

culture of the "poor" (including both blacks and whites) pays more than do affluent consumers. The assertion was made by Caplovitz in a widely circulated report that the poor do pay more.[127] A number of studies were stimulated by this report, focusing upon the retail structure in low-income areas or buying patterns of low-income consumers and some of the results have been equivocal or contradictory.[128]

The conclusion that seems to be emerging is that retailers generally *do not discriminate* between buyers on the basis of income or ethnic characteristics. It has been shown that chain supermarkets do not charge higher prices in the ghetto but in fact may charge lower prices about as often as higher.[129] Sexton found that the costs of operation were actually higher in city areas than suburban areas and slightly higher in black areas than white areas but that prices charged were the same in all stores, creating a situation whereby suburban residents are actually subsidizing the losses in city areas.[130] In a study of appliance buying, discrimination was not found[131] nor was it found in a study of mobile home buying,[132] and among automobile salesman, a pattern was found of charging higher prices to *affluent* persons.[133]

Even though marketing institutions are not overtly discriminating, it does not guarantee that the poor and that ethnic subcultures do not pay more. The shopping behavior of those consumers may create disadvantages that are often based in the environment. In a major study of this problem, Alexis found that poor consumers who shopped in supermarkets were not paying more than more affluent consumers, but a higher proportion of the poor were shopping in neighborhood, independent stores, which charge higher prices than the supermarkets.[134] Most of the studies on this subject have revealed a pattern of smaller, less ably managed, less desirable stores in neighborhoods where poor consumers predominate. Also, consumers may have less access to transportation,

127 David Caplovitz, *The Poor Pay More* (New York: Free Press, 1963).

128 This literature is reviewed in Robert G. Mogull, "Where Do We Stand on Inner City Prices?" *The Southern Journal of Business* 6, pp. 32–40 (July 1971); Donald E. Sexton, "Do Blacks Pay More?" *Journal of Marketing Research*, vol. 9, pp. 420–26 (November 1971); Leonard L. Berry, "The Low-Income Marketing System: An Overview," *Journal of Retailing*, vol. 48 (Summer 1972), pp. 44–63; Loraine Donaldson and Raymond S. Strangways, "Can Ghetto Groceries Price Competitively and Make a Profit?" *Journal of Business*, vol. 46 (January 1973), pp. 61–65; Howard Kunreuther, "Why the Poor May Pay More for Food: Theoretical and Empirical Evidence," *Journal of Business*, vol. 46 (July 1973), pp. 368–83.

129 U.S. Bureau of Labor Statistics, *A Study of Prices in Food Stores Located in Low and Higher Income Areas of Six Large Cities* (Washington, D.C.: U.S. Government Printing Office, 1966); B.W. Marion, L.A. Simonds, and D.E. Moore, "Food Marketing in Low-Income Areas: A Case Study of Columbus, Ohio," *Bulletin of Business Research*, vol. 45, pp. 1–8 (August 1970).

130 Donald E. Sexton, Jr., "Grocery Prices Paid by Blacks and Whites: Further Findings," *Journal of Economics and Business*, vol. 25 (Fall 1972), pp. 39–44.

131 Norman Kangun, "Race and Price Discrimination in the Marketplace: A Further Study," *Mississippi Valley Journal of Economics and Business*, vol. 5, pp. 66–75 (Spring 1970). This study includes Indian families as well as black families.

132 Waylon D. Griffin and Frederick D. Sturdivant, "Discrimination and Middle Class Minority Consumers," *Journal of Marketing*, vol. 37 (July 1973), pp. 65–68.

133 Gordon L. Wise, "Automobile Salesmen's Perceptions of New Car Prospects," *Bulletin of Business Research*, vol. 46, pp. 2–6 (February 1971).

134 Marcus Alexis, "The Effects of Race and Retail Structure on Consumer Behavior and Market Performance," in Jagdish Sheth and Peter L. Wright, eds., *Proceedings of a National Conference on Social Marketing* (Champaign-Urbana: University of Illinois, 1974), pp. 205–40.

less confidence in dealing with retailers outside the neighborhood, less access to credit outside the neighborhood and other characteristics contributing to problems in purchasing choices. These phenomena may lead to consumer dissatisfaction and unfavorable perceptions that present a substantial public policy problem in addition to the physical and economic problems.[135]

Summary

This chapter develops further the basic concept of culture defined in the preceding chapter and describes culture as a learned set of responses that are inculcated in each succeeding generation. When culturally defined responses are dysfunctional (not gratifying) in a society, they change to provide for new, gratifying responses.

Four basic methods of studying culture were described in this chapter. They include intensive field studies, content analysis, cross-sectional studies and longitudinal studies.

Cross-cultural analysis is described in this chapter as a systematic comparison of the similarities and differences in the behavioral and physical aspects of cultures. Cross-cultural analysis provides an approach to understanding market segments both across national boundaries and between groups within a society. The process of analyzing markets on a cross-cultural basis is particularly helpful in deciding which elements of a marketing program can be standardized in multiple nations and which elements must be localized.

Subcultural influences are important because they shape or form market segments. Subcultural influences analyzed in this chapter include nationality, religious, geographic, and racial subcultures. Selected for special analysis because of their importance in North American markets were the French Canadian subculture and the black subculture.

The black subculture has been shaped by a variety of factors such as income deprivation, inadequate educational institutions, differential family characteristics, and discrimination. It appears correct to conclude that there is no "black" market in the United States any more than a "white" market. Rather, there is a heterogeneous group of market segments within the black population that possesses, to varying degrees, some "core" values and consumption patterns. These patterns or influences are described in terms of the environmental influences on consumer behavior, search processes, the process of alternative evaluation, and choice processes as they are related to the retailing structure.

Review and discussion questions

1. Why do values continue to exist in a culture over several generations?

2. Describe four basic types of methodologies used for studying values.

135 Gerald E. Hills, Donald H. Granbois and James M. Patterson, "Black Consumer Perceptions of Food Store Attributes," *Journal of Marketing*, vol. 37 (April 1973), pp. 47–57.

3. Outline a research project using the participant-observer methodology in a way that would be useful in developing a market strategy.

4. What is the primary problem with mass observation techniques or participant-observer techniques?

5. What is meant by cross-cultural analysis? Discuss its relevance in developing marketing strategy.

6. A considerable controversy exists concerning whether or not international advertising can be standardized or whether it must be localized. How can this controversy be resolved?

7. Prepare a report that documents the effects of religious subcultures on consumer behavior.

8. Assume that a French manufacturer of women's apparel is seeking to expand markets by exporting to Canada. What marketing program should be recommended for maximum effectiveness?

9. Assume that a major marketer of soft drinks in the United States receives a marketing research study that indicates low penetration in the rapidly expanding black market. Prepare a marketing program to expand the market position.

10. Do poor consumers pay more for groceries than middle-income or affluent consumers? Document your answer with empirical studies. Prepare a set of recommendations that might be adopted by appropriate government organizations to improve the shopping behavior of low income consumers.

CHAPTER 5

Social stratification

"Birds of a feather flock together," says an old adage. It is more than an idle folk saying, for in this truism lies the concept of stratification of society into groups that feel as if they "belong together." The people in each group recognize or feel that other persons rank above them, often without knowing on what basis the ranking occurs. In India, stratification is called the caste system. In medieval Europe, it was based upon the estate into which one was born. In the United States and much of the rest of the world, stratification of the social system is called the class system, or social class. This chapter describes the nature of stratification, measurement techniques and issues, social-class behavior patterns, and social-class influence on consumer decision making.

When studying social class, it is necessary to maintain an objective, detached viewpoint. It may seem undemocratic to give recognition to the fact that classes exist. Yet, it is a fact that no known society exists or has existed in which social inequality is not present.[1] Even animal societies have stratification and exhibit class behavior.[2]

1 The fact that stratification is ubiquitous is recognized by nearly all sociologists, although there is considerable question whether stratification is "inevitable." The classic article delineating why stratification has arisen in all societies is that by Kingsley Davis and Wilbert E. Moore, "Some Principles of Stratification," *American Sociological Review*, vol. 5, pp. 242–49 (1945). For an opposing view, see Melvin M. Tumin, "Some Principles of Stratification: A Critical Analysis," *American Sociological Review*, vol. 13, pp. 387–93 (1953).

2 This has been verified in studies of insects, deer, mice, wolves, birds, and other animals. One of the most fascinating studies was conducted by a Norwegian zoologist who observed social stratification in a society of hens and found that each hen tends to maintain a definite position in the peck order of the group. (Thus, the existence of what most kinds of workers have known to exist all along: the pecking order.) The researcher concludes, "There are no two hens within the same community who do not exactly know who is superordinate and who is subordinate." See T. Schjelderup-Ebbe, "Social Behavior of Birds," in.C. Murchison, ed., *A Handbook of Social Psychology* (Worcester, Mass.: Clark University Press, 1935).

Social class defined

Social classes may be defined as *relatively permanent and homogeneous divisions in a society into which individuals or families sharing similar values, life styles, interests, and behavior can be categorized.* There is little agreement, however, concerning the nature of those divisions or the criteria for defining them.[3]

Social classes are the largest homogeneous grouping within a society. All of the members *tend* to behave like one another. Social classes therefore *restrict behavior between individuals of differing social classes*, especially in intimate relationships. People have their close social relationships with people who like to do the same things they do, in the same ways and with whom they can feel comfortable. This causes interpersonal communications about products, stores and so forth to be somewhat restricted among social classes.

Restricted behavior

Social classes are hierarchical. When people are asked about other groups of people, they tend to compare themselves in superior or inferior positions. People may not know the basis of the ranking, but they do know that ranking exists in their own minds and in the minds of other people. Social class exists as a *position* without reference to a specific person. A person can be defined as a member of a social *class* even if that member violates the normal behavior of the class.

Hierarchical positions

Social class is based upon many dimensions even though the concept is treated as one, unidimensional variable. When people think of social class, they are actually thinking of a combination of variables that create social class. These may include such things as power, privilege, prestige, influence, good manners, and so forth, which are, in turn, a result of occupation, education, and other variables.

Multidimensional

Social class is *not the same as income,* and should not be confused as such. Truck drivers may average more income than public school teachers or bank tellers, for example, but teachers and bank tellers are usually rated substantially higher in social class. Since it is not possible to identify one variable as social class, marketing research ordinarily uses *proxy variables* to measure social class—such as occupation, place of residence, education, and so forth.

In theory, social classes are discrete divisions in society into which a person might easily be classified, but in practice it does not occur that way for some people. One reason for this is the multidimensional nature of social class characteristics possessed by some persons which may make it difficult to classify an individual. Another reason, however, is the dynamic nature of classes or the movement of individuals, especially those who

Classes are dynamic

3 An excellent discussion of the problems in defining social class, stratification, and status and of the theoretical perspectives that exist in status research is found in Thomas E. Lasswell, *Class and Stratum; An Introduction to Concepts and Research* (Boston: Houghton Mifflin Co., 1965), chaps. 1–4.

are on the fringes of a class. A caste system prohibits movement between divisions in society, but a class system permits people to move into higher classes or drop into lower ones. The classes themselves, therefore, experience change, especially on the fringes, as classes become larger or smaller, adapt to new environmental conditions, and modify existing behavior norms of the class.

Social-class determinants

Sociological theory relating to social class has centered upon two topics. First, sociologists have attempted to answer the question of why social classes develop in a society. Second, they have asked the question, "Given the fact that social classes exist, what determines the social class of a specific individual?" It is the second question that is of most direct relevance to consumer analysts.[4] One very useful schema for understanding the determinants of social class and status has been developed by Kahl. It is used here, with considerable modification, to describe the determinants of an individual's status.[5]

Occupation

Whenever strangers meet, a question soon asked is, "What kind of work do you do?" This question provides a good clue to the social class of the individual. It is used by consumer analysts in measuring social class and is considered the best single indicator available. Hewitt concludes:

> A feature of industrial society is that occupations are the social positions most important for differential evaluation, perhaps because the work that men do intimately affects their life chance and life styles. Even though prestige ideologies often stress the intrinsic worth of all men, occupational status is the single most important basis for according prestige, honor, and respect.[6]

It has been shown that individuals are able to rate abstract occupational titles in terms of prestige, even if they do not know who fills them. These prestige ratings of occupation are central to determining the rank of a person in the social class system. These ratings are also relatively permanent. In a classic study, for example, it was found that the correlation coefficient between ratings in 1947 and in 1963 was 0.99,

4 The reader who is interested in the first question, that of the general sociological theory of stratification, has available a number of excellent sources. See, for example, Davis and Moore, "Some Principles"; also Talcott Parsons, *The Social System* (New York: Free Press, 1955); Bernard Barber, *Social Stratification: A Comparative Analysis of Structure and Process* (New York: Harcourt, 1957); Robert K. Merton, *Social Theory and Social Structure* (New York: Free Press, 1949); Gerhard E. Lenski, *Power and Privilege: A Theory of Social Stratification* (New York: McGraw-Hill, 1966). See p. 439 of Lenski for an attempt to diagram a general theory of stratification. For useful bibliographies, see Donald G. MacRae, "Social Stratification: A Trend Report and Bibliography," *Current Sociology*, vol. 2, no. 1, entire issue (1953–54); Harold W. Pfautz, "The Current Literature on Social Stratification: Critique and Bibliography," *American Journal of Sociology*, vol. 58, pp. 391–418 (1953).

5 Joseph A. Kahl, *The American Class Structure* (New York: Holt, Rinehart and Winston, 1957), pp. 8–10. For an interpretation of these six dimensions of social class in marketing similar to the interpretation presented in this volume, see Edgar Crane, *Marketing Communication* (New York: Wiley, 1966), pp. 326–29.

6 John P. Hewitt, *Social Stratification and Deviant Behavior* (New York: Random House, 1970), p. 25.

indicating that the prestige of occupations had changed very little in this period.[7]

The stability in ratings of prestige associated with occupations exists also on a cross-national basis. Various studies have indicated that physicians rate very high in almost all societies, for example. The correlations for ranks of all occupations tend to exhibit very high correlations (usually above 0.9) among nations in a cross-cultural sample.[8]

Personal performance

A person's social class is determined partially by the degree to which the person performs well within an occupational class. This includes the deference or attitude of respect given to an individual by other persons in the society. Frequently, deference refers directly to job performance. Statements such as, "She is the finest young lawyer in our city," "Frank is the only mechanic I know that I really trust my car to," or "That professor is making the most significant contributions to knowledge of anyone in her field" are examples of evaluations of personal performance. Operationally, job performance is sometimes measured by the amount of income variation *within* an occupation. Thus in one status-rating system, physicians making between $25,000 and $55,000 a year are given a higher than normal rating for their occupation, and physicians earning less than $25,000 a year are lowered from their normal status rating.

Personal performance can relate to activities other than job performance. A person's status may be affected by the prestige or sentiment given for acts that society approves. An individual who is unusually kind and considerate of others may receive the respect of peers. A person who performs some beneficial service such as serving as chairman of a community fund or civic club may receive improved status. Even a reputation as "a good father" or "a good mother" may contribute to one's status.

Interactions

One group of sociologists is sometimes called the "who-invited-whom-to-dinner" school. They believe people feel most comfortable when they are with people of similar values and behavior, and place primary analysis on patterns of association. This indicates which individuals are in the same class, and other members of the community observe status characteristics of persons within such groupings, thereby causing group membership and interactions to be a determinant of one's social class.

Having frequent and intimate association with other occupants of a particular social class is essential to the maintenance of one's social class.

7 Robert W. Hodge, Paul M. Siegel, and Peter H. Rossi, "Occupational Prestige in the United States: 1925–1963," in Reinhard Bendix and Seymour M. Lipset, eds., *Class, Status, and Power*, 2d ed. (New York: Free Press, 1966), pp. 322–34, at p. 326.

8 Alex Inkeles and Peter H. Rossi, "National Comparisons of Occupational Prestige," *American Journal of Sociology*, vol. 61, pp. 329–39 (1956); Robert W. Hodge, Donald J. Treiman, and Peter H. Rossi, "A Comparative Study of Occupational Prestige," in Bendix and Lipset, *Class, Status and Power*, pp. 309–21.

Meredith Willson's unsinkable Molly Brown, for example, could not enter the elite classes of Denver without the proper friends, in spite of her wealth, luxurious residence, and European education.

Interactions may well be the most important key to understanding social classes in spite of the difficulty of measuring them. One commentator has observed, "the essence of social class is the way a man is treated by his fellows and, reciprocally, the way he treats them."[9] The importance of social intimacy as a determinant of social class has been further amplified by Barber:

> The assumption underlying the use of the interactional indicator of social class position is that social intimacy is expressive of social equality. The assumption rests on the fact that the kind of interchange of sentiments and ideas that goes on in intimate association is possible only among people who know each other well and who value each other equally. It is, in other words, possible only among social class equals, and therefore it is an indicator of social class equality.[10]

Limitations on social interaction are rigidly enforced in most social structures. In India, interaction among certain social castes is prohibited on religious grounds.[11] In the United States, restrictions are more subtle but nevertheless are present. The intensive studies of Hollingshead reveal that most marriages—83 percent—occur within the same or adjacent social classes.[12] Hollingshead's investigations of public school behavior reveal definite patterns of restricted association (which he labeled with names such as the elite, the good kids, and the grubby gang) and found that dating tended to be restricted among these classes by parents.[13] Perhaps the most obvious example of restricted interaction is the existence of the *Social Register* in twelve United States cities, which incorporates very rigid criteria for gaining admission to intimate interactions in the top social classes.[14]

Possessions

Possessions are symbols of class membership. They are necessary but not sufficient criteria for class membership. The importance of possessions relates not only to the amount of possessions an individual has but also to the nature of his or her choices. Thus, whether a person chooses wall-to-wall carpeting or an oriental rug, both of equal price, may be an impor-

9 T. H. Marshall, *Citizenship and Social Class and Other Essays* (Cambridge: Cambridge University Press, 1950), p. 92.

10 Barber, *Social Stratification*, p. 122.

11 For examples of the prescriptions for the caste system, see Marc Galanter, "The Problem of Group Membership," in Bendix and Lipset, *Class, Status, and Power*, pp. 628–40, reprinted from *Journal of Indian Law Institute*.

12 A. B. Hollingshead, "Cultural Factors in the Selection of Marriage Mates," *American Sociological Review*, vol. 15, pp. 619–27 (1950).

13 A. B. Hollingshead, *Elmstown's Youth* (New York: Wiley, 1949), p. 483. Another study discovered similar restricted dating patterns and was able to trace them to definite parental influences tending to restrict interaction among classes. See Marvin B. Sussman, "Parental Participation in Mate Selection and Its Effect upon Family Continuity," *Social Forces*, vol. 32, pp. 76–81 (1953).

14 For a description of the *Social Register* and an analysis of the criteria for gaining admission to it, see E. Digby Baltzell, "Who's Who in America and the Social Register," in Bendix and Lipset, *Class, Status, and Power*, pp. 266–75.

tant determinant and symbol of social class. Probably the most important possession in terms of social-class determination is a family's residence, both location and type. Other important "possessions" include the college an individual attends (for upper classes), the type of vacation an individual chooses, the automobile (although its exact importance in the United States is questionable), clothing, furniture, and appliances that are chosen for the home, and the type of wealth possessed by a family.

Cultural values are interpreted and applied differently and thus the value orientations of individuals are determinants and indicators of a person's social class. When a group of people tend to share a common set of abstract convictions that organize and relate a large number of specific values, it becomes relatively easy to observe a person's social class by the degree to which an individual consumer possesses these characteristics.

Value orientations

A crucial issue in analyzing consumer behavior is to determine what value orientations characterize market segments. These beliefs may refer to values about society such as beliefs in capitalism or other political ideals. They also refer to attitudes toward such subjects as child rearing, family structure, sexual behavior, work, and achievement. They may also refer to values about decision making. These value orientations are of central importance in marketing and are discussed later in this chapter.

Another manifestation of social class is the class consciousness of groups within the society and of individuals within those groups. Individuals who are relatively unconscious of class differences in the society tend to perceive less discrepancy between their position and that of others. Thus they may be less motivated toward attaining goods as symbols of class.

Class consciousness

In the United States, most people have some idea of social classes, but those ideas are often nebulous or not strongly held. Some studies have indicated sizable proportions of the population that believe there are no social classes or cannot define specific social classes. The higher an individual's social class, the more class conscious he is likely to be.

Measurement of social classes

Many methods have been developed for measuring social class and describing the values and behavior of social class.[15] For marketing analysts, the purpose is to *identify market segments that may have similar behavior.*

Four principal *types* of methods used for classifying the social class of an individual have been described: (1) reputational, (2) sociometric, (3) subjective, and (4) objective.[16]

15 A discussion of social class measures is found in Thomas E. Lasswell, "Social Stratification: 1964–1969," *Annals of the American Academy of Political and Social Science*, vol. 38, esp. pp. 109–12 (July 1969).

16 David Krech, Richard S. Crutchfield, and Egerton L. Ballachey, *Individual in Society* (New York: McGraw-Hill, 1962), pp. 313–19.

Reputational methods

Reputational methods of measuring social class involve asking people to rank the social position of other persons. Usually, respondents are asked to rank people they know in the particular community in which they live. Even people who say they are not class conscious almost always can divide the community into social groups and tell in which group the people they know belong. The following is an example of a typical interview asking for a description of the social-class structure to which residents of the community belong. This interview is with Mr. George Green, long-time resident of the town and a member of the city government.

You'll find out there's a definite division between the men and the women in the upper stratum in this town. The men are common like us. They'll talk to you at any time. But the women draw the class line, and no one gets over or around it. I can see this just as clearly as I can see you.

We're in a unique position here because of my relation to a couple of families in this group. A cousin of mine married Jim Radcliffe. This relates us to several other people. We've been invited over to their house to parties a few times, and I'm disturbed at how these people look down at others in town. They have several cliques within the larger stratum. Below this stratum is the one composed of prominent business and professional families. Some of these who have money and family are rated in the top group. However, if they have only family and not much money, they rank in the upper-middle class.

The small business men and the foremen out at the mill are in the lower but middle stratum. I mean a lower stratum than the one we have been talking about. I don't know much about their social life, but I know just about where they fit in here in town. The sub-foremen, machinists, several stationary operators, and people like that are in the lowest middle stratum. The ordinary workmen in the foundry and the mill are mostly ranked as lower class around here. But they're not as low as the older Poles, the canal renters, and the people back of the tannery.

The Poles and the poor Americans who work in the mill are on the bottom. These poor Americans and Poles may be working side by side on the same job and getting the same income, but socially they're miles apart. You might say they're each an exclusive group. The several social strata in town are segregated into definite areas, and in each you generally find a class distinction.

Now, that's about the way that the town is divided. That's the way it looks to me, and I am pretty sure that's the way it is.[17]

The reputational method was developed in the United States by Warner and is the basis of much of the most important empirical research on social classes in America. A comprehensive set of instructions for interpreting the interviews and for collaborating social-class ratings has

17 W. Lloyd Warner, Marchia Meeker, and Kenneth Eels, *Social Class in America: A Manual of Procedure for the Measurement of Social Status* (Chicago: Science Research Associates, 1949), pp. 56–57.

been devised and is called the evaluative participation method of establishing the social class of a person.[18]

Jain's conjoint analysis. A variation of the reputational method of measuring social class was developed by Jain and offers considerable potential in understanding the structure of social class. Its purpose is to understand the social class structures explicit in the descriptions of laymen (rather than experts or theorists). Jain employs conjoint analysis, which is a technique for analyzing the contribution of variables to total preferences or results and is used in many other consumer research applications.[19]

Conjoint analysis is used to understand both the relative importance of various levels of socioeconomic characteristics in judgments about social class and to predict the responses of consumers to various product and service attributes. The technique is used by giving each respondent a vignette that contains "core" social class variables. Three levels of the following variables are used: occupation, education, family income and ethnic background. The value of this technique is in its ability to disclose the implicit value system manifest in the choice behavior of decision makers. This might be used in choosing alternative features to be developed in a new product, understanding the importance of multiple attributes in selecting a product, or understanding what kinds of persons would be effective in testimonial or other types of advertising.[20]

Sociometric methods

Sociometric studies involve observing or asking people about their intimate associations with other people. The reports and observations can be analyzed with standard sociometric techniques to determine the cliques and social classes. The most famous study using techniques of this nature is that of Hollingshead.[21] Many social class studies using sociometric methods have been with children.[22] Sociometric methods are useful in theoretical social-class research, but as of the present are untested and too expensive for most consumer research.

Subjective methods

Subjective methods of determining social classes ask respondents to *rate themselves* on social class. Such methods have been used on occasion but are of limited use for consumer analysts for two reasons: (1) respondents tend to overrate their own class position (often by one class rank) and (2) respondents avoid the connotative terms "upper" and "lower" classes and thus exaggerate the size of the middle classes.

---

18 Warner et al., *Social Class*, pp. 47–120.

19 P. E. Green and V. Rao, "Conjoint Measurement for Quantifying Judgmental Data," *Journal of Marketing Research*, vol. 8 (August 1971), pp. 355–63; and Richard M. Johnson, "Trade-Off Analysis of Consumer Values," *Journal of Marketing Research*, vol. 11 (May 1974), pp. 121–27.

20 Arun K. Jain, "A Method for Investigating and Representing Implicit Social Class Theory," *Journal of Consumer Research*, vol. 2 (June 1975), pp. 53–59.

21 Hollingshead, *Elmstown's Youth*.

22 For an example of this type of research, see Celia Burns Stendler, *Children of Brasstown, University of Illinois Bulletin*, vol. 46, no. 59 (Urbana, Ill.: Bureau of Research and Service of the College of Education, 1949).

The problems with a subjective method do not disqualify the method from social-class research. Important findings have been generated by Centers[23] and other investigators using the subjective method, especially with regard to the subject of class consciousness. The value of the method in marketing studies as yet appears to be minimal, however. What is needed is a self-administered rating scale to identify consumer social classes on a subjective basis without actually asking the respondent his or her social class. Such a scale would ask the consumer to choose attitudinal-value statements relating indirectly to social class that he or she agrees with or that characterize the respondent. If such a self-administered scale of social class could be developed, it would be useful in mail questionnaires and other consumer surveys.

Objective methods

Objective methods of determining social classes rely upon the assigning of classes (or status) on the basis of respondents possessing some value of a stratified variable. The most often used variables are occupation, income, education, size and type of residence, ownership of possessions, and organizational affiliations. Most consumer research uses the objective method for classifying respondents into a social class because they yield quantitative results and obviate subjective interpretation. Objective methods can be divided into those that involve single indexes and those that use multiple indexes.

Single-item indexes. Occupation is generally accepted as the single best proxy indicator of social class. Occupational position and individual life styles have demonstrated high correlations for two reasons. People who share similarly ranked occupational levels often share roughly similar access to the means of achieving a particular life style. Leisure time, income independence, knowledge, and power are often common to specific or occupational categories. Second, people in similar occupations are likely to interact with one another. Of particular interest to consumer analysts is the conclusion of social-class researchers Barth and Watson:

> The products of such occupational interaction are likely to be an increased concensus concerning the types of activities, interests, and possessions that are important; some agreement as to how, in general, family resources should be allocated in order to implement the achievement of these goals; and the development of a shared set of norms of evaluation.[24]

23 Richard Centers, *The Psychology of Social Classes* (Princeton, N.J.: Princeton University Press, 1949), esp. pp. 34–54. For other studies using the subjective method, see G. Gallup and S. F. Rae, *The Pulse of Democracy* (New York: Simon and Schuster, 1940); Hadley Cantril, "Identification with Social and Economic Class," *Journal of Abnormal and Social Psychology*, vol. 38, pp. 74–79 (January 1943); Philip E. Converse, "The Shifting Role of Class in Political Attitudes and Behavior," in Eleanor E. Maccoby, Theodore M. Newcomb, and Eugene L. Hartley, eds., *Readings in Social Psychology*, 3d ed. (New York: Holt, Rinehart and Winston, 1958), pp. 388–99.

24 Ernest A. T. Barth and Walter B. Watson, "Social Stratification and the Family in Mass Society," *Social Forces*, vol. 45, p. 394 (March 1967).

An example of an occupational scale, the Trieman scale,[25] which is used on an international basis, is reproduced in Figure 5.1. This scale can be used in consumer research by asking the respondent to write in the exact occupation, which can later be coded numerically according to the scale value of occupational status listed in Figure 5.1. Such a scale has the advantage of providing a precise, numerical estimate of occupational status of each respondent, which can be used in statistical analyses of the other information in the survey.

Figure 5.1 Occupational titles and occupational status scores for seven major occupational groups

Occupational group and title	Occupational status (Treiman's scale)	Occupational group and title	Occupational status (Treiman's scale)
Day labor:		Mechanic	42.9
Day laborer	18.1	Painter	31.0
Farm worker	18.1	Carpenter	37.2
Farm hand	22.9	Mason, bricklayer	34.1
		Miller	32.9
Agriculture:		Woodworker	34.4
Farmer*	37.7	Radio operator	49.2
Farm foreman	40.8	Baker	33.2
Coffee picker	36.7	Printer	40.6
Ranch worker	25.6	Aviation mechanic	49.6
		Craftsman	34.4
Unskilled:		Shoemaker	28.1
Launderer	22.1	Electronics worker	40.9
Milkman	30.7	Watchmaker	39.7
Fruit seller	24.4	Machine operator	38.3
Construction worker	30.0	Plumber	33.9
Carpenter's apprentice	22.6	Aqueduct, sewer installer	37.6
Building caretaker	25.0	Barber	30.4
Tractor driver	28.6	Radio technician	49.2
Processing-plant worker	36.7	Draftsman	54.9
Trashman	12.7	Jeweler	43.0
Wood seller	24.4	Blacksmith	32.2
Egg seller	24.4		
Ticket puncher	35.8	**Semiprofessional:**	
Coal man	29.3	Businessman	50.0
Ox driver	25.6	Accountant	54.6
Coal seller	21.9	Merchant	49.3
		Engineer	45.5
Semiskilled:		Traveling salesman	31.9
Chauffeur	31.5	Sales agent	31.9
Postman	32.8	Tavern owner	48.0
Janitor	32.7	Nurse	53.6
Policeman	30.2	Property owner (real estate)	63.4
Factory worker	40.6	Contractor	59.4
Lumberjack	19.2	Secretary	53.0
Seamstress	39.3	Municipal worker	55.3

25 Nan Lin and Daniel Yauger, "The Process of Occupational Status Achievement: A Preliminary Cross-national Comparison," *American Journal of Sociology*, vol. 81 (1975), pp. 543–61.

Figure 5.1 Occupational titles and occupational status scores
for seven major occupational groups (*continued*)

Occupational group and title	Occupational status (Treiman's scale)	Occupational group and title	Occupational status (Treiman's scale)
Worker foreman	39.3	Inspector	34.7
Sales clerk	33.6	Money lender	15.3
Guard	30.6	Civil clerk	36.8
Office worker	37.5	Sailor	29.0
Promoter	50.0		
Sewer worker	39.5	**Professional:**	
Store attendant	23.2	Schoolteacher	57.0
Head maid	37.2	Doctor	77.9
Municipal foreman	62.8	Schoolmaster	57.0
Presidential guard	34.7	Professional (unspecified)	57.0
Cook	30.9	Lawyer	70.6
Soldier	38.7	Journalist	54.9
Knitter	30.4	Administrator	59.4
Miner	31.5	Health officer	47.6
Agent	39.4	Priest	59.7
		Mathematician	66.9
Skilled:		Economist	60.5
Electrician	44.5	Veterinarian	47.8
Butcher	31.5	Architect	71.8
		Customs official	44.4
		Tax collector	51.6

*Farmers are different from the day laborers in that at least one member of the household owns land.

Source: Maciarlane Smith, *Interviewing in Market and Social Research* (London and Boston: Routledge and Kegan Paul, 1972), pp. 61–63 and app. A. Reprinted by permission.

Several other occupational scales exist. A simple but widely used one is the Edwards scale, which has been adopted by the Bureau of the Census and the American Marketing Association[26] and yields a few simple categories of status. The Duncan scale is a more comprehensive research tool in the sense that it is based on ratings of 425 occupations in the United States and is more objective than the Edwards scale.[27] The Duncan scale has been used successfully in consumer research to delineate social status characteristics of innovators compared to the general population.[28] The social grading scale is widely used in Britain for

26 Alba M. Edwards, *A Social Economic Grouping of the Gainful Workers of the United States* (Washington, D.C.: U.S. Government Printing Office, 1939); U.S. Bureau of the Census, *1960 Census of Population Classified Index of Occupations and Industries* (Washington, D.C.: U.S. Government Printing Office, 1960); American Marketing Association, "Occupation and Educational Scales," *Journal of Marketing*, vol. 15 (April 1951). See comments about this scale in Theodore Caplow, *The Sociology of Work* (Minneapolis, Minn.: University of Minnesota Press, 1954), esp. pp. 42–48.

27 Albert J. Reiss, Jr. et al., *Occupations and Social Status* (New York: Free Press, 1961).

28 Robert J. Kegerreis, James F. Engel, and Roger D. Blackwell, "Innovativeness and Diffusiveness: A Marketing View of the Characteristics of Earliest Adopters," in David T. Kollat, Roger D. Blackwell, and James F. Engel, eds., *Research in Consumer Behavior* (New York: Holt, Rinehart and Winston, 1970), pp. 671–89, esp. pp. 677–78.

readership surveys and endorsed by the British Market Research Bureau. It provides social grading of occupations and includes additional details to determine the classification of borderline cases.[29]

In addition to occupation, some indexes have been constructed on the basis only of possessions. In one famous index, Chapin found that the furniture an interviewer could observe in the living room of respondents was an excellent indicator of more general measures of social class.[30] Chapin was able to measure social class on the basis of observations of the type of floor in the living room, the presence of draperies, the number of armchairs, the number of bookcases, the presence of a sewing machine, the number and type of periodicals displayed, and other items.

Single-item indices of social class are as useful when more complex (and costly) methods are not feasible. Occupation, the best single indicator of social class, does not exhaust the relevant dimensions of class. In addition, the occupational structure does not always parallel the social-class structure; nor does income, the amount or type of possessions, residence, or any single indicator. Consequently the desire for objective methods of measuring social class has brought about a search for *multiple-item indices.*

Multiple-item indices. Multiple-item indices combine several indicators of social class in an attempt to determine the best set of objective predictors of social class as validated by reputational or sociometric methods. Several methods exist.

Warner's ISC. A multiple-item index that has received much empirical investigation is Warner's *Index of Status Characteristics* (ISC). Several advantages accrue to its use:

1. It has been validated with reputational methods.[31]

2. It has been validated with scales of other investigators.[32]

---

29 This scale and discussion of how to use it is in Maciarlane Smith, *Interviewing in Market and Social Research* (London and Boston: Routledge and Kegan Paul, 1972), pp. 61–63 and app. A.

30 F. Stuart Chapin, *Contemporary American Institutions* (New York: Harper & Row, 1935), chap. 19. Chapin's scale was originally a multiple-item index including income, cultural equipment, material possessions, and group activities. The scale for living-room equipment correlated so highly with the combined index that the other variates were dropped from the index. The index was modified for rural use in William H. Sewell, *The Construction and Standardization of a Scale for the Measurement of the Socio-Economic Status of Oklahoma Farm Families,* Technical Bulletin no. 9 (Stillwater, Okla.: Oklahoma A & M Agricultural Experiment Station, 1940). A more recent scale of similar nature has been developed in England and is described in Dennis Chapman, *The Home and Social Status* (London: Routledge, 1955).

31 The correlation between ISC and EP, for example, is greater than 0.97 in Warner's study of Jonesville. For other estimates of the validity of ISC as predictor of social class as measured by EP, see Warner et al., *Social Class,* pp. 163–75.

32 Hollingshead and Warner conducted independent investigations of social classes in Morris, Ill. The two methods were used to classify 134 families measured in both studies, and Hollingshead concluded, "the agreement between the two studies was so high that it should be clear that the two stratification techniques as used by independent investigators produced a valid and reliable index of stratification in the samples studied." *Hollingshead,* pp. 40–41.

3. It has been used in a variety of communities, with modifications, and has been used on a national basis in both large and small cities.[33]

4. It has received considerable theoretical support.[34]

The ISC measures four variables: occupation, source of income, house type, and dwelling area. Originally Warner included amount of income and education in the ISC. Later he concluded that the predictive power of a four-variable ISC was not significantly changed by the deletion of amount of income and education.

After obtaining ratings for each variable for a respondent, the respondent's rating is multiplied by a weight and each product is summated.[35] The weights for each variable, which were obtained by regression analysis, are as follows:[36]

Occupation	Rating × 4
Source of income	Rating × 3
House type	Rating × 3
Dwelling area	Rating × 2

The social-class scores obtained through this method are not equivalent numerically among communities and must be adjusted if they are to be used on a national basis.

Other multiple-item indexes. A number of other multiple-item indexes exist, most of which are related to Warner's ISC. Some of these have received considerable application in consumer research or appear to have the potential of being useful.

Richard Coleman's *Index of Urban Status* (IUS) is used in consumer studies conducted by the Social Research Institute. This index uses the same four variables, and in a similar manner to Warner's ISC. However, the IUS includes two additional variables, education and associational

---

33 The occupation and source of income components of the ISC have been used in modified form for a national sample in Paul K. Hatt, "Occupation and Social Stratification," *American Journal of Sociology*, vol. 55, pp. 533–45 (1950). Social Research, Inc., uses a modified form of the ISC in national samples of metropolitan areas with good results. See the description of methodology in Lee Rainwater, Richard P. Coleman, and Gerald Handel, *Workingman's Wife* (New York: Oceana, 1959), pp. 224–25. The problems of using the ISC in very backward rural areas, however, are described in M. C. Hill and A. N. Whiting "Some Theoretical and Methodological Problems in Community Studies," *Social Forces*, vol. 29, pp. 117–24 (1950).

34 Perhaps the best theoretical validity support is provided by Kahl and Davis' factor analysis of 19 different indicators of social class, in which they found that occupation, quality of house, and residential area are best. These, of course, are central in the ISC. See Joseph A. Kahl and James A. Davis, "A Comparison of Indexes of Socio-Economic Status," *American Sociological Review*, vol. 20, pp. 317–25 (1955). The hypothesis that ISC measures one underlying dimension of social class is tested with positive results in John L. Haer, "A Test of the Unidimensionality of the Index of Status Characteristics," *Social Forces*, vol. 34, pp. 56–58 (October 1955).

35 A methodological question that plagues Warner's research and many other social-class rating techniques is the assumption being made in the data scale. Warner, in his analysis, uses arithmetic averages and parametric tests of significance and measures of correlation such as the test and the Pearsonian product moment. The use of parametric ratings such as 6 and 7 is equal to the distance between 1 and 2, and so forth. It is doubtful, however, that the scale being used by Warner (and others) possesses any more than ordinal properties. Thus, nonparametric statistics are the appropriate form. It appears that Warner and his associates have assumed that the errors from using parametric statistics are not sufficient to warrant use of the less powerful forms of statistical analysis.

36 Warner et al, *Social Class*, p. 124.

behavior.[37] Education of respondent families is rated for both the husband and the wife on a seven-point scale. Associational behavior is rated on the basis of formal club and religious memberships and informal friendships.

Carman has worked on an *index of cultural classes*, specifically for application to marketing problems.[38] He postulates that of the different variables with which class is stratified (power, status, culture), culture is of most relevance to marketing. Carman's research attempts to locate separate subcultures in the United States. These classes, Carman's research indicates, display distinct behavioral characteristics. The purpose of his research is to determine proxy variables that measure these classes. With a factor analysis of 9,318 randomly selected households from the 1960 census of population, Carman isolates occupation, education of household, and expenditures for housing as useful proxy variables for behavioral differences in marketing patterns (home clothes dryer ownership).[39]

Hollingshead's *index of social position* (ISP) is similar to Warner's ISC except that it is a three-variable index with ratings for area of residence, occupation, and education.[40] The index can be reduced to a two-variable index with little loss (by eliminating area of residence) and is useful for making comparisons among communities. Another scale perhaps useful in conducting research on the consumption patterns of college students is the *index of class position*, developed by Ellis, Lane, and Olesen.[41] It is similar to the ISP except that college students are asked to report their *father's* occupation and also to subjectively evaluate their father's position in the class structure.

There are also measures of social class that rely only on demographic information ascertainable without directly involving the respondent. Shevky and his associates produced an index of social rank based only upon *census tract* data.[42] Social rank can be inferred from the ratio of (1) craftsmen, operatives, and laborers in each tract, (2) education as measured by number of persons aged 25 years or more who had completed grade school, and (3) income. Very useful studies relating sales of a product to the social-class characteristics of a geographical area are possible using this index.

Status crystallization. A central problem in the use of all multiple-item indices of social class is what to do about individuals who rate high on one

37 Rainwater et al., *Workingman's Wife.*

38 James M. Carman, *The Application of Social Class in Market Segmentation* (Berkeley, Calif.: Institute of Business and Economic Research, University of California Graduate School of Business Administration, 1965).

39 Carman, *Application of Social Class*, p. 63.

40 Jerome K. Myers and Bertram H. Roberts, *Family and Class Dynamics in Mental Illness* (New York: Wiley, 1959), pp. 24–25.

41 Robert A. Ellis, Clayton Lane, and Virginia Olesen, "The Index of Class Position: An Improved Intercommunity Measure of Stratification," *American Sociological Review*, vol. 28, pp. 271–77 (April 1963).

42 Eshref Shevky and Wendell Bell, *Social Area Analysis: Theory, Illustrative Application and Computational Procedures* (Stanford, Calif.: Stanford University Press, 1955).

variable but low on another. Status crystallization is defined as the consistency that exists among ratings of multiple variables. Lenski devised an index of status crystallization and studied respondents who have a low degree of status crystallization.[43] He concluded that such individuals are more liberal in their political views and more willing to support programs of social change. Individuals such as the black doctor, the successful businessman with little education, and the poorly paid white-collar worker are examples of persons with low status crystallization who are subject to certain pressures from the social order not felt by persons with more highly crystallized status, although the exact effects of status inconsistency are difficult to predict and to measure.[44]

Social classes in America

The need for marketing executives to study social classes is based upon the reality that the audiences for marketing communications are frequently composed of different social classes than the persons who design communications strategies. College-educated executives, for example, may be very inept at designing effective marketing programs for the middle and lower class consumers that comprise mass markets.

Before description and analysis of social class consumption behavior can proceed, however, some consideration should be given to questions about the changing nature of social classes in America.

Is social class vanishing in America?

Some sociologists have questioned the validity of social classes. They maintain that the life styles of middle-class persons have become increasingly representative of the vast majority of Americans. This is sometimes described as the "embourgeoisment" of society or the massification theory. Widespread mass media and increasing incomes with a concomitant dissemination of economic power eliminate many of the differences between working and middle class people, R. A. Nisbet and Gerhard Lenski have concluded.[45]

The massification theory was examined by Glenn, analyzing trends conducted at intervals of eight or more years, and he concluded that differences in attitudes and behavior have *not* diminished.[46] Richard Parker also negates the claim of diminishing social class differentiation and points to 1970 labor force data showing that 57.5 percent of the total

43 Gerhard E. Lenski, "Status Crystallization: A Non-Vertical Dimension of Social Status," *American Sociological Review*, vol. 21, pp. 458–64 (August 1956). A provocative extension of the problem of status incongruence, with some references of potential interest in marketing, can be found in Andrzej Malewski, "The Degree of Status Incongruence and Its Effects," *Polish Sociological Bulletin* (1963), reprinted in Bendix and Lipset, *Class, Status, and Power*, pp. 303–8.
44 James S. House, "Why and When Is Status Inconsistency Stressful?" *American Journal of Sociology*, vol. 81 (1976), pp. 395–411.
45 R. A. Nisbet, "The Decline and Fall of Social Class," in R. A. Nisbet, ed., *Tradition and Revolt* (New York: Random House, 1968); and Gerhard Lensky, *Power and Privilege* (New York: McGraw-Hill, 1966).
46 Norval D. Glenn, "Massification versus Differentiation: Some Trend Data from National Surveys," *Social Forces*, vol. 46 (December 1967); and Norval D. Glenn and Jon P. Alstop, "Cultural Distances among Occupational Categories," *American Sociological Review*, vol. 33 (June 1968).

nonfarm male population was engaged in manual or working class occupation. "Service" jobs are becoming predominantly manual labor, and much of the income increases is due to more spouses joining the labor force rather than to larger salaries.[47]

Children's perceptions. Perhaps one of the best demonstrations of the reality of stratification in America is provided by Simmons and Rosenberg.[48] As part of a larger study, the researchers examined the perception of the stratification system of children. A sample of 1,917 black and white children of varying social backgrounds from grades 3 to 12 were interviewed. Parents of the children were also interviewed on the same questions for comparison with responses of their children.

The children perceived occupation prestige and inequality of opportunity with dramatic awareness. As early as the elementary school stage, children rated 15 occupations in a prestige order almost identical to that of their parents and of the older high-school pupils. Using a Spearman rho rank-order correlation, the rank orders of elementary school children and adults correlated 0.93, well beyond the 0.01 level of significance. The Pearson product moment correlation of absolute scores showed a correlation of 0.96. The high correlations held for all categories of children, whether white or black, middle or working class, and regardless of age.[49] It was also found that both younger and older children reject the doctrine of equality of opportunity in obtaining "the good things in life".[50]

Intergenerational social mobility. A question that arises is whether or not an individual can change his or her social class from that of the previous generation. The answer seems to be that while it is possible the probability is not very high of it actually happening. Furthermore, the chances are not increasing according to some of the most distinguished researchers in this field:

> To put the matter crudely, but correctly, there has been no change in the odds that a man of high status origin will achieve higher rather than lower occupational standing.[51]

Those researchers went on to conclude that the only source of variation in rates of intergenerational occupational mobility were due to changes in the occupational structure. There is a little more hope for change (both upward and downward, however) for women than for men according to research by Ivan Chase, who concluded that women have somewhat

---

47 Richard Parker, "Fact and Fancy about America's Classless Society," *Business and Society Review/Innovation*, No. 10 (Summer 1974).

48 Robert G. Simmons and Morris Rosenberg, "Functions of Childrens' Perceptions of the Stratification System," *American Sociological Review*, vol. 36, pp. 235–49 (April 1971).

49 Simmons and Rosenberg, "Functions," p. 237.

50 Simmons and Rosenberg, "Functions," pp. 239–40.

51 R. Hauser et al., "Structural Changes in Occupational Mobility among Men in the United States," *American Sociological Review*, vol. 40 (October 1975), pp. 585–98.

greater mobility through marriage than do men through occupations, since men are more likely to "inherit" their fathers' statuses.[52]

The process by which some individuals do change their social status is shown in Figure 5.2. A more complete model of the influence is known as

Figure 5.2 Selected influences on intergenerational social mobility

the Wisconsin social-psychological model of socioeconomic achievement.[53] Very simply, however, an individual's intergenerational social mobility is determined by occupational achievement, which is, in turn, heavily influenced by educational achievement and by the willingness

52 Ivan D. Chase, "A Comparison of Men's and Women's Intergenerational Mobility in the United States," *American Sociological Review*, vol. 40 (August 1975), pp. 483–505.

53 W. H. Sewell and R. M. Hauser, *Education, Occupation and Earnings* (New York: Academic Press, 1975); and Karl L. Alexander, B. K. Eckland, and L. J. Griffin, "The Wisconsin Model of Socioeconomic Achievement: A Replication," *American Journal of Sociology*, vol. 81 (1976), pp. 324–41.

(and ability) to engage in geographic mobility.[54] Educational achievement is influenced by two variables—the individual's actual ability and the evaluation of that ability by educational institutions, since educational outcomes depend more on the criteria of selection than on the process within schools.[55] Educational ability is heavily influenced by the self-concept of an individual and it is this motivation or ability to succeed in an academic environment that is transmitted as family advantages regardless of shifts in the economic structure.[56] This process of relying on educational achievement to attain occupational mobility is similar in both the United States and Great Britain although the British stratification system is somewhat more closed than that of the United States.[57]

Social class has been analyzed from a sexist viewpoint in most sociological studies in the sense that a female's status was usually determined by the status of the male head of the household rather than recognizing the contribution of the female to the status of the family or recognizing her own status. Only in recent years has that practice been challenged and some changes implemented.[58]

Social-class overlays. The changing nature of social class is perhaps best characterized as new patterns "overlaying" old patterns. Social-class behavior and attitudes may become more subtle and more complicated but are not disappearing. Old norms are not discarded; rather new ones are added to the old ones to make an even more complicated pattern to confront the sociological or consumer researcher.

> . . . classes do not simply disappear . . . New life styles may replace older ones even while the economic basis of both styles remains the same. More likely, however, new life styles will not completely replace old ones, but will simply become accretions on them. Any innovations in life styles thus increase the complexity of the class system because older classes and styles cannot coexist with the new ones.[59]

The lower middle and upper lower classes are the largest groups of consumers in America. This is the "middle majority"—to which most marketing organizations must sell.

Class distribution

The exact distribution of individuals into separate class categories depends upon the definitions used for each class. The mainstream of

54 Aage B. Sorensen, "The Structure of Intragenerational Mobility," *American Sociological Review*, vol. 40 (August 1975), pp. 456–71.

55 Barbara Heyns, "Social Selection and Stratification within Schools," *American Journal of Sociology*, vol. 79 (1974), pp. 1434–51; and K. L. Wilson and A. Portes, "The Educational Attainment Process: Results from a National Sample," *American Journal of Sociology*, vol. 81 (1976), pp. 343–62.

56 Angela Lane, "The Occupational Achievement Process, 1940–1949: A Cohort Analysis," *American Sociological Review*, vol. 40 (August 1975), pp. 472–82; and Thomas W. Miller, "Effects of Maternal Age, Education, and Employment Status on the Self-Esteem of the Child," *The Journal of Social Psychology*, vol. 95 (1975), pp. 141–42.

57 Donald J. Treiman and Kermit Terrell, "The Process of Status Attainment in the United States and Great Britain," *American Journal of Sociology*, vol. 81 (1976), pp. 563–81.

58 Joan Acker, "Women and Social Stratification: A Case of Intellectual Sexism," *American Journal of Sociology*, vol. 78 (1973), pp. 936–45.

59 Joseph Bensman and Arthur J. Vidich, *The New American Society* (Chicago: Quadrangle Books, 1971), p. 139.

Figure 5.3 Social classes in the United States

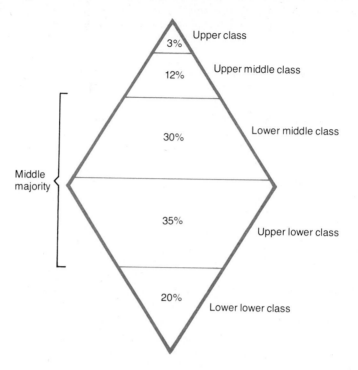

Upper class 3%

Upper middle class 12%

Lower middle class 30%

Middle majority

Upper lower class 35%

Lower lower class 20%

Source: Charles B. McCann, *Women and Department Store Newspaper Advertising* (Chicago: Social Research, 1957), p. 94. Reprinted by permission of the publisher.

social research has commonly used a six-class system. One organization that has dealt with social class extensively is Social Research, Inc., of Chicago. Based upon their continuing studies, they have prepared estimates of class distribution in America. These estimates, which have been used extensively by marketing strategists, are presented in Figure 5.3.

Somewhat similar results have been reported in Carman's study of cultural classes, except that he reports a smaller percentage in the lower lower class. He found 0.38 percent in upper, 10.82 percent in upper middle, 30.82 percent in lower middle, 49.96 percent in upper lower, and 8.02 percent in lower lower class.[60] Numerous studies have been conducted establishing the proportion of individuals in each class, although the categories are generally not directly comparable with each other.[61] An inspection of the studies over time leads to the conclusion, however, that the proportion in middle and upper classes is fairly stable, but that the

60 Carman, *Application of Social Class*, p. 53.

61 W. L. Warner et al., *Yankee City* (New Haven, Conn.: Yale University Press, 1963), p. 43; Richard Centers, *Psychology of Social Class*, p. 77; August B. Hollingshead and Frederick C. Redich, "Social Stratification and Psychiatric Disorders," *American Sociological Review*, vol. 18, pp. 163–67 (1953); Arthur J. Vidich and Joseph Bensman, *Small Town in Mass Society* (Princeton, N.J.: Princeton University Press, 1958, Anchor ed. 1960), p. 52.

proportion in the lower lower class has been declining substantially with corresponding increases in the upper lower class.

The six-class categorization of Warner is used in Figure 5.4 to describe

Figure 5.4 Social class behavior in America

Upper upper

Upper uppers are the social elite of society. Inherited wealth from socially prominent families is the key to admission. Children attend private preparatory schools and graduate from the best colleges.

Consumers in the upper upper class spend money as if it were unimportant, not niggardly but not with display either, for that would imply that money is important. For some products a "trickle-down" influence may exist between social classes. The social position of these individuals is so secure that they can deviate from class norms if they choose to without losing status.

Lower upper

Lower uppers include the very-high-income professional people who have "earned" their position rather than inherited it. They are the *nouveaux riches,* active people with many material symbols of their status. They buy the largest homes in the best suburbs, the most expensive automobiles, swimming pools and other symbols of conspicuous consumption, making them innovators and good markets for luxury marketing offerings.

Upper middle

The key word for upper middles is "career." Careers are based on successful professional or graduate degrees for a specific profession or the skill of business administration. Members of this class are demanding of their children in educational attainment.

The *quality* market for many products is the upper middle class and gracious living in a conspicuous but careful manner characterizes the family's life style. The home is of high importance and an important symbol of the family's success and competence.

Lower middle

Lower middle class families are "typical" Americans, exemplifying the core of respectability, conscientious work habits, and adherence to culturally defined norms and standards. They believe in attending church and obeying the law and are upset when their children are arrested for law violations. They are not innovators.

The *home* is very important to the lower middle family and they want it to be neat, well-painted, and in a respected neighborhood. They may have little confidence in their own tastes and adopt "standardized" home furnishings—perhaps from Levitz or Wickes. This is in contrast to the upper middle housewife who feels freer to experiment with new styles and new arrangements and with the upper lower housewife who is not very concerned about the overall plan for furnishing the home. The lower middle housewife reads and follows the advice of the medium-level shelter and service magazines in her attempt to make her house "pretty."

The lower middle class housewife "works" more at her shopping than other women and considers purchase decisions demanding and tedious. She may have a high degree of price sensitivity.

Upper lower

Upper lower social classes—the largest segment of society—exhibit a routine life, characterized by a day-to-day existence of unchanging activities. They live in dull areas of the city, in small houses or apartments. The "hard hats" are included in this class, with many members working at uncreative jobs requiring manual activity or only moderate skills and education. Because of unions and security, many may earn incomes that give them considerable discreationary income.

The purchase decisions of the working-class wife are often impulsive but at the same

Figure 5.4 Social class behavior in America (continued)

time she may have high brand loyalty to "national" brands. Buying them is one way to "prove" her knowledge as a buyer, a role in which she feels (probably correctly) that she has little skill. She has little social contact outside the home and does not like to attend civic organizations or church activities. Social interaction is limited to close neighbors and relatives. If she takes a vacation, it will probably be a visit to relatives in another city. Upper lowers are concerned that they not be confused with the lower lowers.

Lower lower

The lower lower social class contains the so-called "disreputable" people of the society who may try to rise above their class on some occasions but usually fail to do so and become reconciled to their position in society. An individual in the lower lower class often rejects middle class morality and "gets his kicks" wherever he can—and this includes buying impulsively. This lack of planning causes purchases that cost too much and may result in inferior goods. This person pays too much for products, buys on credit at a high interest rate and has difficulty evaluating the quality or value of a product.

some of the key elements of social-class behavior norms. Figure 5.4 is only a skeleton outline of some of the most important identifying characteristics of each social class and their consumption patterns. These generalizations are developed primarily from the studies of Warner, Coleman, Davis, the Gardners, and Levy, who have all contributed heavily to social class research.[62]

Social class and buying decisions

Much social class research has been concerned specifically with consumption decisions. Consequently, there are a number of empirically based generalizations available concerning social class for marketing decisions and for understanding more fully the stages involved in typical consumption decisions.

Social class and market segmentation

The most direct application of social class to marketing and communications strategy has been in the area of market segmentation where it has been shown to be useful in understanding market segments for a wide variety of products and services[63] although there is considerable skepticism about its universal value in marketing strategy. Frank, Massy and Wind, after assessing social-class studies, concluded that the *potential* is greater than the *realized* value. They point out that lack of success in using social class in marketing studies may be due, among other reasons,

---

62 For more extensive description of these social classes, see the 1973 edition of this textbook.
63 Pierre Martineau, "Social Classes and Spending Behavior," *Journal of Marketing*, vol. 23 (October 1958), pp. 121–30; Sidney Levy, "Social Class and Consumer Behavior," in Joseph W. Newman, ed., *On Knowing the Consumer* (New York: Wiley, 1966), pp. 146–60; Phillip Kotler, "Behavioral Model for Analyzing Buyers," *Journal of Marketing*, vol. 29 (October 1965); Richard P. Coleman and Bernice L. Newgarten, *Social Status in the City* (San Francisco: Jossey-Bass, 1971).

to the inadequacy of using unidimensional measures rather than multidimensional measures in too many social class studies.[64] Part of the problem may also be the failure to use income as a moderating variable within social classes, as was proposed by Coleman when he described some families as "overprivileged" and some "underprivileged" in income when compared to their social class.[65]

Income versus social class. There is a major controversy concerning the efficacy of the variables of income and social class in predicting actual consumer behavior. This controversy was initiated by Chester Wasson who, after studying family budget allocations for food, shelter, and education by both income and by occupational status, concluded that occupational class was a more important determinant of spending allocations than income.[66]

A study by Myers, Stanton, and Haug examined the power of social class compared to income as correlates of buying behavior for a wide variety of consumer household goods. In most cases, income was a far superior indicator of buying behavior than social class except for the product categories of dry instant milk, instant coffee, variety bread, powdered detergent, facial tissues, paper towels and cottage cheese.[67] A later study by Myers and Mount extended the categories to include services and durable goods. Again, income was superior to social class as a segmentation variable except for black and white TV, commercial air travel and possession of a U.S. passport.[68]

A possible resolution to the problems in the Myers and Mount research was offered by Hisrich and Peters, who claim that better results would be obtained if the frequency of use and nature of the product were considered. In their research, using Warner's social class index, social class was a weaker predictor of behavior than life cycle or income when "use or nonuse" was investigated, but social class was a better correlate than income when frequency of use was considered.[69]

Evaluative criteria refer to the specifications that a consumer utilizes to compare products and brands, as noted in Chapter 2. These criteria are a reflection of the individual's goals and basic desires with respect to a purchase related to social class.

Evaluative criteria and product evaluation

64 Ronald E. Frank, William F. Massy, and Yoram Wind, *Market Segmentation* (Englewood Cliffs, N.J.: Prentice-Hall, 1972), pp. 47–49.

65 See Richard P. Coleman, "The Significance of Social Stratification in Selling," in Martin L. Bell, ed., *Marketing: A Maturine Discipline, Proceedings of the American Association* (December 1960), pp. 171–84.

66 Chester R. Wasson, "Is It Time to Quit Thinking of Income Classes?" *Journal of Marketing*, vol. 33, pp. 54–56 (April 1969).

67 James H. Myers, Roger R. Stanton, and Arne F. Haug, "Correlates of Buying Behavior: Social Class vs. Income," *Journal of Marketing*, vol. 35, pp. 8–15 (October 1971).

68 James H. Myers and John F. Mount, "More on Social Class vs. Income as Correlates of Buying Behavior," *Journal of Marketing*, vol. 33 (April 1973), pp. 71–73.

69 R. D. Hisrich and Michael Peters, "Selecting the Superior Segmentation Correlate," *Journal of Marketing*, vol. 38 (July 1974), pp. 60–63.

Clothing. The kind, quality, and style of clothing an individual wears appears to be linked to that individual's social class. Hoult found that clothing furnishes a quick, visual cue to the class culture of the wearer.[70] Ostermeier and Eicher investigated the social-class characteristics of adolescent girls and report that when asked to give the characteristics of the popular girls, "dressed well" was the response most frequently given.[71] More significantly, they found a relationship between clothing, social class, and social acceptance. Earlier, Gordon also found that clothing and appearance become symbols of social differentiation because of their high visibility.[72] In another study, Rich and Jain found high interest in clothing fashions among all social classes, but their data seem to indicate greater attention to fashion information among upper social classes.[73]

Home furnishings. The criteria a family uses to furnish a home appear to be closely related to social class.[74] In a probability survey of 897 respondents, Laumann and House noted the contents and characteristics of the living room on a 53-item checklist inventory. They clustered the living room furniture using a technique called smallest space analysis (SSA). Figure 5.5 depicts how the 53 variables arranged themselves in a two-dimensional space. The clusters reflected style of decor: (1) high status—modern, (2) high status—traditional, (3) low status—traditional, and (4) low status—modern. When people (rather than furnishings) were mapped in a multidimensional scalogram analysis (MSA), interesting conclusions were obtained. Traditional respondents represented the established upper class (white, Anglo-Saxon, Protestants not recently upwardly mobile within the present generation). The modern respondents were generally upwardly mobile within this generation and from non-Anglo-Saxon, Catholic origins. They were the *nouveaux riches*.

Laumann and House propose the theory that the *nouveaux riches* have a strong need to validate their newly found status, yet have not been accepted socially by the traditional upper classes. They turn to conspicuous consumption but with "taste" if it is to validate their claim to high status in respects other than mere money. The researchers conclude that the criteria used by this class reflect the *chic* norms of tastemakers:

> Discovery of such norms is easy in a society that possesses a class of professional tastemakers (e.g., architects, interior decorators, fashion designers) and taste-setting media (ranging from *Better Homes and*

70 Thomas Ford Hoult, "Experimental American Measurement of Clothing as a Factor in Some Social Rating of Selected American Men," *American Sociological Review*, vol. 19, pp. 324–25 (June 1954).

71 Arlene Bjorngaard Ostermeier and Joanne Bubolz Eicher, "Clothing and Appearance as Related to Social Class and Social Acceptance of Adolescent Girls," *Michigan State University Quarterly Bulletin*, vol. 48, pp. 431–36 (February 1966).

72 C. Wayne Gordon, *The Social System of the High School* (New York: Free Press, 1957), p. 114.

73 Stuart U. Rich and Subhash C. Jain, "Social Class and Life Cycle as Predictors of Shopping Behavior," *Journal of Marketing Research,* vol. 5, pp. 41–49 (February 1968).

74 Edward O. Laumann and James S. House, "Living Room Styles and Social Attributes: The Patterning of Material Artifacts in a Modern Urban Community," *Sociology and Social Research*, vol. 54, pp. 321–24 (April 1970).

Figure 5.5 Graphic portrayal of the best two-space solution for living-room objects

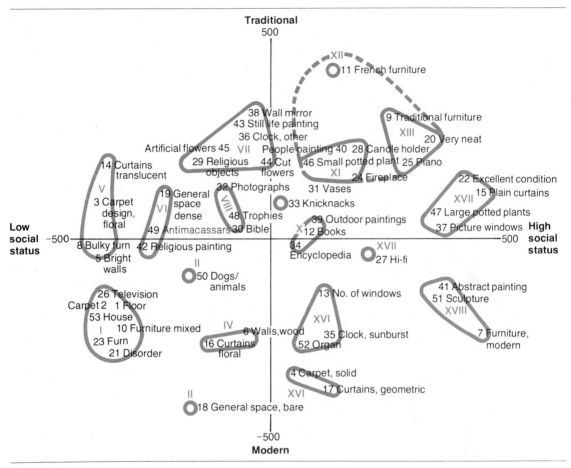

Source: Edward O. Laumann and James S. House, "Living Room Styles and Social Attributes: The Patterning of Material Artifacts in a Modern Urban Community," *Sociology and Social Research*, vol. 54, pp. 321–342, at p. 326 (Apr. 1970). Reprinted by permission of Sociology and Social Research: An International Journal, University of Southern California, Los Angeles, California 90007.

Gardens through the *New Yorker*). Normative consumption trends are evident in styles of decor adopted by business and government for their new offices and stores. In all cases, the norms today favor modern decor.[75]

Leisure. The percentage of family income spent for leisure, independent of income, has not been found to vary much between social classes[76] but the evaluative criteria used in selecting type of recreation is heavily influ-

75 Laumann and House, "Living Room Styles," p. 337.
76 Carman, *Application of Social Class*, p. 31.

enced by social class. Bridge is an upper-class game, while bingo is lower class. Tennis is an upper-class sport, boxing is predominantly lower class. Opera is upper class, roller derby is lower class.[77]

Leisure activities may be characterized within a prestige hierarchy associated with occupational status. In a random sample of males and females, Bishop and Ikeda examined leisure patterns and status (using the North-Hatt occupational scale and Warner's ISC).[78] A multiple discriminant analysis produced three discriminant functions accounting for 53.1 percent of variance. Social status accounted for the most variance in leisure patterns—27.9 percent.

Prestigeful activities such as ice skating, bicycling, swimming, basketball, and tennis involve fairly rapid movement with extreme use of arms and legs, possibly suggesting a compensatory form of leisure for the otherwise sedentary life of many prestige occupations. Bishop and Ikeda also claim that most of these pursuits do not necessarily require a lot of time to the degree that activities such as hunting, fishing, or boating would. Thus, the authors suggest, time may be a critical element in the prestige classes' uses of leisure.[79] (See, also, Chapter 3.)

Choice of leisure activities is also affected by social class–family interaction. There is a linear association between occupational stratum and couple participation in commercial leisure pursuits, with the exception that couples of the very highest occupational stratum reflect a slight decrease in recreation interaction compared to the upper middle class.[80] Rainwater, Coleman, and Handel have characterized the working class wife as not sharing in her husband's recreational activities because she is absorbed in domestic activities and because her husband has no desire for her to participate.[81] Other investigators, however, report an increasing importance of commercial recreation in the lives of lower-status persons.[82]

The heaviest users of both commercial leisure facilities and public facilities (such as parks, museums, and swimming pools) are the middle classes, since upper classes frequently have their own facilities and the lower classes frequently cannot afford them or do not have the propensity to participate in them.[83]

Credit cards. Credit-card acceptance and usage appear to be related to some extent to social class. Mathews and Slocum concluded that the lower classes preferred to use bank credit cards for durable and necessity goods (appliances, furniture, clothing) in contrast to the upper class desire

77 Bert N. Adams and James E. Butler, "Occupation Status and Husband-Wife Social Participation," *Social Forces*, vol. 45, pp. 501–07, at p. 506 (June 1967).

78 Doyle W. Bishop and Masaru Ikeda, "Status and Role Factors in the Leisure Behavior of Different Occupations," *Sociology and Social Research*, vol. 54, pp. 190–208 (January 1970).

79 Bishop and Ikeda, "Status and Role Factors," pp. 200–201.

80 Adams and Butler, "Occupational Status," p. 504.

81 Rainwater et al., *Workingman's Wife*, p. 76.

82 Alfred C. Clarke, "The Use of Leisure and Its Relation to Levels of Occupational Prestige," *American Sociological Review*, vol. 21, p. 304 (June 1956).

83 Lasswell, *Class and Stratum*, pp. 258–64.

to charge luxury items (gasoline, luggage, restaurants).[84] They also found more favorable attitudes toward credit usage among higher social classes. In a later study by the same investigators, however, they concluded that income was equally valuable as a basis for segmentation.[85]

In a study by Plummer, it was found that charge cards were surprisingly widespread and cut across many demographic segments of the population. The most frequent users, however, were of higher income, better education, middle age, and professional occupation.[86] This same pattern of credit card usage was found in the studies of Hawes, Blackwell, and Talarzyk.[87]

Other products. Evaluative criteria for other products have been found to be related to social class. For automobiles, Peters found his measure of relative occupational class income useful. He found that the "average" income group within each social class bought many more foreign, economy, intermediate-sized, and compact cars than would have been expected. The "overprivileged" groups within each social class owned more medium-sized and large cars and fewer foreign economy cars.[88] In another study using Q methodology, Sommers found that lower-class housewives felt appliances represented their "self-concept" in contrast to upper-class housewives who chose clothing as products most symbolic of themselves.[89]

Search processes

The amount and type of search undertaken by an individual varies by social class as well as by product and situation category.[90] Unfortunately, the lowest social classes have limited information sources and are therefore at a disadvantage at filtering out misinformation and fraud in a complex, urbanized society.[91] To compensate, working-class women often rely on relatives or close friends for information about consumption decisions.[92] Middle-class women put more reliance upon media-acquired information and actively engage in external search from the media.[93] Upper-class individuals have far more access to media information than do lower-class individuals.[94]

84 H. Lee Mathews and John W. Slocum, Jr., "Social Class and Commercial Bank Credit Card Usage," *Journal of Marketing*, vol. 33, pp. 71–78 (January 1969).

85 John W. Slocum and H. Lee Mathews, "Social Class and Income as Indicators of Consumer Credit Behavior," *Journal of Marketing*, vol. 34, pp. 69–74 (April 1970).

86 Joseph T. Plummer, "Life Style Patterns and Commercial Bank Credit Card Usage," *Journal of Marketing*, vol. 35, pp. 35–41 (April 1971).

87 Douglass K. Hawes, Roger D. Blackwell, and W. Wayne Talarzyk, "Attitudes toward Use of Credit Cards: Do Men and Women Differ?" *Baylor Business Studies*, no. 110 (January 1977), pp. 57–71.

88 Peters, "Relative Occupational Class," p. 77.

89 Montrose S. Sommers, "The Use of Product Symbolism to Differentiate Social Strata," *University of Houston Business Review*, vol. 11, pp. 1–102 (Fall 1964).

90 Gordon R. Foxall, "Social Factors in Consumer Choice: Replication and Extension," *Journal of Consumer Research*, vol. 2 (June 1975), pp. 60–64.

91 Caplovitz, *Poor Pay More*.

92 Rainwater et al., *Workingman's Wife*, p. 166.

93 Rainwater et al., *Workingman's Wife*.

94 Haer, "Predicting Utility."

Individuals also appear to be more responsive to information sources that they perceive to be compatible with their own social class, and there are good examples of marketers who have customized a basic promotional strategy to the requirements of specific classes.[95] It is clear that sharp differences exist in the class connotations of standard media sources such as newspapers and television, even though all classes have some exposure to them. One study in 15 major cities found, for example, that upper-middle-class people consistently preferred the NBC channel, while lower middles preferred CBS, in keeping with the class images of the networks at that time.[96]

Interpersonal communications vary in other ways. In one study of blue-collar families, the researchers found significant differences between urban and suburban residents. Suburbanites indicated greater neighbor familiarity and displayed a greater sensitivity for their neighbor's work and church activities than did urban counterparts. Conversely, a higher proportion of city dwellers claimed virtually no knowledge of their neighbor's activities, income, or education.[97] The hypothesis generated from such a study would be that personal communications would be more important concerning consumption decisions than media for suburban consumers compared to city dwellers. This topic is explored in other ways in Chapter 19.

Social language

The language patterns of an individual are closely correlated with that individual's social class. Ellis has reported a revealing set of experiments on this topic. In one experiment he measured social class of respondents and had them make a 40-second recording of the fable, "The Tortoise and the Hare." These short recordings were played to groups of 15 to 30 regionally diverse college students who served as judges. The average ratings of social class by these judges correlated 0.80 with the speakers' social classes.[98] When the studies were conducted in such a way that speakers were asked through role playing to "fake" their voices to make them sound upper class, the student judges' correlation with measured actual class was still 0.65.[99] All of the subjects used proper grammer, but their choice of vocabulary, sentence length, sentence structure, and fluency varied by social class. In still another approach, Ellis had the speakers count from 1 to 20 and even in this situation, college students' rankings correlated 0.65 with social class of the speakers.

An additional study by Harms found that the credibility of speakers is

95 Mozell C. Hill, "Ice Cream in Contemporary Society," *New Sociology*, vol. 2, pp. 23–24 (1963).

96 Ira O. Glick and Sidney J. Levy, *Living with Television* (Chicago: Aldine, 1962).

97 Irving Tallman and Romona Morgner, "Life-Style Differences Among Urban and Suburban Blue-Collar Families," *Social Forces*, vol. 48, pp. 334–48 (March 1970); also Rita J. Simon, Gail Crotts, and Linda Mahan, "An Empirical Note about Married Women and Their Friends," *Social Forces*, vol. 48, pp. 520–25 (June 1970).

98 Dean S. Ellis, "Speech and Social Status in America," *Social Forces*, vol. 45, pp. 431–37 (March 1967).

99 Ellis, "Speech."

also associated with status. High-status persons are perceived as being more credible than low-status persons.[100]

Social status appears to have a great deal of influence on where and how people feel they should shop. Evidence indicates that lower-status people prefer local, face-to-face places where they get friendly service and easy credit.[101] Upper middle housewives feel much more confident in their shopping ability and will venture to new places to shop or will range throughout a department store to find what they want. The discount store appeals to the middle classes because they are most careful and economy minded in their buying.[102] The lower classes may not have found what they wanted in the discount stores in the early years because of the initial failure of these stores to carry national brands. It has been found that lower-class women rely on national brands whenever possible to make sure they "are getting a good buy."[103] It has also been found that working-class women are reluctant to try a new store. They limit their shopping to a few stores.[104]

Some important research supports the position that consumers in different socioeconomic segments differ in their patronage of discount stores for some types of products but not for others. Specifically, Prasad found that products with high social, low economic risk and those of high social, high economic risk were products with which social classes differed significantly in their patronage attitudes toward discount stores.[105]

Consumers have an image of what social class a store appeals to, even if a consumer has no shopping experience in that store. Figure 5.6 illustrates this situation. Women were asked to evaluate a department store on various factors that would establish the status group the store served. An interesting feature of this study is that women were able to rate accurately a store they had never seen merely by seeing its advertisements.[106]

Women report that they enjoy shopping regardless of social class, but women in different social classes have varying reasons for their enjoyment. Rich and Jain found that women in upper classes more frequently specify a pleasant store atmosphere and displays with excitement as enjoyable features, but lower classes emphasize acquiring household things or clothing as enjoyable. Upper classes shop more frequently than middle or lower classes.[107]

100 L. S. Harms, "Listener Judgments of Status Cues in Speech," *Quarterly Journal of Speech*, vol. 47, pp. 164–68 (April 1961).

101 Levy, "Social Class," p. 153.

102 Pierre Martineau, "The Pattern of the Social Classes," in Richard Clewett, ed., *Marketing's Role in Scientific Marketing* (Chicago: American Marketing Association, 1957), pp. 233–49, at p. 248.

103 M. Ross, "Uptown and Downtown," *American Sociological Review*, vol. 30, pp. 255–59 (1965).

104 Ross, "Uptown."

105 V. Kanti Prasad, "Socioeconomic Product Risk and Patronage Preferences of Retail Shoppers," *Journal of Marketing*, vol. 39 (July 1975), pp. 42–47.

106 Charles B. McCann, *Women and Department Store Newspaper Advertising* (Chicago: Social Research, 1957), pp. 15–55.

107 Rich and Jain, "Social Class."

Housewife perceptions of department-store status

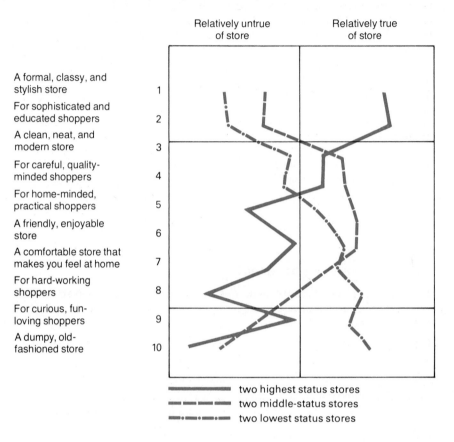

Relatively untrue of store   Relatively true of store

1. A formal, classy, and stylish store
2. For sophisticated and educated shoppers
3. A clean, neat, and modern store
4. For careful, quality-minded shoppers
5. For home-minded, practical shoppers
6. A friendly, enjoyable store
7. A comfortable store that makes you feel at home
8. For hard-working shoppers
9. For curious, fun-loving shoppers
10. A dumpy, old-fashioned store

━━━━━ two highest status stores
━ ━ ━ two middle-status stores
━·━·━ two lowest status stores

Source: Charles B. McCann, *Women and Department Store Newspaper Advertising* (Chicago: Social Research, 1957), pp. 15–55. Reprinted by permission of the publisher.

Shopping by husband and wife together is most likely to occur among lower-middle-class families. Adams and Butler found the greatest propensity to shop together among lower white-collar, skilled, and semiskilled classes.[108] Shopping, especially for the middle-class family, has taken on the characteristics of a form of recreation for many.

Summary

Social classes are relatively permanent and homogeneous divisions in a society in which groups of people are compared with one another. These groups are recognized as having inferior or superior positions by the individuals who comprise the society, although the basis of superiority is not established.

108 Adams and Butler, "Occupation Status," p. 506.

Social classes are discrete groups in theory, but in practice they are treated as continuous. Some people, therefore, exhibit behavior that is partially aligned with one social class and partially aligned with another. One reason for this phenomenon is multidimensionality, which exists when people rank in different positions on the specific determinants of social class.

Occupation is the most important *single* measure of an individual's social class. Other important variables are the personal performance of an individual within his occupational group, the interactions he has with other individuals, his possessions, the value orientations of his group, and his class consciousness. Measurement of social class may involve any or all of these determinants.

Social classes in America are frequently divided into six groups: upper upper, lower upper, upper middle, lower middle, upper lower, and lower lower. Each of these groups displays characteristic values and behaviors that are useful in analyzing consumer decisions.

Review and discussion questions

1. What variables determine an individual's social class? In what order of importance should they be ranked?

2. In what way does income relate to social class? Why is it used so little as an indicator of social class? What should be its proper value as an indicator of social class?

3. Prepare an outline of the major problems involved in the measurement of social classes.

4. Some observers of contemporary America believe that social classes have declined in importance and presence, but others disagree. Outline your analysis of what has happened in recent years to social classes in America.

5. A marketing researcher is speculating on the influence of the upper classes on the consumption decisions of the lower classes for the following products: automobiles, food, clothing, baby care products. What conclusions would you expect for each of those products? Describe a research project that could be used to determine the answer to this question.

6. The leisure products group of a large conglomerate is constantly seeking additional products for expanding markets and additional penetration for existing products. What conclusions that would be helpful in the design of marketing strategy might be reached concerning social class and leisure?

7. The operator of a large discount chain is contemplating a new store in an area of upper lower families. He asks for a consulting report defining the precautions he should take to insure patronage among this group. What would you place in such a report? Assume that the area was mostly lower-lower families. Would you recommend he enter this market?

8. Prepare a research report comparing the search processes of the major social classes of consumers in America.

CHAPTER 6

Reference group and family influences

How important are other persons in influencing the intentions and choices of a consumer? What is the relative influence of the wife, husband, and children in selecting the make of a car, the body style, and other features? Should marketing efforts be directed to all family members or just one member? What are the effects of advertising upon children? How is the demographic structure of the American family changing?

Answers to these types of questions are often essential in designing marketing strategies and programs. This chapter discusses the concept of reference groups, especially the family, the most important reference group in the life of a consumer.

The nature of reference groups

Each consumer is a member of many groups, but those that influence the person's behavior are called *reference groups*. These groups are crucial for marketing managers to understand because they influence the self-conception, attitudes, and behavior of an individual by serving as a point of reference in the presentation of self to others.

Many types of reference groups exist. *Primary groups* are collections of individuals small enough and intimate enough that all the members can communicate with each other face to face.[1] These include the family as the most important primary group but they can also include playmates,

---

1 George Homans, *The Human Group* (London: Routledge, 1961), p. 1.

friendship groups in the neighborhood or on the job, and other types of intimate groupings. *Secondary groups* are social organizations, where less continuous, face-to-face interaction takes place and include professional associations, religious organizations, trade unions, and similar groups. Primary groups often are subsets of the secondary groups, of course.

Reference groups also can be classified as *formal groups* (with a defined structure and usually specified membership requirements) or *informal* groups, which occur on the basis of proximity, interests, or other bases with less specified structure or membership. The former are easier to study, but the latter may be of more influence on consumption decisions because of the likelihood that consumers will see, try, and talk about the products and services used by other members of the informal group.

Other categories of groups may be defined. *Membership groups* are groups in which a person is recognized by others as belonging. An *aspirational group* is one to which an individual wishes or aspires to belong. A *dissociative group* is one with whose values or behavior an individual does not want to be associated. All definitions of a group imply the existence of functional interdependence among people rather than a mere statistical summation of individuals.[2] An example of a nongroup, or statistical summation of people, would be the "youth" market.

Reference groups function in several ways of interest to consumer analysts. First, reference groups create *socialization of individuals*—the process by which individuals become aware of or learn alternative behaviors and life styles. Second, reference groups are important in the process of *developing and evaluating one's self-concept*. Third, reference groups are a *device for obtaining compliance* with norms of society. Each of these is described briefly below and analyzed in more detail in Chapter 11, which describes the use by consumers of nonmarketer-dominated sources in the search process.

Socialization is defined as "the process by which a new member learns the value system, norms, and the required behavior patterns of the society, organizations, or group which the person is entering."[3] Socialization occurs and is necessary because of the individual's need to participate in the social environment. (See Chapters 4 and 8 for additional discussion of socialization, in different contexts.)

Consumer socialization

The process of socialization is accomplished through the influence of various reference groups. A company manual may explain to the new employee, for example, when coffee breaks are to be taken, but informal

2 This is in harmony with a general definition of a social group by Greer, "A social group is an aggregate of individuals who exist in a state of functional interdependence from which evolves a flow of communication, and a consequent ordering of behavior"; Scott A. Greer, *Social Organization* (New York: Doubleday, 1955), p. 18. For amplification of the concept of a group, see James W. Vander Zanden, *Sociology: A Systematic Approach* (New York: Ronald, 1970), pp. 174–95.

3 Edgar H. Schein, "Organization Socialization and the Profession of Management," in David A. Kolb, Irwin M. Rubin, and James M. McIntyre, eds., *Organizational Psychology* (Englewood Cliffs, N.J.: Prentice-Hall, 1971), pp. 1–14, at p. 3.

work groups teach the person when they are actually taken as well as where and how and perhaps whether doughnuts are normally consumed along with coffee. In contemporary societies, individuals are constantly moving among schools, communities, and jobs. Thus, the process of socialization and acculturation (described in Chapter 4) permits an individual to know what behavior is likely to result in stability both for the individual and for the group.

Consumer socialization of children. There is high interest among consumer researchers in understanding the socialization processes of children, within the family and as they are affected by the media, especially television. Scott Ward prepared a review of the literature on this topic in which he concluded that it was necessary to understand socialization for two reasons. First, this may allow consumer researchers *to predict some aspects of adult behavior* by knowing something about childhood experiences. Second, understanding processes by which children acquire consumption-related skills, knowledge, and attitudes is *important to public policy formulation, and the development of consumer education programs.*[4] The study of consumer socialization is also important in understanding intergenerational changes in values and life styles, which were discussed in Chapter 3. "Consumer" socialization is, of course, a special type of socialization and is concerned with the processes by which people acquire skills, knowledge, and attitudes relevant to their functioning as consumers in the marketplace.

Several theories are helpful in understanding the socialization process. A large group of research is related to *learning theory.*[5] In this conceptualization, the acquisition of behavior is a process of trials or activities some of which are reinforced and therefore increase in frequency. Learning can occur personally or vicariously. For example, a child may purchase a particular brand of candy bar and find it very tasty, thereby increasing the child's probability of purchasing the same brand in the future because of the child's personal learning experience. The child may also learn vicariously by accompanying a parent on a shopping trip and observing the behavior of this role model. Other role models may be observed and their reinforcing experiences may be vicariously learned. Experiences with one type of product or a particular brand may be *generalized* to new experiences with other brands. Products or brands of close similarity may be learned to be of different reinforcing values through the process of *discrimination* leading to different behavior on slightly different cues provided by brands that are basically equivalent.

A second group of studies and theories helpful in understanding are *cognitive* or *developmental* theories. In this stream of research the mind of the child is seen as an independent force or organism that interacts with and is influenced by its environment but not entirely controlled

4 Scott Ward,"Consumer Socialization," *Journal of Consumer Research*, vol. 1 (September 1974), pp. 1–14.

5 A more extended discussion of learning theories is contained in an earlier edition of this text (1973), chap. 9.

by the learning environment. The mind of the individual selectively interprets environmental stimuli, reorganizes the new stimuli consistently with existing cognitive structure, and forms a new cognitive structure that controls behavior and continues to interpret selectively environmental stimuli. In the family development literature, these cognitive structures are thought to progress through "stages" of development that are similar among most all children. These theories are most often associated with the French researcher, Jean Piaget.[6] Research is increasingly focusing on these theories, investigating hypotheses that older children have more complex consumer learning skills than younger children, more negative attitudes toward advertising and other related issues. This research is difficult to conduct but generally supports the belief that youthful consumers make decisions progressing through different stages into their adult skills and motivations.[7]

Reference groups fulfill a second important function by developing a person's concept of *self*. (See Chapter 8.) The family is ordinarily the dominant reference group in developing the self-concept in childhood but other reference groups may become dominant in adult life and provide the process by which individuals continuously *evaluate and modify* the self-concept.

Developing and evaluating self-concept

The self is defined by Hewitt as having five components:

> The first component is an organized set of motivations. . . . The second component of the self is a series of social roles to which the person is committed, along with a knowledge of how to play them. Social roles are clusters of norms that are related to particular positions that a person occupies. . . . The third component of the self is a more general set of commitments to social norms and their underlying values. . . . The fourth component of the self is a set of cognitive abilities, including the ability to create and understand symbols, which guide response to the intended meanings of others in social interaction and provide a "map" of the physical and social setting in which the person finds himself. . . . The fifth and final component of the self is a set of ideas about one's qualities, capabilities, commitments, and motives—a self-image—that is developed by the individual in the course of his socialization.[8]

A person's self-concept causes the individual to see herself or himself through the eyes of other persons. In doing so, an individual takes into account the other person's behavior, feelings, and attitudes. This perception or evaluation is closely related to the perceptions of whether other persons in the reference group will approve or disapprove of the "self"

6 Jean Piaget, *The Construction of Reality in the Child* (New York: Basic Books, 1954).

7 Scott Ward and Daniel Wackman, "Family and Media Influences on Adolescent Consumer Learning," *American Behavioral Scientist*, vol. 14 (January–February, 1971), pp. 415–27; and Roy L. Moore and Lowndes F. Stephens, "Some Communication and Demographic Determinants of Adolescent Consumer Learning," *Journal of Consumer Research*, vol. 2 (September 1975), pp. 80–92.

8 John P. Hewitt, *Social Stratification and Deviant Behavior* (New York: Random House, 1970), pp. 32–33.

that is presented to the reference group.[9] For example, a person may chose clothing to be worn on the basis of the "statement" or appearance about that person's self that is being made to important others. A person's clothing may be a nonverbal statement of the manner in which a person wants to be accepted—or rejected. The life style of an individual—including the consumption of goods—is the presentation of "self" which that person hopes to be compatible with that person's own self or "idealized" self.[10]

An example of products as symbols enhancing the self-concept is provided in Figure 6.1 from Grubb and Grathwohl.[11] Assume that an

Figure 6.1 Relationship of the consumption of goods as symbols to self-concept

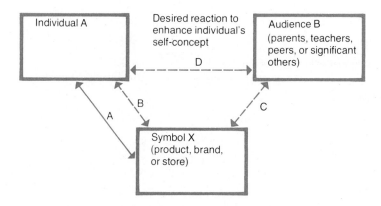

Source: Edward L. Grubb and Harrison L Grathwohl, "Consumer Self-Concept, Symbolism and Market Behavior: A Theoretical Approach," *Journal of Marketing*, vol. 31, p. 25 (October 1967). Reprinted from the *Journal of Marketing* published by the American Marketing Association.

individual A perceives oneself as being thrifty, economical, and practical. The person may purchase a Volkswagen as a symbol of these qualities, thereby achieving internal self-enhancement. The audience B may include peers, parents, and significant others. The double-headed arrows B and C in Figure 6.1 indicate that the Volkswagen is attributed meaning by A and that the audience B is also attributing meaning to it. If the Volkswagen has a commonly understood meaning between A and the reference group B, communication of self has occurred and the reaction of B will provide self-enhancement to individual A. Empirical support for this process in

9 E. L. Quarantelli and Joseph Cooper, "Self-Conception and Others: A Further Test of Median Hypotheses," *Sociological Quarterly*, vol. 7, pp. 281–97 (Summer 1966).

10 Erving Goffman, *The Presentation of Self in Everyday Life* (New York: Doubleday, 1959); and Tamtosu Shibutani, "Reference Groups as Perspectives," *American Journal of Sociology*, vol. 6, pp. 562–69 (May 1955).

11 Edward L. Grubb and Harrison L. Grathwohl, "Consumer Self-Concept, Symbolism and Market Behavior: A Theoretical Approach," *Journal of Marketing*, vol. 31, pp. 22–27 (October 1967).

selection of automobiles is provided by Grubb and Hupp[12] and Birdwell[13]; for beer, soap, cigarettes, and toothpaste by Dolich[14]; and some other brand store selection situations by others.[15] Remember the term self-concept, also, because it will be useful in understanding problem recognition and arousal in Chapter 8.

A third function of reference groups is to achieve individual compliance with group norms. This is sometimes referred to as a *normative* function in that people are caused to behave in similar patterns in contrast to the *evaluative* function of providing a reference point by which an individual evaluates the self-concept and other aspects of behavior.[16] Norms are stable expectations held by a consensus of the group concerning the behavior rules for individual members.[17] They may refer to behavioral expectations of a large segment of society, as was discussed in Chapters 3 and 4, or they may refer to small groups, which are the focus of this chapter.

Compliance with group norms

Normative compliance. The combined effects of social influences lead to a process in the model used in this book called normative compliance. Normative compliance is the effect of perceived social influence on choice behavior plus motivation to comply with those pressures. This influence is shown, as part of the model, in Figure 6.2.

Figure 6.2 Reference group influences on normative compliance

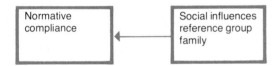

Etzioni formulated three types of compliance systems, which he called coercive, utilitarian, and normative.[18] Each is made up of two components—power and degree of involvement with the group. In

12 Edward L. Grubb and Gregg Hupp, "Perception of Self, Generalized Stereotypes, and Brand Selection," *Journal of Marketing Research*, vol. 5, pp. 58–63 (February 1968).

13 Al E. Birdwell,"A Study of the Influence of Image Congruence on Consumer Choice," unpublished Ph.D. diss. (Austin, Tex.: University of Texas, 1964).

14 Ira J. Dolich "Congruence Relationships between Self Images and Product Brands," *Journal of Marketing Research*, vol. 6, pp. 80–84 (February 1969).

15 The importance of self-concepts in retail store evaluation is presented in Joseph Barry Mason and Morris L. Baker, "The Problem of the Self-Concept in Store Image Studies," *Journal of Marketing*, vol. 34, pp. 67–69 (April 1970). Significant methodological flaws in this study have been suggested, however, by Ira J. Dolich and Ned Shilling, "A Critical Evaluation of the Problem of Self-Concept in Store Image Studies," *Journal of Marketing*, vol. 35, pp. 71–73 (January 1971).

16 Harold H. Kelly "Two Functions of Reference Groups," in C. E. Swanson, T. M. Newcomb, and E. L. Hartley, eds., *Readings in Social Psychology*, rev. ed. (New York: Holt, Rinehart and Winston, 1952).

17 For amplification, see John W. Thibaut and Harold H. Kelly, *The Social Psychology of Groups* (New York: Wiley, 1957), chap. 8.

18 Amitai Etzioni, *A Comparative Analysis of Complex Organizations* (New York: Macmillan, 1961).

marketing, compliance with group norms might be thought of as depending on the ability of the group to allocate rewards to an individual (material, status, or other rewards) as well as the attractiveness of the reference group (source) to the individual whose behavior is being influenced. In informal groups, Festinger hypothesized that the amount of influence on an individual depends upon the similarity or coorientation of an individual with the group on various attributes.[19] Moschis supported Festinger's theory in a marketing study involving consumer decisions about cosmetics.[20]

The reality of reference-group influence on buying intentions was demonstrated in an experiment involving the purchasing of bread. Stafford introduced various "brands" of bread to groups of housewives. The "brands" of bread were all identical and had plain wrappers with no symbols except identifying consonants chosen from the middle of the alphabet. The subjects in the experiment were randomly selected from preexisting reference groups and were unaware that the breads were identical or that the experiment was studying interpersonal influences. The result of the study indicated that preferences formed for each "brand" (letter of alphabet), which could be attributed to the influence of the group upon individual choice. From this study, Stafford concluded that informal groups have a definite influence on their members toward conformity behavior with respect to brands of bread preferred.[21]

An experimental study by Venkatesan also demonstrated the influence of group pressures on consumption decisions. Venkatesan presented business students with three suits (A, B, C) of identical style, color and size and asked them to choose the best suit. Control groups, in which the choices of other members were unknown, were compared to conformity groups in which a naive subject was grouped with confederates who unanimously chose the same suit. In the absence of any group influence, each suit was equally likely to be selected, but in the conformity condition, individuals significantly yielded to the group conformity, choosing the majority preference.[22]

The studies demonstrate in a marketing context well-known studies in the behavioral sciences by Asch and Sherif[23] showing the influence of reference groups on individual choices. While the studies do demonstrate that such effects exist, they have not generally supported the conclusion that the effect was large, at least in the experimental settings in which the

19 Leon Festinger,"A Theory of Social Comparison Processes," *Human Relations*, vol. 7 (May 1954), pp. 117–40.

20 George P. Moschis,"Social Comparison and Informal Group Influence," *Journal of Marketing Research*, vol. 13 (August 1976), pp. 237–44.

21 James E. Stafford, "Effects of Group Influence on Consumer Brand Preferences," *Journal of Marketing Research*, vol. 3, pp. 68–75 (February 1966).

22 M. Venkatesan, "Experimental Study of Consumer Behavior Conformity and Independence," *Journal of Marketing Research*, vol. 3, pp. 384–87 (November 1966).

23 S. E. Asch, "Effects of Group Pressure upon the Modification and Distortion of Judgments," in H. Proshansky and B. Seidenbert, eds., *Basic Studies in Social Psychology* (New York: Holt, Rinehart and Winston, 1965), pp. 393–401; and Muzafer Sherif, "Formation of Social Norms: The Experimental Paradigm," in Proshansky and Seidenberg, *Basic Studies*, pp. 461–70.

research was conducted.[24] Many other variables are affecting brand choice, as the model of consumer behavior indicates. We will need to take a closer look at reference groups as information sources, however, when examining search processes in Chapter 11.

Sociologist George Homans provided a theory to explain why people conform to group norms. Homans' equation of human exchange is built upon the premise that interpersonal activities and sentiments (defined as symbols of approval or esteem for another person) emitted by one individual responding to another are more or less reinforcing or punishing to the behavior of the other individual; that is, they are more or less valuable to him. If someone is asked to join another person for a cup of coffee, for example, there will be rewards (companionship, coffee, esteem indicated by the invitation, etc.) but there may also be costs (time lost, perhaps association with a person of lower status, giving up association with other possibly more valuable persons, and other costs). The nature of interactions will be determined by an individual's perception of the profit of the interaction. Homans defines this in familiar economic terms:

The equation of human exchange

$$profit = rewards - costs$$

Individuals arrange their social relations in such a way as to maximize total profit. The groups a person chooses to belong to and the degree to which the individual adheres to the norms of that group are based upon the net profit figure, not rewards or costs alone.[25]

Pressure to conform to group norms is present in all aspects of life. Of particular interest to marketing strategists is the influence of group norms on conformity in household products and everyday behavior patterns. This is illustrated in a study of the new town, Levittown:

Group pressure in everyday life

> The culture of the block jelled quite rapidly too. Standards of lawn care were agreed upon as soon as it was time to do something about the lawn, and by unspoken agreement, the front lawn would be cared for conscientiously, but the backyard was of less importance. Those who deviated from this norm, either neglecting their lawn or working on it too industriously, were brought into line through wisecracks. When I, in a burst of compulsive concern, worked very hard on my lawn at the start, one of my neighbors laughed and said he would have to move out if I was going to have "that fancy a lawn." Since I was not interested in a "fancy lawn," I found it easy to take the hint but those who wanted a perfect lawn stayed away from the talkfests that usually developed evenings and on Saturday mornings when the men were ostensibly

24 Fleming Hansen,"Primary Group Influence and Consumer Conformity," in Philip R. McDonald, ed., *Marketing Involvement in Society and the Economy* (Chicago: American Marketing Association, 1969), pp. 300–5.
25 George Homans, *Social Behavior: Its Elementary Forms* (New York: Harcourt, 1961). See chap. 3 and 4 for an outline of Homans' theory.

working on the lawns, so as not to be joked about and chastised as ratebusters.[26]

Anomie and deviance A somewhat different but related concept is *anomie*, originally translated from Durkheim to mean "normlessness."[27] The word has various meanings. Generally, a societal use of the term means a weakened respect for the norms of a society rather than complete absence of norms. (See Form's scale in Figure 6.3.) In this sense, anomie means an ambivalence that causes people to conform grudgingly or to nonconform with misgivings or simply for a low concensus to exist in a society about its norms. Where two conflicting norms exist, one for public purposes but another for commonly accepted noncompliance to the public norms, "patterned evasion of norms" is said to exist and include examples such as the following:

> . . . prohibition versus bootlegging; sexual chastity versus clandestine affairs and prostitution; classroom honesty versus established patterns of exam cribbing; impersonal, disinterested, honest government versus political graft, "fixing," and the like; professional codes versus fee splitting among doctors, ambulance chasing among lawyers, and so on; an income tax system versus cheating on tax returns; and concepts of truthful versus fraudulent advertising.[28]

People who score high on anomie scales are poor and uneducated and do not participate in organizations controlled by people in higher strata. People who profit most in a society have low levels of anomie while the deprived have high levels.[29] Thus, theories of anomie are frequently related to social class or cultural alienation. Anomie is also seen then as *deviance* from norms.

The psychological meaning of *anomie* focuses upon the absence of norms or standards for behavior because the *individual* is alienated psychologically from the dominant normative order. This may occur for various reasons. Winch holds, though, that one of the "core functions" of religion is the prevention of a state of normlessness at the societal level and therefore the prevention of alienation at the individual level.[30] Religion provides guidelines for behavior and gives adherents a firm notion that there are right and wrong ways of thinking and acting as well

26 Herbert J. Gans, "The Levittowners: Ways of Life and Politics in a New Suburban Community," in Frank L. Sweetser, ed., *Studies in American Urban Society* (New York: Crowell, 1970), pp. 185–220, at p. 185.

27 Emile Durkheim, *Suicide*, trans. by George Simpson, (New York: Free Press, 1951). For a cultural perspective on anomie, see Robert Merton, "Anomie, Anomia, and Social Interaction: Contexts of Deviate Behavior," in M. B. Clinard, ed., *Anomie and Deviate Behavior* (New York: Free Press, 1964).

28 Vander Zanden, *Sociology*, p. 116. For an excellent discussion of the societal implications of anomie, see pp. 115–31 of this source. Also, see Kenneth R. Schneider, *Destiny of Change* (New York: Holt, Rinehart and Winston, 1968), pp. 81–104.

29 William H. Form, "The Social Construction of Anomie: A Four-Nation Study of Industrial Workers," *American Journal of Sociology*, vol. 80 (1975), pp. 1165–89.

30 Robert F. Winch, *The Modern Family*, 3d ed. (New York: Holt, Rinehart and Winston, 1971), p. 17.

as the specifics of those ways. It appears that religious variables are of greater importance than socioeconomic factors as sources of variance in personal normlessness.[31]

In spite of the large amount of research relating anomie to various aspects of behavior, this variable is just beginning to appear in consumer studies. Examples of "anomie scales" are shown in Figure 6.3. Some of these items have been used in life style studies as AIO (Activity, Interest, Opinion) statements but usually without the conceptual basis in other anomie studies. In one marketing study, however, Pruden and Longman included an anomie scale and found that as anomie increases, so does a tendency to have negative attitudes toward marketing and increased belief in government intervention in the marketplace.[32] Anomie may be a topic of increasing interest in consumer studies in the future.

The preceding pages have discussed various types of reference groups, describing some basic terminology as well as the general functions of reference groups. The reference group of overriding importance for most consumers, however, is the family. The remainder of the chapter, therefore, focuses specifically upon the topic of the family.

Reference groups and the family

The family

The term "family" is used in a wide variety of ways. For the purposes of this book, the following terminology is adequate. *Nuclear* family means the immediate group of father, mother and child(ren) living together. The *extended* family refers to the nuclear family and other relatives, including grandparents, uncles and aunts, cousins, and in-laws. The family one is born into is called the *family of orientation*, while the one established by marriage is the *family of procreation*.[33] The discussion here is concerned primarily with the influence of the nuclear family, although occasional reference is made to the extended family and the family of orientation. When conducting research, an analyst of statistical data will often also encounter the term "household," a term used by the Census Bureau to describe all the persons, both related and unrelated, who occupy a housing unit such as a house or apartment.

Wherever humans live, regardless of the circumstances of life, the family is present. Although family forms and functions vary from culture to culture, the family as an institution is universal.[34] From an individual consumer's point of view, the family differs in a number of respects

Unique aspects of the family

31 Gary R. Lee and Robert W. Clyde, "Religion, Socioeconomic Stature, and Anomie," *Journal for the Scientific Study of Religion*, vol. 13 (March 1974), pp. 35–47.

32 Henry O. Pruden and Douglas S. Longman, "Race, Alienation and Consumerism," *Journal of Marketing*, vol. 36 (July 1972), pp. 58–63.

33 These definitions are widely accepted. See, for example, Bernard Berelson and Gary A. Steiner, *Human Behavior* (New York: Harcourt, 1964), p. 297.

34 William F. Kenkel, *The Family in Perspective* (New York: Appleton, 1966), p. 3.

Figure 6.3 Examples of *anomie* scales

Pruden and Longman

Anomie items (based on Strole)*

1. These days a person doesn't really know who he can count on.
2. Nowadays a person has to live pretty much for today and let tomorrow take care of itself.
3. It's hardly fair to bring children into the world with the way things look for the future.
4. In spite of what some people say, the lot of the average man is getting worse.
5. There's little use in writing to public officials because they aren't really interested in the problems of the average man.

   Anomie Index Construction: For each of the above anomie questions respondents check one of six categories from "strongly agree" to "strongly disagree." "Strongly agree" has an index of one and "strongly disagree" an index value of six. Each respondent's anomie index is the sum of the index value for the five anomie questions.

Form's societal anomie scale†

1. In the everyday problems of life, it is easy to know which is the right path to choose.
2. It is hard to rear children nowadays because what is right today is wrong tomorrow.
3. It seems that nobody agrees on what is right and wrong because everyone is following his own ideas.
4. It is easy to find agreement on what is morally right.
5. There are so many organizations with different goals that it is impossible to trust any of them.
6. The world is changing so fast that it is difficult to be sure that we are making the right decisions in the problems we face daily.
7. The man with morals and scruples is better able to get ahead in this world than the immoral and unscrupulous person.

   (Different sets of the above 7 statements are used as Guttman scales, yielding scores of 0 to 5.)

Rushing's anomie scale‡   Yes   No

Is a person justified in doing almost anything if the reward is high enough?   ____ ____

Some people say you have to do things that are wrong in order to get ahead in the world today. What do you think?   ____ ____

Would you say that the main reason people obey the law is the punishment that comes if they are caught?   ____ ____

Some people say that to be a success it is usually necessary to be dishonest. Do you think this is true?   ____ ____

In your opinion, is the honest life the best regardless of the hardships it may cause?*   ____ ____

In your opinion, should people obey the law no matter how much it interferes with their personal ambitions?*   ____ ____

(Total scores for an individual range from 0 to 6, based on the number of yes answers. Asterisked item is reverse scored.)

*H. O. Pruden and D. S. Longman, "Race, Alienation and Consumerism," *Journal of Marketing* (July 1972), p. 60. Based upon Leo Strole, "Social Integration and Certain Corollaries: An Exploratory Study," *American Sociological Review*, vol. 21 (December, 1956), pp. 709–16.

†William H. Form, "The Social Construction of Anomie" *American Journal of Sociology*, vol. 80 (1975), p. 1170. © 1975 The University of Chicago Press.

‡William A. Rushing, "Class, Culture, and Social Structure and Anomie," *American Journal of Sociology*, vol. 76 (1971), p. 861. © 1971 The University of Chicago Press.

from larger social systems, and these unique aspects are important in understanding the role of the family in influencing individual behavior.

In contrast to larger social systems, the nuclear family is a *primary* group. As such it is characterized by face-to-face intimacy and meaningfulness.[35] This intimacy and association mean, among other things, that the family is often uniquely important in its influence, not merely on normative compliance, but also on individual personality, attitudes, and motives.[36]

The family differs from other reference groups in that it is both an earning and a consuming unit. The consumption needs of each individual as well as family needs, such as a car and home, must be satisfied from a common pool of financial resources. This means that individual needs must sometimes be subordinated to those of other family members or to the needs of the family as a whole.

Because the family is a primary group that both earns and consumes, it differs from larger social systems in the sense that it performs what might be termed a mediating function. The norms of larger social systems—culture, subculture, reference groups, social class, and so on—are filtered through and interpreted by individuals in a family setting. This process of mediation may substantially alter the influences of larger social systems on individual consumption behavior.

There are, then, many ways in which the family differs from larger reference groups. While there are other unique aspects of the family, the above are most relevant for our purposes.[37]

Family influences on individual information and experiences

Family influences are important in two major ways: (1) they form the experience base that influences individual evaluative criteria and beliefs (and indirectly personality and motives), and (2) they affect the decision-making process that is involved in the purchase of goods and services. Figure 6.4 illustrates the relations among larger social systems, the family, and the individual. The nuclear family often performs a mediating function, subject to the complex processes of exposure, attention, and individual reception.

Individuals within the same family may tend to have similar evaluative criteria and purchasing processes because they share a finite amount of financial resources, have many common consumption needs, and are exposed to similar information sources. Consequently, they may have similar personality characteristics, evaluative criteria, attitudes and so forth. Variables and relationships in the buying process tend to converge

---

35 Clifford Kirkpatrick, *The Family as Process and Institution* (New York: Ronald, 1963), p. 4; Kenkel, *The Family in Perspective*, pp. 391–92.

36 See, for example, Gardner Murphy, "New Knowledge about Family Dynamics," *Pastoral Psychology*, vol. 2, pp. 39–47 (1960); William A. Westley and Nathan B. Erstein, "Family Structure and Emotional Health: A Case Study Approach," *Marriage and Family Living*, vol. 22, pp. 25–27 (1960).

37 For other unique aspects of the family, see Kirkpatrick, *The Family as Process*, pp. 4–6.

Figure 6.4 Family influences on individual information and experiences

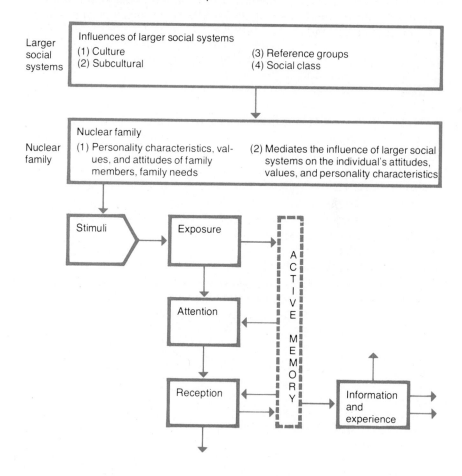

and are typically more homogeneous than would be the case if they were not in the same family.[38]

Family decisions and conflict resolution

Although the generalization that family influences tend to cause family members' psychological characteristics to converge is true in most instances, it leaves many issues unresolved. For example, what is the relative influence of various family members in these processes? Do husbands exert more influence than wives? What is the role of children? What happens when the motives, attitudes, and/or evaluative criteria of family members conflict? How are these conflicts resolved and what is the nature of the conflict resolution process? What happens when they are not resolved?

Many researchers have advanced propositions, hypotheses, and theo-

38 See, for example, Robert Bales and Talcott Parsons, *Family Socialization and Interaction Processes* (New York: Free Press, 1955).

ries concerning the relative importance of family members in influencing these phenomena[39] and the anatomy of the conflict resolution process.[40]

Initially, this research was conducted mostly by sociological researchers in general areas rather than on topics or primary intent to consumer researchers.[41] Recently, however, marketing scholars have begun to examine these topics in the context of buying behavior and these studies are described below.

Analyzing family role structures and decisions

Analyzing the consumption decisions of a family, in contrast to family influences on an individual's buying, requires analysis of the role and influence of family members within the decision-making process. In this context,[42] family role structure means the behavior of nuclear family members at each stage in the decision-making process. Role structures are of fundamental importance to the marketing executive for they often influence the design and packaging of products, the types of retail outlets handling the product, media strategies, creative strategies, and many other types of decisions.

It is difficult to overstate the importance of the family in understanding the purchase of goods. This point is emphasized by Davis after conducting a thorough review of the literature concerning household decision making. Davis concluded:

> Major items of consumer spending such as food, shelter, and transportation are often jointly "consumed." A husband may buy a station wagon, given the reality of having to transport four children, *despite* his strong preference for sports cars. Husbands wear ties, underwear, and socks, yet the purchase of these products is often made by wives. A housewife bases product and brand decisions to some extent on orders or requests from family members and on her judgment of what they like or dislike and what is "good for them." Even preferences for products individually consumed are likely to be influenced by feedback from members of the family—e.g., "Gee, Mom! That dress makes you look fat," or "I like the smell of that pipe tobacco." The number of products that an individual always buys for

---

39 For illustrative investigations, see James N. Morgan, "Household Decision Making" in Nelson Foote, ed., *Household Decision Making* (New York: New York University Press, 1961), p. 91; Robert F. Kelley and Michael B. Egan, "Husband and Wife Interaction in a Consumer Decision Process," in Robert L. King, ed., *Marketing and the New Science of Planning* (Chicago: American Marketing Association, 1969), pp. 250–58.

40 See, for example, Richard W. Pollay,"A Model of Family Decision Making," *British Journal of Marketing*, vol. 2, pp. 206–16 (1968).

41 See, for example, Donald M. Wolfe, "Power and Authority in the Family," in D. Cartwright, ed., *Studies in Social Power* (Ann Arbor, Mich.: Research Center for Group Dynamics, 1958), pp. 98–116; D. Byrne and B. Blaylock, "Similarity of Attitudes between Husbands and Wives," *Journal of Abnormal and Social Psychology*, vol. 67, pp. 636–40 (1973).

42 Role structure is actually considerably more complex than this, since it results from the interaction of a status structure, a communication structure, an attraction structure, and many other structures. See, for example, T. M. Newcomb, R. H. Turner, and P.E. Converse, *Social Psychology* (New York: Holt, Rinehart and Winston, 1965), p. 346. We are concerned with those dimensions of the status and communication structures that influence consumption decisions.

individual consumption must certainly represent a very small proportion of consumer expenditures.[43]

The dilemma facing consumer research is caused by the recognition that although most purchase decisions probably are *family decisions*, most research about consumer behavior has been conducted with *individuals*. It hardly should be expected that an *individual's* attitudes, intentions, or any other variable should be correlated highly with a *family's* purchase decisions. Yet most of the research literature implicitly makes that assumption. Even the model used in this book is a model of individual decision making, showing how the family may influence the individual rather than how the family makes a buying decision. Sheth has attempted to resolve this dilemma with a model of family buying, which is shown in Figure 6.5. While this model is untested empirically and has had little influence on other consumer research, it is valuable as an attempt to translate a model of individual buying behavior into a model of family buying behavior. Figure 6.5, as well as the material supporting it,[44] should be studied in order to understand how family buying may occur.

Types of role structures

While the role of family members in decision making is usually conceptualized as a continuum of influence, practical problems of research make it convenient to utilize role-structure categories. Although considerable variation exists in the categories that are used, one of the more complex but useful is:

1. *Autonomic*, when an equal number of decisions is made by each spouse, but each decision is individually made by one spouse or the other.

2. *Husband dominant*,

3. *Wife dominant*, and

4. *Syncratic*, when most decisions are made by both husband and wife.[45]

Marketing research usually involves simpler categories, such as "husband more than wife," "wife more than husband," "both husband and wife,"[46] or simply husband only, wife only or children only.[47] The use of

43 Harry L. Davis,"Decision Making within the Household," *Journal of Consumer Research*, vol. 2 (March 1976), pp. 241–60, at p. 241.

44 Jagdish N. Sheth, *Models of Buyer Behavior* (New York: Harper & Row, 1974), pp. 17–33.

45 See, for example, P. G. Herbst, "Conceptual Framework for Studying the Family," in O. A. Oeser and S. B. Hammond, eds., *Social Structure and Personality in a City* (London: Routledge, 1954). Also see Elizabeth H. Wolgast, "Do Husbands or Wives Make Purchasing Decisions?" *Journal of Marketing*, vol. 23, pp. 151–58 (October 1958); Paul D. Converse and Merle Crawford, "Family Buying: Who Does It? Who Influences It?" *Current Economic Comment*, vol. 2, pp. 38–50 (November 1949).

46 See, for example, Harry Sharp and Paul Mott, "Consumer Decisions in the Metropolitan Family," *Journal of Marketing*, vol. 21, pp. 149–56 (October 1956); Carl R. Gisler, "Is the Buying Influence of Men Underestimated?" *Printer's Ink*, p. 38 ff (September 24, 1948).

47 "Customer Traffic Patterns: Key to Selling Efficiency," *Progressive Grocer*, pp. k-75–k-106 (January 1967).

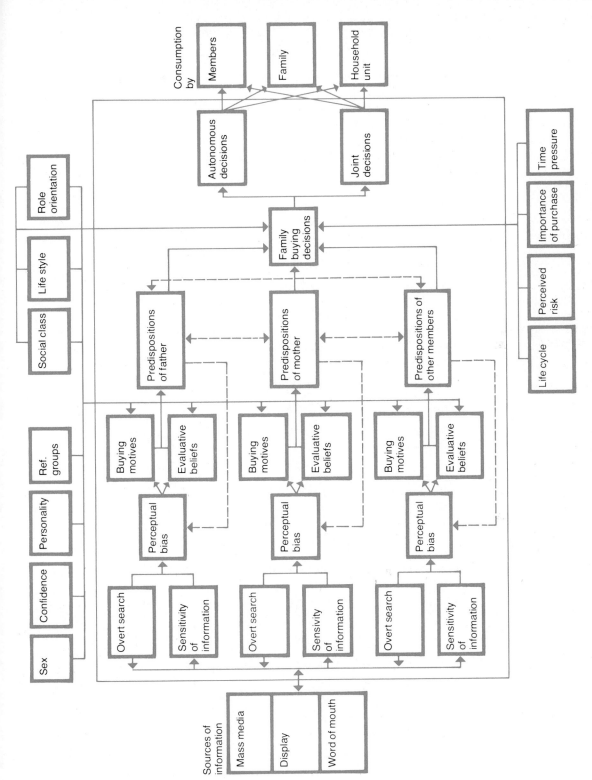

Source: Jagdish N. Sheth, *Models of Buyer Behavior* (New York: Harper & Row, 1974), pp. 22–23. Reprinted by permission of the publisher.

Figure 6.6 Marital roles in 25 decisions

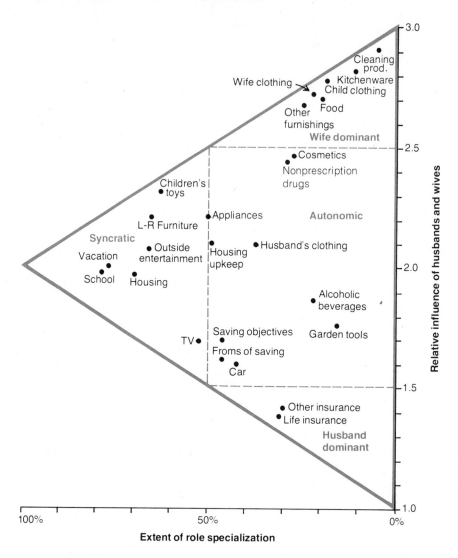

Source: Harry L. Davis and Benny P. Rigaux, "Perception of Marital Roles in Decision Processes," *Journal of Consumer Research*, vol. 1 (June 1974), p. 57. Reprinted from the *Journal of Consumer Research* published by the American Marketing Association.

the more complex role structure categories is shown in Figure 6.6, based upon research by Davis and Rigaux in Belgium.[48] This figure also shows that the role structure varies considerably, depending on the type of product purchased, and this topic is discussed again later.

48 Harry L. Davis and Benny P. Rigaux, "Perception of Marital Roles in Decision Processes," *Journal of Consumer Research*, vol. 1 (June 1974), pp. 51–61.

Most studies find major variation among families in the role of family members in decision-making behavior. While many of these studies have methodological problems, enough of them have been conducted to justify the specification of several tentative bases, or determinants of decision-making role structures. These include sociocultural influences, resource contribution, type of product, and the stage in the decision-making process.

Determinants of decision-process role structures

Sociocultural influences. For a variety of reasons, all societies have somewhat different role specifications for men and women, learned early in life through a process of social conditioning. Role specifications also vary by ethnic and other variables. A list of variables that may influence role specifications includes the following:

1. Cultural influences

2. Subcultural influences

3. Reference group influences

4. Stage in life cycle

5. Social class

6. Employment status of wife

7. Location (urban; rural)

8. Personality of family members

9. Social networks (friends in common).[49]

Resource contributions. The relative contribution hypothesis explains role structures in terms of the relative resources (income, education, decision-making ability) contributed by individuals comprising the nuclear family. This may involve merely *influence* in decisions or the exercise of *power*. Power suggests that there is a *conflict* situation and power is needed to "win out" over another. Not all role structure influence involves conflict situations and influence may be quite different than power.

The resource contribution hypothesis suggests that the greater the relative contribution of an individual, the greater the influence in decision-making. For example, husbands having high income, high occupational prestige, and high social status generally have more decision-making authority or power in the household. This widely-held theory was advanced by Blood and Wolfe[50] but has been challenged more recently in

---

49 Further discussion of these variables is available in the 1973 edition of this textbook. Several of the above variables are investigated also in Donald Hempel, "Family Buying Decisions: A Cross-Cultural Perspective," *Journal of Marketing Research*, vol. 11 (August 1974), pp. 295–302; and Donald J. Hempel, "Family Role Structure and Housing Decisions," in M. J. Slinger, ed., *Advances in Consumer Research* (Association for Consumer Research, 1975), pp. 71–80.

50 Robert O. Blood, Jr., and Donald M. Wolfe, *Husbands and Wives* (New York: Free Press, 1960).

a comprehensive (as well as controversial) review of the literature by Safilios-Rothschild.[51]

In a marketing context, Ferber and Lee investigated the determinants of the member of the family who acts as the family financial officer (FFO). They found that differences in resources such as education or employment, contrary to their original hypothesis, had little effect on whether one member or the other is the FFO. Instead, they found that differences between the wife and the husband on various attitudes (concern with high quality, economy minded, bargain minded) definitely seemed to influence who is more likely to have the most influence or to be the FFO.[52]

A related explanation as to which member possesses the influence in family decisions is the *least-interested-partner* hypothesis, which focuses not on the value to each spouse of the resources contributed by the other, but on the value placed on these resources outside the marriage. The greater the difference between the value to the wife of the resources contributed by her husband and the value to the wife of the resources she might earn outside the existing marriage, the greater the influence of the husband in decision-making.[53]

Of the two, the least-interested-partner hypothesis seems to be the most powerful. It explains as much variation in family role structures as the relative contributions hypothesis, and, in addition, it can accommodate the changing patterns of family-member interaction that occur over the life cycle. However, both hypotheses are limited explanations in the sense that they do not explain differences in role structures attributable to cultural and reference group influences, geographic location, or social networks. Nevertheless, the least-interested-partner hypothesis is a convenient way of summarizing much of what is known about the basis of family role structures.

Type of product

The degree of joint decision making varies considerably from product to product. The extent of joint decision making tends to increase as the price of the product increases. In the purchase of lower price products, there is generally a tendency for purchase decisions to be delegated to the husband and wife according to their respective skills and knowledge about that product.

These skills and knowledge may be actual in the sense that they really exist, or perceived in the sense that cultural and reference group norms prescribe that they *should* exist. For example, as a result of certain cultural prescriptions, a husband is "supposed" to know more about mechanical things and generally plays a more important role in the

51 Constantins Safilios-Rothschild, "The Study of Family Power Structure: A Review 1960–1969," *Journal of Marriage and the Family*, vol. 32 (1970), pp. 539–53. Also see Stephen J. Bahr, "Comment on 'The Study of Family Power Structure: A Review 1960–1969,'" *Journal of Marriage and the Family*, vol. 34 (1972), pp. 239–43. Also, see James L. Turk and Norman W. Bell, "Measuring Power in Families," *Journal of Marriage and the Family*, vol. 34 (1972), pp. 215–22.

52 Robert Ferber and Lucy Chao Lee, "Husband-Wife Influence in Family Purchasing Behavior," *Journal of Consumer Research*, vol. 1 (June 1974), pp. 43–50.

53 David M. Heer, "The Measurement and Bases of Family Power: An Overview," *Marriage and Family Living*, vol. 25, pp. 133–39 (1965).

purchase of products having complex mechanical attributes. On the other hand, cultural and reference group norms as well as other factors operate in such a way that a man is not "supposed" to know much about ironing or irons. Thus, he is likely to be less influential in the purchase of these types of products.

Role differentiation by product category has been clearly shown in numerous marketing studies. The husband was found to be definitely dominant in 69 percent of the decision of when to buy an automobile but decreased to 16 percent in considering when to buy furniture in a study by Shuptrine and Samuelson, replicating earlier research by Davis.[54] In another replication study, variations in role structure by product category were investigated over time. In this study it was found that between 1955 and 1973, family decision making for some products (groceries and life insurance) had become more specialized but that for other products (housing and vacation spots) the trend was toward egalitarianism between spouses.[55] Woodside found dominance in the marital decision-making process to vary significantly across eight product categories and found the concept of power, discussed above, useful in explaining differences. He found that decisions for lawnmowers and beer tend to be highly dominated by the husband, while automobiles, gardening supplies and television sets appear to be more moderately dominated by the husband. Wives tend to dominate the purchase decisions for cheese more than they do for rugs or washing machines.[56]

The marketing implications of these studies are significant. Communications strategies must not only be targeted to different members of the family but probably must stress different product attributes to each spouse. Research must clearly delineate the relative importance of each spouse before marketing strategies are designed and implemented.

There is considerable evidence that the roles of members of the nuclear family vary by stage in the decision process. For example, the husband may recognize the problem while the wife engages in external search, with both the husband and the wife evaluating alternatives and the wife actually purchasing a specific brand.

Stage in the decision process

One of the most thorough studies of role structure through the decision making process is reported by Woodside. For various products, he included questions on who brought up the idea of purchasing the product, discussion of the purchase with friends, neighbors, relatives, obtaining information from mass media, obtaining information from stores (dealers), style or type decisions, who visited stores or dealer showrooms, who selected the specific retail outlet to purchase, who made the actual

54 F. K. Shuptrine and G. Samuelson, "Dimensions of Marital Roles in Consumer Decision Making: Revisited," *Journal of Marketing Research*, vol. 13 (February 1976), pp. 87–91; Harry L. Davis, "Dimensions of Marital Roles in Consumer Decision Making," *Journal of Marketing Research*, vol. 7 (May 1970), pp. 168–77.

55 Sharp and Mott, "Consumer Decisions"; Isabella Cunningham and Robert Green, "Purchasing Roles in the U.S. Family, 1955 and 1973," *Journal of Marketing*, vol. 38 (October 1974), pp. 61–81.

56 Arch G. Woodside, "Dominance and Conflict in Family Purchasing Decisions," *Association for Consumer Research Proceedings*, 1972, pp. 650–59.

purchase, and who experienced dissatisfaction, if anyone.[57] Patterns of influence vary across the decision stages but Woodside found that the likelihood of jointly making the actual purchase of an automobile increases if friends are jointly consulted prior to purchase.

For housing decisions, considerable variation has been found to exist in role structure and stages of the decision. Hempel found that husbands are more likely to be involved as the initiator of the home-buying process but the roles are reversed for the search task. Husbands were more involved in decisions concerning mortgage, price, and when to buy, while wives were more involved in decisions regarding neighborhood and house style.[58] Similar conclusions about housing decisions were reported by Munsinger, Weber, and Hansen.[59]

Variations in spouse influence across the stages of a decision may be most clearly seen by looking at Figure 6.7 and comparing it with Figure 6.6. Davis and Rigaux identified three stages or phases of the family decision making process.[60] Phase I was problem recognition, Phase II was a search for information and Phase III was the final decision. Comparison of the two figures shows that marital roles vary throughout these three phases of the decision process. The authors suggest a number of marketing implications. For example, in the advertising of alcoholic beverages to autonomic decision makers, it would be more justifiable to develop *two* campaigns—one stressing husband-oriented appeals and the other wife-oriented appeals—rather than to use one campaign that tries to "mix" the two. Implications for the timing of messages would require additional information about the length of the decision span from problem recognition to final decision, but perhaps an airline attempting to encourage families to take winter vacations would find decision spans of several months. Such an organization might use a "joint" campaign during September stressing the idea of taking a vacation rather than consuming other forms of leisure, followed by "individual" campaigns (directed to husbands and wives separately) during October which describe alternative vacation plans, and finally, a "joint" campaign during November and December which tries to convince couples that "now is the time to make the final decision."[61]

Measuring family role structure

The first step is to determine whether or not the role and influence of more than one family member should be considered at *any* stage in the decision-making process for a specific product or service. A "no" decision should be made only if the analyst has research data for the specific product. The following paragraphs present guidelines for conducting this research.

57 Arch G. Woodside, "Effects of Prior Decision-Making, Demographics and Psychographics on Marital Roles for Purchasing Durables,"in M. J. Slinger, *Advances*, pp. 81–92.

58 Hempel, "Family Buying."

59 Gary M. Munsinger, Jean E. Weber and Richard W. Hansen, "Joint Home Purchasing Decisions by Husbands and Wives," *Journal of Consumer Research*, vol. 1 (March 1975), pp. 60–66.

60 Davis and Rigaux, *Perception of Marital Roles*.

61 *Ibid,* p. 60.

Figure 6.7 Changes in marital roles between phase 2 and phase 3

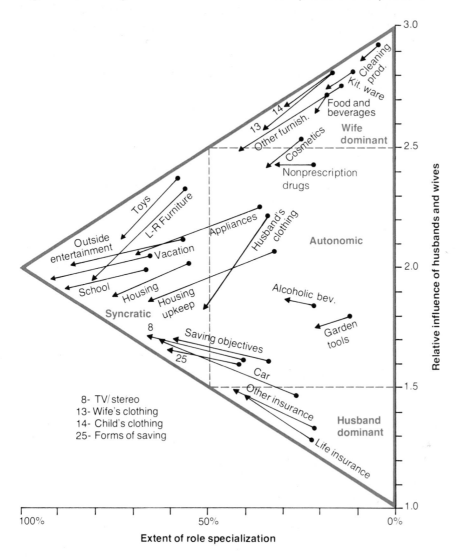

Source: Harry L. Davis and Benny P. Rigaux, "Perception of Marital Roles in Decision Processes," *Journal of Consumer Research*, vol. 1 (June 1974), p. 54. Reprinted from the *Journal of Consumer Research* published by the American Marketing Association.

Choice of product. Role-structure categories can be used to describe: (1) the general pattern of influence in a family, (2) the general pattern of decision making, or (3) the profile of decision making for specific products and brands. As indicated above, the influence of family members often varies from product to product. Hence, it is dangerous to generalize from studies that construct role structures for general decision-making behavior. It is necessary to measure the role and influence of family members for the marketer's specific product or service.

Decision-process framework. Role structure studies in the past usually viewed purchasing as an act rather than a process and based findings on questions such as, "Who usually makes the decision to purchase?" or "Who influences the decision?" Yet the evidence discussed above indicates that the role and influence of family members varies by stage in the decision process. Consequently, meaningless answers are likely to result from the types of questions in the preceding paragraph. What appear to be contradictory results may be caused by respondents' answering in terms of different stages in the decision process.

An example of process methodology is provided in a study by Wilkes, who measured family influence in four stages—problem recognition, search, alternative evaluation (intention), and purchase or choice. His decision process measures of influence included the following:

1. Who was responsible for initial problem recognition?

2. Who was responsible for acquiring information about the purchase alternatives?

3. Who made the final decision as to which alternative should be purchased?

4. Who made the actual purchase of the product?[62]

The research using this methodology produced better results than more global measures of influence. Additionally, husbands and wives within families were found to hold similar perceptions about their relative influence for a given phase of the decision process.

Research designs and questioning techniques. Several methods have been used to identify the roles of family members in making purchase decisions. The most common approaches are as follows:

1. General questions about influence.

2. Direct questions about specific decisions and activities.[63]

3. Questions concerning how conflicts are resolved in the family.[64]

4. Where there is a disagreement among family members, a comparison of the brand purchased and the brand preferred by family members.[65]

5. Given a fixed imaginary income, the proportion of purchases suggested by each family member and the amounts of money other

62 Robert E. Wilkes, "Husband-Wife Influence in Purchase Decisions—A Confirmation and Extension," *Journal of Marketing Research*, vol. 12 (May 1975), pp. 224–27.

63 Examples include Sharp and Mott, "Consumer Decisions"; Wolgast, "Do Husbands or Wives"; Davis (1974), *op. cit.*

64 Wolgast, "Do Husbands or Wives"; pp. 151–8; Martin Gold and Carol Slater, "Office, Factory, Store and Family," *American Sociological Review*, vol. 23, pp. 64–74 (February 1958).

65 "Family Participation and Influence in Shopping and Brand Selection," *Life*, parts 1 and 2 (1964).

family members agree to spend on the items suggested by that individual.[66]

Research indicated that these different measures of the same phenomenon are often not closely related.[67] Answers to direct questions are subject to many biases while direct observations of imaginary decisions sometimes produce different biases[68] because of the hypothetical nature of the decisions.[69] Families interacting in a laboratory setting sometimes differ from those observed at home.[70]

Role-structure categories. The relevant role-structure categories to be included in a research project depend on the specific product or service under consideration. In many product categories only the husband and wife are involved. In this case a defensible approach is to measure the *relative* influence for each specific decision at each stage in the decision process on a five-point Likert scale, where husband decides = 1, husband has more influence than wife = 2, equal influence = 3, wife has more influence than husband = 4, and wife decides = 5.

Children are involved in many types of purchase situations, but the nature of their influence has often been ignored.[71] For example, while it is well known that children influence cereal and soft-drink purchases, other areas of influence are not so well recognized, dog food being an example. In other instances children exert a passive influence in the sense that one of the spouses continues to buy brands until finding one that the children will consume.[72] Many role-structure studies probably grossly underestimate the influence of children.[73]

Respondent selection. In measuring role structures, it is necessary to decide which member(s) of the nuclear family should be asked about the influence of family members in purchasing decisions. The respondent decision is important since the reported influence of family members

66 William F. Kenkel and Dean K. Hoffman, "Real and Conceived Roles in Family Decision Making," *Marriage and Family Living*, vol. 28, pp. 311–16 (November 1956).

67 James G. March, "Influence Measurement in Experimental and Semi-Experimental Groups," *Sociometry*, vol. 19, pp. 260–71 (December 1956); David H. Olson, "The Measurement of Family Power by Self-Report and Behavior Methods," *Journal of Marriage and the Family*, vol. 31, pp. 545–50 (Aug. 1969); D. H. Olson and C. Rabunsky, "Validity of Four Measures of Family Power," *Journal of Marriage and the Family*, vol. 34 (May 1972), pp. 224–34. "Family Power Structure: A Critical Comment," *Journal of Marriage and the Family*, vol. 34 (May 1972), pp. 235–38.

68 Gold and Slater, "Office, Factory," pp. 64–74; William F. Kenkel, "Influence Differentiation in Family Decision Making," *Sociology and Social Research*, vol. 42, pp. 18–25 (September–October 1957).

69 Heer, "Measurement and Basis"; Morgan, "Household," p. 94.

70 John F. O'Rourke, "Field and Laboratory; The Decision Making Behavior of Family Groups in Two Experimental Conditions," *Sociometry*, vol. 27 (December 1963), pp. 422–35; M. Zelditch, Jr., "Experimental Family Sociology," in J. Aldous et al., eds., *Family Problem Solving: A Symposium on Theoretical, Methodological, and Substantive Concerns* (Hinsdale, Ill: Dryden Press, 1971), pp. 55–72.

71 See, for example, Lewis A. Berey and Richard W. Pollay, "The Influencing Role of the Child in Family Decision Making," *Journal of Marketing Research*, vol. 5, pp. 70–72 (February 1968).

72 William D. Wells, "Children as Consumers," in Joseph Newman, ed., *On Knowing the Consumer* (New York: Wiley, 1966), pp. 138–39.

73 Olson and Rabunsky, "Validity of Four Measures," p. 231.

often varies considerably depending on which family members are interviewed.

The most common approach is to interview wives, yet there is disagreement concerning the extent to which their reports accurately report purchase influence. Some researchers have found a substantial or acceptable similarity between husbands' and wives' responses.[74] But others have found that the percentage of couples whose responses agree is unacceptable, perhaps averaging only slightly more than 50 percent.[75]

Granbois and Summers found husbands' responses concerning purchase intentions to be better than wives' as predictors of total planned cost and number of items planned from joint responses, although wives predicted better for certain products such as appliances, home furnishings, and entertainment equipment plans. They concluded that joint responses may be more desirable since they uncover more plans of the family.[76] This suggests that decisions about whether only one spouse can be interviewed or whether both must be interviewed are determined by the circumstances of a specific research project.

Interviewing. It has been demonstrated that the sex of the interviewer or observer influences the roles husbands and wives say they play in a purchase situation.[77] To overcome this bias, either self-administered questionnaires should be used or the sex of the observer should be randomly assigned to respondents.

Analyzing family demographic structure

The demographic structure of a family is also important in understanding the consumption and buying decisions of a family. While the above section was concerned with the roles of family members as they are acted out in buying decisions, it is also necessary to understand some of the realities and constraints that structure the types of products that a family can and is likely to buy because of the demographic structure. It is apparent, for example, that a family of six must buy different quantities of food than a family of two, but in addition to the effect on food purchases, the condition of allowing a larger portion of the budget (assuming the same income in both size families) will constrain the type of purchase for

74 Blood and Wolfe, *Husbands and Wives*, p. 273; Wolgast, "Do Husbands or Wives," p. 153; David M. Heer, "Husband and Wife Perceptions of Family Power Structure," *Marriage and Family Living*, vol. 36, pp. 65–67 (February 1962).

75 Robert Ferber, "On the Reliability of Purchase Influence Studies," *Journal of Marketing*, vol. 19, pp. 225–32 (January 1955); John Scanzoni, "A Note on the Sufficiency of Wife Responses in Family Research," *Pacific Sociological Review*, vol. 8, pp. 109–15 (Fall 1965); Harry L. Davis, "Measurement of Husband-Wife Influence in Consumer Purchase Decisions," *Journal of Marketing Research*, vol. 8, pp. 305–12 (August 1971); J. C. Van Es and P. M. Shingi, "Response Consistency of Husband and Wife for Selected Attitudinal Items," *Journal of Marriage and the Family*, vol. 34 (November 1972), pp. 741–49.

76 Donald H. Granbois and Hohn O. Summers, "Primary and Secondary Validity of Consumer Purchase Probabilities," *Journal of Consumer Research*, vol. 1 (March 1975), pp. 31–38; Donald H. Granbois and Ronald P. Willet, "Equivalence of Family Role Measures Based on Husband and Wife Data," *Journal of Marriage and the Family*, vol. 32, pp. 68–72 (1970).

77 William F. Kenkel, "Sex of Observer and Spousal Roles in Decision-Making," *Marriage and Family Living*, vol. 23, pp. 185–86 (May 1951).

many other products. Other variables that affect the buying behavior of the family include income, age of the family, length of family formation, geographic location, and other variables.

A summary variable for several structural variables is the concept of life cycle. Over time, most consumers pass through a series of stages in their lives known as the *family life cycle*.

Family life cycle

1. Bachelor stage; young single people not living at home.

2. Newly married couples; young, no children.

3. Full nest I; young married couples with youngest child under six.

4. Full nest II; young married couples with youngest child six or over.

5. Full nest III; older married couples with dependent children.

6. Empty nest I; older married couples, no children living with them, household head in labor force.

7. Empty nest II; older married couples, no children living at home, household head retired.

8. Solitary survivor in labor force.

9. Solitary survivor, retired.

The life-cycle concept is useful because several studies indicate that family needs, income, assets and debts, and expenditures vary at different life-cycle stages. Because the life-cycle concept combines trends in earning power with demands placed on income, it is one of the most powerful ways of classifying and segmenting individuals and families. Life cycle is a richer, more productive variable than simply length of marriage.[78] A brief summary of the major dimensions of each stage in the life cycle is presented in Figure 6.8.[79]

The information in Figure 6.8 is a simple, incomplete description of characteristic behavior of families' life cycle stages, but it should provide an adequate background for understanding the kind of information that should be collected in a consumer study for a particular product or organization.

Life cycle information can be *used to segment markets*. Studies of

---

[78] Eli P. Cox, III, "Family Purchase Decision Making and the Process of Adjustment," *Journal of Marketing Research*, vol. 7 (May 1975), pp. 189–95.

[79] The summary of life cycle stages is adapted from William D. Wells and George Gubar, "The Life Cycle Concept" in *Marketing Research*, vol. 3, pp. 355–63 (November 1966); S. G. Barton, "The Life Cycle and Buying Patterns," in Lincoln H. Clark, ed., *Consumer Behavior*, vol. 2 (New York: New York University Press, 1955), pp. 53–57; John B. Lansing and Leslie Kish, "Family Life Cycle as an Independent Variable," *American Sociological Review*, pp. 512–19 (October 1957); John B. Lansing and James N. Morgan, "Consumer Finances over the Life Cycle," in Clark, pp. 36–51; David Riesman and Howard Roseborough, "Careers and Consumer Behavior," in Clark, pp. 1–18; Cox, "Family Purchase Decisions"; Mark R. Bomball, Walter J. Primeaux, and Donald E. Pursell, "Forecasting Stage 2 of the Family Life Cycle," *Journal of Business*, vol. 48 (January 1975), pp. 65–73. The most thorough description of life cycle purchasing influences is probably Fred D. Reynolds and William D. Wells, *Consumer Behavior* (New York: McGraw-Hill, 1977), chaps. 3–7.

Figure 6.8 Life-cycle influences on buying behavior

Bachelor stage

Although earnings are relatively low, they are subject to few rigid demands, so consumers in this stage typically have substantial discretionary income. Part of this income is used to purchase a car and basic equipment and furnishings for their first residence away from home—usually an apartment. They tend to be more fashion and recreation oriented, spending a substantial proportion of their income on clothing, alcoholic beverages, food away from home, vacations, leisure time pursuits, and other products and services involved in the mating game.

Newly married couples

Newly married couples without children are usually better off financially than they have been in the past and will be in the near future because the wife is usually employed. Families at this stage also spend a substantial amount of their income on cars, clothing, vacations, and other leisure time activities. They also have the highest purchase rate and highest average purchase of durable goods, particularly furniture and appliances, and other expensive items, and appear to be more susceptible to advertising in this stage.

Full nest I

With the arrival of the first child, most wives stop working outside the home, and consequently family income declines. Simultaneously, the young child creates new problems that change the way the family spends its income. The couple is likely to move into their first home, purchase furniture and furnishings for the child, buy a washer, dryer, and home maintenance items, and purchase such products as baby food, chest rubs, cough medicine, vitamins, toys, wagons, sleds, and skates. These requirements reduce family savings and the husband and wife are often dissatisfied with their financial position.

Full nest II

At this stage the youngest child is six or over, the husband's income has improved, and the wife often returns to work outside the home. Consequently, the family's financial position usually improves. Consumption patterns continue to be heavily influenced by the children

---

consumer expenditures reveal that the consumption of many products and services varies significantly by stage in family life cycle. Moreover, the qualitative level at which families satisfy basic consumption needs varies from one stage to another. Therefore, life cycle is often a useful tool for identifying heavy buyers of a product category.

The concept of varying rates of consumption by life cycle is illustrated in Figure 6.9. Consumption data in Figure 6.9 are categorized by age of family head, which is not exactly the same as life cycle but represents the closest approximation from government data. These estimates were obtained from diaries kept by 10,000 families, completed by families for two one-week periods, and surveys in which families reported information to interviewers every three months over a 15-month period. The basic data have been recalculated as percentages to facilitate comparison between age levels. Careful study of Figure 6.9 reveals many insights into family consumption patterns by age level. For example, families whose head is aged 65 and over have approximately the same income level as those under age 25. Notice that the proportion of the budget spent for food at home is 15.17 percent for the older families, however, compared to only 8.26 percent for younger families. Similarly, the proportion of

Figure 6.8 Life cycle influences on buying behavior (continued)

as the family tends to buy food and cleaning supplies in larger sized packages, bicycles, pianos, and music lessons.

Full nest III

As the family grows older, its financial position usually continues to improve because the husband's income rises, the wife returns to work or enjoys a higher salary, and the children earn money from occasional employment. The family typically replaces several pieces of furniture, purchases another automobile, buys several luxury appliances, and spends a considerable amount of money on dental services and education for the children.

Empty nest I

At this stage the family is most satisfied with their financial position and the amount of money saved because income has continued to increase, and the children have left home and are no longer financially dependent on their parents. The couple often make home improvements, buy luxury items, and spend a greater proportion of their income on vacations, travel, and recreation.

Empty nest II

By this time the household head has retired and so the couple usually suffers a noticeable reduction in income. Expenditures become more health oriented, centering on such items as medical appliances, medical care products that aid health, sleep, and digestion, and perhaps a smaller home, apartment, or condominium in a more agreeable climate.

The solitary survivor

If still in the labor force, solitary survivors still enjoy good income. They may sell their home and usually spend more money on vacations, recreation, and the types of health-oriented products and services mentioned above.

The retired solitary survivor follows the same general consumption pattern except on a lower scale because of the reduction in income. In addition, these individuals have special needs for attention, affection, and security.

---

budget spent for fuel and utilities is 5.28 percent for families over age 65 but only 2.83 percent for younger families. Younger families spent 7.05 percent of their budget on clothing while older families (over 65) spent only 4.57 percent. These are proportions of the budget, of course, and the absolute amounts of purchases may be higher for the high income, middle-aged families than either the young or older families. (The average amount of expenditures in dollar terms can be computed by multiplying the percentage in a category by the average income of that age group.)

Family life cycle can also be *used to forecast demand* by combining expenditure levels by age group with estimates of future size and age structure of the family population. Although government estimates are usually based on age group categories, Primeaux and Pursell showed that the number of families in categories of life cycle can also be predicted accurately.[80] By identifying the heavy consumption patterns of those age and life cycle segments that are predicted to expand significantly, it is possible to identify products and services that are likely to enjoy above average growth rates in the future. This type of information is useful in

80 Bomball, Primeaux, and Pursell, "Forecasting Stage 2."

Figure 6.9 Percentage of family budget expended on product categories by age of family head

	Total	Under 25	25–34	35–44	45–54	55–64	65 & over
Family Income	11,802	6,855	12,044	14,515	15,645	13,080	6,841
1. Food at Home	11.68%	8.26%	9.61%	13.29%	11.70%	10.98%	15.17%
2. Tobacco	1.08	1.33	1.13	1.10	1.09	1.05	.90
3. Fuel and Utilities	3.63	2.83	3.22	3.62	3.36	3.66	5.28
Gas, Total	.80	.63	.70	.80	.72	.79	1.26
Gas, Piped	.66	.52	.60	.65	.61	.64	.97
Gas, Bottled	.14	.11	.10	.14	.11	.14	.28
Electricity	1.39	1.30	1.39	1.42	1.26	1.29	1.79
Gas and Electricity	.39	.31	.33	.39	.35	.50	.44
Fuel Oil	.47	.26	.32	.40	.46	.51	.92
Other Fuel	.04	.02	.02	.04	.04	.04	.10
Water/Trash	.54	.32	.46	.58	.53	.53	.78
4. House Furnishings	3.90	5.44	4.81	4.35	3.39	2.94	3.28
Textiles	.46	.46	.50	.50	.43	.41	.50
Furniture	1.24	1.98	1.69	1.52	1.02	.73	.82
Floor Coverings	.40	.28	.42	.45	.37	.36	.42
Major Appliances	.80	1.25	1.02	.87	.64	.61	.72
Televisions	.40	.80	.47	.36	.34	.32	.41
Small Appliances	.08	.10	.09	.08	.08	.08	.08
Housewares	.08	.14	.09	.09	.08	.07	.05
Miscellaneous	.43	.44	.53	.48	.43	.37	.28
5. Clothing	5.68	7.05	6.15	6.47	5.60	4.65	4.57
Male	1.88	2.22	2.14	2.33	1.92	1.44	1.05
Female	2.74	2.90	2.68	3.16	2.77	2.36	2.59
Children	.14	.42	.29	.12	.10	.05	.01
Dry Cleaning	.67	1.26	.80	.60	.55	.58	.69
Materials/Services	.24	.24	.24	.26	.25	.21	.22
6. Vehicle Purchases	6.22	11.15	6.64	5.98	6.48	5.78	3.86
7. Vehicle Operation	6.52	9.21	6.59	6.48	6.59	6.18	5.64
Gasoline	3.13	4.38	3.28	3.24	3.17	2.90	2.41
Other	3.38	4.83	3.31	3.23	3.42	3.29	3.22
8. Reading	.41	.44	.47	.42	.37	.37	.46
9. Education	.89	.50	.50	.87	1.68	.91	.14
Private	.53	.22	.34	.60	.94	.53	.06
Public	.36	28	.17	.27	.73	.37	.08
10. Gifts/Contributions	3.66	1.59	2.11	3.13	3.47	4.56	7.38

Source: Authors' calculations based upon 1973 data from "Consumer Expenditure Survey Series; 1973" (Washington: U.S. Department of Labor, Bureau of Labor Statistics, Report 455-2, 1976), Table 4b.

estimating future market potential for a firm's current product line and in making product-line extension decisions. These data could be used at a macro-marketing level, as well, to determine industries with growth or decline in order to understand future employment levels and other macro-economic issues.

Marriage patterns

Markets are affected by marriage patterns and there is evidence that a number of important trends are developing that have direct effect on consumption patterns. Although the divorce rate is increasing substantially, most Americans are choosing and appear likely to continue to choose to live as married couples.[81] Several trends are developing, however, within the structure of marriage. These include a new type of baby boom, later marriages, and rising economic power of individual households compared to married households.

A new type of baby boom. The number of babies born in a society is a function of two statistics—birth *rate* and number of women of child-bearing age. In the United States, the birth *rate* is dropping precipitously and in recent years, even the number of babies has been declining.

The United States experienced the first increase in annual births in recent years in 1974. In that same year the fertility rate reached a record low of 1.862 children per woman. Births were higher, however, because of the large number of young women in the age category likely to give birth to their first baby.

Periodic surveys by the Census Bureau as to the number of children desired by American wives have always reported the same lack of preference by married women to be completely childless. The average number of children expected by young wives aged 18–24 has fallen from 3.1 in 1965 to 2.3 in 1973. The proportion of wives expecting to remain childless, however, remains small at 9.6 percent in 1973. The celebrated decline in births has been due to the recent preference of women to have smaller families rather than any desire for complete childlessness. The number of children in the average family has declined by about 1.5 children in the past decade but there are still few childless couples.

Figure 6.10 A smaller baby boom

	Avg. no. women age 20–29 (000)	Average children per woman	Average first births (000)	Average higher order births (000)	Average total births (000)
1948–1953	12,010	3.1	1.120	2,670	3,790
1954–1959	11,214	3.8	1,111	3,054	4,165
1960–1965	11,726	3.4	1,120	3,015	4,135
1966–1971	14,517	2.4	1,321	2,265	3,585
1972–1977	17,760	1.8	1,300	1,930	3,230
1978–1983	20,000	1.9	1,560	2,200	3,760

Source: John E. Smallwood and Ronald L. Ernst, *Distribution Demographics: Research Report* (Columbus: Management Horizons, Inc., 1975), pp. 42–43. Reprinted by permission.

The net effects of these various fertility forces are shown in Figure 6.10. This figure shows that the real boom will be in *first births*. In 1960, only one child in four was first-born. The projection suggests that by 1980, 40

81 These and other marriage statistics are reviewed in Alan C. Kerckhoff, "Patterns of Marriage and Family Formation and Dissolution," *Journal of Consumer Research*, vol. 2 (March 1976), pp. 261–73.

percent (two of every five children) will be first born. This trend, coupled with much smaller families, will provide an economic boom related to babies as parents spent much higher amounts for baby furniture, enlarged housing, infant supplies and so forth for first-borns than for subsequent children.

Later marriages. Young female consumers continue to show high predispositions for matrimony, although there is a slight decline in the first-marriage rate per 1,000 women aged 20–24. Women in that age bracket account for over 43 percent of all first marriages and when combined with those aged 18 and 19 years, account for about 75 percent of the total. In 1970, less than 36 percent of these females aged 20–24 were found to be single, while 56.2 percent were living with a husband. By 1974 almost 40 percent were single, and only 53 percent were living with a husband. This is difficult to interpret in favor of young Americans staying single forever, however, as the percent of females 25 years and older being classified as single declined from 7.2 percent in 1970 to 6.4 percent in 1974. From these statistics, no clear indication can be found that would indicate anything other than a growing inclination for some young people to postpone marriage but not to forswear it altogether.

More affluent individual households. The most common type of household—defined by the Census Bureau as "an occupied dwelling unit"—has traditionally been those occupied by a husband-wife family. In 1960 these households accounted for exactly three-fourths of the total. By 1974, however, this portion had declined to not quite two-thirds. The growth rate in husband-wife households during this period averaged only 1.2 percent annually, while primary individuals—people not living with other family members—grew at a rate of 3.7 percent, or almost four times as fast. Partially because of this trend, the average household size is projected to fall to a level of less than 2.8 people per household by 1980.

Money makes a market, however, and without income, these new smaller households would not be such an important market. The fact is, though, that these smaller households are not only growing more swiftly in numbers but because of swift income gains are projected to increase their expenditures at a pace more accelerated than that of their population growth. Figure 6.11 summarizes these important trends in household income.

In 1955, the average primary individual household had income only 28 percent of that of the typical family. By 1973, the ratio was more like 43 percent. As these gains continue, the household income difference will narrow still further until, by 1985, the *per capita income* of individual households will be 60 percent *above* that of families. This means that marketing organizations that have historically been oriented toward a traditional family structure will have to adapt to new requirements and potentials of the individual household.

Figure 6.11 Individual households—the growing market

Household income in 1973 dollars

	Primary families				Primary individuals		
	Median income	Number people	Per capita income		Median income	Number people	Per capita income
1955	$ 7,354	3.59	$2,048		$2,053	1.56	$1,316
1960	8,436	3.67	2,299		2,305	1.34	1,720
1965	9,792	3.70	2,646		2,713	1.26	2,153
1970	11,277	3.60	3,133		3,921	1.25	3,137
1973	12,051	3.44	3,503		5,126	1.24	4,134
1980	13,800	3.30	4,200		7,100	1.15	6,200
1985	15,400	3.35	4,600		8,900	1.10	8,100

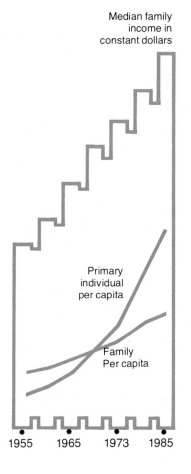

Median family income in constant dollars

Primary individual per capita

Family Per capita

1955 1965 1973 1985

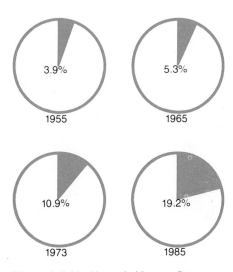

3.9% 1955
5.3% 1965
10.9% 1973
19.2% 1985

Primary individual household expenditures as a percentage of total personal consumption

Source: John E. Smallwood and Ronald L. Ernst, *Distribution Demographics: Research Report* (Columbus: Management Horizons, Inc., 1975), p. 49. Reprinted by permission.

Female households. In 1960, there were 9.6 million households occupied by individual females or by families with a female head of household. These households accounted for 18 percent of the total 52.8 million. By 1980, these independent women will account for 20.7 million households, or more than 25 percent of the total. Income gains at levels well above average should also occur. Although the details of these changes and the reasons (primarily changes in employment status of women) are beyond the scope of this discussion, it is apparent that these individuals are an increasingly important market segment.[82]

Many examples could be developed to illustrate the significance of trends such as this, like marketing opportunities for adaptive organizations, created by households without an adult male household member. Products designed to be a response to these needs might include a "super-lock," combination lock that could be programmed to accept only once—without renewal—a combination made available for delivery of goods or maintenance man entry. The lock would automatically provide a message that the door has been opened and closed since programmed— and how many times. Another example might be a recording device that, when attached to a telephone, can accept messages and delivery instructions in a *masculine* voice, even though the voice *input* was actually feminine. Such a capability would preserve as confidential—when desired—the fact that the household contained no adult male.

Opportunities from changing demographic structure of families

Exciting opportunities are available to marketing organizations as a result of the changing demography of families. Consumer analysts could construct opportunity matrices relating specific demographic changes in the family to strategy opportunities in the area of product development, positioning, and communications. Such analyses might lead to smaller portions in packaged food products for either young markets or the rapidly expanding senior citizen market,[83] furniture and appliances designed for smaller living quarters and capacity requirements, baby boutiques merchandising high quality products for the first baby boom, more convenient store hours and delivery services for the increases in

82 Probably the best single source of statistics on this topic is Bureau of the Census, *A Statistical Portrait of Women in the U.S.*, Special Studies, Series P-23, No. 58. Also see U.S. Department of Labor, *U.S. Women: A Chartbook*, 1975; Mary Dublin Keyserling, "The Economic Status of Women in the United States," *American Economic Association* (May 1976), pp. 205–12; Fabian Linden, "Woman, Worker," Conference Board *Record* (March 1977), pp. 25–27; Allyson Sherman Grossman, "The Labor Force Patterns of Divorced and Separated Women," *Monthly Labor Review* (January 1977), pp. 48–53; Barbara E. Bryant, "Respondent Selection in a Time of Changing Household Composition," *Journal of Marketing Research*, vol. 12 (May 1975), pp. 129–35; Beverlee B. Anderson, "Working Women versus Non-Working Women; A Comparison of Shopping Behaviors," in Boris W. Becker and Helmut Becker, eds., Combined Proceedings of the American Marketing Association, 1972 (Chicago: American Marketing Association, 1972), pp. 355–59; Susanne McCall, "Analytical Projections of Lifestyle Identification in Consumer Behavior," In K. L. Bernhardt, *Marketing: 1776–1976 and Beyond* (Chicago: American Marketing Association, 1976), pp. 354–59.

83 For information on the important senior citizen markets, see Joyanne E. Block, "The Aged Consumer and the Market Place: A Critical Review," *Marquette Business Review* (Summer 1974), pp. 73–80; John A. Reinecke, "Supermarkets, Shopping Centers and the Senior Shopper," *Marquette Business Review* (Fall 1975), pp. 105–7; Joseph B. Mason and Brooks E. Smith, "An Exploratory Note on the Shopping Behavior of the Low Income Senior Citizen," *The Journal of Consumer Affairs*, vol. 8 (Winter 1974), pp. 204–9; Frederick E. Waddell, "Consumer Research and Programs for the Elderly—the Forgotten Dimension," *Journal of Consumer Affairs*, vol. 9 (Winter 1975), pp. 164–75.

individual households and employed women, more exciting apparel or special purpose garments to fit the life styles of premarriage independent females, and so forth.[84]

Summary

As a primary group, the family is perhaps the ultimate in face-to-face interaction, and from the individual consumer's point of view, it differs from larger reference groups in that these family members must satisfy their unique and joint consumption needs for a common and relatively fixed amount of financial resources. As a consequence of these and other factors, family influences affect individual personality characteristics, attitudes, evaluative criteria and consumption patterns, and these influences change as the individual proceeds through the family life cycle.

Family role structures—or the behavior of nuclear family members at each stage in the decision-making process—are of fundamental importance to marketers. Types of role structures, determinants of role structures, and methods of measuring role structures were analyzed, thereby laying the foundation for the discussion of role structure on consumer decision processes in the remainder of the book.

Family demographic structures are of high importance in understanding consumption choices, and panel data indicate substantially different proportions of the family budget spent on various product categories. Other important trends in marriage patterns are developing in U.S. markets. These include a new type of baby boom which is founded on an increasing proportion of first order babies, later marriages, more affluent individual households and an increase in female households. All of these create exciting opportunities for marketing organizations that are sensitive and adaptive to changing demographic characteristics of families.

Review and discussion questions

1. Define the following terms and assess their importance in consumer analysis: (a) reference group, (b) membership group, (c) aspirational group, (d) dissociative group, and (e) primary group.

2. In what ways are reference groups associated with adult socialization? Describe some examples of this that might affect consumer decisions.

3. Why is the concept of "group norms" of relevance to marketing strategists?

4. Explain the Homans equation of human exchange and critically assess its importance in understanding the formation of reference groups.

84 Additional materials relating to future trends in the family and marketing opportunities include the following: Robert H. Myers, "Profiles of the Future," *Business Horizons*, vol. 15 (February 1972), pp. 5–16; Rudolf Dreikurs, "Equality: The Life-Style of Tomorrow," *Futurist*, vol. 6 (August 1972), pp. 153–57; Gary Gappert, "Post-Affluence," *Futurist*, vol. 8 (October 1974), pp. 212–16; Ben J. Wattenberg, "The Forming Families," paper presented at the International Marketing Conference of the American Marketing Association, Montreal, 1974; James W. Ramey, "Intimate Networks," *Futurist*, vol. 9 (August 1975), pp. 175–81; James Ramey, "Multi-Adult Household: Living Group of the Future?" *Futurist*, vol. 10 (April 1976), pp. 78–83.

5. Assume that a large manufacturer of living room furniture has asked for an analysis of the term "self-concept" as it relates to his marketing problems. Outline your analysis of the relevance of the term.

6. What is meant by the term "family?" What type of family is most relevant in the study of consumer behavior?

7. From an individual's point of view, how does the family differ from larger reference groups?

8. According to the text, a family is a mediating social system. What does this mean and of what importance is it?

9. Many students of consumer behavior maintain that the family rather than the individual should be the unit of analysis. What are the advantages and disadvantages of using the family as the unit of analysis?

10. In a given purchase situation, assuming that the motives of other family members are operative, how would marketing strategy differ depending on whether the motives of other family members are compatible with an individual's motives? Using an actual product of your own choice, compare and contrast the types of marketing strategies that could be used when motive compatibility prevails as opposed to when it does not.

CHAPTER 7

Life style research and marketing strategy

As a reader, you may wish to consider whether you would agree or disagree with the following statements:

1. A woman's place is in the home.

2. Generally speaking, women should not have positions of authority over men.

3. Liquor is a curse on American life.

4. If it was good enough for my mother, it is good enough for me.

5. I usually stay at home on Saturday night.

6. Premarital sex is immoral.

7. Sex is more important to men than it is to their wives.

8. To buy anything, other than a house or car, on installment credit is unwise.

If you "agree" or "agree strongly" with most of the above statements, you probably would be classified by your life style as "middle-America." If you disagree with these statements more than most people who are "middle America," you would be in a different life style segment.

Consider further how you would respond to the following questions:

1. I get more satisfaction from my job or other outside activities than I do from being a housewife.

2. The use of marijuana should be made legal.

3. A husband and wife should not conceive more than two children.

4. My idea of housekeeping is once over lightly.

5. I like to go to parties where there is lots of music and talk.

6. I generally have sex three or more times per week.

7. I will probably have more money to spend next year than I have now.

8. I buy many things with a credit card or charge card.

If you "agree" or "strongly agree" with most of the above statements, however, you are more likely to be classified as a "younger trendsetter."

In the study from which these statements are excerpted, about 44 percent of women were classified as "Middle America" and about 25 percent were classified as "Younger Trendsetters." Another group of 20 percent were "Middle-Age Affluents," and about 11 percent were "Older Sophisticates."[1] This is an example of "life style research." The theory and techniques involved in life style research as well as their application to the development of marketing strategy are the concern of this chapter.

Life style concepts and measures

Life styles can be defined as the *patterns in which people live and spend time and money.* The concept of life style has become widely diffused in the marketing literature and among marketing practitioners even though its use was not common until about 1969 or 1970. To some degree, the term life style is an outgrowth of the concept known as personality and also is related to research that was done in the 1950s called motivation research. Life style research also yields many of the kind of insights described in Chapter 5 as social class and is especially similar to the social class studies of Pierre Martineau and Lloyd Warner.

Life style influences on consumer decisions

The process of life style influence on consumer decisions is shown in Figure 7.1. Life styles are learned by individuals as the result of many influences such as culture, social class, reference groups, and the family. More specifically, however, life styles are derivatives of a consumer's personal value system and personality. Thus, there is great overlap in meaning between the terms values, personality, and life styles. Life style can be considered a derivative concept combining the influences of personality and social values that have been internalized by an individual.

The theory of life styles is based upon a theory of human behavior

---

1 David T. Kollat, *Profile V Survey of American Households* (Columbus: Management Horizons, Inc., 1976).

Figure 7.1 Life style influences on consumer decisions

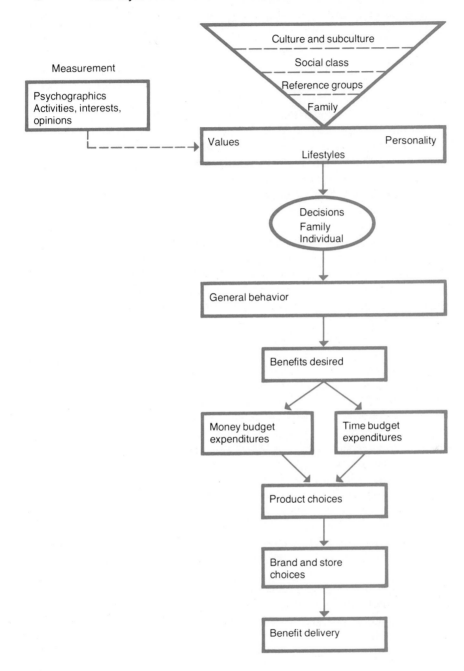

proposed by George Kelly,[2] which states that people try to predict and control their lives. To do this, people form "constructs" or patterns to construe the events happening around them and use such constructs to interpret, conceptualize, and predict events. Some persons will have constructs or patterns for interpreting their universe different from other individuals—accounting for differences in life styles. Kelly noted that this construct system is not only personal but it is also continually changing in response to a person's need to conceptualize cues from the changing environment to be consistent with one's personality.

People develop their set of constructs *to minimize incompatibilities or inconsistencies,* which is why a person who agrees with the statement "I buy many things with a credit card" is also likely to agree with the statement "I will probably have more money to spend next year." Although less obvious, perhaps, this "construct" theory also explains why the same person is likely to agree with the statements "A husband and wife should not conceive more than two children," and "The use of marijuana should be made legal." Only a limited part of a person's life style is visible or measurable by the consumer researcher, but from that portion that is measured, conclusions are made about their "type" or overall pattern. The failure to comprehend fully or measure the whole life style may account for apparent inconsistencies in a person's style of life or pervasiveness in the person's personality. This, of course, complicates prediction of consumer choices related solely to life style measures.

Psychographics

Psychographics is the principal technique used by consumer researchers as an *operational measure of life style* as shown in Figure 7.1. A function of psychographics is to provide *quantitative measures* of consumer life styles, in contrast to "soft" or qualitative research from focused group interviews, depth interviews, and similar techniques.

In reaction to the small samples of most qualitative research, consumer analysts previously tried to explain consumers' life patterns in terms of demographics—income, education, place of residence, and so forth. While demographics are very important in explaining consumer behavior—because they define and constrain the life patterns that are possible for most people—they do not go far enough. The concept and name of psychographics were originated by Demby to describe a technique that added the richness of the behavioral and social sciences to demographics.[3]

The term psychographics has come to mean about the same as AIO measures and will be used interchangeably in this discussion. AIOs refer to measurements of activities, interests, and opinions.[4] Keep in mind when

2 George A. Kelly, *The Psychology of Personal Constructs,* vol. 1 (New York: W.W. Norton & Co., 1955). The following discussion is drawn heavily from Fred Reynolds and William Darden, "Construing Life Style and Psychographics," in William D. Wells, ed., *Life Style and Psychographics* (Chicago: American Marketing Association, 1974), pp. 71–96.

3 Emanuel Demby, "Psychographics and from Whence It Came," in Wells, *Life Style,* pp. 11–30.

4 William Wells and Doug Tigert, "Activities, Interests and Opinions," *Journal of Advertising Research,* vol. 11 (August 1971), pp. 27–35; and Joseph T. Plummer, "Life Style Patterns and Commercial Bank Credit Card Usage," *Journal of Marketing,* vol. 35 (April 1971), pp. 35–42.

reading the literature in this field that some people use the term "activities and attitudes"[5] rather than AIO measures and sometimes AIO is used to mean "attitudes, interests, and opinions." In the rest of this book, however, the term AIO will be used to mean activities, interests, opinions, the same as the term psychographics. Definitions of the three components have been formulated by Reynolds and Darden as follows:

> An *activity* is a manifest action such as viewing a medium, shopping in a store, or telling a neighbor about a new service. Although these acts are usually observable, the reasons for the actions are seldom subject to direct measurement.
>
> An *interest* in some object, event, or topic is the degree of excitement that accompanies both special and continuing attention of it.
>
> An *opinion* is a verbal or written "answer" that a person gives in response to stimulus situations in which some "question" is raised. It is used to describe interpretations, expectations, and evaluations—such as beliefs about the intentions of other people, anticipations concerning future events, and appraisals of the rewarding or punishing consequences of alternative courses of action.[6]

When researchers use AIO measures, variables such as income, life cycle, education and other demographics are also included. Plummer describes variables typically included in life style research as:

> . . . measures of people's activities in terms of (1) how they spend their time; (2) their interests, what they place importance on in their immediate surroundings; (3) their opinions in terms of their view of themselves and the world around them; and (4) some basic characteristics such as their stage in life cycle, income, education, and where they live.[7]

General and specific AIOs. Two basic types of AIO statements are used in life style research. One type—probably the most common—uses general life style items that are intended to determine the overall patterns of living or basic constructs that affect a person's activities and perceptual processes. Examples of such statements would include those given in the opening paragraphs of this chapter. General statements allow the consumer researcher to define overall patterns such as satisfaction with life, family orientation, price consciousness, self confidence, religious beliefs and so forth.

The specific approach to life style research includes items that measure product-related activities, interests and opinions. This approach may include such items as attitudes toward the product class or brands, frequency of use of a product or service, media in which information is sought and so forth. Frequently, product-specific AIO statements relate

5 Thomas P. Hustad and Edgar A. Pessemier, "The Development and Application of Psychographic Life Style and Associated Activity and Attitude Measures," in Wells, *Life Style* (1974), pp. 33–70.

6 Reynolds and Darden, "Construing Life Style," p. 87.

7 Joseph T. Plummer, "The Concept and Application of Life Style Segmentation," *Journal of Marketing*, vol. 38 (January 1974), pp. 33–37, at p. 33.

to the *benefits desired* which result from more general behavior. (Refer to Figure 7.1.)

Current research practice often includes both general and specific AIO statements in the same study. In a survey of consumer attitudes toward health care issues, for example, the following general statements were included, accompanied by an agree-disagree scale:

1. I usually have a good tan each year.

2. It seems that I am sick a lot more than my friends are.

3. I generally approve of abortion if a woman wants one.

4. I generally do exercises at least twice a week.

Although these are related to health care, they are quite general and designed to discover the overall patterns that exist in reference to health care. This study also had as its purpose a very specific objective of predicting what types of consumers were likely to bring malpractice suits. Since attitude theory indicates that consumers will try to behave in such a way as to achieve consistency between their behavior and their attitudes, it was necessary to determine specific attitudes toward physicians as well as specific attitudes toward malpractice. Thus, statements such as the following were included:

1. I have a great deal of confidence in my own doctor.

2. About half of the physicians are not really competent to practice medicine.

3. Most physicians are overpaid.

4. In most malpractice suits, the physician is not really to blame.

In this study, respondents who indicated that they have a great deal of confidence in their doctors also reported a much lower likelihood of bringing a malpractice suit. Respondents agreeing with the statement that physicians are not really competent and they are overpaid and *dis*agreeing with the statement that physicians are not really to blame in malpractice suits had a much greater likelihood of filing a malpractice suit. Thus, these specific AIO statements could be used to profile specific behaviors and opinions associated with malpractice suits. However, analysis of the general statements also revealed that persons who agree with the general statements, "I generally do exercises" and "I am sick a lot more than my friends are" were found also to be more likely to bring malpractice suits—supporting the position that both general AIOs and specific AIOs can be used to profile consumers and relate their life styles to behavior.[8]

There is considerable concern about the differences in usefulness between general and specific AIO statements. Some researchers believe

8 The above research is summarized from Roger Blackwell and Wayne Talarzyk, *Consumer Attitudes toward Health Care and Malpractice* (Columbus: Grid Publishing, Inc., 1977), Chapter 5.

that specific AIOs may be better for *predicting* actual consumer choices of products or brands but that general AIOs may yield better *understanding* of consumer behavior.[9] This suggests that the *use* of the research must influence whether general or specific AIOs will be best. Additional considerations in the measurement of life styles will be discussed in the latter part of this chapter.

If life styles were a static phenomenon, research would be greatly simplified. Under static conditions, once a research study was conducted it could be placed in the file and simply retrieved when additional decisions were to be made concerning marketing strategy and programming. Such a scenario does not describe reality, however, because American life styles are changing substantially. Firms or other organizations that hope to survive must monitor closely changing life styles and proportions of the population adopting specific life styles.

Sources of life styles

Life styles result from the interaction of social and personal variables. Individuals are bombarded with influences from their environment. The most important of these occur during childhood through the process of socialization, described in Chapter 6. Social influences continue to surround the individual throughout life, however, originating in the family, reference groups, social classes, important subcultures and the overall culture. Economic influences also provide constraints and opportunities in the manifestation of one's life style.

Values. Life styles are a result, in a sense, of all the influences discussed in the previous four chapters in Part II. These are represented as *values* in Figure 7.1. In the next section of this chapter, we will try to draw together some of the most important of these social influences that are forces for *changing* consumer life styles. The purpose of this is two-dimensional. The first dimension is *descriptive*, describing the basic life forces that are likely to influence consumer decisions in the next decade. This is important as background for relating to much of the rest of the book. All of the research reported in the rest of the book has been done in the *past*. While the basic relationships and variables are likely to remain constant in the future, the *specific parameters are constantly changing*. Thus, while reading the rest of the book, you may want to keep in mind how some of the specifics that are reported in research studies may change over time, partly because of changes in the fundamental forces that create consumer life styles.

The second dimension or reason for analyzing changes in life style forces is *analytical*; that is, what are the structural elements common to all or most consumer behavior that can be applied to various circumstances? In the following section, a paradigm for sociocultural analysis will be presented that can be used to collect information on changes in the environment beyond the times described in the following pages.

9 This issue is investigated in Michel A. Zins, "An Exploration of the Relationship between General and Specific Psychographic Profiles," in Kenneth L. Bernhardt, ed., *Marketing 1776–1976 and Beyond* (Chicago: American Marketing Association, 1976), pp. 507–11.

Personality. Personality provides an explanation for why two individuals receiving the same social influences have different life styles. This topic will be described and analyzed following the discussion of changing influences on values.

Fundamental forces shaping American life styles

From the time a baby looks up and begins "cooing" and smiling, the process of socialization begins. In this process, a person is being shaped and influenced into what is thought to be "human" behavior, or what will become an individual's "personality." The influences continue throughout a lifetime, causing people to adopt general values that influence consumption—such as thrift, pleasure, honesty, and so forth. These life forces also produce specific preferences—such as color preferences, packaging and convenience preferences, preferred hours of shopping, characteristic interactions with sales persons, and so forth.

Values
Values are generalized beliefs or expectations about behavior, it will be remembered from Chapter 4. Values are important determinants of life styles and are broader in scope than attitudes or the types of variables contained in AIO measures. Values serve as a basic, integrating framework for our attitudes.[10]

Individuals are not born with their values. Rather, values are learned or passed on from generation to generation in a society or from member to member in a subcultural group. Many values are relatively permanent from generation to generation but others are undergoing considerable change in the contemporary environment. The values most in transition frequently are of most interest to marketing strategists because they provide the *basis for differences between life style market segments*. They may hold the key to growth for marketing strategists seeking to understand and predict future opportunities or challenges for a particular company or industry.

Two types of forces may be isolated and analyzed in understanding values in a society. The first type of values source is the *triad of institutions*: families, religious institutions, and schools. The second source of values is *early lifetime experiences* and includes a wide range of diversified experiences while a person is growing up and forming values. Such experiences include wars, civil rights movements, economic factors and many other events, and of course diversified institutions such as government and the media are important in transmitting these influences on values.

The transmission of values from generation to generation is shown in Figure 7.2. The following pages describe some important trends in the

---

10 Milton Rokeach, "A Theory of Organization and Change within Value-Attitude Systems," *Journal of Social Issues* (January 1968), pp. 13–33; Milton Rokeach, "The Role of Values in Public Opinion Research," *Public Opinion Quarterly* (Winter 1968–69), pp. 547–49; Milton Rokeach, *The Nature of Human Values* (New York: The Free Press, 1973).

Figure 7.2 Intergenerational value transmission

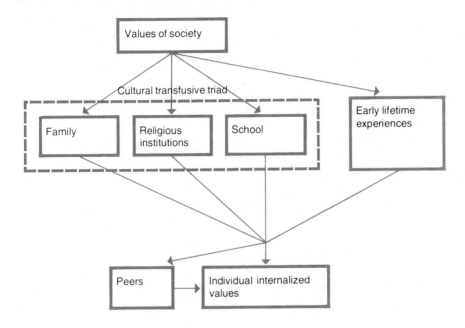

family, religious institutions, and schools as well as some contrasts in the value influencing experiences of pre-World War II consumers and post-World War II consumers. This exhibit also shows that peers exhibit influence on an individual in the process of internalizing values of a group. These peer or reference group influences were discussed in Chapter 6.

Institutional influences on values

The triad of institutions shown in Figure 7.2 plays a key role in understanding the values of a society. As long as these institutions are stable, the values transmitted are likely to be relatively stable. When these institutions change rapidly, however, the values of consumers also change rapidly, causing serious discontinuity in the effectiveness of communication and marketing strategies.

Some of these dislocative changes are presented in the following paragraphs. While the changes are described in the context of the United States, many of them are also applicable in many other countries of the world.

Declining family influences

In most cultures, the family is the dominant transfusive agent of values. Several trends indicate a decline in this influence with the effect that values change toward more flexibility. Since the family was a major topic of discussion in Chapter 6, only a few additional trends that relate specifically to value transmission are discussed here.

A *decreasing amount of time is available for in-home or parent-child influences among the very young.* This is largely due to increased enrollments in pre-school or day care facilities. Among three to four year olds, only 5.7 percent were enrolled in schools in 1965. By 1974, U.S. census figures reveal, the number had increased to 28.8 percent. In the past, children spent the formative years of zero to six with their parents. More recently, this parent-child interaction has decreased markedly, permitting values to be learned outside the family to an increasing extent.

Increased *divorce rates* also contribute to decreased family or one-parent influence on values. Between 1960 and 1974, the divorce rate per 1,000 married women increased by 110 percent, U.S. census figures reveal. About one out of every 2.5 marriages ended in divorce in 1977 compared to one in 13 in 1900. Rather than learning the stable values that accompany traditional parent roles, children are faced with changed value systems.

Weekend parents cause values to be transmitted to children by substitute parents such as babysitters, schools, and media. In an older, agrarian society and even in a blue-collar economy, children spent time with their fathers but this all changed in a post-World War II society with the enormous rise in white collar or professional occupations. The elite of white-collar fathers frequently have extensive travel as well as longer, irregular working hours leaving less opportunity to implant their values among children. The dramatic rise in working wives also leaves children open to value transmission by persons and institutions other than the family. In 1940, for example, only 20 percent of married women were employed outside the home, but by 1976, according to the U.S. Department of Labor, about 48 percent were employed outside the home.

The *isolated nuclear family* or geographical separation of the immediate (nuclear) family from the grandparents and other relatives (extended family) also contributes to a substantial decline in family influences on value transmission. Massive increases in the proportion of young people attending college has created a condition where a much higher percentage of families take career positions geographically separated from where the family grew up and from the influence of the extended family. This removes an important stabilizing or traditionalizing influence on values and perhaps results in more basic conditions of lack of heritage identity or a yearning for "roots."

Some companies have responded to the diminished influence of the extended family. A notable example is provided by the advertising of telephone companies, which offers communication and expression of love by the telephone "as the next best thing to being there." Figure 7.3 is an example of such a communication.

Changing religious influences

Judaic-Christian religious institutions have historically played an important role in transmitting values from one generation to another. In recent years, these institutions appear to have declined in influence on individuals and their values. Church membership hit a peak of 64 percent in 1960

Figure 7.3 Communication strategy based
upon the emergence of the isolated nuclear family

The telephone can fly you back again in seconds.

No matter whether you're going or coming, the telephone can fly you right back
for a quick visit with the people you just left behind. An international phone call costs less
than you think. And it's almost as easy to make as a call across town.
Long Distance is the next best thing to being there. **Bell System**

Source: Courtesy of AT&T.

but has been declining slightly since then.[11] Church membership is one
thing; attendance is another. Gallup polls indicate that the proportion of
the nation's adults attending services has declined from about 49 percent
in 1958 to 42 percent in 1969 and 40 percent in the '70s. In this sample, 35

11 *Yearbook of American Churches*, annual editions (New York: National Councils of the Churches of
Christ.)

percent of Protestants attended services in a week, 64 percent of Catholics attended and 13 percent of Jews attended.[12]

The role of religious institutions is further diminished by the *secularization of religious institutions*—or loss of function. Religion has become compartmentalized and lost its capacity to judge secular values and structure. This thesis is articulately presented by Francis Schaeffer[13] who describes how religion historically provided the values by which justice, science, the arts, and all other relevant dimensions of a culture were evaluated. In contemporary society this world-view has been replaced with a system in which religion is, at most, only relevant to a limited portion of life and, at least, not relevant to any of life. The view of Herberg that traditional religion has lost its impact on "the American way of life" is summarized in the following passage:

> Religiousness in America has become a "religiousness without religion," lacking real inner commitment and stressing social adjustment and legitimation of secular value orientations. Religion becomes a reactive system; it is shaped by secular values rather than shaping them. It no longer exerts creative leverage for judging and influencing secular life.[14]

There is considerable empirical evidence of the secularization of society as perceived by consumers themselves. In a nationwide Gallup sample in 1957, 76 percent felt religion was increasing its influence in daily life but by 1969, only 14 percent did so. While nearly every socioeconomic stratum changed to the same extent, young people changed more.[15] In a comprehensive study of college students from 1931 to 1968 using the Thurstone Attitude Scales, Jones concluded:

> It would seem that whatever weakening in students' favorable attitudes toward religion that occurred in the last 37 years has not been so much a decrease in belief in the Diety—although there has been some of that—as a disillusionment with the church establishment and the use of its beliefs and preachments in the solution of current social, civic, and economic problems.[16]

Although religion as an institution appears to be declining in influence in American and other cultures, it is still possible for it to be very important for individuals and for subgroups in the culture. There have been many studies that attempt to relate socioeconomic and other

12 Jon P. Alston, "Social Variables Associated with Church Attendance, 1965 and 1969: Evidence from National Polls," *Journal for the Scientific Study of Religion*, vol. 10 (Fall 1971), pp. 233–36.

13 Francis A. Schaeffer, *How Should We Then Live?* (Old Tappan, New Jersey: Fleming H. Revell Company, 1976).

14 Judith R. Porter, "Secularization, Differentiation, and the Function of Religious Value Orientation," *Sociological Inquiry*, vol. 43 (1973), pp. 67–74, at p. 70.

15 J.P. Alston and R.C. Hollinger, "Review of the Polls," *Journal for the Scientific Study of Religion*, vol. 11 (1972), pp. 401–03.

16 Vernon Jones, "Attitudes toward the Church," *Genetic Psychology Monographs* (1970), pp. 5–53, at p. 52. Also see Angelo Danesion and William A. Layman, "Catholic Attitudes and Beliefs in Transition: A Decade Study of a Jesuit College," *Psychological Reports*, vol. 28 (1971), pp. 247–50.

variables to religious belief and involvement, although a review of such research is beyond the present scope.[17] It also appears that a new sense of religious commitment and understanding may be emerging in the United States and many other countries of the world. Following the presidential campaign of Jimmy Carter and the popularity of books such as that of Charles Colson, presidential advisor convicted in Watergate litigation,[18] nearly one out of every three Americans indicated they were born again according to a 1976 Gallup Poll.[19]

The net effect of changing religious institutions is to allow values of the new consumer of the '80s to be established in more personal, more diversified, and less traditional ways. In many instances, these values will be different from a previous generation and will be based upon new religions in the United States such as Transcendental Meditation (which is a religion although its adherents sometimes do not describe it as such) or other Eastern religions and new forms of Judaic-Christian beliefs. The interest in some of these diverse and nontraditional religious movements is displayed in Figure 7.4, which reports the results of a nationwide, youthful survey of *Psychology Today* readers.

Figure 7.4 Interest in new religious movements

Reactions to Various Sects	Taken part	Interested	Neutral	Opposed	Never heard of group
TM	8	45	32	8	7
Hare Krishna	2	18	45	21	15
Scientology	2	12	33	20	33
Zen	4	36	41	8	12
Campus Crusade	4	17	37	26	17
Jews for Jesus	1	12	43	14	31
Children of God	1	9	37	21	31
Yoga	10	46	36	7	3
Satanism	1	2	31	59	7
Hassidism	1	6	26	7	60

Source: Robert Wuthnow and Charles Y. Glock, "The Shifting Focus of Faith: A Survey Report," *Psychology Today* (November, 1974), pp. 131–36, at p. 133. Reprinted by permission.

17 Milton Rokeach, "Value Systems in Religion," *Review of Religious Research*, vol. 11 (Fall 1969), pp. 3–23; Bruce L. Warren, "Socioeconomic Achievement and Religion: The American Case," *Sociological Inquiry*, vol. 40 (Spring 1970), pp. 130–55; Waldo W. Burchard, "Denominational Correlates of Changing Religious Beliefs in College," *Sociological Analysis*, vol. 31 (Spring 1970), pp. 36–45; Armand L. Mauss, "Dimensions of Religious Defection," *Review of Religious Research*, vol. 10 (Spring 1969), pp. 128–35; John Photiadis and William Schweiker, "Attitudes toward Joining Authoritarian Organizations and Sectarian Churches," *Scientific Study of Religion*, vol. 9 (Fall 1970), pp. 227–34; Harold E. Quineley, "The Dilemma of an Activist Church: Protestant Religion in the Sixties and Seventies," *Scientific Study of Religion*, vol. 13 (1974), pp. 1–21; Ralph Van Roy, Frank Bean, and James Wood, "Social Mobility and Doctrinal Orthodoxy," *Scientific Study of Religion*, vol. 13 (1974), pp. 427–39; Stephen M. Sales, "Economic Threat as a Determinant of Conversion Rates in Authoritarian and Nonauthoritarian Churches," *Journal of Personality and Social Psychology*, vol. 23 (1972), pp. 420–28.

18 Charles Colson, *Born Again* (Old Tappan, New Jersey: Fleming H. Revell Company, 1976).

19 George Plagenz, "1 in 3 Americans said 'born again' Christians," Scripps-Howard News Service, Inc., November 1976.

The impact of religious values will be felt more rather than less on some segments of the population because some religious organizations have been willing to adapt their strategies to a marketing orientation.[20] One example is provided by the Garden Grove Community Church in California. It was started in a drive-in theatre and in 20 years became a church of 8,000 members with massive community impact programs and a sponsor of the top rated religious television program in nearly every city in America. The senior minister of this church practices a marketing orientation and states the church is "a shopping center for God; it's part of the service industry."[21] In the conduct of consumer research, it appears that attention must increasingly be given to individualized measurement of religious beliefs and participation rather than assuming that most of the market shares a common value system. In religious research, a number of scaling devices and other research techniques have been developed recently that may be included in the future in consumer studies attempting to segment the market on meaningful dimensions of life styles.[22]

Rising influence of educational institutions

The third major institutional influence on values is schools and it appears that the influence of schools is rising. In part, this is due to the increased participation of Americans in formal education and in part it is due to filling the vacuum left by families and religious institutions.

The proportion of 18–21 year old persons enrolled in college is shown in Figure 7.5 to have increased from 15.6 percent in 1940 to 45.8 percent in 1973. A substantial part of this increase occurred in 2-year institutions, which may provide less influence toward discontinuity in values than institutions in which students are more likely to be living away from home. Nevertheless, this dramatic rise in college enrollment must be interpreted as indicating a high value on education by young consumers and their parents. At the same time that the proportion of young people in college is increasing, however, many universities and colleges are enrolling more "older" consumers, especially in the 25–34 age group, but also even among retirees. All of this is an indication of the value consumers place on education.

Other factors occurring within the educational system contribute to

20 James F. Engel and H. Wilbert Norton, *What's Gone Wrong with the Harvest?* (Grand Rapids: Zondervan Publishing House, 1975); Donald McGavran, *Understanding Church Growth* (Grand Rapids: William B. Eerdmans, 1970).

21 Robert H. Schuller, *Your Church Has Real Possibilities!* (Glendale, California: Regal Books, 1974). Also see "Possibility Thinking and Shrewd Marketing Pay Off for a Preacher," *The Wall Street Journal* (August 26, 1976), p. 1 ff.

22 Morton King and Richard Hunt, "Measuring the Religious Variable: Replication," *Journal for the Scientific Study of Religion,* vol. 13 (1974), pp. 240–51 (this reference lists 10 religious scales believed to be of most relevance to social scientists in measuring religious beliefs and involvement); Floyd L. Jennings, "A Note on the Reliability of Several Belief Scales," *Journal for the Scientific Study of Religion,* vol. 13 (1974), pp. 157–297; N.J. Demerath III and Richard M. Levinson, "Baiting the Dissident Hook: Some Effects of Bias on Measuring Religious Belief," *Sociometry,* vol. 34 (1971), pp. 346–59; Robert D. Coursey, "Consulting and the Catholic Crisis," *Journal of Consulting and Clinical Psychology,* vol. 42 (1974), pp. 519–28 (although in a Catholic context, this reference provides a scale of liberalness-conservatism); Bernard Lazerwitz, "Religious Identification and Its Ethnic Correlates: A Multivariate Model," *Social Forces,* vol. 52 (December 1973), pp. 204–20 (this reference provides a useful illustration of the path-analysis technique); Charles Y. Glock, Benjamin Ringer, and Earl Babbie, *To Comfort and to Challenge* (Berkeley: University of California Press, 1967).

Figure 7.5 College enrollment in the United States

	Percentage of 18–21 year olds in college	Percentage in	
		4-Year institutions	2-Year institutions
1940	15.6%	91%	9%
1950	29.6	91	9
1960	34.9	88	12
1970	44.4	79	21
1973	45.8	78	22

Source: U.S. Bureau of the Census.

discontinuity in value systems. Prior to World War II, teachers and professors originated primarily from the middle class. Upper-class parents sent their children to college also but not to become teachers, and most lower-class families did not have the opportunity to send their children to college at all. Thus, historically, most teachers had middle- or upper middle-class backgrounds and reflected in their teaching what have come to be known as the traditional American values. During the 1950s, a new breed of teachers emerged as college enrollments from all social classes soared. While the middle classes still dominated teaching, teachers and professors now came to some extent from the entire spectrum of society. Students could reasonably expect to encounter teachers with values different from their own—and in some cases radically different.[23]

Another trend occurred involving the emergence and proliferation of new teaching techniques. Teaching methods previously emphasized description and memorization. This approach to "learning" implicitly, if not explicitly, says, "This is the way things are; just learn it," with no latitude for questioning. During the past two decades, however, there has been a gradual but steady trend away from description and memorization in favor of analytical approaches emphasizing questioning of the old and the formulation of new approaches and solutions. In many instances this approach concludes that there is no one correct answer. The case method in business school is an example of this analytical, questioning approach.

The result is a "spillover" of questioning and rejection of rigid definitions of "right and wrong" from the educational system into the basic values of life. To paraphrase a statement attributed to Archibald MacLeish, "The central reality of our time is that individuals, particularly younger people, are no longer willing to lead unexamined lives." This important influence leads to the aggressive consumerism discussed in the last part of this book. Marketing organizations must develop new types of sales programs and product information formats when a substantial number of consumers are more militantly asking "why" and "why not" to marketing offerings. More basically, this questioning of old values permits

23 For an expansion of these ideas, see Harvey C. Burke, "The University in Transition," *Business Horizons*, vol. 12, pp. 5–17 (August 1969).

the rise of contemporary and diverse life styles for substantial portions of a society, requiring a thorough understanding of marketing segmentation in the design of communication and marketing strategies.

All three of these institutions—family, religion, and school—contribute both to transmitting some traditional values and at the same time transmitting conditions among some consumers for receptivity to changed life styles. In addition to the influence of this cultural transfusive triad, early lifetime experiences are also important in creating the values of a generation of consumers.

Intergenerational motivating factors

"Every person is a product of his or her environment" is a familiar truism. A less familiar one is that, "People strive to achieve as adults what they feel they were deprived of in early stages of life." These generalizations suggest another set of reasons why values are changing—namely, that the lifetime experiences of young consumers are fundamentally and qualitatively different from those of previous generations.

Pre-World War II consumers. Over 70 percent of contemporary American consumers were not yet born during the Great Depression of the 1930s. For most Americans, even World War II predates their personal history. Yet, the severity of these two events had a profound and indelible impact on the lives of consumers who experienced them. The fact that the effects of these events were so pervasive made their impact a national experience as well as a private one. Hence there is a marked tendency for consumers who experienced the Depression and World War II to hold values that emphasize *job security*, *patriotism*, and the acquisition of wealth and *material goods*. These were the things they were deprived of as children.

What have come to be known as conventional values and life styles, reflected in many older consumers, were a logical consequence of the experiences of the Depression and World War II. Many of the persons who lived through these experiences are managers of organizations—but to act upon their own value systems could lead to ineffective results in the communications strategies of those organizations, which attempt to deal with the new consumer.

Post-World War II consumers. Instead of the ravages of the Depression, the strategic consumer markets of the '80s will have experienced during childhood the greatest period of prolonged economic expansion in the history of the United States. During the 1950s, the economy nearly doubled and repeated the growth again in the '60s and not until the mid-'70s did this expansion lose momentum. Even though a substantial amount of this growth represented inflation, there remained a tremendous proliferation of affluence.

The critical lifetime experiences of the growth segments of the markets in the 1980s vary greatly, but among the prominent influences are the following: the nuclear age, the civil rights movement, pockets of poverty amidst mass affluence, questionable space exploration, the Viet Nam War, concern about ecology, pervasive university experiences, campus disorders and protests, the ecology crisis, inflation, Watergate, and a revolution in communication technology.[24]

From an analysis of intergenerational influences, it is predicted that the market for products could be segmented to some extent on the basis of values derived from lifetime experiences. Older, depression-oriented consumers should place greater emphasis upon material things, financial security and more economic criteria, whereas younger consumers should place greater emphasis on interpersonal or relationship values, noneconomic criteria and pleasure now rather than in the future. In a study related to this topic, Vinson and Munson measured the values of students and compared them to similar measures of values of parents, particularly as they related to product attributes in an automobile. The results confirmed the above analysis and the researchers concluded that parents emphasized attributes signifying utilitarian or functional characteristics associated with automobile ownership (e.g., quality of warranty, service required, handling) while students were more concerned with aesthetic and socially observable features (styling, prestige, luxury interior).[25]

Values impact life styles in very substantial ways. Although it has been recognized for some time that values have pervasive influence on consumer life styles and consumption patterns,[26] it has been difficult for marketing executives to relate these broad based values to the specifics of marketing strategy and programming.

Marketing strategy and programming—a case example

Figure 7.6 is presented as a case example of how changing values are manifested in life styles specific enough to be used for developing marketing programs. This figure is presented in the next several pages of the text and requires the reader to expend considerable effort to study the relationship between life style and strategy. It would be possible to describe in general terms that strategies can be based upon life styles but we believe you will grasp how this is done more readily with a comprehensive case example than with an abstract description.

The case example presented in Figure 7.6 contains descriptions of key life styles emerging as a result of the forces described in the preceding pages of this text. The trends were measured through repeated measures in surveys conducted by national polling services amplified by a psychographic study of 10,000 households selected from families in the market facts panel base. The names given the trends are significant only to the extent that they help communicate in a few words the meaning of this

24 These are adapted from several sources. Many are discussed in Margaret Mead, "The Generation Gap That Has No Parallels," The Providence Sunday *Journal* (October 4, 1970), p. N–43. Also see CBS News, *Generations Apart* (New York: Columbia Broadcasting System, 1969); Elizabeth Herzog et. al., "Teenagers Discuss the 'Generation Gap.'" Youth Reports no. 1 (Washington: U.S. Department of Health, Education and Welfare, 1970); and "What They Believe," *Fortune* (January 1969), pp. 70 ff; Daniel Bell, "Social Trends of the 70's," *Conference Board Record* (June 1970), pp. 70–71 ff.

25 Donald E. Vinson and J. Michael Munson, "Personal Values: An Approach to Market Segmentation," in Kenneth Bernhardt, ed., *Marketing: 1776–1976 and Beyond* (Chicago: American Marketing Association, 1976), pp. 313–17.

26 William Lazer, "Life Style Concepts and Marketing," in Stephen Greyser, ed., *Toward Scientific Marketing* (Chicago: American Marketing Association, 1963), pp. 140–51.

Figure 7.6 Case example of marketing strategy and programming based on life style trends

Trend	Description of trend	Illustrative product implications for manufacturers and retailers	Illustrative additional manufacturer strategy implications	Illustrative additional retailer strategy implications
More casual life styles	Desire to live a less traditional, conservative, formalized life style in terms of behavior, dress, eating, entertainment, and so on.	Potential increase in sales of furniture that is more comfortable. More casual, perhaps rugged, case goods. Potential long-term reduction in sales of formal living and dining room furniture. Good growth prospects for indoor/outdoor furniture.	Consider advertising featuring furniture and home furnishings in more realistic and casual life style settings. Think about emphasizing comfort where appropriate.	Same as manufacturer.
Desire for elegance and personalization	Growing interest in a personalized life style that is different from others and consistent with one's self-concept.	Growing market for uniquely designed furniture that is visibly different from what is widely available. Growing market for old, second-hand furniture including antiques. Increasing tendency to mix styles between and/or within rooms. Potential increase in sales of "refinish-it-yourself" furniture, including kits.	Consider advertising featuring unique furniture and furniture settings that mix styles and designs harmoniously. Evaluate distribution through retailers having a reputation for uniqueness; brochures and sales promotion pieces that recommend what goes with what.	Consider devoting some inventory dollars to unique and unusual merchandise that is not available elsewhere. Some room settings and advertising might mix styles and designs harmoniously.
Flexibility of roles/women's liberation	Men and women perform multiple roles—mother, hostess, wife, maid. Greater exchange of many roles between sexes.	Growing market for interchangeable (room-to-room) furniture as well as furniture that can serve a variety of purposes (multiple purpose).	Consider advertising and sales promotion featuring the interchangeability and multiple purpose features of appropriate items.	Same as manufacturer. Add interchangeability and multiple purpose features to sales presentations where applicable. Avoid double standards (male, female) in extending credit.
Instant gratification	Living more for today and planning and living less for the future. Desire for instant standard of living, instant career achievement. Interest in "solutions to problems" rather than parts of problems. Growing intolerance of incompetence—waiting in line, etc.	Enlarging market for low cost, reasonable quality, and well-designed furniture and home furnishings analogously, the Mustang (or "fun watches"). Greater interest in groupings (packages) of furniture that go together—not necessarily the same style.	Continue to reevaluate delivery time. Evaluate advertising and sales promotion for complete rooms using themes like "decorate your family room by bedtime."	Same as manufacturer. Also consider trying to speed up the time required to process a customer transaction. For regular customers, think about maintaining a file containing room layout, items purchased, including swatches, and so on.

			Manufacturer	Retailer
New theology of pleasure	Interested in having fun and in products, services, and other experiences that make life fun. This is a reaction to the boredom of life emanating partly from job tedium and dissatisfaction.	Favors unique, interesting furniture and furnishings that are conversation pieces. Also fun items like bean bag chairs and water beds.	Consider advertising and promoting furniture and furnishings in unique, fun settings. Evaluate distribution through retailers having a unique, fun image.	Create store excitement through unique displays. Reevaluate how frequently they are changed. Consider music and other techniques that are consistent with your market. Think about establishing a play area for children, refreshment center, etc. Advertise and promote furniture in unique, fun settings.
Life simplification	Removing or reducing the time and/or energy required to perform what are perceived by some to be mundane, undesirable tasks. Examples include self-cleaning ovens, trash compactors, power lawnmowers, etc.	Furniture and home furnishings that are easy to care for, easy to repair, and require less frequent cleaning, dusting, and so on. Minimum maintenance wall coverings. Opportunity for services such as furniture and carpet cleaning and repair, complete interior cleaning, painting, refurbishing, and so on.	Consider advertising and promoting easy maintenance features.	Same as manufacturer.
Changing morality	Growing tendency to believe that premarital sex, extramarital sex, homosexuality, etc., are not morally wrong. Increasing tendency to live together without being married.	Creates new needs for "temporary" furniture and home furnishings, including rental. Growing market for modular sofa and chair units that can be pushed together to create a large "lounging area." Opportunity for unique beds, headboards, and bedroom furniture designs that create atmosphere and facilitate "lounging" as well as sleeping. Emphasis on products of minimum deterioration or obsolescence for rental programs.	Think about advertising and promoting the modular features of sofa and chairs, if applicable. Also emphasize the "lounging" features of beds and bedroom furniture. Feature bedroom and other furniture in tastefully sensual settings. Potential opportunity for diversification into furniture rental.	Same as manufacturer, depending upon local market characteristics and opportunities.

Figure 7.6 Case example of marketing strategy and programming based on life style trends (continued)

Trend	Description of trend	Illustrative product implications for manufacturers and retailers	Illustrative additional manufacturer strategy implications	Illustrative additional retailer strategy implications
Concern about appearance and health	Partial outgrowth of youth orientation. Concern about health, weight, physical appearance—often youthful appearance. Illustrations include wigs, hair dye, face lifts, vitamins, bust development, diet foods, etc.	Potential market for health and exercise equipment that has good design and is like furniture so that it looks well in bedrooms and/or other furnished areas, or which can be marketed as an accessory item, to be attached to or used with some item of furniture.		
Novelty, change, and escape	Reaction to the perceived boredom of life, resulting partly from the absence of meaningful work. Interest in products, services, and experiences that provide for novelty, change, and escape.	Potential market for less long-lasting, relatively low-priced, furniture and furnishings provided they are well-designed—i.e., the Timex concept. Growth potential for novelty items. Growing market for furniture and home furnishings for camping, camping vehicles and trucks, second homes, and so on. Potential opportunity for multiple coverings for upholstered goods.	Through advertising and promotion, evaluate positioning the home (apartment) as a place to "get away from it all." Also show how furniture and furnishings can be rearranged to create a fresh change and new feeling.	Same as manufacturer. Also include in merchandise presentations and sales presentations.
Naturalism	Growing desire to have the best of both worlds—the advantages of technology and the standard of living that it makes possible on the one hand—and naturalism, return to nature on the other. Rejection of artificial forms of behavior and dress.	Continuing market for natural woods and other materials. Earth tones should be popular. Designs that facilitate "openness" and "bring the outdoors" inside should do well. Less demand for wall-to-wall carpeting; more for area and throw rugs. Potential growth of patterns and materials using natural scenes and outdoor living.	Through advertising and sales promotion, consider featuring the natural characteristics of the product—natural woods, natural wool, etc.	Same as manufacturer. Include naturalness in sales presentations. Consider expanding assortment of area rugs.

Personal creativity	For reasons of economy and/or self-expression, desire to make selected things and perform certain functions that have historically been purchased—i.e., crafts, home sewing, home repair and improvement, etc.	Growing market for products that allow final accessorization by the purchaser. Sales of unfinished furniture should increase, including higher quality furniture and knock-down pieces that require finishing as well as assembling. Growing market for used furniture that is unique. Opportunity for carpeting and floor covering products with "do-it-yourself" installation. Limited, but growing opportunity for high cost gourmet cookware. Opportunity for "do-it-yourself" wall covering kit.	Advertising and promotion that shows consumers how to finish, assemble, refinish, upholster, reupholster furniture, install carpeting, wall coverings, etc. Potential theme might be: "If we can do it, so can you."	Same as manufacturer. Consider offering refinishing, reupholstering, cleaning, and similar services to customers. Also consider conducting classes in things like finishing and upholstering and sell kits.
Changing attitudes toward credit	Expectation that credit will be available to finance the "good life."	Increasing stability of sales.		Process credit applications quickly and politely. If third parties are involved, develop a mechanism to make the transition as smooth as possible.
New work ethic	Having fun is not necessarily something to be minimized. Trend toward "working to live" rather than "living to work."	More time at home to enjoy furniture. Growing market for indoor/outdoor casual furniture and furnishings.	Think about advertising and promotion emphasizing "you deserve to relax." Utilize background settings in which people are relaxing and having fun. Where possible, adjust personnel policies to changing work ethic—flexible work hours, limited night and weekend commitments, and so on.	Same as manufacturer.
Institutional reliance	Reliance on institutions—particularly government and business—to solve society's "problems" and a growing number of consumption needs.	Potential increase in the number of furniture and home furnishings items that are built in at the time of construction.	Consider developing working relationships with large builders, developers, architects, etc.	Same as manufacturer.

Figure 7.6 Case example of marketing strategy and programming based on life style trends (continued)

Trend	Description of trend	Illustrative product implications for manufacturers and retailers	Illustrative additional manufacturer strategy implications	Illustrative additional retailer strategy implications
Eroding confidence in institutions	Dramatic reductions in the confidence people have in major institutions, particularly business.		Develop consumerism program.	Same as manufacturer.
Consumerism	Increasing concern over price/quality/quantity relationships. Increasing product and service expectations.	Growing need to tighten quality control. Guarantees and warranties will become more important.	Use guarantee/warranty cards to monitor who is buying your product(s) and where. Set up system to encourage customer complaints and to respond honestly and fairly. Periodically conduct studies of your customers and other people to measure your image.	Same as manufacturer. Also think about encouraging salespeople to talk in "customer-oriented" rather than technical terms. For example, the difference between wool and nylon carpeting is _____. What this means to you, Mrs. Consumer, is _____.
International orientation	Gradual emergence of a "one world" orientation resulting from political and trade relationships and increasing travel, education, and communications. Early manifestations likely to be the gradual assimilation of selected Western European traditions and life styles—particularly among younger, higher educated, more affluent segments.	Monitor trends in Europe to identify items that are popular there, particularly those that appeal to people under 35 years of age. Pay particular attention to furniture and home furnishings in countries having high density and smaller size (square footage) housing—such as Sweden and Holland.		
Energy/ecological/ environmental orientation	Gradual proliferation of energy conservation ethic, which in turn may be generalized into natural resources conservation, and then into "anti-waste" in general.		Consider publicizing how your company buys wood only from resources that have an acceptable restoration program. Follow same policy for other natural resources that you use—including energy.	Same as manufacturer.

Price/value orientation	Emanating from the loss of real income and rising prices, growing concern about the value received for the price.	Products should have "visible" price-quality relationships. Greater attention should be placed on engineering products that give good value for the price. Warranties and guarantees will become more important. Potential decline in middle price points compared to upper and lower.	Think about emphasizing that furniture and many other home furnishings are one of the best investments that can be made. Reevaluate pricing strategy in the context of achieving a "visible" price-quality relationship. If applicable to your company, develop a contingency strategy for the potential erosion of middle price points.	Same as manufacturer.
Eclecticism	Trend away from homogeneous fashion and life styles toward the acceptance of a multiplicity of acceptable styles. Decline of fashion and life style dictatorship toward more individualistic, often peer group influence.	Eclectic product line and assortment (that goes together) may become more effective. Comfort may become a more important criterion in selecting items. Growing market for accessories based on astrology, the occult, mysticism. Also accessory collections—medals, stamps, etc.	Through advertising and promotion, show eclectic furniture groupings, and dramatize comfort. Where appropriate, emphasize maintenance/durability aspects; for example, "(brand name) lets kids be kids."	Same as manufacturer.
Time conservation	Growing recognition that time is a critical resource and constraint in many consumers' lives.	Furniture and home furnishings that are easy to care for, easy to repair, require less frequent cleaning, dusting, and so on.	Consider featuring ease of cleaning and maintenance in advertising and promotion.	Same as manufacturer. Also include in sales presentations. Also, improve ability of consumer to buy some items without visiting store.

Source: David T. Kollat, *Profile V Management Report* (Columbus: Management Horizons, Inc., 1976); David T. Kollat and Roger D. Blackwell, *Direction 1980* (Columbus: Management Horizons, Inc., 1970), and other related materials.

trend to the executives who must make marketing strategy decisions. This particular study, which is representative of similar projects by other organizations, was funded by the Home Furnishings Marketing Institute, to be used by a number of their member firms.

Many observations can be made after studying this case example. Perhaps the most important, however, is the possibility of an *integrated marketing program* based upon information about consumer life styles. Figure 7.6 gives examples of how both *manufacturers* and *retailers* can develop strategic implications from life style data. Additionally, the reader should note, in the third and fourth columns, the range of marketing decisions that are affected by life style trends. These include product, price, and advertising elements of the program as well as many distribution elements.[27]

Personality and life style

If all consumers in a society are exposed to the same basic life forces in a society, does that mean they should all have the same life styles? The answer is unmistakably "no." It is unlikely that all consumers would be exposed to the same influences, of course, but even if they were, differences in life styles would exist between individuals. The reason this is true is due to what is called *personality*.

Most definitions of personality are quite general and the term is frequently used in different ways by various types of researchers. Generally, however, personality is linked to the concept of *consistent* responses to environmental stimuli.[28] This concept has been embodied in most personality theories utilized in contemporary marketing research. Three of these theories—psychoanalytic, social-psychological, and trait-factor—are discussed in more detail below.

Psychoanalytic theory

The psychoanalytic theory[29] posits that the human personality system consists of the id, ego, and superego. The id is the source of psychic energy and seeks immediate gratification for biological and instinctual needs. The superego represents societal or personal norms and serves as an ethical constraint on behavior. The ego mediates the hedonistic demands of the id and the moralistic prohibitions of the superego. The dynamic interaction of these elements results in unconscious motivations that are manifested in observed human behavior.

The psychoanalytic theory served as the conceptual basis for the motivation research movement that was the precursor to life style studies.

27 For additional discussion of the impact of changing life styles on marketing strategy, see Robert H. Myers, "Profiles of the Future: Marketing Opportunities," *Business Horizons*, vol. 15 (February 1972), pp. 5–16.

28 H.H. Kassarjian, "Personality and Consumer Behavior: A Review," *Journal of Marketing Research*, vol. 8 (November 1971), pp. 409–18, at p. 409.

29 For a marketing level view of psychoanalytic theory, see W.D. Wells and A.D. Beard, "Personality and Consumer Behavior," in Scott Ward and T.S. Robertson, eds., *Consumer Behavior: Theoretical Sources* (Englewood Cliffs, N.J.: Prentice-Hall, 1973); C.S. Hall and G. Lindzey, *Theories of Personality*, 2d ed. (New York: Wiley, 1970); R.J. Markin, *The Psychology of Consumer Behavior* (Englewood Cliffs, N.J.: Prentice-Hall, 1969).

According to the philosophy of motivation researchers, consumer behavior was the result of unconscious consumer motives. These unconscious motives could be determined only through indirect assessment methods that included a wide assortment of projective and related psychological techniques.

The motivation research movement produced some extraordinary findings. Kotler reports the following hypotheses as typical psychoanalytic explanations of consumer purchase motivations:

1. A man buys a convertible as a substitute "mistress."

2. A woman is very serious when she bakes a cake because unconsciously she is going through the symbolic act of birth.

3. Men want their cigars to be odiferous in order to prove that they (the men) are masculine.[30]

These examples are interesting but others may be more valuable. Competent marketing researchers use motivation research very productively in many instances to provide a thorough, in-depth understanding of life styles, personality, and decision-making. Frequently, however, there is a need for more quantitative methods, a need that was later achieved by AIO and other measures.

Social-psychological theory[31] differs from psychoanalytic theory in two important respects. First, social variables,[32] not biological instincts, are considered to be the most important determinants in shaping personality. Second, behavioral motivation is conscious. People know their needs and wants and behavior is directed to meet those needs.[33]

Social-psychological theory

A representative example of social-psychological personality theory is the Horney paradigm. This model suggests that human behavior results from three predominant, interpersonal orientations—compliant, aggressive, and detached.[34]

For marketing research purposes, Cohen developed a research methodology using the Horney paradigm to explain some aspects of consumer

30 Philip Kotler, *Marketing Management* (Englewood Cliffs, N.J.: Prentice-Hall 1967), p. 88.

31 Social-psychological personality theory specifically recognizes the interdependence of the individual and society. The individual strives to meet the needs of society, while society helps the individual to attain his goals. The theory is, therefore, not exclusively sociological or psychological, but rather a combination of the two (review Chapter 6). This theoretical orientation is most widely associated with Adler, Horney, Fromm, and Sullivan. For a more complete explanation of this approach, see Hall and Lindzey, *Theories of Personality*, chap. 4, pp. 117–59.

32 There was no general agreement among the social theorists as to the relative importance of social variables. Fromm emphasized the importance of social context, while Sullivan and Horney stressed interpersonal behavior, and Adler eclectically employed many different variables (Hall and Lindzey, *Theories of Personality*, pp. 154–55.

33 Hall and Lindzey, *Theories of Personality*, pp. 155–56.

34 Compliant people are dependent on other people for love and affection, and are said to move toward others. Aggressive people are motivated by the need for power, and move against others. Detached people are self-sufficient and independent, and move away from others. For a marketing-level explanation of the Horney paridigm, see J.B. Cohn, "An Interpersonal Orientation to the Study of Consumer Behavior," *Journal of Marketing Research*, vol. 4, pp. 270–78 (August 1967); J.B. Cohen, "Toward an Interpersonal Theory of Consumer Behavior," *California Management Review*, vol. 10, pp. 73–80 (1968).

behavior. The CAD scale[35] is used to measure predominant interpersonal orientation in a sample of consumers. Some consumer behavior response measures (such as product usage) are collected. The consumer's interpersonal orientation, measured by the CAD scale, is then used as a predictive variable. Although significant differences are sometimes found between these measures of personality and product choice, marketing relevance is limited to date.

Trait-factor theory

Trait-factor theory represents a quantitative approach to the study of personality. This theory postulates that an individual's personality is composed of definite predispositional attributes called traits. A trait is more specifically defined as "any distinguishable, relatively enduring way in which one individual differs from another."[36] Traits, therefore, can alternatively be considered individual difference variables.

Three assumptions delineate this theory. It is assumed that traits are common to many individuals and vary in absolute amounts between individuals.[37] It is further assumed that these traits are relatively stable and exert fairly universal effects on behavior regardless of the environmental situation.[38] It follows directly from this assumption that a consistent functioning of personality variables is predictive of a wide variety of behavior. The final assumption asserts that traits can be inferred from the measurement of behavioral indicators.

The most commonly used measurement technique is the standard psychological inventory such as the California Psychological Inventory or the Edwards Personal Preference Scale (EPPS). Borrowing standard scales that were designed for clinical purposes may produce poor results for marketing purposes.[39] A better practice is to modify standard tests for marketing usage. An example of such a test is shown in Figure 7.7, measuring the traits of "sociable, relaxed, and internal control." The research of Villani and Wind indicates that such tests are reliable measures of such traits.[40]

Trait-factor theory has been used almost exclusively as the conceptual basis of marketing personality research. In this research, the typical study attempts to find a relationship between a set of personality variables and assorted consumer behaviors such as purchases, media choice, innovation, fear and social influence, product choice, opinion leadership, risk taking, attitude change, and so forth.[41] Personality has been found to relate to specific *attributes* of product choice.[42] Research also indicates

35 The CAD scale is a 35-item Likert scale developed by Cohen. The scale and scoring procedure appear in Cohen, "An Interpersonal Orientation," pp. 277–78.

36 Guilford, *op. cit.*, p. 6.

37 W. Mischel, *Personality and Assessment* (New York: Wiley, 1968), p. 6.

38 N. Sanford, *Issues in Personality Theory* (San Francisco: Josey-Bass, 1970), pp. 8–9.

39 Raymond L. Horton, "The Edwards Personal Preference Schedule and Consumer Personality Research," *Journal of Marketing Research*, vol. 11 (August 1974), pp. 335–37.

40 Kathryn E.A. Villani and Yoram Wind, "On the Usage of 'Modified' Personality Trait Measures in Consumer Research," *Journal of Consumer Research*, vol. 2 (December 1975), pp. 223–28.

41 Kassarjian, "Personality," p. 409.

42 Mark I. Alpert, "Personality and the Determinants of Product Choice," *Journal of Marketing Research*, vol. 9 (February 1972), pp. 89–92.

Figure 7.7 Test items in the modified personality instrument

Sociable

I am always glad to join a large gathering.
I consider myself a very sociable, outgoing person.
I find it easy to mingle among people at a social gathering.
When I am in a small group, I sit back and let others do most of the talking.
I have decidedly fewer friends than most people.
I am considered a very enthusiastic person.

Relaxed

I get tense as I think of all the things lying ahead of me.
Quite small setbacks occasionally irritate me too much.
I wish I knew how to relax.
I shrink from facing a crisis or a difficulty.

Internal Control

Sometimes I feel that I don't have enough control over the direction my life is taking.
Many times I feel that I have little influence over the things that happen to me.
What happens to me is my own doing.
Becoming a success is a matter of hard work; luck has nothing to do with it.
Getting a good job depends mainly on being in the right place at the right time.

Source: Kathryn E. A. Villani and Yoram Wind, "On the Usage of 'Modified' Personality Trait Measures in Consumer Research," *Journal of Consumer Research*, vol. 2 (December 1975), pp. 223–28. Reprinted from the *Journal of Consumer Research* published by the American Marketing Association.

that people can make relatively good judgments about other people's traits and how they relate to such choices as automobile brands, occupations, and magazines.[43]

Predicting buyer behavior

Research studies that have a common objective of predicting consumer behavior through the use of various types of personality measures have appeared in the marketing literature. These studies fall into two general classifications: (1) susceptibility to social influence, and (2) product and brand choice.

The rich literature on personality in psychology and other behavioral sciences has led many researchers in marketing to theorize that personality characteristics should predict brand or store preference and other types of buyer activity.

The study that stimulated much of the interest among marketing personnel in the topic of personality was a study by Evans in which he attempted to test the assumption that automobile buyers differ in personality structure.[44] He administered a standard personality inventory, the Edwards Personal Preference Schedule, to owners of Chevrolets and Fords. There were only a few statistically significant differences between the two groups. Using discriminant analysis, he was able to predict correctly a Ford or Chevrolet owner in only 63 percent of the cases, not

43 Paul E. Green, Yoram Wind, and Arun K. Jain, "A Note on Measurement of Social-Psychological Belief Systems," *Journal of Marketing Research*, vol. 9 (May 1972); pp. 204–8.
44 F.B. Evans, "Psychological Objective Factors in the Prediction of Brand Choice: Ford versus Chevrolet," *Journal of Business*, vol. 32, pp. 340–69 (1959).

much better than the 50 percent that would be expected by chance. Using 12 objective variables, such as age of car, income, and other demographics, a correct prediction was made in 70 percent of the cases. Evans concluded, therefore, that personality is of relatively little value in predicting automobile brand ownership.

A number of studies investigated the hypothesis that personality could be directly related to product choice. Some of these studies reported some relation between product use and personality traits.[45] Most other studies found only very small amounts of variance in product choice explained by personality.[46] Looking back from today's vantage, it is not surprising that these studies found little relationship between personality and overall brand or product choice. After all, personality is but one variable even in the concept of life style, and life style is only one variable in the overall model of consumer decision making.

But even if personality traits were found to be valid predictors of buyer behavior, would they be useful as a means of market segmentation? In order for a positive answer to be given, the following circumstances must prevail:

1. People with common personality dimensions must be homogeneous in terms of demographic factors such as age, income, and location so that they can be reached economically through the mass media. This is necessary because data are available on media audiences mostly in terms of demographic characteristics. If they show no identifiable common characteristics of this type, there is no practical means of reaching them as a unique market segment.

2. Measures that isolate personality variables must be demonstrated to have adequate reliability and validity. The difficulties in this respect have already been pointed out.

3. Personality differences must reflect clear-cut variations in buyer activity and preferences that, in turn, can be capitalized upon meaningfully through modifications in the marketing mix. In other words, people can show different personality profiles yet still prefer essentially the same product attributes.

4. Market groups isolated by personality measures must be of a sufficient size to be reached economically. Knowledge that each person varies on a personality scale is interesting but impractical for a

45 M.J. Gottlieb, "Segmentation by Personality Types," in L. H. Stockman, ed., *Advancing Marketing Efficiency* (Chicago: American Marketing Association, 1959), pp. 148–58; W.T. Tucker and J.J. Painter, "Personality and Product Use," *Journal of Applied Psychology*, vol. 45, pp. 325–29 (1961); D.M. Ruch, "Limitations of Current Approaches to Understanding Brand Buying Behavior," in J.W. Newman, ed., *On Knowing the Consumer* (New York: Wiley, 1966), pp. 173–86.

46 Ralph Westfall, "Psychological Factors in Predicting Product Choice," *Journal of Marketing*, vol. 26, pp. 34–40 (1962); F.B. Evans, "Ford versus Chevrolet: Park Forest Revisited," *Journal of Business*, vol. 41, pp. 445–59 (1968); A. Koponen, "Personality Characteristics of Purchasers," *Journal of Advertising Research*, vol. 1, pp. 6–12 (1960); W.F. Massy, Ronald Frank, and T. Lodahl, *Personal Behavior and Personal Attributes* (Philadelphia: University of Pennsylvania Press, 1968); "Are There Consumer Types?" (New York: Advertising Research Foundation, 1964).

marketing firm, which, of necessity, must generally work with relatively large segments.

It seems that the evidence to date falls short of these criteria, and personality has not been demonstrated convincingly as a useful means of market segmentation. There is no reason to assume, for example, that individuals with a given personality profile are homogeneous in other respects; nor does it seem reasonable to expect that they have enough in common to be reached easily through the mass media without attracting a large number of nonprospects.

Therefore, it appears that future research that attempts to predict buyer behavior or identify market segments based on personality dimensions is destined to a low practical payout. There are, however, some significant applications of personality theory where the outlook is much brighter. These applications are described below.

Many theorists now believe that personality and the environment interact to shape behavior, as pointed out previously. An extension of this view leads to the prediction that a set of personality characteristics may be a better predictor of behavior in one situation than in another. In other words, it may be useful to distinguish situations in advance in which sample subgroups are differentially affected by specific personality traits. If these differentials are operative, then these personality traits are said to "moderate" the situation.[47] The resulting predictions from the use of personality inventories should then be more accurate.

Personality as a moderator variable

Brody and Cunningham proposed a theoretical framework to predict the situational importance of consumer decision variables. In this conceptualization, the situational importance of any decision variable depends upon the choice situation.[48] Brody and Cunningham postulated that situational variables will moderate the choice situation when performance risk and specific self-confidence are perceived as being high. Thus, in *some* product buying situations and in some kinds of situations, personality will be an intervening variable. In other situations, it will not be. This hypothesis was tested with a reanalysis of Koponen's data on coffee purchases. Sample subgroups were isolated on the pertinent dimensions and regression equations were recomputed. The predictions obtained increased strikingly from virtually no variance accounted for by personality to as much as 32 percent.[49]

Fry cast self-confidence as a moderator variable in cigarette brand

---

47 For a more thorough discussion of the concept of moderator variables, see D.R. Saunders, "Moderator Variables in Prediction," *Educational and Psychological Measurement*, vol. 16, pp. 209–22 (1956); E.E. Ghiselli, "The Prediction of Predictability," *Educational and Psychological Measurement*, vol. 20 (1960), p. 308; E.E. Ghiselli, "Moderating Effects and Differential Reliability and Validity," *Journal of Applied Psychology*, vol. 47, pp. 81–86 (1963).

48 Specifically, situational importance depends on the consumer's perception of the choice situation. The perceptual filters include performance risk, specific self-confidence, and social risk.

49 The greatest amount of explained variance was recorded for persons who were 100 percent brand loyal. Explained variance decreased directly with brand loyalty.

choice. He hypothesized greater explanation of cigarette brand choice among the subset of buyers high in self-confidence. Regression equations for a combination of socioeconomic and personality variables explained between 20 percent and 30 percent of the purchase variance.[50] This increase in predictive ability is equivalent to the Brody and Cunningham result.

Both of these studies demonstrate empirical advantages in utilizing personality as a moderator variable. This usage, however, raises three pertinent issues. First, the selection procedure for useful moderator variables is not intuitively clear. Several authors have noted this problem[51] and Brody and Cunningham readily admit the deficiency of their model in this area. Second, only a fraction of explained variance is accounted for in either study. Fry indicates refinements in measurement procedures are needed. Finally, research is still needed to determine situations in which personality variables are, or are not, relevant moderators. Solutions to these questions present formidable methodological problems.

The use of personality as a moderator variable shows promise as a means of explaining conflicting results. It is, however, an area that needs considerably more experimentation before a definitive assessment can be made.

Personality as an intervening variable

Personality may be useful if the market is first segmented on some objective variable other than personality. Then each isolated subgroup is studied to determine any differences in psychological attributes. Any number of variables could be used for the initial market segmentation, including age, income, degree of product use, or others depending upon the nature of the problem. One approach that has proved useful is to differentiate buyers by the extent to which they use both the product and the brand. Then the inquiry focuses on why one person uses the brand while others do not.

One manufacturer followed this procedure, and it is useful to discuss briefly conclusions that resulted.[52] The Flavorfest Company (the company is real, but the name is fictitious) manufactures and distributes a well-known bottled condiment product. The firm has long dominated the market for this product line, which includes other spices and seasoning items.

Flavorfest could base a marketing program on the assumption that all potential customers are equally valuable prospects, but such an assumption must be verified by research to be successful. It is more likely that

50 J.N. Fry, "Personality Variables and Cigarette Brand Choice," *Journal of Marketing Research*, vol. 8, pp. 298–304 (August 1971). Self-confidence was selected as a moderator variable because of its presumed influence on more specific personality dimensions. Fry readily admits the arbitrariness of this choice.

51 R.P. Brody and S.M. Cunningham, "Personality Variables and the Consumer Decision Process," *Journal of Marketing Research*, vol. 5, pp. 50–57 (February 1968); Fry, "Personality Variables."

52 James F. Engel, Hugh G. Wales, and Martin R. Warshaw, *Promotional Strategy* (Homewood, Ill.: Irwin, 1971), pp. 160–62.

substantial consumer differences exist. Subsequent research disclosed three distinct market segments, each of which offered very different prospects for marketing success. These research findings were as follows:

Heavy users (39 percent of the market)

1. Demographic attitudes. Housewives aged 20–45; well educated; higher income categories; small families with most children under five; concentration in Northeast and Midwest regions and in suburban and farm areas.

2. Motivational attributes.

   a. Strong motivation not to be old-fashioned and a desire to express individuality through creative action and use of exciting new things.

   b. The traditional role as a housewife is viewed with displeasure, and experimentation with new foods is done to express her individuality, not to please her family.

   c. The image of Flavorfest suggests exciting and exotic taste, and the product is reacted to favorably in terms of taste, appearance, and food value. It is highly prized in experimental cooking. Hence, there is substantial compatibility between values of the user and product image.

Light to Moderate Users (20 percent of the market)

1. Demographic attributes. Housewives aged 35–54; large families with children under 12; middle-income groups; location mostly in Southeast, Pacific states, and Southwest.

2. Motivational attributes.

   a. A strong desire to express individuality through creative cookery, but this desire is constrained somewhat by a conflicting desire to maintain tradition and subvert herself to her family's desires.

   b. The desire to experiment with new foods is also constrained by a lack of confidence in the results of her experimental cooking.

   c. The image of Flavorfest is favorable. The product is liked in all respects, but it is confined largely to use with one type of food. It is viewed as unacceptable in other uses. Hence, her vision is limited regarding new uses for Flavorfest.

Nonusers (41 percent of the market)

1. Demographic attributes. Older housewives; large families; lower

income brackets; location mostly in the Eastern states and some parts of the South.

2. Motivational attributes.

    a. A strong motive to maintain tradition and emotional ties with the past; identification with her mother and her role in the home.

    b. A conservative nonventuresome personality.

    c. Her role as a mother and housewife discourages experimental cookery, and Flavorfest is thus looked upon unfavorably. The image of Flavorfest connotes exotic flavors and a degree of modernity that is unacceptable.

    d. No interest is expressed in new uses and experimentation with Flavorfest, for the product does not represent the values embraced by these housewives.[53]

From this research it is clear that there are important demographic differences between users and nonusers. Therefore, it is possible through skillful use of advertising media to avoid certain segments if this is deemed desirable. Specially designed questions also isolated some important personality differences.

The heavy-user segment is relatively large, and the product is well regarded by these housewives. Because of the product's use in experimental cookery and its role in expressing individuality, the potential exists for stimulating greater use.

The nonuser segment, on the other hand, presents a different marketing situation. While this segment now tends to be large, it is made up largely of people with relatively little purchasing power living in areas where population growth is stagnant. In addition, the potential for stimulating use of Flavorfest is not at all favorable. The existence of strong negative values increases the probability of selective perception of persuasive messages, and there would seem to be little market opportunity.

The light-to-moderate-user segment represents the greatest opportunity for increased sales. The desire for creative cookery is present but is constrained by a desire to maintain tradition and by a lack of confidence in results of experimental efforts. Yet the product is liked in nearly all respects. Lack of confidence, for example, might be minimized by stressing "nonfail" recipes. The interest in pleasing the family can be shown as compatible with creative cookery by stressing favorable family reaction to new tastes and recipes. Finally, Flavorfest can be featured as an ideal accompaniment to a variety of foods.

As an intervening variable, personality is more properly categorized as it should be—a variable that accounts for individual differences within broader categories of economic and social influence. As such, it may be a significant variable in a total model of consumer behavior in some buying

53 Engel et al., *Promotional Strategy.*

situations and consequently should be measured and studied in more detail in consumer research.[54]

Measurement of life styles

This final section of the chapter deals with some of the practical issues of measuring life styles. It is one of the simpler methodologies in consumer research and should readily be understood by examining an example from several perspectives.

Large surveys

The measurement of life styles, or psychographics, generally involves surveys of fairly large size. The surveys frequently have been administered by mail, often to families who have agreed to return questionnaires as part of nationwide panels operated by firms such as Market Facts in Chicago or National Family Opinion in Toledo. Typically, such surveys involve 1,000 or more respondents in order to provide ample cell sizes for analysis by specific classifications such as age, geographic region, and so forth. In the Profile V study discussed earlier in this chapter, questionnaires were sent to 10,000 families.

Self-administered questionnaires (usually by mail) are often preferred because of the time required to fill out surveys which may have 200 to 300 or more AIO questions. It is possible to give smaller questionnaires in person or to hand them to consumers stopped in shopping centers (known as "intercept" studies) by interviewers asking that the AIO questions be mailed later. It is possible to administer AIO questions by telephone although the number of questions must be reasonably small and care must be taken to write short, clear questionnaire items.[55]

Likert items

The most frequently used type of questionnaire items are known as "Likert scales" named after the researcher who popularized the method of response in which individuals indicate whether they strongly agree, agree, are neutral, disagree, or strongly disagree. Numerous variations are possible, sometimes resulting in seven, nine, or some other number of response categories to the AIO questions.

The content of typical AIO studies is shown in Figure 7.8, compiled by Plummer. In addition to activities, interests, and opinions, Plummer included demographics as a separate category. In such studies, other measures than Likert scales would be used, conforming to standard practice in marketing research. Some researchers include media as a separate category, rather than include it under interests as Plummer does.

An example of the specific format for questions and categories of response is shown in Figure 7.9. This example includes mostly specific

54 Much of this section is adapted from James F. Engel, David T. Kollat, and Roger D. Blackwell, "Personality Measures and Market Segmentation," *Business Horizons* (June 1969), pp. 61–70. For additional materials from relevant marketing literature on this topic, see John Walton, *Personality Research and Consumer Decisions*, unpublished A.M. thesis (Columbus, Ohio: Ohio State University, 1972).

55 An example of a telephone administered AIO study is found in Blackwell and Talarzyk, *Consumer Attitudes*.

Figure 7.8 Life style dimensions

Activities	Interests	Opinions	Demographics
Work	Family	Themselves	Age
Hobbies	Home	Social issues	Education
Social events	Job	Politics	Income
Vacation	Community	Business	Occupation
Entertainment	Recreation	Economics	Family size
Club membership	Fashion	Education	Dwelling
Community	Food	Products	Geography
Shopping	Media	Future	City size
Sports	Achievements	Culture	Stage in life cycle

Source: Joseph T. Plummer, "The Concept and Application of Life Style Segmentation," *Journal of Marketing*, vol. 38 (January 1974), p. 34. Reprinted from the *Journal of Marketing* published by the American Marketing Association.

AIO statements relating to leisure and related activities although a few general statements are presented in the lower portion of the figure.

Methods of analysis The simplest and often the most actionable form of analysis of AIO measures is simple cross-classification techniques. By that, it is meant that responses to a question are tabulated by a particular classification such as age, income or some other variable—including other AIO questions.

Notice that the responses in Figure 7.9 were classified by sex. Some questions have very different responses by sex, such as "I like to go and watch sporting events." Other questions, such as "Our family travels together quite a bit" have almost identical responses for males as for females. This particular cross-tabulation illustrates a very important problem in relating AIOs (or any type of consumer research) to behavior. The *behavior* may be determined by the entire family or influenced heavily by one member but the responses of a specific spouse—who may or may not be the decision maker—are the measures of life styles. Similarly, measures may be obtained about television or radio preferences, but these may be unrelated to actual viewing if other members of the family dominate the media decisions.

Multivariate techniques. Most AIO studies also use some multivariate techniques of analysis in addition to cross-classification. Typically, factor analysis is used to reduce a great amount of data into its more basic structure. Factor analysis is a mathematical procedure for analyzing the high amount of correlation almost always existent in items into its most basic components or "factors."[56] An example of the output of such analysis is presented in Figure 7.10. This consolidation into eight male groups is based upon about 300 psychographic questions completed in a

56 A good introduction to factor analysis and other multivariate techniques is available in David A. Aaker, *Multivariate Analysis in Marketing: Theory & Application* (Belmont, Calif: Wadsworth, 1971).

Figure 7.9 An example of AIO questions, classified by sex

Activity statements	Females (N = 594)					Males (N = 490)				
	SA	A	N/O	D	CD	SA	A	N/O	D	CD
Vacation related										
Our family travels together quite a lot	38%	30%	7%	16%	9%	37%	33%	7%	15%	8%
A cabin by a quiet lake is a great place to spend the summer	44	28	10	11	7	45	30	9	11	5
On a vacation, I just want to rest and relax	31	30	7	23	9	34	30	4	21	11
I like to spend my vacations in or near a big city	6	13	12	30	39	4	10	11	28	47
On my vacations, I like to get away from mechanization and automation	23	33	16	19	9	28	37	14	16	5
Vacations should be planned for children	17	39	16	20	8	18	38	19	18	7
Entertainment related										
Television is our primary source of entertainment	26%	26%	6%	23%	19%	24%	31%	6%	19%	20%
I would rather spend a quiet evening at home than go out to a party	24	30	8	25	13	30	31	8	23	8
We do not often go out to dinner or the theater together	20	22	8	19	31	15	25	6	22	32
Sporting related										
The best sports are very competitive	13%	21%	31%	21%	14%	28%	28%	20%	15%	9%
I prefer to participate in individual sports more than team sports	11	18	39	18	14	16	29	25	17	13
Whenever possible, I prefer to participate in sporting activities, rather than just watch them	15	27	15	19	24	25	29	12	18	16
I like to go and watch sporting events	18	40	13	15	14	34	37	10	12	7
Leisure time related										
I have enough leisure time	14%	23%	8%	28%	27%	13%	14%	8%	31%	34%
I tend to spend most of my leisure time indoors	16	35	6	29	14	7	22	7	32	32
Basically, I'm satisfied with my present leisure time activities	21	45	7	20	7	25	39	7	22	7
My leisure time tends to be boring	4	14	8	26	48	4	12	8	27	49
Specific activity related										
I do a lot of repair work on my car	1%	4%	23%	7%	65%	24%	24%	5%	16%	31%
I often work on a do-it-yourself project in my home	37	34	15	7	7	36	31	13	11	9
I am active in one or more service organizations	12	11	19	17	41	8	10	23	18	41
General statements										
When it comes to my recreation, time is a more important factor to me than money	23%	29%	17%	21%	10%	25%	30%	15%	19%	11%
When it comes to my recreation, money is a more important factor to me than time	9	19	16	34	22	10	20	18	34	18
I watch television more than I should	21	28	7	23	21	20	29	9	24	18
My major hobby is my family	49	30	9	9	3	35	32	14	14	5

Note: SA = Strongly agree; N/O = Undecided or no opinion; D = Disagree somewhat; CD = Completely disagree.
Source: Douglass K. Hawes, W. Wayne Talarzyk, and Roger D. Blackwell, "Consumer Satisfactions from Leisure Time Pursuits," in M. J. Schlinger, ed., *Advances in Consumer Research* (Chicago: American Marketing Association, 1975), p. 833. Reprinted by permission.

Figure 7.10 Eight male psychographic segments

Group I. *"The quiet family man"* (8% of total males)

He is a self-sufficient man who wants to be left alone and is basically shy. Tries to be as little involved with community life as possible. His life revolves around the family, simple work, and television viewing. Has a marked fantasy life. As a shopper he is practical, less drawn to consumer goods and pleasures than other men.

Low education and low economic status, he tends to be older than average.

Group II. *"The traditionalist"* (16% of total males).

A man who feels secure, has self-esteem, follows conventional rules. He is proper and respectable, regards himself as altruistic and interested in the welfare of others. As a shopper he is conservative, likes popular brands and well-known manufacturers.

Low education and low or middle socioeconomic status; the oldest age group.

Group III. *"The discontented man"* (13% of total males)

He is a man who is likely to be dissatisfied with his work. He feels bypassed by life, dreams of better jobs, more money and more security. He tends to be distrustful and socially aloof. As a buyer, he is quite price conscious.

Lowest education and lowest socioeconomic group, mostly older than average.

Group IV. *"The ethical highbrow"* (14% of total males)

This is a very concerned man, sensitive to people's needs. Basically a puritan, content with family life, friends, and work. Interested in culture, religion, and social reform. As a consumer he is interested in quality, which may at times justify greater expenditure.

Well educated, middle or upper socioeconomic status, mainly middle aged or older.

Group V. *"The pleasure oriented man"* (9% of total males)

He tends to emphasize his masculinity and rejects whatever appears to be soft or feminine. He views himself a leader among men. Self-centered, dislikes his work or job. Seeks immediate gratification for his needs. He is an impulsive buyer, likely to buy products with a masculine image.

Low education, lower socioeconomic class, middle aged or younger.

Group VI. *"The achiever"* (11% of total males)

This is likely to be a hardworking man, dedicated to success and all that it implies, social prestige, power, and money. Is in favor of diversity, is adventurous about leisure time pursuits. Is stylish, likes good food, music, etc. As a consumer he is status conscious, a thoughtful and discriminating buyer.

Good education, high socioeconomic status, young.

Group VII. *"The he-man"* (19% of total males)

He is gregarious, likes action, seeks an exciting and dramatic life. Thinks of himself as capable and dominant. Tends to be more of a bachelor than a family man, even after marriage. Products he buys and brands preferred are likely to have "self-expressive value," especially a "man of action" dimension.

Well educated, mainly middle socioeconomic status, the youngest of the male groups.

Group VIII. *"The sophisticated man"* (10% of total males)

He is likely to be an intellectual, concerned about social issues, admires men with artistic and intellectual achievements. Socially cosmopolitan, broad interests. Wants to be dominant, and a leader. As a consumer he is attracted to the unique and fashionable.

Best educated and highest economic status of all groups, younger than average.

Source: William D. Wells, "Psychographics: A Critical Review," *Journal of Marketing Research*, vol. 12 (May 1975), pp. 196–213. Reprinted from the *Journal of Marketing Research* published by the American Marketing Association.

national sample of 4,000 respondents.[57] This tremendous quantity of data must be reduced into a concise form to be useful to managers, and techniques such as factor analysis are useful in such situations. Other sophisticated techniques are available to increase the predictability and usefulness of psychographics as a segmentation tool.[58]

The most frequent and perhaps useful application of life style measurement currently is for market segmentation strategies. This application is based upon the premise that the more you know and understand about customers, the more effectively a communications and marketing program can be developed to reach that market target. Plummer analyzes the value of market segmentation and concludes that it provides a new view of the market, assists in product positioning, leads to more effective communication, helps develop total marketing and media strategies, suggests new product opportunities and, overall, helps explain the "why" of a product or brand situation.[59]

Market segmentation

Overall, life style research is most appropriate for products whose function includes psychological gratification, or whose performance cannot be evaluated objectively, products with high involvement, or those that are designed for a minority market segment, are relatively expensive, or symbolic.[60] Life style research is particularly helpful where advertising is a major tool in the product's marketing mix, where consumers are willing to switch brands when they are not completely satisfied, and where the category is not dominated by one or two brands. It is not so appropriate for commodities, for products that are purchased on the basis of price primarily, or which have low involvement on the part of the consumers.

For appropriate products and market segments, the most productive use of marketing programming based upon life style research is probably in determining the style of communications, in developing new products, positioning them, or developing new packaging.[61]

A concluding perspective

This concludes Chapter 7 and it also concludes the first major part of this text. This chapter on lifestyles, in a sense, serves the purpose of "summarizing" much of the material in Part 2 because all of the influences from the economic, cultural, family, and reference group are manifested in consumer life styles—which in turn, are measured through the technique of psychographics or AIO measures. All of these external or environmental variables become internalized through time to

---

57 Newspaper Advertising Bureau study quoted in Wells (1975), *op. cit.*

58 William R. Darden and William D. Perreault, Jr., "A Multivariate Analysis of Media Exposure and Vacation Behavior with Life Style Covariates," *Journal of Consumer Research*, vol. 2 (September 1975), pp. 93–103.

59 Plummer, "Concept and Application."

60 Rudolph W. Struse, "Lifestyle Research Inappropriate for Some Categories of Products," *Marketing News*, vol. 10 (June 17, 1977), p. 9.

61 Ibid.

become a part of the decision-making influences within an individual. The sum of all of these and other influences is often described or thought of as personality. Traditionally, personality has been considered as an "internal" variable while influences such as family have been considered "external" variables. Yet, it can easily be concluded that all of the external variables cumulate and become a part of the life ways or patterns of an individual. In a sense, the term "personality" reflects an individual's characteristic ways of behaving or responding to these varied external and internal influences.

The discussion of personality in this chapter also provides a "bridge" to the rest of the book, for now we are ready to leave our analysis of environmental influences in Part 2, which, even though they are internalized within an individual, are basically external in measurement and analysis procedures. Now, we will turn our attention directly on the individual and will not return to these types of external topics until Parts 6 and 7 of the book. This part of the text in Part 2, however, is of critical importance in understanding the consumer because it focuses on the fact that *consumers purchase within the context of a life setting learned through socialization and interaction with others.*

Summary

Life styles are the patterns in which people live and spend time and money. Life styles are the result of the total array of economic, cultural, and social life forces that contribute to a person's human qualities. Most directly, life style is a derivative of the social values a person internalizes and an individual's personality.

The concept of life style is built upon the social-psychological theory that people develop constructs with which to interpret, predict, and control their environment. These constructs or patterns result in behavior patterns and attitude structure maintained to minimize incompatibilities and inconsistencies in a person's life—thus, it is possible to measure patterns among groups of people called life styles. Psychographics or AIO measures are the operational form of life styles, which marketing researchers measure. AIO stands for activities, interests, and opinions, and may be either general or product-specific.

The fundamental forces creating life styles include the *cultural transfusive triad* and *early lifetime experiences*. The former refers to the influence of institutional influences such as the family, religion, and schools while the latter refers to basic intergenerational influences such as depressions, wars, and other major events.

Personality is linked to the concept of consistent responses to environmental stimuli and explains the differences in life style that may be observed in individuals. Three theories of personality affecting consumer research include psychoanalytic, social-psychological, and trait-factor theories. Of these, trait-factor is most frequently used in marketing research, and it appears most useful as an intervening variable rather than a direct predictor of product or brand choice.

In this chapter, lifestyles are analyzed from the perspective of: the society as a whole, groups of people within the society (segments), and individuals. Understanding the market through the analysis of life styles has many applications to the development of product and communication strategies and the development of an integrated marketing strategy and program.

Review and discussion questions

1. Clearly distinguish among the following terms: life styles, values, psychographics, AIO measures, benefits, personality.

2. Why do people have "life styles"? Why are consistent patterns observable in a society, within groups of people, and between individuals?

3. Explain the difference between a general life style measure and a specific life style measure. Give two examples of each for a research project involving a soft drink.

4. Select from the topics of family, religious institutions, or schools and prepare a report documenting the changes that are occurring in these institutions.

5. Describe ways in which advertising directed to consumers raised during the Depression era might differ compared to that directed at consumers of the post –World War II era.

6. In what way is the rise of urbanism related to the changing values described in this chapter?

7. Assume that you are a marketing official for a large furniture manufacturer. Prepare a marketing program that would be successful in reaching consumers who might be young trendsetters. How should the manufacturer integrate retailers into this marketing program?

8. Describe the trait-factor theory of personality and assess its importance in past and future marketing research.

9. Assume that the marketing research director of a large consumer package goods firm is investigating the potential of personality variables as a basis for segmentation strategies. The director is familiar with several standardized psychological tests of personality but has been advised that tailor-made inventories might also be helpful. Citing the research in this chapter and other studies you may find in the literature, which approach would seem to have the highest probability of being useful?

10. Assume that you have recently been employed by a large department store and have been asked to prepare an analysis of the market for furniture in your city. The president of the store is interested in doing a psychographic study and has asked you to prepare a questionnaire that could be used in this city. Prepare a preliminary form of this questionnaire. Be sure to indicate the specific content of the questionnaire, some sample questions, the method of data collection, and methods of analysis.

PART 3

PROBLEM RECOGNITION & SEARCH

Part 3 considers the first two stages of the process consumers follow when making purchase decisions—problem recognition and search for information.

Chapter 8 is concerned with the first stage in the process. This is the point at which consumers recognize that some decision is necessary. The nature and determinants of problem recognition are discussed, followed by an analysis of procedures and techniques used for measurement and appraisal. The chapter also centers on the dilemma faced by marketers in triggering problem recognition.

After a problem is recognized, the consumer may or may not engage in an external search for information in order to learn about and to evaluate the characteristics and attributes of the alternatives available as potential solutions to the problem that has been recognized. Chapter 9 centers on the nature of this search process, with particular emphasis on those conditions and factors that are likely to precipitate search. Chapters 10 and 11 then describe the available information sources. The marketer-dominated influences (advertising, personal selling, and point-of-sale influence) are the subject of Chapter 10. Chapter 11 analyzes the nature and marketing impact of interpersonal communications (i.e., nonmarketer-dominated sources), the characteristics of opinion leaders and methods of identifying them, and alternative models of interpersonal communication and personal influence.

Chapter 12, on the diffusion of innovations, serves as a relevant integration of much that has been said in the preceding chapters. It reviews in depth the manner in which new products and other forms of innovations become accepted and adopted in a social setting. There is a vast literature on this subject, and the marketing implications abound.

CHAPTER 8

Problem recognition

The first stage in decision-process behavior is problem recognition—*a perceived difference between the ideal state of affairs and the actual situation sufficient to arouse and activate the decision process.* When problem recognition occurs, the human system is energized and goal-oriented behavior ensues. Seemingly unrelated activities now become organized to satisfy this state of arousal, and the individual becomes distinctly more sensitive to relevant information from the environment. In short, the system is "turned on" and triggered to engage in purposeful activity.

Figure 8.1 Determinants of problem recognition

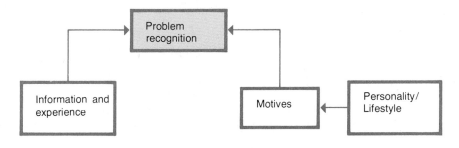

The abbreviated model of the consumer decision process in Figure 8.1 depicts two principal determinants of problem recognition: (1) motives and (2) information and experience. Motives are enduring predispositions to strive to attain specified goals and, hence, determine, to a large degree, the "ideal" for an individual at any point in time. New information, on the other hand, often serves to reveal the extent to which the present circumstance deviates from the ideal. Once this perceived deviation reaches a certain point, the individual then is aroused to restore the disturbed balance.

This chapter begins with an analysis of the nature of problem-recognition processes. The discussion then shifts to the determinants of the ideal state. Motives are the principal determinant and insights are gained through reference to theories of motivation and learning. Then the determinants of perceived inadequacy of the actual state are discussed. While there is emphasis on the marketing implications throughout, the chapter concludes with an expanded consideration of the problems of measurement and strategy.

The nature of problem-recognition processes

Problem recognition results when the consumer recognizes a difference of sufficient magnitude between what is perceived as the desired state of affairs and what is perceived as the actual state of affairs.

The desired state

In a given situation, the desired state may be shaped by many variables. By definition, one or more motives underlie this state, and motive must be considered as the primary influence. But other factors enter as well. Since the consumer usually has several alternative ways of satisfying motives, other personality characteristics, attitudes, values, and evaluative criteria may affect the desired state. Internalized social influence may have a similar effect. Finally, exposure to such marketing efforts as advertising, displays, and salesmen may have an effect, but this usually is relatively small, as later sections will indicate.

The actual state

The actual state may be perceived as inadequate and thereby trigger problem recognition. Marketing efforts certainly can lead to this outcome as can the influences of friends, relatives, and family members. There are a number of other causes as well, such as depletion, wear out, and so on.

Examples of problem-recognition processes

The way in which problem recognition can function as well as variations in the process hopefully will become more clear from the following three examples.

Case 1: Simple problem-recognition processes. Many, and perhaps even the majority, of the problems that consumers perceive result from the depletion of the product being used to satisfy the problem. Assume, for example, a housewife is in the process of preparing dinner and discovers that she is out of coffee. In her family, coffee is always served with dinner. In this case having coffee is the desired state, and out of coffee is the actual state; thus a problem is perceived. Although perhaps not arising in the same way, this general type of situation has occurred many times in the past, with the result that problem recognition is a rather simple and strongly learned type of process.

Case 2: More complicated problem-recognition processes. Assume that a housewife has been purchasing brand X coffee for several months and is completely satisfied with it. She sees a commercial for brand Z coffee but does not think much about it and continues to purchase brand X. She continues to see commercials for brand Z, and a few months later she has brand Z while visiting a friend. She thoroughly enjoys it. On her next trip she notices that brand Z coffee is several cents cheaper than brand X. All of these events may have changed because of the advertisements, the consumer noticing that her friend uses brand Z, her enjoyment of brand Z, and/or the price of brand Z. In this situation, problem recognition is a more complex process than in Case 1.

Case 3: Highly complex problem-recognition processes. Assume that several years ago a consumer purchased a 12-inch black and white television set. The set has worked well and the consumer is satisfied with it. He has seen advertisements for color television but feels that the quality of reception is poor and the price is excessive. One evening he watches one of his favorite programs on a friend's new 25-inch color set. He is amazed at the quality of the picture and enjoys the program. This feeling is intensified considerably during subsequent evenings when he watches television on his small black and white set. During the next few months he spends several evenings watching color television at his friend's house. He also pays closer attention to advertisements for color television and occasionally stops at various retail outlets to watch color television and sometimes asks salesmen about prices and financing arrangements.

Finally he comments to his wife about the possibility of buying a color set. She reacts negatively, pointing out that a color set costs far too much and that she would much rather use the money for a vacation or to redecorate the den, to say nothing of the new washer and dryer that she needs.

A few weeks later the old black and white set breaks down, and it is estimated that it will cost $75 to repair it. Both husband and wife are upset, and the husband points out that after spending $75 to have it fixed they will still have the same old set; so why not go ahead and buy the color set. The wife still wants to use the money for other purposes, so nothing is done. Several weeks pass, and both husband and wife become increasingly irritable because they cannot watch their favorite programs.

At work the next day the husband learns that he has received a $50-a-month raise. During dinner he informs his wife of the raise and again brings up the color set. She agrees that something needs to be done but still thinks that the color set costs too much money. After nearly a two-hour discussion they agree to buy a smaller color television in an inexpensive cabinet and a new washer and dryer.

In this hypothetical although not unrealistic situation, it is obvious that problem recognition is a far more complex process than in cases 1 and 2. Problem recognition has occurred over a considerable period of time as the result of the interaction of many factors, including perhaps advertisements, seeing color television at a friend's house, the breakdown of the old set and the cost of repairing it, the raise, and the discomfort of not having a set. The situation is further complicated because the spouses have different, and somewhat conflicting, attitudes and motive hierarchies.

Unique aspects of problem-recognition processes

The nature of problem recognition and the examples just cited indicate that these processes differ in many respects from the concepts discussed elsewhere in this text. An explicit discussion of the unique aspects of problem recognition is necessary for a clear understanding of the nature of the process.

First, it is apparent that problem-recognition processes may simultaneously involve many variables, including perception, learning, attitudes, personality characteristics, and various reference-group influences. The number of concepts involved varies considerably from situation to situation, as illustrated by the increasing complexity of the three examples presented above. In this sense, problem recognition may be a more comprehensive process than many concepts discussed previously.

It is also obvious that problem recognition is a more complex process than motivation. Although problem recognition involves motives, it may also involve attitudes, values, and other influences, as illustrated by cases 2 and 3. Problem recognition is, therefore, not just another name for motivation; it embraces many other concepts and processes.

Third, problem recognition may involve complex comparisons and weighting of such things as the relative importance of various needs, attitudes about how limited financial resources should be allocated to alternative uses, and attitudes about the qualitative level at which needs should be satisfied. Moreover, these need hierarchies and attitudes may differ from one family member to another, so that conflict resolution processes may be necessary before problem recognition occurs. Case 3 illustrates this aspect of problem recognition.

Finally, as used here, problem recognition differs from the concepts of awareness and interest that are used in many studies of consumer behavior, particularly the diffusion of innovations.[1] Problem recognition involves an awareness of a difference between an actual and a desired state. The consumer may or may not be aware of products and brands, and an awareness of, or exposure to, products and/or brands may or may not precipitate problem recognition. Thus, "awareness" is a much more general term than "problem recognition" and, as such, bears no necessary relation to this phenomenon. Similarly, the concept of interest does not have any necessary relation to problem recognition. Problem recognition

---

1 For a discussion of much of the literature in which awareness and interest are used, see Everett M. Rogers, *Diffusion of Innovations* (New York: Free Press, 1962); Everett M. Rogers, *Bibliography on the Diffusion of Innovations,* Diffusion of Innovations Research Report No. 4 (East Lansing, Mich.: Department of Communications, Michigan State University, July 1966).

can occur without any interest on the part of the consumer in a product or brand. Or the consumer can be interested in a product or brand without recognizing a problem (a new car or home being among the more common examples).

The ideal state

Perceptions of the ideal state can change, of course, for many reasons as was noted above, but there are five determinants that warrant special discussion: (1) the influence of other decisions; (2) reference group influence; (3) novelty; (4) marketing efforts; and (5) motive activation. Of these, motive activation is most important, but it is discussed last because of the need for a more lengthy consideration.

The influence of other decisions

Problem recognition, chiefly through changed perception of the desired state, is often the outgrowth of other purchase decisions. For example, a new residence or remodeling tends to affect perceptions of the desirability of carpeting and various pieces of furniture, even though present options are not worn out.[2] In fact, there is growing evidence that one purchase follows from another, thus resulting in a distinct pattern of product acquisition. Using factor analysis, Wells, Banks, and Tigert showed that homemakers who are heavy purchasers of ready-to-eat cereal also purchase peanut butter, laundry detergent, toothpaste, shampoo, gelatin desserts, adhesive bandages, and certain other products in large quantities.[3]

In the case of durable goods, consumers tend to arrange purchases according to acquisition priorities.[4] Here again it is possible to predict a future action if one has information on present purchases and established purchase intentions.[5]

Reference group influence

It was stressed clearly in Chapter 6 that important reference groups, especially those that perform a normative function, can be a powerful determinant of the ideal state. In fact, their normative expectations can set a rigid standard that makes deviation difficult unless a degree of social rejection can be tolerated.[6] Many college freshmen quickly learn, for instance, that there is a vast difference between the types of clothing suitable on the high school campus and those acceptable at college.

Novelty

Novelty or the desire for change is a frequently overlooked factor in

2 Donald H. Granbois, "A Study of the Family Decision Making Process in the Purchase of Major Durable Household Goods," unpublished doctoral diss., Indiana University Graduate School of Business, 1962, p. 84.

3 William D. Wells, Seymour Banks, and Douglas Tigert, "Order in the Data," in Reed Moyer, ed., *Changing Marketing Systems* (Chicago: American Marketing Association, 1962), pp. 263–66.

4 See J. Paroush, "The Order of Acquisition of Consumer Durables," *Econometrica*, vol. 33, pp. 225–35 (January 1965) and Hugh M. Sargent, *Consumer Product Rating Publications and Buying Behavior* (Urbana, Ill.: Bureau of Business and Economic Research, University of Illinois, 1959).

5 John McFall, "Priority Patterns and Consumer Behavior," *Journal of Marketing*, vol. 33, pp. 50–55 (October 1969).

6 Granbois, "Study of the Family," p. 84.

problem recognition.[7] In one study, for example, about one-third of those who switched to a new brand did so simply because they wanted a change, even though they were satisfied with the present alternative.[8] Another researcher discovered that 15 percent of those studied bought a new product because it was new.[9] A desire for novelty and change, then, really affects the desired state. Unfortunately it has largely been ignored in consumer research and further inquiry is warranted.

Marketing efforts

Promotion often is designed to appeal to a dominant motive or set of motives. This then reinforces the desired state and triggers problem recognition. Aside from the obvious benefits of financial protection for one's family, one study disclosed an interesting pattern of motivations underlying the purchase of life insurance.[10] First, such a purchase represents an emancipation from childhood and thereby serves as a mark of entry into the adult world. In addition, it is alleged that life insurance presents a symbol of adult love which circumvents selfishness of youth and even extends beyond death. Large amounts of insurance may, in addition, enhance feelings of potency and power in much the same manner as boasting of sexual achievements. Finally, insurance purchased during the years of striving is a positive achievement, a symbol of power and success, so to speak, representing that one's family will be provided for adequately. The advertisement in Figure 8.2 builds upon these motives and also stresses the desire of many contemporary women to take their rightful place in what was once strictly a man's world.

Motive activation

A lifetime of learning and experience obviously will serve to reinforce certain patterns of behavior that are beneficial either in giving pleasure or reducing discomfort and pain. These, in turn, become embedded in one's basic personality (Figure 8.1) as motives—enduring predispositions that direct behavior toward attaining certain generic goals. Motives function both to arouse behavior initially and to direct it toward desired outcomes.

To underscore the significance of motives, it should be stressed that *purposeful behavior is motive-satisfying behavior.* The implication of this basic premise is that motive patterns are not likely to be changed through persuasive activity of any type, especially that undertaken by the commercial marketer. One essential role for marketing research, therefore, is to uncover dominant motives and thereby provide clues for the development of products and sales appeals that will be regarded as motive satisfying by the consumer.

Before proceeding further, it is well to stop and ask the important question of the relevance of *individual* motives to the marketer who must,

7 See M. Venkatesan, "Cognitive Consistency and Novelty Seeking," in Scott Ward and Thomas S. Robertson, eds., *Consumer Behavior: Theoretical Sources* (Englewood Cliffs, N.J.: Prentice-Hall, 1973), pp. 354–84.

8 Elihu Katz and Paul Lazarsfeld, *Personal Influence* (New York: Free Press, 1955).

9 George H. Haines, "A Study of Why People Purchase New Products," in R. M. Haas, ed., *Science, Technology and Marketing* (Chicago: American Marketing Association, 1966), pp. 685–97.

10 Ernest Dichter, *The Strategy of Desire* (New York: Doubleday, 1960), pp. 215–20.

Figure 8.2 An appeal to dominant motives

Find the $25,000 executive without life insurance.

She's the working woman. And she needs life insurance as much as anyone else in the picture.

If you're single, life insurance is a solid, sensible way to get ready for the future. Because The Equitable's whole life insurance plans give guaranteed cash values that you can borrow against. For a house. For retirement. For emergencies.

And if you're married, you also need life insurance to protect your contribution to your family's income and lifestyle.

The Equitable has a booklet for you that talks life insurance. Woman to woman. It's filled with quotes from a recent panel discussion. And it could answer some of your questions about life insurance.

It's free. And it's important you read it.

Because you need life insurance as much as a man.

EQUITABLE

It's time you figured out how much your life is worth.

To: Corporate Relations Department
The Equitable Life Assurance Society
1285 Avenue of the Americas
New York, New York 10019

Please send me a free copy of *Life Insurance...*
"*Women Speak their Minds*."

Name_____

Address_____

City_____State_____Zip_____

The Equitable Life Assurance Society of the United States, New York, N.Y.

Source: Courtesy of the Equitable Life Assurance Society of the United States.

of necessity, deal with *masses* in most situations. Fortunately, it usually is possible to uncover market segments with common strivings and goals. One authority puts it this way:

> Motives are individually acquired but certain situations will produce pleasure or pain with such regularity either through biological or cultural arrangements that the probability of certain common motives developing in all people is very high.[11]

11 David C. McClelland, *Personality* (New York: William Sloane Assoc., 1951), p. 474.

Motive arousal or activation occurs in three primary ways: (1) arousal of drive; (2) autistic thinking; or (3) environmental stimulation.

Arousal of drive. A college student studying for a final examination suddenly says to his roommate, "I'm thirsty; I need to get a drink." He then rises and gets a drink of water. What has happened to activate this sequence of behavior? Clearly he felt discomfort that was recognized as thirst. It has become conventional in learning theory to explain that he felt a *need*, which then activated *drive* (a sense of discomfort or tension).

There is no general agreement on the causes of drive activation. Some postulate that it is generated by an internal disturbance of equilibrium stemming from physiological or even hereditary causes. Whatever the reason, drive leads to a change in the level of activity which then is channeled by motive patterns toward goals that have satisfied the aroused state in the past. It is in this sense that motive has both an arousing and a directing function.

Autistic thinking. The human being possesses the unique capability of thinking about a person or object not present at the immediate time or of imagining the desirable consequences of engaging in some type of activity. This thought process, referred to as autistic thinking, can serve as a source of arousal in and of itself. Most people, for example, have been motivated to eat merely by thinking about a food object, even though no hunger drive was felt prior to that time.

Environmental stimulation. As we saw in the example of the life insurance ad, a motive can be triggered by information coming from the environment. The smell of food can stimulate a desire to eat. In this instance the food smells activate an expectancy that pleasure will be forthcoming, and the result is arousal of drive.

In other instances, the information provides cues about the probability of success if a desired course of action is pursued. This also can activate a motive. Assume that a consumer has a strong motive to succeed in situations in which it is known that behavior will be evaluated by others. In this case the person possesses a strong achievement motive.[12] Assume further that the person is exposed to the ad in Figure 8.3. Notice that success is virtually guaranteed each time a picture is taken using this advanced camera. Excellence in photography can be a real source of pride for some, with the result that the images of success stimulated by this appeal can activate the achievement motive.

Atkinson makes the important point that motives are *stable* because of the fact that they are established in childhood.[13] A motive will not be altered by outside influence, but persuasion from various sources *can* change the perception of success in motive satisfaction in a given

---

12 See David C. McClelland, *The Achieving Society* (Princeton, N. J.: D. Van Nostrand Company, Inc., 1961).
13 Atkinson, p. 435.

Figure 8.3 An appeal to the achievement motivation

The key, of course, was 110 film. Which had gotten to the stage where color slides and enlargements were comparable to 35mm.

Except for its cameras. Some of which were more advanced than others.

But all of which were limited. And most of which were toys. This single lens reflex eliminates the limitations.

It's 5.3 inches wide, 4.3 inches deep.

And only 2.1 inches high.

We've created a 15-ounce single lens reflex camera that can do what you usually do with a big two-pounder.

It weighs just 15.1 ounces.

The lens is a zoom.

Which goes from 25 to 50mm. From normal to 2X telephoto. It's like being able to choose from more than 25 focal lengths.

Except that they're all on the camera, not in a camera bag.

The lens is also a "macro."

Just turn the collar on the zoom and you can focus as close as 11.3 inches from your subject.

Automatic electronic exposure system.

You set the lens and the shutter sets itself automatically.

For anything from time exposures at 10 seconds to a fast 1/1000th.

The shutter is metal (not cloth). And "stepless," so that it gives you the exact shutter speed you need, not a compromise.

You can override the auto-exposure system if you like, for special effects or more control in unusual lighting.

You view and focus through the lens.

What you see is what you get on film. The microprism center spot keeps the image "fractured" until it's razor-sharp. And focusing is always with the lens wide open for maximum brightness.

Light emitting diodes in the finder tell you when not to shoot.

And when to.

One tells you your batteries are O.K.

(If they're not, the finder blacks out.)

Another, that the light's not enough or too much.

Another, if the shutter's on B (bulb) or X (electronic flash) instead of A (automatic).

Some other interesting advances.

The camera has a hot shoe for electronic flash at 1/150th of a second. That means there's less chance you'll get "ghost images" in action shots.

Safeguards: the shutter release locks. The shutter selector dial's locked until you unlock it. All to keep you from taking a picture you don't want to take.

Instant loading, of course. 4 supports hold the drop-in 110 cartridge rigidly for maximum sharpness. And the exposure system sets itself automatically for the right film speed.

The one-pounder vs. the two-pounder.

No contest.

For literature, see your dealer or write Minolta Corporation, 101 Williams Drive, Ramsey, New Jersey 07446.

Minolta 110 Zoom SLR

There's never been a camera like it.

Source: Provided by courtesy of Minolta Corp., Ramsey, N.J.

situation. As a broad generalization, it is safe to conclude that one major role for marketing communication is to show a product or service in the most favorable light in terms of the motive or motives it is designed to satisfy.

Classification of motives. Psychologists and marketing people alike have tried their hand at classification and some lists attain great length. This often is little more than an exercise in ingenuity, however, because 100 people no doubt would produce 100 different lists. When an attempt is made to determine motive patterns on a more analytical basis, this is a different matter. A. H. Maslow brought important clarity to this difficult question.[14] While his thinking is based more on an intuitive than on an empirical foundation, it is worthy of note.

Maslow hypothesizes that motives are organized in such a way as to establish priorities and hierarchies of importance (prepotency). Through this means, internal conflict is avoided by one motive taking precedence over another. The following classification was suggested, proceeding from the lowest order to the highest:

1. Physiological—the fundamentals of survival, including hunger and thirst.

2. Safety—concern over physical survival, ordinary prudence, which might be overlooked in striving to satisfy hunger or thirst.

3. Belongingness and love—striving to be accepted by intimate members of one's family and to be an important person to them. This also can include nonfamily members.

4. Esteem and status—striving to achieve a high standing relative to others, including desires for mastery, reputation, and prestige.

5. Self-actualization—a desire to know, understand, systematize, organize, and construct a system of values.

Three essentially different categories are comprehended in this classification: (1) motives related to survival needs; (2) motives related to human interaction and involvement; and (3) motives related to competency and self. Each higher order of motive will not function until lower levels are satisfied, at least to some degree. The hungry person will care little about understanding nuclear physics. Undoubtedly it is reasonable to assume that some motives in each category are never fully satisfied, thus remaining as a continued source of problem recognition. A strong desire for status, for example, can be virtually insatiable.

The higher-order motives are of particular significance in understanding cross-cultural differences in consumer behavior. They generally will not be activated among the mass of people living in highly underdeveloped countries in which bodily survival is the primary concern. On the other hand, they will tend to predominate in the affluent societies of the Western world in particular. Witness the incidence of striving for individuality through the inventory of consumer goods typical in suburban American homes—stereo sets, hobby activities of all types, a resurgence of interest in art and serious music, and so on. It is interesting also to point out that those who engage in such socially-conscious activities as the consumerism movement or civil rights are motivated to a large degree by self-actualization.[15]

14 A.H. Maslow, *Motivation and Personality* (New York: Harper & Row, 1954).

15 George Brooker, "The Self-Actualizing Socially Conscious Consumer," *Journal of Consumer Research*, vol. 3, pp. 107–12 (September 1976).

Life obviously is more complex at these higher levels; greater individuality is exerted; and, accordingly, it becomes more difficult to isolate the motives underlying a particular buying action. Yet, this knowledge is all the more crucial for the business firm. This is because the exercise of individuality by buyers requires that all components of marketing strategy be precisely on target if sales potentials are to be attained.

It is unlikely that a classification such as Maslow's will prove very useful in explaining the specific motives in a given purchase. But the concept of prepotency (ordered relationships of motive strength) is of conceptual value. It has been verified that prepotency is reflected in consumer buying to the extent that previously ignored desires often exert themselves only after a purchase has satisfied a predominant (and perhaps lower order) motive.[16]

Unity and stability of motive patterns. A major thesis of this book is that the consumer behaves in a consistent and purposeful manner. This implies that motives are integrated into a meaningful whole. As was stressed in Chapter 6, there is widespread agreement in the behavioral sciences that one's entire psychological makeup is organized around the *self-concept*. It is not a governor against which behavior is referred. Rather, it is a means whereby social values and controls become internalized as behavioral standards. Rogers puts it this way:

> The self-concept, or self-structure, may be thought of as an organized configuration of perceptions of the self which are admissible to awareness. It is composed of such elements as the perceptions of one's characteristics and abilities; the percepts and concepts of the self in relation to others and to the environment; the value qualities which are perceived as associated with experiences; and objectives, goals, and ideas which are perceived as having positive or negative valence.[17]

The self becomes a value to be enhanced, with the result that certain goal objects become internalized as permanent incentives. As Maslow indicated, self-actualization, self-esteem, and belongingness and love are all motives keyed to self-maintenance and enhancement.[18]

The self-concept integrates motives into a purposeful pattern that is reflected in purchasing behavior. To take one example, cranberry sauce long has been a staple of the American diet, especially at Thanksgiving, Christmas, and other holidays. The heavy user of this product, however, uses it throughout the year as well. The heavy user was found through marketing research to have a very interesting self-concept and life style. The core of her self concept was found to lie in service to her family, and the same had been true of her mother and grandmother. Not surprisingly, her dominant values are highly traditional, and she adamantly rejects the modern liberation movement. The image of cranberry sauce, in turn, is remarkably consistent with her outlook on life in that it connotes tradition

16 George Katona, *The Powerful Consumer* (New York: McGraw-Hill, 1960), p. 132.
17 Carl R. Rogers, *Client-Centered Therapy* (Boston: Houghton Mifflin Company, 1951), p. 492.
18 Maslow, *Motivation and Personality.*

and engenders happy associations of family life, well being, and the "horn of plenty." Use of the product, then, represents highly self-approved behavior.

Quite an opposite life style was found when the nonuser of cranberry sauce was studied. Her values reflect the now familiar concept of the liberated woman, even though this study was undertaken prior to the onset of the feminist movement. Traditional values, by and large, are rejected, and cranberries are rejected as well because of their old-fashioned image. Here is an example of a contradiction between self-concept and product image that will not be overcome through marketing effort, no matter how skillful. It is interesting to note, however, that this same person proved to be a heavy user of cranberry juice, which reflects quite a different image. Its values in nutrition, dieting, and modern cookery make it compatible with the life style of those in this market segment.

The ad in Figure 8.4 is an interesting appeal to the housewife who no longer is tied to the home. The product offered by Stouffer's facilitates her self expression.

There have been some attempts in the literature on consumer behavior to measure self-concept and relate it to particular aspects of buying behavior.[19] This type of research is not likely to be a part of the arsenal of those who are on the marketing firing line, however, because measurement and analysis of this type lie more in the domain of psychoanalysis. Furthermore, the now standard techniques of psychographic research discussed in Chapter 7 to a large extent reveal those aspects of self-concept that are reflected in purchasing behavior.

In summary, it is a basic principle that nonself-approved behavior is atypical in the market place, even though one writer has argued somewhat unconvincingly to the contrary.[20] Sometimes behavior appears to be irrational simply because it violates the observer's own standards and criteria. Two decades ago, Snygg and Combs stated a philosophy of inquiry that should be assumed by all who claim to be objective analysts of consumer behavior.[21] This was cited in Chapter 1, and it points out that behavior always is purposeful if analyzed from the point of view of the person in question. The problem enters when the analyst looking from the outside cannot fully grasp all of the relevant determinants of the behavior.

The measurement of motives. A number of pervasive motives such as achievement and affiliation have been studied in the literature. It is now

---

19 Much of this literature has been summarized in E. Laird Landon, Jr., "Self Concept, Ideal Self Concept, and Consumer Purchase Intention," *Journal of Consumer Research*, vol. 1, pp. 44–51 (September, 1974). Also see Ira J. Dolich, "Congruence Relationships between Self Images and Product Brands," *Journal of Marketing Research*, vol. 6, pp. 80–84 (1969); E. L. Grubb and G. Hupp, "Perception of Self, Generalized Stereotypes, and Brand Selection," *Journal of Marketing Research*, vol. 5, pp. 58–63 (1968); and E. L. Grubb and B. L. Stern, "Self-Concept and Significant Others," *Journal of Marketing Research*, vol. 8, pp. 382–85 (1971).

20 Edward C. Bursk, "Opportunities for Persuasion," *Harvard Business Review*, vol. 36, pp. 114–15 (September-October, 1958).

21 Donald Snygg and Arthur W. Combs, *Individual Behavior* (New York: Harper & Row, 1949), p. 12.

Figure 8.4 An appeal to the self-concept of the modern housewife

THE JOY OF NOT COOKING.

4:42—Your serve is beautiful today. And you've got the advantage.

When your game is going good, don't rush home. Let Stouffer's do the cooking.

Try Green Pepper Steak with Rice, ready after just 15 minutes in boiling water. Tender steak strips, savory sauce, delicious flavor. Or Salisbury Steak, grilled beef and onions, tasty beef broth gravy.

Or Chicken Stuffed Shells, big pasta shells chockful of chicken, blanketed with cheese sauce.

They're just some of the more than 40 good foods we make. To give you the time to do the things you want. And still put a good meal on the table.

That's the joy of Stouffer's.

© 1976, Stouffer's

STOUFFER'S, ANYTIME.

generally felt, along with McClelland, that the following methodological criteria must be met:

1. The measure should reflect the presence or absence of a motive, as well as variations in its strength. This generally requires an indepen-

dent measure of the motive against which the measure in question can be compared and validated. Needless to say, this can be extraordinarily difficult to attain.

2. The measure should reflect variations only in the motive under analysis, without contamination from other psychological variables. The various tests used often are not pure indicators in this sense and, as a result, contain considerable bias.

3. The measure should give the same reading for an individual at many points in time under approximately the same conditions. If this criterion is met, the measuring instrument can be said to be *reliable*.[22]

One of the most common methods is a self-rating in which the individual verbally gives responses that indicate the presence or absence of a motive. Another method is observer rating. Some of the best results have been obtained with various types of behavioral measures. McClelland, for example, measures achievement motivation through responses in which an individual is asked to "tell a story" about a situation he sees, thus revealing important underlying motivations.

The marketing researcher usually does not make use of these standardized measures, which have been developed largely for purposes of clinical diagnosis of the individual. Rather, motives are assessed most frequently through psychographic research discussed in Chapter 7. Interest in a product or particular type of behavior is isolated at the outset. Then a battery of AIO (activity, interest, and opinion) questions is administered to explore a variety of dimensions of life style. These psychographic measures then are correlated with the behavior under analysis to reveal the underlying motivations.

A leading publishing house, for example, had to discover the motives satisfied through purchase of a Bible if a modern language version of the Bible were to be marketed successfully to the nonchurch-going public.[23] It was discovered that interest in the Bible in general and *The Living Bible* in particular was highest among housewives in the middle income and average education bracket with children still living at home. The psychographic profile revealed a basic conservative outlook toward life characterized by a traditional value profile and high premium placed on the family and child raising. *The Living Bible* thus was presented as an ideal guide for the concerned parent in raising children as they should be in today's world. *The Living Bible* quickly outdistanced its competition and found its way into nearly 40 percent of American homes.

The reader may well inquire at this point about so-called *motivation research*—an approach to consumer analysis much ballyhooed in the 1950s through the popularized writings of Vance Packard and others. Claims were made that researchers had discovered a set of miracle tools

22 David C. McClelland, "Methods of Measuring Human Motivation," in John W. Atkinson, ed., *Motives in Fantasy, Action and Society* (Princeton, N. J.: D. Van Nostrand Company, 1958), pp. 7–42.

23 See Roger D. Blackwell, James F. Engel, and W. Wayne Talarzyk, *Contemporary Cases in Consumer Behavior* (Hinsdale, Ill.: Dryden Press, 1977), pp. 350–59.

that could be used to plumb the depths of the consumer's psyche in some mysterious way so that he or she could be manipulated by the marketer. Actually the term was a real misnomer. The tools used at that time were not especially applicable to the measurement of motives any more than to attitudes, life style, or a host of other influences on consumer behavior.

There were some, however, who designated motivation research as the use of certain techniques pioneered in the psychological clinic, including depth interviewing and projective tests. Depth interviewing is nothing more than nonstandardized questions and probes into reasons underlying behavior. Much can be learned, but the unconscious certainly cannot be penetrated in a one hour consumer interview. This might be possible following months of psychoanalysis, but even this is a debatable point.

The other tool of "motivation research," the projective technique, is based on the accurate assumption that people can easily avoid such direct questions as "why do you shop at Kroger's?" and give an evasive or even deceptive answer. The projective question utilizes some type of indirect format, which elicits a response in such a way that the respondent is not completely aware that the answer given reflects his or her own feelings. There is no proof, however, that this method is superior to the more traditional direct question. Fortunately, the term "motivation" research has generally passed out of common use.

Dissatisfaction with the actual state

Many factors can function to change an individual's perception of the present state of affairs in comparison with the desired state. These influences on problem recognition fall into two categories: (1) changed circumstances and (2) marketing efforts.

Depletion of previous solution. Looking at the total spectrum of consumer behavior, the most common trigger to buying action is depletion of the previous solution. The housewife runs out of laundry detergent, shampoo, milk, and so on. The actual state is now seen to be inadequate, and a purchase decision is required.

Changed circumstances

Dissatisfaction. A problem often is perceived when the present alternative is evaluated as being unsatisfactory. Perhaps the product is broken, run down, worn out, or even seen to be overpriced.[24] Price, for example, is a particularly important factor motivating the purchase of a home or town house in comparison with a continuation of renting.[25]

Altered family circumstances. Problem recognition often occurs as the outcome of changes within the nuclear family. The birth of a child, for

24 Granbois, "Study of the Family," p. 84.
25 Ruby T. Norris, "Processes and Objectives of House Purchasing in the New London Area," in, Lincoln Clark, ed., *The Dynamics of Consumer Reaction* (New York: New York University Press, 1955), pp. 25–29; Peter Rossi, *Why Families Move* (New York: Free Press, 1955); William T. Kelly, "How Buyers Shop for a New Home," *Appraisal*, vol. 25, pp. 209–14 (1957).

instance, results in modified requirements for food, clothing, furniture, and perhaps a house instead of an apartment.[26] New needs and redefinitions of desired states thus occur as the size and age composition of the family change.[27] Even a change in the husband's place of employment can affect the desirability of the present home, thereby evoking problem recognition.[28]

A changed financial status or anticipated change also can have the same effect. Salary increases, tax refunds, temporary or unusual employment, cash gifts, and the retirement of debts all serve to activate a new set of desires.[29] The opposite also can happen, of course. In addition, financial expectations are quite important in the period immediately preceding the purchase of durable goods. A favorable outlook is an incentive for purchase and vice versa.[30]

As an example of the effect of anticipated change in financial status, many students in the senior year of college purchase clothing, cars, or other items before they actually have a job. This may trigger other purchases as well either during the recruiting process or after the job has been accepted. One leading life insurance company maintains a highly developed sales force on campuses primarily to sell insurance to those who are graduating on the anticipation of future earnings.

Marketing efforts

One role of marketing activity is to underscore the inadequacy of the present solution and thereby trigger problem recognition. The obvious strategy is to develop new products or to improve existing products so as to offer features not available from competitors. This is precisely the strategy of the Olivetti Corporation in marketing the "world's only electric portable with interchangeable typing balls" (Figure 8.5).

Marketing efforts and consumer problem recognition

While marketing implications have been stressed at various points throughout the chapter, there is more yet to be said. In particular, it is necessary to discuss (1) the measurement of problem recognition; (2) formulation of general marketing strategy; (3) identification of market targets; and (4) the payoff in attempting to trigger problem recognition.

Measurement of problem recognition

Problem recognition is most commonly measured with various types of purchase intention scales. These usually are relatively global in nature and assess whether or not the person or family intends to make a purchase within a product category. This is in sharp contrast to brand

---

26 Granbois, "Study of the Family," p. 84.

27 See, for example, William D. Wells and George Gubar, "The Life Cycle Concept of Marketing Research," *Journal of Marketing Research*, vol. 3, pp. 355–63 (November, 1966).

28 Norris, "Processes and Objectives," p. 26.

29 Granbois, "Study of the Family," p. 84.

30 Eva Mueller, "The Desire for Innovations in Household Goods," in, Lincoln Clark, ed., *Consumer Behavior: Research on Consumer Reactions* (New York: Harper & Row, 1958), p. 37.

Figure 8.5 Appeal to trigger problem recognition through product improvement

The Big Gift!
Olivetti's Lexikon 82

World's only electric portable with interchangeable typing balls.

Give the world's only electric portable with interchangeable typing balls. Give someone a lasting writing companion. One that lets people change type styles (in seconds) to fit their mood. Formal for business, informal for personal letters.

Choose your color from a rainbow of ribbon cartridges. Fast as you read this sentence, switch your cartridge, change your color. Your fingers never touch the black, red, blue, green or brown ribbons.

Look at its sleek, flawless design. Give somebody this typewriter-of-the-future, beautifully designed by Mario Bellini. And the Lexikon 82's graceful exterior encases a precisely engineered interior for smooth, crisp, trouble-free performance. Complete with its own carrying case, $299 suggested retail.

Free.
This extra typing ball, worth $13, when you buy a Lexikon 82 electric portable. Present this coupon to any participating Olivetti dealer (he's in the Yellow Pages) and receive one extra typing ball. Offer expires Dec. 24, 1976.

olivetti
OLIVETTI CORPORATION OF AMERICA
500 PARK AVE. NEW YORK CITY 10022

Source: Used by permission of Olivetti Corporation of America, New York, New York.

specific buying intentions, which are a variable in the consumer behavior model used in this text.

The accuracy of purchase intention measures of this type depends in part on the length of the forecasting period. As Howard and Sheth pointed out:

> . . . To the extent . . . that the lag is greater between the measure of Intention and the Act of Purchase, greater discrepancies between Intention and Purchase would be expected because the buyer must *anticipate* environmental changes that will occur after the Intention measure and before Purchase. The longer the period of anticipation, the greater we would expect the anticipation to err.[31]

The most commonly used forecasting periods have been 6, 12, and 24 months.[32] Occasionally the period is three months.[33] The choice of a forecasting period is usually a compromise of many considerations, including cost. In making this compromise, it should be remembered that accuracy increases as the length of the forecasting period decreases.

Although it is possible to obtain purchase intentions from conventional surveys, it is preferable to interview the same people more than once over time. This is referred to as *longitudinal analysis.* The reason is that a repeated measure research design provides an accurate indication of whether or not stated intentions actually are fulfilled.

The General Electric Company provides an example of the use of a longitudinal design to measure purchase intentions. General Electric maintains an area probability panel of 5,000 households. Interviews are conducted by an independent agency and are in no way associated with G.E. Panel members are asked many questions about household possessions other than appliances. Interviewing is conducted continuously throughout the year, with a new cohort entering the panel each month. Each panel member is interviewed a minimum of three times at six-month intervals.

During the first interview respondents are asked about their intentions to buy a large number of consumer durables, ranging from automobiles to relatively inexpensive housewares and radios. Respondents are also asked about brand intentions. When reinterviewed they are asked a number of questions that refer directly to their earlier statements of intent.[34]

The Bureau of the Census has probably had the most experience with these types of surveys. Their estimates are based on the quarterly household survey in which housing units are interviewed for six quarters

31 John A. Howard and Jagdish N. Sheth, *The Theory of Buyer Behavior* (New York: Wiley, 1969), p. 133.

32 See, for example, Gertrude S. Weiss, Tynan Smith, and Theodore G. Flechsig, "Quarterly Survey of Consumer Buying Intentions," *Federal Reserve Bulletin*, vol. 46, pp. 977–1003 (September, 1960); James C. Byrnes, "An Experiment in the Measurement of Consumer Intentions to Purchase," in *Proceedings of Statistical Association* (Washington, D.C., 1965), pp. 265–79; Robert Ferber and R. Piskie, "Subjective Probabilities and Buying Intentions," *Review of Economics and Statistics*, vol. 47, pp. 322–25 (August, 1965).

33 C. Joseph Clawson, "How Useful Are 90-Day Purchase Probabilities?" *Journal of Marketing*, vol. 35, pp. 43–47 (October, 1971).

34 For a more detailed description see Robert W. Pratt, Jr., "Using Research to Reduce Risk Associated with Marketing New Products," in Reed Moyer, ed., *Changing Marketing Systems* (Chicago: American Marketing Association, 1967), pp. 98–104.

with one sixth of the sample retired and a new sixth introduced each quarter. Respondents are asked to estimate the probability of purchasing a new car, a number of appliances, furniture, and carpeting. The accuracy of these data is not affected by the type of respondent (husband, wife, or other).

Using panel data, Pratt showed that it is possible to estimate the average length of the planning process, that is, the time between intentions and purchase. The estimating equation used for durable goods is

Formulating a general marketing strategy

$$
\begin{array}{l}
\text{average length} \\
\text{of the planning} \\
\text{process}
\end{array}
=
\left[
\dfrac{
\begin{array}{c} \text{plans at time 1} \\ \text{fulfilled by time 2} \end{array}
}{
\begin{array}{c} \text{total} \\ \text{purchases} \end{array} \times \begin{array}{c} \text{purchases} \\ \text{recorded} \\ \text{at time 2} \end{array}
}
\right]
\times
\left[
\begin{array}{c} \text{time} \\ \text{between} \\ \text{interviews} \end{array}
\right]
$$

Those durables having relatively short planning periods require marketing programs characterized by relatively heavy emphasis on wide distribution, local advertising, and point-of-purchase displays. Durables with relatively long planning periods usually require a marketing strategy involving limited distribution, heavy use of national media, and less frequent advertising.[35] Thus planning periods provide a quantitative measure of buying behavior that can be used to array products in the product line and assist in the formulation of a general marketing strategy.[36]

Some people tend to respond to innovations sooner than others, thus underscoring individual differences in proneness to recognize a problem and undertake appropriate buying action. If they can be identified, these innovators are an excellent target for marketing efforts. The subject of diffusion of innovations is discussed in Chapter 12, but it is worth noting at this point that the early adopter tends to possess the following characteristics:[37]

Identifying market targets

1. More education

2. Higher income

3. Higher standard of living

4. More relevant product knowledge

5. A positive outlook toward change in general

35 Robert W. Pratt, Jr., "Consumer Buying Intentions as an Aid in Formulating Marketing Strategy," in Robert L. King, ed., *Marketing and the New Science of Planning* (Chicago: American Marketing Association, 1968), pp. 296–302.

36 Joseph W. Newman and Richard Staelin, "Multivariate Analysis of Differences in Buyer Decision Time," *Journal of Marketing Research*, vol. 8, pp. 192–98 (May 1971).

37 Everett M. Rogers and J. David Stanfield, "Adoption and Diffusion of New Products: Emerging Generalizations and Hypotheses," in Frank M. Bass et al., eds., *Applications of the Sciences in Marketing Management* (New York: Wiley, 1968).

6. A strong achievement motivation

7. High aspirations for children and their success

8. Cosmopolitan interests

9. Higher than average exposure to the mass media

10. A tendency to deviate from group norms, accompanied by greater than average participation in groups

11. Higher than average exposure to interpersonal communication

12. Frequent service as an opinion leader to others

13. Possession of needs, attitudes, and behavioral patterns that are compatible with the innovation chosen.

Also it was stressed in Chapter 6 that various family members interact and assume different roles in the purchase process. The role of husband and wife will vary considerably from product to product, especially in terms of initial problem recognition. Once again, the member recognizing the problem first will be the most responsive market target. From the data accumulated thus far, the following generalizations appear to be warranted:

1. The higher the price of the item, the greater the tendency for the husband to dominate in problem recognition.

2. The extent of husband-wife involvement in problem recognition tends to vary according to cultural norms of specialization. Husbands will dominate, for instance, when the product is technically or mechanically complex.

3. Younger and higher income husbands play a greater role in problem recognition than their older and middle-to lower-income counterparts.

4. Working wives are more involved in problem recognition than those whose primary role is within the home.

Attempts to trigger problem recognition

It has been pointed out that marketing efforts can play a role in triggering problem recognition either by highlighting the ideal state or by showing the inadequacies of the present state. Nevertheless, the stimulation of problem recognition through any type of marketing activity is far more difficult than it might seem from the discussion thus far. Keep in mind that each person has an ability to be completely oblivious to persuasion, to see and hear what he or she wants to see and hear. In fact, filters tend to be closed when problem recognition is not active. The very existence of an aroused motive, per se, makes one decidedly more responsive to relevant information. The reverse is also true, as Chapter 13 will stress at length.

In the final analysis, *problem recognition most frequently is triggered by factors beyond the control of the marketer.* Advertisements and other forms of promotion assume their greatest effectiveness *following* problem recognition. The best strategy, then, is to uncover those who, for one reason or another, are dissatisfied with their present solution and are open to something different. Then appropriate changes can be introduced in product, package, price, promotion, and distribution to capitalize upon a responsive segment of prospective customers. The payout from this approach usually is greater than that achieved from attempts designed to stimulate problem recognition in a frequently indifferent consumer audience that is inundated with persuasion from all sides.

Summary

Behavior begins with the triggering of problem recognition. A problem is recognized when there is an intolerable gap perceived to exist between the ideal state of affairs and the present state of affairs.

Problem recognition can arise when something happens to highlight the ideal state and thus make the discrepancy between ideal and actual more apparent. One cause is the influence of other decisions in which one purchase often makes another necessary. Reference group members can stress only the allowable behavior and therefore make that the ideal through normative social influence. Sometimes problem recognition even occurs through novelty as the consumer seeks to bring about a change simply for the sake of change. Marketing efforts can trigger problem recognition as well when dominant motives are aroused by the appeals used. The most important factor, however, is motive activation.

Motives serve as the primary determinant of the ideal state. These learned predispositions embody goals that have been shown to be rewarding by past experience. As such, they are deeply imbedded in basic personality and are beyond change through marketing efforts. The best strategy is to uncover the motives associated with a particular purchase, highlight them, and demonstrate how the particular product or service is an adequate alternative to reduce the aroused drive.

Problem recognition also occurs when the present state is seen to be inadequate. Changes in circumstances (income, family life cycle, financial expectations, and so on) are one important cause. Marketers also can show the present solution to be inadequate by stressing the benefits of improved products.

Problem recognition most frequently is measured through general intentions to purchase a type of product or service. This information then can prove useful in defining marketing strategy and in identifying promotional or market targets.

Review and discussion questions

1. A consumer goes into an automobile showroom planning to buy a four-door sedan and emerges with an air-conditioned hardtop costing $1,000 more than he intended to pay. When he was asked why he made this purchase, he was at a loss other than to say that he liked the car. He did

mention, however, that he could not afford the extra cost. A professor from a nearby university observed this scene and concluded in disgust that this was just another example of "irrational behavior." The implication was that this consumer acted in a nonpurposeful manner. Do you agree?

2. Can motives be changed through advertising? Why or why not?

3. Using Great Britain and India as examples, indicate how the concept of motive prepotency might explain certain cross-cultural differences in consumer behavior.

4. Discuss the problem-recognition process that occurred before you purchased your last bottle of soft drink. How did this differ from the one that preceded the purchase of a suit of slacks? What role, if any, did marketing activity play in problem recognition?

5. How did problem recognition underlie your decision to attend college or graduate school? Describe the process.

6. Use examples from your own experiences to illustrate how problem recognition resulted from: a depletion of previous solution, b dissatisfaction with present solution, c change in family characteristics or status, d change in reference groups, and (e recognition of other problems.

7. What is the self-concept? How is it formed? Would measurement of self-concept be of any use to a brand manager who has full responsibility for the marketing of a new brand of household detergent? Would it be of greater use to the executive responsible for marketing stereo sets? Explain fully.

8. A manufacturer has developed a line of new power tools and has discovered that the husband is far more likely to feel the need for such a product and hence more apt to recognize the problem initially than is the wife. Of what use, if any, is such information in marketing strategy?

9. Assume that you are a consultant to a national manufacturer of air conditioners. Your firm has 60 percent of the market. The remainder is divided among seven competitors. Your firm wants to stimulate problem recognition among those who own second homes for vacation and weekend purposes. What are your recommendations concerning, first of all, the desirability of such a strategy and, secondly, the techniques that should be used for this purpose?

CHAPTER 9

The search process

Brad Jones entered the busy expressway on his way home from work. Suddenly his car began to miss, and he pulled off as soon as he could. Fortunately there was a garage close at hand. The mechanic reported that he had a burned valve and that a major overhaul was needed. This news threw Brad into an immediate state of problem recognition. Now what was he to do? He was going to trade the old chariot in anyway, but he had not even begun to look at the new models which had just been introduced. Brad knew without much introspection that additional information was needed before he could make a new car buying decision. In short, search for additional information became a necessity. Prechoice search is often a part of decision-process behavior, and it is defined as motivated exposure to information with regard to a given alternative.

Broadly speaking, search results when existing beliefs and attitudes are found to be inadequate—i.e., they are based on insufficient information. This is depicted in Figure 9.1. Other factors also enter into the search decision, however, and Brad must determine which, if any, of the available information sources will be used. This chapter focuses on the determinants of search and presents a broad overview of the information sources and the role of each. Following chapters elaborate the nature of each source in more detail.

Determinants of search

It should be stressed at the outset that search does not precede the majority of consumer purchases. More often than not, a past solution to

A model of the search process

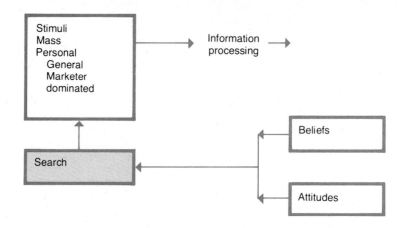

the recognized problem is remembered and implemented.[1] This, of course, is the essence of habitual or routine response behavior, and the marketer faces a formidable challenge indeed when the objective is to introduce change in established buying and consuming patterns.

Search, on the other hand, represents a *motivated* decision to seek new inputs. If the marketer can identify preferred information sources, there is a good opportunity to increase the probability that a brand will be considered.

In general, the decision to search as well as the extent of search depends upon the consumer's perception of the *value* to be gained in comparison with the *costs* of obtaining and using that information.[2] New insights into product characteristics, financing arrangements, and the opinions of others are just a few of the many benefits that may be obtained.[3] Costs of search may include time, travel, parking, psychological frustrations, time away from more pleasurable pursuits, and so on.[4]

Perceived value

Somehow Brad manages to make it home that night, and he discusses his dilemma with the family over the supper table. Brad and his wife Ann soon decide that a new car must be purchased, but neither have paid much

1 George Katona, *Psychological Analysis of Economic Behavior* (New York: McGraw-Hill, 1951), p. 47.

2 See, for example, Louis P. Bucklin, "Retail Strategy and the Classification of Consumer Goods," *Journal of Marketing*, vol. 27, pp. 50–54 (January 1963); Richard H. Holton, "The Distinction between Convenience Goods, Shopping Goods, and Speciality Goods," *Journal of Marketing*, vol. 69, pp. 213–25 (June 1961); Louis P. Bucklin, "Testing Propensities to Shop," *Journal of Marketing*, vol. 30, pp. 22–27 (January, 1966); Donald F Cox, "The Audience as Communicators," in Stephen Greyser, ed., *Toward Scientific Marketing* (Chicago: American Marketing Association, 1963), pp. 58–72; Donald H. Granbois, "The Role of Communication in the Family Decision Making Process," in Greyser, pp. 44–57; John U. Farley, " 'Brand Loyalty' and the Economics of Information," *Journal of Business*, vol. 37, pp. 370–81 (October 1964).

3 See, for example, W. Phillips Davidson, "On the Effects of Communication," *Public Opinion Quarterly*, vol. 3, pp. 343–60 (1959).

4 Wesley C. Bender, "Consumer Purchase Costs—Do Retailers Recognize Them?" *Journal of Retailing*, pp. 1–8 (Spring 1964).

attention to the ads which have inundated them lately. Their son Greg tries his best to convince them that *any* brand of foreign car is superior to an American make, but Brad dismisses that argument quickly by pointing out the imported "lemon" he had shortly after World War II. Ann complicates the problem by stressing their precarious financial situation at the time: "Make sure you do the right thing, honey." Brad's dilemma is intensified by the unmistakable fact that an engine is a complete mystery to him. All three realize that they must do a good bit of looking before a decision can be made.

Brad and his family to one degree or another illustrate the major factors that can serve to motivate search: (1) the quantity and quality of existing information; (2) ability to recall that information; (3) perceived risk; and (4) confidence in decision-making ability.

Quantity and quality of existing information. First of all, the more the person knows, the lower the propensity to search, all things being equal. Research findings support the obvious conclusion that search is much less probable when a product has been bought repeatedly over time.[5] Similarly, the greater the number of brands of the generic product that have been purchased previously, the lower the likelihood of search.[6] Thus, both the presence and the extent of search vary inversely with the length and breadth of experience.[7]

The quality of stored information also is a major factor, and there are three variables that affect perceived relevance:

1. Satisfaction. The greater the satisfaction with the results of past purchases, the lower the probability that search will occur in the future when the same problem is recognized.[8]

2. Interpurchase time. The amount of time that elapses between purchases affects the appropriateness of stored information. The greater the interpurchase time, the higher the probability that search will occur.[9]

3. Changes in the mix of alternatives. The appropriateness of stored information is also affected by the rate of price and style changes as

5 George Katona, *The Mass Consumption Society* (New York: McGraw-Hill, 1964), pp. 289–90; and Joseph W. Newman and Richard Staelin, "Prepurchase Information Seeking for New Cars and Major Household Appliances," *Journal of Marketing Research*, vol. 9, pp. 249–57 (August 1972). See also Peter D. Bennett and Robert M. Mandell, "Prepurchase Information Seeking Behavior of New Car Purchasers—The Learning Hypothesis," *Journal of Marketing Research*, vol. 6, pp. 430–33 (November 1969) and Robert D. Woodruff, "Measurement of Consumers' Prior Brand Information," *Journal of Marketing Research*, vol. 9, pp. 258–63 (August 1972).

6 Katona, *Mass Consumption*; and Newman and Staelin, "Prepurchase."

7 Paul E. Green, Michael Halbert, and J. Sayer Minas, "An Experiment in Information Buying," *Journal of Advertising Research*, vol. 4, pp. 17–23 (September 1964); also G. David Hughes, Seha M. Tinie, and Philippe A Naert,"Analyzing Consumer Information Processing," in Philip R. McDonald, ed., *Marketing Involvement in Society and the Economy* (Chicago: American Marketing Association, 1969), pp. 235–40.

8 Peter D. Bennett and Robert Mandell, "Prepurchase Information Seeking Behavior of New Car Purchasers—The Learning Hypothesis," *Journal of Marketing Research*, vol. 6, pp. 430–33 (November 1969).

9 Katona, *Mass Consumption* , pp. 289–90.

well as by the frequency of new product introductions. The greater the rate of change of these variables, the higher the probability that search will occur.[10]

Ability to recall information. The ability to recall stored information depends in part on the degree to which the present problem is perceived to be similar to those which have arisen in the past.[11] It will be stressed in Chapter 13 that ability to retrieve information from memory is affected to a large extent by the degree to which present circumstances mirror those of the past.[12] Often this will not be the case, and existing information is rendered largely inaccessible.

Recall ability also is affected by the time that has elapsed since the problem was last faced. The greater the interpurchase time, the higher the probability that external search will occur.[13]

Perceived risk. Brad's wife evidenced a phenomenon occasionally experienced in consumer decision making—perceived risk that a wrong decision will be made. In her case the cause of this concern was financial, but there are other roots as well. Information search is a major way of reducing risk to tolerable levels.[14] As a generalization, the greater the degree of perceived risk from the sources described below, the greater the propensity to search.[15] It should be noted, however, that most purchase situations activate little or no perceived risk.

Perceived risk and the resulting search can be triggered by one or more of these factors:

1. Price. The higher the price, the greater the financial consequences of making an incorrect decision.[16]

10 George Katona, *Psychological Analysis of Economic Behavior*, pp. 67–68.

11 Frederick E. May, "Adaptive Behavior in Automobile Brand Choices," *Journal of Marketing Research*, vol. 6, pp. 62–65 (February 1969); John E. Swan, "Experimental Analysis of Predecision Information Seeking," *Journal of Marketing Research*, vol. 6, pp. 192–97 (May 1969). For more detailed relationships including some findings that contradict the above generalization, see Donald J. Hempel, "Search Behavior and Information Utilization in the Home Buying Process," in McDonald, *Marketing Involvement*, pp. 241–49.

12 See, for example, Peter H. Lindsay and Donald A. Norman, *Human Information Processing* (New York: Academic Press, 1972).

13 Katona, *Mass Consumption*, pp. 289–90.

14 Raymond A. Bauer, "Consumer Behavior as Risk Taking," in Robert S. Hancock, ed., *Dynamic Marketing for a Changing World* (Chicago: American Marketing Association, 1960), pp. 389–98.

15 Paul E. Green, "Consumer Use of Information," in Joseph Newman, ed., *On Knowing the Consumer* (New York: Wiley, 1966), pp. 67–80; Scott M. Cunningham, "Perceived Risk as a Factor in Product Oriented Word of Mouth Behavior: A First Step," in L. George Smith, ed., *Reflections on Progress in Marketing* (Chicago: American Marketing Association, 1964), pp. 229–38; Scott M. Cunningham, "Perceived Risk as a Factor in the Diffusion of New Product Information," in Raymond M. Haas, ed., *Science Technology and Marketing* (Chicago: American Marketing Association, 1966), pp. 698–721.

16 William P. Dommermuth, "The Shopping Matrix and Marketing Strategy," *Journal of Marketing Research*, vol. 2, pp. 128–32 (May 1965); George Katona and Eva Mueller, "A Study of Purchasing Decisions," in Lincoln H. Clark, ed., *Consumer Behavior: The Dynamics of Consumer Reaction* (New York: New York University Press, 1955), pp. 30–87, at p. 46; Henry Towery, "A Study of the Buying Behavior of Mobile Home Purchasers," *Southern Journal of Business*, vol. 5, pp. 66–74 (July 1970). For an exception, see Ruby T. Norris, "Processes and Objectives in Home Purchasing in the New London Area," in Clark, pp. 25–29.

2. Length of commitment. The greater the period of time the consumer is committed to use the product, the higher the risk and the greater the intensity of search.[17]

3. Social influences. Recalling the discussion of reference groups in Chapter 6, the more "visible" a product is to others, the greater the risk of rejection by them and the need for additional information.[18]

4. Physiological considerations. The consumption of some products may produce harmful or undesirable physiological effects, with the result that information is sought to reduce this type of risk.[19]

5. The presence of competing decisions. Some purchases require multiple decisions on brand, color, size, style, and so on. To the degree that this is true, perceived risk and propensity to search both increase.[20]

Confidence in decision-making ability. Brad Jones is not a mechanic and hence has real doubt in his abilities to make the correct choice. Confidence as a determinant of search and choice behavior has been studied in two dimensions: (1) the degree of certainty perceived toward a brand[21] or (2) confidence in ability to judge or evaluate brand or product attributes.[22] Search is obviously more likely when confidence is low, all things being equal. Yet, it is interesting to note that concern or anxiety of this nature was evidenced by fewer than one-third of those in the process of buying a major appliance and by only 10.6 percent of those who had just made a purchase.[23]

Confidence, by the way, is a major component of the Howard-Sheth model of consumer behavior, but the evidence on its role in buying decisions is still meager.[24] For this reason, the present authors treat it as just one aspect of life style and prefer not to single it out for special emphasis.

---

17 Katona and Mueller, "Study of Purchasing Decisions," pp. 30–80; Donald H. Granbois, "A Study of the Family Decision Making Process in the Purchase of Major Household Durable Goods," unpublished doctoral diss. (Bloomington, Ind.: Indiana University Graduate School of Business, 1962).

18 Katona, *Mass Consumption*, pp. 289–90.

19 See, for example, James F. Engel, David A. Knapp, and Deanne E. Knapp, "Sources of Influence in the Acceptance of New Products for Self-Medication: Preliminary Findings," in Haas, *Science Technology*, pp. 776–82. This relation can also be inferred from Sidney P. Feldman and Merlin C. Spencer, "The Effect of Personal Influence in the Selection of Consumer Services," in Peter D. Bennett, ed., *Marketing and Economic Development* (Chicago: American Marketing Association, 1965), pp. 44–52.

20 Donald F. Cox and Stewart Rich, "Perceived Risk and Consumer Decision-Making—A Case of Telephone Shopping," *Journal of Marketing Research*, vol. 1, pp. 32–39 (November 1964); Dommermuth, "Shopping Matrix," p. 130.

21 John A. Howard and Jagdish N. Sheth, *The Theory of Buyer Behavior* (New York: Wiley, 1969).

22 Peter D. Bennett and Gilbert Harrell, "The Role of Confidence in Understanding and Predicting Buyers' Attitudes and Purchase Intentions," *The Journal of Consumer Research*, vol. 2, pp. 110–17 (September, 1975).

23 "Consumer Satisfaction in the Purchase Decision Process," (unpublished study reviewed by the authors).

24 See Donald R. Lehmann et al., "Some Empirical Contributions to Buyer Behavior Theory," *Journal of Consumer Research*, vol. 1, pp. 43–55 (December, 1974).

The costs of search Brad and Ann Jones obviously need more information, but they also must weigh the costs of search in terms of decision delay, expenditure of time and money, psychological considerations, and information overload.

Decision delay. Bauer suggested that some buyers may shorten the decision process in order to reduce unpleasantness.[25] He refers to an unpublished study now nearly two decades old, which also has been examined by the authors, that demonstrates that the automobile buyer seems to go into a kind of panic as the point of decision is reached. A rush into the purchase thus is an escape from the problem. There is no doubt that the predecision period can be one of frustration,[26] and the delay required for search can only compound the dilemma. All things considered, the greater the perceived decision delay, the lower the intensity of search.[27]

Expenditure of time and money. Some forms of search, particularly visits to retail outlets, require the consumer to spend considerable amounts of time. Moreover, a retail visit also tends to include a number of other decisions as well. Assuming that time is limited, search is markedly reduced under such circumstances.[28]

The expenditure of money also may loom large as a factor in the decision to search. Travel and parking costs easily can offset any gains from the information acquired. In fact, telephone shopping is growing in importance largely for this reason alone.

Information overload. Even if perceived risk is present as an incentive for search, providing people with additional information may actually *increase* uncertainty rather than decrease it. The discussion of consumer information processing in Chapter 13 will demonstrate the existence of finite limits on ability to utilize information. Once this limit is passed, frustrations mount and decision-making ability may be deterred rather than assisted as one might otherwise have assumed.[29]

The public policy implications of these findings are substantial. All too

25 Bauer, "Consumer Behavior."

26 Leon Festinger, *Conflict, Decision, and Dissonance* (Palo Alto, Calif.: Stanford University Press, 1964), esp. pp. 152–56.

27 John T. Lanzetta and Vera Kanareff, "Information Cost, Amount of Payoff and Level of Aspiration as Determinants of Information Seeking in Decision Making," *Behavioral Science*, vol. 7, pp. 459–73 (1962); Green, "Consumer Use," p. 75; Green et al., "Experiment in Information," p. 23.

28 Robert W. Chesnut and Jacob Jacoby, "The Impact of 'Time' Costs on Acquisition of Package Information" (Purdue Papers in *Consumer Psychology*, no. 155, 1976).

29 These findings come from a large number of studies by the Purdue consumer psychology group. See, for example, Jacob Jacoby, "Consumer Reaction to Information Displays: Packaging and Advertising" (Advertising and Public Interest Workshop, American Marketing Association, May 1973); Jacob Jacoby, Donald Speller, and Carol Kohn, "Brand Choice Behavior as a Function of Information Load," *Journal of Marketing Research*, vol. 11, pp. 63–69 (February 1974); Jacob Jacoby, Donald Speller, and Carol Kohn Berning, "Brand Choice Behavior as a Function of Information Load: Replication and Extension," *The Journal of Consumer Research*, vol. 1, pp. 33–42 (June, 1974); and Jacob Jacoby et al., "Information Acquisition Behavior in Brand Choice Situations: A Cross-Cultural Extension" (Purdue Papers in *Consumer Psychology*, no. 162, 1976). For a dissenting point of view, see J. Edward Russo, "More Information Is Better: A Reevaluation of Jacoby, Speller and Kohn," *The Journal of Consumer Research*, vol. 1, pp. 68–72 (December 1974).

often it is naively assumed that consumer welfare will be increased as information is increased. This completely ignores the costs of information acquisition and use and assumes unlimited information capacity on the part of the consumer. The error of such assumptions simply underscores that strategies for consumer welfare must be based on legitimate research in the same manner as marketing decisions.

Psychological costs. Search requiring a dealer visit also may carry certain psychological costs. The consumer may experience frustration, tension, and annoyance for several reasons, including fighting traffic, finding a place to park, standing in line to be waited upon, and dealing with incompetent sales personnel.[30] These factors alone are a strong deterrent to search.

Finally, it is known that some types of consumers are more likely to engage in search than others. These are the characteristic attributes known to be associated with search:

Some individual differences in the propensity to search

1. Personality characteristics:

   a. Those who are information sensitive tend to have a higher confidence in the degree of control they have over their environment, whereas their counterparts tend to be more fatalistic.[31]

   b. Consumers demonstrating an open mind are more information sensitive than those with a closed mind.[32]

   c. The greater the tendency toward dependence on others, the lower the sensitivity to information.[33]

2. Family role structure:

   a. "Liberal" women (those interested in politics and uninterested in household chores) and "traditionalist" women (those basing their cooking and meal choices on their parents' patterns) have low proclivities to engage in search. The "mother" type (concerned with welfare of husband and children) is just the opposite.[34]

   b. Women are more likely to engage in search in the decision processes for major durable goods than are men.[35]

3. Demographic characteristics

   a. "Transient" households living in a temporary status tend to

30 For a discussion of these and other costs, see Anthony Downs, "A Theory of Consumer Efficiency," *Journal of Retailing*, pp. 6–12 (Spring 1961); and Bender, pp. 1–8.

31 Green, "Consumer Use," p. 76.

32 Green, "Consumer Use," p. 76; also, Gerald D. Bell, "Developments in Behavioral Study of Consumer Action," in Smith, *Reflections on Progress*, pp. 272–82.

33 Orville Brim et al., *Personality and Decision Processes* (Stanford, Calif.: Stanford University Press, 1962), p. 122.

34 Louis P. Bucklin, "Consumer Search, Role Enactment, and Market Efficiency," *Journal of Business*, vol. 42, pp. 416–38 (October 1969).

35 Newman and Staelin, "Prepurchase Information Seeking."

withdraw from search. "Aging, bleak future" households (older and perceive current social and economic position to be deteriorating) are most prone to search.[36]

b. Those in the highest social status have a lower tendency than average to engage in search.[37]

c. Consumers with education less than high school search the least, but there are no differences among those with varying degrees of education beyond high school.[38]

d. Intensity of search is likely to be greater when the consumer is under 35 years of age and in the middle-income category as opposed to a higher or lower category.[39]

Implications

It is now obvious that search for information is not the simple process it might appear to be on the surface. While there are definite benefits to be gained, there also are very real costs the consumer must weigh before taking this step.

The marketer cannot make any assumptions one way or another about the search process in a given decision situation. Strategy must be based on consumer research. In those instances in which it is verified that the benefits outweigh the costs from the consumer's perspective, then appropriate information can be provided at the time and place desired by the target audience. Usually the marketer can predict the necessity of this communication strategy by a largely common sense analysis. For example, search is most probable when the product is new or when, for other reasons, existing consumer beliefs and attitudes will prove to be inadequate. Furthermore, certain types of people are more likely to search than others (those under 35, etc.). Thus, it is possible to identify both the types of products and segments of consumers for which additional information is most necessary.

Again it must be stressed that the addition of more information does not necessarily lead to greater consumer confidence or satisfaction, regardless of the assumption of some who are concerned about consumer welfare. The necessity for more information can be determined *only* from the point of view of the user. As a case in point, unit pricing was advocated for many years before it was adopted by various retailers. In this method price is stated per ounce, per serving, and so on. It was widely alleged at the outset that the consumer would be an immediate beneficiary, but this does not appear to have taken place. Fewer than one-third of consumers actually have been found to use prices when stated in this manner, and those who do are mostly in the higher income and wealth

36 Bucklin, "Consumer Search," pp. 416–38.
37 This relationship does not always hold. See, for example, Joseph N. Fry and Frederick H. Siller, "A Comparison of Housewife Decision Making in Two Social Classes," *Journal of Marketing Research*, vol. 7, pp. 333–37 (August 1970).
38 Newman and Staelin, "Prepurchase Information Seeking."
39 Katona and Mueller, "Study of Purchasing Decisions," pp. 30–87; Hempel, "Search Behavior," pp. 241–49.

segments.[40] Furthermore, actual buying behavior appears to be largely unaffected. Hopefully the future will witness increased use by those who need it most, but appear to be least aware of it—the poor.

Sources of information

Once it has been determined that search indeed does take place, the next question of importance to a marketer concerns the sources used and the importance of each. Four different categories are depicted in Figure 9.2 based on whether or not the source is marketer dominated or general in nature, utilizing face-to-face or mass communication.

Figure 9.2 Categories of consumer information sources

	Face-to-face	Mass media
General	Word-of-mouth influence	General content media
Marketer-dominated	Personal selling	Advertising and point-of-sale influence

This section discusses the major issues involved in isolating the importance of one medium in comparison with another. Some of the research problems inherent in this task can be difficult indeed.

Determining the importance of information sources

Criteria of importance. One way of expressing the importance of a source is in terms of exposure and subsequent attention. This is probably the most commonly used criterion.[41] One must be cautious, however, in judging one medium to be more important than another simply because a greater percentage of people report attending to it. This does not necessarily indicate that the source under consideration proved to be helpful in making the purchase decision. As a consequence, there can be a significant difference between *exposure* and *attention* and *effectiveness* (i.e., actually using the information provided).

Furthermore, consumers will often perceive sources as having varying degrees of effectiveness. The following typology can be helpful when comparing one source with another:[42]

1. **Decisive effectiveness.** The source was evaluated by the consumer as being most important to the decision.

40 See "Dual Pricing," *Progressive Grocer*, pp. 46–50 (February 1971).
41 Frederick C. May, "An Appraisal of Buying Behavior Research," ed., Peter D. Bennett, *Marketing and Economic Development*, p. 397.
42 This is a slight modification of the typology used by Elihu Katz and Paul Lazarsfeld, *Personal Influence* (New York: Free Press, 1955), chap. 4.

2. Contributory effectiveness. The source has played some specific role such as reducing uncertainty[43] but was not the *most* important source.

3. Ineffective. The source did not play any particular role in the decision even though the consumer was exposed to it.

Regardless of the typology used, importance always should be stated in *relative* rather than absolute terms (i.e., importance relative to degree of attention given each source). This is necessary because sources may vary widely in terms of exposure value, with the result that an absolute measure may reflect this fact alone and little else. Therefore it is best to use a relative measure that holds coverage or exposure constant. This can be done by computing an index such as the ratio of decisive effectiveness of a particular source to total exposure to that source.[44] When this index is less than 1.00, it means that exposure exceeded effectiveness. The higher the ratio, the better.

Research methodology. There are three ways of measuring the importance of one source versus another: (1) retrospective questioning; (2) protocol records; and (3) observation.

1. Retrospective questioning. The most common method is to survey people after a decision has been made.[45] Often this requires nothing more than an interview with consumers during or following the purchase. Another common approach is to use warranty card registration forms. Although this is relatively inexpensive, it has some limitations. First, and probably most important, is that in-depth questioning cannot be utilized because of the very nature of the form itself. Furthermore, those who return warranties may differ in important ways from those who do not; finally, not all products offer warranties. Therefore, the warranty card should be viewed only as a supplementary method.

Careful attention should be given to the type, content, and sequencing of questions. One recommended approach is to utilize a series of *specific influence* questions, followed by *assessment* questions, followed by *exposure* questions:[46]

Influence questions should emphasize the process of decision, and the wording should not favor one channel of information over another. Considerable experimentation is needed to develop appropriate questions for the specific product, and it is often advisable to ask several questions. Examples of influence questions that have been used include: (1) "How did you happen to find out about the new brand?" (2) "How did you happen to choose this particular brand?" and (3) "How did you happen to start using the new brand of food?"

---

43 Woodruff, "Measurement of Consumers' Prior Brand Information."
44 Katz and Lazarsfeld, *Personal Influence*.
45 This is the method used by Newman and Staelin.
46 Katz and Lazarsfeld, *Personal Influence*, ch. 4.

Assessment questions should be asked after specific influence questions have been administered. This increases the probability that the consumer will give some thought to the matter before answering. Relatively simple assessment questions seem appropriate, the following being examples: (1) "Summing up now, what was most important in causing you to purchase X?" or (2) "Summing up now, what do you think was the most important thing in causing you to change to this new brand?" While more sophisticated approaches to assessment are often necessary in other settings, this one appears sufficient for determining the effectiveness of information sources.

Exposure questions should be asked after the two preceding types of questions have been administered. It is appropriate to give consumers a check list itemizing sources of information and ask them to indicate whether they were exposed to various information sources. Representative questions are: (1) "Did you hear someone talk about it?" (2) "Did you read about it in a magazine?" and (3) "Did you see it on TV?"

2. Protocol records. In this method the individual actually performs shopping choice behavior, usually in some type of laboratory setting. He or she may then be asked to think out loud during the process, and a verbal record called a protocol is developed, which reveals the way in which information is used. Bettman has used this approach to construct what he calls *decision nets* depicting a flow chart of how consumers combine attribute and situational influence.[47] More is said about this in later chapters, especially Chapter 13. Jacoby and his associates, on the other hand, provide an actual array of information consumers may use if they wish in a simulated shopping situation. A protocol is developed by observing the information actually selected.[48]

3. Observation. To a limited degree actual field observation has been employed to reveal information selection and use in a retail store setting.[49] Evidence thus far indicates that the incidences of information seeking are higher when observed than they prove to be when sole reliance is placed on retrospective questioning.[50] Undoubtedly recall ability fades quite quickly.

It is difficult to determine the relative importance of various information sources from the empirical studies undertaken to date. They differ in the use or nonuse of a criterion of importance, and indexes of effectiveness, if employed at all, are rarely directly comparable. Nevertheless, Figure 9.3 provides a useful summary of the evidence obtained from some of the major investigations. These studies have been classified according to

The relative importance and roles of major information sources

47 James R. Bettman, "Toward a Statistics for Consumer Decision Net Models," *Journal of Consumer Research*, vol. 1, pp. 71–80 (June 1974).

48 Jacob Jacoby et al., "Pre-Purchase Information Acquisition: Description of a Process Methodology, Research Paradigm, and Pilot Investigation," in Beverlee B. Anderson, ed., *Advances in Consumer Research*, vol. 3 (Atlanta, Ga.: Association for Consumer Research, 1976), pp. 306–14.

49 Joseph W. Newman and Bradley D. Lockeman, "Measuring Prepurchase Information Seeking," *Journal of Advertising Research*, vol. 11, pp. 216–22 (December 1975).

50 Newman and Lockeman, "Measuring Prepurchase."

Figure 9.3 Rankings of the relative importance of major sources of information obtained from major studies of information seeking

Type of choice	Exposure — Information Source				Effectiveness — Information source			
	Mass media	Personal sources	Advertisements	Dealer visits, salesmen	Mass media	Personal sources	Advertisements	Dealer visits, salesmen
			(Marketer dominated)				*(Marketer dominated)*	
Major durables[a]		3	2	1	2	1		
Major durables and furniture[b]		2	3	1		1	3	
Major and small durables[c]		2	1	3		1		3
Small appliances[d]				2	3	1	2	
Fashion** items[e]			1	2		1	2	
Nylons, dacron[f]						1	3	2
Movies**[g]			1	2		1	2	
Food** and household products[h]			1	2		1	3	2
Food* products[i]		3	2	1		3	2	1
Food** and toiletries[j]						2	1	
Choice of supermarket[k]						1	*Sampling* 2	
Farmers' choice of hybrid seed[l]		1		*Salesman*	2	1	2	*Salesman* 2

Farmers' choice of new products[m]	3	1	2 *Salesman*		1
Doctors' choice of drugs[n]	3	2	1 *Salesman*		
Food and household products**[o]	3	1	2	1	
Automobiles and major appliances**[p]	3	2	1		1	1
Number of first rankings	1	6	5	10	1	1

Notes: *Study used an effectiveness index; **Study used an effectiveness index and a typology of effectiveness.

Sources:[a]George Katona and Eva Mueller, "A Study of Purchasing Decisions," in Lincoln H. Clark (ed.), *Consumer Behavior: The Dynamics of Consumer Reactions* (New York: New York University Press, 1955), pp. 30–87.
[b]Bruce Le Grand and Jon G. Udell, "Consumer Behavior in the Market Place," *Journal Retailing*, pp. 32–40 (Fall 1964).
[c]Hugh W. Sargent, *Consumer Product Rating Publications and Buying Behavior* (Urbana. Ill.: University of Illinois Bureau of Economic and Business Research, 1959).
[d]Jon G. Udell, "Prepurchase Behavior of Buyers of Small Electrical Appliances," *Journal of Marketing*, vol. 30, pp. 50–51 (October 1966).
[e]Elihu Katz and Paul Lazarsfeld, *Personal Influence* (New York: Free Press, 1955), chap. 5.
[f]George M. Beal and Everett M. Rogers, "Informational Sources in the Adoption Process of New Fabrics," *Journal Home Economics*, vol. 49, pp. 630–44 (1957).
[g]Katz and Lazarsfeld, *Personal Influence*, chap. 5.
[h]Katz and Lazarsfeld, *Personal Influence*, chap. 5.
[i]George Fisk, "Media Influence Reconsidered," *Public Opinion Quarterly*, vol. 23, pp. 83–91 (1959).
[j]George H. Haines, Jr., "A Study of Why People Purchase New Products," in Ramond M. Haas, ed., *Science, Technology and Marketing* (Chicago: American Marketing Association, 1966), pp. 665–85.
[k]Kenward L. Atkins, "Advertising and Store Patronage," *Journal Advertising Research*, vol. 2, pp. 18–23 (December 1962).
[l]B. Ryan and N. C. Gross, "The Diffusion of Hybrid Seed Corn in Two Iowa Communities," *Rural Sociology*, vol. 8, pp. 15–24 (1943).
[m]Robert G. Mason, "The Use of Information Sources in the Process of Adoption," *Rural Sociology*, vol. 29, pp. 40–52 (March 1964); Everett M. Rogers and George M. Beal, "The Importance of Personal Influence in the Adoption of Technological Changes," *Social Forces*, vol. 36, pp. 329–35 (May 1958).
[n]Herbert Menzel and Elihu Katz, "Social Relations and Innovation in the Medical Profession: The Epidemiology of a New Drug," *Public Opinion Quarterly*, vol. 19, pp. 337–52 (Winter 1955–56); Raymond A. Bauer, "Risk Handling in Drug Adoption: The Role of Company Preference," *Public Opinion Quarterly*, vol. 25, pp. 546–59 (Winter 1961).
[o]Carol A. Kohn Berning and Jacob Jacoby, "Patterns of Information Acquisition in New Product Purchases," *The Journal of Consumer Research*, vol. 1, pp. 18–22 (September 1974).
[p]Joseph W. Newman and Richard Staelin, "Prepurchase Information Seeking for New Cars and Major Household Appliances," *Journal of Marketing Research*, vol. 9, pp. 249–57 (August 1972).

whether or not exposure, effectiveness, or both have been used as the criterion of effectiveness. Asterisk combinations depict the utilization of an effectiveness typology and/or an effectiveness index.

These data reveal, first of all, that consumers rarely rely exclusively on one source. Rather, search tends to be a cumulative process in that those who seek information from one source also turn to others and vice versa. This would suggest that the various media are *complementary* rather than *competitive*.[51]

If *exposure* is used as the criterion of importance, the marketer-dominated sources (advertising, point-of-sale influence, and personal selling) are usually preponderant. The general mass media also will rank well on this criterion in some instances. This suggests that the mass media, whether dominated by the marketer or not, perform an *informing* function.[52] They play an important role in providing data about the availability and attributes of various alternatives.[53] This informing function generally prevails regardless of the type of purchase or choice that is being made.

When effectiveness is used as the criterion, on the other hand, the nonmarketer-dominated sources, especially word-of-mouth, assume the primary role. Contact with friends and relatives typically assumes a legitimizing or evaluating function because of greater credibility and clarity.[54] This is not to say that personal sources never perform an informing function or that the mass marketer–dominated media never perform a legitimizing or evaluating function. But, as a general rule, the following provides a good practical guideline to remember when assessing the relative impact of the media: consumers often use friends and relatives for information about quality, but personal sources such as these will seldom perform an informing function about price, particularly if the price of the product is high.[55]

Determinants of the relative importance of information sources

There is a growing body of evidence documenting why some information sources are more important than others, and the following factors play an important role: (1) the type of information desired, (2) perceived risk, (3) characteristics of the decision-making unit, and (4) the stage of market development.

51 See, for example, George Katona and Eva Mueller, "A Study of Purchase Decisions," in Lincoln H. Clark, ed., *The Dynamics of Consumer Reactions* (New York: New York University Press, 1955), pp. 30–87, at p. 46; Bernard Berelson and Gary Steiner, *Human Behavior* (New York: Harcourt, 1964), p. 532; Cox, "The Audience as Communicators."

52 Elihu Katz, "The Two Step Flow of Communication: An Up-to-Date Report on an Hypothesis," *Public Opinion Quarterly*, vol. 20, pp. 61–78 (1957); Eugene A. Wilkining, "Joint Decision Making as a Function of Status and Role," *American Sociological Review*, vol. 23, pp. 187–192 (1958); Kenward L. Atkin, "Advertising and Store Patronage," *Journal of Advertising Research*, vol. 2, pp. 18–23 (December 1962).

53 See, for example, Bruce Legrand and Jon Udell, "Consumer Behavior in the Market Place," *Journal of Retailing*, pp. 32–40 (Fall 1964).

54 Carol A. Kohn Berning and Jacob Jacoby, "Patterns of Information Acquisition in New Product Purchases," *Journal of Consumer Research*, vol. 1, pp. 18–22 (September 1974); John P. Robinson, "Mass Communication and Information Diffusion," in N. F. Gerald Kline and Phillip J. Tichenor, eds., *Current Perspectives in Mass Communication Research* (Beverly Hills, Calif.: Sage Publications Inc., 1972), ch. 2.

55 Legrand and Udell, "Consumer Behavior."

Type of information. Figure 9.4 summarizes part of a study of decision-making in the purchase of a home, and it illustrates that the type of information needed will, in part, determine the source to be consulted.

The data suggest the following:[56]

1. Personal sources, particularly friends and co-workers, were most important for decisions regarding the social dimensions of the purchase, preferred neighborhood, and location.

2. Personal sources as well as newspapers were also used frequently in the selection of other information sources, such as the choice of a real estate broker.

3. Commercial sources of information—agents, bankers, builders, and contractors—were more influential for decisions regarding technical matters such as valuation of the house and where to obtain a mortgage loan.

4. Real estate agents, bankers, and newspapers were most important for decisions regarding the price range considered.

Perceived risk. It has already been demonstrated that the occasional incidence of perceived risk of one type or another is a stimulus for search activity. It also affects the sources chosen, however. There is, for example, evidence that financial risk is a consideration, in that the role of personal sources increases as the cost of the item increases.[57] Second, the greater the visibility and social significance of a product (and hence the greater the perceived risk), the more likely that word-of-mouth influence will be dominant.[58] Finally, physiological risk can have an effect. As the severity of a disease increases, the need for authoritative information also increases, and the importance of marketer-dominated sources declines.[59]

Characteristics of the decision-making unit. The focus here is on the social status of the family (or decision-making unit if it is not a family in the usual sense). Word-of-mouth tends to dominate under these circumstances:

---

56 Donald J. Hempel, "Search Behavior and Information Utilization in the Home Buying Process," in McDonald, ed., *Marketing Involvement*, pp. 24–49.

57 Granbois, p. 106. The data in Figure 9.3 also appear to support this hypothesis, although there are not enough lower priced products to be certain.

58 See, for example, Michael Perry and B. Curtis Hamm, "Canonical Analysis of Relations between Socioeconomic Risk and Personal Influence in Purchase Decisions," *Journal of Marketing Research*, vol. 6, pp. 351–54 (August 1969); Robert B. Settle, "Consumer Attributional Information Dependence," unpublished paper (Gainesville, Fla.: University of Florida, September 1971).

59 James F. Engel, David A. Knapp, and Deanne E. Knapp, "Sources of Information in the Acceptance of New Products for Self-Medication: Preliminary Findings," in Haas, *Science Technology*, pp. 776–82, at p. 781. For additional studies dealing with the relationship between risk and the relative importance of information sources, see Scott M. Cunningham, "Perceived Risk as a Factor in Product-Oriented Word-of-Mouth Behavior: A First Step," in L. George Smith, ed., *Reflections on Progress in Marketing* (Chicago: American Marketing Association, 1964), pp. 229–38; Ted Roselius, "Consumer Rankings of Risk Reduction Methods," *Journal of Marketing*, vol. 35, pp. 56–61 (January 1971).

Figure 9.4 Relative importance of information sources for selected decisions in the home-buying process

Decision for which information was obtained	Percent exposed to information source and index of effectiveness							
	Friends and business associates	Relatives	Real estate agents	Bankers	Builders and contractors	Newspapers	Other	N
Preferred neighborhood or location	54%* 0.66	19% 0.52	35% 0.33	8% 0.00	8% 0.21	30% 0.22	7% 0.00	244
Price range to be considered	16% 0.41	11% 0.48	38% 0.43	34% 0.52	13% 0.42	30% 0.34	8% 0.33	240
Which real estate agents to contact	51% 0.64	10% 0.57	3% 0.43	4% 0.38	3% 0.71	59% 0.65	3% 0.33	215
Which builders to contact	42% 0.71	9% 0.54	24% 0.70	4% 0.50	12% 0.53	40% 0.69	1% 0.00	139
What characteristics of a house should be used to estimate its value	34% 0.45	26% 0.42	40% 0.43	22% 0.39	24% 0.47	16% 0.22	17% 0.54	227
Fair value or price for house purchased	34% 0.33	20% 0.33	32% 0.59	36% 0.53	14% 0.55	27% 0.24	9% 0.62	232
Where to apply for a mortgage loan	33% 0.66	11% 0.62	38% 0.69	27% 0.70	8% 0.90	3% 0.29	5% 0.67	236
Terms and conditions for mortgage loan	25% 0.48	12% 0.61	26% 0.53	52% 0.68	5% 0.50	4% 0.44	15% 0.56	236
Which firm to contact for property insurance	44% 0.87	13% 0.74	13% 0.10	6% 0.43	1% 0.67	3% 0.43	22% 0.90	232

*The first number in each set indicates the proportion of respondents reporting that they referred to the information source in making the decision listed. The second number is an index measure representing the ratio of the number designating the sources as that having the "most influence" for each decision to the total number referring to that source. For example, 54 percent of the respondents mentioned friends and business associates as sources of information they referred to in decision making concerning their preferred neighborhood or location; 66 percent of those using this source also designated it as the most influential source of information for this decision. The exposure percentages do not always total 100 percent because some respondents mentioned several sources or their own personal evaluations.

Source: Donald J. Hempel, "Search Behavior and Information Utilization in the Home Buying Process," in Philip R. McDonald (ed.), *Marketing Involvement in Society and the Economy* (Chicago: American Marketing Association, 1969), pp. 241–49, at p. 247.

1. The consumer is socially isolated rather than integrated into primary and/or secondary groups.[60]

2. Husband and wife's friends constitute separate social networks.[61]

3. The decision-making process is performed independently by both parties in a family or by one spouse alone.[62]

Stage of market development. The relative importance of information sources also varies, depending, in part, on the length of time the product has been on the market. In the case of some farm products and practices, for instance, market-dominated sources tend to decline and personal sources increase in impact as the product matures.[63] This is covered in more depth in Chapter 12 under the subject of the diffusion of innovations.

It is obvious that much is now known about the relative impact of the four **Implications** major sources of information delineated in Figure 9.2. Yet, there still is progress to be made in terms of present understanding. Various studies have employed differing definitions and research designs, thus making direct comparison difficult. Furthermore, it is common to focus on only one or a limited subset of the total options open to the consumer. It is anticipated that research of a more inclusive nature such as that undertaken by Jacoby and his associates will assume a higher priority in the future as a part of current interest in consumer information processing.[64]

Obviously one can use the discussion here only as a general guide in a specific consumer buying situation. There is no substitute for research in each instance, which always will have its own elements of uniqueness. Retrospective questioning no doubt will continue as the most common research method, but there is merit in the precision of the protocol technique. It offers greater benefits in basic research, however, as opposed to the more applied focus of the marketer or consumer economist.

Marketing research and diagnosis of the impact of search behavior

The marketer always must ask what impact, if any, consumer search has had on the relative impact of the firm's brand. There are some methods of data analysis that can be of real help in answering this question.

60 E. H. Schein, "Interpersonal Communication, Group Solidarity, and Social Influence," *Sociometry*, vol. 24, pp. 148–61 (June 1960); Harold L. Wilensky, "Orderly Careers and Social Participation," *American Sociological Review*, vol. 26, pp. 521–39 (August 1961); Harold L. Wilensky, "Social Structure, Popular Culture and Mass Behavior: Some Implications for Research," *Public Opinion Quarterly*, vol. 24, pp. 497–99 (Fall 1960).

61 Granbois, "Study of Purchasing Decisions," p. 105.

62 Granbois, "Study of Purchasing Decisions," pp. 104, 106.

63 Everett M. Rogers and George M. Beal, "The Importance of Personal Influence in the Adoption of Technological Changes," *Social Forces*, vol. 36, pp. 329–35 (1958); Bruce Ryan and Neal Gross, "The Diffusion of Hybrid Seed Corn in Two Iowa Communities," *Rural Sociology*, vol. 8, pp. 15–24 (March 1943).

64 Jacoby et al., "Pre-Purchase Information."

Before-after analysis

This procedure requires the measurement of brand preference before and after information seeking. Assuming that all other factors are held relatively constant, the difference between the two measurements roughly indicates the effect of information search on brand preference.

Examine the data in Figure 9.5. In this situation, information search is hindering brand A, helping brand C, and having no particular effect on preference for brand B. The essential question now is *why* this pattern exists, but further analysis is required before the answer can be given.

Figure 9.5 Before-after analysis of the impact of information-seeking on brand preference

Brand	Consumers preferring brand before information seeking (%)	Consumers preferring brand after information seeking (%)
A	30	15
B	40	40
C	30	45
	100	100

Information utilization analysis

The methodological requirements for information utilization analysis are less exacting than those discussed above. Figure 9.6 illustrates the first phase in which brand A is compared with the average for all other brands (AOB) in terms of exposure to sources of information. Exposure is classified into three categories: decisive, contributory, and ineffective.

Brand A appears to be enjoying reasonable success in terms of *total exposure.* Compared with AOB, brand A has received better total exposure in radio and television, and it is about average in terms of personal contacts and salesmen's influence. Purchasers are considerably less exposed than the average purchaser to magazines and newspapers.

Figure 9.7 carries this analysis into a second phase. Brand A is now compared with AOB in terms of effectiveness indices (decisive exposure versus total exposure) for the sources used by purchasers. This indicates that the brand is reasonably competitive with AOB for radio, television, magazines, and newspapers. Personal contacts and salesmen seem to be the major reasons why the brand is being hurt during the search process.

Figure 9.8 extends the analysis by disclosing the relationship between the brand recommended through word-of-mouth influence and purchasing behavior. Compared with AOB, brand A suffers from a low recommendation-fulfillment rate. This means that consumers have a lower than average tendency to purchase brand A once it is recommended by another person. Furthermore, consumers have a below average tendency to switch to brand A when other brands are recommended. As Figure 9.9 indicates, brand A loses 1.55 customers for each one who switches to it, and the other brands are doing much better.

Figure 9.6 Exposure to sources of information

Type of exposure by type of information source	Brand purchased	
	Brand A (%)	Average for all other brands (%)
Personal contacts		
Decisive exposure	28	34
Contributory exposure	18	25
Ineffective exposure	16	6
Total	62	65
Radio		
Decisive exposure	1	1
Contributory exposure	2	2
Ineffective exposure	6	4
Total	9	7
Television		
Decisive exposure	3	2
Contributory exposure	7	7
Ineffective exposure	8	2
Total	18	11
Magazines		
Decisive exposure	15	21
Contributory exposure	22	29
Ineffective exposure	8	12
Total	45	62
Newspapers		
Decisive exposure	3	4
Contributory exposure	15	22
Ineffective exposure	11	10
Total	29	36
Salesmen		
Decisive exposure	23	33
Contributory exposure	35	54
Ineffective exposure	37	10
Total	95	97

In summary, information seeking adversely affects brand A, and there is evidence that it is receiving poor word-of-mouth advertising. It has a low recommendation-fulfillment rate, and it is doing poorly at the point of sale even though it has achieved average exposure. Several steps are now required to complete the analysis:

1. The data should be analyzed by such characteristics as age, income, and life style to determine which types of consumers are showing the most adverse reactions. There quite likely will be differences between segments.

Figure 9.7 Effectiveness indices for information sources*

Information source	Purchasers of brand A	Average for purchasers of all other brands
Personal contacts	45.2	52.3
Radio	11.1	14.3
Television	16.7	18.2
Magazines	33.3	33.9
Newspapers	10.3	11.1
Salesmen	42.2	34.0

*These indices are computed by calculating the ratio of decisive exposure to total exposure for each information source.

Figure 9.8 Relationship between brand recommended through personal contacts and purchasing behavior

Brand recommended	Purchasing behavior

Brand A
- → 35% Purchased the brand recommended
- → 65% Purchased a different brand

Average for all other brands
- → 60% Purchased the brand recommended
- → 40% Purchased a different brand

Figure 9.9 Net gains and losses resulting from switching from the brand recommended through personal contacts

Brand	Number of customers switching to the brand for each 100 switchings from the brand	Net gain or loss (%)
A	45	−55
Average for all other brands	99	−01

2. Further analysis should determine why word-of-mouth is benefiting the other brands and hurting Brand A.

3. The reasons for the relative ineffectiveness of salesmen must be uncovered. There could be any number of reasons such as low commission, and so on.

Summary

Search refers to the process whereby the consumer seeks information to learn about the advantages and disadvantages of the various alternatives to satisfy a problem that has become recognized. Whether search will occur or not and the extent to which it occurs depend on the consumer's perceptions of the benefits and costs involved. The perceived benefit will be affected by the amount and appropriateness of existing information, the ability to recall that information, the type and degree of risk seen to be accompanying the purchase, and confidence. Costs include time, money, psychological discomforts, the satisfaction foregone by delaying purchase, and the dangers of information overload.

The information sources chosen vary from individual to individual and from one situation to the next. In general, it can be said that marketer-dominated sources (advertising, personal selling, and point-of-sale influence) are important in providing information in earlier stages of decision processes, but personal sources (word-of-mouth advertising) are most important in terms of effectiveness. The research techniques required to isolate the impact of one source versus another were presented.

Finally, a case history was presented to illustrate what can be learned from diagnosis of the impact of search behavior on the purchase. Without such information the marketer will be at a loss to evaluate the dynamics underlying consumer decision.

Review and discussion questions

1. Define or otherwise describe the relevance of the following concepts: (a) external search, (b) interpurchase time, (c) physiological risk, (d) pyschological costs, (e) changes in the mix of alternatives.

2. A product has a long interpurchase time, a low amount of social risk, a high degree of financial risk. Will external search occur? Discuss.

3. What are the consequences of external search?

4. "The majority of purchases a consumer makes are not preceded by external search." Why?

5. "Since consumers typically visit only one store before purchasing a product, store visits are not an important information source." Evaluate.

6. What problems, if any, are involved in determining the relative importance of information sources? How should these problems be overcome?

7. How does the type of information desired affect the utilization of information sources?

8. Select a product and discuss how you would go about determining the information-seeking role structure associated with that product.

9. What is the difference between effectiveness and exposure?

10. When you last bought an item of clothing, what was the relative importance of the information sources that you consulted? Why was this source most important? What type of information did you obtain from this

source and how does it compare with the type of information generally obtained from the most important source?

11. Assume you are a consultant to the research director of a large manufacturer of middle-priced ($1,000–$4,000) boats. The research director wants to know the relative importance of information sources and asks you to prepare a statement indicating how you would go about it.

12. Assume that your research recommendation was accepted and the research done. With the use of an index of relative effectiveness it was found that personal sources were five times more effective than advertising. Seeing this finding, the marketing vice president has asked the advertising manager to justify the amount of money being spent on advertising. You are the advertising manager. What do you say?

13. The research director for brand C presents you with the following data based on a rigorously controlled study:

Brand	Preferring brand before information-seeking (%)	Preferring brand after information-seeking (%)
A	30	35
B	30	35
C	40	30
	100	100

The research director is uncertain as to what the problem is and does not know how to proceed. As a consultant to Company C, prepare an outline indicating what procedure will allow the company to determine what the problems are.

14. Your company manufactures a full line of mobile homes in all price ranges. Several studies have indicated that personal sources of information are considerably more effective than other sources. Prepare a statement indicating (a) the alternative strategies that can be used to utilize effectively consumers' use of personal information sources, (b) the alternative that you prefer and why.

CHAPTER 10

Marketer-dominated information sources

Chapter 9 delineated the role of marketer-dominated information sources as compared with the mass media in general and word-of-mouth communication. This chapter extends the discussion by focusing in greater depth on the functions of media advertising and retail store visitation in the search process.

Media advertising

It has been stressed that advertising most often has an informative role as compared with the legitimizing role of word-of-mouth influence. Thus, one primary task of advertising is to communicate relevant product information and hopefully to persuade the consumer to purchase the product or service offered. At other times, however, advertising plays a much more decisive role and actually triggers the decision. The marketing implications of these functions are sharply different.

Once consumers recognize a problem, they generally become more receptive to advertising they previously might have ignored entirely.[1] Advertisements are consulted to learn about such product attributes as price and color, to compare various brands on the basis of these attributes, to visualize the product in use, to learn about possible financing arrangements, and so on. Although the informative role of

The informative role

---

1 See, for example, Robert W. Pratt, Jr., "Understanding the Decision Process for Consumer Durable Goods: An Example of the Application of Longitudinal Analysis," in Peter D. Bennett, ed., *Marketing and Economic Development* (Chicago: American Marketing Association, 1965), pp. 244–60.

advertising varies widely between products[2] and types of consumers,[3] the following are illustrative findings:

1. Of those consumers who purchased major durable goods, 21 percent claimed to have obtained information from reading advertisements and circulars.[4]

2. Of those who bought a small electrical appliance, 25 percent consulted newspaper advertisements, 15 percent read magazine advertisements, 14 percent saw the product advertised on television, and 7 percent acquired information from radio commercials.[5]

3. 26 percent of consumers purchasing food products claimed to have obtained information from advertising.[6]

It was just such evidence as this that led Russell Colley in 1961 to state forthrightly that advertising performs primarily an informative function.[7] In his words:

> Advertising's job purely and simply is to communicate to a defined audience information and a frame-of-mind that stimulates action. Advertising succeeds or fails depending on how well it communicates the desired information and attitudes to the right people at the right time and at the right cost.[8]

This philosophy has since become known as DAGMAR (*D*efining *A*dvertising *G*oals, *M*easuring *A*dvertising *R*esults).

This seemingly commonsense point of view has not been universally accepted, and it still generates controversy today. One of the primary criticisms is that advertising may accomplish communication goals yet have no influence whatsoever on buyer behavior. Assume, for instance, that 60 percent of potential customers are found to be unaware of a new detergent product. Assume further that advertising has then communicated product benefits to 50 percent of this group. Does this automatically mean that the advertising has been successful? The answer may be negative because it is possible to convey facts without having any

---

2 See, for example, Elihu Katz and Paul F. Lazarsfeld, *Personal Influence* (New York: Free Press, 1955), chap. 5; Hugh W. Sargent, *Consumer Product Rating Publications and Buying Behavior* (Urbana, Ill: Bureau of Economic and Business Research, University of Illinois, 1959), p. 41; K. L. Atkin, "Advertising and Store Patronage," *Journal of Advertising Research*, vol. 2, pp. 18–23 (December 1962); and George H. Haines, Jr., "A Study of Why People Purchase New Products," in Raymond M. Haas, ed., *Science, Technology and Marketing* (Chicago: American Marketing Association, 1966), pp. 665–85.

3 Donald H. Granbois, "The Role of Communication in the Family Decision Making Process," in Stephen Greyser, ed., *Toward Scientific Marketing* (Chicago: American Marketing Association, 1963), pp. 44–57.

4 George Katona and Eva Mueller, "A Study of Purchasing Decisions," in Lincoln H. Clark, ed., *Consumer Behavior: The Dynamics of Consumer Reaction* (New York: New York University Press, 1955), pp. 30–87.

5 Jon G. Udell, "Prepurchase Behavior of Buyers of Small Electrical Appliances," *Journal of Marketing*, vol. 30, pp. 50–52 (October 1966).

6 George Fisk, "Media Influence Reconsidered," *Public Opinion Quarterly*, vol. 23, pp. 83–91 (1959).

7 Russell H. Colley, ed., *Defining Advertising Goals* (New York: Association of National Advertisers, Inc., 1961).

8 Colley, *Defining Advertising*, p. 21.

influence at all in terms of persuasion.[9] In fact, people can even be made *less* likely to buy after awareness has been stimulated. In such instances, the information actually conveyed and that needed by the consumer have little or no relationship. Great care must be exercised to verify that the information truly is relevant in terms of consumer decision processes.

Contrast the difference in this case example. A pilot study disclosed in sharp clarity that housewives over the age of 35, with children at home, with average income and education were interested in modern language versions of the Bible.[10] The greatest felt need was to find help in establishing the moral and spiritual values of their children. At that point awareness of the *Living Bible*, one of several modern language versions, was only 18 percent. An advertising campaign then stressed the readability of this version and its role in the upbringing of children. Soon, awareness values quadrupled, and one out of two Bibles purchased in a recent year was a *Living Bible*.

Advertising, then, can change beliefs and attitudes, assuming that the information provided is relevant in terms of the consumers' evaluative criteria. Effectiveness cannot be measured, however, unless advertising objectives state the hoped for change in quantitative terms. Here is an example of a well stated objective: increase the number mentioning brand A when asked "What brand of all-purpose flour claims it gives you a feeling of confidence when you use it?" from 35 percent to 45 percent.[11] All things being equal, this change in awareness should lead to a sales increase.

There are instances in which advertising will play a decisive role in the decision. At times, for example, the consumer has decided to make a purchase but is waiting for a price reduction on one of several acceptable brands. Price advertising then will trigger a sale and this is its primary role.

The decisive role

Advertising also has a decisive function when the planning period for purchase is short—perhaps even a matter of seconds. Relatively little thought, for example, will precede trial of a new soft drink advertised by direct mail with a price coupon. Stimulation of an immediate sale was the objective of an advertising campaign designed to present the Goodyear Christmas album at its $1 price so forcefully that consumers would make a special trip to the dealer for that purpose.[12]

Point-of-sale influences

Consumers also obtain information by shopping in retail outlets. Although this may be a relatively expensive method of search from the point of

9 Jack B. Haskins, "Factual Recall as a Measure of Advertising Effectiveness," *Journal of Advertising Research*, vol. 4, pp. 2–8 (1964).

10 See "The Living Bible" case in Roger D. Blackwell, James F. Engel, and W. Wayne Talarzyk, *Contemporary Cases in Consumer Behavior* (Hinsdale, Ill.: Dryden Press, 1977), pp. 350–59.

11 National Industrial Conference Board, *Setting Advertising Objectives* (New York, 1966).

12 "The Goodyear Christmas Album Campaign," in *Outstanding Advertising Case Histories* (Southport, Conn.: Thomas E. Maytham, 1967), p. 46.

view of costs versus benefits, it is widely used to obtain information on price, quality, performance, style, appearance, and other product features, as well as the conditions of sale. Point-of-sale advertising and display and personal selling, of course, are the two principal information sources.

The extent of shopping behavior

The frequency and intensity of information search at the retail level is rather surprising. The following are illustrative findings:

1. Of those consumers purchasing major durable goods, 47 percent visited only the store in which the item was purchased; 15 percent visited two or three stores; and 26 percent visited more than three.[13] In an updating of this study 70 percent were found to have shopped at two or more outlets.[14]

2. Of those purchasing small electrical appliances, 60 percent shopped only in the store where the purchase was made, 16 percent shopped in two, and 22 percent visited three or more.[15]

3. Another study of electrical appliances found that the percentage of purchasers shopping in only one outlet was: for refrigerators, 42.4 percent; for television sets, 58.3 percent; for washing machines, 62.4 percent; for vacuum cleaners, 79.4 percent; for electric irons, 82.4 percent.[16]

Although the majority confine their efforts to the store where the product is purchased, some will visit that outlet more than once. Nearly one-fourth of the buyers of small electrical appliances, for example, made more than one shopping trip to the same store.[17]

Multiple shopping trips are most likely, first of all, when the price of the product is high.[18] And, as might be expected, the amount of information already in possession will affect shopping behavior, but the form of this relationship may be surprising. It seems that those who have the most or, conversely, the least information shop least extensively, whereas those in the middle do the most.[19] This may be explained by the fact that those with the least information also have the highest incomes. Consumers with higher incomes, in turn, often minimize search behavior on the basis that the costs outweigh the benefits.

It is interesting to speculate about consumer behavior of this type in the future. On the one hand it is possible to make a case for increased shopping because of the remarkable growth of specialty stores of all

13 Katona and Mueller, "Study of Purchasing," pp. 45–46.

14 Joseph W. Newman and Richard Staelin, "Prepurchase Information Seeking for New Cars and Major Household Appliances," *Journal of Marketing Research*, vol. 9, pp. 249–57 (August 1972).

15 Udell, "Prepurchasing Behavior," p. 52.

16 William P. Dommermuth, "The Shopping Matrix and Marketing Strategy," *Journal of Marketing Research*, vol. 2, pp. 128–32 (May 1965).

17 Udell, "Prepurchasing Behavior," p. 52.

18 Louis P. Bucklin, "Retail Strategy and the Classification of Consumer Goods," *Journal of Marketing*, vol. 27, pp. 50–54 (January 1963); also Dommermuth and Udell have found this relationship.

19 Bucklin, "Retail Strategy."

types. This, in turn, is accompanied by pressures to economize brought on by increased inflation and diminished growth of disposable income. On the other hand, the competing demands on leisure time are great, and these can reverse the balance between the benefits and costs of search, in which case shopping will diminish. Whatever the situation, changes are imminent, and there is a growing need for consumer research of this type. Far too much of the present evidence is becoming increasingly outdated.

In one recent study nearly one-third of the prospective buyers of major appliances interviewed at the retail level expressed a need for more information.[20] While this will, of course, vary widely from product to product, much can be learned from the package itself and from the various forms of point-of-purchase display and advertising.

Point-of-sale advertising and display

The package. No doubt every reader has consulted a package, on occasion, to obtain additional information. Surprisingly this very commonplace activity has only rarely been investigated by consumer researchers with any degree of sophistication. Jacoby and his associates have demonstrated that consumers indeed do refer to package information, but there is a definite point at which this type of search ceases.[21] This point is when the number of separate bits of information exceeds 12, and this is further evidence of the costs of information overload mentioned in Chapter 9.

The type of information and labeling used can shift consumer preference. For example, nutritional labeling clearly improves consumer perception of quality attributes such as "wholesomeness" and "tender."[22] Vague labels, on the other hand, have no such effect. It also was found that strictly promotional terms such as "sweet" and "succulent" leave consumers with an assurance of quality comparable to that of the more detailed nutritional information. This underscores the opportunity provided for outright deception, and one cannot help but wonder the extent to which consumers have been misled by this means.

Point-of-purchase display. This term is usually meant to refer to such devices as counter cards, banners, window streamers, shelf extenders, wire racks, merchandise displays, easel back displays, and others. Studies of the effects vary in purpose and sophistication. One study attempted to evaluate *awareness* of these materials and their effect on sales. Nearly 82 percent of the more than 5,000 respondents surveyed indicated that they had recalled seeing at least two of the test displays during their shopping

20 "Consumer Satisfaction in the Purchase Decision Process" (unpublished study reviewed by the authors).

21 Jacob Jacoby, "Consumer Reaction to Information Displays: Packaging and Advertising" (paper delivered at the Advertising and Public Interest Workshop, American Marketing Association, May 1973). Also see Jacob Jacoby, George J. Szybillo, and Jacqueline Busato-Schach, "Information Acquisition Behavior in Brand Choice Situations," *Journal of Consumer Research*, vol. 3, pp. 209–16 (March 1977).

22 Edward H. Asam and Louis P. Bucklin, "Nutritional Labeling for Canned Goods: A Study of Consumer Response," *Journal of Marketing*, vol. 37, pp. 32–37 (April 1973).

trip, 44 percent said they had used displays to assist in the purchase decision, and 33 percent purchased one or more of the displayed items.[23]

The degree to which point-of-purchase display *induces brand switching* has also been investigated. Interviews were conducted with 2,803 consumers in 16 drugstores located in nine major metropolitan areas geographically scattered from Boston to Los Angeles. Approximately 18 percent of the consumers interviewed said that they decided to try a new brand after entering the store, and 30 percent of these brand switches were allegedly made because the selected item was given point-of-purchase display treatment.[24]

Another study interviewed 2,055 customers shopping in 36 package liquor stores across the country. Point-of-purcase displays were reputed to be responsible for 39 percent of the brand switches.[25]

The above are illustrative of studies that have relied on customers' assessments of the influence of point-of-purchase displays on postpurchase outcomes. Other studies have used experimental designs and other more sophisticated techniques in an attempt to determine the effect of point-of-purchase materials. The following studies are examples:

1. Using a before-after with control group design, tests were conducted in supermarkets on juice, beer, and cigarettes; in grocery stores, on beer; in package stores, on blended whiskey and bourbon; in drugstores, on personal care items; in stationery stores, on pens; and in camera stores, on cameras. Displays without motion averaged a gain of 37 percent above normal shelf sales, while a display with motion increased sales by 83 percent above the no-display treatment.[26]

2. Another study utilized five supermarkets in Wilmington, Delaware, to test five different types of point-of-purchase materials over a five-week period. The results indicated that point-of-purchase materials influenced the sales of spices. The percentage increase varied considerably depending on the type of point-of-purchase material used—shelf extenders and floor bins were more effective than spotters and recipes.[27]

3. Tests were conducted in four drugstores and four stationery stores in Boston. The purpose was to determine the effect of a new countertop wire carrousel display on the sales of dacron felt tip marker pens. The new display had a positive influence on sales.[28]

A series of display merchandising tests were conducted by *Progressive*

23 *Awareness, Decision, Purchase* (New York: Point-of-Purchase Advertising Institute, 1961), p. 14.

24 *Drugstore Brand Switching and Impulse Buying* (New York: Point-of-Purchase Advertising Institute, 1961), p. 14.

25 *Package Store Brand Switching and Impulse Buying* (New York: Point-of-Purchase Advertising Institute, undated).

26 *Motion Moves More Merchandise* (New York: Point-of-Purchase Advertising Institute, undated), p. 3.

27 *Increasing Spice Sales with Point-of-Purchase Advertising* (New York: Point-of-Purchase Advertising Institute, undated), p. 9.

28 Peter J. McClure and E. James West, "Sales Effects of a New Counter Display," *Journal of Advertising Research*, vol. 9, pp. 29–34 (March 1969).

Grocer magazine using a panel of test supermarkets over a five-month period during mid-1970. All test stores were matched in terms of volume, layout, size, and demographics. Display experiments were conducted in pairs of stores with comparison control stores retaining normal operating procedures during the length of each specific test. These tests also demonstrate the power of displays in generating sales.[29]

1. Displays of new health and beauty-aid items increased sales from 100 percent to 400 percent more than normal shelf movement.

2. One of the most effective sales producers among displays was the related item presentation. Individual items sold as much as 418 percent more in combination arrangements than when presented by themselves elsewhere in the store.

3. Added sales also resulted from relating mid-aisle displays to neighboring products rather than competing with them. For example, a salad dressing display was related by means of crepe paper streamers to an adjacent section of salad greens. Sales of individual items increased from 29 to 250 percent more than regular shelf movement.

4. Displays featuring interdepartmental tie-ins also increased sales. For example, stores using a display combining fresh lemons and instant tea sold $23.24 more product than stores not using this display technique.

5. "As advertised" signs, "cents-off" signs, and "product identification" signs increased sales by 124, 23, and 18 percent, respectively.

6. The average display tended to decrease in sales after the first week, but items constantly promoted or seasonally related and kept well stocked were productive for much longer periods.

End-aisle displays differ from those discussed up to this point in that they are located in one specific position—at the end of a selling counter. These displays are used almost exclusively in self-service outlets, particularly supermarkets and drugstores.

The following are illustrative of some of the more sophisticated attempts to determine the effect of end-aisle displays on in-store behavior:

1. Using ten experimental and ten control stores, a before-after with control group design was used to measure the sales effectiveness of 36-inch, three-dimensional displays in supermarkets. The displays increased sales for three of the four products tested. The test brand of coffee experienced a gain in share of market of 125 percent in the test stores as compared with 10 percent in the control stores. The sales of competing brands declined. The test brand of gelatin gained 177

29 "How In-Store Merchandising Can Boost Sales," *Progressive Grocer,* pp. 94–97 (October 1971); "How the Basics of Special Display Affect Sales and Profits," *Progressive Grocer,* pp. 34–45 (January 1971); "How to Make Displays More Sales Productive," *Progressive Grocer,* pp. 34–45 (February 1971).

percent in the test stores, 15 percent in the control stores, and the sales of competing brands declined. The test brand of bathroom tissue gained 8 percent in the test stores and 3 percent in the control stores while competitive brands declined. Sales of the test brand of beer declined less in the test stores than in the control stores.[30]

2. A before-after with control group design was used to test the effect of end-aisle displays on the sales of the following products: pancake mixes, flour, shortening, coffee, condiments, canned fruits, luncheon meat, cereals, tuna fish, foil wrap, paper napkins, snacks, peanut butter, syrup, and canned corn. End-aisle displays increased the sales of all products included in the study. Sales of substitute items generally decreased during the display week. The week after the display, total sales of displayed items decreased relative to their normal weekly sales. Finally, even if the price of a displayed item were increased, unit sales still increased.[31]

3. Another study audited 734 displays of 360 grocery items in five supermarkets. Unit sales of items on special display increased significantly over normal shelf position.[32]

4. A before-after with control group design was used to test the effectiveness of end-aisle displays in 12 super drugstores. Displays increased the number of units sold by from 142 percent to 217 percent. Moreover, displays with signs produced better results than displays without signs, and fluorescent and larger signs were more effective than regular and smaller signs.[33]

5. Tests were conducted in six Vancouver, Canada, supermarkets over a four-week period to determine how displays affected sales of carton cigarettes. End-aisle displays produced greater sales increases than displays in an island shelving unit located in front of one of the store checkouts, or regular shelving.[34]

On the basis of these and other studies,[35] it appears legitimate to conclude:

1. Displays typically increase the sales of items displayed.

30 Mary L. McKenna, "The Influence of In-Store Advertising," in Joseph Newman, ed., *On Knowing the Consumer* (New York: Wiley, 1966), pp. 114–15.

31 George J. Kress, *The Effect of End Displays on Selected Food Product Sales* (New York: Point-of-Purchase Advertising Institute, undated).

32 George E. Kline, "How to Build More Profit into Your Display Programs," *Progressive Grocer*, pp. 48–72 (January 1960).

33 Bert C. McCammon and Donald H. Granbois, *The Super Drugstore Customer* (New York: Point-of-Purchase Advertising Institute, 1962), pp. 12–18.

34 John R. Kennedy, "The Effect of Display Location on the Sales and Pilferage of Cigarettes," *Journal of Marketing Research*, vol. 7, pp. 210–15 (May 1970).

35 For other studies, see B. A. Dominick, Jr., *Research in Retail Merchandising of Farm Products* (Washington, D.C.: U.S. Department of Agriculture, Agricultural Marketing Service, 1960); "Display Ideas for Supermarkets," *Progressive Grocer* (1958); *Triggering Plus Sales and Profits* (New York: Point-of-Purchase Advertising Institute, undated); *The Tavern Study: Parts I, II* (New York: Point-of-Purchase Advertising Institute, undated).

2. The sales of some products increase to a greater extent than others. Reasons for interproduct variation to displaying are largely unexplored.[36]

3. Displays often cause the sales of substitute, nondisplayed items to decrease.

4. The effectiveness of displays is often overstated.

There are two basic reasons why the effectiveness of displays is exaggerated. First, most studies do not determine the extent to which consumers respond by accumulating inventory rather than increasing the rate of consumption. Second, many studies do not determine the extent to which customers purchase from the display instead of from the product's regular location. Despite these factors, the evidence is clear that displays of various types *do* increase sales in most situations.

One explanation is that exposure to display can trigger consumer problem recognition on the spot. Mere exposure to the product in question can either serve as a reminder of a previously-recognized need or activate a latent need. Furthermore, it can stimulate conscious recall of previous advertising or other forms of influence and hence activate buying behavior. In these instances, the consumer usually will not have entered the store with a specific intent to buy this product or brand.

Displays also have the effect of leading the consumer to believe that prices have been lowered. Discussion in the next section will demonstrate that most consumers do not know the prices of products, particularly those sold in supermarkets. Therefore, they can easily be misled when a particular item stands out from its competitors. The tendency for sales of display items to increase even when price is increased lends support to this hypothesis. The manufacturer and retailer, of course, are beneficiaries, but the effect on the consumer is little less than outright deception. Since this practice is completely legal at this point in time, the only remedy is consumer education stressing the value of price comparison shopping.

Point-of-sale pricing. As has been stressed above, many studies document that most people do not have accurate price perceptions. This is true even for the widely advertised convenience items sold in supermarkets and drugstores. A *Progressive Grocer* study, for example, focused on 59 items that industry executives considered to be frequently advertised and highly price competitive.[37] These items were clustered into groups of six. Tables were set up in Colonial test stores, and a different group of items was placed on each table. Several thousand people were asked to state the

---

36 Some studies have investigated some of the reasons why end-aisle displays increase the sales of some products more than others. See, for example, "Displays Add Sales, Profit, and Personality to Kroger of Bay Village," *Progressive Grocer*, pp. 63–70 (January 1967); Kress, *Effect*, pp. 18–22; Robert Kelley, "An Evaluation of Selected Variables of End Display Effectiveness," unpublished doctoral diss. (Cambridge, Mass.: Harvard University, 1965).

37 "Colonial Study," *Progressive Grocer*, pp. C-81–C-96 (January 1964).

prices, and less than half could estimate the price within five percent of the true price. The authors have undertaken similar studies, which verify that consumers really do not know the prices of drug store items and major appliances. Furthermore, the incidence of misperception seems to be widespread among all types of people.[38]

(1) Dual Pricing. Knowing that price misperception exists and that many people search for price information at point-of-sale, a number of mass merchandising retailers have instituted a practice of dual pricing. This is where conventional prices are also accompanied by unit price—price stated per ounce, per serving, and so on. Presumably unit pricing will help the consumer in this search process.

Three major studies have documented the effects of dual pricing.[39] In October 1970, Jewel Tea supermarkets released a study of the effects of their Compar-A-Buy (CAB) program, then seven months old. About 45 percent of the respondents had used the system one or more times, 41 percent considered it worthwhile, but only 30 percent said they used it on a regular basis. Most importantly, only 5 percent said they had changed a shopping decision on the basis of CAB. Finally, while the device was originally intended as an aid for lower income shoppers, use appeared to increase with income and education.

Another study, conducted under the auspices of the Consumer Research Institute, took place in six Kroger stores over a 16-week period. The percentage of those polled who had actually used the unit pricing system in shopping was about 31 percent, close to Jewel's 30 percent. As with the Jewel tests, the Kroger study also found higher use among the more educated and affluent and negligible changes in buying patterns. Product movement analysis showed that most product categories displayed no tendencies to shift toward lower or higher price points.

A third study was cosponsored by the National Association of Food Chains and Safeway supermarkets. It was found that 31 percent of respondents used dual pricing—exactly the same as in Kroger stores. The study also concluded:

> . . . that shoppers are not able to make many price comparisons of supermarket packages effectively without the aid of dual-price labels . . . indeed our figures indicate that label usage may increase the number of correctly made cost comparisons involving such packages by factors ranging from 2.5 to 7.

The above studies as well as other information suggest that some of the worst fears about dual pricing—that it would benefit private label to the detriment of brand name sales, and that it would cause a mass movement to size—appear to be overstated. Buying decisions involve more than cost considerations.

38 F. E. Brown, "Who Perceives Supermarket Prices Most Validly?" *Journal of Marketing Research*, vol. 8, pp. 110–13 (February 1971).
39 This section was adapted from "Dual Pricing," *Progressive Grocer*, pp. 46–50 (February 1971).

Costs of establishing and maintaining dual pricing programs are not excessive. Estimates range from over $2,000 a year per store down to negligible costs offset partly by system benefits, such as lower costs for stocking, reordering, and inventory control.

Finally, by demonstrating an interest in consumer information techniques and a willingness to experiment, the industry may avoid restrictive legislation.

(2) Multiple-unit pricing. As its name implies, multiple-unit pricing refers to the practice of pricing items in quantities, such as 5/89¢ or 3/69¢. The effects were investigated in *Progressive Grocer's* panel of supermarkets during a six-month period.[40] In general, it proved to be quite effective in increasing immediate sales. This could, of course, merely be an indication that consumers are stocking up at a point in time assuming that prices have been reduced. Or, conversely, it is equally possible that sales of the product in question indeed are increased over time.[41]

Experience has demonstrated, first of all, that the price has to be easy to understand. Complicated multiple prices—i.e. 6/59¢ or 8/79¢—are usually less effective in increasing sales than a more simple multiple such as 2/18¢. Second, one dollar seems to be about the limit for the price range. Third, the check-out operator must be able to calculate prices accurately when less than the full number of units is purchased. In one test of 80 transactions, 14 percent were rung incorrectly. Given the fact that after-tax profit margins of the average supermarket seldom exceed 1.5 percent of sales, such mistakes can be costly indeed.[42]

Once again we have a situation in which the benefits for the retailer are undeniable, but the potential for consumer deception looms large. There is no denying the fact that the effect is to create the impression of a bargain. Furthermore, the consumer is hampered in calculating the price per unit. Without a genuine price saving or, alternatively, a desire for the greater convenience of buying multiple items in one package, this practice is hard to defend from the consumer's perspective. Unless remedial legislation is forthcoming, the only remedy once again is strengthened consumer education. One would be naive indeed to presume that manufacturers and retailers will voluntarily drop a profitable practice on their own volition.

Personal selling

The discussion to this point has centered primarily on products that are presold by advertising. While point-of-sale stimuli do convey some additional information, there is relatively little negotiation per se. Many purchases are not accompanied by this degree of information closure, however, and there still is a role for personal selling.

Despite the fact that salespeople are among the most extensively studied members of the business world, surprisingly little is known about

40 "How Multiple-Unit Pricing Helps . . . and Hurts," *Progressive Grocer,* p. 55 (June 1971).

41 See "Multiple-Pricing Makes the Most of the Moment of Purchase," *Progressive Grocer,* pp. C-128–C-132 (March 1964).

42 How Multiple Unit Pricing Helps . . . and Hurts," *Progressive Grocer.*

the role and impact of the salesperson in the ultimate sale of consumer goods as opposed to industrial goods.[43]

Until recently most research centered on predicting the salesperson's performance on the basis of background characteristics and a broad spectrum of personality, interest, and ability factors measured by various psychological testing instruments.[44] The purpose was to discover predictor variables that prove useful in selecting and recruiting qualified personnel. The results have been mixed. Occasionally predictor variables are found, but this often does not prove to be the case.[45] Even when predictors have been uncovered, this research strategy has contributed very little to understanding of why or how a salesperson becomes effective. Davis and Silk put it this way:

> In attempting to predict sales performance, this research has concentrated almost entirely on the characteristics of salesmen and has failed to take explicit account of who the salesman interacts with in attempting to make a sale. The assumption tacitly made is that differences among salesmen with respect to the types of prospects they contact are minimal, and hence variations in performance must be due to differences among the salesmen themselves . . . such an assumption seems tenuous for many if not most types of selling.[46]

Insights have been gained from research focusing directly on customer-salesperson interaction (often referred to more technically as "dyadic interaction").[47] It is explicitly recognized that the outcome is the result of the interaction between the salesperson and customer rather than a result of the individual qualities of either party considered in isolation.[48] The following types of questions are then investigated:

1. The nature and content of the interaction.[49]

43 James G. Hauk, "Research in Personal Selling," in George Schwartz, ed., *Science in Marketing* (New York: Wiley, 1965), at p. 217.

44 For an excellent review of this literature, see James C. Cotham, III "Selecting Salesmen: Approaches and Problems," *MSU Business Topics*, vol. 18, pp. 64–72 (Winter 1970).

45 See, for example, James C. Cotham, III, "Predicting Salesmen's Performance by Multiple Discriminant Analysis," *Southern Journal of Business*, vol. 4, pp. 25–34 (January 1969); James C. Cotham, III, "Job Attitudes and Sales Performance of Major Appliance Salesmen," *Journal of Marketing Research*, vol. 5, pp. 370–75 (November 1968).

46 Harry L. Davis and Alvin J. Silk, "Behavioral Research on Personal Selling: A Review of Some Recent Studies of Interaction and Influence Processes in Sales Situations" (Cambridge, Mass.: Marketing Science Institute, 1971), p. 4.

47 This conceptualization is based on Ronald P. Willett and Allan L. Pennington, "Customer and Salesman: The Anatomy of Choice and Influence in a Retail Setting," in R. M. Haas, ed., *Science, Technology and Marketing* (Chicago: American Marketing Association, 1966), pp. 598–616. For an alternative conceptualization, see James H. Bearden, "Decision Processes in Personal Selling," *Southern Journal of Business*, vol. 4, pp. 189–99 (April 1969).

48 Franklin B. Evans, "Selling as a Dyadic Relationship—A New Approach," *American Behavioral Scientist*, vol. 6, pp. 76–79 (May 1963).

49 "Content" refers to the categories used in Bales's interaction-process analysis. The observation categories are (1) shows solidarity, (2) shows tension release, (3) agrees, (4) gives suggestion, (5) gives opinion, (6) gives orientation, (7) asks for orientation, (8) asks for opinion, (9) asks for suggestion, (10) disagrees, (11) shows tension, (12) shows antagonism. These observational categories are usually collapsed into four interaction-process categories. The Bales system is by far the most highly developed and widely used method of describing interaction. See Robert F. Bales, *Interaction Process Analysis: A Method for the Study of Small Groups* (Reading, Mass.: Addision-Wesley, 1950).

2. The roles played by each of the participants.[50]

3. The changes occurring during the transaction, which culminate in an eventual sale.

The nature of the customer-salesperson transaction. In one major investigation, customer-salesperson interaction was analyzed in terms of length, velocity, content, interaction roles, and change in content of interactions over time.[51] Here are the major findings:

1. Length. The average retail transaction observed lasted 23 minutes, with the length of time varying from one minute to over two hours.

2. Velocity. Over 50 percent of all transactions generate rates of between six and 11 acts per minute, and the average for all transactions was ten acts per minute.

3. Content.[52] The most frequent type of interaction was the giving of orientation (information, clarification, and so on), followed by the giving of opinion. These two categories accounted for over 75 percent of the interaction.

4. Interaction roles. Interaction roles designate the relative contribution of interaction behavior[53] by both parties. In general, customers performed half as many acts as the salesperson. Attempted answers were primarily the domain of the salesperson while in the question categories, customer acts outnumbered salesperson acts by a multiple of four. Interestingly, customers were more likely to give positive reactions, whereas salespeople were almost completely responsible for disagreement, tension, and antagonism.

In general it was found that the salesperson controlled the interaction by patterns of response. The customer rarely achieved the upper hand.

Interaction and outcomes. There are, of course, many factors in addition to the structure and characteristics of interaction that determine whether or not customers will make a purchase. There is some evidence, however, that a sale differs from a nonsale in terms of the pattern of interaction.

Figure 10.1 presents some additional findings from the Willett-Pennington study of appliance shoppers. These 11 factors, taken together in a multiple discriminant analysis, permitted prediction of purchase outcomes in 80 percent of the cases. Thus, the transaction characteristics accurately predicted whether or not a person would become a buyer. The salesperson, in turn, was more likely to generate a sale through these types of interaction behaviors: frequent reference to concession limits

---

50 In this case, roles are measured as ratios of customer to salesman acts for each of the interaction-process categories.
51 Willett and Pennington, "Customer and Salesmen," pp. 598-616.
52 For an itemization of interaction categories, see footnote 49.
53 For an itemization of interaction behaviors, see footnote 49.

Figure 10.1 Relationships between key shopping and bargaining variables and purchase at time observed

Shopping or bargaining variable	Correlation of variable with purchase at time observed (point-biserial r)
1. Number of stores shopped by customer	−0.27*
2. Frequency of direct offers	+0.18†
3. Relative frequency of attempts to change concession limits	−0.25*
4. Frequency of commitment to concession limits	+0.33*
5. Frequency of attempts to change concession limits by devaluating other's product	−0.17‡
6. Frequency of reference to product quality	−0.17‡
7. Frequency of reference to delivery	+0.25*
8. Frequency of reference to styling	+0.21†
9. Relative frequency of reference to price	−0.24*
10. Relative frequency of reference to warranty	+0.18†
11. Relative frequency of reference to brand	−0.16‡

*Significant at 0.001 level.
†Significant at 0.01 level.
‡Significant at 0.05 level.

Source: Allan L. Pennington, "Customer-Salesman Bargaining Behavior in Retail Transactions," *Journal of Marketing Research*, vol. 5 (August 1968), pp. 255–62, at p. 261. Reprinted from the *Journal of Marketing Research* published by the American Marketing Association.

(bargaining ranges), reference to delivery, reference to styling, and reference to warranty. On the other hand, negative effects resulted when the salesperson knocked a competitive product, attempted to change concession limits, made frequent reference to quality, or continually mentioned price. This can provide some invaluable clues to sales training in this type of interaction.

In a related study Engel analyzed the interaction between the salesperson and buyer in furniture outlets.[54] One of the most interesting findings was the distinction between dollar sales volume by the individual salesperson and his or her ability to convert a shopper into a buyer. Some salespeople achieve large volumes by "highspotting"—centering only on those who have pretty well decided what to purchase when approached. This type of retailing, however, often entails advice giving and negotiation. Many who excelled in this dimension had lower total sales volumes but, in the long run, were more useful in building a permanent clientele for the store. The problem was aggravated in this situation by compensation solely on the basis of commission. This serves only to encourage highspotting, whereas a combination of salary and commission will facilitate a greater focus on helpful information giving.

By the way, it is interesting to note that a highly dependent consumer tends to be suggestible and hence prefers assistance by a salesperson in

54 See "The Columbia Furniture" case in Blackwell et al., *Contemporary Cases*, pp. 247–56.

decision making, whereas an independent person prefers a minimum of suggestion and assistance.[55] The independent person, in turn, seems to respond more positively to aggressive selling.[56] Women, on the other hand, are more likely to be negative to aggressive salespersons than their male counterparts.[57]

Customer-salesman similarity. The key to the interaction patterns discussed above seems to lie in the extent to which the two parties are similar to one another. Most of the evidence on this point comes from research in nonmarketing areas,[58] but some studies also have been conducted in a marketing context.

In one of the early investigations of this subject, Evans focused on 168 sold and 183 unsold insurance prospects.[59] He demonstrated, first of all, that attitudinal, personality, or demographic characteristics will not differentiate a buyer from a nonbuyer. Much of the difference was explainable by the fact of great similarity between the buyer and salesperson in terms of age and height and a number of other personal characteristics. As Evans pointed out:

> The successful salesman was seen by sold prospects as (1) an expert on insurance, (2) similar to themselves in outlook and situation, (3) a person they would like to know better, and (4) interested in them personally, not just as a source of revenue.[60]

His conclusions were reinforced by Gadel, who found that insurance salesmen sell most of their policies to people who were in the same age group as themselves.[61]

Further light was shed by Brock's experiment undertaken to determine the relative importance of salesman expertise and customer-salesman similarity in influencing sales.[62] Although the expert salesman was perceived as more knowledgeable about the product (paint), he was less effective than the salesman who identified his own paint consumption as similar to that of his customers. This seems to verify the fact known by most successful communicators that their success is always in proportion to their empathy or ability to put themselves in another's shoes.

55 M. Zuckerman and H. J. Grosz, "Suggestibility and Dependency," *Journal of Consulting Psychology*, vol. 26, pp. 32–38 (October 1958).

56 James E. Stafford and Thomas V. Green, "Consumer Preference for Types of Salesmen: A Study of Independence-Dependence Characteristics," *Journal of Retailing*, pp. 27–33 (Summer 1965).

57 Stafford and Greer, "Customer Preference," p. 32; and Gilbert Burck, "What Makes Women Buy?" *Fortune*, pp. 93–94, 174–94 (August 1956).

58 See, for example, Dana Bramel, "Interpersonal Attraction, Hostility and Perception," in Judson Mills, ed., *Experimental Social Psychology* (New York: Macmillan, 1969), pp. 1–120; Fritz Heider, *The Psychology of Interpersonal Relations* (New York: Wiley, 1961); George C. Homans, *Social Behavior: Its Elementary Forms* (New York: Harcourt, 1961).

59 Evans, "Selling."

60 Evans, "Selling."

61 M. S. Gadel, "Concentration by Salesmen on Congenial Prospects," *Journal of Marketing*, vol. 28, pp. 64–66 (April 1964).

62 Timothy C. Brock, "Communicator-Recipient Similarity and Decision Change," *Journal of Personality and Social Psychology*, vol. 1, pp. 650–54 (June 1965).

The impact on consumer search processes. There is no question that the consumer *can* benefit greatly from an honest, empathetic salesperson. But all too frequently the information transmitted (or not transmitted) has an opposite effect. Engel found, for example, that many furniture salespersons knowingly permitted customers to make a purchase that, for one reason or another, was very wrong for their own circumstances.[63] Couples had been specially trained for this project to pose as shoppers who offered a variety of situations to each salesperson who, by the way, had been formally trained in how to contend with each situation. More often than not the content of sales training never found its way to the sales floor. Outright indifference was not uncommon.

This problem becomes especially acute when one's physical well being is threatened. In one unpublished study, shoppers visited many retail pharmacists in a major city and presented this question to one of the registered pharmacists: "I am on insulin, but I am having trouble with allergies and sinus. Would it be ok if I take Dristan?" The usual answer was, "Fine, go ahead," even though directions on the label clearly indicated that Dristan was *not* to be taken by those on insulin. A pharmacist of any repute should have known this, and failure to alert the consumer of the dangers is outright irresponsibility.

In a more recent study, pharmacists in various cities were evaluated to determine whether or not information on side effects of prescription drugs was ever communicated to the customer.[64] Most indicated that this was not their responsibility at all and that the doctor should do so. Not surprisingly it was verified that the physician also largely ignored this critical information. So where does this leave the consumer who must trust the professional in the field of health?

Unfortunately, personal selling is more difficult to regulate than media advertising. Nevertheless, the consumerism movement has taken important steps both in legal action and in consumer education. Still, the best strategy is "let the buyer beware."

Attraction-conversion analysis

Some consumers shop retail outlets because they believe the store carries the brand they are looking for. Other consumers do not have brand preferences prior to shopping. The sequence of these decisions—brand choice followed by store choice or store choice followed by brand choice—has important implications for manufacturers and retailers.

Attraction-conversion analysis is based on two basic concepts:

1. Attraction power. The number of consumers who visit a retail outlet because they want to purchase a specific brand.

2. Conversion power. The percentage of consumers shopping a retail outlet for a brand that actually purchase the brand.

Figure 10.2 illustrates how attraction and conversion indices can be con-

63 "The Columbia Furniture" case in Blackwell et al., *Contemporary Cases.*
64 James C. McCullagh, "Is Your Medicine Chest a Relic from the Dark Ages?" *Prevention*, vol. 28, pp. 95–113 (December 1976).

Figure 10.2 Attraction and conversion
indices for hypothetical brands and stores

	Brands		
Stores	A	B	C
Store 1			
Attraction power	120	102	98
Conversion power	80	98	105
Store 2			
Attraction power	100	107	94
Conversion power	100	102	102
.			
.			
.			
Store N			
Attraction power	90	95	93
Conversion power	120	97	94

Note: For attraction and conversion, 100 is the average for all brands and all stores. For example, for brand A, Store 1's attraction power is 20 percent above average while store N's is 10 percent below average.

structed for hypothetical brands in various stores. In constructing the indices, 100 equals the average for all brands and all stores. Thus in store 1, brand A is 20 percent above average in terms of attraction power, but 20 percent below average in conversion power.

Retailers can use attraction and conversion indices in several ways. However, in all instances, these measures must be interpreted within the context of the retailer's merchandising strategy. Attraction power is useful because it allows retailers to evaluate the relative effectiveness of brands in generating store traffic. In store 1, for example, brand A is drawing a greater number of customers than are brands B or C. In evaluating relative effectiveness, the retailer must make certain that differences in attraction power are not due to *his* advertising and sales promotion emphasis.

Conversion power must also be interpreted cautiously. If the retailer is giving equal sales and merchandising emphasis to each brand, then conversion power is a true measure of the ability of a brand to convert shoppers into purchasers. On the other hand, if the retailer is emphasizing a brand, then variations in conversion power may simply reflect his merchandising strategy for the product category.

Retailers can also compute other measures that might be termed *sales power* indices. For a given brand, sales power could be (1) the percentage of shoppers that purchase any brand in the product category, or (2) the gross margin, or direct product profits, resulting from the fact that consumers are attracted to the store by the brand. The latter measure incorporates the profit resulting from all purchases made by the customer during the shopping trip.

Manufacturers can use attraction, conversion, and sales power measures to demonstrate the importance of their brands to retailers. Again, however, these measures can be used for this purpose only if retailers' sales and merchandising emphasis do not vary across brands in a product category.

Manufacturers can also use variations of this type of analysis. First, the percentage of purchasers who decide on a brand prior to shopping is a rough measure of the effectiveness of the manufacturer's promotion program, as well as an indication of the relative importance of retail support.

Second, conversion power provides the manufacturer with a gross measure of how effectively distribution strategy is converting preferences into purchases. Moreover, it is possible to assess strengths and weaknesses further by determining how conversion power varies by type of retail outlet, as well as by individual retailers.

Third, the manufacturer can perform the type of gain-loss analysis previously described in Chapter 9. Using brand preference before shopping as the base statistic, the manufacturer can determine the number of consumers switching to the brand as the result of shopping for each one that switches away from the brand. This allows the manufacturer to identify the brands the company is gaining from and those that are making inroads.

The next step is to obtain ratings of brands on the relevant evaluative criteria. Economic, demographic, psychographic, and media-usage profiles can be constructed for consumers who switch away from and switch to the manufacturer's brand. Armed with this information the manufacturer can determine whether it is possible to improve conversion ratios and, if so, the target market, the product benefits that should be emphasized, and the media vehicles that should be used.

Summary

This chapter continued the discussion of search processes by focusing on the role and functioning of the marketer-dominated stimuli. The first to be discussed was media advertising. It was stressed that the primary role of advertising is informative. The impact in terms of changing beliefs and attitudes can be great, and this predisposes the consumer to make a purchase at a later time. Only in certain instances will advertising actually trigger a purchase, and in those instances the purchase was imminent anyway.

The remainder of the marketer-dominated stimuli were evaluated within the context of the retail store. First it was demonstrated that people do shop extensively and that point-of-sale is a significant source of information. Some of the specific means include point-of-sale display, packages, pricing, and personal selling. Attraction, conversion, and sales power measures were examined, and it was shown how both retailers and manufacturers can use this analysis to increase the effectiveness of point-of-sale communication.

Review and discussion questions

1. Under what circumstances would a sales objective be appropriate for advertising? Under what circumstances would it be more appropriate to attempt to stimulate changes in awareness, attitude, or other so-called communication responses?

2. A leading manufacturer of recreational vehicles based its advertising campaign on this statement of objectives: "Our goal is to tell as many people as possible that travel and camping is fun for the family and that it is easier when you are traveling in your own 'motel.'" Evaluate.

3. "Since consumers typically visit only one or at most two stores before purchasing a product, store visits are not an important information source." Do you agree?

4. What is the relation between point-of-purchase display and sales response? What are the implications for retailers? For manufacturers?

5. When multiple-unit pricing is used, why do sales often increase even when the single unit price is higher than normal?

6. Does the customer-salesperson similarity hypothesis describe your own preferences and responses when you have contact with salespeople? If not, is there an alternative hypothesis?

7. Of what use is the customer-salesperson similarity hypothesis in marketing planning?

8. Describe the manner in which both a manufacturer and a retailer can make use of attraction and conversion indices.

CHAPTER 11

Nonmarketer-dominated information sources

To what extent do consumers rely on the opinions and experiences of other individuals in making purchasing decisions? What kinds of people do consumers look to for advice? Are there generalized opinion leaders or tastemakers in America? These are the major issues that are discussed in this chapter.

Interpersonal communications

Hundreds of studies have found that consumers obtain information about products and services from other people, particularly family members, friends and neighbors, and other acquaintances. This exchange of information between consumers is called *interpersonal communications*, while the effect of this behavior is termed *personal influence*. Individuals who influence the general and purchasing behavior of other people are called *opinion leaders*. Opinion leadership may be *positive* in its effect on promoting the purchase of a product or it may be *negative* and lead to the discouragement of others from buying a product. This section discusses the impact and dynamics of interpersonal communication.

The marketing impact of interpersonal communications

It is quite common for interpersonal communications to be influential in purchasing decisions. Consider the following illustrative examples:

1. Almost 50 percent of male and female students at Florida State University discussed with their friends clothing brands, styles, retail outlets, and prices.[1]

---

1 John R. Kerr and Bruce Weale, "Collegiate Clothing Purchasing Patterns and Fashion Adoption Behavior," *Southern Journal of Business*, vol. 5 (July 1970), pp. 126–33, at p. 129.

2. A study of the diffusion of a new food product in a married students' apartment complex revealed that exposure to favorable word of mouth was found to increase the probability of purchase, while exposure to unfavorable comments decreased the probability.[2]

3. A large-scale study of Indianapolis housewives revealed that nearly two-thirds of those interviewed told someone else about new products they had purchased or tried.[3]

4. Another study found that the source of information most frequently consulted by durable goods buyers was friends and relatives. ". . . more than 50 percent of our buyers turned for advice to acquaintances and in most instances also looked at durable goods owned by them." Even more striking is the finding that one-third of durable goods buyers bought a brand or model that they had seen at someone else's house, often the house of relatives.[4]

5. A study of consumer attitudes toward health care found that the largest segment of consumers state the most important reason for choosing their doctor was a recommendation by a friend or relative.[5]

Other studies have also found interpersonal communications to be very important in the purchase of food items, soaps, and cleansing agents, in motion picture selections, hairdo styles, makeup techniques,[6] general fashions,[7] dental products and services,[8] farming practices,[9] physicians,[10] man-made fabrics,[11] and new products,[12] to mention just a few.

2 Johan Arndt, "Role of Product-Related Conversations in the Diffusion of a New Product," *Journal of Marketing Research*, vol. 4 (August 1967), pp. 291–95.

3 Charles W. King and John O. Summers, "Technology, Innovation and Consumer Decision Making," in Reed Moyer, ed., *Consumer, Corporate and Government Interfaces* (Chicago: American Marketing Association, 1967), pp. 63–68, at p. 66.

4 George Katona and Eva Mueller, "A Study of Purchasing Decisions," in Lincoln H. Clark, ed., *Consumer Behavior: The Dynamics of Consumer Reaction* (New York: New York University Press, 1955), pp. 30–87, at p. 45.

5 Roger D. Blackwell and W. Wayne Talarzyk, *Consumer Attitudes toward Health Care and Malpractice* (Columbus: Grid Publishing, Inc., 1977).

6 Elihu Katz and Paul F. Lazarsfeld, *Personal Influence* (New York: Free Press, 1955).

7 Charles W. King, "Fashion Adoption: A Rebuttal to the Trickle Down Theory," in Stephen A. Greyser, ed., *Toward Scientific Marketing* (Chicago: American Marketing Association, 1963), pp. 108–25.

8 Alvin J. Silk, "Overlap among Self Designated Opinion Leaders: A Study of Selected Dental Products and Services," *Journal of Marketing Research*, vol. 3 (August 1966), pp. 255–59.

9 Elihu Katz, "The Social Itinerary of Technical Changes: Two Studies in the Diffusion of Innovation," *Human Organization*, vol. 20 (1961), pp. 70–82; E. M. Rogers and G. M. Beal, "The Importance of Personal Influence in the Adoption of Technological Changes," *Social Forces*, vol. 36 (May 1958), pp. 329–35.

10 James Coleman, Elihu Katz, and Herbert Menzel, "The Diffusion of an Innovation among Physicians," *Sociometry* (December 1957), pp. 253–70; Herbert Menzel and Elihu Katz, "Social Relations and Innovation in the Medical Profession: The Epidemiology of a New Drug," *Public Opinion Quarterly*, vol. 19 (Winter 1955–56), pp. 337–52.

11 George M. Beal and Everett M. Rogers, "Informational Sources in the Adoption Process of New Fabrics," *Journal of Home Economics*, vol. 49 (October 1957), pp. 630–34.

12 *Rare Research Opportunity in Word of Mouth Advertising* (New York: Advertising Research Foundation, 1967), p. 10.

Interpersonal communication dyads

Although considerable research has been conducted on the importance of interpersonal communication, research on the transmitter-receiver dyad is scarce. After reviewing the literature, King and Summers concluded that although the dimensions of analyses and the methodologies used have varied between studies, the research findings are remarkably consistent.[13]

1. The interaction dyad appears to be relatively homogeneous across many interaction contexts. In other words, studies comparing the social status and age of participants in an interaction dyad indicate that people tend to exchange information with other age and social status peers.

2. Perceived credibility and/or expertise of the person giving information on a topic is an important dimension in information-seeking behavior. Seekers search for referents "more qualified" than themselves on a topic. In contexts where expertise is not perceived available within the seekers' peer level, sources higher or lower in age and social status may be consulted.

3. The family plays an important role in interpersonal communication in the socialization of children and in interaction within the extended family. The specific functions of family versus nonfamily interactions may be different, but this area has not been explored.

4. Proximity is important in facilitating interaction. Proximity as a variable is two-dimensional, including physical proximity and social proximity. Obviously, physical proximity, for example, living in the same neighborhood, makes possible physical contact and the settings for interpersonal exchange. Physical proximity also suggests a minimum social proximity in terms of some overlap of social status, interests, life style, etc.

Decision process variations. The influence of interpersonal communications varies by stages of consumer decision making. While much of the research on interpersonal communications starts with models that recognize that consumer decisions are *processes*, in practice much of the research has failed to incorporate the process approach into the research design when implementing research. Berning and Jacoby have noted this problem and set about to deal with it by analyzing one stage in decision making, the use of sources of information, both for new products and for established products. They concluded that the decision-making process preceding the purchase of new products is different than that in the purchasing of established products and that the difference lies primarily in the search for information from friends.[14]

13 Charles W. King and John O. Summers, "Dynamics of Interpersonal Communication: The Interaction Dyad," in Donald F. Cox, ed., *Risk Taking and Information Handling in Consumer Behavior* (Boston: Division of Research, Graduate School of Business Administration, Harvard University, 1967), pp. 240–64, at p. 261.

14 Carol A. Kohn Berning and Jacob Jacoby, "Patterns of Information Acquisition in New Product Purchases," *Journal of Consumer Research*, vol. 1 (September 1974), pp. 18–22.

This brief summary of the salient characteristics of interpersonal communications dyads provides an introduction to a more detailed and rigorous discussion of the nature and dynamics of personal influence.

A recent development in understanding interpersonal influence is *attribution theory*. Attribution is a theoretical construct referring to cognitive processes through which an individual infers the cause of the behavior of others or even of himself or herself. Individuals come to know their own attitudes, emotions, and other internal states partially from inferring them from observations of their own behavior as "actors" in the circumstances in which the behavior occurs. To some degree, attribution theory (or self-perception theory, as it is also called) postulates that the individual is functionally in the same position as an outside observer who must rely on external cues to infer the individual's inner state.

Attribution theory

Attribution theory presents considerable potential for understanding the *dynamics* of interpersonal influence because it attempts to explain how cognitive processes are modified by behavior. Attributions amount to judgments or inferences about a consumer which shape an observer's actions with respect to the consumer. The observer's actions may directly affect the consumer's behavior, and thus these attributions provide psychological reasons for the actions of influencers. A comprehensive review of attribution theory and its applications to consumer research is available in a seminal paper on the topic by Scott.[15] While the topic is embryonic in its development, it provides the possibility of a far-ranging explanation for the process by which the effects of behavior are fed back into and influence cognitive processes.

Personal influence

It is one thing to conclude that consumers use other persons as sources of information, but for the marketer the question becomes: "How is this fact useful in designing marketing programs?" The ultimate purpose of this chapter is to answer that question, but to do so, some intermediate steps are necessary. If it is determined that personal sources are important in consumer decisions about a specific category, then the first step is to identify what individuals or types of people are opinion leaders. To do that requires research, of course, including consideration of how that research might be conducted. The following pages describe, first, the research techniques used to identify leaders and second, the conclusions that have been drawn from such research about the characteristics of opinion leaders.

Opinion leadership refers to the degree to which an individual influences others in a given choice situation. Those who do a disproportionately

Identifying opinion leaders

15 C. A. Scott, "Self-perception Processes in Consumer Behavior: Interpreting One's Own Experiences," in Keith Hunt, ed., *Advances in Consumer Research*, vol. 5 (Chicago: Association for Consumer Research, 1978). See also B. J. Calder and R. F. Burnkrandt, "Interpersonal Influence on Consumer Behavior: An Attribution Theory Approach," *Journal of Consumer Research*, vol. 4 (June 1977), pp. 29–38.

large amount of influencing others are called "opinion leaders" in those situations in which they exert influence.

Three basic types of techniques are used to measure opinion leadership:

1. The sociometric method involves asking respondents from whom they get advice and to whom they go to seek advice or information in making a specified type of decision.[16]

2. The key informant method involves the use of informed individuals in a social system to identify opinion leaders in a given situation.[17]

3. The self-designating method relies on the respondent to evaluate his own influence in a given topic area.[18]

King and Summers studied and evaluated the advantages and disadvantages of these methods.[19] The sociometric method has face validity but it is not effective when the social system to be investigated is not self-contained in terms of the flow of influence on the topic area of interest or when the social system is too large to permit the interviewing of all of its members. For example, a retail store might wish to determine opinion leaders for fashion and appearance in a high school. The sociometric methods might be ideal from a theoretical perspective but not practical because of the cost and difficulty of the research.

The key informant method is useful when the objective is to study only opinion leaders, when financial and other constraints prohibit interviewing a large number of people, and/or when the social system is small and key informants can provide accurate information on the interaction process.

Since the conditions favoring these two methods do not usually exist in marketing settings, most consumer studies use the self-designating method. This technique is a compromise between the other two methods, being simple to administer in survey research and not limited to small, self-contained social systems where a census is required.

An example of the self-designation scales typically used in marketing studies is provided in Figure 11.1. In practice, marketing researchers may

16 For example, see Robert K. Merton, *Social Theory and Social Structure* (New York: Free Press, 1957); John C. Myers, "Patterns of Interpersonal Influence in the Adoption of New Products," in Haas, *Science*, pp. 750–57.

17 See, for example, Alvaro Chaparro, "Role Expectation and Adoption of New Farm Practices," unpublished Ph.D. diss. (University Park: Pennsylvania State University, 1955).

18 For examples, see Francesco M. Nicosia, "Opinion Leaders and the Flow of Communication: Some Problems and Prospects," in L. G. Smith, ed., Reflections on Progress in Marketing (Chicago: American Marketing Association, 1965), pp. 340–59; James S. Fenton and Thomas R. Leggett, "A New Way to Find Opinion Leaders," *Journal of Advertising Research*, vol. 11 (April 1971), pp. 22–25; Fred D. Reynolds and William R. Darden, "Mutually Adaptive Effects of Interpersonal Communication," *Journal of Marketing Research*, vol. 8 (November 1971), pp. 449–54; Stephen A. Baumgarten, "The Innovative Communicator in the Diffusion Process," *Journal of Marketing Research*, vol. 12 (February 1975), pp. 12–18.

19 Charles W. King and John O. Summers, "Generalized Opinion Leadership in Consumer Products: Some Preliminary Findings," paper no. 224 (Lafayette, Ind.: Institute for Research in the Behavioral, Economic, and Management Sciences, Krannert Graduate School of Industrial Administration, January 1969).

Figure 11.1 Example of self designation scales of opinion leadership

(1) In general, do you like to talk about _____ with your friends?

Yes _____ —1   No _____ —2

(2) Would you say *you give very little information, an average amount of information,* or *a great deal of information* about _____ to your friends?

You give very little information   _____ —1
You give an average amount of information _____ —2
You give a great deal of information   _____ —3

(3) During the *past six months,* have *you told anyone* about some _____?

Yes _____ —1   No _____ —2

(4) Compared with your circle of friends, are you *less likely, about as likely,* or *more likely* to be asked for advice about _____?

Less likely to be asked   _____ —1
About as likely to be asked _____ —1
More likely to be asked   _____ —3

(5) If you and your friends were to discuss _____, what part would *you* be most likely to play? Would you *mainly listen* to your friends' ideas or would *you try to convince them* of your ideas?

You mainly listen to your friends ideas _____ —1
You try to convince them of your ideas _____ —2

(6) Which of these happens more often? Do *you tell your friends* about some _____, *or* do *they tell you* about some _____?

You tell them about _____ —1
They tell you about _____ —2

(7) Do you have the feeling that you are generally regarded by your friends and neighbors as a good source of advice about _____?

Yes _____ —1   No _____ —2

Source: Charles W. King and John O. Summers, "Generalized Opinion Leadership in Consumer Products: Some Preliminary Findings," paper no. 224 (Lafayette, Ind.: Institute for Research in the Behavioral, Economic and Management Sciences, Krannert Graduate School of Industrial Administration, January 1969), p. 16. Reprinted by permission.

only use one or two questions similar to those in Figure 11.1 along with many other questions or may use several questions about opinion leadership. Generally, longer scales have greater validity and reliability[20] than methods involving fewer questions.[21]

The continuous scores from self-designating opinion leadership scales are divided into dichotomous categories of opinion leaders and non–opinion leaders. The criteria used to establish these categories include (1) comparability with previous studies, (2) comparability across product categories, and (3) reasonable categories given the distributions of the

20 Everett M. Rogers and David G. Cartano, "Methods of Measuring Opinion Leadership," *Public Opinion Quarterly,* vol. 26 (Fall 1962), pp. 43–45.

21 The relative strengths and problems of alternative methods are reviewed in George Brooker and Michael J. Houston, "An Evaluation of Measures of Opinion Leadership," Kenneth L. Bernhardt, ed., *Marketing 1776–1976 and Beyond* (Chicago: American Marketing Association, 1976), pp. 564–71.

opinion leadership scores for each product category. Typically, the opinion leadership scores are arrayed, and the upper 23 to 30 percent of the respondents are classified as opinion leaders.[22] Sometimes, opinion leadership is defined as including more than two categories into something such as low, medium, and high opinion leadership.[23]

Who are opinion leaders?

Marketing organizations would like to know who the opinion leaders are—those having such importance in determining the acceptance or rejection of the marketing organization's products or services. If opinion leaders can be identified, the possibility exists they might be influenced by more or better mass media directed toward them. Considerable research has been directed toward determining the characteristics of opinion leaders. This has focused on demographic characteristics, social activity, general attitudes, personality characteristics, life styles, and product-related characteristics as well as the general question whether opinion leadership is generalized or specific.

Demographic characteristics. There has been much effort devoted to determining if persons with certain demographic characteristics—such as high income, education, and so forth—would be opinion leaders. The answer seems to be that opinion leadership depends very much on the product category. In a product category where relatively high income is needed to purchase the product, people in higher income categories are likely to consider the product more feasible to buy, have higher ownership and experience, and therefore be opinion leaders for others. In other product categories, wives with large families may dominate opinion leadership for household cleaning or maintenance items because they have greater experience with the product category. On the other hand, young women dominate for fashion products and movie-going.[24] Some research has found that young persons are slightly more influential across many different products and have found some other demographic relationships. For the most part, however, demographic relationships are usually too weak to be very helpful.[25]

One of the reasons why opinion leaders are not from specific demographic groups is that interpersonal communications tend to be homogeneous in terms of social class, age, and income. This is known as *homophily*, or the principle that the sources of communications and the receivers of communications tend to have similar attributes. *Homophilious* or highly similar communication dyads tend to interact with greater frequency than *heterophilious*, or highly dissimilar dyads. Thus, influence (mass media or personal) tends to occur when source and receiver have

22 Katz and Lazarsfeld, *Personal Influence*; King and Summers, "Dynamics."

23 Baumgarten, "Innovative Communicator."

24 See, for example, Katz, "Social Itinerary"; Katz and Lazarsfeld, *Personal Influence*; Rogers, op. cit.; W. L. Warner and P. S. Lunt, *The Social Life of a Modern Community* (New Haven, Conn.: Yale University Press, 1941).

25 James H. Myers and Thomas S. Robertson, "Dimensions of Opinion Leadership," *Journal of Marketing Research*, vol. 9 (February 1972), pp. 41–46.

similar or shared attitudes, meanings of language, belief structure and so forth.[26]

Social activity. Opinion leaders usually participate in more social activities and are more gregarious than non–opinion leaders.[27] In all of the factors used to identify opinion leaders, gregariousness is often one of the most important.

General attitudes. In the case of new products, opinion leaders tend to have more favorable attitudes toward both new products as a concept and new products within their specific areas of influence. Where the norms of the population as a whole reflect positive attitudes toward new products, opinion leaders reflect even greater commitment to new products than do their counterparts. Thus leaders are usually more innovative than other individuals.[28]

Personality characteristics. Robertson and Myers studied the relationship between personality characteristics and opinion leadership. Using the California Psychological Inventory to measure personality characteristics in eighteen major areas, they concluded that none of the basic personality variables related substantially to opinion leadership for any of the product areas studied (appliances, clothing, food).[29]

Other studies have found that opinion leaders do have some distinguishing personality characteristics. For example, Summers found that women's clothing fashion opinion leaders are more emotionally stable, assertive, likeable, less depressive or self-deprecating, and tend to be leaders and more self-confident.[30] Others have also found that opinion leaders tend to be more self-confident.[31] Thus it appears that the relationship between personality characteristics and opinion leadership depends on the type of personality characteristic studied and the product under investigation. Tailor-made personality variables are probably more effective discriminators than are general personality characteristics.

Life style characteristics. Tigert and Arnold constructed lifestyle profiles of general, self-designated opinion leaders, both in the United States and Canada. Using activity, interest, and opinion variables, they were able to

26 E. M. Rogers and D. K. Bhomik, "Homophily-Heterophily: Relational Concepts for Communication Research," *Public Opinion Quarterly*, vol. 34 (Winter 1970), pp. 523–38; George P. Moschis, "Social Comparison and Informal Group Influence," *Journal of Marketing Research*, vol. 13 (August 1976), pp. 237–44.

27 For contemporary examples, see Reynolds and Darden, "Mutually Adaptive," pp. 449–54; John O. Summers, "The Identity of Women's Clothing Fashion Opinion Leaders," *Journal of Marketing Research*, vol. 7, pp. 178–85 (May 1970); Baumgarten, "Innovative Communication." This was not found to be a significant relationship, however, in Myers and Reynolds, op. cit.

28 John O. Summers and Charles W. King, "Interpersonal Communication and New Product Attitudes," in McDonald, op. cit., pp. 292–99.

29 Thomas S. Robertson and James H. Myers, "Personality Correlates of Opinion Leadership and Innovative Buying Behavior," *Journal of Marketing Research*, vol. 6, pp. 164–68 (May 1969).

30 Summers, "Identity," pp. 180–81.

31 See, for example, Reynolds and Darden, "Mutually Adoptive," p. 450.

construct a rich portrait of opinion leaders. Factor analysis revealed that eight factors—leadership, information exchanges, innovation, community and club involvement, independence, price consciousness, occupation, and fashion consciousness—were able to explain 27 percent in the variance of opinion leadership in Canada.[32]

The Tigert and Arnold study was concerned with a composite opinion leader for a broad variety of product categories. Had they constructed profiles of opinion leaders for specific products, or products in the same interest category, they probably would have been more successful. Nevertheless, their study points up the potential value of life style profiles.

Product-related characteristics. Opinion leaders tend to have certain additional distinguishing characteristics related to the type of decision being made. First, they perceive themselves as more interested in the topic area. For example, in women's fashions, opinion leaders are more interested in fashions than are non–opinion leaders.[33]

Second, opinion leaders are more active in receiving interpersonal communications about products within their area of influence. In other words, other consumers talk to opinion leaders more than they do to non–opinion leaders about things that are related to the leaders' alleged area of expertise.[34] This varies by product category and between cultural groups and subgroups. In the United States, people tend to discuss grocery products more than in France. While word-of-mouth communications about grocery products was relatively low in France, it was relatively high with respect to retail services.[35]

Finally, opinion leaders are usually more exposed to certain additional sources of information. They may be more exposed to the mass media in general although not in every instance.[36] However, they are almost always more exposed to specific types of mass media that are relevant to their area of interest. Thus, for example, opinion leaders in women's fashions may not be more exposed to television in general, but they are usually more exposed to women's fashion magazines.[37]

Opinion leadership overlap. There is a great deal of interest in the question of whether opinion leadership is *monomorphic*—product specific—or *polymorphic*—overlapping many product areas. Much of the early literature supported the concept of monomorphic opinion leader-

32 Douglas J. Tigert and Stephen J. Arnold, *Profiling Self-Designated Opinion Leaders and Self-Designated Innovators through Life Style Research* (Toronto: School of Business, University of Toronto, June 1971).

33 Summers, "Identity," pp. 178–85.

34 Summers and King, "Interpersonal Communication," pp. 292–99.

35 Robert T. Green and Eric Langeard, "A Cross-National Comparison of Consumer Habits and Innovator Characteristics," *Journal of Marketing*, vol. 39 (July 1975), pp. 35–41.

36 See, for example, Robert Mason, "The Use of Information Sources by Influentials in the Adoption Process," *Public Opinion Quarterly*, vol. 27, pp. 455–66 (1963).

37 See, for example, Katz and Lazarsfeld, *Personal Influence*, pp. 309–20; Summers, "Identity," pp. 178–85; Reynolds and Darden, "Mutually Adoptive," pp. 449–54.

ship,[38] but more recently this has been clarified to support the conclusion that the same persons will be opinion leaders for related products but not for all products. For example, influence for women's clothing was found to be highly related to that for cosmetics. Also, personal care and influence for household furnishings correlated highly with that for household appliances in the research of Myers and Robertson.[39] Although the same persons may be opinion leaders for fashions and cosmetics, little overlap appears to exist between cosmetics and appliances.[40]

Montgomery and Silk found overlap in opinion leadership across most but not all of the categories studied. They also found that the patterns of overlap appeared to parallel the manner in which housewives' interests in these categories clustered together.[41] Further work by Montgomery and Silk found that patterns of association in opinion leadership for sixteen topics corresponded to the structure of interrelationships among measures of interest in the same topics.[42]

Thus research to date indicates that there are quasi-generalized opinion leaders. The nature of interest patterns seems to be one of the important factors that determine what constitutes their sphere of influence.

In summary, opinion leadership is an important phenomenon and marketing organizations need to understand what types of people are leaders in a specific product category. Leaders are usually—although not always—similar to those they influence, and they typically differ from one sphere of interest to another. They tend to be more gregarious and innovative, are more interested in the area in question, and both receive and transmit more information about the topic.

Models of personal influence

A number of theories or models have been developed in an attempt to help marketers and others understand how the process of personal influence occurs. This section describes some of these models and the research that has developed from the models.

The two-step flow of communications is the traditional model of the link between mass media and interpersonal communication. Despite some

The two-step flow hypothesis

38 See, for example, Silk, "Overlap," p. 257; Katz and Lazarsfeld, *Personal Influence*, p. 334; Everett M. Rogers, *Diffusion of Innovation* (New York: Free Press, 1962), pp. 30–36; Elihu Katz, "The Two Step Flow of Communication: An Up-to-Date Report on a Hypothesis," *Public Opinion Quarterly*, vol. 21, pp. 61–78 (Spring 1957).

39 Myers and Robertson, "Dimensions," p. 45.

40 Charles W. King and John O. Summers, "Overlap of Opinion Leadership across Consumer Product Categories," *Journal of Marketing Research*, vol. 7, pp. 43–50 (February 1970). For additional evidence see Edwin J. Gross, "Support for a Generalized Marketing Leadership Theory," *Journal of Advertising Research*, vol. 9, pp. 49–52 (November 1969).

41 David B. Montgomery and Alvin J. Silk, "Patterns of Overlap in Opinion Leadership and Interest for Selected Categories of Purchasing Activity," in Philip R. McDonald, ed., *Marketing Involvement in Society and the Economy* (Chicago: American Marketing Association, 1969), pp. 377–86. For supporting evidence in other areas, see Herbert F. Lionberger, *Adoption of New Ideas and Practices* (Ames, Iowa: Iowa State University Press, 1960), pp. 65–66.

42 David B. Montgomery and Alvin J. Silk, "Clusters of Consumer Interests and Opinion Leaders' Spheres of Influence," *Journal of Marketing Research*, vol. 8, pp. 317–21 (August 1971).

revisions and modifications, the essential elements of the hypothesis remain unchanged from its original formulation in 1948. Briefly, this model states that influences and ideas flow from the mass media to opinion leaders and from them to the less active sections of the population.[43] The link between the passive masses and the mass media is the opinion leader.

Although the two-step flow was a historic breakthrough in understanding communications, it is no longer an accurate and complete model of the process. For one thing, it views the audience as passive receivers of information. Yet several studies have found that up to 50 percent of word-of-mouth communications are initiated by consumers seeking information from opinion leaders.[44] Moreover, at least in some instances, word-of-mouth communication is affected by selective exposure and selective response.[45]

Multi-stage interaction models

A more contemporary view of personal influence is built upon a multi-stage interaction approach. Much of this research is derived from the diffusion of innovations literature showing differences in personal communication and influence, depending upon whether consumers are earlier triers or later adopters of a product. A longitudinal study of Maxim coffee concluded that early adopters followed a pattern close to the two-step flow hypothesis but that later adopters engaged in a more conversational form of word-of-mouth that appeared to be devoid of opinion leadership.

Other studies have questioned the accuracy of a two-step flow. For example, King and Summers found in the case of women's apparel:[46]

1. About 39 percent of those who reported involvement in interpersonal communication mentioned participation as both a transmitter and a receiver.

2. Nearly 53 percent of those who reported participation as a receiver also reported participation as a transmitter.

3. Approximately 60 percent of those who reported participation as a transmitter also reported participation as a receiver.

Katz has also suggested that in some instances there may be chains of

---

43 Paul F. Lazarsfeld, Bernard R. Berelson, and Hazel Gaudlet, *The People's Choice* (New York: Columbia University Press, 1948), p. 151. Many of the concepts and techniques utilized in this study were orginated by Merton. See Robert K. Merton, "Patterns of Influence: A Study of Interpersonal Influence and of Communications Behavior in a Local Community," in P. F. Lazarsfeld and F. Stanton, eds., *Communications Research* (New York: Harper and Brothers, 1949). An earlier exploratory study was conducted by Frank Stewart, "A Sociometric Study of Influence in Southtown," *Sociometry*, vol. 10, pp. 11–31, 273–86 (1947).

44 Johan Arndt, "Selective Processes in Word-of-Mouth," *Journal of Advertising Research*, vol. 8, pp. 19–22 (June 1968).

45 Russell W. Belk and Ivan Ross, "An Investigation of the Nature of Word of Mouth Communication across Adoption Categories for a Food Innovation," paper presented at the Association for Consumer Research Conference, University of Maryland, September 1971.

46 Charles W. King and John O. Summers, "Dynamics of Interpersonal Communication," in Cox, *Risk Taking*, pp. 253–54.

personal influence rather than simple dyads.[47] Sheth's study of the diffusion of stainless steel blades indicated that there may exist a three-or-more-step flow of communication.[48]

These findings suggest the need for more complex multistep, multisituation models that focus on consumers' needs for information, opinion leaders' motives for transmitting information, and situational determinants of the processes.

In general, opinion leaders will not talk about products or services unless such a conversation produces some type of satisfaction. Motivations to talk about products or services appear to fall into one or more of the following categories: (1) product involvement, (2) self-involvement, (3) concern for others, (4) message involvement,[49] or (5) dissonance reduction.

Why do people become opinion leaders?

First, the *more interested an individual is in a given topic* or product or service, the more likely he or she is to initiate conversations about it. For example, Katz and Lazarsfeld found that public affairs and fashion leaders were more interested in their areas than were nonleaders. Similarly, marketing leadership was concentrated in wives of large families who were more interested and more experienced than were the "girls" or the small-family wives.[50] Apparently, in these and other situations, conversations serve as an outlet for the pleasure and/or excitement caused by or resulting from the purchase and/or use of the product or service.

Second, *self-involvement* may also play a major role in motivating opinion leaders to comment about a product or service. Dichter's research indicated that talking about a product or service often performs such functions as gaining attention, showing connoisseurship, suggesting status, giving the impression that the opinion leader has inside information, and asserting superiority.[51] Whyte found in a classic study of the diffusion of air conditioners, that some respondents subscribed to *Consumer Reports* to acquire conversational material.[52]

Concern for others may also precipitate talk by opinion leaders. Some conversations are motivated by a desire to help the listener make better purchasing decisions. In other instances, talking about a product or service allows the opinion leader to share the satisfactions resulting from the use of the product or service.

Advertising involvement is another type of opinion-leader motivation. Some people find it entertaining to talk about certain advertisements such as those for Volkswagen and Alka-Seltzer. Other people like to make

47 Katz, "Two Step Flow," pp. 61–78.

48 Jagdish N. Sheth, "Word-of-Mouth in Low-Risk Innovations," *Journal of Advertising Research*, vol. 11, pp. 15–18 (June 1971).

49 This typology was developed by Ernest Dichter, "How Word-of-Mouth Advertising Works," *Harvard Business Review*, vol. 44, pp. 147–66 (November–December 1966).

50 Katz and Lazarsfeld, *Personal Influence*, pp. 249–52, 274–75, 239–42.

51 Dichter, "How Word of Mouth," pp. 147–66.

52 William H. Whyte, Jr., "The Web of Word-of-Mouth," in Lincoln H. Clark, ed., *The Life Cycle and Consumer Behavior* (New York: New York University Press, 1955), pp. 113–22.

jokes about advertising symbols such as the Jolly Green Giant, Mrs. Olson, or "flicking your Bic."

Finally, some research suggests that under certain conditions word of mouth is used *to reduce cognitive dissonance* following a major purchase decision. Presumably the buyer attempts to reduce dissonance by persuading other people to buy the same product.[53] This motivation does not exist in all instances, however, as Engel, Kegerreis, and Blackwell failed to find significant amounts of this behavior following the usage of an automotive diagnostic service.[54]

Why do people accept opinion leadership?

The conditions that are likely to cause consumers to seek information from opinion leaders are similar to general search determinants and include (1) small amount of stored information, (2) stored information not appropriate, (3) high degree of perceived risk, and (4) low cost involved in using this source of information. Of those mentioned, perceived risk has received the most *empirical* attention. Situational determinants and product visibility are also relevant determinants.

Perceived risk. Studies investigating the relation between perceived risk and information seeking from personal sources indicate that those consumers high in perceived risk are more likely to initiate conversations, and when they do, they are more likely to request information than those who are felt to be low in perceived risk.[55] In other words, there appears to be a flow of information from those low in perceived risk to those high in perceived risk.[56]

A model for use by marketing organizations to analyze the relationship between perceived risk and word-of-mouth advertising has been proposed by Woodside and Delozier and is presented in Figure 11.2. It portrays the structure and mechanism they believe occurs in acquiring, transmitting and processing information from word-of-mouth advertising. The model (in box 14) indicates that if informal groups consider a product to be a risk, this may cause consumers to search other sources of information such as professional organizations, noncommerical literature, personal salespersons and so forth, and to need different types of advertisements. They suggest that sellers of a product such as a Zenith color television—a relatively risky purchase for consumers—might want to inform consumers, "Tom has one, I have one, everyone has one."[57] It

53 Much of this section was based on a comprehensive literature review in Johan Arndt, "Word-of-Mouth Advertising," in Cox, *Risk Taking*, pp. 188–239.

54 James F. Engel, Robert J. Kegerreis, and Roger D. Blackwell, "Word-of-mouth Communication by the Innovator," *Journal of Marketing*, vol. 33 (July 1969), pp. 15–19. See also James F. Engel, Roger D. Blackwell, and Robert J. Kegerreis, "How Information Is Used to Adopt an Innovation," *Journal of Advertising Research*, vol. 9 (December 1969), pp. 3–8.

55 Raymond A. Bauer, "The Initiative of the Audience," *Journal of Advertising Research*, vol. 3, pp. 2–7 (1963).

56 Scott M. Cunningham, "Perceived Risk as a Factor in the Diffusion of New Product Information," in Haas, *Science*, pp. 698–721; Johan Arndt, "Perceived Risk, Sociometric Integration and Word-of-Mouth in the Adoption of a New Food Product," in Haas, *Science*, pp. 644–49.

57 Arch G. Woodside and M. Wayne Delozier, "Effects of Word of Mouth Advertising on Consumer Risk Taking," *Journal of Advertising*, vol. 5 (Fall 1976), pp. 12–19.

Figure 11.2 Model of word-of-mouth advertising and consumer risk taking

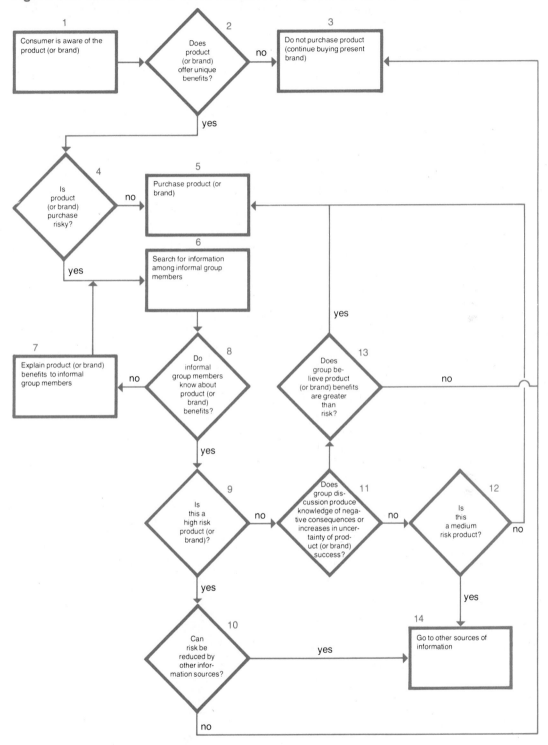

Source: Arch G. Woodside and M. Wayne DeLozier, "Effects of Word of Mouth Advertising on Consumer Risk Taking," *Journal of Advertising*, vol. 5 (Fall 1976), p. 17. Reprinted by permission.

might also be possible for the company to arrange group discussions among influentials for the purpose of decreasing perceived risk.

Situational determinants. Various situational and conversational determinants of word-of-mouth communication are important. Belk found that for both senders and receivers, food-related cues (drinking coffee, general conversations concerning food, shopping for food) were present in at least three-fourths of the reported incidents of word-of-mouth activity. Spontaneous word-of-mouth was rare. Based on the Maxim study and his previous research Belk concluded that:[58]

1. Much informal conversation regarding a new product does not involve opinion leader/follower pairs, and often such communications are exchanges of views and information.

2. The probabilistic occurrence of specific word-of-mouth conversations is more dependent upon the conversational and environmental context (cues) than upon the particular assemblage of persons present.

The first conclusion rejects the conventional concept of opinion leadership in favor of a more conversational form in which leader-follower role playing does not seem to occur. The second conclusion maintains that while spontaneous word-of-mouth may occur, a relevant context facilitates most word-of-mouth. An appropriate context may be created conversationally (that is, a relevant setting for discussing a certain type of product).

Product-social visibility. Interpersonal influence also varies by the social visibility of product categories. An early study by Bourne has come to be regarded as the classic example of how some products are more conspicuous and therefore subject to reference group influences than are others.

Figure 11.3 presents the Bourne research, showing that some products have significant interpersonal dimensions. These are called the product-plus, brand-plus categories.[59] People talk about and have norms concerning the purchase of automobiles, cigarettes, beer, and drugs and about specific brands of these products. To say that one drinks "Coors" may have a different effect on one's opinion leadership than if a person states a preference for "Blatz," as an example of a product that has strong brand and product reference group dimensions.

The Bourne research indicates that product conspicuousness is the most important of the various determinants of whether or not products will be strongly influenced by reference groups. The authors conclude:

58 Russell W. Belk, "Occurrence of Word-of-Mouth Buyer Behavior as a Function of Situation and Advertising Stimuli," paper presented at the American Marketing Association Fall Conference, August 1971.

59 Foundation for Research on Human Behavior, *Group Influence in Marketing and Public Relations* (Ann Arbor, Mich.: The Foundation, 1956).

Figure 11.3 Reference-group influence on product decisions

	Weak −	Strong +		
Strong +	Clothing Furniture Magazines Refrigerator (type) Toilet soap	Cars Cigarettes Beer (prem. vs. reg.) Drugs	+	*Brand or Type*
Weak −	Soap Canned peaches Laundry soap Refrigerator (brand) Radios	Air conditioners Instant coffee TV (black and white)	−	
	−	*Product*	+	

Source: Foundation for Research on Human Behavior, *Group Influence in Marketing and Public Relations* (Ann Arbor, Mich.: The Foundation, 1956), p. 8. Reprinted by permission.

The conspicuousness of a product is perhaps the most general attribute bearing on its susceptibility to reference-group influence. There are two aspects to conspicuousness in this particular context that help to determine reference-group influence. First, the article must be conspicuous in the most obvious sense that it can be seen and identified by others. Secondly, it must be conspicuous in the sense of standing out and being noticed. In other words, no matter how visible a product is, if virtually everyone owns it, it is not conspicuous in this second sense of the word.[60]

Other studies have also shown the effects of interpersonal communications even though they made little attempt to determine the reasons for opinion leadership. A famous study by Whyte in Philadelphia of early usage of room air conditioners indicated that interpersonal communication and imitation occurred next door and across the back yard but not across the street.[61] Other studies of beer, deodorant, after-shave lotion, and cigarettes show the variation that exists in group influence among product categories.[62] Even for a product such as bread, however, an opinion leader may exist whose choice of bread may influence others in the influence group. In the bread study, Stafford found that the increased cohesiveness of the informal group leads to an agreeable environment in which informal opinion leaders can operate.[63]

60 Foundation for Research on Human Behavior, *Group Influence*, pp. 7–8.

61 W. H. Whyte, Jr., "The Web of Word of Mouth," *Fortune*, vol. 50 (November 1954), pp. 146 ff.

62 Robert E. Witt and Grady D. Bruce, "Purchase Decisions and Group Influence," *Journal of Marketing Research*, vol. 7, pp. 533–55 (November 1970); Robert E. Witt, "Group Influence on Consumer Brand Choice," in McDonald, *Marketing Involvement*, pp. 306–9.

63 James E. Stafford, "Effects of Group Influence on Consumer Brand Preferences," *Journal of Marketing Research*, vol. 3 (February 1966), pp. 68–75.

Strategy implications of personal influence processes

The above pages show the importance of the personal influence process for marketing organizations and indicate some of the variables and techniques that are available to analyze the process of influence as it applies to the products or services of an individual firm or other organization. The remaining task in this chapter is to analyze what marketing organizations can do to capitalize on this information about personal influence.

When discussing marketing implications, it is necessary to take an integrated view of the mass media and of personal influences. In the previous chapter on marketer dominated sources of information, the information was discussed so that the person might design advertising, sales personnel, point-of-sale materials and so forth more effectively. In this chapter, however, the title implies that the material discussed is not controlled or dominated by marketing organizations. So, how can marketing organizations do anything about "nonmarketer-dominated" influences?

The answer is often a blend of efforts, combining mass media dominated by marketing (i.e., *advertising*) and mass media not dominated by marketing but which can be influenced through public relations. If a marketing organization understands how mass media and personal influences interact, it may be possible to develop an integrated marketing program including these influences even though they are not controlled by marketing organizations. Several possibilities are discussed in the following pages.

Reaching opinion leaders

The most formidable problem lies in identifying opinion leaders. Opinion leaders, it will be recalled, exist in all strata of society; they differ from other consumers in terms of competence, social location, the personification of certain values, and exposure to mass media; and they are only quasipolymorphic. Thus a marketer must conduct research to identify opinion leaders.

Even when opinion leaders are identified, it may not be profitable to direct advertising to them. For example, Tigert and Arnold found that opinion leaders in the U.S. could not be reached through print media any more effectively than the average consumer in the population. However, in Canada they found that it was possible to reach general opinion leaders through several television and print vehicles.[64]

In situations where opinion leaders can be identified and reached effectively, several strategies are possible. First, as mentioned above, advertisements in the mass media or direct mail—if not too expensive—can be directed to them. It is possible to buy very specific "mailing lists" of groups such as high school coaches, physicians by specialties, church members of various denominations, and so forth. A number of organizations sponsor research that has a high probability of being read in journals

---

64 Tigert and Arnold, *Profiling Self-Designated*, pp. 28–29.

or through press releases in order to reach key opinion leaders. Effective use of press conferences and releases can thus generate information directed toward opinion leaders, if a company's marketing research has provided a good profile of the opinion leaders for a product.

Second, many companies maintain advisory committees or "boards of reference" to help evaluate new products and programs. Knowing some of the reasons why people like to be opinion leaders, which were discussed earlier in this chapter, it could be predicted that if members of these advisory boards were carefully selected, they could be very important as opinion leaders when the product is introduced or when a consumer asks about a store or other aspect of the marketing program. Many sales organizations and many charitable organizations maintain advisory boards that are important adjuncts to the marketing dominated efforts of the organization.

A third way of using opinion leaders is to give them, or loan them, a product for usage in a natural setting (where they are likely to be opinion leaders). Chevrolet and other auto manufacturers have sponsored projects in which students are loaned a new car. Ostensibly the car is for research, but it is also driven by students and professors in the business school who may be active as information transmitters to others on campus. In some instances, retailers have given products that were not selling well to opinion leaders in a community and have observed large quantities of the product sold later.

Finally, opinion leaders can be hired by a firm, as sales clerks or in other positions. Department stores and clothing retailers sometimes hire the most popular young people as clerks and give large discounts on the clothing they purchase, knowing of their influence as opinion leaders. Sometimes persons who are obvious opinion leaders are hired as "vice-president of community affairs" or "director of special projects" to capitalize on their influence in interpersonal relationships.

In situations where it is not possible or practical to identify real opinion leaders, an alternative strategy is to simulate them. One technique is to use advertising to replace or reduce the need for personal influence. Advertisements can communicate the idea that the consumer's reference group buys the product and that buying it is therefore appropriate for him. A related technique is to use testimonial advertising by a famous person who is perceived as competent to give advice about the product or service.

Reaching proxy opinion leaders. Since opinion leadership and innovativeness are often highly correlated, it is sometimes possible to use innovators as quasileaders, or a proxy variable for leaders. This strategy is appealing when innovators can be effectively reached through the mass media but opinion leaders cannot.

Using people who have a high degree of public exposure is another potential method of reaching proxy opinion leadership. In the introduction of the Mustang, for example, the Ford Motor Company used several promotional approaches where college newspaper editors, disc jockeys, and airline stewardesses were loaned Mustangs.[65] Similarly, the Chrysler Corporation tried to generate conversations about the new Plymouth by offering 5,000 cab drivers in 67 cities $5 if they asked Chrysler mystery riders if they had seen the 1963 Plymouth.[66] Some restaurants and bars offer cab drivers and bellhops meals and drinks at cost if they refer traveling executives and other "out-of-towners" to their establishments.

Creating new opinion leaders. An alternative or complementary strategy is to create opinion leaders. This may be an attractive approach when it is impossible to identify and/or reach real opinion leaders.

This approach has been used to transform unknown songs and unknown singing stars into hits. The initial step was to seek out social leaders among the relevant buyers, public high school students. Class presidents, secretaries, sports' captains, and cheerleaders were selected from geographically diverse high schools. Later research revealed that most of these students were not opinion leaders for phonograph records.

The social leaders were contacted by mail and invited to join a select panel to help evaluate rock-and-roll records. The introductory letter stressed several major points:

1. The recipient had been carefully selected, and the organizers felt that he or she, as a leader, should be better able to identify potential rock-and-roll hits than fellow students.

2. In return for his help, he would receive a token of appreciation for his cooperation—free records.

3. He was encouraged to discuss his choices with friends and to weigh their opinions before submitting a final vote.

4. He would be told something about each specific record and the singing star. In addition, *Billboard Magazine* and record stores were suggested as sources of information to verify his attitudes and eventual choices.

5. He was a member of a panel of leaders, and after the panel members had voted he would be informed of the outcome.

6. He was under no obligation to join the panel and he could withdraw from it at any time.

7. The experiment was essentially unstructured, but he would be informed of any expected or unexpected results.

8. An informal two-way atmosphere was encouraged and any new ideas or suggestions would be welcomed and, if appropriate, adopted.

65 Frederick D. Sturdivant et al., *Managerial Analysis in Marketing* (Glenview, Ill.: Scott Foresman, 1970), p. 233.
66 The *Wall Street Journal* (September 27, 1962), p. 5.

9. He would be asked also to answer a few simple questions each month, and the results of the previous month's questionnaire would be made available to respondents the following month.

The total cost of the experiment was less than $5,000. The results were impressive: several records reached the top ten charts in the trial cities but did not make the top ten selections in any other cities. Thus, without contacting any radio stations or any record stores, rock-and-roll records were pulled through the channels of distribution and made into hits.[67]

Stimulating information seeking. Another family of strategies consists of various techniques designed to stimulate information seeking. These techniques may be used instead of, or in addition to, those mentioned above.

One approach is to generate curiosity and interest in products through planned secrecy. This technique was apparently successful for the new Mustang which was "the most talked about—and least seen—auto of this year."[68]

Another technique is to use advertisements that capture the imagination of the public through various techniques, particularly slogans or phrases that become part of the everyday language. For example, early Volkswagen ads were thought to stimulate conversations. Alka-Seltzer's "try it, you'll like it" advertisements also appeared to generate considerable word of mouth.

Another approach is to use advertisements that ask consumers to seek information. "Tell your friends," "ask your friends," and "ask the man who owns one" are examples of this technique.

Demonstrations, displays, and trial usage are methods that can be used to encourage consumer experience with more expensive products. For example, color television manufacturers sell their sets to hotels and motels at low prices partly because they feel it increases the chances that consumers will purchase their brands. Similarly, new types of telephones are placed in public locations because the practice is thought to accelerate adoption.

Summary and evaluation. In spite of the impressive amount of research that has been done on how consumers use personal sources of information, little attention has been given to the problems involved in practically implementing these processes. Specific questions about how to combine mass media and word-of-mouth advertising are rarely raised, let alone studied. Yet the potential benefits to marketers can be impressive. Consider:

1. Advertising of a certain type for a household product was able, over a period of several months, to increase steadily word-of-mouth activi-

---

67 Joseph R. Mancuso, "Why Not Create Opinion Leaders for New Product Introductions?" *Journal of Marketing*, vol. 33, pp. 20–25 (July 1969).
68 *Time* (March 13, 1964), p. 91.

ty, particularly among people who might be regarded as prospective users of the product.

2. A study of a novel consumer service found that 73 percent of consumers who had tried the service as the result of direct-mail advertising, and who had responded to a mail questionnaire, indicated that they had recommended the service to friends and relatives. Furthermore, 8 percent of these respondents claimed that they had told at least ten people about the new service.

3. One company in a highly competitive consumer product category regularly spent only one-third as much on advertising as its two major competitors, yet retained a market share roughly equal to that of the two leading competitors. The apparent reason for their ability to succeed with relatively little advertising was the fact that their brand received vastly more word-of-mouth activity than did the other two brands, which had about the same market shares. The other brands were moved by muscle. The word-of-mouth brand had developed an advertising program that apparently aroused curiosity, which, in turn, stimulated some of the information seeking. In addition, the company had a good product that was well regarded by certain opinion leaders, and this resulted in favorable word-of-mouth activity.[69]

Research designed to discover the success requirements for the above types of strategies is necessary if the gap between research findings and operational strategies is to be bridged.

At the present stage of development it seems appropriate to conclude that whatever use is made of personal sources of information, it is necessary that advertising and distribution strategies be coordinated and consistent with personal communication. The firm needs to monitor informal channels to determine how actively they are being used, as well as the content of the communications.

Summary

This chapter discussed the personal-sources component of the search and alternative evaluation stage in the decision-making process. The first part of the chapter documented the fact that interpersonal communications are very influential in many purchasing decisions. These conversations usually occur between consumers who have similar characteristics, providing the referent is perceived to be competent and there is sufficient proximity to facilitate the interaction.

The second part of the chapter discussed communications interactions in greater detail, noting both the consistencies and inconsistencies with the generalizations advanced earlier. Techniques for isolating opinion leaders were identified and evaluated and the characteristics of opinion leaders were described.

69 Cox, *Risk Taking*, pp. 185–186.

Alternative "models" of interpersonal communications and personal influence were presented in the last section of the chapter. It was concluded that the two-step flow hypothesis is no longer an accurate depiction of the processes involved. Consequently, an effort was made to synthesize the relevant literature into a provisional multistep interaction model and to identify some ideas and guidelines for future research projects.

Finally, this chapter concludes that there are a number of programs that marketing organizations can implement to capitalize on "nonmarketer dominated" influences on consumer search processes. These include various ways of reaching opinion leaders, ways of reaching proxy opinion leaders, and methods for stimulating information seeking.

Review and discussion questions

1. Can personal influence be negative as well as positive? Explain your answer.

2. Assume that you are a consultant for a manufacturer of men's clothing. Discuss how you would go about identifying campus opinion leaders.

3. Describe the two-step flow hypothesis. Is this hypothesis a complete model of communication flows? Why or why not?

4. Recall the last time you volunteered information to someone about a product or service. What caused you to talk about the product or service? How does this compare with the general reasons that opinion leaders pass on information?

5. How do opinion leaders differ from those they influence?

6. Why do consumers seek information from opinion leaders?

7. Your company manufactures a full line of mobile homes in all price ranges. Several studies have indicated that personal sources of information are considerably more effective than other sources. Prepare a statement indicating (a) the alternative strategies that can be employed to utilize effectively consumers' use of personal information sources, (b) the alternative that you prefer and why.

8. Assume that you are a public relations consultant for a state medical association that is concerned about the attitudes of the general public about malpractice claims. Specifically, the concern is that a general view may be developing that filing a malpractice claim against a doctor is an easy way to pay one's medical bills or to get something for nothing. Using the knowledge from this chapter, what advice would you give the state medical association?

CHAPTER 12

The diffusion of innovations

Almost everyone has watched a stone fall into a pool of water. From the initial splash concentric circles move out through the rest of the pool. At first the small waves reach only the area immediately surrounding the splash, but with time the widening waves reach across the expanse of water into nearly every area of the pool.

The acceptance of a new product by large numbers of people is in some ways analogous to the waves caused by a stone dropped into the pool. A few people purchase a product. Those around the initial purchasers then try the product, and eventually the acceptance of the product may diffuse throughout the entire population.

From this simple illustration, however, there are a number of questions that can be asked about the diffusion of new products:

1. How is the initial "splash" accomplished? Are certain types of people more likely than others to accept new products? Can we predict ahead of time who these people will be?

2. How rapidly do the "waves" of acceptance of new products move from those who are the first to adopt to other members of the population?

3. What is the pattern of the "waves" of acceptance that move through the population?

4. How can the diffusion process be influenced by marketing activity?

These questions illustrate the importance of understanding the diffusion process and form the basis of the discussion in this chapter.

The topic of diffusion has spawned considerable research in the past few decades. This research has been prompted by a variety of macro and microsocietal problems. Three specific problems have caused economists, sociologists, and marketing researchers to recognize the importance of learning how consumers react to new ideas and products.

Importance of new product decisions

The first problem is the economic waste caused by investing resources in the introduction of new products that are rejected by consumers. Estimates vary concerning the proportion of new products that are successful, but nearly all report that the majority fail. A study of leading companies by Booz-Allen & Hamilton reported that only one new product is successful out of each 58 ideas.[1] In the food-processing areas, Buzzell and Nourse found that only about two out of each 58 ideas are successful new products.[2] These failures are expensive; a single product failure can cost from $75,000 to $20,000,000.[3] Furthermore, firms often make serious errors in their prediction of sales levels of products that do succeed. Tull found in a study of 63 new products an average error of sales forecasts of 65 percent and an average error for profit forecasts for 53 new products of 128 percent.[4]

The second reason for concern with diffusion research might be termed the desire to influence human behavior into accepting socially desirable ideas and products. Rural sociologists have been particularly interested and helpful in obtaining acceptance of new ideas that contributed to increased efficiency in farming practices or the health of a community. The motivation for such studies stems from the notion that people should change so that they more closely conform to some norm of what is good for society. This had led to research (with the goal of changing behavior) on improved sanitation techniques, birth control methods, and increased use of political information. This is sometimes referred to as "social marketing."

A third reason for interest in diffusion research lies in the criticality of new product acceptance in the survival and growth of contemporary business firms. Historically, growth industries in the American economy have used new products as a major part of their growth strategy. Additionally, profits are heavily influenced by new products. Profit margins peak during the latter state of the growth phase in the product life cycle and then continuously decline during subsequent stages. This means that a company must systematically introduce new products and/or modified products that can command better margins. As the life cycle of products continues to shorten, profits can be sustained in the long run only by a continuing flow of successful new products, not

1 *Management of New Products* (New York: Booz-Allen & Hamilton, 1965).

2 Robert D. Buzzell and Robert E. M. Nourse, *Product Innovation in Food Processing 1954–1964* (Boston: Division of Research, Harvard Business School, 1967).

3 Theodore L. Angelus, "Why Do Most New Products Fail?" *Advertising Age*, pp. 85–86 (March 24, 1969).

4 Donald S. Tull, "The Relationship of Actual and Predicted Sales and Profits in New-Product Introductions," *Journal of Business*, vol. 40, pp. 233–50 (July 1967).

only to replace sales volume, but also to sustain and increase profit margins.[5]

Consumer decisions and the diffusion research tradition

This chapter deals with consumer decisions to buy new products that are innovations. The question can be asked, "Why have a special chapter on new products? Does not the consumer model in this book apply to new products as well as all other decisions?" Those are very reasonable questions.

There are several reasons for studying the diffusion of innovations as a separate topic. The first is the emphasis of diffusion research on "adoption," which refers to the acceptance and continued use of a product or brand. Adoption is a behavioral variable but most of the diffusion research is built upon an "adoption process," which includes the mental and behavioral sequence through which consumers progress, potentially leading to acceptance and continued use of a product or brand.[6] This is in contrast to the consumer behavior models that focus on a single buying decision and the influences that are operative in that decision. The two are not incompatible because the consumer behavior model in this book includes feedback (satisfaction or dissonance) from purchase outcomes that determines future behavior. In diffusion research, however, the final outcome is not the purchase of a specific product but rather the decision to continue to use (or reject) a product. Usually, also, diffusion research focuses on adoption of a generic product rather than a specific brand or store, as does a more comprehensive model of consumer behavior. Thus, while diffusion models and more general models of consumer behavior are not contradictory to each other, there is considerable difference in points of emphasis.

A second reason for studying diffusion research is the emphasis placed upon the *social structure of communication rather than on the individual.* This relational approach to consumer decisions places the emphasis upon the flow of information between consumers rather than on the processing of the information by an individual consumer. A *relational* approach to how new products are adopted examines how social-structural variables affect diffusion flows in a system, analyzes the networks of communication flows on a sociometric basis and is concerned about the attitudes and behavior of other persons (nonadopters) in the social structure. A *monadic* approach, in contrast, focuses upon the personal and social characteristics of individual consumers.[7] Although the theory used in diffusion research is relational, much of the research, reported later in this chapter, is monadic in approach.

A third reason for studying diffusion of innovations as a special topic is

---

5 For amplification of these ideas, see David T. Kollat, Roger E. Blackwell, and James Robeson, *Strategic Marketing* (New York: Holt, Rinehart and Winston, 1972), chap. 11.

6 Thomas S. Robertson, "A Critical Examination of 'Adoption Process' Models of Consumer Behavior," in Jagdish Sheth, ed., *Models of Buyer Behavior* (New York: Harper & Row, 1974), pp. 271–95.

7 Everett M. Rogers, "New Product Adoption and Diffusion," *Journal of Consumer Research*, vol. 2 (March 1976), pp. 290–301, especially see Table 2 on p. 298.

the quantity of research that has accumulated about this subject and the diversity of disciplines that have contributed to that research. At least 12 identifiable disciplines have studied the diffusion of innovations. These include anthropology, sociology, rural sociology, education, medical sociology, communication, marketing, agricultural economics, psychology, general economics, geography, and industrial engineering.

The most influential researcher in the diffusion literature is Everett Rogers, whose book *Diffusion of Innovations*[8] provided the basic structure for diffusion research in marketing and other disciplines. Over 400 empirical studies on the adoption of new products existed before Rogers wrote his book, so he did not "originate" the field. Nevertheless, his book brought together research from many disciplines and served to publicize the topic as a "respectable" academic discipline. Later publications and revisions[9] have continued to summarize the more than 2,000 studies of diffusion and have provided guidelines for research in marketing and other disciplines to "branch out" from this basic framework. Rogers once wrote a fascinating "personal history" of diffusion research, which shows the evolution of this area of inquiry as a separate discipline during the past few decades.[10]

Many diffusion studies completed outside the marketing discipline are of interest to consumer analysts because they involve consumer products. Some of the products studied in well-known diffusion studies include health-care practices, child-rearing practices, health insurance, leisure and recreational activities, new synthetic fabrics, fluoridation, self-medication, new food products, durable goods, auto insurance, women's apparel, the selection of a physician, new drug products, new retail stores, automobiles and automobile services, vacations, furniture, movies (such as "In Cold Blood"), and new types of telephones.[11]

The importance of diffusion research for consumer analysts is not derived solely from the fact that these studies dealt with products of specific interest. Rather, the importance derives from the conclusion that throughout the diffusion studies of many disciplines, generalizations can be made that demonstrate a consistency of pattern independent of the disciplinary affiliation, the specific type of respondents studied, or the nature of the innovation. Although marketing strategists must use care in applying detailed findings of the diffusion traditions to marketing prob-

8 Everett Rogers, *Diffusion of Innovations* (Glencoe, Ill.: The Free Press, 1965 and 1971).

9 Everett Rogers and F. Floyd Shoemaker, (New York: The Free Press, 1971); Everett Rogers, *Communication Strategies for Family Planning* (New York: The Free Press, 1973); Everett Rogers and Rehka Agarwala-Rogers, *Communication in Organizations* (New York: The Free Press, 1976).

10 Everett M. Rogers, "A Personal History of Research on the Diffusion of Innovations," in Alan R. Andreasen and Seymour Sudman, eds., *Public Policy and Marketing Thought* (Chicago: American Marketing Association, 1976), pp. 43–63.

11 For a review of diffusion research by marketing researchers as well as studies in other disciplines of interest to marketing analysts, see Charles W. King, "Adoption and Diffusion Research in Marketing: An Overview," in Raymond M. Haas, ed., *Science, Technology and Marketing* (Chicago: American Marketing Association, 1966), pp. 665–84; and Johan Arndt, "New Product Diffusion: The Interplay of Innovativeness, Opinion Leadership, Learning, Perceived Risk and Product Attributes," in Sheth, *Models*, pp. 327–35.

lems,[12] the general consistency among disciplines is one of the basic reasons for the importance diffusion research has attained.

Elements of the diffusion process

The diffusion process is conceptualized as having four basic elements, or analytical units. These elements or structural variables have been identified as (1) the innovation, (2) the communication of the innovation among individuals, (3) the social system, and (4) time.[13]

The innovation

An innovation can be defined in a variety of ways. In a search of the literature, one researcher found 51 different concepts of innovation, defined either explicitly or by implication.[14] The most commonly accepted definition of an innovation, however, appears to be any idea or product perceived by the potential innovator to be new.[15] This may be called a subjective definition of innovation, since it is derived from the thought structure of a particular individual.[16]

Innovations can also be defined objectively on the basis of criteria external to the potential adopter. The anthropologist Barnett described innovations in such a way, defining them as "any thought, behavior, or thing that is new because it is qualitatively different from existing forms."[17] In consumer behavior, classifying an innovation using this definition focuses upon product characteristics to determine if differences occur between new products and previously existing ones. The question that arises is how "different" a new product must be to be considered "qualitatively different." References are sometimes found in the marketing literature that emphasize that substantial technological change must be present in a product for it to be considered an innovation. One marketing scholar, for example, denies that the new products brought out by a food company in a given year are innovations and limits the term to products with such a magnitude of change that they produce a significant effect upon the economy.[18]

The operational definition of innovation that appears to have been

12 Some researchers have produced evidence to demonstrate, for example, that significant differences exist in the communication of information concerning new products from what has been found to be true in rural sociology. See William Lazer and William E. Bell, "The Communications Process and Innovation," *Journal of Advertising Research*, vol. 6, pp. 2–7 (September 1966).

13 Everett Rogers, *Diffusion of Innovations*, pp. 12–20. This conceptualization is retained in the later edition by Rogers and Shoemaker, op. cit.

14 Douglass K. Hawes, "An Inspection of Innovation," unpublished paper submitted for a graduate course in consumer behavior (Columbus, Ohio: Ohio State University, 1968).

15 This definition is used by Rogers, *Communication*, p. 13; King, "Adoption and Diffusion," p. 666.

16 There are many examples of how products are perceived to be "new" even though they may reflect no new physical characteristic or process. See Chester R. Wasson, "What Is 'New' about New Products," *Journal of Marketing*, vol. 24, pp. 52–56 (1960).

17 H. G. Barnett, *Innovation: The Basis of Cultural Change* (New York: McGraw-Hill, 1953), p. 7.

18 Paul D. Converse, "Marketing Innovations: Inventions, Techniques, Institutions," in Frederick E. Webster, Jr., ed., *New Directions in Marketing* (Chicago: American Marketing Association, 1965), pp. 35–41. This view of innovation has its roots in the economic theory of innovations contained in Joseph A. Schumpeter, *Business Cycles*, vol. 1 (New York: McGraw-Hill, 1939).

most used by consumer researchers is any form of a product that has recently become available in a market. According to this definition, an example of an innovation is a brand of coffee that was not previously available in a given geographical area.[19] Other examples are modifications of existing products, such as new features in the annual model change on automobiles[20] or a new package for a food. An innovation can also be, of course, a totally new product such as television, the electric toothbrush, or automobile diagnostic centers. It can also be the opening of a new retail store.[21] Additionally, an innovation in some marketing studies has been defined as any product that has achieved less than x percentage of market penetration.[22]

The variety of definitions of innovations dictates an important caveat: diffusion findings developed in varied research traditions do not necessarily apply to all types of new-product purchase decisions. Most of the research in the diffusion tradition was conducted on major technological innovations. It is reasonable to expect that the details of the process may differ considerably when the innovation is a product of less consequence than a major technological change, although this area needs further investigation.

There is thus a need for a classification system to handle widely differing types of product innovations. One such classification system is based on the impact of the innovation on the social structure accepting the innovation. In this taxonomic system, innovations may be classified as (1) continuous, (2) dynamically continuous, and (3) discontinuous.

1. A continuous innovation has the least disrupting influence on established patterns. Modification of an existing product is characteristic of this type rather than the establishment of a totally new product; examples: adding fluoride to toothpaste, new-model automobile changeovers, adding menthol to cigarettes.

2. A dynamically continuous innovation has more disrupting effects than a continuous innovation, although it still does not generally alter established patterns of customer buying and product use. It may involve the creation of a new product or the alteration of an existing

19 An example is the introduction of Folgers coffee to the Chicago market reported in Ronald E. Frank, William F. Massy and Donald G. Morrison, "The Determinants of Innovative Behavior with Respect to a Branded, Frequently Purchased Food Product," in L. George Smith, ed., *Reflections on Progress in Marketing* (Chicago: American Marketing Association, 1964), pp. 312–23. See also a study of new brands of toothpaste and deodorants by George H. Haines, Jr., "A Study of Why People Purchase New Products," in Haas, *Science*, pp. 685–97.

20 John B. Stewart, "Functional Features in Product Strategy," *Harvard Business Review*, pp. 65–78 (March–April 1959).

21 Robert F. Kelly, "The Diffusion Model as a Predictor of Ultimate Patronage Levels in New Retail Outlets," in Haas, *Science*; also Robert F. Kelly, "The Role of Information in the Patronage Decision: A Diffusion Phenomenon," in M. S. Moyer and R. E. Vosburgh, eds., *Marketing for Tomorrow . . . Today* (Chicago: American Marketing Association, 1967), pp. 119–29. This work is based upon Fred C. Allvine, *The Patronage Decision*, unpublished doctoral dissertation (Bloomington, Ind.: Indiana University, 1966).

22 An example is found in Lazer and Bell, "Communications Process," p. 4, where they use the operational definition: "A product is an innovation if less than 10 percent market penetration exists in a given geographic location." This definition is common in marketing studies.

product; examples: electric toothbrushes, the Mustang automobile, touch-tone telephones.

3. A discontinuous innovation involves the introduction of an entirely new product that causes buyers to alter significantly their behavior patterns; examples: television, computers.[23]

Many of the conflicting findings that exist in the diffusion literature stem from the fact that diffusion models developed for dynamically continuous or discontinuous innovations are being applied to research on continuous innovations. This may be appropriate in developing a broad conceptual framework for analyzing innovations, but when applied to such details as the amount of decision making involved in a purchase, the sources of information, or other important details, the assumption that the same generalizations are applicable to each type of innovation is tenuous. Unfortunately, research on the marketing of new products often has not clarified these issues.

Communication

The role of communications is a central issue in the study of diffusion and may be of two types, informal and formal. *Informal* communications are nonmarketer dominated, such as reference-group and family influences. There is a temptation to assume that the people who first adopt a product are the ones who influence others to purchase and that their communications are therefore instrumental in the diffusion process. Interpersonal influence appears to be much more complex, however.[24]

Formal communications are those dominated by marketers. They include advertising, various forms of reseller support, and personal salespersons. When control of communications is possible, questions arise such as these: What types of media are most likely to transmit messages to those persons who are most likely to be the first adopters of an innovation? What media are most likely to be considered authoritative? What messages are most likely to influence new product acceptance?

Understanding the role of communications in the diffusion process is sufficiently important to justify a special section later in the chapter describing what is known about this topic.

The social system

The diffusion of innovations is a social phenomenon. The word "diffusion" has little meaning except as it relates to a group of people. Acceptance or rejection of a product can apply to an individual person, but diffusion is a concentration gradient and refers to some group of individuals. Consequently, diffusion research should focus not only on characteristics of a decision-making unit (individual or family) but also on the environment provided by the social system.

23 Thomas S. Robertson, "The Process of Innovation and the Diffusion of Innovation," *Journal of Marketing*, vol. 31, pp. 14–19, at p. 15 (January 1967).

24 Thomas S. Robertson, "Group Characteristics and Aggregate Innovative Behavior: Preliminary Report," in Sheth, *Models*, pp. 310–26.

Adoption of new products is a temporal phenomenon and needs to be analyzed as such. The decision to adopt a new product, like all other consumption decisions described by the model in this book, is a process rather than an event. People recognize problems, search for alternatives, evaluate new products as potential alternatives, decide to purchase the new product, and perhaps eventually purchase it. The adoption process is not considered complete, however, until postpurchase evaluation and repeat usage or purchases are generated. This is because adoption implies the decision to continue full use of an innovation.[25] To study the rate of diffusion in a social structure, it is necessary to evaluate the exact position of individual consumers in the process that leads to adoption. **Time**

There is a striking incongruity between the theoretical concept of adoption as a process and the way it is often measured. The theoretical concept of adopter should be measured by determining the intention of the consumer to incorporate the new product into his habitual pattern of consumption. In actual practice, the measurement of adoption is usually a "has or has not purchased" measure. If a consumer is observed to have purchased a new product or patronized a new store, the person is considered to be an adopter. Those who have not done so at the time of the study are considered to be nonadopters. This may cause misleading results when the product has been purchased as well as when it has not been purchased. This can happen because of some variable unrelated to the consumer's long-run intention to adopt the product (such as an out-of-stock situation for the consumer's true preference) or when the consumer has begun the process that leads to adoption (such as deciding in the mind to try the product at the next purchase occasion) but has not yet purchased the new product.

The innovation-decision process

The process that individuals move through in adopting a new product has been conceptualized as multistage in nature, as shown in Figure 12.1, with several kinds of variables that influence each stage.[26] The stages described below are knowledge, persuasion, decision (which may lead to adoption or rejection), and confirmation.

The knowledge stage begins when a consumer receives physical or social stimuli that give exposure and attention to the innovation's existence and some understanding of how it functions. The consumer becomes aware of the product but has made no judgment concerning the relevance of the product to an existing problem or need. **Knowledge (awareness)**

Knowledge is a result of selective perception, but beyond this many questions remain unanswered. The marketing analyst needs to know more about the antecedents or what creates knowledge. Do some consumers have more knowledge of new products in general than do other consum-

25 Rogers, *Communication*, p. 17.
26 This section is a condensation of Rogers and Shoemaker, op. cit., pp. 100–33.

Figure 12.1 Paradigm of the innovation-decision process (for simplicity, only consequences of process are shown, not of innovation)

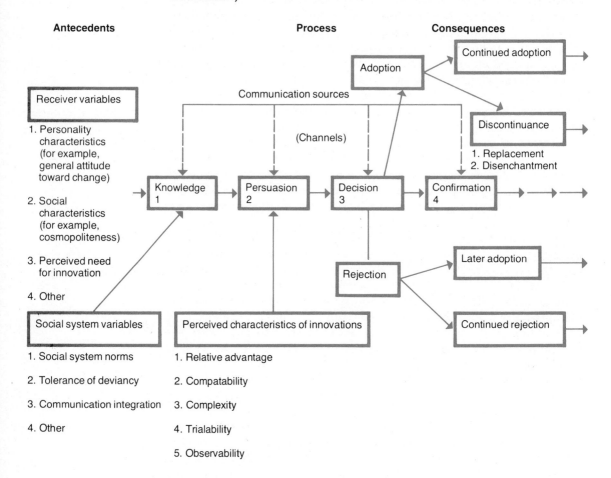

Source: Reprinted with permission of Macmillan Publishing Co., Inc., from *Communication in Innovations* by Everett M. Rogers and F. Floyd Shoemaker. Copyright © 1971 by The Free Press, a division of the Macmillan Company.

ers? Of all the stimulus sets that are constantly being sampled by the consumer, what makes one set have an impact and be remembered while another appears to have no impact and be lost to consciousness? Is increased knowledge of new products necessarily associated with early adoption of that product?

Persuasion   Persuasion, the Rogers-Shoemaker paradigm, refers to the formation of favorable or unfavorable attitudes toward the innovation. The individual may mentally imagine how satisfactory the new idea might be in some anticipated future use situation before deciding whether to try it. This might be called "vicarious trial." All of the influences on consumer decision making described in previous chapters are brought to bear in the evaluation of the innovation that leads to the rejection or acceptance (the evaluation) of the idea of the innovation.

The persuasiveness of the innovation may be related to the perception of risk in the new product, with uncertainty reduction as a determinant of evaluation. This notion may be stated in the following manner: When an individual considers a new product, he or she must weigh the potential gains from adopting the product with the potential losses from switching from the product now used. The consumer recognizes that if the new product is adopted, it may be inferior to a present product, or the cost (price of the product plus possible disadvantages) may be greater than the increased value. Thus, adopting the new product has a risk that can be avoided by postponing acceptance until the value has been clearly established. If, however, the product is designed to solve a problem that is of significant concern to the consumer, there is also the risk that value may be lost by delaying adoption of a product that is truly superior to the present product.

The consumer can reduce the risk of adopting the new product—and therefore uncertainty about the buying situation—by acquiring additional information. A person may seek out news stories, pay particular attention to advertising for the product, subscribe to product-rating services, talk with individuals who have already tried the product, talk with experts on the subject, or in some instances, even try the product on a limited basis. Each of these information search and evaluation strategies, however, has an economic and/or psychological cost. Moreover, they are unlikely to yield information that will completely reduce uncertainty.

Some laboratory experiments at the University of Pennsylvania support the risk-reduction information theory of new product adoption. In these experiments, housewives and graduate students were asked to make decisions on the basis of incomplete information. Their decisions could be altered through use of information they could acquire at a cost. The following generalizations have emerged from this set of experiments:

1. In general, consumers seek more information about options as their uncertainty about the options increases.

2. The more ambiguous their perceptions of a situation, the more likely consumers are to accept new information.

3. When new information conflicts with previous beliefs and attitudes, previous information will tend to prevail.

4. Large interpersonal differences exist in the amount of information sought and used in evaluating decisions.

5. A large proportion of consumers—at least in the laboratory situation—do not differentiate between relevant and irrelevant information.

6. The valuation of information appears to be higher early in the decision process than late in the process.

7. There appear to be some personality variables that differentiate information seekers and information avoiders. Respondents who were information sensitive tended to have open mindedness and adaptable attitudes, while those who were not information sensitive tended to be rigid in their attitudes and exhibit fatalism with regard to the future and control over one's destiny.[27]

Decision

The decision stage involves activities that lead to a choice between adopting or rejecting the innovation. The immediate consideration is whether or not to try the innovation, which is often influenced by the ability to try the innovation on a small scale (including vicarious trial by observing the use of the innovation by others). Innovations that can be divided are generally adopted more readily. Trial can sometimes be stimulated by the use of free samples or other small units with low risk.

Figure 12.1 shows that the output of decision can be either rejection or adoption. Rejection can be continuous or may be reversed by later adoption. Conversely, adoption may be continuous or may lead to later discontinuance.

Confirmation

Confirmation refers to the process postulated by Rogers and Shoemaker of consumers seeking reinforcement for the innovation decision that has been made and of the situation in which consumers sometimes reverse previous decisions when exposed to conflicting messages about the innovation. This state involves the issue of cognitive dissonance, which will be discussed in Chapter 18.

Discontinuance is, of course, as serious a concern to marketers as the original process of adoption. The rate of discontinuance may be just as important as the rate of adoption, with the corresponding need for marketing strategies to devote attention to preventing discontinuance of innovations. Rogers and Shoemaker report that later adopters are more likely to discontinue innovations than earlier adopters and are generally likely to have the opposite characteristics (in education, social status, change agency contact, and the like) to those of the innovators. Discontinuance is most likely to occur when the innovation is not integrated into the practices and way of life of purchasers, suggesting the need for after-the-sale reinforcement activity by marketing strategists designed to ensure continued acceptance and use.

Marketing and the Rogers paradigm

The early Rogers paradigm and the revised Rogers-Shoemaker paradigm serve as theoretical models for diffusion research by consumer analysts. In spite of its emphasis on the process approach, however, the Rogers approach has generated limited amounts of process research in the consumer behavior field. Instead, diffusion research typically has treated adoption as dichotomous (that is, adopt or reject).

27 Paul E. Green, "Consumer Use of Information," in Joseph W. Newman, ed., *On Knowing the Consumer* (New York: Wiley, 1966), pp. 67–80.

A more serious problem is that the Rogers paradigm deals mostly with discontinuous innovations, whereas most marketing decisions involve continuous or dynamically continuous innovations. Conceptually, it is probably helpful to use a general model of consumer behavior that permits analysis of all types of products. The determination of when a product is sufficiently different to be an innovation fitting the conditions of the Rogers paradigm and when it is merely a modification of an existing product appears to be an arbitrary decision.

Correlates of new product adoption

Marketing analysts are concerned with the task of predicting whether or not a new product will be adopted by consumers or, even better, of discovering how to influence the adoption process. This has led consumer researchers to concentrate considerable energy on the question of what variables are correlated with new product adoption—either for the purpose of predicting adoption or stimulating it.

Researchers have focused on the types of variables suggested by the Rogers paradigm of the diffusion of innovations. The findings from these studies are described in the following pages. They are categorized as consumer variables (such as personality, attitude, income, and so forth), product variables, and variables that relate to the social structure of the communication process. Some of this research is relational in nature but the bulk of it is monadic.

Over 2,700 publications have reported studies on the diffusion process. Of these, 1,800 report empirical research and 900 report nonempirical analyses or discussions.[28] These reports are compiled in a diffusion documents center and have been subject to considerable analysis by Rogers and others. The following section of this chapter relies heavily on findings from this compilation.[29] In these studies, innovativeness is operationally defined as (1) the adoption or nonadoption of one new idea or a set of ideas or (2) the degree to which the unit of adoption is relatively earlier in adopting new ideas than other members of the social system.

Sociodemographic variables. A few variables emerge fairly consistently as associated with the kinds of people who are likely to be early adopters of innovations. Figure 12.2 summarizes the results of studies relating to these consumer characteristics. The table indicates that sociodemographic variables most often associated with early adoption are education, literacy, income, and level of living. These findings, it should be noted, and those that follow are primarily based upon correlational studies. Thus they indicate only associations between the variable and innovativeness.

Consumer characteristics associated with innovativeness

28 Everett Rogers and P. C. Thomas, *Bibliography on the Diffusion of Innovations* (Ann Arbor: Department of Population Planning, University of Michigan, 1975).

29 Everett M. Rogers and J. David Stanfield, "Adoption and Diffusion of New Products: Emerging Generalizations and Hypotheses," paper presented at the Conference on the Application of Sciences to Marketing Management, Purdue University (July 12–15, 1966); also in Bass et al., op. cit.

Figure 12.2 Consumer characteristics related to innovativeness

Number of empirical findings indicating
relation to innovativeness (%)

	Positive	None	Negative	Condi-tional	Total	Total number of published findings
Sociodemographic						
(1) Education	74.6	16.1	5.2	4.1	100	193
(2) Literacy	70.4	22.2	3.7	3.7	100	27
(3) Income	80.3	10.7	6.3	2.7	100	112
(4) Level of living	82.5	10.0	2.5	5.0	100	40
(5) Age	32.3	40.5	17.7	9.5	100	158
Attitudinal						
(6) Knowledgeability	78.8	16.7	1.5	3.0	100	66
(7) Attitude toward change	73.6	14.5	8.2	3.8	100	159
(8) Achievement motivation	64.7	23.5	0.0	11.8	100	17
(9) Aspirations for children	82.6	8.7	4.3	4.3	100	23
(10) Business orientation	60.0	20.0	20.0	0.0	100	5
(11) Satisfaction with life	28.6	28.6	42.8	0.0	100	7
(12) Empathy	75.0	0.0	25.0	0.0	100	4
(13) Mental rigidity	20.8	25.0	50.0	4.2	100	24

Source: Modified with special permission from Everett M. Rogers and J. David Stanfield, "Adoption and Diffusion of New Products: Emerging Generalizations and Hypotheses," paper presented at the Conference on the Application of Sciences to Marketing Management, Purdue University (July 12–15, 1966), Tables 4 and 5.

They should not be construed as causation. In many cases they indicate to the marketer only that these variables facilitate understanding and buying new products when other reasons also exist for buying them.

Attitudinal variables. Some attitudinal variables emerge as consistently associated with innovativeness, as indicated in Figure 12.2. Many parents apparently want to provide the latest and best products to enable their children to compete with others. This is may be related to consistent findings that the variable "aspirations for children" is associated with innovativeness. Related to this is achievement motivation. Both of these indicate the individual's desire to better the life of his family, especially in his children's education and occupation. Knowledgeability refers to the awareness that an individual has of the external world and events in general that occur about him. Also associated with innovativeness is attitude toward change. Mental rigidity or satisfaction with life, conversely, lead to rejection of innovations.

Marketing applications. A great deal of research in recent years has been directed toward the profiling of innovators in a manner helpful to marketing strategists.[30] Like most general innovation studies, the marketing studies have almost always indicated the importance of income in profiling the innovator. Robertson found that out of thirteen studies where this variable was examined, nine show higher income level to be associated with higher innovativeness, while four show a lack of relationship.[31] It may be more useful to use the concept of "privilegedness" than income. This refers to the amount of income an individual has relative to the other individuals with whom he or she normally associates.[32] When the product is a frequently purchased low-priced product, however, income (and education and occupation) may have little relation to early adoption.[33] In one study a curvilinear relationship was found between income and innovativeness, with the middle-income group containing fewer innovators because of unwillingness to take risks.[34]

Marketing strategists probably should assume that income will be important in profiling the innovator but that it should be weighed in direct proportion to the price of innovation. Also, the ability to try or to sample the new product with little risk may mitigate the importance of income in innovation.

Social status appears also to be positively related to consumer innovation. Using the Reiss index of occupational status, one study revealed that among the earliest adopters of a new automobile service, one in three had an occupational index higher than 75. This is compared to a ratio of only one in seven for the population at large (or noninnovators). The 75-point level of the socioeconomic index consists only the highest status professions such as architects, scientists, lawyers, doctors, engineers, auditors, and top management positions.[35]

Highly mobile people also appear to be more likely to be early adopters of new products. Shaw found that people who traveled extensively, had advanced in their jobs and income, and moved around were more likely to accept new products than stay-at-homes, even with income held constant.[36] Heavy users of the product were found by King[37] to be more likely to accept a new style of millinery, although this was not found to be

30 An excellent summary and synthesis of this literature is available in Thomas S. Robertson, *Innovative Behavior and Communication* (New York: Holt, Rinehart and Winston, 1971). The authors express their gratitude for Professor Robertson's kind permission to rely heavily on his book in the revision of this chapter.

31 Robertson, *Innovative Behavior*, p. 104.

32 Richard P. Coleman, "The Significance of Social Stratification in Selling," in Martin L. Bell, ed., *Marketing: A Maturing Discipline* (Chicago: American Marketing Association, 1960), pp. 171–84.

33 Frank et al., "The Determinants of Innovative Behavior," p. 318.

34 Frank Cancian, "Stratification and Risk-Taking: A Theory Tested on Agricultural Innovation," *American Sociological Review*, vol. 32, pp. 912–27 (December 1967).

35 Robert J. Kegerreis, James F. Engel, and Roger D. Blackwell, "Innovativeness and Diffusiveness: A Marketing View of the Characteristics of Earliest Adopters," in Kollat et al., *Strategic Marketing*, pp. 671–89, at p. 678.

36 Stephen J. Shaw, "Behavioral Science Offers Fresh Insights on New Product Acceptance," *Journal of Marketing*, vol. 29 (January 1965), pp. 9–14, at p. 10.

37 Charles W. King, "The Innovator in the Fashion Adoption Process," in Smith, *Reflections*, pp. 324–39, at p. 335.

true for heavy coffee users when faced with a new brand of coffee.[38] There is a need, however, for more research relating consumer characteristics to specific product categories.

Of various personality or attitudinal variables that explain early adoption by consumers, one of the most explanatory appears to be venturesomeness. Robertson and Kennedy found that the trait of venturesomeness was able to explain about 35 percent of the difference between innovators and noninnovators for a new telephone product.[39] Jacoby found in a study of 15 product categories that "openmindedness" was significantly related to innovative reponses.[40] Scores on "dogmatism" have also been investigated as a variable in innovativeness. Jacoby found that persons low in dogmatism were most likely to be innovators and the findings of Jacoby have been substantially supported in a replication by Coney.[41]

In a study of Ford Maverick buyers, when that car was first introduced, the early adopters were found to be more "inner directed" than "other directed." This study used Kassarjian's I.O. Social Preference Scale and is also significant in that it found that the early adopters of a new product may be significantly different in social character than later adopters of the same "new product."[42]

Innovation proneness. Early in diffusion research, an assumption was sometimes made that some individuals were "innovation prone" and that consequently the person who was an innovator for one product would also be the innovator of other products. Robertson and Myers found that appliance, clothing, and food innovators were statistically related but with such a low level (of correlation) as to dispute the notion that innovativeness is a general trait possessed by consumers.[43] Arndt concluded that a general receptiveness to innovation exists, but his investigation was in closely related product lines related to food consumption.[44]

The earliest adopters of a new automobile service, compared to the population as a whole, were found to be

1. Much more willing to experiment with new ideas

2. More likely to buy new products (in general) earlier

38 Frank et al., "The Determinants of Innovative Behavior," pp. 318–20.

39 Thomas S. Robertson and James N. Kennedy, "Prediction of Consumer Innovators: Application of Multiple Discriminant Analysis," *Journal of Marketing Research*, vol. 5 (February 1968), pp. 64–69.

40 Jacob Jacoby, "A Multiple-Indicant Approach for Studying Innovators," Purdue Papers in Consumer Psychology, no. 108 (Lafayette, Ind.: Purdue University, 1970).

41 Jacob Jacoby, "Personality and Innovation Proneness," *Journal of Marketing Research*, vol. 8 (May 1971), pp. 244–47; Kenneth A. Coney, "Dogmatism and Innovation: A Replication," *Journal of Marketing Research*, vol. 9 (November 1972), pp. 453–55. Inconclusive results were obtained, however, in Brian Blake, Robert Perloff, and Richard Heslin, "Dogmatism and Acceptance of New Products," *Journal of Marketing Research*, vol. 7 (November 1970), pp. 483–86.

42 James H. Donnelly, Jr. and John M. Ivancevich, "A Methodology for Identifying Innovator Characteristics of New Brand Purchasers," *Journal of Marketing Research*, vol. 9 (August 1974), pp. 331–34.

43 Thomas S. Robertson and James H. Myers, "Personality Correlates of Opinion Leadership and Innovative Buying Behavior," *Journal of Marketing Research*, vol. 6 (May 1969), pp. 164–68.

44 Johan Arndt, "Profiling Consumer Innovators," in Johan Arndt, ed., *Insights into Consumer Behavior* (Boston: Allyn and Bacon, 1968), pp. 71–83.

3. Less likely to switch brands because of a small price change

4. Less interested in low price per se

5. Less likely to try new convenience items if the innovation represented only minor changes.[45]

In this study, it was concluded that innovators were the best informed sector of the population and that they engaged in considerable planning before purchasing innovations. It is not surprising (because of better information and planning) that innovators are more willing to experiment with new ideas and that they are not willing to be classified as hasty purchasers just because a product is new. The superior education, occupational status, and purchasing planning are likely to contribute to innovativeness for other types of products, but the desire for "newness" per se does not seem to be a reason for innovation proneness.

After a rigorous assessment of the literature in this area, Robertson concluded that "the consistency of innovativeness cannot be expected across product categories, but can be expected within product categories and, sometimes, between related product categories.[46]

The acceptance of a new product by innovators is determined to a large degree by characteristics of the product itself. It is more correct to say that the product's acceptance is determined by what consumers perceive the product to be. Diffusion research indicates a number of product characteristics associated with the early adoption of the product. Those that have been investigated in multiple studies are presented in Figure 12.3 and are described briefly below.[47]

Product characteristics associated with innovativeness

Relative advantage of the new product is an important determinant of a product's success. The product must be perceived by consumers to be superior to the product it supersedes or to offer a "benefit" recognized as more attractive than present products. Similarly, research indicates the stronger the fulfillment of felt needs is perceived by the consumer, the more readily he seeks information about a new product, maintains interest, and undertakes trial and adoption. Some evidence indicates that the more immediate the benefit, the more likely the consumer is to try the product. This same principle applies in the adoption of innovations by organizations, it appears. A review of the literature concluded that the rate of innovation in organizations is directly associated with perceived profitability. The more profitable is an innovation, the greater the rate of adoption.[48]

The *compatibility* of a new product is the degree to which the product is consistent with existing values and past experiences of the adopter, and is an important determinant of a new product's acceptance. The norms of the relevant reference group will retard acceptance of products that are

45 Kegerreis et al., "Innovativeness," p. 687.
46 Robertson, *Innovative Behavior,* p. 111.
47 The following section is based upon Rogers and Shoemaker, op. cit., pp. 137–57.
48 Joseph P. Martino, "Adopting New Ideas," *The Futurist,* vol. 8 (April 1974), pp. 88–89.

Figure 12.3 Product characteristics related to innovativeness

		Number of empirical findings indicating relation to innovativeness (%)					Total number of published findings
		Positive	None	Negative	Condi-tional	Total	
(1)	Relative advantage	78.8	15.2	3.0	3.0	100	66
(2)	Compatibility	86.0	14.0	0.0	0.0	100	50
(3)	Fulfillment of felt needs	92.6	3.7	3.7	0.0	100	27
(4)	Complexity	18.8	37.5	43.7	0.0	100	16
(5)	Trialability	42.9	42.9	14.3	0.0	100	14
(6)	Observability	75.0	25.0	0.0	0.0	100	8
(7)	Availability	55.6	22.2	16.7	5.6	100	18
(8)	Immediacy of benefit	57.1	28.6	14.3	0.0	100	7

Source: Modified with special permission from Everett M. Rogers and J. David Stanfield, "Adoption and Diffusion of New Products: Emerging Generalizations and Hypotheses," paper presented at the Conference on the Application of Sciences to Marketing Management, Purdue University (July 12–15, 1966), Table 7.

not compatible with the social system. If the consumer perceives the product to be too similar to previously tried and rejected products, however, acceptance of the new product will also be retarded. The color and design of the package, product, and promotional material accompanying the product act as a symbol to the consumer, communicating the compatibility of the new product with existing values and cognitive structure.

The *observability* (or communicability) of an innovation influences its rate of acceptance. Products that are visible in social situations or that have significant impact upon the social system appear to be those that are most communicable.

Products must have *perceived newness* to be attractive to early triers, Lambert found.[49] Promotional messages often stress "newness," of course, but it is important for marketers to assess empirically consumers' perceptions of newness before committing substantial resources to the introduction of a product which management perceives to be "new."

Some product characteristics have been identified that appear to *inhibit the rate of adoption.* One such characteristic is *complexity,* or the degree to which a new product is difficult to understand and use. Products that require detailed personal explanation, for example, are unlikely to diffuse rapidly. Although the research is far from conclusive, it appears that the trialability of a product affects the rate of acceptance. This is due to the desire of consumers to try the product in a small quantity before deciding to adopt it. When the consumer is forced to buy a large unit at one time,

49 Zarrel V. Lambert, "Perceptual Patterns, Information Handling, and Innovativeness," *Journal of Marketing Research*, vol. 9 (November 1972), pp. 427–31.

he is likely to perceive more risk in the purchase than if he were able to purchase a little at a time.

The relations between a consumer and other members and objects of the social system influence the rate of adoption of new products. The relations that affect new product acceptance are of two basic types: marketing dominated and nonmarketing dominated. The effectiveness of one is often influenced by the other.

Social and communication variables associated with innovativeness

Marketer dominated influences. Intensive contact with the mass media and commercial change agents tends to produce individuals who accept innovations more readily than others. This fact is indicated in items 2 and 3 of Figure 12.4. The majority of research on diffusions indicates that

Figure 12.4 Social and communications variables related to innovativeness

	Number of empirical findings indicating relation to innovativeness (%)					Total number of published findings
	Positive	None	Negative	Conditional	Total	
(1) Cosmopolitaness	80.8	11.0	2.7	5.5	100	73
(2) Mass media exposure	85.7	12.2	0.0	2.0	100	49
(3) Contact with change agencies	91.9	6.6	0.0	1.5	100	136
(4) Deviancy from norms	53.6	14.3	28.6	3.6	100	28
(5) Group participation	78.8	10.3	6.4	4.5	100	156
(6) Interpersonal communication exposure	70.0	15.0	15.0	0.0	100	40
(7) Opinion leadership	64.3	21.4	7.1	7.1	100	14

Source: Modified with special permission from Everett M. Rogers and J. David Stanfield, "Adoption and Diffusion of New Products: Emerging Generalizations and Hypotheses," paper presented at the Conference on the Application to Sciences of Marketing Management, Purdue University (July 12–15, 1966), Table 6.

communications from the mass media affect the adoption process most strongly at the awareness stage, the most important function being to inform the public of new products or ideas.[50] This research indicates that at later stages in the adoption process—interest and evaluation—personal influences become more important. These conclusions have been challenged by Lazer and Bell, however, who present some contradictory findings. They found that only 13.8 percent of consumers in one study of appliances used mass media in the awareness stage and that 96 percent of

50 Rogers, *Communication*, p. 99.

those seeking information at the interest and evaluation stages turned to the mass media.[51] Engel, Knapp, and Knapp, however, found that advertising is an effective communication in creating awareness of new drug products when coupled with other sources,[52] and King found that mass media sources were the most important sources of information to early adopters of millinery.[53] The more experience with a product category a potential adopter has, the more the person is likely to use advertising as an information source.[54]

Effective use of the media by marketers is complex because of the interactions of variables. In a study by Eskin, it was found that both advertising and price were important determinants of the sales levels for a new food product but that the effectiveness of the advertising in stimulating adoption depended upon the level of price charged.[55]

The type of product or service affects the role of media also. Green, Langeard and Favell found that the print media were more important as a source of innovation for innovators of a new *service* than for innovators of a new *product*. These investigators found that heavy television viewing was a characteristic of innovators in both categories, however.[56]

Other activities under the control of the marketing organizations have a significant impact on adoption. Sampling has been shown to be one of the most effective techniques for informing consumers of a new product.[57] Also, the research of Willett and Pennington on the nature of the salesman-customer problem-solving process is consonant with the view that personal salesmen play a very important role in providing information to the consumer.[58] Stefflre and Barnett have advanced a technique called cognitive mapping to determine how consumers view a product category with the objective of determining how effective advertising should be developed for new products.[59]

Word-of-mouth communications

Word-of-mouth, or personal, communications play a critical role in the adoption of new products. Numerous studies have indicated such a finding, as indicated in item 6 of Figure 12.4. Traditionally, it has been

51 Lazer and Bell, "Communication Process," pp. 4–5.

52 James F. Engel, David A. Knapp, and Deanne F. Knapp, "Sources of Influence in the Acceptance of New Products for Self-Medication: Preliminary Findings," in Haas, *Science*, pp. 776–82, at p. 778.

53 Charles W. King, "Communicating with the Innovator in the Fashion Adoption Process," in Peter D. Bennett, ed., *Marketing and Economic Development* (Chicago: American Marketing Association, 1965), pp. 425–39, at p. 435.

54 Kjell Gronhaug, "How New Car Buyers Use Advertising," *Journal of Advertising Research*, vol. 15 (February 1975), pp. 49–53.

55 Gerald J. Eskin, "A Case for Test Market Experiments," *Journal of Advertising Research*, vol. 15 (April 1975), pp. 27–33.

56 Robert T. Green, Eric Langeard, and Alice C. Favell, "Innovation in the Service Sector: Some Empirical Findings," *Journal of Marketing Research*, vol. 11 (August 1974), pp. 323–26.

57 Haines, "A Study," p. 689.

58 Ronald P. Willett and Allan L. Pennington, "Customer and Salesman: The Anatomy of Choice and Influence in a Retail Setting," in Haas, *Science*, pp. 598–616. The influence of salesmen in distributing information about new drugs to physicians is also well documented. See Theodore Caplow, "Market Attitudes: A Research Report from the Medical Field," *Harvard Business Review*, vol. 30, pp. 105–12 (November–December 1952).

59 Volney Stefflre, "Market Structure Studies: New Products for Old Markets and New Markets (Foreign) for Old Products," in Bass et al., op. cit., pp. 251–68; Norman L. Barnett, "Developing Effective Advertising for New Products," *Journal of Advertising Research*, vol. 8, pp. 13–18 (December 1968).

postulated that as an individual moves through early stages and toward adoption, the individual increasingly turns to other individuals for confirming information. The individual seeking information turns either to someone who has already purchased the new product or to an "expert"—someone who by reason of training or experience has superior ability to judge the product. For example, a consumer interested in buying a new model of a camera may ask a photographer or a serious camera hobbyist to help evaluate the new model.

Individuals apparently turn to personal sources of influence as the amount of perceived risk in the new product increases.[60] Generally it has also been found that individuals turn to personal sources of information when the choice between products is ambiguous.[61]

Word-of-mouth influence about new products is a two-way information flow. A study of adoption of a new automobile service demonstrated that word of mouth was the most important influence in the trial stage leading to adoption (as differentiated from awareness and interest), and that the innovators actively sought opinion from a variety of personal sources.[62] Myers and Robertson in a study of household products found that opinion leadership for these products was a two-way phenomenon. They concluded that the opinion leader is moderately more innovative than nonopinion leaders and is only relatively more influential than the average person. The housewife who is an opinion leader and innovator is also a "recipient of influence, not a dominant leader influencing a passive set of followers."[63]

Marketing strategists should also be concerned about the potential of unfavorable as well as favorable word-of-mouth communications. Arndt found that consumers who received unfavorable word-of-mouth comments were 24 percentage points less likely to purchase a new product than other consumers, while persons who received favorable word-of-mouth comments were only 12 percentage points more likely to buy.[64]

60 Herbert Menzel and Elihu Katz, "Social Relations and Innovation in the Medical Profession: The Epidemiology of a New Drug," *Public Opinion Quarterly*, pp. 337–52 (Winter 1955–56). For an overview of the physician studies, see Raymond A. Bauer and Lawrence H. Wortzel, "Doctor's Choice: The Physician and His Sources of Information about Drugs," *Journal of Marketing Research*, vol. 3, pp. 40–47 (February 1966). For additional research concerning the role of perceived risk in innovative behavior, see Johan Arndt, "Perceived Risk, Sociometric Integration, and Word of Mouth in the Adoption of a New Food Product," in Donald F. Cox, ed., *Risk Taking and Information Handling in Consumer Behavior* (Boston: Division of Research, Graduate School of Business Administration, Harvard University, 1967), pp. 289–316; also Donald T. Popielarz, "An Exploration of Perceived Risk and Willingness to Try New Products," *Journal of Marketing Research*, vol. 4, pp. 368–72 (November 1967).

61 James Coleman, Herbert Menzel, and Elihu Katz, "Social Processes in Physicians' Adoption of a New Drug," *Journal of Chronic Diseases*, vol. 9, pp. 1–19 (January 1959).

62 James F. Engel, Roger D. Blackwell, and Robert J. Kegerreis, "How Information Is Used to Adopt an Innovation," *Journal of Advertising Research*, vol. 9, pp. 3–10 (December 1969).

63 James H. Myers and Thomas S. Robertson, "Dimensions of Opinion Leadership," *Journal of Marketing Research*, vol. 9, pp. 41–46 (February 1972).

64 Johan Arndt, "Role of Product Related Conversations in the Diffusion of a New Product," *Journal of Marketing Research*, vol. 4 (August 1967), pp. 291–95, at p. 292. Arndt has conducted numerous other studies of personal influence upon innovativeness. Among his conclusions is the finding that some overlap occurs in opinion leadership, especially for closely related product categories. See Johan Arndt, "New Product Diffusion: The Interplay of Innovativeness, Opinion Leadership, Learning, Perceived Risk and Product Characteristics," *Markedskommunikasion*, vol. 5 (1968), pp. 1–9; Johan Arndt, "Exploring Consumer Willingness to Buy New Products," *Markedskommunikasion*, vol. 8 (1971), pp. 1–12.

Social integration. There is a considerable body of research attempting to determine the role that social integration of an individual plays in his decision to adopt a new product. In general, persons who are well integrated into the social system and who are respected by a group appear to adopt new products more rapidly than those who are less integrated.[65] An example of empirical research in this area is shown in Figure 12.5. A

Figure 12.5 Relation between time of first purchase of new food product and number of choices received by housewives as "relatively close friend"

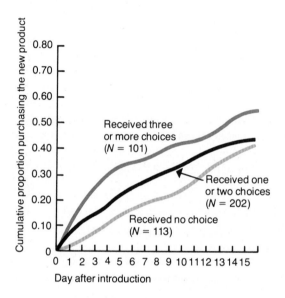

Source: Johan Arndt, "Role of Product-Related Conversations in the Diffusion of a New Product," *Journal of Marketing Research*, vol. 4, pp. 291–295, at p. 293 (August 1967). Reprinted from *Journal of Marketing Research* published by the American Marketing Association.

new food product was introduced into a social system; the figure shows that housewives who were named most often as "a relatively good friend" were also among the earliest adopters of the product.[66] Coleman and co-workers, in their studies of physicians, have demonstrated that the reliance upon highly respected members of the group increases markedly with the amount of risk perceived to be associated with adopting a new product.[67]

Gregariousness is a trait usually associated with innovativeness, both

65 For a review of the literature supporting this statement, see Rogers, *Communication*, pp. 237–47.
66 Johan Arndt, "Role of Product," pp. 291–95, at p. 293.
67 James Coleman, Elihu Katz, and Herbert Menzel, "The Diffusion of an Innovation among Physicians," *Sociometry*, vol. 20 (December 1957), pp. 253–69.

on the part of the opinion leader and the individual being influenced.[68] King found that the fashion innovator is characterized by an active life style in which innovators were likely to visit or entertain friends frequently, attend church or synagogue frequently, attend spectator sports, eat at restaurants frequently, and attend teas, concerts, plays, and club meetings.[69] An additional observation is that individuals who adhere fairly closely to the norms of their group in other forms of social behavior may perform similarly with regard to innovations.[70] Exceptions may be those who have achieved very high status in their reference group and are freer to deviate from the norms of behavior and those so low in status that they no longer observe the group norms. Presumably, it might be reasoned, these exceptions may be expected to deviate from norms more readily than others when considering the acceptance of a new product.

Marketing as a change agent

The marketing organization plays the role that traditionally in diffusion studies has been described as a "change agent"—stimulating the adoption of a new idea or product in a social system. The process of bringing about acceptance of a new product does not occur instantly, however. It is a process that occurs *over time.*

The process of adoption over time is illustrated in Figure 12.6 as a classical normal distribution. Although not all products may follow this distribution, it is useful in making the point that some persons are

Figure 12.6 Market segments identified by time of adoption of new product (as proportion of total who eventually adopt product) ($\overline{X}$ = mean time for adoption)

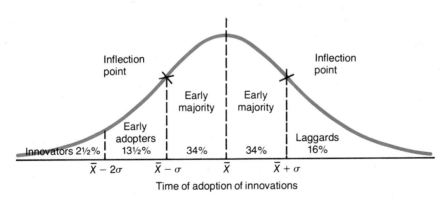

Source: Reprinted with permission of Macmillan Publishing Co., Inc., from *Diffusion of Innovations* by Everett M. Rogers. Copyright © 1962 by The Free Press.

68 The classic documentation of this finding is Elihu Katz and Paul F. Lazarsfeld, *Personal Influence* (New York: Free Press, 1955), esp. chaps, 10 and 11; also W. Erbe, "Gregariousness, Group Membership and the Flow of Information," *American Journal of Sociology*, vol. 67 (March 1962), pp. 502–16.
69 King, "Communicating," p. 335.
70 George C. Homans, *Social Behavior: Its Elementary Forms* (New York: Harcourt, 1961), chap. 5.

"innovators," others are "early adopters," others fall in the early or late majority, and some persons who eventually adopt a product may be called "laggards."

Acceptance of a new idea does not come all at once in a social system. The idea is transmitted to a few innovators who must pass through various stages of awareness, persuasion, trial and decision leading to adoption or rejection. After some innovators have adopted the product, others may follow, depending on the value of the innovation and other characteristics of the product. The process continues throughout the social system and its speed as well as eventual penetration of the system will be determined by many factors.

It should be concluded that the acceptance of new products does not occur for "one" reason or because of a "single" influence. A variety of forces are necessary to stimulate adoption. Some of these influences are marketer dominated such as advertising, sampling, and the sales force. Effective utilization of these marketing forces depends upon knowledge of the diffusion characteristics of the product category. At the same time, other variables which are beyond the control of the marketing strategist influence the adoption process. In the latter instance, the consumer analyst provides information helpful in adapting to consumer realities rather than trying to change them.

Predicting diffusion and adoption success

Marketing strategists are interested in predicting the behavior of aggregates of consumers rather than individual behavior. There are a number of models that, with varying degrees of success, have been used to predict market acceptance of new products. The output of these models usually involves predictions of the number of consumers who will accept a new product and the timing of acceptance.

New product models can be placed into two categories.[71] The first category can be called diffusion models, which are based upon fitting a mathematical curve to new product sales, using a parsimonious set of parameters. The parameters may or may not have definite behavioral content. The mathematical curves are determined from historical situations or theoretical propositions and applied to current problems. The variables in diffusion models are such things as the time the product has been introduced and number of persons in the market (with assumptions about interaction between consumers). Numerous types of diffusion or *stochastic* models are possible.

The second category of models is adoption models. These focus upon variables that describe consumer decision making concerning the new product and are called *deterministic* models. Some of them also include variables that describe marketer activity. Both kinds of models are included in the following discussion.

---

71 This categorization is from Philip Kotler, *Marketing Decision Making: A Model Building Approach* (New York: Holt, Rinehart and Winston, 1971). See chap. 17 of this source for an excellent overview of new product models.

The most basic stochastic models of new product acceptance permit predictions of the level of penetration by a new product in a given time period based upon early sales results. These models require data with which the analyst can separate the initial purchasers in early time periods from repeat purchasers. Thus these models separate the "triers" from the "adopters."

Penetration models assume some "ceiling" penetration—a percentage of households that represents the maximum proportion that can be expected to purchase a product of this type. The ratio of repeat purchasers in a period to triers can be represented by r, and the ceiling proportion can be represented by x. The penetration in the first period would be rx. The penetration in the second period would be equal to rx less those first-period triers who did not repeat their purchase. The penetration in period two, therefore, would be $rx(1-r)$. In period three, penetration would be $rx(1-r)^2$, and similarly for other periods until the ceiling is reached. Frequently, the effects of some external force (such as advertising) are added to the model as K. If this model were realistic, the marketer could project the total number of adopters at any point of time. Figure 12.7 shows how the penetration curve is calculated. In Figure 12.8 an application of this model is presented. Kelly found that the model was

Figure 12.7 Explicit character of the penetration model

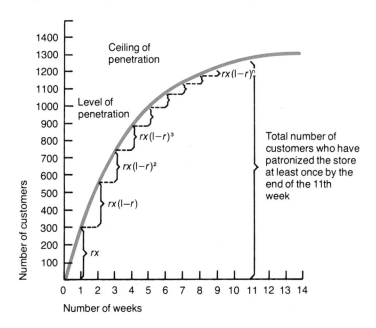

Source: Robert F. Kelly, "Estimating Ultimate Performance Levels of New Retail Outlets," *Journal of Marketing Research*, vol. 4 (February 1967), pp. 13–19, at p. 18. Reprinted from the *Journal of Marketing Research* published by the American Marketing Association.

Figure 12.8 Comparison of estimated and actual penetration curves for a retail store (based on the first three weeks data)

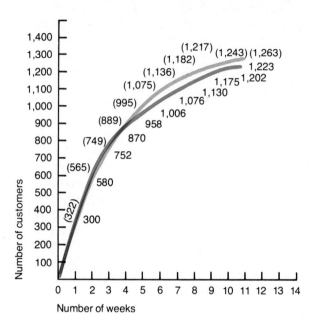

Note: Colored curve—actual penetration; gray curve—estimated penetration.

Source: Robert F. Kelly, "Estimating Ultimate Performance Levels of New Retail Outlets," *Journal of Marketing Research*, vol. 4 (February 1967), pp. 13–19, at p. 17. Reprinted from the *Journal of Marketing Research* published by the American Marketing Association.

useful in predicting the penetration of the market area for a new dairy store.[72]

The penetration model was introduced by Fourt and Woodlock.[73] It depends upon adequate data (usually from a consumer panel) to ascertain early penetration ratios and stability of these ratios over time. In spite of the impracticality of many of its assumptions for most innovations, it is one of the general group of brand share models[74] that has influenced diffusion thought and research.

Epidemiological models A number of models have been developed that view new product diffusion as a process of social interaction about the product in which

72 Robert F. Kelly, "Estimating Ultimate Performance Levels of New Retail Outlets," *Journal of Marketing Research*, vol. 4 (February 1967), pp. 3–19.

73 L. A. Fourt and J. W. Woodlock, "Early Prediction of Market Success for New Grocery Products," *Journal of Marketing*, vol. 25 (October 1962), pp. 31–38; also William D. Barclay, "Probability Model for Early Prediction of New Product Market Success," *Journal of Marketing*, vol. 27 (January 1963), pp. 63–68.

74 For a description of the fundamentals underlying these early brand-switching models, see David W. Miller and Martin K. Starr, *Executive Decision and Operations Research* (Englewood Cliffs, N. J.: Prentice-Hall, 1960), pp. 173–82.

innovators and early adopters "infect" the rest of the population. Thus, these models, which are based upon social-interaction assumptions, have been compared to disease epidemics that move through the population. Predictions are usually based upon acceptance-rejection criteria in a time setting. The assumptions of these models and the number of variables are usually simple, although the mathematics involved may be sophisticated. The new product models of this type that are useful to marketing strategists have precedent in other areas of social science.[75]

One model that has yielded good predictions of actual data was developed by Bass.[76] The assumptions underlying this model are that initial purchases of a new product will be made both by innovators and imitators, the distinction between the two being buying influence. Innovators are influenced in their initial purchase by marketing-controlled communications, but imitators are influenced by the number of previous buyers; imitators "learn" from the experiences of those who have already bought. Bass defines p as the coefficient of innovation and r as the coefficient of imitation. The importance of innovators is greater at first and diminishes monotonically with time.

The Bass model is described in the following manner:[77]

$$S(T) = mf(T) = [P(T) \, m - Y(T)] = [p + q \int_0^T S(t)dt/m] \, [m - \int S(t)dt]$$

where

q/m = initial purchase rate (a constant)

p = probability of initial purchase (a constant)

$f(T)$ = likelihood of purchase at T

$Y(T)$ = total number purchasing in the (O,T) interval

$S(T)$ = sales at T

Using standard maximization techniques, it is possible to predict the peak and timing of peak sales for the product. Bass has applied this model to sales of eleven durable goods and it has generally yielded excellent predictions. Using regression analysis with data for three years, Bass was able to predict sales of room air-conditioners that coincided with actual sales with a coefficient of determination of $R^2 = 0.92$. For color television, the predictions of sales through 1970 using the Bass model apparently were more accurate than the forecasts made by the manufacturers of color television. An example of the closeness of fit between actual and predicted sales is shown in Figure 12.9 for power lawnmowers.

An advance in epidemiological models recently was developed by Midgley in Australia, who dealt explicitly with the problem that interpersonal contacts or "contagion" can be either positive or negative or

75 Representative models include Stuart C. Dodd, "Diffussion Is Predictable: Testing Probability Models for Laws of Interaction," *American Sociological Review*, vol. 20 (December 1955), p. 392; A. Rapoport, "Spread of Information through a Population with Socio-Structural Bias: I. Assumption of Transivity," and "II Various Models with Partial Transivity," *Bulletin of Mathematical Biophysics*, vol. 15 (1953), pp. 523–33, 534–44; Melvin H. DeFleur and Otto N. Larsen, *The Flow of Information* (New York: Harper & Row, 1958).

76 Frank M. Bass, "A New Product Growth Model for Consumer Durables," *Management Science*, vol. 15 (January 1969), pp. 215–27.

77 Bass, "New Product," p. 217.

Figure 12.9 Actual sales and sales predicted by Bass model of new product diffusion (power lawn mowers)

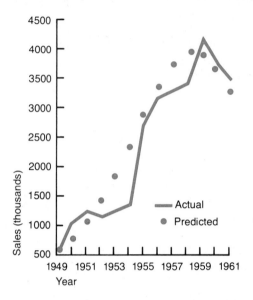

Source: Frank M. Bass, "A New Product Growth Model for Consumer Durables," *Management Science*, vol. 15, no. 5 (January 1969), p. 223, Figure 7. Reprinted by permission.

neutral, with regard to new product information.[78] Figure 12.10 displays the Midgley model, which relates four categories of the population. The number of *potential adopters* is represented as X and from that group, which is the total population before the new product is introduced but becomes a smaller number as some *potential* adopters become *adopters*, some will become *active adopters* (Y), some active rejectors (Z), and some *passives* (P). The cumulative number of adopters (C) is then:

$$C = Y + Z + P$$

In a fixed population size of N, it will be true that

$$N \text{ (population size)} = X + Y + Z + P$$

At the time a new product is launched, Y, Z and P must equal zero and the number of potential adopters therefore equals the population size (X = N). This means that the process must be initiated by the marketing mechanisms (B in Figure 12.10) since the influences (A, C, D) must be zero before the product is introduced. It is possible to derive the equations for such influences. Midgley tested the theory with some data from a consumer panel for toothpaste, candy, detergent, and biscuits and found support for the theory from the data.

While the Midgley model must still be regarded as exploratory, it

78 David F. Midgley, "A Simple Mathematical Theory of Innovative Behavior," *Journal of Consumer Research*, vol. 3 (June 1976), pp. 31–41.

Figure 12.10 Mathematical model of innovative behavior

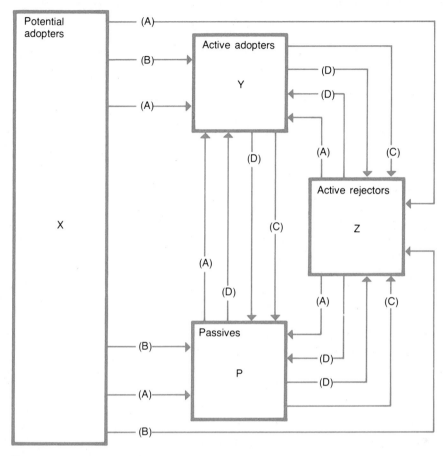

Key
(A) Due to the influence of active adopters
(B) Due to the influence of marketing activities
(C) Due to the influence of active rejectors
(D) Other state change mechanisms

Source: David F. Midgley, "A Simple Mathematical Theory of Innovative Behavior," *Journal of Consumer Research*, vol. 3 (June 1976), pp. 33–34. Reprinted from the *Journal of Consumer Research* published by the American Marketing Association.

indicates the potential that is developing for forecasting new product adoption. The fact that the methodology is at least partially successful indicates the possibilities for future consumer researchers to derive better and better estimates of the parameters needed for use of such models by marketers in a wide range of product categories and marketing programs.[79]

79 For other stochastic approaches to new product acceptance, see William F. Massey, "Forecasting the Demand for New Convenience Products," *Journal of Marketing Research*, vol. 6 (November 1969), pp. 405–12; and David H. Ahl, "New Product Forecasting Using Consumer Panels," *Journal of Marketing Research*, vol. 7 (May 1970), pp. 160–67.

Deterministic (adoption) models

Various mathematical models have been developed that relate adoption of a new product to specific consumer variables, which, if they can be measured, determine outcome variables of intermediate stages leading to trial of a new product.

The DEMON model is an example of the multistage model in which an assumption is made that consumers pass through stages of decision making leading to purchase of a new product. As each stage is reached, it is assumed that a higher probability of purchase results than in the preceding stage.[80]

DEMON was developed at the advertising agency of Batten, Barton, Durstine, and Osborne to predict acceptance of new products and to improve management decisions concerning marketing strategy for new products. DEMON is represented in Figure 12.11. The figure shows the stages involved in acceptance of a product new to a consumer. In the model, awareness is an important variable. Awareness is predicted by measuring the ratio of advertising dollars spent to the number of delivered gross impressions and the ratio of impressions to level of attained reach and frequency.[81]

In the DEMON model, each variable is first dependent, then independent.[82] Thus, trial depends on awareness but once activated, trial becomes the independent variable for prediction of *usage*. Each of these variables is influenced in turn by variables (such as advertising) which are marketer dominated. Although Figure 12.11 does not show the relationships between variables, the computer program for DEMON does contain such explicit equations. Components of this model have been further refined by Light and Pringle, using a set of recursive regression equations called NEWS (new product, early warning system).[83]

A number of other deterministic models have been developed and some of these have been used by marketing organizations with a reasonable amount of success. The N.W. Ayer Advertising Agency uses a model that includes recall of advertising claims as an important determinant of initial purchases of new products.[84] The most ambitious of these models is probably one developed by Amstutz, which was used to obtain a good simulation of physician adoption of new drugs.[85] One other model

80 David B. Learner, "Profit Maximization through New-Product Marketing Planning and Control," in Frank Bass, ed., *Application of the Sciences in Marketing Management* (New York: Wiley, 1968), pp. 151–67.

81 "Reach" and "frequency" are commonly used terms in advertising. Reach is the percentage of the population contacted at least once by an advertisement. Frequency is the average number of times each person is reached, or gross impressions divided by reach.

82 James K. DeVoe, "Plans, Profits, and the Marketing Program," in Webster, *New Directions*, pp. 473–88.

83 Lawrence Light and Lewis Pringle, "New Product Forecasting Using Recursive Regression," in David et al., *Research in Consumer Behavior*, (New York: Holt, Rinehart and Winston, 1970), pp. 702–9; and Abraham Charnes et al., "NEWS Report: A Discussion of the Theory and Application of the Planning Portion of DEMON," in Sheth, *Models*, pp. 296–309.

84 Henry J. Claycamp and Lucien E. Liddy, "Prediction of New Product Performance: An Analytical Approach," *Journal of Marketing Research*, vol. 6, pp. 414–20 (November 1969).

85 Arnold Amstutz, *Computer Simulation of Competitive Market Response* (Cambridge, Mass.: M.I.T. Press, 1967); and Henry J. Claycamp and Arnold E. Amstutz, "Simulation Techniques in the Analysis of Marketing Strategy," in Frank M. Bass, Charles W. King, and Edgar Pessemier, eds., *Applications of the Sciences in Marketing Management* (New York: Wiley, 1968), pp. 113–50.

Figure 12.11 DEMON model of new product acceptance

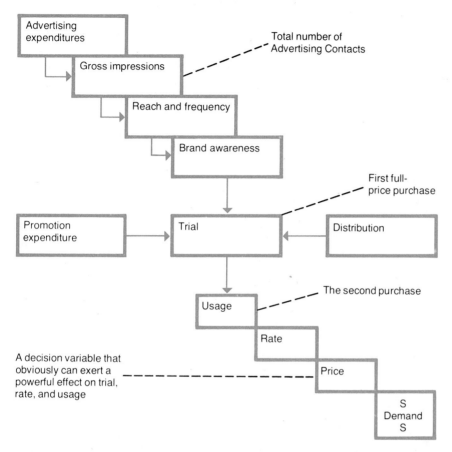

Source: James K. DeVoe, "Plans, Profits, and the Marketing Program," in Frederick E. Webster, Jr., ed., *New Directions in Marketing* (Chicago: American Marketing Association, 1965). Reprinted by permission.

that has received considerable managerial attention is SPRINTER developed by Urban. This model simulates new product adoption based upon an assumption of buying activity leading to trial in the following stages: (1) awareness, (2) intent, (3) search, (4) selection, and (5) postpurchase behavior.[86]

There has been a rapid expansion of knowledge in recent years concerning the development of models for new product acceptance. In many cases, extensive data have been presented to show the efficacy of respective models. To date there has been little application of a model developed by one individual or group to data or problems faced by other

Evaluation of models of diffusion and adoption

86 Glen L. Urban, "A New Product Analysis and Decision Model," *Management Science*, vol. 14 (April 1968), pp. 490–517; also David B. Montgomery and Glen L. Urban, *Management Science in Marketing* (Englewood Cliffs, N.J.: Prentice-Hall, 1969).

individuals or groups. That is the ultimate test of a model's generality. This type of testing is occurring (with NEWS and the Ayer model, for example), but the situations involved are mostly proprietary business applications, which do not lend themselves to widespread publication of the results. Perhaps also, if the results were more conclusive, publication of the results would be more widespread.

It must be concluded, however, that new product models appear to be one of the most successful applications of mathematics to consumer behavior problems. The Bass model has been shown to be more useful than conventional methods of forecasting (for color television, for example), and other models have been demonstrated to be useful. It is clear that the adoption models have more behavioral assumptions made explicit and presumably should have more general applicability to many types of new product introductions. The diffusion models, however, are generally more parsimonious. Data collection is generally more feasible with the diffusion models. The more simplistic, curve-fitting types of models appear to have been more feasible and economical to date than the complex models.

Summary

The diffusion of innovations is a topic of study and research that grew rapidly in the past few decades, dealing with how a new product is adopted in a society. It is a topic of immense importance to marketing organizations because of their necessity to bring out new products continuously in order to survive.

The purchase of a new product is analyzed as a special category of consumer decision for three reasons. First, much of the research in the diffusion tradition has focused upon the decision to *continue or discontinue* future use of a product rather than upon the individual decision for a product or brand that is more typically analyzed with general consumer behavior models. A second reason for the special nature of diffusion studies is their emphasis upon the *social structure of communication* rather than individual processing of information. Thus, diffusion theory is generally *relational* rather than monadic. A third reason for an emphasis upon diffusion research is the simple volume of research to be assimilated. Over 2,700 publications exist in this field, reporting over 1,800 empirical investigations.

The elements of the diffusion process to be studied are (1) the *innovation*, (2) the *communication* of the innovation among *individuals*, (3) the *social system*, and (4) *time*. The most commonly accepted definition of an innovation is *any idea or product perceived by the potential innovator to be new*. Most marketing studies simply consider an innovation to be any form of a product that has recently become available in a market. Innovations may be classified as continuous, dynamically continous and discontinous.

Everett Rogers is the most influential analyst of the diffusion process. His model has become well-known in many disciplines, including consumer research. This model describes the adoption process as one of *knowledge* or awareness by the consumer, *persuasion* that the new product is valuable and worth the risk of trying it, a *decision* to adopt or reject the product, and *confirmation* of the trial and decision.

Marketing studies have focused on several correlates of new product adoption and the results of these studies are described in this chapter. The variables analyzed may be grouped together as *consumer characteristics* related to innovativeness, product characteristics, and social and communication variables.

The final section of this chapter described some of the mathematical models that are currently being developed in an attempt to predict levels and timing of new product acceptance. Some of these are stochastic in that they represent aggregate behavior with relatively simple mathematical equations. Examples include models by Bass and by Midgley as well as early penetration models by others. Deterministic models attempt to explain product acceptance (outcome) as determined by intermediate stages (inputs). One of the most developed of these models is DEMON. Although the deterministic models are probably more realistic and helpful in advancing knowledge about how consumers make decisions, the stochastic models are currently more feasible and economical than the complex models.

Review and discussion questions

1. The interest of a marketing manager in the topic of diffusion of innovations is rather obvious. Why might an economist concerned with macroeconomic problems be interested in this topic?

2. Several definitions of innovation are presented in this chapter. Which would you use to conduct research in marketing or in another discipline? Defend your choice.

3. Explain as precisely as possible the differences between continuous, dynamically continuous, and discontinuous innovations.

4. What is meant by *relational* and *monadic* approaches to diffusion studies? Explain how research would be affected by one approach compared to the other.

5. A new bakery product is being introduced by a large firm. The company believes that it should obtain about 20 percent penetration in a market of 20 million people. In a test market, it was found that 3 percent of the people tried the product within the first week of introduction and that of those who tried it about half purchased the product again. However, of those who repurchased, usage was only one unit every two weeks. The bakery has asked you to help estimate the amount of production that will be needed each week until the product reaches a stable market position. Prepare a method to use.

6. The manufacturer of a new product is attempting to determine who the innovators for the product might be. The product is a game that requires players to answer each other with phrases from various foreign languages. Who would you identify as the most likely innovators? What appeals would you suggest be used in promoting the product?

7. A large manufacturer of drug and personal grooming products wants to introduce a new toothpaste brand in addition to the three he already markets. Evaluate for the firm what information might be used from innovation studies to guide in introducing the product.

8. A large pharmaceutical firm has successfully marketed an infant formula for several years. This product has good acceptance among pediatricians, who recommend the product for babies up to six months. In an attempt to expand their market, the firm has developed a new liquid food for babies between the ages of six and eighteen months. The new food is flavored with vegetables, fruits, or cereal, yet is fed through a bottle. It will compete directly with regular strained baby food, and the firm knows that competition will be keen. However, the firm is prepared to release an authoritative report by a well-known medical school to show that morbidity rates among liquid-fed babies are significantly lower than among strained-food-fed babies. This report indicates that it takes 100 spoonfuls of strained food each day to give a baby a nutritionally sound diet. Since babies tend to throw the food on the floor they often receive a deficient diet and the liquid food will remedy this. The firm is convinced it must receive the endorsement of the liquid food by pediatricians to be successful. Your job is to outline a program to gain adoption of liquid food as the food recommended by pediatricians.

PART 4

ALTERNATIVE EVALUATION

Once search has been finished and relevant information has been procured, the next stage of the decision process is alternative evaluation. First the information must be processed so that it is in usable form. This is the subject of Chapter 13. A considerable body of evidence is reviewed documenting that the consumer, to a large extent, sees and hears what he or she wants to see and hear. There are some significant implications of this fact for marketing planning as will be stressed in other chapters in this unit.

Evaluative criteria play an important role in alternative evaluation. These are the specifications or expectations the consumer has formed and against which various alternatives are assessed. They are a reflection of underlying motives and hence resist change. As such, they usually are accepted as a given in marketing strategy, as the discussion in Chapter 14 will reveal.

When incoming information is evaluated in terms of these criteria, the outcome will be a belief that a given alternative expresses certain desired attributes. Beliefs, in turn, lead to attitudes that are the evaluation of the "goodness or badness" of the belief. Beliefs and attitudes are the subject of Chapter 15. The underlying principle is that a change in belief will, all things being equal, lead to a change in attitude, which leads to a corresponding change in behavioral intentions and finally in behavior itself. This relationship has only recently been clarified, and much of Chapter 15 is devoted to the significance of what have become known as "expectancy-value" models of attitude and attitude change. This discussion is continued in Chapter 16 in which the focus is more directly on the manner in which changes occur in beliefs and attitudes and some of the ways in which this change can best be accomplished.

This unit is concluded with a discussion of brand loyalty in Chapter 17. Much of consumer behavior research has focused on ways to achieve shifts in brand preference, with the result that models of brand loyalty assume some importance. By necessity this chapter is somewhat technical, because there have been a number of attempts to construct quantitative models of this phenomenon. Those without much background in quantitative models may wish to skip the more difficult portions of the chapter.

CHAPTER 13

Information processing

In the early 1970s CBS introduced a program that was destined to become one of the most popular in its long history—"All in the Family," featuring Archie Bunker. Assuming that the program would be perceived as a satire on bigotry, it seemed reasonable to predict that most people would see Archie for what he is—highly prejudiced and narrow minded. Yet, an audience survey indicated that many saw Archie as a hero.[1] These people, on the whole, embraced the same patterns of prejudice, whereas those who were not prejudiced had quite an opposite reaction.

Now what happened here? Both groups received exactly the same message, but their responses were polar opposites. One thing becomes clear immediately and that is the fact that the audience is *not* just a group of passive recipients. Each person actively processes and interprets that information in a unique way. In fact, they tend to see and hear what they want to see and hear, as is demonstrated by the fact that only 44 percent of those exposed to the thousands of print advertisements analyzed by the Starch readership service notice a particular ad, 35 percent read enough to identify the brand, and only 9 percent said they read most of the ad.[2] Obviously, only a small proportion of advertising is fully perceived at any given point in time, thus demonstrating the *selectivity* of information processing.

In order to understand information processing it will be necessary to delve into the broader subject of cognitive processes by which an

1 Neil Bidmar and Milton Rokeach, "Archie Bunker's Bigotry: A Study in Selective Perception and Exposure," *Journal of Communication*, vol. 24 (Winter 1974), pp. 36–47.
2 Herbert Krugman, "What Makes Advertising Effective?" *Harvard Business Review*, vol. 53 (March–April 1975), pp. 96–102.

information input is "transformed, reduced, elaborated, stored, recovered, and used."[3] The organization and functioning of memory assumes special importance. It will be shown that response to communication is multistaged, beginning with exposure and progressing to attention, message reception, and attitudinal or behavioral change. Moreover, it will be demonstrated that the individual is fully capable of resisting persuasion and there is no "magic power" available for the seller or advertiser to use. This chapter provides the undergirding rationale for the basic proposition of this book that marketing success comes *only* through creative adaptation of the entire strategy to the consumer.

Cognitive processes

Cognitive processes describe some of man's most significant activities. Our senses are constantly besieged with stimuli of all types, and complex mechanisms exist to interpret sensory information and extract content. It is the purpose of this section to describe the ways in which people "make sense" of their world.

Memory

"Why study such things as memory when my need is for research to help me meet my sales goals?" The authors often encounter such questions, and they are logical indeed from the perspective of the practitioner. In one sense we are entering the basic research domain of the academic psychologist. But the purpose is quite pragmatic—to discover, if possible, why people respond as they do to commercial persuasion. For this and other reasons, McGuire has designated analysis of the organization of memory as one of the highest priorities of consumer research.[4]

Figure 13.1 represents the *traditional* conception of memory organization in graphic form. It has been widely embraced until recently by both psychologists and writers in consumer behavior.[5] Briefly, memory was assumed to function as follows:[6]

1. Information input enters and is then altered by the central nervous system through extracting information about color, contour, and so on. This simplified information then is passed on to a higher level analysis.

3 Ulrich Neisser, *Cognitive Psychology* (New York: Appleton, 1966), p. 4.

4 William J. McGuire, "Some Internal Psychological Factors Influencing Consumer Choice," *Journal of Consumer Research*, vol. 2 (March 1976), pp. 302–19.

5 Donald A. Norman, *Memory and Attention* (New York: Wiley, 1969); Peter H. Lindsay and Donald A. Norman, *Human Information Processing* (New York: Academic Press, 1972); A. Newell and H. A. Simon, *Human Problem Solving* (Englewood Cliffs, N.J.: Prentice-Hall, 1972); J. W. Payne, "Heuristic Search Processes in Decision Making," in Beverlee B. Anderson, ed., *Advances in Consumer Research*, vol. 3 (Association for Consumer Research, 1976), pp. 321–27; and James R. Bettman, "Issues in Designing Consumer Information Environments," *Journal of Consumer Research*, vol. 22 (December 1975), pp. 169–77.

6 There are two excellent summaries to which the reader is referred. See Leo Postman, "Verbal Learning and Memory," in Mark R. Rosenzweig and Lyman W. Porter, eds., *Annual Review of Psychology*, vol. 26 (Palo Alto, Calif.: Annual Reviews, Inc., 1975), pp. 291–335; and Robert W. Chestnut and Jacob Jacoby, "Consumer Information Processing: Emerging Theory and Findings" in Arch G. Woodside, Jagdish N. Sheth, and Peter Bennett, eds: *Consumer and Industrial Buying Behavior* (New York: Elsevier North-Holland, 1977).

Figure 13.1 The traditional conception of memory organization

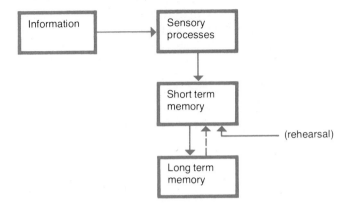

2. The information enters *short term memory* (sometimes referred to as primary memory) which is distinctly limited in capacity.

3. Information does not stay in the short term storage without rehearsal, a type of inner speech by which the memory trace is strengthened and embedded. Without rehearsal, the information fades from memory.

4. Information that is rehearsed then is transferred to *long term memory* (or secondary memory). It may be retrieved if it is successfully integrated within the existing memory organization. Forgetting occurs when means of retrieval are lost or when new information provides interference.

No theory of memory ever really can be proved, of course, because memory per se cannot be observed directly. Rather, the contents of storage must be inferred from some type of test, and most of the data until recently tended to favor the existence of two separate and distinct types of memory.[7] It now appears, however, that there is only one memory with differing internal functions.[8]

The reader certainly is familiar by now with the model of consumer behavior utilized in this book. The central processing unit reproduced in Figure 13.2, in effect, depicts memory in its totality. Notice, however, that there is one component labeled as *active memory* following the suggestion of Posner.[9] Active memory is similar to a desk top. All sorts of things are

7 See Michael J. Watkins, "Concept and Measurement of Primary Memory," *Psychological Bulletin*, vol. 81, pp. 695–711 (October 1974).

8 For some of the evidence leading to this revised perspective, see Michael I. Posner, *Cognition: An Introduction* (Glenview, Ill.: Scott Foresman, 1973); F. I. M. Craik and R. S. Lockhart, "Levels of Processing: A Framework for Memory Research," *Journal of Verbal Learning and Verbal Behavior*, vol. 11 (1972), pp. 671–684; Wayne A. Wickelgren, "The Long and Short of Memory," *Psychological Bulletin*, vol. 80, (December 1973), pp. 425–438; Watkins, "Concept and Measurement"; Postman, "Verbal Learning"; and Chestnut and Jacoby, "Consumer Information Processing."

9 Posner, *Cognition*.

Figure 13.2 The components of a consumer's memory

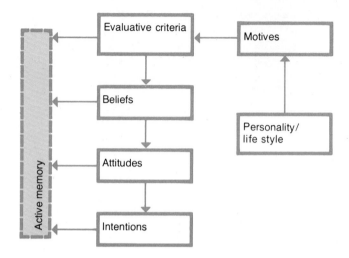

assembled on the desk surface when one is working on a problem and later are put away. In active memory, incoming information and that already stored in long term or permanent memory are brought together. It is here that the new input is categorized and interpreted.

Not everything within long term memory will be available for use within the active memory. There appear to be two basic determining factors. First, there are differences in the depth with which new information is analyzed. The greater the depth, the higher the probability of long term retention.[10] The second consideration is the extent to which the contents of memory are recirculated and used both in problem solving and in the process of interpreting new information.[11] If there is little or no recirculation, a particular item will become increasingly irretrievable.

Rehearsal (silent, inner speech[12]) is still felt to be the necessary condition for new information to move into long term memory. Rehearsal implies an active, conscious interaction with the incoming material. Mere repetition, however, does nothing to enhance subsequent recall. Repetition of nonsense syllables is an example, because it is usually found that such information is quickly forgotten. Active processing and thought, however, are another matter.[13] The new input is likely to be retained if it is put to the constructive use suggested by Posner:

> We must be able to reorganize information in order to solve
> problems, develop new structures, and interpret the world around us. To

10 Watkins, "Concept and Measurement."
11 Craik and Lockhart, "Levels of Processing."
12 Norman, *Memory and Attention*, p. 86.
13 See Postman, "Verbal Learning," for further elaboration of the difference between mere repetitive rehearsal and what he terms to be "maintenance rehearsal" (p. 301).

accomplish this we must operate upon the structures stored in our memories in a way analogous to the carpenter's shaping of wood.[14]

Memory, then, is dynamic and continually changing. The practical problem for anyone concerned with influencing consumer behavior, whether for purposes of education or for commerical gain, is to ascertain that the information presented indeed does move from active memory into long term storage where it has a chance of shaping future behavior.

Figure 13.3 The stages in information processing

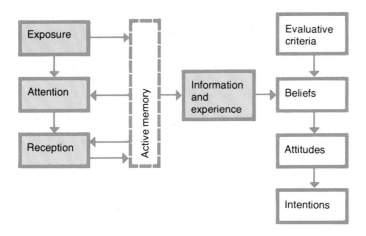

The expanded model in Figure 13.3 shows what happens as new information is processed and analyzed.[15] The first step, of course, must be actual *exposure* and activation of sensory processes. The stimulus moves from there into conscious active memory, and it can then be said that *attention* has been attracted. This does not guarantee, however, that the message will actually be *received and comprehended* in the manner intended by the sender. In fact, quite a different item may enter into long term memory as the stimulus is elaborated, attenuated, and otherwise changed in the process of active analysis. Furthermore, as was stressed earlier, those inputs that do not receive rehearsal will never even be retained. Finally, the last stage will be some type of *response*, depicted here primarily in terms of new information and experience leading to changes in beliefs, attitudes, or intentions. Each of these phases is elaborated in the following sections.

The dynamics of information processing

14 Posner, *Cognition*, p. 92.

15 This is consistent with the multiple stage model suggested by McGuire. See William J. McGuire, "Some Internal Psychological Factors Influencing Consumer Choice" and "Persuasion, Resistance and Attitude Change," in Ithiel de Sola Pool et al., eds., *Handbook of Communication* (Chicago: Rand McNally, 1973), chap. 9.

Exposure

Information processing begins when patterns of energy in the form of stimulus inputs reach one or more of the five senses. For this to happen, of course, it is necessary for the communicator to select media, either interpersonal or mass, which reach that individual at the time and place where he or she happens to be. Exposure occurs from physical proximity to a stimulus input such that the individual has direct opportunity for one or more senses to be activated. This very commonsense principle of media selection is more difficult to implement than it might appear, however, because the first step is a very precise definition of audience target. It will not do, for example, to say that the target market for Friskie's dry cat food is all families who have a cat as a pet. Obviously any consumer has a variety of options in feeding a pet, and it will be necessary to determine beforehand exactly the type of person who prefers both a dry food and this particular brand. Next, research must disclose the types of media that actually will reach this particular audience. Now, all things being equal, the marketer at least stands a chance of delivering the message to the potential customer.[16]

The central nervous system possesses a vast capability to transmit information about numerous energy variations to the brain.[17] In vision, for example, the retina of the eye is stimulated by electromagnetic waves, and the result is optic nerve activity.[18] The perception of different hues, on the other hand, results from changes in wave length.

Vibrations of the basilar membrane of the inner ear provide the basic sensations of hearing. Variations in experience of loudness, pitch, and timber, in turn, are a function of similar variations in the amplitude, frequency, and complexity of these vibrations.

Taste and smell seem to be activated by chemical interactions between stimuli and the membranes of the nose and taste buds. There is little else known about the physiology of these senses, other than the fact that different regions of the tongue detect one or more of four basic tastes—bitter at the base of the tongue, sour along the side, salty on the sides and top, and sweet along the top.

The skin senses provide information about pressure, pain, and temperature. Different receptors seem to exist for each type of sensation, and the types of energy submitted by each to the central nervous system are quite divergent.

Finally, there also are sensory receptors that provide information about internal states. Examples are the kinesthetic impulses, impulses from muscles or tendons, feelings of motion generating from the semicircular canals, an orientation to gravity resulting from the vestibular sacs, and various other types of pressure and pain.

16 For a detailed review of the principles of media selection, see James F. Engel, Hugh G. Wales, and Martin R. Warshaw, *Promotional Strategy*, 3d ed. (Homewood, Ill.: Richard D. Irwin, 1975), chap. 12.

17 For a useful but technical source on the sensory process, see S. S. Stevens, ed., *Handbook of Experimental Psychology* (New York: Wiley, 1951), chaps. 3–11.

18 Daniel J. Weintraub, "Perception," in Rosenzweig and Porter, eds., *Annual Review of Psychology*, vol. 26 (Palo Alto, Ca.: Annual Reviews, Inc., 1976), pp. 263–89.

Nearly a century ago, the famous psychologist William James defined attention as: **Attention**

> . . . the taking possession by the mind, in clear and vivid form, of one out of what seems several simultaneously possible objects or trains of thought. Focalization, concentration, of consciousness are of its essence. It implies withdrawal from some things in order to deal effectively with others.[19]

This is precisely the meaning still attributed to attention by the leading theorists of today[20] with one essential difference: it is now viewed as the conscious *end product* of a complex process whereby an incoming stimulus is categorized and given initial meaning. More formally, attention is the active processing of exposed information stimuli such that a conscious impression is made.

Transforming sensations into meaning. It now seems probable that all stimuli that activate one or more of the senses enter into active memory for further processing.[21] The first phase is a preliminary classification based largely on physical properties of the stimulus. The second phase is an analysis for pertinence at which time active memory functions to admit some stimuli for further analysis and to reject others on the basis of their utility to that individual at that point in time.[22] The first screening is based mostly on sensory factors, whereas the second brings the entire range of the individual's central processing unit (Figure 13.2) into consideration.

(1) Preliminary classification. At this stage, referred to as preattentive processing by Neisser,[23] stimuli receive an initial analysis for meaning based largely on such physical properties as loudness, pitch, and so on.[24] The correct classification of a stimulus is aided materially by past experience and learning in the form of *categories of meaning.*[25]

Learning begins in childhood as the individual begins to group stimulus patterns along a number of dimensions. Common physical characteristics and functions are especially useful in this regard. The child comes to recognize, for example, that a thin object consisting of many pages between two covers that is usually longer than it is wide is some type of

---

19 William James, *The Principles of Psychology*, vol. 1 (New York: Henry Holt and Co., 1890), pp. 403–4.

20 See especially Neisser, *Cognitive Psychology*; and Norman, *Memory and Attention.*

21 Donald A. Norman, "Toward a Theory of Memory and Attention," *Psychological Review*, vol. 75 (1968) pp. 522–36.

22 Norman, "Toward a Theory," pp. 526–29.

23 Neisser, *Cognitive Psychology.*

24 For a good review, see Hershel W. Leibowitz and Lewis O. Harvey, Jr., "Perception," in Mark R. Rosenzweig and Lyman W. Porter, eds., *Annual Review of Psychology*, vol. 24 (Palo Alto, Ca.: Annual Reviews, Inc., 1973), pp. 200–40.

25 A classic source on the nature of categories of meaning is J. S. Bruner, "On Perceptual Readiness," *Psychological Review*, vol. 64, pp. 123–52 (1957). Also see Posner, *Cognition*; Chestnut and Jacoby, "Consumer Information Processing"; Norman F. Dixon, *Subliminal Perception—The Nature of the Controversy* (Maidenhead-Berkshire, England: McGraw-Hill Publishing Co., Ltd., 1971); and Ezra Stotland and Lance K. Canon, *Social Psychology: A Cognitive Approach* (Philadelphia, Pa.: W. B. Saunders, 1972), chap. 3.

book. When he or she sees such an object, then, these basic stimulus properties will assist in selection of the correct category. In addition, all of these stimulus properties blend into an intrinsic whole rather than just a collection of individual parts. This broader pattern, or *gestalt*, also leads to more accurate categorization. Finally, motives and other personal influences will help determine the appropriate category. The person might have a strong achievement need reflected in a desire to learn. Books will be important, therefore, and the category "book" should stand out.

The mature individual would have thousands of such stored categories. Once a new stimulus is received, Bruner hypothesizes that preliminary meaning is assigned through a four stage comparison process:[26]

1. Primitive categorization. The basic characteristics of the stimulus are isolated.

2. Cue search. Analysis begins of input attributes so that the proper category of meaning can be determined.

3. Confirmation check. A category is tentatively selected.

4. Confirmation completion. A decision is made regarding meaning.

Obviously this takes place virtually instantaneously without conscious awareness. The categories chosen, in large part, are determined on the basis of accessibility. Accessibility, in turn, determines the amount of stimulus input necessary to provoke a response. The higher the accessibility, the less the stimulus input needed, the wider the range of input characteristics that will be accepted, and the greater the likelihood that other possible categories will be ignored or masked.

Classification is an ongoing process in that categories at times are disconfirmed by experience. For example, the person discovers that the long, thin object is a magazine rather than a book. In such instances it is less likely that the category "book" will be called forth again under similar stimulus and background conditions.

(2) Analysis for pertinence. An incredible number of stimuli vie for classification at any given moment. One authority gives the following estimates: (1) information comes into the central nervous system from over 260 million visual cells alone; (2) 48,000 cells are available for auditory perception; (3) the other senses each have at least 78,000 receptor cells; and (4) it would take a brain the size of a cubic light year to process just the information received by the eyes alone.[27] Obviously there are distinct limits on processing capacity, and the analysis for pertinence functions to restrict entry only to those that have relevance.

Selective attention has been extensively documented in the psychological literature, and some representative evidence will be reviewed on

---

26 Bruner, "Perceptual Readiness."

27 Wilbert J. McKeachie and Charlotte L. Doyle, *Psychology* (Reading, Mass.: Addison-Wesley, 1966), p. 171.

three topics: (1) the influence of needs; (2) perceptual defense and vigilance; and (3) maintenance of cognitive consistency.

Everyone is well aware that the presence of need affects those stimuli that are received and those that are rejected. Hungry people, for example, are more likely to give food-related responses when the actual stimulus to which they are exposed is ambiguous. Psychological need can have the same effect as was demonstrated by the fact that those with a strong affiliation motive are more likely to identify pictures of people from a larger grouping of pictures than do their counterparts with a weaker affiliation drive.[28] The implications are quite apparent for consumer behavior. The hungry person will be far more receptive to food stimuli than he or she would be on other occasions; in fact, it is said by consumer economists that the worst time for food shopping is just prior to a meal because of the sharp increase in food buying expenditures. Similarly, those who fear social rejection are likely to respond to an appeal that stresses social acceptance through avoidance of body odor.

It has been found consistently that important values influence the speed of recognition for value-related words. For example, words that connote important values often are perceived more readily, and this form of selective attention has come to be called perceptual vigilance.[29] It would seem reasonable to hypothesize, as a result, that preferred brand names will be recognized more quickly than nonpreferred brands. This was confirmed in two studies, and this may shed light on why certain advertisements are noticed more readily than others.[30] The key may lie in the extent to which the brand name itself is featured.

The opposite of perceptual vigilance is *perceptual defense*, whereby recognition of threatening or low-valued stimuli is delayed or even avoided altogether.[31] Presumably the word has negative pertinence, and the evidence seems to indicate that real barriers are erected to further information processing.[32] It is possible that consumers avoid promotion for nonpreferred brands in this way, although there is no direct evidence on this point.

Finally, human beings have a persistent tendency to resist changes in strongly held attitudes and beliefs, especially those that are related in some way to an individual's self concept. This cognitive structure functions, therefore, to enable the individual to cope with his or her environment, and it is not surprising that change is resisted in order to

28 J. W. Atkinson and E. L. Walker, "The Affiliation Motive and Perceptual Sensitivity to Faces," *Journal of Abnormal and Social Psychology*, vol. 53 (1956), pp. 38–41.

29 L. Postman and B. Schneider, "Personal Values, Visual Recognition, and Recall," *Psychological Review*, vol. 58 (1951), pp. 271–84. There has been some methodological controversy that may be of interest to some readers. See D. E. Broadbent, "Word-Frequency Effect and Response Bias," *Psychological Review.*, vol. 74 (1967), pp. 1–15.

30 Homer E. Spence and James F. Engel, "The Impact of Brand Preference on the Perception of Brand Names: A Laboratory Analysis," in P. R. McDonald, ed., *Marketing Involvement in Society and the Economy* (Chicago: American Marketing Association, 1970), pp. 267–71.

31 D. P. Spence, "Subliminal Perception and Perceptual Defense: Two Sides of a Single Problem," *Behavioral Science*, vol. 12 (1967), pp. 183–93.

32 This literature is thoroughly reviewed in D. P. Spence, "Subliminal Perception."

maintain this organization.[33] For purposes of illustration, assume that a person has arrived at the conclusion that the addition of fluoride to water can be harmful. He or she then is exposed to a radio news announcement of current local study that seems to show no ill effects. If this message is fully processed it could introduce a state of psychologically uncomfortable inconsistency within the belief structure. It is quite possible that it would be rejected in the analysis for pertinence for this reason.

(3) The issue of discrimination without awareness. One of the raging controversies of the 1950s and 1960s was over the question of whether or not people could be influenced without any awareness on their part. More technically, this has been referred to as *subliminal perception*.[34] The issue has been dormant for some time because of evidence which appeared to indicate that there were no effects without at least some awareness.[35] It has come to life again, however, because of the influential book by Dixon in which he presents new evidence and argues convincingly that subliminal perception *is* a reality.[36] He states unequivocally that this implies lack of awareness on the part of the individual.

If Dixon is correct, then the analyses described above take place on a preconscious level. This means that the individual does not consciously censor the intake of information and that attraction of attention does not necessarily require awareness. This immediately raises the spector of the "hidden persuader" and images of "Big Brother." These fears of unconscious manipulation of people are groundless, however, because the evidence does *not* indicate that people can be induced to do something they would not consciously do. All it says is that both the preliminary processing and the analysis for pertinence take place without conscious awareness. The entry of unwanted stimuli still appears to be barred, and that should put the fears to rest.

The attraction of attention. Once the stimulus receives preliminary categorization and survives the analysis for pertinence it stays within active memory. Its fate from here on depends entirely on whether or not it is given further analysis and rehearsal. One of the outcomes is triggering of the so-called *orientation reaction*, which functions to prepare the individual to contend with a novel stimulus.[37] Activities previously underway are altered, and there are some specific additional physical manifestations:

1. An increase in the sensitivity of the sensory organs. This occurs as

33 For a cogent analysis, see E. E. Jones and H.D. Gerard, *Foundations of Social Psychology* (New York: Wiley, 1967), chap. 7.

34 See J. V. McConnell, R. L. Cutler, and E. B. McNeil, "Subliminal Stimulation: An Overview," *American Psychologist,* vol. 11 (1958), p. 230 ff.

35 See, for example, M. Wiener and P. H. Schiller, "Subliminal Perception or Perception of Partial Cues," *Journal of Abnormal and Social Psychology,* vol. 61 (1960), pp. 124–37.

36 Dixon, *Subliminal Perception.*

37 R. Lynn, *Attention Arousal and the Orientation Reaction* (Oxford: Pergamon, 1966).

pupil dilation and photomechanical changes, which lead to lowered reaction times for stimuli.

2. Changes in skeletal muscles that direct the sense organs. Turning the head is an example.

3. Changes in general skeletal musculature in the form of increased muscle tone and greater readiness for activity.

4. Generation of a state of arousal as indicated by electroencephalogram scores.

5. Elevation in galvanic skin response accompanied by a reduction in heart rate.

The problem of sensory overload. As Toffler pointed out so graphically in *Future Shock*, this is an over-communicative era in which persuaders of all types outdo themselves to attract attention.[38] Literally the consumer is bombarded on all sides. Estimates of the number of commercial messages confronting the average individual each day range from 250 to 2,000! This gives rise to what is known more technically as *sensory overload*.[39] It is quite possible that a given message will not capture attention simply because it is "lost in the noise."

Most commercial persuaders also make use of repetition, and this only accentuates the problem. As stimulation occurs repeatedly, the ability to attract attention fades; when this occurs the stimulus is said to be habituated. Certain factors interact to bring about habituation:[40]

1. Stimulus intensity. The lower the intensity, the more rapidly habituation occurs.

2. Duration of stimulus. An extremely brief stimulus is less likely to habituate.

3. Difficulty of discrimination. The more difficult it is to grasp stimulus details, the less the likelihood of habituation.

4. Time. Habituation occurs more rapidly as time between exposures decreases.

5. Conditioning. A stimulus that has become conditioned so that it is of personal significance to the recipient will not habituate even when it is repeated.

Advertising readily habituates. Most products are highly familiar, and oftentimes little can be said in a message which is truly novel or new.

To avoid being lost in the crowd the advertiser often must resort to

38 Alvin Toffler, *Future Shock* (New York; Random House; 1970).
39 For a more extensive discussion, see William J. McGuire, "Some Internal Psychological Factors Influencing Consumer Choice."
40 D. E. Berlyne, *Conflict, Arousal and Curiosity* (New York: McGraw-Hill, 1960).

some real creative ingenuity. There are various attention attracting devices that may, on the surface, appear just to be gimmicks, but their sole purpose is to do nothing more than capture attention. The message itself then takes over and determines the degree of success in the remaining stages of information processing. Here are three possible means: (1) novelty and contrast; (2) manipulation of intensity through variations in size and position of the message; and (3) use of color.

(1) Novelty and contrast. Notice the Chiquita brand banana advertisement in Figure 13.4, because it makes effective use of novelty and contrast. The appearance of the banana in such a way that it stands on its end is quite unusual, with the result that attention is likely to be captured. This, of course, says nothing about the persuasive power of the message itself.

Numerous other illustrations could be given, only several of which are suggested here:

1. A black and white advertisement featuring an unusual amount of white space with no print or illustration can stand out clearly when competitive messages are in color.

2. A unusually shaped package captures attention when all others on a shelf are similar in design, shape, and color.

3. The announcer's voice advertising a product during a break in a classical music program is likely to be noticed because of the sharp stimulus contrast.

(2) Size and position of the message. There have been a number of studies on the effects of increasing the size of an advertisement on the printed page; it has been found that doubling the size does not double the impact. Readership tends to increase in proportion to the square root of the increase in space.[41]

It also is possible to generalize on the relative value of different positions on the page in print media:

1. There is little variation in readership of advertisements appearing on the left- and right-hand pages in magazines or newspapers. The primary factor in readership is what the message says and how it says it.[42]

2. The greatest readership in magazines is usually attracted by advertisements on the covers or in the first 10 percent of the pages, but beyond this point location is a minor factor.[43]

3. Position within a newspaper does not appear to be crucial because of high page traffic throughout the paper.[44]

41 R. Barton, *Advertising Media* (New York: McGraw-Hill, 1964), p. 109.
42 "Position in Newspaper Advertising: 2," *Media/scope,* pp. 76–82, (March 1963).
43 "Position in Newspaper Advertising: 2."
44 "Position in Newspaper Advertising: 1," *Media/scope,* p. 57 (Feb. 1963).

Figure 13.4 An illustration of novelty and contrast.

4. Readership tends to be highest when the message is placed adjacent to compatible editorial features.

5. Position in the gutter (the inside fold) offers little advantage in print media. In fact, position on the page itself has no effect except when competing advertisements become especially numerous, in which

case the upper right-hand position offers an advantage in newspapers.[45]

Position in broadcast advertising has received less research, although it is known that commercials generally perform better when inserted as a part of the regular program rather than during the clutter of a station break.[46] It also appears that commercials at the beginning and end of a program suffer a disadvantage because of the clutter of announcements and other distracting nonprogram material.

(3) The use of color. It is widely recognized that color can add significantly to the effectiveness of an advertisement for a number of reasons:

1. The attention-attracting and holding power of the message may be sharply increased.

2. Contemporary social trends have encouraged experimentation with color in all phases of life, ranging from the factory to the home. Thus people have become responsive to innovative color stimuli.

3. Most products look better in color, especially food.

4. Color can be used to create moods, ranging from the somber appeal of dark colors to the freshness of greens and blues.

Numerous studies have demonstrated that color is a significant aid in attracting attention. For example, it appears to be the one outstanding factor in high readership of newspaper advertisements, undoubtedly because of the relative infrequency of color in that medium.[47] Moreover, data show that color commercials on the average are at least 50 percent more effective than the same television messages in black and white.[48]

Reception

The fact that a stimulus has successfully attracted attention by no means implies that it will be processed further in the manner intended by the sender. Whether or not it will actually be received and processed into long term memory depends upon *reception* (accurate comprehension of the meaning of incoming stimuli and acceptance of that input into long term memory).

Comprehension. The preliminary analysis required for attention attraction also can affect the degree to which a stimulus is correctly comprehended. In fact, physical stimulus properties can actually be distorted in the process. A study was undertaken in 1947 that proved to be a landmark because of its influence on later research.[49] It was discovered that

45 "Position in Newspaper Advertising: 1."
46 Barton, *Advertising Media*, p. 255.
47 "What Stirs the Newspaper Reader?" *Printers' Ink* (June 21, 1963), pp. 48–49.
48 *Are Color Television Commercials Worth the Extra Cost?* (New York: Association of National Advertisers, 1966).
49 J. S. Bruner and Cecile C. Goodman, "Value and Need as Organizing Factors in Perception," *Journal of Abnormal and Social Psychology*, vol. 42 (1947), pp. 33–44.

children from the lowest economic classes overestimate the size of coins. The assumption is that economic deprivation affects the process of perception. There is some contradictory evidence also, but most authorities now accept that need and other personal characteristics can affect cognitive processes in this way.[50]

This type of physical stimulus distortion also occurs in consumer decision making. A soft-drink company introduced a new product that fell far short of its sales potential.[51] A taste test was conducted in which samples of this brand and competitors' were compared with and without labels. The findings disclosed that the brand under analysis received excellent ratings in comparison with others when it was unlabeled. The ratings were completely reversed, however, when labels were in place. It thus appears that the product image, name, or some other consideration affected taste ratings. As a result, the promotional program was totally revamped while product formulation was left unchanged.

Miscomprehension can enter in another way. Each person has certain expectations about the content of new information, and it is known that the reaction often reflects the expectation rather than the stimulus itself.[52] For example, a liquid cold remedy was introduced in a test market in the attempt to make inroads into the market share of Vick's Nyquil, and there was considerable evidence that consumers thought they were viewing Nyquil ads. The competitor's ads were quite similar to those used by Nyquil and the result was miscomprehension.

Acceptance. Correct comprehension also does not guarantee that the message will be accepted into long term memory where it will have the opportunity to modify existing cognitive structures. In fact, the process of rehearsal can function as a blockage. For example, supporters of former President Richard Nixon tended for a long period after the Watergate disclosures to remain unchanged in their convictions regarding the president regardless of the contradictory evidence.[53] There are literally hundreds of studies of this type that could be cited, and the implications are so significant for the marketer that a major later section of the chapter is devoted to the subject of resistance to persuasion.

The mechanism at work here is counter argumentation.[54] The message is accepted if the recipient rehearses thoughts which are consistent with its theme and conclusions. Similarly, it will be rejected if counter arguments oppose the position that is advocated.[55]

50 Noel Jenkin, "Affective Processes in Perception," *Psychological Bulletin*, vol. 54 (1957), pp. 100–27.

51 "Twink: Perception of Taste," in Roger D. Blackwell, James F. Engel, and David T. Kollat, *Cases in Consumer Behavior* (New York: Holt, Rinehart and Winston, 1969), pp. 38–43.

52 For a classic study on this subject, see A. L. Edwards, "Political Frames of Reference as a Factor Influencing Recognition," *Journal of Abnormal and Social Psychology*, vol. 36 (1941), pp. 34–50. Also it is discussed in Norman, *Memory and Attention*.

53 Garrett J. O'Keefe, Jr., and Harold Mendelsohn, "Voter Selectivity, Partisanship and the Challenge of Watergate," *Communications Research*, vol. 1 (October 1974), pp. 345–67.

54 A. G. Greenwald, "Cognitive Learning, Cognitive Response to Persuasion and Attitude Change," in A. G. Greenwald, T. C. Brock, and T. M. Ostrom, eds., *Psychological Foundations of Attitudes* (New York: Academic Press, 1968).

55 Peter L. Wright, "The Cognitive Processes Mediating Acceptance of Advertising," *Journal of Marketing Research*, vol. 10, (February 1973), pp. 53–62.

The most convincing evidence comes from studies in which individuals are presented with a message advocating a particular point of view. They then are asked to record their thoughts concerning the issue, judge the favorability of each thought, and classify each thought. It now seems quite clear that acceptance is much higher when the recipient's initial beliefs and attitudes are consistent with those contained in the message.[56] One can image the responses that might be generated when the opposite is true: "oh yeah?" "says who?" and so on.

This counter argumentation has some interesting effects. First, it can cause the person to miss the point altogether, as was illustrated by the "Archie Bunker" study described at the beginning of the chapter. A second response is to dismiss the source as being entirely biased and not worthy of further consideration. This is particularly common in response to advertising, which tends to have low public credibility compared with other forms of communication. Furthermore, the message itself can be distorted in two ways.[57] First, it can be sharpened by adding new elements to the message to make it more consistent with present beliefs. A second form of distortion is *leveling*, whereby some details are blurred to make it more consistent with the content of memory. In either case, the net effect will be quite different from what the communicator intended.

While the distorting effect of counter argumentation is increasingly well documented, there still is a question regarding the extent to which a contradictory message is actually prevented from entering into long term memory. Common sense would argue that this indeed does happen, and most readers can point to examples from their own lives. There has been some experimental verification,[58] but others have produced contradictory findings.[59] The most defensible conclusion at this point is that a probable blocking relationship does indeed exist, but its functions are not well understood.[60]

Response

The final stage is entry of the new information into long term memory. This is designated in Figure 13.3 by the box labeled stored information and experience. Obviously this can lead to changes in any of the components of memory, but the marketer is most interested in changing beliefs, which in turn leads to changes in attitudes and intentions, as is

56 Wright, "Cognitive Processes." Also W.J. McGuire, "Inducing Resistance to Persuasion: Some Contemporary Approaches," in L. Berkowitz, ed., *Advances in Experimental Social Psychology*, vol. 1 (New York: Academic Press, 1964), pp. 191–229.

57 Thomas R. Donohue, "Impact of Viewer Predispositions on Political TV Commercials," *Journal of Broadcasting*, vol. 18 (Winter 1973–74), pp. 3–16.

58 J. M. Levine and G. Murphy, "The Learning and Forgetting of Controversial Material," in T. M. Newcomb and E. L. Hartley, eds., *Readings in Social Psychology* (New York: Henry Holt, 1947), pp. 108–15.

59 A. G. Greenwald and J. S. Sakumura, "Attitude in Selective Learning: Where are the Phenomena of Yesteryear?" *Journal of Personality and Social Psychology*, vol. 7 (1967), pp. 387–97; Patricia Waly and S.W. Cook, "Attitude as a Determinant of Learning and Memory: A Failure to Confirm," *Journal of Personality and Social Psychology*, vol. 4 (1966), pp. 280–88; S. S. Smith and B. D. Jamieson, "Effects of Attitude Ego Involvement on the Learning and Retention of Controversial Material," *Journal of Personality and Social Psychology*, vol. 22 (1972), pp. 303–10.

60 J. C. Brigham and S. W. Cook, "The Influence of Attitude on the Recall of Controversial Material: A Failure to Confirm," *Journal of Experimental Social Psychology*, vol. 5 (1969), pp. 240–43.

designated by the arrows connecting these variables. The barriers preventing this type of change have already been discussed, but they seem to operate prior to entry of the stimulus into memory. The probability of changes occurring can be evaluated through computing a net counter argumentation score (positive thoughts minus negative thoughts). The higher the ratio of the positive to the negative, the greater the probability of changes in beliefs and attitudes.[61]

Because changes in belief, attitude, and intentions are the subject of a later chapter, this section focuses only on measurement of exposure, attention, and reception.

The measurement of information processing

Exposure. In a laboratory setting, exposure can be measured by what Bettman refers to as "information monitoring approaches."[62] People are provided with information on some type of display device and are allowed to make their choice. This approach has been used by Jacoby and his associates in a number of studies.[63] Obviously it suffers from a high degree of artificiality since behavior is being directly observed in a nonreal world situation.

Apart from the laboratory, exposure is difficult to measure directly, and it usually is inferred from data on radio or television listenership or readership of various forms of print media.[64] The problem, of course, is that exposure to the medium does not necessarily reflect exposure to the advertising. There have been a few experimental efforts using such devices as photo sensitive pages to isolate actual advertising exposure, and it appears that there is quite a gap between exposure measured in this way and actual recall of advertising content, thus documenting the existence of selective information processing.

Attention. The most common method used to measure attention attraction is exposure of a group of prospects to one or more messages under conditions ranging from presentation of three or four test advertisements in some type of booklet to full-scale exposure to actual television or radio shows or print publications. Respondents then are questioned sometime after exposure and are asked to indicate what messages they recall or recognize. Obviously this measures *retention* rather than attention. It is to be expected that many more people attend to the message than will be revealed in this manner, because recall scores reflect the effects of

61 J. L. McCullough, "The Use of a Measure of Net Counterargumentation in Differentiating the Impact of Persuasive Communications," unpublished doctoral diss. (Columbus, Ohio: Ohio State University, 1971).

62 James R. Bettman, "Data Collection and Analysis Approaches for Studying Consumer Information Processing," in William Perreault, ed., *Advances in Consumer Research*, vol. 4 (Atlanta: Association of Consumer Research, 1977), pp. 342–48.

63 See, for example, Jacob Jacoby, Harold A. Kohn, and Donald E. Speller, "Time Spent in Acquiring Product Information as a Function of Information Load and Organization" (Purdue Papers in Consumer Psychology, no. 127, 1973).

64 For a review of media research methods, see James F. Engel, Martin R. Warshaw, and Hugh G. Wales, *Promotional Strategy*, 3rd ed. (Homewood, Ill.: Richard D. Irwin, 1975), chap. 12.

selective information processing. For that reason considerable interest has been shown in recent years in laboratory measures that analyze attention without making use of verbal responses.[65] Attention is, after all, a largely unconscious physiological process. Among the methods attracting the most interest are (1) galvanic skin response (GSR) and pupil dilation response (PDR), (2) the eye movement camera, (3) the tachistoscope, and (4) binocular rivalry.

(1) GSR and PDR. Galvanic skin response (GSR) and pupil dilation response (PDR) seem to be measuring different aspects of information processing.[66] GSR measures two phenomena: (1) a decline in the electrical resistance of the skin to a passage of current and (2) a change in the potential difference between two areas of body surface.[67] When it elevates upon exposure to a stimulus, it is now felt to be an indicator of *arousal.* PDR, on the other hand, measures minute differences in pupil size as it dilates and contracts. Recent studies document that it is a sensitive measure of the amount of information or load processed within the central control unit from the incoming stimulus.[68] At one time it was felt that PDR measured affective or emotional response to a stimulus,[69] and several studies were published which purported to document that relationship in response to marketing stimuli.[70] The weight of later evidence, however, makes the load processing interpretation of PDR far more plausible.

A series of studies was undertaken at the Ohio State University using both GSR and PDR with a variety of audio and print stimuli.[71] The most consistent finding was that when GSR and and PDR were both high, the stimulus in question generated good short-term and long-term retention. In other words, the high score on attention attraction was reflected by a correspondingly high score on retention, thus indicating that the stimulus had not been screened out in information processing. In addition, there was some tentative evidence that the GSR score also correlates with

65 J.S. Hensel and D.T. Kollat, "Present and Projected Uses of Laboratory Equipment for Marketing and Advertising Research," paper presented at the American Marketing Association (September 1970). Also see "Oculometer Is Finding Out What Viewers See in Those TV Commercials," *Advertising Age* (April 11, 1977), p. 56; and the following two papers presented at the annual meetings of Division 23 of the American Psychological Association, September 5, 1976; Norman B. Leferman, "Current Uses of the Tachistoscope in Advertising Research," and Edmund W. J. Faison, "Validating Recognition Speed as an Indicator of Package Design Effectiveness."

66 J. S. Hensel, "Physiological Measures of Advertising Effectiveness: A Theoretical and Empirical Investigation," unpublished doctoral diss. (Columbus, Ohio: Ohio State University, 1970).

67 R. D. Blackwell et al., *Laboratory Equipment for Marketing Research* (Dubuque, Iowa: Kendall Hunt, 1970), p. 42.

68 For an extensive literature review see R. D. Blackwell, J. S. Hensel, and B. Sternthal, "Pupil Dilation: What Does it Measure?" *Journal of Advertising Research*, vol. 10 (1970), pp. 15–18.

69 E. H. Hess and J. M. Polt, "Pupil Size as Related to Interest Value of Visual Stimuli," *Science*, vol. 132 (1960), pp. 349–50.

70 See, for example, H. E. Krugman, "Some Applications of Pupil Measurement," *Journal of Marketing Research*, vol. 1 (1964), pp. 15–18.

71 Most of these are reviewed in Hensel. Also see R. D. Blackwell and B. Sternthal, "Physiological Measurement of Communication Variables: Empirical Results," paper presented at the American Marketing Association (September 1970).

attitude change, but this relationship needs further investigation under a variety of circumstances.[72]

If further replication verifies the relationship reported here, there are some significant practical implications. Different messages can be analyzed prior to the investment of funds in production to see which offers the greatest probability of attracting and holding attention. The great advantage is that reliance need not be placed on verbal recall, which can be highly inaccurate.

It is hard to predict whether or not such equipment will see widespread commercial use. In the first place it can be quite expensive. The pupilometer alone can cost as much as $20,000.[73] Moreover, findings have to be interpreted both with caution and with a measure of common sense. One advertiser, for example, used the pupilometer to test an ad for frozen french fries. The designers were pleased with the amount of pupillary dilation recorded until they learned that the people were looking at the steak in the picture instead of the french fries.[74]

(2) The eye movement camera. For many years it has been possible to track eye movement through advertising copy using a camera especially designed for this purpose. This shows which parts of the message capture and hold attention and whether or not various elements are perceived in the intended order. It never has achieved especially wide use, because viewing must be done under highly unnatural conditions using awkward equipment. Nevertheless, it is a useful diagnostic tool.

(3) The tachistoscope. The tachistoscope is basically a slide projector with attachments that permit the presentation of stimuli under varying conditions of speed and illumination. It can be used to assess the rate at which a message conveys information.[75] Response speed is recorded for various elements of the message (illustration, product, or brand name), and it has been found that high readership scores usually correlate with the speed of recognition of the elements under analysis. The writer or designer thus has a useful basis to evaluate that the message is being processed as intended.

(4) Binocular rivalry. The binocular rivalry technique is used to measure which of two competing stimuli first attracts attention.[76] The stimuli are viewed through a stereoscopic device with an eye piece, and a different stimulus is projected to each eye. The basic underlying theory is that the

72 Two unpublished studies at the Ohio State University under the direction of J. F. Engel.

73 Berkeley Rice, "Rattlesnakes, French Fries, and Pupil-ometric Oversell," *Psychology Today*, pp. 55–59 (February 1974).

74 Rice, "Rattlesnakes."

75 C. Leavitt, "Intrigue in Advertising—The Motivational Effects of Visual Organization," in *Proceedings of the 7th Annual Conference* (New York: Advertising Research Foundation, 1961), pp. 19–24.

76 J. M. Caffyn, "Psychological Laboratory Techniques in Copy Research," *Journal of Advertising Research*, vol. 4 (1964), p. 48.

stimulus exerting the greatest potential for attention attraction will dominate, and this has been verified experimentally.[77]

Reception. Reception, it will be recalled, has two aspects: (1) comprehension and (2) acceptance. Comprehension is widely tested by advertisers through some type of recall procedure. The preferred method is to place test messages within, for example, a magazine or television program and then to allow for exposure under completely natural conditions. Recognition or recall is then assessed at some period after exposure, usually within 24 hours.

Grey Advertising, Inc. often will pretest the communicative ability of a piece of copy by placing it along with other material in a fictitious magazine entitled *Today*.[78] This magazine was created to duplicate the format of a new general-interest magazine. Interviewers place it in homes, and people are asked to read it as they would any other magazine. Telephone interviews on the following day measure comprehension and recall as follows:

1. *Related recall.* The percentage of actual readers who can give: (1) aided or unaided identification of the brand and (2) some playback on the message (either some specific detail or a general correct description).

2. *Comprehension and impact.* Ability to state the actual intended content of the copy correctly.

Analysis of the counter argumentation process is probably the only way to detect the probability that a message will be accepted or rejected. At the present time this has primarily been done only experimentally, but its use on a more widespread basis would shed considerable light on both comprehension and acceptance. Admittedly it is artificial in that people are asked to vocalize their thoughts, but it is one promising way of detecting success prior to actual investment of funds in space or time. The net counter argumentation score suggested by McCullough would seem to be the logical approach.[79]

Resistance to persuasion

When the words *persuasion* or *propanganda* are mentioned, many people have a decidedly uneasy feeling. There is a widespread fear that skillful propagandists will succeed in causing us to do things we would not otherwise do. Basically it boils down to this question: is the audience sovereign or not?

From the discussion thus far it is apparent that the consumer indeed

77 Caffyn, "Psychological Laboratory."
78 See "W. T. Grant Company (B): Attitude Change through Advertising," in Blackwell, Engel, and Kollat, *Cases in Consumer Behavior*, pp. 88–94.
79 McCullough, "Use of a Measure."

does have a system of defense against unwanted persuasion. The conditions under which it functions and its mechanisms have not been spelled out in other than general terms, however. The key point to be elaborated below is this: *people resist change in strongly held beliefs and attitudes* and do so through selective information processing. Beliefs and attitudes are strongly held, in turn, under conditions of *commitment*—the subject matter is related to one's self concept. The response under conditions of low commitment can be quite different.

High commitment is most likely in a marketing setting first of all when there are a high number of distinguishing characteristics among alternatives and secondly when there is a high level of importance attached to these characteristics or attributes.[80] Under such conditions, active memory can function as a *filter* and trigger selective exposure, selective attention, and selective reception.

Resistance to change when commitment is high

Selective exposure. It came as a surprise to political observers in the 1940 presidential campaign to discover that "exposure to political communications during the presidential campaign is concentrated in the same group of people not spread among the people at large."[81] It has since been found repeatedly that Democratic rallies and telethons attract mostly Democrats and vice versa.[82] It seems to a commonplace thing for people to avoid contradictory information simply by not being in the audience when they are forewarned.[83] Katz argues that we maintain cognitive consistency in this way:

> . . . (a) . . . an individual self-censors his intake of communications so as to shield his beliefs and practices from attack; (b) . . . an individual seeks out communications which support his beliefs and practices; and (c) . . . the latter is particularly true when the beliefs or practices in question have undergone attack or the individual has otherwise been made less confident of them.[84]

Not all authorities agree with Katz on his assessment,[85] but the balance of the evidence certainly points this way. Also, every reader no doubt has

80 Thomas S. Robertson, "Low-Commitment Consumer Behavior," *Journal of Advertising Research*, vol. 16 (April 1976), pp. 19–26.

81 P. F. Lazarsfeld, B. B. Berelson, and H. Gaudet, "Radio and the Printed Page as Factors in Political Opinion and Voting," in W. Schramm, ed., *Mass Communications* (Urbana, Ill.: University of Illinois Press, 1949), p. 484.

82 Garrett J. O'Keefe, Jr., and Harold Mendelsohn, "Voter Selectivity, Partisanship, and the Challenge of Watergate"; Dorthy L. Barlett et al., "Selective Exposure to a Presidential Campaign Appeal," *Public Opinion Quarterly*, vol. 38 (Summer 1974), pp. 264–70; and Stuart H. Surlin and Thomas F. Gordon, "Selective Exposure and Retention of Political Advertising," *Journal of Advertising*, vol. 5 (Winter 1976), pp. 32–37.

83 See, for example, M. T. O'Keefe, "The Anti-Smoking Commercials: A Study of Television's Impact on Behavior," *Public Opinion Quarterly*, vol. 35 (1971), pp. 242–48; David L. Paletz et al., "Selective Exposure: The Potential Boomerang Effect," *Journal of Communication*, vol. 22 (March 1972), pp. 48–53.

84 E. Katz, "On Reopening the Question of Selectivity in Exposure to Mass Communications," in R. P. Abelson et al., eds., *Theories of Cognitive Consistency: A Sourcebook* (Chicago: Rand McNally, 1968), p. 789.

85 See D. O. Sears, "The Paradox of De Facto Selective Exposure without Preferences for Supportive Information," in Abelson et al., *Theories of Cognitive Consistency*, pp. 777–87.

practiced selective exposure frequently, if not daily, in controlling the intake of mass media. Therefore it must be accepted as a fact of life, and selective exposure is one cornerstone in the proposition that the audience *is* sovereign.

Selective attention. It was pointed out earlier that the typical advertising message is attended to by only a subset of those who are exposed. Bogart notes that "Advertising research data accurately reflect the fact that many messages register negative impressions or no impression at all on many of the people who are exposed to the sight or sound of them."[86] Assume, for example, that a consumer who at one time was considering the purchase of a microwave range has become alarmed at adverse publicity regarding possible radiation effects. This would most likely result in a negative attitude toward that product. Now what will happen if he or she is exposed to the ad in Figure 13.5? While it would receive preliminary processing for its physical properties, the analysis for pertinence could function to prevent further information processing. This would be done to prevent disturbance of cognitive consistency, and it is a fairly common-place phenomenon.[87]

When beliefs and attitudes are strongly held, as is assumed to be the case here, there is little the communicator can do to overcome selective attention. This is especially true when mass media are used, because there is no way to modify the message and, in effect, try again. In face-to-face communication, on the other hand, there is instant feedback of response and the opportunity to rephrase the content. A skillful salesman, then, can be successful in countering a strongly held belief, but this is not possible through advertising.

The logical strategy for the mass marketer is to direct efforts, insofar as possible, to those who already are neutral or even sympathetic toward the content and to avoid those who are not. The probability of inroads into this latter group usually is not worth the effort. This fact is the underlying rationale for the concept of market segmentation. Another possibility is to search for those whose beliefs are wavering for one reason or another. Perhaps there is dissatisfaction with a competitor because of poor performance. This could underscore a profitable market opportunity and signify an "open perceptual filter."

Another way for marketing organizations to overcome the problem of selective attention is through the practice of what might be called "controlled exposure." With this technique, consumers are placed in situations in which they have little or no choice but to give their attention to the message. In one such example, a real estate firm invites potential customers to a free meal and then makes a highly concentrated presentation during the meal concerning the real estate development in Florida. The consumer is in a room with no windows and few distractions other

86 Leo Bogart, "Where Does Advertising Research Go from Here?" *Journal of Advertising Research*, vol. 9 (March 1969), p. 6.
87 See Jones and Gerard, *Foundations of Social Psychology.*

Figure 13.5 Appeal to strongly held beliefs and attitudes

the Roper Microwave does it all . . . your way!

**WARMS
LO-SIMMERS
HI-SIMMERS
ROASTS
RE-HEATS
DEFROSTS**

Step right into the exciting world of microwave magic . . . but don't change your cooking style! The Roper Micro-Select control matches the cooking speed to what your recipe calls for . . . to make fast micro-wave cooking even more efficient. You can warm rolls, sandwiches, snacks in seconds. Lo-simmer your soups. The browning dish gives steaks and chops that beautifully-browned appearance. Special defrost cycle makes freezer-to-table preparation fast . . . with no fuss or muss. Big, bright interior even holds a 22-pound turkey. If you haven't experienced the delightful difference of microwave magic . . . try the Roper Microwave, *your way!*

Your Roper Dealer has three countertop Roper Microwaves, a combination wall oven, and an eye-level Microwave with a self-cleaning lower oven to show you.

America's cooking specialists with a century-plus tradition for quality and reliability!

KANKAKEE, ILLINOIS 60901

than the sales presentation itself. While this tactic may be highly debatable from an ethical point of view given the frequency of fraudulent real estate deals, many variants exist in the form of beauty seminars, cooking schools, sewing classes, and other situations in which consumers are brought into a situation in which attention can be controlled.

Selective reception. It is a curious fact that the possibility of miscomprehension and lack of acceptance of a persuasive message was largely overlooked until about the time of World War II. It came as a surprise that propaganda films did not succeed in producing a greater desire to fight among members of the allied forces.[88] Many other studies began to document the same reactions, especially in the political arena:

> In the course of the campaign . . . strength of party support influences the perception of political issues. The more intensely one holds a vote position, the more likely he is to see the political environment as favorable to himself, as confirming his own beliefs. He is less likely to perceive uncongenial and contradictory events or points of view and hence presumably less likely to revise his own original position. In this manner perception can play a major role in the spiraling effect of political reinforcement.[89]

It was discovered that strong party members consistently comprehended the stand of a preferred candidate on issues as being in harmony with their own viewpoints, regardless of reality. Conversely, those less interested in partisan politics showed a reduced tendency to misinterpret a candidate's stand. The same phenomena still hold true today.[90]

Some of the most clear-cut examples of miscomprehension were reported by Cooper and Jahoda in the famous predecessor of the "Archie Bunker" study cited at the beginning of the chapter.[91] They analyzed reactions to a booklet designed to help prejudiced persons to see their own shortcomings in the person of Mr. Biggot. Yet many people missed the point by ridiculing him, transforming him into a foreigner, making him appear inferior, and otherwise sidetracking the issue to avoid any application to their own prejudiced beliefs. Some of the other means of miscomprehension were:

1. Admitting the point of the message while claiming that it did not depict the situation correctly.

2. Alleging that everyone is entitled to their prejudices.

3. Failing to get the point because the message was "too difficult."

As was mentioned earlier, another common means of avoiding the implications is to reject the source, the content, or both as being biased. In one landmark study favorable reactions to a message were expected to increase as the distance decreased between the viewpoint of the recipient

---

88 C. I. Hovland, A. A. Lumsdaine, and F.D. Sheffield, *Experiments in Mass Communication*, vol. 3 (Princeton, N.J.: Princeton University Press, 1949).

89 B. R. Berelson, P. F. Lazarsfeld, and W. N. McPhee, *Voting* (Chicago: University of Chicago Press, 1954), p. 223.

90 See Surlin and Gordon, "Selective Exposure and Retention"; Donohue, "Impact of Viewer Predispositions"; and Barlett et al., "Selective Exposure."

91 Eunice Cooper and Marie Jahoda, "The Evasion of Propaganda: How Prejudiced People Respond to Anti-Prejudice Propaganda," *Journal of Psychology*, vol. 23 (1947), pp. 15–25.

and the point of view advocated in the message itself.[92] Opinions were measured toward the controversial issue of repeal of prohibition in Oklahoma, and subsequent communications were administered that differed from subjects' own positions on the topic in varying degrees. When the discrepancy was large, the message was perceived as less fair, less informed, less grammatical, less logical, and so on.

Although the persuasive intent of a communication may be short circuited during information processing, the conveying of facts may be unaffected. Baur, for example, reported that an intensive propaganda campaign by a watershed association changed knowledge and awareness without changing beliefs.[93] Similarly, it was concluded that the major result of orientation films intended to influence willingness of soldiers to fight during World War II was noticeable gain in specific information.[94] To cite one example, soldiers recalled much about how Britons were able to withstand Nazi bombings, but opinions of the British as allies were unaffected.

Now to return to our consumer and the ad for microwave ranges, it is possible that he or she will attend to the ad but completely distort the message to conclude that the product is inferior. Moreover, acceptance certainly could be prevented by concluding that "advertisers are always biased anyway." Thus, exposure and attraction of attention by no means infer that the message will be perceived as the advertiser intends.

Marketers are increasingly recognizing that a need exists for additional tools to overcome the problem of miscomprehension. One possibility is the use of materials to reinforce learning after the initial exposure. This includes the utilization of "hang-tags" on products to reinforce messages appearing in advertising or given through personal selling. Also, one trade association found that people were miscomprehending messages given in public meetings. As a result, they prepared concise, informative brochures that restated the oral message. These brochures were attractive and were designed to fit into a coat pocket or a woman's purse. The intent was to induce the person to take the brochure home and discuss it with others in the hopes that miscomprehension of the oral presentation would be minimized.

In personal selling situations, firms also attempt to reduce miscomprehension through use of media involving both sight and sound. The oral presentation is either augmented or supplanted through use of a flip chart, a video cassette, a written outline, or some other similar tool.

The selective processing of advertising is clearly documented in the data reproduced in Figure 13.6. But is this happening as consumers protect

Response to persuasion when commitment is low

92 C. I. Hovland, O. J. Harvey, and M. Sherif, "Assimilation and Contrast Effects in Reactions to Communication and Attitude Change," *Journal of Abnormal and Social Psychology*, vol. 55 (1957), pp. 244–52.

93 E. J. Baur, "Opinion Change in a Public Controversy," *Public Opinion Quarterly*, vol. 24 (1962), pp. 212–26.

94 Hovland et al., "Assimilation and Contrast."

Figure 13.6 Registration of featured idea; recall after 24 hours

Magazines		Television	
Number of ads	Recall range (%)	Number of ads	Recall range (%)
Tires			
13	0– 3.9	13	0– 3.9
21	4– 7.9	5	4– 7.9
11	8–11.9	5	8–11.9
2	12–15.9	4	12–15.9
3	16–19.9		
2	24–27.9		
2	28–31.9		
Automobiles			
20	0– 1.9	49	0– 1.9
33	2– 3.9	29	2– 3.9
47	4– 5.9	19	4– 5.9
27	6– 7.9	6	6– 7.9
12	8– 9.9	4	8– 9.9
7	10–11.9	2	10–11.9
7	12–13.9	2	12–13.9
1	14–15.9	4	14–15.9
1	16–17.9	1	16
1	18–19.9		
3	20–21.9		
3	22–23.9		
1	24		
Life insurance			
24	0– 1.9	8	0– 1.9
23	2– 3.9	13	2– 3.9
10	4– 5.9	7	4– 5.9
2	6– 7.9	5	6– 7.9
1	8– 9.9	3	8– 9.9
		1	10–11.9
		1	14–15.9
		1	18–19.9
		1	20–21.9
TV sets			
5	0– 1.9	6	0– 1.9
6	2– 3.9	9	2– 3.9
4	4– 5.9	4	4– 5.9
4	6– 7.9	3	6– 7.9
3	8– 9.9	1	8– 9.9
1	10–11.9	3	10–11.9
2	12–13.9	2	12–13.9
1	14–15.9	1	14–15.9
1	18–19.9	3	16–17.9
Aftershaves, colognes			
2	0– 3.9	7	0– 3.9
10	4– 7.9	4	4– 7.9

Figure 13.6 (continued)

Magazines		Television	
Number of ads	Recall range (%)	Number of ads	Recall range (%)
3	8–11.9	3	8–11.9
1	12–15.9	2	12–15.9
1	16–19.9	1	16–19.9
1	20–23.9	3	24–27

Source: *Advertising Age*, p. 52 (April 12, 1971). Reprinted with permission from the April 12, 1971 issue of *Advertising Age*. Copyright 1971 by Crain Communications Inc.

their beliefs against cognitive inconsistency? Is it likely, for example, that a housewife would avoid or misperceive an ad because of her commitment to a competitive brand? The point is that commitment in the sense discussed above is *not* common in consumer buying.[95] In fact, apathy and outright boredom are more likely. Leo Bogart, a well-known leader in the field of advertising, took quite a strong position on this issue:

> Perhaps the main contribution that advertising research can make to this study of communications is in the domain of inattention to low-key stimuli, as exemplified by the ever increasing flow of unsolicited and unwanted messages to which people are subject in our ever communicative civilization.[96]

Yes, there is selective exposure, attention, and response, but it by no means is done to protect existing beliefs. Messages are rejected because of indifference and *lack* of commitment. Bear in mind that hundreds of commercial stimuli are vying for each person's attention daily. Given restrictions on information processing capability, most are simply lost in the noise. Small wonder that word-of-mouth communication rates so much higher in its impact, as was stressed in Chapter 9.

While people have full capability of screening out unwanted persuasion, this does not mean that the media are without power to deceive. Gardner offers a definition of deception that states the issue with precision:

The issue of deception

> If an advertisement (or advertising campaign) leaves the average consumer within some reasonable market segment with an impression(s) and/or belief(s) different from what would normally be expected if the average consumer within that market segment had reasonable

95 Robertson, "Low Commitment."
96 Bogart, "Where Does Advertising Research," p. 6.

knowledge and that impression(s) and/or belief(s) is factually untrue or potentially misleading, then deception is said to exist.[97]

Gardner's purpose here is to give a definition that will be accepted by legal authorities, but it makes a simple point—deception enters when people are left with an understanding that deviates from the truth. The emphasis is on how the message is comprehended and not only on the literal content of the message itself.

There is still another dimension of deception, however, and that refers to the use of devices which inhibit an individual's freedom of action.[98] Examples would be appeal to a strong but irrelevant emotion, use of such distractions as soft lighting or music, and so on. The person is deceived if he or she is somehow deterred from pursuing a course of action that would have been taken without the distorting effect of the message. When deception has entered, then the effects of audience sovereignty are blunted, and the communicator has opted for deliberate falsification and manipulation.

There also has been fear of manipulation through the use of so-called *subliminal perception*. This was discussed earlier under the subject, discrimination without awareness. It was pointed out that the analysis, which precedes attraction of attention, indeed takes place without awareness. The first test of this in an advertising context was in the late 1950s. The words DRINK COKE and EAT POPCORN were presumably flashed on a movie screen at speeds well beyond the conscious awareness of audience members.[99] Technically it would be said that the presentation was subliminal, or below the threshold at which conscious discrimination is possible. Hence the term subliminal perception. The sales of Coca Cola allegedly increased 57.7 percent, whereas sales of popcorn increased 18.1 percent. In reality, these findings have unanimously been dismissed as being invalid, and all attempts at replication of that particular experiment have failed.

More recently, Hawkins has verified that people can be motivated through a subliminally presented stimulus.[100] This is also what Dixon has alleged in his influential book referred to earlier.[101] Once again, however, this does not say that the ability of the individual to filter out unwanted content truly is circumvented. Furthermore, Dixon goes on to point out that only a fractional stimulus is given, which can easily be swamped by those stimuli presented under more normal conditions. As a result, the commercial persuader has nothing to gain by resort to this means. Fears of a new-found tool of manipulation are without justification.

97 David M. Gardner, "Deception in Advertising: A Receiver Oriented Approach to Understanding," *Journal of Advertising*, vol. 5 (November 1976), p. 7.
98 Emory Griffin, *The Mind Changers* (Wheaton, Ill.: Tyndale, 1976).
99 J. J. Bachrach, "The Ethics of Tachistoscopy," *Bulletin of Atomic Scientists*, vol. 15 (1959), pp. 212–15.
100 Dell Hawkins, "The Effects of Subliminal Stimulation on Drive Level and Brand Preference," *Journal of Marketing Research*, vol. 7 (August 1970), 322–26.
101 Dixon, *Subliminal Perception*.

The consumer *is* sovereign. He or she has full powers to screen out any message that contradicts a strongly held disposition. The only way this filtering ability can be overcome is if we can gain full control of their lives such as would be true in a prison camp setting.[102] Then we would have access to such tools of manipulation as hypnosis, psychotherapy, sensory deprivation (perhaps from solitary confinement), stimulation with drugs, the inducing of stress, or brain implantation with electrodes.[103] Needless to say, such means are not available to the business firm. Therefore, the only strategy is to design messages in such a way that they are (1) directed toward those whose dispositions and need states are consistent with the action being suggested and (2) oriented toward reinforcing these tendencies, thereby leading to the desired action. As one authority observes,

A concluding word

> . . . to the social scientist, A's influence of B is not a matter of art, but of the witting or unwitting application of known or unknown scientific principles, and must be looked upon as such. The scientific analysis of human behavior is perhaps the single most potent weapon in A's arsenal. If he fails to make use of this powerful tool, he does so at his own risk.[104]

Summary

The purpose of this chapter has been to clarify how people process information. It was pointed out initially that memory is a coherent whole, but it does seem to have two differing components: long-term memory, which may or may not be fully accessible to consciousness, and active memory. It is in active memory that incoming stimuli are compared with existing beliefs and dispositions stored in long-term memory.

The process begins with exposure and activation of one or more senses. Then the stimulus is given a preliminary analysis for its physical properties as well as its pertinence for the individual. Those stimuli judged to have pertinence then undergo further information processing through a type of subvocal speech referred to as rehearsal. It is at this stage that the stimulus is either received or not received into long-term memory. It is completely possible for incoming information to be blocked or screened out at any stage through selective exposure, selective attention, and selective reception. In every sense of the word, the consumer is sovereign and is in full control of the input into long-term memory. Because of this, the burden is placed upon the persuader to be an accurate analyst of the individual and to direct messages to those who are at best neutral and to attempt to bring about modifications rather than drastic change in existing beliefs, attitudes, and intentions.

102 J. V. McConnell, *Persuasion and Behavioral Change,* mimeograph (Ann Arbor, Mich: University of Michigan, 1959).

103 A. D. Biderman and H. Zimmer, eds., *The Manipulation of Human Behavior* (New York: Wiley, 1961).

104 McConnell, *Persuasion,* p. 73.

Review and discussion question

1. Define the term "cognitive processes." What is its relevance for the study of consumer behavior?

2. A reader's attention is attracted by a center-fold advertisement in a news magazine. The advertisement is in four colors and features the new model of a popular compact automobile. What does it mean to say that attention is attracted? What are the stages in this process? How might they have taken place? Is there anything the artists and writers can do to influence preattentive processing? Analysis for pertinence?

3. Assume that a housewife cannot recall seeing advertisements for any brand of hair spray other than her preferred brand even though she had the opportunity in a given day to see 20 or more competing ads. What explanations can be given?

4. What is meant by the "boredom barrier"? What influence does it have on response to marketing stimuli?

5. A leading critic of advertising contends that advertising has the power to influence people to buy unwisely—to act in a way which they would not otherwise do. In other words, advertising is a tool for manipulation of the consumer. What would your response be to this criticism?

6. Under what conditions is it possible for perceptual defense to affect the perception of brand names?

7. Assume that you have been given the assignment to investigate the possibility of subliminal presentation of advertisements on television for canned soup. What problems would occur? What would happen if a similar attempt were to be made with advertisements designed to appear in women's magazines?

8. A reader's attention is attracted by a two-page spread in *Time* advertising a new automobile. The advertisement is in four colors and features three pretty girls. What does it mean to say that attention is attracted? How does this happen?

9. The creative director of a leading New York advertising agency claims that creativity cannot be measured. He refuses to make any use of pretests of his copy and layouts and claims that his creative intuition is his best guide. If you were the director of research, what would your answer be?

10. Many critics contend that too much advertising today is "grimmicky" and "cute." The argument is that creative people are carried away by flashy attention-attracting devices and are forgetting that good advertising must sell. How would you analyze this criticism?

11. What is meant by rehearsal and counter argumentation?

12. Studies often show that recall is the most widely used measure of communication effectiveness on a pretest basis. Many refuse to measure other stages of the communication process, such as attitude change. Why does this occur? What arguments could you present in behalf of attitude and/or behavior measurement?

13. Do you agree that laboratory measures will see more use in the future? Why or why not? What is their unique advantage? Disadvantage?

CHAPTER 14

Alternative evaluation:
The role of evaluative criteria

Information has now been processed and is part of long-term memory. It is available for use in alternative evaluation—a process that consists of the comparison of various alternatives for purchase and consumption against those criteria or product attributes felt by the consumer to be important in the decision. The outcome will be formation of or change in beliefs, attitudes, and intentions, all of which are the subject of the next two chapters. While an overview of alternative evaluation will be provided below, the primary purpose of this chapter is to consider the nature and function of evaluative criteria—*desired outcomes from choice or use of an alternative expressed in the form of the attributes or specifications used to compare various alternatives.*

An overview of the alternative evaluation process

Brad Jones, whom we first met in Chapter 10, has recognized a problem that has led to a family decision to purchase a new car. He and his wife have shopped extensively, looked at ads, talked with friends, and consulted such product rating services as *Consumer's Reports*. Most of this information has survived information processing intact without much distortion or change and is now available for use in the decision.

Brad is different from some car buyers in that his concern is primarily with functional considerations. Furthermore, price considerations have placed him in the market for a compact- or intermediate-sized car. His primary interest is to acquire respectable transportation without excess expenditure. As such he finds himself as part of the 54 percent of the compact car market and 34 percent of the intermediate and standard car market whose evaluative criteria are not oriented toward styling, prestige, luxury, and sporty appeal.[1]

As he and other family members weigh the information they have acquired, Brad quickly forms some beliefs about the various makes. These beliefs serve to specify the consequences of purchasing a particular make in terms of each criteria he feels to be significant. For example, is it likely that Brand A really will give economical performance and offer low maintenance? Once that belief has been established (or an existing belief modified), he cannot help arriving at an evaluation that states whether the consequence is good or bad. Each evaluative criterion, then, is accompanied by a belief that states the anticipated outcome of purchasing one make over another and an evaluation of that outcome. The sum total of these beliefs and evaluations represents Brad's attitude, either favorable or unfavorable, toward the act of purchasing and using each make.

Now, all things considered, Brad will purchase that make toward which his attitude is most positive. Perhaps in this case it will be the Ford Granada, which was specifically designed to meet the criteria for members of this segment with particular emphasis on shape, price, mileage, comfort, space, and size.[2] Usually a positive attitude toward the act of purchase will be accompanied by an intention to act. Intentions are a statement of the subjective probability that a specified action (purchase of a Granada) will be undertaken. Again, all things being equal, this intention will culminate in an actual purchase.

This example has illustrated the central concepts in the consumer behavior model referred to earlier, a portion of which is reproduced in Figure 14.1. While omitting some detail to be discussed in the next chapter, it shows the functional relationship among evaluative criteria, beliefs, attitudes, intentions, and choice.

The starting point is the consumer's own evaluative criteria. As will be elaborated below, these generally must be accepted as a given by the marketing planner. The response of the business firm is to adapt product, price, promotion, and distribution to these important buying determinants. It can be a fatal mistake to proceed otherwise, as some later examples will prove.

The nature of evaluative criteria

Evaluative criteria find their specific representation in the form of those physical product attributes as well as strictly subjective factors the consumer considers to be important in the purchase decision. They can either be *objective* (i.e., specific physical features such as low price or long

1 Norman Krandall, "Fewer Arrows: More Moving Targets," *Proceedings of the 20th Annual Conference* (New York: Advertising Research Foundation, 1974), pp. 9–10.
2 Krandall, "Fewer Arrows."

Figure 14.1 The functional relationship between evaluative criteria, beliefs, attitudes, intentions, and choice

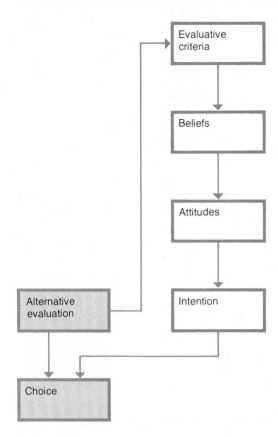

service life) or *subjective* (i.e., symbolic values or benefits such as the perceived "youthfulness" of the product).[3] It is not uncommon for virtually identical products to receive widely varying evaluations because of perceived subjective differences. One airline may be preferred over another, for example, because it is evaluated as being more exciting and energetic than its more conservative counterpart.

The diagram in Figure 14.2 indicates that evaluative criteria are shaped by two basic factors: (1) motives and (2) information and experience. Motives, of course, are important personal goals that find their roots in personality and life style, which, in turn, are strongly affected by cultural norms and values.

Psychological foundations

We have already discussed the importance of motives in arousal and stimulation of problem recognition. In the present context, motives function in a highly specific manner to shape those product attributes and

3 Irving S. White, "New Product Differentiation: 'Physical and Symbolic Dimensions,'" in B. A. Morin, ed., *Marketing in a Changing World* (Chicago: American Marketing Association, 1960), p. 100.

Figure 14.2 The determinants of evaluative criteria

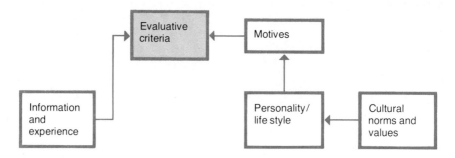

benefits that will contribute most to motive satisfaction. While many examples could be given, consider the studies on achievement motivation by McClelland and his colleagues. Some of the major findings of more than 20 years of research are as follows:

1. American males with a high achievement need most often come from the middle class, have a good memory for incompleted tasks, and are active in college and community affairs.[4]

2. Those high in achievement are more likely to take risks in situations where achievement is possible through individual efforts.[5] Furthermore, they stay at a task longer than the average person if they perceive a chance for success.[6]

3. A need for achievement is reflected in development of internal standards; there is little desire to conform to social pressure in situations where internal and external standards conflict.[7]

The marketer would never measure achievement motivation directly, but its effects might clearly be observed in the criteria utilized to evaluate types and brands of cameras. These are just a few of the possible ways in which it might be reflected: "allows me to take the best pictures," "allows me to make my own settings and adjustments without automatic gadgets," "gives pictures I can be proud of." The nonachievement-oriented consumer, on the other hand, might place far greater importance on automatic features that would guarantee an acceptable picture with fewer risks. Here are two distinct market segments with widely variant product specifications, and such data cannot be ignored in marketing planning. It is unlikely that either could be induced to switch the evaluative criteria used without changes first taking place in the underlying motive pattern.

4 D. C. McCelland, *The Achieving Society* (Princeton, N.J.: Van Nostrand, 1961), pp. 43–46.
5 McClelland, *Achieving Society*, pp. 43–46.
6 N. T. Feather, "The Relationship of Persistence at a Task to Expectation of Success and Achievement-Related Motives," *Journal of Abnormal and Social Psychology*, vol. 63 (1961), pp. 552–61.
7 R. M. deCharms et al., "Behavioral Correlates of Directly and Indirectly Measured Achievement Motivation," in D.C. McClelland, ed., *Studies in Motivation* (New York: Appleton, 1955), pp. 414–23.

Evaluative criteria are not static, however. They will undergo modification and change based on new information and experience. Products enter the market, for example, with previously unheard-of features. Friends mention various attributes which they have found to be helpful in decision, and so on. It should not be assumed at this point that these desired product attributes may be easily changed by advertising and promotion. For reasons elaborated later, quite the opposite is likely to be the case, and this has some potent implications for marketing strategy.

The two most important characteristics of evaluative criteria include the number used in reaching a decision and the relative strength (salience) of each.

Characteristics

Number used. It is obvious from the discussion of information processing capacity limitations in the previous chapter that there are limitations on the number of criteria that can enter into any decision. Most studies show that six or fewer generally are used by most consumers, although Fishbein suggests that the number may go as high as nine.[8] Here are two illustrative examples:

1. Nylon stockings are selected on the basis of high quality and potential for long wear.[9]

2. Detergent manufacturers have found that housewives tend to judge the cleaning power of a detergent on the basis of suds level and smell. Similarly, the color of the detergent and its package is a cue often used to judge mildness.

Salience. Frequently one or two criteria will stand out above all others as being critical in that they must be satisfied before a purchase will be made. In fact, there are times in which choice is made on a single criterion.[10] Judging quality by price is an example. Usually these will be highly routinized purchases in which conscious evaluation is minimized or absent altogether.

Evaluative criteria, of course, are expressed in terms of desired product attributes. Some of the more common are low price, package design and size, performance, material, color, and durability. Several deserve special comment because of the attention afforded them in published research.

Types of criteria

Reputation of brand. Brand reputation frequently emerges as a dominant criterion as it did in a study of purchases of toothpaste, dress shirts, and

8 This is a cardinal principle of the Fishbein extended behavior model to be discussed in the next chapter. For a general review, see Martin Fishbein, "Attitude, Attitude Change, and Behavior: A Theoretical Overview," in Philip Levine, ed., *Attitude Research Bridges the Atlantic* (Chicago: American Marketing Association, 1975), pp. 3–16.

9 Donald H. Cox, "The Measurement of Information Values: A Study in Consumer Decision Making," in W. S. Decker, ed., *Emerging Concepts in Marketing* (Chicago: American Marketing Association, 1962), pp. 414–15.

10 Flemming Hansen, "Psychological Theories of Consumer Choice," *Journal of Consumer Research*, vol. 3 (December 1976), p. 133.

suits.[11] It also proved to be significant in use of over-the-counter drugs.[12] The brand name appears to serve as a surrogate indicator of product quality, and its importance as a criterion seems to vary with the ease by which quality can be judged objectively. If ease of evaluation is low, the consumer sometimes will perceive a high level of risk in the purchase.[13] Reliance on a well-known brand name with a reputation of long-standing quality thus can be an effective way to reduce risk.

In the case of headache and cold remedies, there is no way in which the average consumer can judge purity and quality. Brand thus becomes especially crucial as a surrogate indicator of quality. It is such a dominant factor with many consumers, for example, that they will pay many times more for a branded item even though they are aware that government regulations require all aspirin products to contain the same basic therapeutic formulation.[14]

Price. There has been considerable interest in the role and significance of price, perhaps because of the relation of marketing to its parent field of economics. A number of recent studies have focused on the price-quality relationship, and there is additional evidence on the ways in which price is used as an evaluative criterion.

(1) The price-quality relationship. One premise of economic theory is that price can be used as a surrogate indicator of quality, in which case the demand curve will show a backward slope. In his review of 76 studies, Monroe reports that the findings tend to be mixed; the most he could conclude was that there are indications that this positive relationship does exist, at least over some ranges of prices in some product categories.[15] Additional recent supportive evidence has been reported by Shapiro[16] and by Cimball and Webdale.[17]

It now seems quite clear that there is a definite range of prices people are willing to pay as well as a reference price that influences price judgments.[18] Consumers appear to group unacceptably low and unacceptably high prices into categories and completely disregard price differences when they fall outside of what they consider to be the acceptable

11 D. M. Gardner, "Is There a Generalized Price-Quality Relationship?" *Journal of Marketing Research*, vol. 8 (1971), pp. 241–43.

12 J. F. Engel, D. A. Knapp and D. E. Knapp, "Sources of Influence in the Acceptance of New Products for Self-Medication: Preliminary Findings," in R.M. Haas, ed., *Science, Technology and Marketing* (Chicago: American Marketing Association, 1966), pp. 776–82.

13 R.A. Bauer, "Consumer Behavior as Risk Taking," in *Dynamic Marketing for a Changing World* (Chicago: American Marketing Association, 1960), pp. 389–98.

14 Engel, Knapp, and Knapp, "Sources of Influence."

15 Kent B. Monroe, "Buyer's Subjective Perceptions of Price," *Journal of Marketing Research*, vol. 10 (February 1973), pp. 70–80.

16 Benson P. Shapiro, "Price Reliance: Existence and Sources," *Journal of Marketing Research*, vol. 10 (August 1973), pp. 286–94.

17 Richard S. Cimball and Adrienne M. Webdale, "Effects of Price Information on Consumer-Rated Quality," (paper presented at American Psychological Association, 1973).

18 Kent B. Monroe, "The Influence of Price Differences and Brand Familiarity on Brand Preferences," *Journal of Consumer Research*, vol. 3 (June 1976), pp. 42–49.

range.[19] This zone of acceptable prices may be the result of the consumer's perception of prices asked or paid in the past, his or her attitude about what the fair price should be, and the price that will allow the seller to cover costs and earn a reasonable profit.[20]

Most of the above studies have looked at price in isolation as the sole criterion of quality judgments. This has tended to overstate the effects on quality perceptions.[21] Stafford and Enis report, for example, that quality judgments are affected by an interaction of price and store image.[22] In other situations, price has relatively little influence on perceived quality, especially when other information cues are available such as the merchandise itself, product ratings, and brand familiarity.[23]

It appears that a positive price-quality relationship is most probable under these conditions:

1. When the consumer has confidence in price as a predictor of quality.[24]

2. When there are real and perceived quality variations between brands.[25]

3. When quality is difficult to judge in other ways, especially when there are no quality-connoting criteria such as brand name or store location.[26]

(2) Other factors affecting price. Apart from the price-quality question, the use of price as an evaluative criterion varies from product to product.[27] One study, for example, found that concern with price was high for detergents but low for cereal.[28] In some cases, price is of greater significance when the product is felt to be socially visible.[29]

---

19 P. S. Raju, "Product Familiarity, Brand Name and Price Influences on Product Evaluation" (Working Paper no. 38, College of Business Administration, Pennsylvania State University, 1976).

20 A. O. Oxenfeldt, *Establishing a New Product Program: Guides for Effective Planning and Organization* (New York: American Management Association, 1958), pp. 17–18.

21 R. A. Peterson, "The Price-Perceived Quality Relationship: Experimental Evidence," *Journal of Marketing Research*, vol. 7 (1970), pp. 525–28.

22 James E. Stafford and Ben M. Enis, "The Price-Quality Relationship: An Extension," *Journal of Marketing Research*, vol. 6 (1969), pp. 456–58.

23 David M. Gardner, "Is There a Generalized Price-Quality Relationship?" *Journal of Marketing Research*, vol. 8 (1971), pp. 241–43; J. Jacoby, J. C. Olson, and R.A. Haddock, "Price, Brand Name, and Product Composition Characteristics as Determinants of Perceived Quality," *Journal of Applied Psychology*, vol. 55 (1971), pp. 570–80; and V. R. Rao, "Salience of Price in the Perception of Product Quality: A Multidimensional Measurement Approach," paper presented at the American Marketing Association, 1971.

24 Z. V. Lambert, "Product Perception: An Important Variable in Price Strategy," *Journal of Marketing*, vol. 34 (1970), pp. 68–76.

25 Lambert, "Product Perception."

26 Monroe, "Influence of Price Differences."

27 A. Gabor and C. W. J. Granger, "Price Sensitivity of the Consumer," *Journal of Advertising Research*, vol. 4 (1964), pp. 40–44; A. Gabor and C. W. J. Granger, "Price as an Indicator of Quality: Report on an Enquiry," *Economica*, vol. 33 (1966), pp. 43–70.

28 W.D. Wells and L.A. LoSciuto, "Direct Observation of Purchasing Behavior," *Journal of Marketing Research*, vol. 3 (1966), pp. 227–33.

29 Lambert, "Product Perception."

Second, the role of price is often overrated. Consumers are not always looking for the lowest possible price or even the best price-quality ratio; other factors often assume greater importance.[30] In addition, consumers frequently are completely unaware of the price when decisions are made. In one study, for example, 25 percent of those interviewed did not know the relative price of the brand of toothpaste they had just purchased.[31]

Finally, there is some indication that the importance of price is affected by the number of alternatives under consideration. The greater the number of available options, the less important price tends to become.[32]

Packaging. The package often is an important evaluative criterion, especially for products purchased on impulse.

(1) The role of packaging in in-store decisions. During 1970 *Sales Management* magazine sponsored a major study of the role of packaging on consumer decisions in drugstores.[33] Interviews were confined primarily to housewives. More than 38 percent indicated that the package design had a great influence on their choice of brands when they first purchased a cosmetic or toiletry product, and 30 percent claimed to have switched brands for a better package. Over 50 percent said they would pay more for a more convenient or more efficient package.

At the same time it was found that the package itself will not rescue a product that is mediocre in other respects. In fact, only 9 percent assumed that the best looking packages contain quality products.

The ten best liked packages were handbag-sized dispensers for breath fresheners and other toiletries, metal boxes for adhesive bandages, aerosol dispensers as well as other types of spray-top containers for toiletries, individually-wrapped tablets, and five different plastic containers. In contrast, glass was most frequently rated poorly.

(2) Package-size proneness. In an analysis of purchases of 31 different products it was found that smaller-sized packages were preferred by the following types of people: (1) families with large numbers of adults as compared with children; (2) households living in high-rise apartments; (3) single male households; and (4) those purchasing higher than average priced products.[34]

Other criteria. The literature on other criteria used is quite meager, with the exception of isolated studies documenting the influences in a specific

30 Monroe, "Buyer's Subject Perceptions."

31 George Haines, "A Study of Why People Purchase New Products," in Haas, *Science*, pp. 665–85, at p. 683.

32 L. K. Anderson, J. R. Taylor, and R. J. Holloway, "The Consumer and His Alternatives: An Experimental Approach," *Journal of Marketing Research*, vol. 3 (1966), p. 64.

33 "Drugstore Packages," *Sales Management*, pp. 41–52 (September 15, 1970).

34 Ronald E. Frank, Susan P. Douglas, and Rolando E. Polli, "Household Correlates of Package-Size Proneness for Grocery Products," *Journal of Marketing Research*, vol. 4 (November 1967), pp. 381–84.

decision. For example, it was found that the selection of a bank is based primarily on five criteria: (1) friends' recommendations; (2) reputation; (3) availability of credit; (4) friendliness; and (5) service charges on checking accounts.[35] Obviously there are substantial variations between products and between consumers.[36] It is worth emphasizing once again that consumers do not always use physical or objective criteria to evaluate alternatives; indeed subjective factors easily can be the dominant consideration.[37]

Measuring evaluative criteria

Because of the growing recognition of the importance of understanding the evaluative criteria that consumers use,[38] considerable attention must be paid to the problems of measurement. There are three categories of research methods: (1) direct approaches, (2) indirect approaches, and (3) inference techniques. In addition, it usually is necessary to utilize some type of measure of attribute saliency.

It is possible to come right out and ask what considerations were used in comparing various products in a recent purchase decision. The assumption is made that the individual is aware of salient criteria and will state them when asked. Those that receive the most frequent mention or highest ranking then are considered to be the dominant or determinant factors. But what if the consumer really has given the matter little thought? It is quite possible that only some very obvious and socially acceptable product features will be mentioned. The validity of the data gathered in this way thus can be suspect.

Direct approaches

Assume, for example, that a housewife says that price is the most important consideration in the purchase of an electric iron. She might mean one or more of several things: (1) "I will not pay $8–$10 more for the built-in sprinkling mechanism," (2) "I will not purchase an iron costing more than $25," (3) "I will seriously consider a brand only if it is within the $8–$14 range," or (4) "I know there are price differences between stores, so I will shop around." Obviously the questioning procedure should go into depth and probe the meaning of attribute labels. This can be done through a free-form guided (depth) interview in which respondents, either individually or collectively, expand on their answers.

Another difficulty with the direct questioning approach is that a criterion such as "style" may not be mentioned for the reason that all

35 W. Thomas Anderson, Jr., Eli P. Cox III, and David G. Fulchur, "Bank Selection Decisions and Market Segmentation," *Journal of Marketing*, vol. 40 (January 1976), pp. 40–45.

36 S.A. Smith, "How Do Consumers Choose between Brands of Durable Goods?" *Journal of Retailing*, pp. 18–26 (Summer 1970).

37 White, "New Product Differentiation."

38 Evaluative criteria are found, in one form or another, in most of the major models of consumer behavior. See, for example, John A. Howard and Jagdish N. Sheth, *The Theory of Buyer Behavior* (New York: Wiley, 1969), esp. pp. 118–26.

available alternatives are esentially similar.[39] Under different circumstances it might well be quite significant. This can be detected by dual questioning that calls for a two-phase query: (1) indication of the attribute and its importance in the decision and (2) the extent of perceived differences between alternatives along the dimension in question.[40] These two ratings then are combined into one overall score.

Indirect approaches

Sometimes a marketer may believe that the consumer will not verbalize the true reasons for a choice when asked directly.[41] One proposed remedy is to elicit a response in "third person" through some type of *projective question*. An example would be, "What product features do most of the people around here consider to be important in buying a dishwasher?" Response biases presumably are overcome through a feeling by the respondent that he or she is not revealing personal opinions. The underlying premise of the projective method has not been verified experimentally,[42] so it is seldom used.

Inference techniques

It is an undeniable fact that many find great difficulty in spelling out the reasons underlying their actions. Therefore, a research approach that can avoid this type of questioning has intuitive appeal. There has been some use in recent years of a family of research techniques grouped under the label of *nonmetric multidimensional scaling* (MDS).[43] Respondents are asked only to rate similarities between alternatives, two at a time, usually on a 10–12 point scale ranging from similar to dissimilar. The computer then takes over and generates a visual output indicating the extent to which the various alternatives are seen to be similar. Usually they will be depicted graphically in two dimensions as the example in Figure 14.3 indicates. The two dimensions or axes of this so-called perceptual space are assumed to be the evaluative criteria along which the ratings of similarity were made. Now the analyst must infer the nature of these criteria and label these axes. That can be a demanding task indeed.

Looking at Figure 14.3, the problem here was to evaluate the success of a company that opened ten fast-food outlets in two midwest cities. An attempt was made to gain competitive advantage through a higher-price, higher-quality menu. After one year of operation it was felt that a survey was needed to evaluate the success to date. Part of the study focused on

39 T.T. Semon, "On the Perception of Appliance Attributes," *Journal of Marketing Research*, vol. 6 (1969), p. 101.

40 M. I. Alpert, "Identification of Determinant Attributes: A Comparison of Methods," *Journal of Marketing Research*, vol. 8 (1971), pp. 184–91.

41 See, for example, E. Dichter, *The Strategy of Desire* (New York: Doubleday, 1960).

42 J. F. Engel and H. G. Wales, "Spoken versus Pictured Questions on Taboo Topics," *Journal of Advertising Research*, vol. 2 (1962), pp. 11–17.

43 For a definitive introduction, see P. E. Green and J. J. Carmone, *Multidimensional Scaling and Related Techniques in Marketing Analysis* (Boston: Allyn and Bacon, 1970). For practical examples, see Larry Percey, "An Application of Multidimensional Scaling and Related Techniques to the Evaluation of a New Product Concept," in Beverlee B. Anderson, ed., *Advances in Consumer Research*, vol. 3 (Atlanta: Association for Consumer Research, 1976), pp. 114–18; and Russell I. Haley, "Strategy Research, 1976," in *Proceedings of the 22nd Annual Conference* (New York: Advertising Research Foundation, Inc., 1977), pp. 23–33.

Figure 14.3 Two-dimensional MDS configuration
of ten quick-service restaurants
(Axis 1–quality/price: 63 percent; axis 2–service: 18 percent)

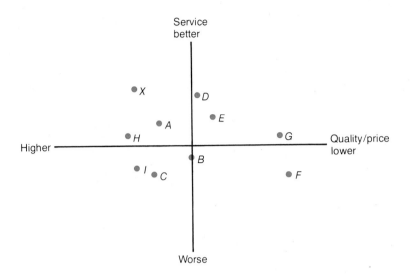

the ratings of the ten leading competitors, as well as Company X, the company under consideration here.

Consumers were asked to rate the similarity between each of these 11 competitors, two at a time, on a ten-point scale ranging from "very similar" to "very dissimilar." The appropriate computer program was used,[44] and the result was the output in Figure 14.3. Originally there were no labels whatsoever on these axes. Rather these must be provided by the analyst who infers their content either by his or her own subjective intuition or by the presence of other data. In this case it appeared from prior research that the dimensions were *service* and *quality/price*. There was no way to be sure, however, and this is one of the real disadvantages of this technique. If the inferences were correct, the computer computation revealed that the price/quality criterion was most important in the perceived similarity ratings (it explained 63 percent of the variance).

MDS was most helpful in this instance in verifying that management had indeed been successful in differentiating its restaurants from others in the fast-food field. Notice that it stands alone in terms of higher quality and better service as was intended. MDS is no panacea, however, in revealing the evaluative criteria that were used. The labeling of axes can be quite subjective and even erroneous. Another disadvantage is that the evaluative criteria cannot be determined until after the alternatives are rated, thus necessitating a cumbersome research process just to arrive at

44 See F. W. Young and W. S. Torgerson, "TORSCA, A Fortran IV Program for Shepard-Kruskal Multidimensional Scaling Analysis," *Behavioral Science,* vol. 12 (1967), pp. 498–99.

this type of output. For this reason and others its use has not been especially widespread.

Which method is best?

Some light was shed on the comparative usefulness of several of the above methods in one study that directly compared the predictions offered by direct questions, projective questions, and dual questions.[45] In order, it was found that dual questioning, direct questioning, and projective questioning were most useul in isolating product attributes in preference ratings. Obviously a definitive answer to this question awaits further methodological research of this type.

Measuring attribute importance (salience)

The following chapter will introduce the controversy over whether or not it is necessary to utilize a separate measure of attribute importance. Some argue that it is,[46] whereas others contend that the methods used to determine beliefs and attitudes have a built-in importance component.[47] In this later instance, a measure of importance would, of course, be redundant. Given that this controversy is not fully settled (see the following chapter), many still prefer to utilize an importance rating, and there are two methods: (1) rating scales and (2) conjoint analysis.

Rating scales. The most common procedure is to ask respondents to assess the salience of each criterion using some type of scaling approach. In the fast food restaurant example given earlier it was known from a previous study that consumers by and large make use of nine criteria when evaluating alternatives. They were asked to rate the importance of each of these attributes in the following manner:

	Important							Unimportant	
Good products	1	2	3	4	5	6	7	8	9
Good service	1	2	3	4	5	6	7	8	9
Low prices	1	2	3	4	5	6	7	8	9
Clean facilities	1	2	3	4	5	6	7	8	9
Open 24 hours	1	2	3	4	5	6	7	8	9
Well-known company	1	2	3	4	5	6	7	8	9
Wide range of choices	1	2	3	4	5	6	7	8	9
Convenient location	1	2	3	4	5	6	7	8	9
Many outlets	1	2	3	4	5	6	7	8	9

45 Alpert, "Identification of Determinant Attributes."

46 See Frank M. Bass and W. Wayne Talarzyk, "An Attitude Model for the Study of Brand Preference," *Journal of Marketing Research*, vol. 9 (February 1972), pp. 93–96. There is a definitional problem, however. See James H. Myers and Mark I. Alpert, "Semantic Confusion in Attitude Research: Salience vs. Importance vs. Determinance," in William D. Perreault, ed., *Advances in Consumer Research*, vol. 4 (Atlanta: Association for Consumer Research, 1977), pp. 106–10.

47 Fishbein, "Attitude."

An alternative is to employ paired adjectives such as "nutritious" and "not nutritious" using a similar numerical rating scale.[48] Also, some prefer to ask respondents to allocate 100 points across the categories to reflect their ranking of importance.

There always is the question of proper phrasing for the scale intervals. Only one study has specifically focused on methods for assigning weights to evaluative criteria, and the following results are reported:[49]

1. Rank orders of attribute importance appear to be quite stable across versions; simple "yes–no" or "1–6" judgments work as well as a more difficult task such as assigning points to attributes ranging from 0 to 100.

2. The use of a "1–6" gradient scale seems to generate finer distinctions when used alone than an arbitrary dichotomy for importance such as "yes–no."

3. There are some differences between these versions, which raises the question of the wisdom of using a single measuring device.

Further research obviously is needed. Not only must it be determined how relative rankings of attribute importance change from one method to another, but further inquiries also must employ some type of external criterion of importance against which each approach can be assessed. In the absence of this type of evidence, it is recommended that a nondichotomous rating scale be used, and the number of scale positions is apparently a matter of the researcher's personal preference.

Conjoint analysis. Rating scales require a respondent to rate each criterion one at a time, and the possibility of interaction effects between criteria is overlooked. A mouthwash that provides both taste and germ-killing power, for example, may be rated more positively when both factors are considered than it would be if either criterion were considered by itself. A relatively new development in mathematical psychology called conjoint measurement permits assessment of "bundles of benefits" as well as part-worth contributions of each benefit to an overall rating of preference.[50]

The data required are rank-ordered ratings of various benefit combinations taken two or more at a time. This methodology was used to determine the existence of possible market segments for aerosol hard-

48 For useful insights into the wording of these adjectives, see J. H. Myers and W. C. Warner, "Semantic Properties of Selected Evaluation Adjectives," *Journal of Marketing Research*, vol. 5 (1968), pp. 409–12.

49 D. E. Schendel, W. L. Wilkie, and J. M. McCann, "An Experimental Investigation of 'Attribute Importance,'" in D. M. Gardner, ed., *Proc. 2nd Annual Conf. of the Association for Consumer Research* (College Park, Md.: College of Business and Public Administration, University of Maryland, 1971), pp. 404–16.

50 P. E. Green and V. R. Rao, "Conjoint Measurement for Quantifying Judgmental Data," *Journal of Marketing Research*, vol. 8 (1971), pp. 355–63. Also see Richard M. Johnson, "Trade-off Analysis of Consumer Values," *Journal of Marketing Research*, vol. 11 (May 1974), pp. 121–27; and John O'Neill, "The Use of Conjoint Measurement for Product Planning," in William Locander, ed., *Marketing Looks Outward* (Chicago: American Marketing Association, 1977), pp. 96–100.

surface floor cleaners.[51] Preliminary research had verified that the following criteria were most salient: (1) makes the floor covering seem fresh and new, (2) does not take out color or fade the floor covering, (3) restores the floor covering to like-new brightness, (4) cleans away deep-down ground-in soil, and (5) protects the floor covering against resoiling. Cards were made up for all pairs of benefits (10), all quadruples of benefits (5), and one quintuple of benefits, a total of 16 cards. Respondents were asked to rank these 16 combinations in terms of what they would most like to see in this type of product. The computer then takes over and shows the importance of each benefit and each combination.[52] In this example, it was found that a cluster of two highly valued benefits emerged—"cleans away deep-down, ground-in soil" and "protects the floor covering against resoiling." The other benefits were valued about equally and well below these two.

One of the problems associated with conjoint analysis is that the data collection process becomes unwieldy, especially if the number of attributes being studied is large.[53] Also data collection costs can be high, although it is possible to reduce these outlays by confining the analysis only to those evaluative criteria already known to have at least a measure of importance in the choice process.[54]

Can evaluative criteria be changed?

It was pointed out earlier that evaluative criteria have their roots in personality and life style. As a result, they often resist change, especially if they are related closely to the individual's self concept. If this is the case, the criteria are said to have *centrality*. The difficulty of bringing about change raises a real dilemma for the marketer. In the final analysis this question becomes one of consumer education.

The marketer's dilemma

A market research study was undertaken and results indicated that the following criteria are used by a large segment of people to evaluate headache remedies (on a scale of 1–6, where 1 represents very important and 6 represents very unimportant):

Speed of relief	1.5
Reputation of brand	1.7
Quality of ingredients	2.3
Price	4.3
No side effects	4.8
Used by friends	5.6

51 See P.E. Green, Y. Wind, and A.K. Jain, "Benefit Bundles Analysis and Market Segmentation" (unpublished working paper, University of Pennsylvania, 1971).

52 J. B. Kruskal, "Analysis of Factorial Experiments by Estimating Monotone Transformations of the Data," *Journal of Royal Statistical Society,* vol. 27 (March 1965), pp. 251–63.

53 Herb Hupfer, "Conjoint Measurement—A Valuable Research Tool When Used Selectively," *Marketing Today,* vol. 14 (1976), p. 1 ff.

54 See Hupfer, "Conjoint Measurement," for more practical suggestions on use of this method.

Brand *A* was found to rate relatively well on most criteria, especially on price, but it rated poorly on reputation of brand. The brand has a six-percent share of market and sells at a price roughly 40 percent below that of the three leading competitors.

Management now is faced with a dilemma. Its price advantage is of comparative unimportance to most buyers, and reputation of the brand is weak. This latter factor is especially critical because, as was discussed earlier, reputation of brand often is a surrogate indicator of product quality.

One alternative for remedial action is to convince buyers that all brands are identical; hence, the "rational" consumer should buy on the basis of price. From a strictly objective point of view, this could be in the best interest of consumers since government ratings (USP) do guarantee that all products sold contain the same chemical formulation. An advertising message with this theme, however, probably would prove ineffective with most of the members of this market segment. Reputation of brand is a strongly held evaluative criterion, and, similarly, there are strong negative views regarding the importance of price. The message probably will be screened out in the information-processing stage through selective attention. Even if the consumer is aware of the advertisement, he will probably distort the content and retain his views unchallenged. The reasons for this selective screening were discussed earlier, and it can be a major inhibitor to promotional success.

Others have tried this first option with minimal success. Aluminum manufacturers tried for many years to convince consumers that a light-weight cooking utensil could be as high in quality as the more traditional heavier product. It was found that this belief was exceedingly difficult to change. Similarly, a manufacturer of ceiling tile found that it was impossible to sell a tile without holes. The reason was a deep-seated conviction that sound absorption capability was in proportion to the numbers of holes per square foot. Many other examples could be given. It should not be concluded that evaluative criteria *never* change; rather, change is most likely when the underlying life style determinants of the criterion change.

Appeal to benefits, not attributes. In a recent study of new product introductions in the United Kingdom, 70 percent of those test marketed never were introduced nationally and thus could be classified as failures.[55] The most common reason was that the product was nothing more than an indistinctive "me too," which offered no significant price or performance advantage to the consumer. Chin points out that one of the most common marketing errors is to advertise product attributes that may not be a real benefit to the consumer.[56] In his words, "After all is said

55 J. Hugh Davidson, "Why Most New Consumer Brands Fail," *Harvard Business Review*, vol. 54 (March–April 1976), pp. 117–22.
56 Theodore G. N. Chin, "New Product Success and Failures—How to Detect Them in Advance," *Advertising Age* (September 24, 1973), pp. 61–64.

and done, consumers are only interested in one thing, 'What's in it for me?' "[57]

The obvious strategy, then, is to make the consumer's evaluative criteria the starting point of marketing strategy. Advertising should feature only *true* benefits. If there are no such distinctives, then it is time for a marketing overhaul of some type to remedy the deficiencies.

Following the end of the Viet Nam War, the United States Army was faced with the need to recruit an all-volunteer force.[58] In previous years, the traditional benefits of army service (getting out on your own, gaining maturity, meeting people, travel, job training, challenge, and adventure) often were met with the response, "Yeah, but I might have to die for it." That objection now has diminished, but what are the perceived benefits of army service in the post–Viet Nam era? Certainly patriotism as an appeal will not have the potency it once did.

The Defense Department undertook a series of interviews with prospects, and it seemed that advertising should be positioned explicitly to demonstrate that army service is a natural, beneficial step between high school and adulthood for many—not just something to be done in wartime. Rather, the goal was to show the military as something you do as part of life, to test yourself, to grow mentally and in other ways, and to present a way to serve one's country while serving one's self. A multiple-media campaign followed featuring 23 magazines to reach men between 18 and 24 years of age, outdoor advertising, newspapers and newsweeklies, and television spots. Recruitment goals were fully met.

Benefit segmentation. Often good marketing opportunities are discovered by analysis of consumer attribute preferences; it is not unusual to uncover one or more segments not being adequately served by existing alternatives. This is referred to as *benefit segmentation*.[59]

Benefit segmentation lies at the heart of most of the new product successes in recent years. It is helpful to look at several examples. The pet food market must rank as one of the most competitive in terms of the number of product offerings. Not surprisingly, sales are made by appealing to the pet owner; the pet's preferences are decidedly secondary in spite of the claims of some advertisers. Ralston Purina, for example, successfully focused on convenience and introduced its Whisker Lickins soft moist cat food in single serving pouches.[60] Presumably the cats also will eat the stuff, but the greatest benefit is to the owner who avoids both touching and smelling it.

Interest in convenience also extends into many other product catego-

57 Chin, "New Product Success," p. 61.

58 "The United States Army: Recruiting Program," in Roger D. Blackwell, James F. Engel, and W. Wayne Talarzyk, *Contemporary Cases in Consumer Behavior* (Hinsdale, Ill.: Dryden, 1977), pp. 52–56.

59 R. I. Haley, "Benefit Segmentation: A Decision-Oriented Research Tool," *Journal of Marketing*, vol. 32 (1968), pp. 30–35; R. I. Haley, "Beyond Benefit Segmentation," *Journal of Advertising Research*, vol. 11 (1971), pp. 3–8.

60 *The Gallagher Report*, vol. 24 (November 15, 1976).

ries. A major market research study in the 1960s disclosed that users of traditional ground coffee were having some problems in its usage:

1. Measurement. Spilling of grounds, losing count, etc.

2. Grounds disposal. Messy, time-consuming.

3. Cleaning the pot. Oils and sediment, untidy.

4. Time-consuming preparation.

A new product concept then was developed and described both in flavor and in convenience terms. A concept test among prospects disclosed that a majority definitely or probably would purchase a new coffee offering these benefits:

> A totally new ground coffee offering you the easiest, fastest way ever to prepare coffee in your percolators. It's premeasured and packed in a disposable filter. No measuring, no mess in preparation or disposal. The filtered coffee keeps your percolator clean. And, it tastes good.

The new product was called Max-Pax, and it was introduced in 1971.[61] It has found a distinct niche in the market.

The marketing problem becomes especially acute when efforts are made to attack an entrenched leader. The $460 million tooth care market was dominated by Crest and Colgate (controlling 73 percent) in 1971 when Lever Brothers began initial development of Aim.[62] Cue, Fact, Ipana-Plus, and Stripe all were notable product failures of previous years. The cause of failure was pure and simple—they offered no advantage whatso-ever over the leading brands. Lever Brothers' strategy was to introduce Aim with a therapeutic level of stannous fluoride and a gel formulation offering greater incentives to brush—better color, flavor, texture, and appearance. With its advertising theme, "Take Aim Against Cavities," this new product soon achieved third place in most markets—quite an achievement in view of the history of new product failures.

Finally, it seems that the United States of the 1970s is characterized by fast-food outlets. One of the authors recently counted 24 in a two-mile stretch of highway leading into his community. The success of McDonald's Corporation, of course, has been legendary, with hamburger sales alone totalling nearly $8 billion in 1974. But marketing research disclosed that many customers disliked having to wait for special orders.[63] A leading competitor, Burger King, offered the capability of making sandwiches fresh and handling specials without the necessity of waiting. It has achieved a good measure of success (a 38 percent sales increase) with its "Have it your way" campaign. The importance of quick response to special orders also is indicated by the rapid growth of Wendy's Old

61 "Max-Pax," in Blackwell, Engel, and Talarzyk, *Contemporary Cases*, pp. 11–15.
62 Charles Fredericks, "Aim Toothpaste vs. Crest and Colgate," *How Do You Tackle the Leaders?* (New York: American Association of Advertising Agencies, 1975), pp. 3–13.

Fashioned Hamburgers, which features immediate service on hamburgers available "256 ways."

Skillful personal selling. The discussion thus far has assumed that use will be made mostly of the mass media that offer the greatest opportunities for selective avoidance by the consumer. Another approach, however, is to utilize personal selling. At times consumers will be receptive to help from a salesperson, especially when they have had little relevant past experience, when something has happened to change previous beliefs, or when there is high perceived risk surrounding the purchase. Training of salespeople to suggest more appropriate evaluative criteria has proved highly successful for the EMBA Mink Company, the Royal Worcester Porcelain Company, and many others.[64] Unfortunately personal selling all too often has become a lost art.

Consumer education

There are a number of instances in which the consumer does not get maximum value for his or her outlays. The headache remedy example cited earlier in this section is a good case in point. A lower purchase expenditure will provide comparable therapeutic effects. Unfortunately, many consumers tend to be ignorant of such facts, especially those with minimal educational backgrounds. This is the situation in other product categories as well.[65] Therefore, there is a real need for consumer education, especially to provide help in the use of objective criteria, where possible, instead of subjective criteria.

Former Federal Trade Commissioner Mary Gardiner Jones points to yet another factor which underscores the need for consumer education.[66] It is her contention (and the authors' as well) that advertisers will provide consumer information only with respect to those evaluative criteria over which they have some competitive advantage. The consumers will be left in ignorance on other factors that quite often are of greater significance in their welfare.

Consumers' Union has been in the vanguard of the consumer education movement for many years, and the circulation of *Consumers' Reports* now approaches two million. This magazine publishes product tests that compare alternatives on many dimensions which are impossible for the consumer without extensive testing equipment. He or she thus is able to make a decision on a more objective basis. The purchaser of a high-fidelity speaker, for instance, can make a selection on the basis of performance curves, compatibility with various types of inputs, and other objective considerations in addition to the way in which it "sounds."

There is increasing emphasis on the consumer in the schools. It seems

63 Richard Mercer, "Burger King vs. McDonald's," in *How Do You Tackle the Leaders?* pp. 27–39.

64 James F. Engel, W. Wayne Talarzyk, and Carl M. Larson, *Cases in Promotional Strategy* (Homewood, Ill.: Irwin, 1971), pp. 361–66, 373–80.

65 Arch G. Woodside and James L. Taylor, "Predictive Values of Product Information: An Application of the Brunswick Lens Model to Consumer Behavior" (unpublished working paper, University of South Carolina, 1976).

66 Mary Gardiner Jones, "A Critical Analysis of the Howard Report" (Advertising and Public Interest Workshop, American Marketing Association, 1973).

especially appropriate to offer this subject so that the young consumer can learn how to be a wise buyer before actually entering the market in a major way.

It is not the purpose to discuss consumer education fully at this point, since it is considered in one of the concluding chapters. Rather, the intent is to point out that evaluative criteria can be changed through education. In a world in which the pace of change is almost overwhelming, the role of this type of education will increase.

Summary

This chapter is the first of two which analyze the process whereby consumers evaluate alternatives and form new beliefs, attitudes, and intentions. An overview of this process was provided at the outset, and the remainder of the discussion focused on evaluative criteria—desired outcomes from choice or use of an alternative expressed in the form of the attributes or specifications used to compare various alternatives. These desired product attributes are formed largely by the individual's personality and life style and reflect important motives. Because of these roots in such basic dispositions, they are difficult to change through marketing influences and usually must be accepted as given and adapted to accordingly. Examples were given of price, product reputation, and package size and design. Considerable emphasis was placed on measurement and several different methodologies were discussed. Finally, several marketing strategies were suggested, and the need for consumer education was underscored.

Review and discussion questions

1. What are evaluative criteria? What criteria did you use when you purchased your last pair of shoes? How did these differ, if at all, from those used by others in your family?

2. It is frequently alleged that the consumer is irrational and fails to buy wisely if he or she does not make maximum use of objective criteria in purchasing decisions. Evaluate.

3. One of the major criteria mentioned by many college girls in the purchase of an underarm deodorant is that "it makes me feel more confident in the presence of others." From your understanding of psychological and social influences on behavior, assess the probable underlying determinants of this evaluative criterion.

4. How important is reputation of brand as an alternative criterion in each of these product classes: Hand soap, toilet paper, panty hose, men's shirts, china and glassware, and gasoline? What are the reasons for your answers?

5. Summarize the evidence on the price-quality relationship. Would you expect this relationship in each of the types of products mentioned in question 4? Why or why not?

6. Before World War II, the Customer Research Department of the General Motors Corporation regularly asked people to appraise the relative impor-

tance of certain product attributes using direct questions. It usually was found that highest marks were given to dependability and safety; styling was rated lower, and price was somewhere in between. What uses, if any, can be made of these data in marketing planning?

7. What are surrogate indicators? Why are they used?

8. Using a product of your own choice, prepare a research proposal indicating how you would determine the evaluative criteria which are being used in the purchase process.

9. Today considerable importance is being placed on consumer education. What are the causes of the so-called "consumer movement?" What is the role of the business firm in educating consumers on how to buy wisely?

CHAPTER 15

Alternative evaluation:
Beliefs, attitudes, and intentions

Given the existence of evaluative criteria, the next step in alternative evaluation is formation or modification of beliefs, attitudes, and intentions. In effect, these variables define a consumer's knowledge, evaluation, and disposition to act toward a product or brand. As such, they are a major determinant of choice.

Attitude has been the most researched variable of these three, and it is necessary to begin with a historical note documenting the enormous recent developments in theory and measurement. Without this background it will be difficult for the reader to appreciate the significance of current thinking with respect to the manner in which beliefs and attitudes are formed initially, the distinction between attitude toward an object itself and attitude toward the act of actually purchasing and using that object, and the extended models that introduce several additional variables. The recent leap in understanding has cleared up much of the fuzziness in models of consumer behavior, and there also are some significant implications for marketing and for consumer education.

Historical perspective

Until the 1970s, attitude was the single most important variable in the literature of social psychology. In fact, many agreed that an understanding of the nature and functioning of attitudes was the greatest contribution of social psychology to its parent field.

The classic definition is that an attitude is a mental and neural state of readiness to respond, which is organized through experience and exerts a directive and/or dynamic influence on behavior.[1] It soon became popular to theorize that there are three underlying attitude components: (1) *cognitive*—the manner in which the attitude object is perceived, (2) *affective*—feelings of like or dislike, and (3) *behavioral*—action tendencies toward the object. Unfortunately, most methods of measurement concentrated only on the second aspect, and this fact has some important ramifications as will soon become apparent. In reality these three components are interrelated as later discussion will indicate.

From the outset, the assumption has been that a change in attitude will be followed by a change in behavior. The entire theory of persuasion to be discussed in the next chapter rests on this premise. Yet, it remained unverified for many years, and two camps soon formed. One alleged, largely without evidence, that behavior change indeed does follow attitude change. The other, acting on an equally shaky foundation, held strongly to the contrary. Some even dismissed attitude as a "phantom variable."

On the negative side, it was shown as early as 1934 that behavior was not predicted from written statements which presumably reflected attitudes toward minority groups.[2] Festinger was unable to find any consistent published evidence that attitudes and behavior are related in any direct way, although it must be pointed out that his review neglected vast numbers of relevant findings.[3] A similar review led Deutscher to state that "disparities between thought and action are the central methodological problem of the social sciences."[4] Fishbein concluded that:

> After more than 70 to 75 years of attitude research, there is still little, if any, consistent evidence supporting the hypothesis that knowledge of an individual's attitude toward some object will allow one to predict the way he will behave with respect to that object. Indeed, what little evidence there is to support any relationship between attitude and behavior comes from studies that a person tends to bring his attitude into line with his behavior rather than from studies demonstrating that behavior is a function of attitude.[5]

Those on the positive side of this argument tended, almost without exception, to come from the applied fields of public opinion or consumer research. There are a number of studies clearly documenting that a change in attitude, usually through some type of persuasive campaign, is

1 G. Allport, "Attitudes," in C. Murchison, ed., *Handbook of Social Psychology* (Worcester, Mass.: Clark University Press, 1935), pp. 798–884.

2 R. T. LaPiere, "Attitudes vs. Actions," *Social Forces,* vol. 13 (1934), pp. 230–37.

3 Leon Festinger, "Behavioral Support for Opinion Change," *Public Opinion Quarterly,* vol. 28 (1964), pp. 404–17.

4 L. Deutscher, "Words and Deeds: Social Science and Social Policy," *Social Problems,* vol. 3 (1966), p. 235.

5 M. Fishbein, "Attitude and the Prediction of Behavior," in M. Fishbein, ed., *Attitude Theory and Measurement* (New York: Wiley, 1967), p. 477.

followed by behavioral change among large numbers of people.[6] In fact, many marketing researchers feel that attitude change should be a primary goal of promotional strategy. DuBois, for example, reported that the better the level of attitude, the more users you hold and the more nonusers you attract.[7] Studies at Grey Advertising, Inc. over a number of years led to this conclusion:

> More and more psychologists are coming to the conclusion that to result in a sale an advertisement must bring about a positive change in the *attitude* of the reader or viewer . . . . That there is a definite relationship between *change of attitude* toward a brand and buying action is not only a logical conclusion but is supported by a preponderance of *evidence.*[8]

There are three basic reasons for the divergence of viewpoint on this vitally important subject:

1. Varying conceptions and definitions. Fishbein and Ajzen reviewed 750 articles published between 1968 and 1970 and found almost 500 different ways of conceptualizing this variable.[9] The upshot is that published studies often are studying different phenomena.

2. Varying measurement methods. The variety of measurement approaches used in the published literature is virtually endless. Only in recent years have there been serious attempts to compare various approaches to determine those that appear to have the greatest validity.[10]

3. Assignment of too much predictive weight to a single variable. Common sense ought to indicate that attitude alone cannot fully explain a complex behavioral act, yet this often has been the expectation. Consideration also must be given to the moderating effect of social pressure,[11] economic circumstances, and expectations;[12] attitude toward the situation in which the behavior takes place;[13] and a variety of other factors such as exposure to new information, opportunity to make brand choice, the influence of competing brands, the effect of

6 For just a few of the current references, see Alvin A. Achenbaum, "Advertising Doesn't Manipulate Consumers," *Journal of Advertising Research*, vol. 12 (April 1972), pp. 3–14; and "Ads Can Change Attitudes, Hike Sales; Effects Are Measurable," *Marketing News* (February 13, 1976), p. 5; and Steven J. Gross and C. Michael Niman, "Attitude-Behavior Consistency: A Review," *Public Opinion Quarterly*, vol. 39 (Fall 1975), pp. 358–68.

7 C. DuBois, "Twelve Brands on a Seesaw," in *Proceedings of the 13th Annual Conference* (New York: Advertising Research Foundation, 1968).

8 *Grey Matter,* vol. 39 (November 1968), p. 1.

9 Martin Fishbein and Icek Ajzen, "Attitudes and Opinions," in P. H. Mussen and M. R. Rosenzweig, eds., *Annual Review of Psychology*, vol. 23 (Palo Alto, Calif.: Annual Reviews, Inc., 1972), pp. 188–244.

10 See, for example, Joel N. Axelrod, "Attitude Measurements That Predict Purchases," *Journal of Advertising Research*, vol. 8 (March 1968), p. 3.

11 Icek Ajzen and Martin Fishbein, "Attitudes and Normative Beliefs as Factors Influencing Behavioral Intentions," *Journal of Personality and Social Psychology*, vol. 21 (1972), pp. 1–9.

12 George Katona, *The Powerful Consumer* (New York: McGraw-Hill, 1960).

13 Milton Rokeach, "Attitude Change and Behavioral Change," *Public Opinion Quarterly*, vol. 30 (1966–67), pp. 529–50.

store environment, price and financial constraints, and family decision processes.[14]

The first edition of this text was published in 1968, and the authors could do little more than cite the evidence to that point and leave unanswered the all-important question of whether or not attitude change is a valid communication goal. During that period, however, the writings of Milton Rosenberg came into vogue,[15] and Martin Fishbein rose to prominence with his fresh viewpoints.[16] Fishbein, in particular, introduced *beliefs* as the cognitive building block on which attitudes are built.[17] Attitudes are functionally related to behavioral intentions, according to Fishbein, which, in turn, will predict behavior. Both Rosenberg and Fishbein also contributed methodological innovations that quickly were adopted by academically-oriented marketing researchers.

The reader will recall the relationship between beliefs, attitudes, and intentions from Figure 14.1, which is reproduced here for ease of reference. It seemed for a period that Rosenberg and Fishbein were largely ignored by their fellow psychologists, but this certainly was not the case in consumer research. In fact, the Fishbein model, in particular, dominated published consumer research in the 1970s, with the outcome that needed light has been shed on the attitude-behavior relationship.

Because the remainder of the chapter makes extensive use of the variables in Figure 15.1, it is necessary to define them with precision at the outset:

1. Evaluative criteria: *desired outcomes from choice or use of an alternative expressed in the form of the attributes or specifications used to compare various alternatives.*

2. Beliefs: *Information that links a given alternative to a specified evaluative criterion, specifying the extent to which the alternative possesses the desired attribute.*

3. Attitude: *A learned predisposition to respond consistently in a favorable manner with respect to a given alternative* (referred to earlier as the affective dimension).

4. Intention: *the subjective probability that beliefs and attitudes will be acted upon.*

It should be pointed out that Figure 15.1 is, as yet, not a complete model

---

14 George Day, *Buyer Attitudes and Brand Choice Behavior* (New York: Free Press, 1970).

15 Milton J. Rosenberg, "Cognitive Structure and Attitudinal Effect," *Journal of Abnormal and Social Psychology,* vol. 53 (1956), pp. 367–72.

16 Martin Fishbein, "The Relationships between Beliefs, Attitudes and Behavior," in Shel Feldman, ed., *Cognitive Consistency* (New York: Academic Press, 1966), pp. 199–223.

17 See Martin Fishbein and Icek Ajzen, *Belief, Attitude, Intention and Behavior: An Introduction to Theory and Research* (Reading, Mass.: Addison-Wesley, 1975), p. 12.

Figure 15.1 The relationships among evaluative criteria, beliefs, attitudes, and intention

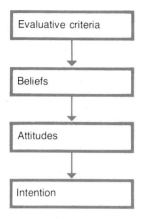

of the attitude-behavior link, because it fails to take account of situational influences of various types. These refinements are introduced later in the discussion of the extended Fishbein model.

The formation of beliefs and attitudes

The process by which consumers form beliefs and attitudes toward products and brands has only recently received much attention in the literature on consumer behavior. The evidence is tentative at best, but it is well worthy of review.

Consumers appear to use two different types of strategies in arriving at these judgments. The first has been conceptualized in the *compensatory* type of attitude model. If the compensatory strategy is used by the consumer, perceived strength of a given alternative on one or more evaluative criteria (referred to in this context more explicitly as product attributes) can compensate for weaknesses on other attributes. With the *noncompensatory* strategy, on the other hand, the weakness of a product or brand on one attribute cannot be compensated by its strength on another attribute, with the result that the alternative will be eliminated from consideration. There are several variations within each of these categories which are discussed below.

Research methods[18]

Before discussing compensatory and noncompensatory models, it is necessary to review once again the various ways in which consumer information processing is analyzed. Some of these methods were dis-

18 This section closely follows the discussion of James R. Bettman, "Data Collection and Analysis Approaches for Studying Consumer Information Processing" (Working Paper no. 41, Center for Marketing Studies, University of California, Los Angeles, July 1976).

cussed briefly in Chapter 9, but more background is needed to understand why some of the findings appear as they do.

Information integration. This method was pioneered by Bettman and his colleagues.[19] It begins with the specification of items of information an individual can use to arrive at a judgment, usually about a brand. Each piece of data is conceived to be a factor in an analysis of variance with several levels such as degrees of belief ranging from very unlikely to very likely. The person then is given the information to be used and is asked to make a response, perhaps a rating of attitude. Computer methods then analyze the ways in which the individuals combined the data to arrive at the judgments.

Protocol methods. In this approach the consumer is asked to think out loud as he or she actually is performing some type of behavior such as shopping or selection from various alternatives.[20] The resulting verbal record is termed a protocol. In most of the research to date, these models have been in the form of decision nets in which attributes are displayed in a type of branching structure that specifies the specific rules that may be applied in judging an alternative.[21] While the analysis methods have gained in sophistication,[22] many people find it difficult actually to verbalize their thoughts during the process itself. It may be much easier to give a retrospective report.

Information monitoring. Originally pioneered by Jacoby and his associates at Purdue, consumers are provided with information on a display board consisting of a matrix with information cards available for both brand and attribute.[23] The person chooses a brand after selecting as many cards as desired. The sequence of information selected is of primary importance. This has been extensively used, but it is apparent that the task is artificial. The actual decision rule used can only be inferred, and the task permits processing of information by brand or by attribute. This is in contrast to an actual shopping environment in which the information is most often organized by brand through exposure to commercials, shelving, and so on.

Eye movement analysis. Only recently applied to consumer research, eye movement analysis involves presenting information on a screen or in

19 See James R. Bettman, Noel Capon, and Richard J. Lutz, "Cognitive Algebra in Multi-Attribute Attitude Models," *Journal of Marketing Research,* vol. 12 (May 1975), pp. 151–64.

20 James R. Bettman, "Information Processing Models of Consumer Behavior," *Journal of Marketing Research,* vol. 7 (August 1970), pp. 370–76.

21 James R. Bettman, "Decision Net Models of Buyer Information Processing and Choice: Findings, Problems, and Prospects," in G. David Hughes and Michael L. Ray, eds., *Buyer/Consumer Information Processing* (Chapel Hill: University of North Carolina Press, 1974), pp. 59–74.

22 John W. Payne, "Heuristic Search Processes in Decision Making," in Beverlee B. Anderson, ed., *Advances in Consumer Research,* vol. 3 (Chicago: Association for Consumer Research, 1976), pp. 321–27.

23 See Jacob Jacoby et al., "Prepurchase Information Acquisition: Description of a Process Methodology, Research Paradigm, and Pilot Investigation," in Anderson (ed.), *Advances in Consumer Research,* pp. 306–14.

tabular format.[24] The sequence of eye movements undertaken in examining the information array then is analyzed by an eye movement camera. This device is cumbersome and serves to make the choice situation highly artificial.

All of the above methods have been used singly or in combination to attempt to isolate the actual manner in which consumers arrive at brand evaluations.

Consumer judgment rules

Compensatory models. Compensatory models (a weakness on one attribute may be compensated for by strengths on others) fall into two main categories: (1) expectancy-value models and (2) attribute adequacy models. Some other possibilities have also been explored in the literature, but there is insufficient evidence to warrant their inclusion here.[25]

(1) The expectancy-value model. This model assumes from the outset that there will be more than one evaluative criterion or attribute along which the alternative will be evaluated. Judgments are based on beliefs that assess whether or not the object actually possesses the attribute in question plus an evaluation of the "goodness or badness" of that belief. This, in effect, is the Fishbein multiattribute attitude model described in much more depth later. It is hypothesized that brands are evaluated one at a time along all attributes and that the total evaluation or judgment is the sum of the ratings along each attribute. The brand with the highest sum wins, and a relatively poor rating on one attribute may be offset by higher ratings on the others.

(2) The attribute adequacy model. The expectancy-value model makes no particular assumptions about the degree to which the rating of a brand or product along an attribute approaches or even exceeds the "ideal" the consumer has in mind for that attribute. In the attribute adequacy model, the evaluation is arrived at in a similar manner to that discussed above, with the exception that an explicit assessment is made of the difference between "ideal and actual" on each attribute.[26] While there has not been much research to report, this may be a closer approximation of actual consumer behavior in extended problem-solving situations.

Noncompensatory models. The noncompensatory model (weakness on one attribute is not compensated for by strength on another) have received much less attention in the literature, but it now appears that there are three variations: (1) conjunctive; (2) disjunctive; and (3) lexicographic.

24 See Edward J. Russo and Larry D. Rosen, "An Eye Fixation Analysis of Multi-Alternative Choice," *Memory and Cognition*, vol. 3 (May 1975), pp. 267–76. Also W. Fred van Raaij, "Consumer Information Processing for Different Information Structures and Formats," in William D. Perreault, ed., *Advances in Consumer Research*, vol. 4 (Atlanta: Association for Consumer Research, 1977), pp. 176–84.

25 For more extensive discussion, see Flemming Hansen, "Psychological Theories of Consumer Choice," *Journal of Consumer Research*, vol. 3 (December 1976), pp. 132–37.

26 For one illustration see James L. Ginter and Frank M. Bass, "An Experimental Study of Attitude Change, Advertising, and Usage in New Product Introduction," *Journal of Advertising*, vol. 1 (1972), pp. 33–39.

(1) The conjunctive model. When this model is used, the consumer establishes a minimum acceptable level for each product attribute. A brand will be evaluated as acceptable only if *each* attribute equals or exceeds that minimum level. A lower than acceptable rating on one attribute will lead to a negative evaluation and rejection. For example, a stereo component system may be evaluated as completely satisfactory in terms of sound reproduction and mechanical characteristics yet be rejected because it is not compact in size.

(2) The disjunctive model. When following the disjunctive approach, the consumer establishes one or more attributes as being dominant. A brand will be evaluated as acceptable only if it exceeds the minimum specified level on these key attributes. The other attributes really are of little significance. To continue with the example of the stereo component set, assume that sound reproduction and mechanical characteristics are the dominant considerations. Any set measuring up to expectation on these attributes will be regarded as acceptable no matter what its size, color, and so on. The basis of final choice is unclear given that there is a *set* of acceptable alternatives.

(3) The lexicographic model. Now the consumer has ranked product attributes from most important to least important. The brand that dominates on the most important criterion receives the highest evaluation.[27] If two or more brands tie, then the second attribute is examined and so on until the tie is broken.

Evaluation and implications. It is likely that any of the above methods will be used by consumers in certain circumstances, and the evidence seems to confirm that this indeed is the case. The variables that underlie choice of processing strategy are not yet understood, but it is helpful to note that all but one, the lexicographic, assume that consumers process information in terms of the brand, looking at all attributes of importance in determining choice. The lexicographic, on the other hand, encourages processing by attribute first rather than brand as a primary consideration. Bettman argues that processing by attribute is much simpler from the consumer's point of view.[28] Therefore, it might be utilized most frequently in routinized buying decisions or in those situations in which evaluative criteria are fixed and the consumer already possesses some understanding of the various alternatives. True extended problem-solving, on the other hand, would most likely favor either the expectancy-value or the attribute adequacy approach.[29]

In a comparative study of processing strategies people were asked to

27 A. Tversky, "Intransitivity of Preferences," *Psychological Review,* vol. 76 (January 1969), pp. 31–48.
28 Bettman, "Data Collection and Analysis."
29 This is the conclusion of Hanson. A similar position has been reached by C. Whan Park and V. Parker Lessing, "Judgmental Rules and Stages of the Familiarity Curve: Promotional Implications," *Journal of Advertising,* vol. 6 (Winter 1977), pp. 4–9. Also, James R. Bettman, "Issues in Designing Consumer Information Environments," *Journal of Consumer Research,* vol. 2 (December 1975) pp. 169–77.

rank order ten automobiles evaluated on seven dimensions.[30] They then were presented with a written description of judgment and evaluation strategies people could follow. These described the expectancy-value, lexicographic, conjunctive, and disjunctive models. Then those participating in the study indicated which, if any, was closest to the method they actually followed. By far the majority indicated they followed the lexicographic approach, with the expectancy-value a distant second. The conjunctive and disjunctive were chosen only by a tiny handful. While this study did not actually isolate and observe the actual processing strategy, it does support Bettman's conclusion that most people prefer the simpler strategy of processing by attribute.[31]

It should be noted in this context that the research strategies followed often have inadvertently favored processing by brand. The reasons for this conclusion are too detailed for inclusion here,[32] but there should be greater attention paid to the structuring of a research environment that truly reflects the task at hand. Only then can the hypothesized effects of extended problem-solving versus routinized decision-making actually be evaluated.

From the viewpoint of marketing strategy, the apparent tendency to prefer processing by attribute has interesting implications. As was pointed out earlier most advertisements and retail shopping situations structure information only by brand category. Given the current incidence of consumer overload discussed in Chapter 13, ads and other types of promotional stimuli may be screened out by the consumer if they do not prominently feature the preferred attribute and use that has the lead appeal. The tendency *all too often is to talk about the product first and to stress the benefit second.*

Attitudes toward alternatives: Expectancy-value models

The expectancy-value model discussed above has become the dominant focus of consumer researchers in recent years. The authors estimate that the Fishbein model, in particular, has accounted for more published research in consumer behavior than any other subject in the past several years. Yet, in a more important sense, attitudes play a key role in marketing strategy in that most advertising is undertaken on the assumption that a change in attitude will be accompanied by a change in behavior. The expectancy-value models, in turn, have represented a large step forward in both conceptual understanding and in research methodology.

Two names are clearly dominant: Milton Rosenberg and Martin

30 Michael D. Reilly, Rebecca H. Holman, and Roger Evered, "Individual Differences in Information Processing: An Exploratory Report" (Working Paper no. 50, College of Business Administration, Pennsylvania State University, November 1976).

31 Bettman, "Issues in Designing."

32 See Bettman, "Data Collection and Analysis." Also, James R. Bettman and Pradeep Kakkar, "Effects of Information Presentation Format on Consumer Information Acquisition Strategies," *Journal of Consumer Research*, vol. 3 (March 1977), pp. 233–40.

Fishbein. Their models have provided the impetus for expectancy-value research. Both are described first, followed by discussion of some of the "hybrid" models and the methodological issues which have emerged.

The Rosenberg model

Rosenberg's model, as initially published, contained two variables: (1) values (equivalent to the term "evaluative criteria" used in this book) and their importance in arriving at an attitude and (2) perceived instrumentality (a complex term that simply estimates the degree to which the taking of a point of view or following an action will either enhance or block the attainment of a value).[33] Assume that "low price" is an important value (evaluative criterion) and that the consumer has come to believe that brand A offers low price. The perceived instrumentality of brand A thus would be high.

His attitude model took this form:

$$A_0 = \sum_{i=1}^{N} (VI_i)(PI_i)$$

where:

A_0 = the overall evaluation of the attractiveness of alternative 0
VI_i = the importance of the ith value
PI_i = the perceived instrumentality of alternative 0 with respect to value i
N = the number of pertinent or salient values

In its pure form, the Rosenberg model calls for the measurement of value importance on a scale containing 21 categories ranging from "gives me maximum satisfaction" (+10) to "gives me maximum dissatisfaction" (−10). Using our earlier example, "low price" might receive a rating of +10. Perceived instrumentality is assessed using 11 categories ranging from "the condition is completely attained through a given action" (+5) to "the condition is completely blocked through undertaking the given action" (−5).[34] Perhaps brand A in the above example would be given a score of +5.

Probably the best test of this approach in its pure form was published by Hansen in 1969.[35] He successfully predicted choices among modes of travel, menu items, hairdryers, and restaurants. He also found that the two basic terms (value importance and perceived instrumentality) are independent and will not predict response when used separately. Similar results were reported by Bither and Miller.[36]

The Fishbein model

The Fishbein model is similar in many ways to Rosenberg's formulation, but there are subtle differences.[37] His first component is belief, defined as

33 Rosenberg, "Cognitive Structure."

34 Rosenberg, "Cognitive Structure."

35 Flemming Hansen, "Consumer Choice Behavior: An Experimental Approach," *Journal of Marketing Research,* vol. 4 (November 1969), pp. 436–43.

36 Stewart W. Bither and Stephen Miller, "A Cognitive Theory of Brand Preference," in Philip R. McDonald, ed., *Marketing Involvement in Society and the Economy* (Chicago: American Marketing Association, 1969), pp. 210–16.

37 Martin Fishbein, "An Investigation of the Relationships between Beliefs about an Object and the Attitude toward That Object," *Human Relations,* vol. 16 (1963), pp. 233–40.

the probability that an object does or does not have a particular attribute. The second component is an "affective term" normally stated in terms of "good or bad." It specifies whether or not the possession or failure of possession of the attribute in question is positive or negative. The model takes this form:

$$A_0 = \sum_{i=1}^{N} B_i a_i$$

where:

A_0 = attitude toward the object
B_i = the ith belief about the object
a_i = the evaluation of the belief
N = the total number of beliefs

In his initial research, Fishbein measured attitudes toward Negroes.[38] It was his hypothesis that attitudes are a function of beliefs about the characteristics of members of this race (B_i) and the evaluative aspects of those beliefs (a_i). For example, the characteristic "uneducated" was rephrased into the belief statement "Negroes are uneducated." The belief statements were measured with a five point scale with the poles labeled with such terms as "probable-improbable" and "likely-unlikely." A five point scale also was used to measure evaluative aspects of each belief with such terms as "good-bad."

The formula calls for belief (B_i) and evaluation (a_i) scores to be multiplied for each belief. Then these scores are summed to arrive at a single attitude ranking. While this model has seldom been applied to marketing in its pure form as the next section points out, Bettman and his associates verified through the integration method discussed in the last section that people do multiply beliefs in their evaluation as Fishbein has hypothesized.[39] Whether or not these are then summed was less clear. It also was found that both the B_i and the a_i terms make substantial contribution to the evaluation and hence must be retained in this type of research. They feel, however, that both should be scored with a scale ranging from -3 to $+3$.[40]

Hybrid models

Most of the marketing applications have not followed Rosenberg or Fishbein to the letter. Rather, there have been some substantial modifications. The attribute adequacy model mentioned in the last section is one example. It will be recalled that belief is compared with the "ideal" with respect to a given attribute. Another formulation is quite close to the Rosenberg model, but its measurements are different.[41]

38 Fishbein, "An Investigation of the Relationships."

39 James R. Bettman, Noel Capon, and Richard J. Lutz, "Multi-Attribute Measurement Models and Multi-Attribute Attitude Theory: A Test of Construct Validity," *Journal of Consumer Research,* vol. 1 (March 1975), pp.1–15.

40 Bettman, Capon, and Lutz, "Multi-Attribute Measurement Models."

41 W. W. Talarzyk and R. Meinpour, "Comparison of an Attitude Model and Coombsian Unfolding Analysis for the Prediction of Individual Brand Preference," paper presented at the Workshop on Attitude Research and Consumer Behavior, University of Illinois (December 1970).

$$A_b = \sum_{i=1}^{n} W_i B_{ib}$$

where

A_b = attitude toward a particular alternative b
W_i = weight or importance of evaluative criterion i
B_{ib} = evaluative aspect or belief with respect to
  utility of alternative b to satisfy evaluative criterion i
n = number of evaluative criteria important in selection
  of an alternative in category under consideration

In this formula W_i is the weight or importance of the evaluative criterion, and B_{ib} is the evaluation of the alternative along that criterion. This rating is performed for each evaluative criterion, and the summed score is attitude toward the alternative.

The determination of evaluative criteria was discussed in the preceding chapter. It will be recalled that the usual procedure is to isolate the appropriate dimensions and then to assess the importance of each W_i through some type of scale. The next step is to measure beliefs about the utility of individual brands through use of a scaling technique such as that shown below.[42] The score criterion B_{ib} times the importance of that criterion W_i.

		Very satisfactory				Very unsatisfactory	
Decay	Brand A	1	2	3	4	5	6
prevention	Brand B	1	2	3	4	5	6
Taste	Brand A	1	2	3	4	5	6
	Brand B	1	2	3	4	5	6

Data from one study utilizing this formula appear in Figure 15.2. Five brands of mouthwash were rated along five criteria, of which germ-killing power and effectiveness were perceived as being of greatest importance. No summary score of A_b is provided, but the detailed ratings often are of greater use in marketing planning. From these data, for example, it is apparent that Listerine holds first place in preference, and correspondingly, it has the highest ratings on the two most important evaluative criteria. Cepacol, on the other hand, is least preferred and has consistently the lowest ratings across all criteria. Additional data from this study showed that Cepacol is most preferred by those with a masters or doctor degree but, unfortunately, mouthwash consumption is lowest in this segment. Management now must determine what must be done to improve these ratings. If the product, in fact, is competitive in terms of germ killing and

---

42 F. M. Bass and W. W. Talarzyk, "Relative Contribution of Perceived Instrumentality and Value Importance in Determining Attitudes towards Brands," paper presented at American Marketing Association (August 1970).

Figure 15.2 An example of brand attitudes computed as a rating along evaluative criteria

(a) Frequency of attribute-importance ranking

Attribute	Ranking (in percent)				
	1st	2nd	3rd	4th	5th
Kills germs	49.3	31.9	11.9	5.9	1.0
Taste/flavor	15.1	22.6	43.0	18.5	0.7
Price	4.7	12.2	22.9	52.8	7.4
Color	0.2	0.3	1.1	9.3	89.1
Effectiveness	30.9	33.1	21.0	13.4	1.6

(b) Average consumer ratings of mouthwash brands on relevant attributes

Brands	Average score on				
	Kills germs	Taste/ flavor	Price	Color	Effective- ness
Micrin	2.22	2.46	2.60	1.85	2.21
Cepacol	2.40	2.92	2.70	2.29	2.36
Listerine	1.63	2.86	2.29	2.27	1.64
Lavoris	2.31	2.38	2.50	1.81	2.27
Colgate 100	2.35	2.52	2.68	1.87	2.32

Source: "General Consumer Products," in J. F. Engel, W. W. Talarzyk, and C. M. Larson, eds., *Cases in Promotional Strategy* (Homewood, Ill.: Irwin, 1971), pp. 90–91. Reprinted by permission of the publisher.

the other attributes, the solution may be to advertise this fact. In any event, useful information has been provided for marketing planning.

Other variations of the expectancy-value model have been reported as well.[43] Much of the early research attempted to validate the approaches through correlating the attitude scores produced through the Rosenberg, Fishbein or hybrid model of various types with some other independently derived measure of attitude. This did serve to prove what is technically known as *convergent validity*, and there are some excellent summaries for the reader to refer to.[44] Unfortunately *predictive validity* (the hypothesized correlation between beliefs, attitudes, intentions, and behavior) was yet to be proved, but more about that later.

There has been quite a debate of whether or not the so-called "value importance" component adds to the predictive power of the model. It is important conceptually, but it may not facilitate prediction of choice. The literature is too voluminous to describe in detail except to cite some of the

The controversy over the "importance component"

43 Jagdish N. Sheth, "An Investigation of Relationships among Evaluative Beliefs, Affect, Behavioral Intention, and Behavior" (Working Series in Marketing Research, Pennsylvania State University, 1970).

44 See especially M. B. Holbrook and J. M. Hulbert, "Multi-Attribute Attitude Models: A Comparative Analysis," in Mary Jane Schlinger, ed., *Advances in Consumer Research*, vol. 2 (Chicago: Association for Consumer Research, 1975), pp. 375–88; and W. L. Wilkie and E. A. Pessemier, "Issues in Marketing's Use of Multi-Attribute Attitude Models," *Journal of Marketing Research*, vol. 10 (November 1973), pp. 428–41.

authorities who claim it is unnecessary[45] and those who claim that it is.[46] Bettman attempted to isolate conditions under which importance will contribute to prediction.[47] The obvious conclusion is that it will add to explanatory power only when the evaluative criteria are widely differing in their significance to the individual. Perhaps this is most likely in an extended problem-solving situation.

Part of the difficulty has entered by straying from the original form of the expectancy-value models. Fishbein argues convincingly that importance does not need to be measured separately.[48] Rather, it will show up in the polarity of the (a_i) evaluation. Highly positive or highly negative attributes generally are those that have attained some importance to the individual, and a separate measurement of this factor adds nothing to predictive power.

Which model is "best"?

There have been various attempts to assess which of the models discussed here performs best in terms of predicting attitude when measured independently, intention or behavior. Not surprisingly the results have been widely varying. Sheth found superiority for the Fishbein model.[49] Mazis, Ahtola, and Klippel documented superiority for the adequacy importance model.[50] Other findings could be cited as well,[51] and there is no clear winner.

There are several reasons why ability to predict behavioral response is low. First, attitude toward an object takes no account whatsoever of the situation in which the behavior is undertaken. Situational influence has now been documented thoroughly, and it must be given proper emphasis in behavioral prediction.[52] Consider Burdus's words on this subject:

45 See, for example, Jagdish N. Sheth, "Brand Profiles from Beliefs and Importances," *Journal of Advertising Research,* vol. 13 (February 1973), pp. 37–42; and Jagdish N. Sheth and W. Wayne Talarzyk, "Perceived Instrumentality and Value Importance as Determinants of Attitudes," *Journal of Marketing Research,* vol. 9 (February 1972), pp. 6–9.

46 See, for example, J. B. Cohen, M. Fishbein, and O. T. Ahtola, "The Nature and Uses of Expectancy-Value Models in Consumer Attitude Research," *Journal of Marketing Research,* vol. 9 (November 1972), pp. 456–60; and P. Sampson and J. Palmer, "The Importance of Being Earnest about Importance," *Market Research Society Conference,* 1973, pp. 157–89.

47 James R. Bettman, "To Add Importance or Not to Add Importance: That is the Question," in Scott Ward and Peter Wright, eds., *Advances in Consumer Research,* vol. 1 (Urbana, Ill.: Association for Consumer Research, 1974), pp. 291–301.

48 Fishbein and Ajzen, *Belief, Attitude, Intention and Behavior,* p. 221.

49 See J. N. Sheth and C. W. Park, "Equivalence of Fishbein and Rosenberg Theories of Attitudes" (Working Paper no. 108, College of Commerce and Business Administration, University of Illinois at Urbana, 1973); and S. Tuncalp and J. N. Sheth, "Prediction of Attitudes: A Comparative Study of the Rosenberg, Fishbein and Sheth Models, in Schlinger, *Advances in Consumer Research,* pp. 384–404.

50 Michael B. Mazis, Olli T. Ahtola, and R. Eugene Klippel, "The Comparison of Four Multi-Attribute Models in the Prediction of Consumer Attitudes," *Journal of Consumer Research,* vol. 2 (June 1975), pp. 38–52.

51 J. B. Cohen and O. T. Ahtola, "An Expectancy X Value Analysis of the Relationship between Consumer Attitudes and Behavior," paper presented at the Association for Consumer Research (September 1971).

52 For some of the recent literature, see Russell W. Belk, "The Objective Situation as a Determinant of Consumer Behavior," in Schlinger, *Advances in Consumer Research,* pp. 427–37; Richard J. Lutz and Pradeep Kakkar, "The Psychological Situation as a Determinant of Consumer Behavior," in Schlinger, *Advances in Consumer Research,* pp. 439–53; Russell W. Belk, "Situational Variables in Consumer Behavior," *Journal of Consumer Research,* vol. 2 (December 1975), pp. 157–64; and Richard J. Lutz and Pradeep Kakkar, "Situational Influence in Interpersonal Persuasion," in Anderson, *Advances in Consumer Research,* pp. 370–78.

When my colleagues talk about my ideal cigarette, I am tempted to ask them whether they mean ideal for work or ideal for play, ideal for the beginning of the month when I'm rich or ideal for the end when I am poor. When they talk about shampoos, another so called homogeneous market, I want to know whether the ideal they are asking me about is my ideal when I am on holiday sea-bathing, my ideal when the shopping has to be done as quickly as possible. The markets may be homogenous—it seems I am not.[53]

A second major omission is failure to consider the existence of conformity pressures from various reference groups and family. These often can dominate beliefs and attitudes as a determinant of both intention and behavior.[54]

Finally, there is a host of both anticipated and unanticipated circumstances that will affect intentions and choice. Examples are financial circumstances, assumed availability of goods, and so on.

The net result is that beliefs and attitudes, defined in terms of attitudes toward an object, have been expected to carry an impossible weight of prediction. This fact has led to the development of the extended Fishbein model discussed in the next section.

The extended Fishbein model

As his research program matured, Fishbein soon came to realize that attitude toward an object was a limited concept. Consider his own words:

> . . . it really doesn't make a lot of difference how much a person likes a given product, or how good that product's "brand image" is—if the consumer doesn't believe that buying that product will lead to more "good consequences" (and fewer "bad consequences" than buying some other product, they will tend to buy the other product. Thus, one of the factors that contributes to a person's intention to engage in some behavior is the attitude toward engaging in that behavior . . . not the attitude toward the object of the behavior. Fortunately, however, everything we know about attitudes toward objects also applies to attitudes toward actions.[55]

Therefore, the first modification is to substitute *attitude toward the act* (A_{act}) for attitude toward the object (A_O). This is quite consistent with the viewpoint articulated throughout this book that consumers purchase *benefits*, not product attributes per se.

The second modification is to take explicit account of the norms governing behavior and the person's motivation to comply with those norms.[56] It is his contention that A_{act} and the normative component, taken

53 J. A. Burdus, "Attitude Models—The Dream and the Reality," in Philip Levine, ed., *Attitude Research Bridges the Atlantic* (Chicago: American Marketing Association, 1975), p. 161.

54 Herbert C. Kelman, "Attitudes Are Alive and Well and Gainfully Employed in the Sphere of Action," *American Psychologist,* vol. 29 (May 1974), pp. 310–24.

55 Martin Fishbein, "Attitude, Attitude Change, and Behavior: A Theoretical Overview," in Levine, *Attitude Research,* p. 12.

56 Fishbein and Ajzen, *Belief, Attitude, Intention and Behavior,* esp. p. 301 and following.

together, will provide an accurate prediction of intentions, which, in turn, will give an approximate prediction of behavior, all things being equal. The resulting general model appears as follows:

$$B \approx BI = (A_{act})\, w_o + (NB)\,(Mc)\, w_1$$

where:

B = overt behavior
BI = behavioral intentions
A_{act} = attitude toward undertaking a given action in a particular set of circumstances
NB = normative beliefs—those norms that govern the situation
Mc = the individual's motivation to comply with those social norms active in the situation
w_o = the weights reflecting the importance of each component (derived
w_1 statistically through a regression analysis)

A_{act}, NB, and Mc all must be measured, whereas the weights reflecting the importance of these factors are estimated statistically.

Notice that Fishbein makes no claim to be able to predict behavior perfectly. The most he will say is that behavioral intention (BI) will approximate behavior. This is a deficiency in this formulation we will remedy later.

Attitude toward the action (A_{act})

Attitude toward the act is estimated with the following formula, which bears some real similarities to the attitude toward the object (A_o) formulation described earlier:

$$A_{act} = \sum_{i=1}^{N} B_i a_i$$

where:

A_{act} = attitude toward the act under consideration
B_i = the ith belief toward the act
a_i = the evaluation of the ith belief
N = the total number of beliefs

The differences between A_O and A_{act} are not in the formulation but in the questions utilized to assess the B and a components. The questions here focus on one specific purchase and use situation and attempt to evaluate the consequences. Belief may now be interpreted as the probability that a product attribute will exist or that the act of purchase will give certain consequences. The a_i component evaluates that belief along a "good-bad" dimension.

For purposes of illustration, assume that a consumer is about to purchase a camera and is involved in alternative evaluation. Assume, further, that "ease of use," "guarantees good pictures every time," and "price" are known to be the most frequently utilized evaluative criteria among those in this particular market segment. The belief statements appear as follows based on this prior knowledge:

The camera does not require me to make my own settings for light and distance.

The camera works in such a way that I cannot overexpose or under-expose a picture.

The camera costs $150 or less.

Attitudes toward the act of purchasing brand X now would be evaluated with scales such as these:[57]

Brand x does not require me to make my own settings for light and distance.

(B_i) Probable ____ ____ ____ ____ ____ ____ Improbable
(a_i) Good ____ ____ ____ ____ ____ ____ Bad

Brand x works in such a way that I cannot overexpose or underexpose a picture.

(B_i) Probable ____ ____ ____ ____ ____ ____ Improbable
(a_i) Good ____ ____ ____ ____ ____ ____ Bad

Brand x will cost less than $150.

(B_i) Probable ____ ____ ____ ____ ____ ____ Improbable
(a_i) Good ____ ____ ____ ____ ____ ____ Bad

The attitude now is derived by multiplying the (B_i) and (a_i) components for each belief and then summing across the total number of beliefs (N). The a_i component only must be measured once, whereas (B_i) must be computed for each brand.

The normative component

Social norms have been discussed extensively in an earlier chapter, and they were defined, in general, as internalized, socially sanctioned forms of behavior. The existence of such norms, however, is of no consequence unless the individual is motivated to comply with these social pressures. There are a number of ways to measure normative beliefs, and the following are only illustrative questions for the camera buying example:

The local camera club believes that brand x offers the best buy for the money.

Probable ____ ____ ____ ____ ____ ____ Improbable

Most of the better photographers in the camera club use brand x and consider all other brands to be inferior.

Probable ____ ____ ____ ____ ____ ____ Improbable

My best friends and picture-taking partners believe that brand x is the best brand to buy and use.

Probable ____ ____ ____ ____ ____ ____ Improbable

57 These questions and those on the normative component are derived following the general models in Fishbein and Ajzen, *Belief, Attitude, Intention, and Behavior.*

Motivation to comply would be revealed by questions such as these:

I intend to follow the thinking of other members of the camera club.

True _____ _____ _____ _____ _____ _____ False

I intend to follow the leadership of the better photographers in the camera club.

True _____ _____ _____ _____ _____ _____ False

I intend to follow the advice of my picture-taking friends.

True _____ _____ _____ _____ _____ _____ False

The second component of the extended model now is computed by multiplying the two values for each normative statement and summing them across all possible statements. The total estimate of behavioral intention then is the combined sum of these two factors.

The validity of the extended model

It should be stated once again that Fishbein is measuring only *intentions* and not behavior itself. Therefore, the validity of this model must be assessed by comparison against an independently derived measure of intentions. Preliminary research of this type has been undertaken, but it is necessary first to say something about the manner in which intentions themselves should be measured.

The measurement of intentions. While a number of different methods have been used over the years,[58] recent research evidence reported by Pavasars and Wells indicates that intentions predict behavior best when they are defined as "the probability of buying a particular brand relative to the probabilities of buying competitive brands on the next purchase."[59] This definition encompasses both intentions toward the brand itself and toward purchase of that brand relative to other offerings. Wells recommends that these probabilities be assessed by the constant sum method in which a fixed number of points, say 100, is allocated by the consumer to a set of brands in proportion to the estimated likelihood of buying that brand on the next purchase. The number of points allocated to each, divided by the total number of points, then represents the probability of purchase.[60]

The measurement of intentions in this way, of course, will not guarantee a perfect prediction of purchase on the next store visit, but it should accurately reflect the proportions of various brands purchased over a period of time. Furthermore, the accuracy of prediction is increased when individual estimates are aggregated to reflect a total market segment. Under those conditions, estimates attain high precision.

58 See, for example, Susan P. Douglas and Yoram Wind, "Intentions to Buy as Predictors of Buying Behavior," paper presented at the Association for Consumer Research (September 1971).

59 John Pavasars and William D. Wells, "Measures of Brand Attitudes Can Be Used to Predict Buying Behavior," *Marketing News* (April 11, 1975), p. 6.

60 Pavasars and Wells, "Measures of Brand Attitudes."

The predictive power of the extended model. In one major test of this conceptualization, Wilson, Mathews, and Harvey measured both intentions and behavior with respect to toothpaste purchases in comparison with the estimates derived from the extended Fishbein model.[61] The BI model was found to predict intention across all six brands of toothpaste. Also a strong association between behavior and intention was reported, thus suggesting that the BI model indirectly predicts behavior as well. A_{act} and the normative component both entered as important predictors of intention, thus verifying that they should be retained in the model. Good preliminary results also were reported by Harrell[62] and Wilson, Mathews, and Monoky.[63]

Ryan and Bonfield report a series of studies, however, that are not as optimistic.[64] In a review of evidence conducted in both the United States and Great Britain, some of which is proprietary, the average correlation between intention and behavior was .435. The average multiple correlation of A_{act} and the normative component on behavioral intention, in turn, was .62. It was their conclusion that the predictive power obtained in marketing studies has been lower than those reported by Fishbein and others working in a less "real world" situation.

All that can be said with certainty thus far is that the behavioral intention model predicts both intentions and behavior far better than the A_0 model discussed earlier. This, in itself, is encouraging, but greater predictive accuracy certainly is desired by anyone working in an applied context.

Part of the problem might lie in the formulation of the model itself. Lutz has raised a number of detailed questions that should be confronted in future research.[65] In particular, he challenges the "additive assumption" of the model and feels, instead, that people are more likely to arrive at an average judgment across beliefs. If so, different results would be obtained.

The authors feel that the root of the problem really is quite simple. We still have not taken account of the full range of situational influence, even though A_{act} can be made situationally specific and the normative component is included. In the first place, *anticipated circumstances* such as financial status, availability of goods, access to retail stores, and general

61 David T. Wilson, H. Lee Mathews, and James W. Harvey, "An Empirical Test of the Fishbein Behavioral Intention Model," *Journal of Consumer Research*, vol. 1 (March 1975), pp. 39–48.

62 Gilbert D. Harrell, "Physician Prescribing: Behavioral Intention, Attitudes, Normative Beliefs, Risk and Information" (unpublished doctoral diss., Pennsylvania State University, 1977).

63 David T. Wilson, H. Lee Mathews, and John F. Monoky, "Attitude as a Predictor of Behavior in a Buyer-Seller Bargaining Situation: An Experimental Approach" (Working Series in Marketing Research, Pennsylvania State University, February 1972).

64 Michael A. Ryan and E. H. Bonfield, "The Fishbein Extended Model and Consumer Behavior," *Journal of Consumer Research,* vol. 2 (August 1975), pp. 118–36; and Michael J. Ryan and E. H. Bonfield, "The Extended Fishbein Model: Additional Insights . . . Problems," in Schlinger, *Advances in Consumer Research,* pp. 265–83.

65 Richard J. Lutz, "Conceptual and Operational Issues in the Extended Fishbein Model," in Anderson, *Advances in Consumer Research,* pp. 469–76. Also, see Richard J. Lutz, "An Experimental Investigation of Causal Relations among Cognitions, Affect, and Behavioral Intention," *Journal of Consumer Research,* vol. 3 (March 1977), pp. 197–208.

attitudes of optimism or pessimism toward the future financial picture all function to shape intentions. A change in any of these will result in a change in intentions. Thus, anticipated circumstances should enter as a third factor in the BI equation along with A_{act} and the normative component. Similar, *unanticipated changes* in any of these considerations and others will prevent the fulfillment of intentions. Choice, then, is a function of both the intention and unanticipated circumstances. These predictions have been verified by Sheth[66] and Woodside,[67] although both used widely differing methodologies.

   While further research obviously is required, the authors believe that a total model of the belief, attitude, and intention relationship should take the form diagrammed in Figure 15.3.

Figure 15.3 A model of the relationship between beliefs, attitudes, and intentions

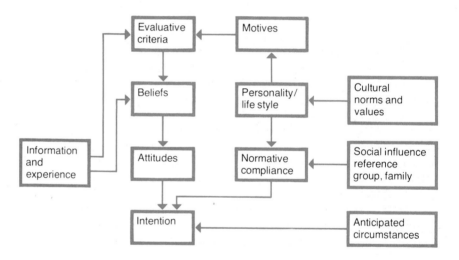

Notice, first of all, that beliefs are a function of evaluative criteria and information and experience. Attitudes, in turn, are a function of beliefs (plus, of course, the evaluative aspect) as Fishbein claims. Finally, intention is hypothesized to be a function of attitude (A_{act}), normative compliance (computed as specified in the Fishbein extended model using measures of both the existence of norms and the motivation to comply), and anticipated circumstances. Normative compliance, by the way, also is affected by life style, since motivation to comply is a personality variable.

   The model in Figure 15.3 is a part of the basic model of consumer behavior in this book. It is the authors' contention along with Belk and

66 Jagdish N. Sheth, "An Investigation of Relationships among Evaluative Beliefs, Affect, Behavioral Intention, and Behavior."

67 Arch G. Woodside and William O. Bearden, "Longitudinal Analysis of Consumer Attitude, Intention, and Behavior toward Beer Brand Choice," in Perreault, *Advances in Consumer Research*, pp. 349–56.

others that circumstances must be given a more explicit recognition in our conceptualization of decision processes.[68] If this is done with more rigor, the accuracy of behavioral prediction should increase sharply.

Implications for marketing strategy

The various forms of expectancy-value models, ranging from the more simple A_O model to the complex extended Fishbein conceptualization, all can be of value in marketing planning.[69] While the subject of change in beliefs and attitudes is considered in depth in the next chapter, it is helpful to discuss briefly the marketing uses of (1) aggregated models; (2) disaggregated models; and (3) intention to purchase indexes.

Use of the aggregated model

The Rosenberg model or the two versions of the Fishbein model all result in a single computed value that may, on the surface, appear to have little meaning. Yet this score can provide a useful measure of the effectiveness of marketing efforts if it is correlated with market share and computed over a period of time. Once the index-share relationship is known, changes in the index can serve as a forecasting tool. If it declines, this is a signal that a diagnosis of marketing strategy is needed. If it increases, on the other hand, this may provide a useful forecast of gains in share.

This type of computation also can be extended to competitors. The (a_i) score (evaluation of the "goodness or badness" of an attribute in the consumer's life style) only must be measured once. Beliefs about a given brand and its possession of these attributes, of course, must be collected for each alternative. If this is done, advance warnings may be provided of potential competitive inroads or decline. A gain in the index is a warning signal that a competitor may have gained an edge, which must be countered if market share is to be retained.

Finally, expectancy indexes can be computed for new products in test marketing. An accurate indication then can be gained of the probable market success in comparison with existing competitive alternatives.

Use of disaggregated models

Much also can be gained by using the disaggregated scores for each component of the index. The (B_i) (a_i) terms of the Fishbein model, for example, provide a sharp indication of those evaluative criteria or attributes most determinant in the purchase decision. When evaluated in terms of market segments (i.e., age, income, and so on), clues can be provided for benefit segmentation strategies discussed in the preceding chapter.

The disaggregated index also allows for diagnosis of marketing strategy variables. Let's return to the example of a camera purchase. Assume that the (a_i) computations show that two attributes are most important in the purchase:

68 See the various sources on situational influence cited in footnote 52.

69 This section builds upon many of the various ideas advanced in an unpublished article, "Uses and Misuses of Expectancy Attitude Models in Marketing," which has been reviewed by the authors.

The camera does not require me to make my own settings for light and distance.

The camera works in such a way that I cannot overexpose or underexpose the picture.

Assume further that most of those in the market segment of interest rated brand x as follows:

Brand x does not require me to make my own settings for light and distance.

Probable _____ _____ _____ _____ _____ __x__ Improbable

Brand x works in such a way that I cannot overexpose or underexpose a picture.

Probable _____ _____ _____ _____ __x__ _____ Improbable

Management now is faced with a dilemma. Consumer perceptions are clearly unfavorable. The first question to ask is "are we, in fact, failing to measure up in product design to meet the attributes desired by our market?" If the answer is "yes," then there are at least two possibilities. One is to shift to a different market segment that will respond more favorably to the brand as it is. The second is to make major changes in the existing product or to introduce an altogether new product to become more competitive.

If the answer to the above question is "no," then the problem is one of market awareness. The strategy now is to use advertising, personal selling, and other forms of promotion to change the (B_i) values on these two evaluative criteria in a more favorable direction. Some of the procedures for changing beliefs, attitudes, and intentions are discussed in the following chapter.

One possible approach is to convince the consumer that he or she is using the wrong evaluative criteria. Here an attempt would be made to change the (a_i) rating for the two important attributes, and it was shown in the last chapter that this is a near impossibility for the business firm. That can be done most readily through consumer education.

Use of indexes of intentions

The use of aggregated indexes in forecasting sales was already mentioned. There also is much to be learned, however, from an analysis of the relationship between stated purchase intentions, measured either directly or through the extended Fishbein model, and actual purchase behavior.

Figure 15.4 presents hypothetical data summarizing the actual buying behavior of those who expressed an intention to purchase one of the three brands listed. Notice, for example, that only 40 percent of those intending to purchase brand A proceeded to make a purchase of any kind. Assuming that the product under consideration is an expensive durable good, lack of fulfillment of intentions is quite common because of changes in anticipated circumstances (income, etc.). But, in addition, 40 percent of those who planned on buying brand A actually switched brands, thus

Figure 15.4 Relationships between purchase intentions and purchasing behavior

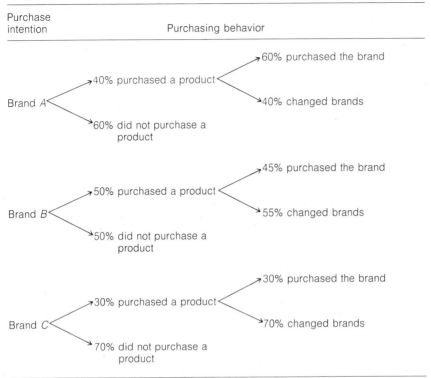

| Purchase intention | Purchasing behavior |

Brand *A*
- 40% purchased a product
  - 60% purchased the brand
  - 40% changed brands
- 60% did not purchase a product

Brand *B*
- 50% purchased a product
  - 45% purchased the brand
  - 55% changed brands
- 50% did not purchase a product

Brand *C*
- 30% purchased a product
  - 30% purchased the brand
  - 70% changed brands
- 70% did not purchase a product

Source: Adapted from Robert W. Pratt, Jr., "Understanding the Decision Process for Consumer Durable Goods: An Example of the Longitudinal Approach," in Peter D. Bennett, ed., *Marketing and Economic Development* (Chicago: American Marketing Association, 1965), pp. 244–60. Reprinted by permission.

indicating only a 24 percent actual fulfillment of original intentions (40% × 60%).

Figure 15.4 does not reveal the whole process, however, because it only shows the percentage of those who changed their intention and

Figure 15.5 Net gains and losses resulting from stated brand intentions

Stated brand intention	Number of consumers switching to the brand (listed at left) for each 100 switchings away from the brand	Net gain or loss (%)
Brand *A*	145.6	+45.6
Brand *B*	125.2	+25.2
Brand *C*	47.2	−52.8

Source: Adapted from Robert W. Pratt, Jr., "Understanding the Decision Process for Consumer Durable Goods: An Example of the Longitudinal Approach," in Peter D. Bennett, ed., *Marketing and Economic Development* (Chicago: American Marketing Association, 1965), pp. 244–60. Reprinted by permission.

purchased a different brand. Each of the three products suffers from a loss from stated intentions, especially brand C, which loses 70 percent of its potential market in the process. Figure 15.5 adds new light and shows which of three brands is making the greatest inroads into its competitors, based on erosion and shifts in intention rates. Brand A gained 1.45 customers for each intender who changes to an alternative, while brand B gained 1.25. Brand C, on the other hand, loses more than two intenders for each person who changes to C.

Overall it would appear that brand A has a more effective marketing program than its counterparts. Perhaps its superiority resides in distribution policy; size, location and attractiveness of displays; self-space allotment; point-of-purchase advertising; salesman influence; or other programs. By interviewing those who switched brands and by comparing the firm's marketing approach with that of competitors, it is possible to identify the reasons for these differences and to take needed remedial action.

The gap between academic and applied attitude research

Before concluding this chapter, it must be stated forthrightly that the popularity of the Fishbein type model has been confined by and large to academic ranks. The industrial applications, at least insofar as the published literature, have been few indeed.

Why does this gap exist? One possible reason simply lies in the fact that the expectancy-value, multiattribute models have to some degree become a fad of the 1970s. Much of the published research splits hairs to such a degree that those with a more applied interest quickly dismissed the output as irrelevant. In part this always will be a problem when the focus of one group lies more on basic research than does the other, but this is not a complete explanation.

It already has been pointed out that industry researchers have been greatly concerned over issues of methodological validity, and there have been some fairly notable breakthroughs in ability to predict behavior from modified attitude scales[70] or through such methods as multidimensional scaling[71] and conjoint analysis.[72] Industry researchers have quietly moved ahead on these fronts, and there has been less explicit interest in the Fishbein type of model. This may change, however, given the demonstrated utility of the extended Fishbein model.

It also should be noted that the gap may be more apparent than real. The authors have kept a foot in both camps, so to speak, for many years. Much of the research undertaken in the so-called "real world" is designed to measure evaluative criteria, assess the strengths and weaknesses of competitive alternatives in these terms, and to predict behavioral intentions. While there may be some differences in methods used, the basic

70 Axelrod, "Attitude Measurements."

71 Paul E. Green and Vithala R. Rao, *Applied Multidimensional Scaling: A Comparison of Approaches and Algorithms* (New York: Holt, Rinehart and Winston, 1972).

72 Herb Hupfer, "Conjoint Measurement—A Valuable Research Tool When Used Selectively," *Marketing Today*, vol. 14 (1976), p. 1 ff.

approach is often surprisingly similar to that suggested by Fishbein and others. The perspectives may differ, therefore, but the final outcomes have a high degree of similarity.

The only logical approach, in the final analysis, is to experiment with these models in industrial settings. Only then can there be a definitive evaluation of the extent to which existing methodology is improved. Hopefully this degree of cooperation will soon be forthcoming (see Chapter 21 for more suggestions).

Summary

This chapter examined an important phase of alternative evaluation: the formation and function of beliefs, attitudes, and intentions. It began with a historical perspective of the progress that has occurred in the years since the first edition of this book was published. Previously the nature of the relationship between attitudes and choice, if any, was an open question. But recent years have seen a concentration of research on the expectancy-value models pioneered by Rosenberg and Fishbein. Now it can be said with some certainty that attitudes predict intentions, which in turn will predict buying action, all things being equal. Attitudes are the outcome of beliefs, which state the probability that an alternative under consideration actually possesses the desired attributes specified by the evaluative criteria discussed in the preceding chapter.

It was shown that consumers form beliefs and attitudes through use of two different methods: (1) the compensatory strategy (failure of a brand or product to measure up to specifications on one attribute will be compensated by favorable ratings on others) and (2) the noncompensatory strategy (failure to measure up on an important attribute results in elimination of the brand from consideration). There are several variations in approach under each category.

Until recently, most attention was directed toward attitude toward an object (A_o). The models used for this purpose and some of the methodological and conceptual questions were analyzed. Deficiencies in the predictive power of the A_o model has led to widespread acceptance of the extended Fishbein model, which predicts buying intentions through a combination of attitude toward the act of purchasing a brand (A_{act}) plus the existence of normative social pressures and a motivation by the individual to comply. This model has resulted in much sharper predictive power, but it also was shown that predictions can be increased if specific account also is taken of anticipated circumstances. These factors then were combined in a model that is part of the consumer behavior model used in this book. The chapter concluded with a review of implications for marketing strategy.

Review and discussion questions

1. Consult five basic textbooks in introductory social psychology and list the definitions of attitude. What differences can you detect? Why do different authorities offer varying definitions of such a familiar concept?

2. What explanations can you give for the contradictory evidence in the literature until recently regarding the relationship of a change in attitude to a change in behavior? Is attitude change a valid marketing goal?

3. What are the relationships among evaluative criteria, beliefs, attitudes, and intentions?

4. Contrast the Rosenberg and Fishbein models of attitude toward an object (A_0). Are they really measuring the same thing as some authorities have contended? Or are there some basic differences?

5. Think of the last time you made a purchase that required some thought and contemplation. Did you use a compensatory or a noncompensatory strategy in arriving at your final judgment?

6. Ask a friend to think out loud regarding a recent purchase that also required some thought and contemplation. In effect you will be using a retroactive protocol method of research. Was the judgment strategy compensatory or noncompensatory? Can you be more specific and use such labels as expectancy-value, disjunctive, conjunctive, or lexicographic?

7. What are some of the reasons why measures of A_0 often are not very good predictors of both intention and purchase?

8. In what specific ways does Fishbein's extended model differ from his earlier model of A_0? In your estimation, is this an improvement or not?

9. Reviewing the camera purchasing example discussed in the text, why is it easier to change a (B_i) component than the (a_i) component? You may need to refer to the preceding chapter to answer this question with precision.

10. One leading New York advertising agency refuses to use attitude change as a criterion of advertising success or failure. Another agency uses *only* attitude change for this purpose. What reasons could be given for such a major difference?

11. A marketing research study undertaken for a major appliance manufacturer disclosed that 30 percent plan on purchasing a trash compactor in the next three months and 15 percent plan on purchasing a new iron. How much confidence should be placed in the predictive accuracy of these intention measurements? Are there differences in predictive accuracy between products? Why or why not?

CHAPTER 16

Changing beliefs and attitudes*

This chapter continues the emphasis of the preceding chapter on the implications of the expectancy-value models of belief and attitude. The fundamental underlying proposition is that a change in beliefs will lead to a change in attitude, which, in turn, is reflected in changed intentions and behavior, all other things being equal. The immediate purpose is to explore the literature on persuasion to discuss ways in which beliefs can be changed. Unfortunately, this literature is enormous, and some selectivity must be exercised. McGuire, for example, cited over 800 studies in his review of the evidence through 1967,[1] and Fishbein and Ajzen reviewed 790 articles published between 1968 and 1970.[2] The one redeeming factor is that the volume of relevant literature on attitude change dropped between January 1971 and December 1973 and in the years since that time as well. Kiesler and Munson concluded that persuasion and attitude change is not the thriving field it was at one time in the behavioral sciences, partly because of decline in popularity of the theory of cognitive dissonance and controversy over the nature of attitude itself.[3] Obviously they did not have the benefit of the recent research centering on the Fishbein and Rosenberg models, which, interestingly enough, has appeared more in the literature on consumer behavior than it has elsewhere.

*The authors continue to acknowledge the contribution of Dr. Brian Sternthal of Northwestern University in reviewing the literature and preparing this chapter for the second edition of this book. Many of his contributions are retained in this edition.

1 William J. McGuire, "The Nature of Attitudes and Attitude Change," in Gardner Lindsey and Eliot Arsonsen, eds., *Handbook of Social Psychology* (Reading, Mass.: Addison-Wesley, 1968), pp. 136–314.

2 Martin Fishbein and Icek Ajzen, "Attitudes and Opinions," in P. H. Mussen and M. R. Rosenzweig, eds., *Annual Review of Psychology,* vol. 23 (Palo Alto, Calif.: Annual Reviews, Inc., 1972), pp. 188–244.

3 Charles A. Kiesler and Paul A. Munson, "Attitudes and Opinions," in Rosenzweig and Lyman Porter, eds., *Annual Review of Psychology,* vol. 26, pp. 415–56.

The chapter begins with a discussion of the general strategies required to change beliefs and attitudes in the context of the expectancy-value models. This will provide needed conceptual understanding in the *message content*. Design and structure of appeals are considered later. The most important factor in this latter context is discrepancy between the beliefs of members of the target audience and the position advocated by the communicator. Then additional variations in message content and structure are reviewed, including such topics as the fear appeal, one-sided versus two-sided messages, and so on. Also it is necessary to touch briefly on whether there ever will be a definitive science of persuasion complete with rules and theorems. The chapter concludes with a discussion of postchoice attitude change.

General strategies to change beliefs and attitudes

The reader will recall that Fishbein's formula for either attitude toward an object (A_O) or attitude toward an act (A_{act}) is identical:

$$Attitude = \sum_{i=1}^{N} (B_i)(a_i)$$

where B refers to particular beliefs about a product and its attributes and/or performance in a particular situation, and "a" represents the individual's evaluation of the "goodness or badness" of those beliefs. Attitudes can be changed in three basic ways: (1) changing an existing B element;[4] (2) changing an existing "a" element; and (3) adding a new (B) (a) combination.[5] For purposes of simplicity the A_O model is used here as opposed to the more complex extended model.

Changing an existing "B" element

Let's return once again to the camera-buying example used in the previous chapter. The reader will recall that there were two important beliefs underlying attitudes, and brand x received an unfavorable evaluation:

Brand x does not require me to make my own settings for light and distance.

Probable _____ _____ _____ _____ __X__ _____ Improbable

Brand x works in such a way that I cannot overexpose or underexpose a picture.

Probable _____ _____ _____ _____ _____ __X__ Improbable

It was suggested that the first question always must be to verify whether or not consumer perceptions are true. If so, changes may be called for in product design. If they are not true, however, the company faces the

4 James L. Ginter, "An Experimental Investigation of Attitude Change in Choice of a New Brand," *Journal of Marketing Research*, vol. 11 (February 1974), pp. 30–40.

5 All three of these options were suggested by Lutz. See Richard J. Lutz, "Changing Brand Attitudes through Modification of Cognitive Structure," *Journal of Consumer Research*, vol. 1 (March 1975), pp. 49–59.

problem of remedying weakness in awareness on these important dimensions.

Here the goal would be to undertake a strategy with the objective of moving a large number of people in a more positive direction on both attributes. Usually it is possible to state such objectives in quantifiable terms. An example might be "to convince 60 percent of those in this market segment that brand x does not require them to make their own settings for light and distance." A similar goal might be set for the second attribute. Changes then would be detected by actually measuring the number of prospects rating these statements as being highly probable after the marketing strategy has been implemented.

This type of objective is quite common in advertising management.[6] It is based on the premise, first of all, that the attributes in question are salient to the individual. If not, it matters little whether movement in the desired direction occurs or not, because attitudes and behavior will remain unchanged. One of the authors once served as a consultant to a manufacturer of refrigerators. In that year, the only distinctive feature of this brand was "unexposed cooling coils." Unfortunately consumers did not care one way or another about this product feature. An advertising campaign might have been undertaken that successfully communicated this attribute, but it would represent utter waste.

Fishbein also points out that systems of beliefs are interrelated.[7] If you change one, you often will change another in an unexpected fashion. For instance, an advertiser might succeed in convincing a large part of the market that brand x is low in price. In so doing, however, this may lead to the conclusion that it also is low in quality. This can be avoided by awareness of the interrelationship between these attributes and stressing that low price does not mean low quality.

Changing an existing "a" element

The manufacturer in our camera example could perhaps examine the poor ratings on the belief statements and conclude that the best strategy is to tell prospects that it is wrong to purchase a fully automatic camera that prevents overexposure or underexposure. The message might read like this: "the really expert photographers always make their own settings. In that way, they know the picture is their own creation. Brand x allows you to achieve this high degree of fulfillment."

Such a strategy may completely overlook that evaluative criteria often have their roots in life style, and that they are a reflection of important motives. In this case the average prospect may, in effect, be manifesting real fear that he or she cannot operate a complex camera. In this case, such an appeal is likely to fall on deaf ears because of the difficulties any manufacturer faces in trying to change evaluative criteria. Usually they are strongly held and must be taken as a given.

6 For further discussion, see James F. Engel, Hugh G. Wales, and Martin R. Warshaw, *Promotional Strategy,* 3d ed. (Homewood, Ill.: Richard D. Irwin, Inc., 1975), chap. 9.

7 This is particularly stressed in Martin Fishbein, "Attitude, Attitude Change, and Behavior: A Theoretical Overview," in Philip Levine, ed., *Attitude Research Bridges the Atlantic* (Chicago: American Marketing Association, 1975), p. 9.

Adding a new (B) (a) combination

Another strategy could be to attempt to introduce an altogether new attribute in the hopes of increasing the overall attractiveness of the brand. This assumes, of course, that such benefits do, in fact, exist. One example might be to feature the company's brand of camera as having small size and lighter weight (see Figure 8.3 for an example). This may not have previously been a criterion used by the prospect, but it easily could be, especially if the messages stressed "automatic performance and fool proof pictures" as well as small size and light weight.

Maintenance of belief levels

A great deal of advertising and selling is undertaken simply to maintain present levels of consumer belief. This assumes a routine buying situation as opposed to the extended problem-solving example discussed above. Often this strategy is referred to as "share of mind." The hypothesis is that competitive advertising over time will erode present levels of awareness and belief if the company does not retain a rough parity in promotional expenditures. Brand switching does, in fact, occur, especially when loyalty levels are low. Therefore, there is some validity to this strategy. Unfortunately it can lead to such a level of repetitive clutter on the air waves that the noise problem referred to earlier reaches excessive levels. But, from the manufacturer's perspective, share of mind cannot be ignored. Perhaps the only solace to the over-saturated consumer is that this is one of the "wages" of a competitive system that must be endured if we also are to benefit from product innovation.

General principles of message content

Continuing with the camera-buying example, the manufacturer has two general goals: to convince prospective buyers that (1) the brand does not require the user to make settings for light and distance and (2) the brand works in such a way that it is impossible to overexpose or underexpose a picture. At the moment, the vast majority do not believe either of these facts to be true of brand x.

Now the issue is one of message content required to bring about the desired change in beliefs (and, of course, in attitude toward the brand, which will be the consequence of belief change). Assume that the primary issue for the moment is focused on the advertising campaign. Should the advertising aimed at these prospects clearly assert the superiority of the brand on these two attributes, hence making a frontal attack on beliefs? Or should a more moderate position be taken, with the expectation that beliefs will gradually change over time? The problem boils down to the degree of allowable *discrepancy* between the person's present beliefs and the content of the message. Two factors will now have to be weighed seriously: (1) the degree to which the prospect is ego involved in his or her beliefs and (2) the credibility of the company in the eyes of the market.

Ego involvement

A general principle of persuasion theory is that attitudes are more resistant to change when the object of the individual's attitudes and beliefs is anchored in his or her conception of self-worth. If this anchoring is strong, the attitude is said to have high *centrality*.

It has been stressed in earlier chapters that beliefs and attitudes toward most products and brands do not attain high centrality, in which case brand loyalty is not very high. Yet there are those instances, and the camera purchase is one, in which the decisions made are ego anchored.

Sherif and his colleagues discovered that involvement is indicated by the degree to which the individual will tolerate or accept a position that is different from his own along a scale of belief.[8] The range of positions felt to be acceptable is referred to as the *latitude of acceptance.* Conversely, the range of unacceptable belief statements is the *latitude of rejection*. Ego involvement is reflected by the degree to which the latitude of acceptance is very low and the latitude of rejection is large. In fact, ego involvement may be so high that the individual says, in effect, "nothing you say can change me." In that case the latitude of acceptance includes only the present belief, and all other possibilities are in the latitude of rejection.

To illustrate this somewhat abstract concept, one of the authors undertook a study of brand loyalty toward various brands of headache remedies. It was suspected that brand loyalty in this product category was undergirded by ego involvement. All possible brands were listed, and the consumer was first asked to indicate his or her preference. Then a hypothetical situation was presented. "Assuming this brand is not available, what other brands, if any, would you choose?" The number of acceptable brands mentioned constituted the latitude of acceptance. Respondents also were asked to choose those they considered to be unacceptable. This, of course, was the latitude of rejection. Some listed only their preferred brand and no other, thus indicating strong loyalty. Others were much more prone to use a variety of alternatives. By the way, actual brand choices were predicted quite accurately from this analysis. In other words, those with a narrow latitude of acceptance confined their choices to preferred brands and vice versa.

Evidence is increasingly verifying that the best strategy to stimulate belief change is to design the message in such a way that it falls at the outer edge of the latitude of acceptance.[9] If this latitude is exceeded, it is highly probable that the message will not be accepted and will be filtered out in information processing. It will take some skillful marketing research to discover just how great this level of discrepancy can be.

---

8 C. W. Sherif, M. Sherif and R. E. Nebergall, *Attitude and Attitude Change* (New Haven, Conn.: Yale University Press, 1961). For an alternate approach, see N. T. Hupfer and D. M. Gardner, "Differential Involvement with Products and Issues: An Exploratory Study," paper presented at the Association for Consumer Research (September 1971).

9 This is the fundamental tenet of belief change stressed in Martin Fishbein and Icek Ajzen, *Belief, Attitude, Intention, and Behavior: An Introduction to Theory and Research* (Reading, Mass.: Addison Wesley, 1975), chap. 11. Also see C. Insko, F. Murashima, and M. Saiyadain, "Communicator Discrepancy, Stimulus Ambiguity and Influence," *Journal of Personality*, vol. 34 (1966), pp. 52–66; H. Johnson, "Some Effects of Discrepancy Level on Responses to Negative Information about One's Self," *Sociometry*, vol. 29 (1966), pp. 52–66; J. Whittaker, "Opinion Change as a Function of Communication–Attitude Discrepancy," *Psychological Reports*, vol. 13 (1963), pp. 763–72.

About the only way it can be detected in a practical fashion is to design a series of messages ranging from a hard sell attack on beliefs to a much softer, perhaps testimony oriented, approach that makes the same points without being so blatant. Prospects then should be questioned on which they find to be most believable and acceptable.

What will tend to happen is that the various latitudes change over time. In other words, the consumer may be moved a position or two on the belief scale now. A new belief position is thus established, accompanied by a new set of latitudes. Then reexposure takes place, hopefully accompanied by another shift up to the limits of the latitude of acceptance and so on until the desired goal is achieved.

It is necessary to pause here and point out that there is a school of thought with roots in the theory of cognitive dissonance that attitude change is a linear function of the extent of discrepancy between the individual's position and message content.[10] In other words, the more the message deviates, the greater the probability of change in the desired direction. It is now generally recognized, however, that this principle *only* holds true under conditions of low ego involvement.[11]

The reader no doubt has sensed the real difficulties that will be faced in changing a negative attitude that has high centrality. Figure 16.1 may help to make the implications more apparent. Notice that we now have introduced another factor—the *latitude of noncommitment.* Common sense will indicate that usually there is likely to be a range of positions lying between acceptance and rejection, especially when centrality is low.

Figure 16.1 The effect of latitudes of acceptance and rejection on the probability of change in beliefs and attitudes

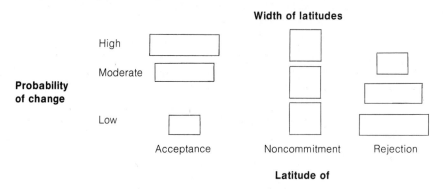

10 See, for example, S. Goldberg, "Three Situational Determinants of Conformity to Social Norms," *Journal of Abnormal and Social Psychology,* vol. 49 (1964), pp. 325–29; H. Helson, R. Blake, and J. Mouton, "An Experimental Investigation of the 'Big Lie' in Shifting Attitudes," *Journal of Social Psychology,* vol. 48 (1958), pp. 51–60; R. Tuddenham, "The Influence of a Distorted Group Norm upon Influential Judgment," *Journal of Psychology,* vol. 46 (1956), pp. 227–41; P. Zimbardo, "Involvement and Communication Discrepancy as Determinants of Opinion Conformity," *Journal of Abnormal and Social Psychology,* vol. 60 (1960), pp. 86–94.

11 For a pertinent illustration, see Frederick W. F. Winter, "A Laboratory Experiment of Individual Attitude Response to Advertising Exposure," *Journal of Marketing Research,* vol. 10 (May 1973), pp. 130–40.

The probability of change is shown as a function of the size of these three latitudes.

All things being equal, people with a negative attitude accompanied by a narrow latitude of acceptance (indicating high centrality) are poor prospects. Whenever possible, efforts should concentrate on those who show the highest probability of change. The likelihood of profitable return on substantial marketing investment directed toward the former group is too low. In effect, this type of thinking is the root principle of market segmentation—"fish where the fishing is good."

It should be pointed out, by the way, that the discussion thus far has assumed that primary use will be made of the mass media. A negatively disposed prospect can be changed much more readily through personal selling. In fact, one of the attributes of a good sales person is ability to detect the limits of the latitude of acceptance and work skillfully up to that point by countering objections and stressing product strong points. Beliefs frequently will change in a tangible manner right on the spot as the sales person keeps moving toward the objective. The key, of course, is the opportunity for feedback and interaction provided by the face-to-face communication situation.

Source credibility

It also has been found that there can be a greater discrepancy between a prospect's present belief position and message if the source is perceived as being credible.[12] In other words, people seem to place greater confidence in a trustworthy source and hence are more receptive to what is said, even when there is a substantial deviation from their own position. Similarly, there is a marked reduction in willingness to accept a discrepant message when the source is of moderate or low credibility.

The moderating effect of source credibility has distinct managerial significance. It is quite difficult to make an advertisement credible when it is obvious that the whole intent of the message is to persuade. The recipient generally recognizes that the source is anything but impartial and unbiased. Therefore, a message that deviates substantially from the recipient's own position is likely to be screened out as he or she processes the stimulus. Given this relationship it becomes necessary to predict the boundary of acceptable discrepancy, but attempts to predict this point have repeatedly failed to date.[13]

Admittedly much in this area is pure speculation not based on research undertaken under natural field conditions using commercial messages as the variable. Nevertheless, the importance of impartiality is verified. Undoubtedly the image of certain commercial spokesmen is largely attributable to this type of reputation. Arthur Godfrey, for example, was often mentioned as a credible source who would not recommend a product that did not perform as claimed. Spokesmen who capitalize upon credibility, however, are infrequent in the mass media.

12 This literature is thoroughly reviewed in Brian Sternthal, "Persuasion and the Mass Communication Process," unpublished doctoral diss. (Columbus, Ohio: Ohio State University, 1972), chap. 4.

13 See, for example, H. Johnson and I. Steiner, "The Effects of Source on Reponses to Negative Information about One's Self," *Journal of Social Psychology*, vol. 74 (1968), pp. 215–24.

It is interesting to speculate regarding the extent to which salespersons are perceived as being expert and trustworthy—the essential requirements of credibility. It would seem that most consumers feel that the salesperson has a high intent to persuade and thus would show a strong reaction against what he or she has to say. Nevertheless, a properly trained salesperson can serve as a valuable source of information, and there is no reason why credibility cannot be improved in personal selling situations. Unfortunately this point is often overlooked, especially by retailers, and sales staffs are not properly trained to become a credible source.

Implications

It now seems apparent that the effects of message discrepancy on attitude change are moderated by source credibility and ego involvement. Two recent studies that manipulated both of these moderating variables confirmed this conclusion.[14] In each instance highly involved subjects changed their attitude significantly less upon exposure to a discrepant message than did those who were less involved, and there was a greater tendency for this group to disparage the communication source.

Given that marketing communications usually are not perceived as highly credible, the message should deviate from the attitude position of members of the target audience only to a small extent. Attitude change is best achieved by successive exposures, each of which encompasses only small discrepancy. This generalization is especially critical when recipients' attitudes are based on ego involvement.

Variations in message content and structure

The remainder of the chapter focuses selectively on the vast literature of persuasion. It should be noted at the outset that not all of these studies pertain to attitude change per se. Rather, the intent has been to clarify various stages of the communication process itself, which, as the reader will recall, fall into four broad categories: (1) exposure; (2) attention; (3) reception; and (4) response. Attitude change, in turn, is just one type of response. Moreover, it makes little sense to analyze attitude change and disregard the earlier steps, all of which are part of one process.

The first part of this section looks at several broad categories of studies on variations in message content: (1) fear appeals, (2) humor; (3) drawing a conclusion; (4) distraction; and (5) nonovert appeals. Then discussion shifts to another major consideration in communication strategy—manipulation of such structural factors as one-sided versus two-sided messages, order of presentation, degree of internal structure, and repetition.

14 H. Johnson and J. Scileppi, "Effects of Ego-Involvement Conditions on Attitude Change to High and Low Credibility Communicators," *Journal of Personality and Social Psychology,* vol. 13 (1969), pp. 31–36; K. Sereno, "Ego-Involvement, High Source Credibility and Response to a Belief-Discrepant Communication," *Speech Monographs,* vol. 35 (1968), pp. 476–481.

The fear appeal. A study undertaken in 1953 by Janis and Feshbach indicated that a communication stressing the unfavorable physical consequences (fear) of not taking the suggested course of action can have an adverse effect on attitude if this fear appeal is too intense.[15] This negative relationship between fear arousal and persuasion was confirmed in several subsequent investigations undertaken between 1953 and 1963,[16] with the result that fear appeals were used only in such isolated instances as promotion of medical products and sale of life insurance.[17] More than 100 studies have been undertaken since 1953, however, and the great majority contradict the early findings and show a positive relationship between fear and persuasion.[18] In fact, of 16 relevant experiments undertaken between 1965 and 1971, all reported positive findings.[19] Not surprisingly, Ray and Wilkie concluded that marketers have neglected a promising area of inquiry.[20]

(1) The effect of source credibility. It now appears that an increased threat of physical consequences enhances a persuasion only when credibility of the source is high.[21] When this is not the case, counter argumentation seems to be generated, with the outcome that the source is rejected as being biased.

It has been stressed earlier that the credibility of advertising, in general, is not high. This fact, in itself, should be a warning light to those who would use this type of appeal indiscriminately. Furthermore, there are wide variations in credibility between manufacturers. The credibility of both medium and communicator must be established, therefore, before serious consideration is given to this type of strategy.

(2) Type of fear. Almost without exception, the published studies have centered on threats of physical consequences. Thus marketing applications are pretty much limited to those purchase situations in which physical fear is a potential motivator. Yet, social disapproval can be an even more powerful motivation, but only one study has examined the consequences of fear of disapproval.[22] The findings were that threat of

---

15 I. L. Janis and S. Feshbach, "Effects of Fear-Arousing Communication," *Journal of Abnormal and Social Psychology,* vol. 48 (1953), pp. 78–92.

16 See, for example, I. L. Janis and R. Terwilliger, "An Experimental Study of Psychological Resistance to Fear Arousing Communications," *Journal of Abnormal and Social Psychology,* vol. 65 (1962), pp. 403–10.

17 J. Stuteville, "Psychic Defenses against High Fear Appeals: A Key Marketing Variable," *Journal of Marketing,* vol. 34 (1970), pp. 39–45.

18 There have been a number of literature reviews. See K. Higbee, "Fifteen Years of Fear Arousal: Research on Threat Appeals: 1953–1968," *Psychological Bulletin,* vol. 72 (1969), pp. 426–44; I. Janis, *The Contours of Fear* (New York: Wiley, 1968); H. Leventhal, "Findings and Theory in the Study of Fear Communications," in L. Berkowitz, ed., *Advances in Experimental Social Psychology,* vol. 5 (New York: Academic Press, 1970), pp. 119–86; W. McGuire, "Nature of Attitudes"; and Brian Sternthal and C. Samuel Craig, "Fear Appeals: Revisited and Revised," *Journal of Consumer Research,* vol. 1 (December 1974), pp. 22–34.

19 Sternthal, "Persuasion," chap. 5.

20 M. Ray and W. Wilkie, "Fear: The Potential of an Appeal Neglected by Marketing," *Journal of Marketing,* vol. 34 (1970), pp. 59–62.

21 These studies are reviewed in Sternthal, "Persuasion," chap. 5.

22 Ray and Wilkie, "Fear."

disapproval is even more persuasive than a promise of social approval. This clearly warrants further investigation.

(3) The need for further research.[23] While there is merit in considering use of this type of message in appropriate situations, caution must be exercised in generalizing too extensively from published evidence to date. First, the range of topics investigated has been quite narrow, encompassing mainly such issues as health and politics. Furthermore, most investigations have employed only two levels of fear (referred to variously as "minimal-high," "weak-strong," and so on), and there is no confirmation that the full range of fear has been explored. Finally, the effects of temporal delay on response should be investigated more fully. It is quite possible that different results will be achieved through the passage of time.

Humor. At one point in time, particularly during the 1950s and 1960s, there was a tendency to avoid the use of humor on the pretext that it can quickly overwhelm the product message and fail to achieve creative objectives.[24] While this is always a possibility, it has been used much more frequently in recent years. In fact a content analysis of 2,000 television commercials discovered that 15 percent made use of humorous appeals, especially in the form of animation.[25] Some of today's great product successes arrived in a dominant market position through humor; most North American readers will quickly identify these product themes:

"With a Name Like Smucker's . . ."

"Flick of My Bic . . ."

"Please Don't Squeeze the Charmin . . ."

"Butter . . . Parkay . . ."

"The Noisiest Potato Chip in the World . . ."

Sternthal and Craig reviewed the literature on the role of humor in persuasion and concluded that humorous messages particularly excel in terms of attention attraction.[26] Furthermore, humor can serve to enhance source credibility, something the advertiser certainly can benefit from.

More can be learned from the study of the effectiveness of 40 different factors in television commercial content and execution.[27] Humor appeals

23 For a more extensive discussion see Sternthal and Craig, "Fear Appeals."

24 David Ogilvy, "Raise Your Sights! 97 Tips for Copywriters, Art Directors and TV Producers—Mostly Derived from Research" (internal publication, Ogilvy & Mather, Inc.).

25 J. Patrick Kelly and Paul J. Solomon, "Humor in Television Advertising," *Journal of Advertising,* vol. 4 (Summer 1975), pp. 31–35.

26 Brian Sternthal and C. Samuel Craig, "Humor in Advertising," *Journal of Marketing,* vol. 37 (October 1973), pp. 12–18.

27 Harold L. Ross, Jr., "How to Create Effective Humorous Commercials, Yielding above Average Brand Preference Changes," *Marketing News* (March 26, 1976), p. 4.

can produce above average change in brand preference if these precautions are observed:[28]

1. The brand must be identified in the opening 10 seconds, or there is the real danger that humor can inhibit recall of important selling points.[29]

2. The type of humor makes a difference. Subtlety is more effective than the bizarre.

3. The humor must be relevant to the brand or key idea. Recall and persuasion both are diminished when there is not this linkage. An example of especially effective strategy in this sense is Life cereal's "Mikey" in Figure 16.2. Most readers will recall the two kids who said, in effect, that a "cereal which is good for you can't taste good. Let's try it on Mikey. Hey! Mikey, *he likes it*!"

Figure 16.2 Life cereal's "Mikey."
An example of humor integrated with the main selling point

Source: Courtesy of the Quaker Oats Company.

28 Ross, "How to Create."
29 This danger also was found by Sternthal and Craig, "Humor in Advertising."

4. Humorous commercials that entertain by belittling the potential user usually do not perform well. A better strategy is to make light of the brand, the situation, or the subject matter.

Drawing a conclusion. In recent years, growing use has been made of what some now refer to as *cool commercials*.[30] A cool message is unstructured; the viewer is told a fragment of the story or impressions are invoked so that he or she must fill in from his or her own imagination (see Figure

Figure 16.3 A cool commercial

Courtesy of the Dr Pepper Company and Young & Rubicam of New York, New York.

30 The authors are indebted here to Bill Taylor of Ogilvy & Mather, Inc.

16.3). The hot message, on the other hand, is more structured and tells a complete story logically and sequentially, with a definite conclusion stated (see Figure 16.4).

Figure 16.4 A hot commercial

1. GRANDMOTHER: Helen, what are you doing to my grandson...
2. what's this blue stuff?
3. HELEN: It's Aim, Mother. A new toothpaste. You probably haven't heard about it yet.
4. GRANDMOTHER: Yeah. What about stannous fluoride? You know little Billy is cavity-prone...
5. just as you were. HELEN: But Aim has stannous fluoride.
6. GRANDMOTHER: But so has the toothpaste we always used.
7. HELEN: That toothpaste has been around since I was a girl!
8. GRANDMOTHER: If it was good enough for you...
9. HELEN: Mother. Aim is a gel. It tastes better. GRANDMOTHER: Oooo, it looks funny.
10. HELEN: (VO) And this gel spreads that good taste faster...
11. spreads faster than paste in the normal brushing time.
12. Aim is low in abrasion, too.
13. BILLY: And I like it. It tastes good.
14. HELEN: And he likes it, Mother.
15. GRANDMOTHER: Well, I don't know...
16. HELEN: Oh Mother. Aim is new. It's got stannous fluoride. It's low in abrasion.
17. And Billy likes it.
18. GRANDMOTHER: Well, if he likes it, he might brush longer.
19. ANNCR: (VO) If your children are in the cavity-prone years, have them brush often...see the dentist
20. regularly...and take Aim against cavities!

Courtesy of Lever Brothers Company.

From the results of a number of communication studies, the unstructured approach of the cool commercial would appear to be ineffective. This is because experimental research has determined repeatedly that explicit conclusion-drawing is more persuasive than allowing the audience to draw its own conclusions.[31] Presumably the audience is not sufficiently motivated or intelligent enough to draw conclusions on its own.

There is contradictory evidence, however, that the message that states a conclusion only implicitly *over time* approaches the structured message in persuasive impact.[32] When the audience is highly intelligent or motivated, this approach may be particularly effective. As Brehm has pointed out, many people seem to react negatively when a conclusion is stated and feel that an attempt is being made to influence and thereby limit their freedom of choice. When this is the reaction a boomerang effect can occur in the form of solidification of initial opinion.[33]

Given that the net persuasive effect of explicit versus implicit conclusion drawing does not appear to differ, the choice between the two approaches must be resolved on the basis of other considerations.[34] The cool commercial, for example, appears to be used more appropriately to build a long-range image. Also it is effective when a product has no apparent advantage; when competitors are running hot commercials; and when the basic product appeal is primarily emotional rather than logical (as is the case with cosmetics, for example).

Distraction. People counterargue with a message that contradicts their present attitudes, and change is impeded. Therefore, any strategy that serves to interfere with or reduce counterargumentation is worthy of consideration from the perspective of ensuring correct comprehension. The potential for deception and consumer manipulation is high, however, and the authors would be hard put to defend such a strategy from an ethical point of view.

There is some evidence that counterargumentation can be reduced if distraction of some type is introduced during exposure.[35] This can be done through the use of humor, for example.[36] Or competing stimuli such

31 E. Cooper and H. Dinerman, "Analysis of the Film 'Don't Be a Sucker': A Study of Communication," *Public Opinion Quarterly,* vol. 15 (1951), pp. 243–64; B. Fine, "Conclusion-Drawing, Communicator Credibility and Anxiety as Factors in Opinion Change," *Journal of Abnormal and Social Psychology,* vol. 54 (1957), pp. 369–74; H. Hadley, "The Non-Directive Approach in Advertising Appeals," *Journal of Applied Psychology,* vol. 37 (1963), pp. 496–98; C. Hovland and W. Mandell, "An Experimental Comparison of Conclusion-Drawing by the Communicator and by the Audience," *Journal of Abnormal and Social Psychology,* vol. 47 (1952), pp. 581–88; N. Maier and R. Maier, "An Experimental Test of the Effects of 'Developmental' versus 'Free' Discussion on the Quality of Group Decisions," *Journal of Applied Psychology,* vol. 4 (1957), pp. 320–23; and "Ads without Answers Make the Brain Itch," *Psychology Today,* vol. 9 (November 1975), p. 78.

32 A. Cohen, *Attitude Change and Social Influence* (New York: Basic Books, 1964), p. 10; W. McGuire, "A Syllogistic Analysis of Cognitive Relationships," in C. Hovland and M. Rosenberg, eds., *Attitude Organization and Change* (New Haven, Conn.: Yale University Press, 1960); E. Stotland, D. Katz and M. Patchen, "The Reduction of Prejudice through the Arousal of Self-Insight," *Journal of Personality,* vol. 27 (1959), pp. 507–53.

33 Jack W. Brehm, *A Theory of Psychological Reactance* (New York: Academic Press, 1966), chap. 6.

34 Engel, Wales, and Warshaw, *Promotional Strategy,* p. 317.

35 J. Allyn and L. Festinger, "The Effectiveness of Unanticipated Persuasive Communications," *Journal of Abnormal and Social Psychology,* vol. 62 (1961), pp. 35–40; L. Festinger and N. Maccoby, "On Resistance to Persuasive Communications," *Journal of Abnormal and Social Psychology,* vol. 68 (1964), pp. 359–366; J. L. Freedman and D. O. Sears, "Warning, Distraction, and Resistance to Influence," *Journal of Personality and Social Psychology,* vol. 1 (1965), pp. 262–266.

36 Sternthal and Craig, "Humor in Advertising."

as background music or noise might be utilized.[37] Unfortunately, experiments conducted under varying conditions of distraction in an advertising context show that distraction also can reduce attention and reception and thereby overpower any positive effect on attitude itself.[38]

From the studies to date distraction would appear to be a possible strategy under circumstances in which the recipient is committed to attitude and hence resists change.[39] Counterarguing apparently can be reduced through this means, although this has not been conclusively demonstrated. Brand attitudes, however, seldom attain this degree of commitment; hence counterargumentation is less likely to occur. Therefore, distraction may only serve to inhibit attention and comprehension. The deliberate manipulation of distraction in a marketing context thus appears to be unwarranted unless attitudes to be changed are based on ego involvement (commitment).

Nonovert appeals. Walster and Festinger reported success in producing changes under conditions in which recipients felt they were "overhearing" a message.[40] Presumably it was felt that those who were speaking were making no conscious attempt to persuade. This may suggest that the "slice of life" commercial,[41] ostensibly showing real-life situations with ordinary people who normally would not be commercial spokesmen, stands a better chance of success than a more overt attempt to persuade. This hypothesis, however, can only be tentative, because the Walster and Festinger study did not possess the degree of experimental control normally required for verified findings.

One-sided versus two-sided messages. In a variety of studies undertaken in a noncommercial context, it has been found that a two-sided message (that is, information and persuasive arguments favorable and unfavorable to the advocated position are contained in the message) induces more attitude change than a one-sided appeal. In a widely quoted study, Hovland and others reported the following findings:[42]

Use of structural variables

1. Giving both sides produced greatest attitude change in those instances where individuals were initially opposed to the point of view advocated.

37 In an unpublished study undertaken as part of the research program in consumer decision making at the Ohio State University in 1966 it was found that distraction in the form of varied background music enhanced attitude change.

38 M. Venkatesan and C. A. Haaland, "The Effect of Distraction on the Influence of Persuasive Marketing Communications," in J. Arndt, ed., *Insights into Consumer Behavior* (Boston: Allyn and Bacon, 1968), pp. 55–66; D. M. Gardner, "The Distraction Hypothesis in Marketing," *Journal of Advertising Research,* vol. 10 (1970), pp. 25–30; S. W. Bither, "Effects of Distraction and Commitment on the Persuasiveness of Television Advertising," *Journal of Marketing Research* (1972), pp. 1–5.

39 Bither's results would suggest this conclusion, but his data are far from definitive.

40 E. Walster and L. Festinger, "The Effectiveness of 'Overheard' Persuasive Communications," *Journal of Abnormal and Social Psychology*, vol. 65 (1962), pp. 395–402.

41 Kenneth Roman and Jane Maas, *How to Advertise* (New York: St. Martin's Press, 1976), pp. 23–24.

42 C. I. Hovland, A. A. Lumsdaine, and F. D. Sheffield, *Experiments on Mass Communication*, vol. 3 (Princeton, N.J.: Princeton University Press, 1948), chap. 8.

2. For those convinced of the main argument, presentation of the other side was ineffective.

3. Those with higher education were most affected when both sides were presented.

More recent evidence documents that the two-sided appeal may have a positive effect on perceived source credibility. Walster and others, for example, showed that presentation of both pro and con arguments appeared to increase audience perception of source credibility sufficiently to allow for successful utilization of a widely discrepant communication message.[43] Similar results were reported by Chu, who also found that the one-sided message induced significantly more counterargumentation than a two-sided version.[44]

While it may appear that advertisers never could capitalize upon these findings, Faison suggests that such a conclusion is premature.[45] He presented both favorable and unfavorable product attributes in advertisements for automobiles, ranges, and floor waxes. The influence of the two-sided appeal was significantly greater, and this suggests a previously overlooked way to increase promotional effectiveness. It might be quite a task, however, to convince a manufacturer that his advertising campaign also should mention product flaws.

It is interesting to point out that the policy of corrective advertising instituted by the Federal Trade Commission in 1971 may have some unintended effects. The basic premise is that manufacturers should be required to admit blame publicly in their advertisements once they have been found guilty of false and misleading appeals. This admission in a certain percentage of its future messages presumably will serve to offset past misleading efforts, and there is evidence that counteradvertising works in this way.[46] The opposite also can happen, however, in that the admission of blame will enhance the present credibility of the advertiser in the consumer's eyes and hence increase promotional effectiveness. This, of course, would be contrary to the result intended by the Federal Trade Commission.

Order of presentation. There now is a considerable body of evidence on the subject of the order in which dominant appeals should be presented. This assumes, of course, that there are two or more main arguments either related to each other or pro and con. Some say that the argument presented first will prove to be most effective (*primary*), whereas others

43 E. Walster, E. Aronson, and D. Abrahams, "On Increasing the Persuasiveness of a Low Prestige Communicator," *Journal of Experimental Social Psychology*, vol. 2 (1966), pp. 325–42.

44 G. Chu, "Prior Familiarity, Perceived Bias, and One-Sided versus Two-Sided Communications," *Journal of Experimental Social Psychology*, vol. 3 (1967), pp. 243–54.

45 E. W. Faison, "Effectiveness of One-Sided and Two-Sided Mass Communications in Advertising," *Public Opinion Quarterly*, vol. 25 (1961), pp. 468–69.

46 H. T. Hunt, "Measuring the Impact and Effectiveness of Counter Messages" (Conference on Advertising and the Public Interest, American Marketing Association, May 1973); and Michael B. Mazis and Janice E. Adkinson, "An Experimental Evaluation of a Proposed Corrective Advertising Remedy," *Journal of Marketing Research*, vol. 13 (May 1976), pp. 178–83.

say that the most recently presented argument will dominate (*recency*). Research investigations have focused both on the order of two-sided appeals as well as the order of major arguments in a one-sided message.

(1) Two-sided appeals. The available evidence of order of presentation of two-sided appeals presents an equivocal picture. Roughly equal numbers of studies report primacy, recency, or no significant order effect.[47] Attempts to explain these wide differences to date have been unfruitful, with the result that no firm generalizations can be advanced.

(2) One-sided appeals. Should the strongest argument in a commercial message be presented first or last? Again the empirical evidence is contradictory. Although one experimenter reports that presentation of the strong argument first is most effective,[48] the majority of published studies report no differences whatsoever.[49]

While there is no empirical resolution of the question at this point in time, there are some logical guidelines for strategy. First, initial presentation of the strongest argument may have a stronger effect on attention attraction and receptiveness to subsequent arguments. Moreover, material presented first usually is best learned.[50] On the other hand, presentation of successively weaker arguments may tend to diminish the overall persuasive effect of the message. Therefore, saving the strongest arguments for last may boost reception when it is most needed.

Repetition. The benefit of repetition is a fundamental tenet of learning theory. Most authorities agree that repetition of a persuasive message generally is beneficial. It is argued that preceding advertisements may have made too weak an impression to stimulate much buying interest. Later ads, then, can be effective in strengthening weak impressions, with the result that a prospect's disposition to think and act favorably is enhanced.

In addition, markets are not static; people continually enter and leave. Therefore, a repeated message will reach new prospects. If this fact is overlooked a firm can quickly experience erosion of its market share as loyal buyers diminish.

Once one goes beyond a general agreement on the benefits, the issues become less clear. What effect does multiple exposure have on each stage of the communication process? Can repetition be overdone to the point that a reverse or boomerang effect occurs? In short, decision makers perceive an acute need for knowledge of the effects of repeated messages,

---

47 This evidence is reviewed in Sternthal, "Persuasion," chap. 8.

48 H. Sponberg, "A Study of the Relative Effectiveness of Climax and Anti-Climax Order in an Argumentative Speech," *Speech Monographs,* vol. 13 (1946), pp. 35–44.

49 H. Gilkinson, S. Paulson, and D. Sikkink, "Effects of Order and Authority in an Argumentative Speech," *Quarterly Journal of Speech,* vol. 40 (1954), pp. 183–92; H. Gulley and D. Berlo, "Effect of Intercellular and Intracellular Speech Structure on Attitude Change and Learning," *Speech Monographs,* vol. 23 (1956), pp. 288–97.

50 Sternthal, "Persuasion," chap 8.

but available evidence is inconclusive. Nevertheless, some tentative generalizations are possible.

(1) The manner in which repetition functions. Mitchell and Olson advanced some hypotheses on the role of repetition, which are quite consistent with the general perspective of this book:[51]

1. Due to situational distractions or because of message complexity, it may be necessary to repeat a message a number of times before information is completely processed.

2. Information is moved from short-term memory into long-term memory through repetition, which enhances cognitive rehearsal.

3. Repetition creates a new belief linking attribute and brand, which in turn functions to change attitude.

4. The continued pairing of an attribute and a brand through repetition increases strength of belief.

5. Repetition reduces or stops forgetting by continually activating the process of information retrieval from long-term memory.

(2) Effects of repetition on awareness and reception. There is extensive evidence that a repeated message, all things being equal, increases awareness and comprehension.[52] The following are representative findings:

1. The NBC Hofstra study in 1951 showed that the percentage of television set owners recalling a brand's advertising went from 33 to 65 percent as cumulative viewing minutes increased from 2 to 20.[53]

2. Spontaneous awareness of the name Tyrex (a type of tire cord) was exhibited by 20 percent of those not exposed to spot television advertisements, by 65 percent of viewers, and by 92 percent of those viewing three or more commercials.[54]

3. An advertised brand was mentioned by 15.2 percent of those interviewed prior to an advertising campaign in *Post* magazine; after one exposure the brand came to mind to 18.1 percent; and the percentage of awareness increased to 20.7 percent following two exposures.[55]

4. A McGraw-Hill study in 1961 covered a six-year campaign period,

---

51 Andrew A. Mitchell and Jerry C. Olson, "Cognitive Effects of Advertising Repetition" (Working Paper no. 49, College of Business Administration, Pennsylvania State University, October 1976).

52 This is demonstrated conclusively in Sawyer's review of over 200 published studies. See Alan G. Sawyer, "The Effects of Repetition: Conclusions and Suggestions about Experimental Laboratory Research" (paper presented at the Workshop on Consumer Information Processing, University of Chicago, November 1972).

53 "Frequency in Broadcast Advertising: 1," *Media/scope* (February 1962).

54 "Frequency in Broadcast Advertising: 1," *Media/scope* (February 1962).

55 "Frequency in Print Advertising: 1," *Media/scope* (April 1962).

and it was reported that recognition of the company name increased from 34 percent in 1955 to 44 percent in 1957. Then advertising was ceased, and name recognition slumped to 31 percent by 1960.[56]

5. In a similar study it was reported that recognition of the brand name Eversharp increased from 15 to 38 percent after only five months of advertising. Then the campaign was ceased for two months and recognition slumped to 29 percent. It was then reinstated, and it took 10 months to bring awareness up to 36 percent.[57]

In one of the most definitive investigations in the published literature, Stewart found that considerable repetition is necessary if high brand awareness is to be achieved, and the prime benefit of repeated advertising for a well-known brand is to sustain awareness.[58] In more detail:

1. Advertising causes a rapid initial rise in awareness and then levels off in its effects. While repeat messages sustain awareness, it tends to fall once promotion is stopped.

2. At least 15 consecutive exposures are needed to produce the lowest costs in terms of attracting additional prospects per dollar of advertising. Only three or four insertions proved to be inefficient.

3. One of the two products studied was a failure primarily because of the content of the advertising and the product itself rather than the duration of repetition.

It also must be stressed, however, that increased frequency tends to result in diminishing returns per exposure, due, in part, to the large effects of initial exposures on cognitive measures.[59] This can lead to a significant loss of meaning referred to as *semantic satiation*.[60] Satiation was first discovered when the meaning of a familiar monosyllabic noun repeated aloud for several seconds dropped away.[61] More recently it was found that the meaning of a stimulus word as measured by an attitude scale disappears with repetition.[62]

The explanation for satiation seems to be that continuous repetition calls into effect various associations with the meaning of a stimulus that sooner or later no longer are elicited. In fact, these associations (an

56 "Recognition Increased with Advertising . . . Dropped When Advertising Stopped" (New York: McGraw-Hill Advertising Laboratory Publication, May 1961).

57 E. Pomerance and H. A. Zielske, "How Frequently Should You Advertise?" *Media/scope* (September 1958), pp. 25–27.

58 J. B. Stewart, *Repetitive Advertising in Newspapers: A Study of Two New Products* (Boston: Harvard Business School, 1964).

59 Sawyer, "Effects of Repetition," p. 10.

60 Harriett Amster, "Semantic Satiation and Generation: Learning? Adaptation?" *Psychological Bulletin*, vol. 62 (1964), pp. 273–86; D. E. P. Smith and A. L. Raygor, "Verbal Satiation and Personality," *Journal of Abnormal and Social Psychology*, vol. 52 (1956), pp. 323–26.

61 M. F. Basette and C. J. Warne, "On the Lapse of Verbal Meaning with Repetition," *American Journal of Psychology*, vol. 30 (1919), pp. 415–18.

62 W. E. Lambert and L. A. Jakobovits, "Verbal Satiation and Changes in the Intensity of Meaning," *Journal of Experimental Psychology*, vol. 60 (1960), pp. 376–83.

association between pride of appearance and a brand of clothing, for example) become reduced or suppressed.[63] That this can occur in advertising was shown by Capitman.[64] As further evidence, the competitive preference scores for various commercials analyzed by the Schwerin Research Corporation generally were lower on the second test.[65] In addition Grass found that a satiation pattern emerges upon repetition in which attention is maximized at two to four exposures and is followed by a decline as the total number of exposures increases.[66] He observed a similar effect on extent of learning, but attitude formation and change do not seem to satiate in the same manner.

(3) Effects of repetition on changes in beliefs and attitudes. In his definitive literature review, Sawyer reports that repetition can result in increased liking for a repeated stimulus.[67] To a lesser extent, repetition may result in a more positive attitude, but it also is possible that there will be no effect whatsoever or even a negative effect over time.

On the favorable side, Zajonc marshalled data from a variety of published research studies, most of which are only indirectly related to the subject under consideration; his conclusion was that "mere exposure" (that is, repeated exposure) is a sufficient condition for attitude modification and change.[68] Since most of the data he cited traditionally have not been considered as pertinent to an understanding of repetition, this conclusion must be accepted only as tentative. More recently, it was demonstrated that overexposure can lead to a boomerang effect in which the initial effects on attitudes are largely offset by diminution.[69]

More definitive positive evidence is provided by several published studies. It is reported, for example, that positive evaluations toward a brand increased from 29.2 percent prior to advertising exposure to 38.2 percent after two exposures.[70] Similarly, the findings from the Schwerin Research Corporation indicate that repetition helps a strong campaign,[71] Gardner reports that successive repetition causes the audience to move in the direction intended by the message;[72] the Grey Advertising Agency found that frequent exposure to television shows carrying a brand's advertising is reflected in a higher attitude level and in a greater likelihood

---

63 L. A. Jakobovits and W. E. Lambert, "Stimulus Characteristics as Determinants of Semantic Changes with Repeated Presentation," *American Journal of Psychology*, vol. 77 (1964), pp. 84–92.

64 "Frequency in Broadcast Advertising: 2," *Media/scope* (March 1962).

65 Personal communication from a Schwerin user to one of the authors.

66 R. C. Grass, "Satiation Effects of Advertising," in *Proceedings of the 14th Annual Conference of the Advertising Research Foundation* (New York: Advertising Research Foundation, 1968), pp. 20–28.

67 Sawyer, "Effects of Repetition," p. 17.

68 R. Zajonc, "The Attitudinal Effects of Mere Exposure," *Journal of Personality and Social Psychology*, monograph supplement, vol. 9 (1968), pp. 1–27.

69 Richard L. Miller, "Mere Exposure, Psychological Reactance and Attitude Change," *Public Opinion Quarterly*, vol. 40 (1976), pp. 229–33.

70 "Frequency in Print Advertising:1," *Media/scope* (February 1962).

71 "Frequency in Broadcast Advertising:2," *Media/scope* (March 1962).

72 As cited in H. Cromwell and R. Kunkel, "An Experimental Study of the Effect on Attitude of Listeners of Repeating the Same Oral Propaganda," *Journal of Social Psychology*, vol. 35 (May 1952), pp. 175–84.

of positive attitude change;[73] and McCullough demonstrated that exposure of individuals to print messages five times produced greater attitude change than did a single exposure.[74] Finally, it may be a general phenomenon that consumers attribute higher quality to a heavily advertised brand than to its less frequently advertised counterpart.

Repetition also can have negative effects, however. Capitman reported that a decline in preference often occurs after the fourth exposure to the same commercial.[75] This is especially likely if the claim is perceived by consumers as debatable and open to challenge. Similarly, continued acceptance of a commercial probably is associated with the level of good taste; a weak commercial seems to be especially vulnerable to a negative result.[76] Ray and Sawyer also found that attitudinal responses toward certain products were not influenced by repetition of the message.[77] A possible explanation for these results is that Ray and Sawyer reexposed subjects immediately after first exposure, and the effects of reexposure have been found to be most effective after sufficient time has elapsed to allow some decay in the impact of the original message.[78]

The factor of density (the proportion of the firm's messages to all messages received by the consumer) also is important. In his study, Light discovered a negative relation between frequency and attitude when density is high, thus showing the effects of saturation from many messages.[79]

The key also lies in the message itself, with favorable results occurring when a strong message is repeated, and vice versa. What, however, is the essential ingredient of a "good" message? While it is difficult to generalize, it appears that too frequent repetition without reward leads to loss of attention, boredom, and disregard of the communication.[80] The consumer, in other words, must perceive the appeal favorably and glean from its content some continuing positive reinforcement of his own predispositions. A commercial that stresses product improvement and continued excellence, for example, is likely to be rewarding to a prospective purchaser of color television.

It is unlikely that any message, no matter how strong, can be repeated ad infinitum without variation. The reward from the twelfth exposure to the same beer advertisement is likely to be minimal, for example, and it probably will be negative. Capitman's warning of wearout following approximately the fourth exposure is worthy of note. The best strategy is

73 "How Advertising Works: A Study of the Relationship between Advertising, Consumer Attitudes, and Purchase Behavior," unpublished study (Grey Advertising, 1968).

74 J. L. McCullough, "The Use of a Measure of Net Counterargumentation in Differentiating the Impact of Persuasive Communications," unpublished doctoral diss. (Columbus, Ohio: Ohio State University, 1971).

75 "Frequency in Broadcast Advertising: 2," *Media/scope* (March 1962).

76 "Frequency in Broadcast Advertising: 2," *Media/scope* (March 1962).

77 Sawyer, "Effects of Repetition,"

78 T. Cook and C. Insko, "Persistance of Attitude Change as a Function of Conclusion Reexposure: A Laboratory-Field Experiment," *Journal of Personality and Social Psychology,* vol. 9 (1968), pp. 243–64.

79 M. Lawrence Light, unpublished paper, Ohio State University.

80 C. I. Hovland, I. L. Janis, and H. H. Kelley, *Communication and Persuasion* (New Haven, Conn.: Yale University Press, 1953), p. 249.

to *repeat the basic theme with variation* so that the reward level can remain high.[81] Product excellence can be demonstrated in many ways, and a campaign can clearly register the theme by varying the message and thus avoiding boredom and loss of attention from overexposure. The proper strategy, of course, is unique to each situation.

(4) Effects of repetition on behavior. Much of the evidence gathered in a laboratory setting indicates that repetition has less effect on buying action than it does on brand evaluation or intention to purchase.[82] Sawyer's findings are reproduced in Figure 16.5, and it will be noticed that recall was affected far more than behavior as measured by coupon return after five or six exposures.

Figure 16.5 Effects of repetition on recall, brand evaluation, purchase intention, and coupon redemption

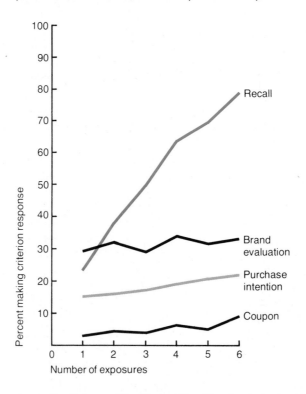

Source: Alan G. Sawyer, "The Effects of Repetition: Conclusions and Suggestions about Experimental Laboratory Research" (paper presented at Workshop on Consumer Information Processing, University of Chicago, November 1972), p. 26. Reprinted by permission.

81 C. Samuel Craig, Brian Sternthal, and Clark Leavitt, "Advertising Wearout: An Experimental Analysis," *Journal of Marketing Research,* vol. 13 (November 1976), pp. 365–72.
82 Sawyer, "Effects of Repetition," p. 24.

The findings from actual field studies are more positive, however, as the following examples indicate:

1. From a series of investigations at NBC, a generalization emerged that the probability of purchasing an advertised brand increases with the frequency of exposure to television commercials.[83]

2. Findings from the McGraw-Hill Advertising Laboratory indicate that sustained, continuous advertising results in increased recognition of a company name, which, in turn, is positively correlated with increased sales.[84]

3. Before exposure to an advertising campaign in *Post* magazine, 9.1 percent of those interviewed stated that they would buy the product in question. The percentage increased to 13.8 percent, however, after two exposures.[85]

4. Starch reported that failure to advertise in a given year results, on the average, in a 6.0-percent decrease in sales, whereas use of 13 pages in magazines and other publications leads to a 6.8-percent increase.[86] A similar relation between advertising and sales was discovered by Mullen.[87] Four advertising insertions a year seem to be the minimum needed on the average to sustain sales, according to Starch,[88] and others agree with this generalization.[89]

5. In the Stewart study referred to earlier, the following results were reported:[90]

   a. When no advertisements were used, few tried the two new products that were studied (Lestare and Chicken Sara Lee).

   b. Four weekly insertions served to encourage some people to buy sooner than they otherwise would.

   c. Eight advertisements doubled the number of customers, but 15 insertions produced the best results per dollar of advertising investment.

   d. Twenty advertisements produced the most customers, but costs of advertising exceeded the gains in sales.

6. In a methodologically sophisticated investigation, duPont researchers conclusively verified the negative effect of discontinued advertising

83 "More Exposure Means More Effectiveness," *NBC Research Bulletin* (1960).

84 "Advertisers with Greater Continuity Achieved Greater Readership" (New York: McGraw-Hill Advertising Laboratory, 1963).

85 "Frequency in Print Advertising: 1," *Media/scope.*

86 D. Starch, "What Is the Best Frequency of Advertisements?" (Daniel Starch Tested Copy, 1962).

87 W. H. Mullen, "The Matter of Continuity," *Advertising Agency and Selling,* vol. 49 (1949).

88 Starch, "What Is the Best Frequency."

89 R. Barton, *Media in Advertising* (New York: McGraw-Hill, 1964).

90 Stewart, "Repetitive Advertising."

on sales.[91] Purchases of Teflon cookware were significantly higher in those cities where high advertising expenditures were maintained.

It is probable that the above findings are based on the assumption that the message itself is of high quality. If this were not so, a definite boomerang effect could occur.[92]

(5) Implications. The review of the literature here has been extensive. In a general way, it has been verified that repetition is helpful at all phases of the communication process. Yet, there is that ever present problem of wearout in which the point of maximum return is exceeded. Perhaps it will be helpful to provide a summary of the known ways in which wearout can be minimized or avoided altogether:

1. Repetition aids consumer learning and hence can be effectively utilized at the start of a new campaign.

2. Repetition can help establish products or brands that are new to a particular medium.

3. A pool or group of commercials should not wear out as quickly as a single commercial, given the same frequency of exposure.

4. When it is not possible to produce a number of varied commercials, introduce several claims within the message to lengthen the learning process.

5. When several commercials are produced, introduce significant variations, or are they likely to be perceived as the same and hence wear out more quickly.

6. A commercial with humor or a single point wears out quickly.

7. Commercials for infrequently purchased products wear out more slowly for the reason that only a fraction of the audience are prospects at any given point of time.

8. The greater the time span between repetition, the longer a message can be run.

9. A message can be reintroduced after a period of absence from the air and hence be perceived as new.

10. Wearout is greatest among heavy television viewers.

11. If the budget is limited, a single commercial spread out over a period of time may produce greater learning than airing of a pool of commercials.

91 J. C. Becknell and R. W. McIsaac, "Test Marketing Cookware Coated with Teflon," *Journal of Advertising Research*, vol. 3 (1963), pp. 2–8.

92 Valentine Aopel, "On Advertising Wear-Out," *Journal of Advertising Research*, vol. 11 (February 1971), pp. 11–13.

12. Commercials that involve the viewer wear out more slowly than those with a straightforward message.

13. Copy testing predicated on a single exposure can shed little light on wearout.

14. Performance must be tracked over time to assess wearout.

15. Only good commercials wear out—those that are ineffective to begin with will lose nothing.[93]

It is obvious that wearout must be monitored in the couse of a campaign. This is easiest to do in terms of awareness. Once knowledge of, say, a brand name of product attribute peaks, serious consideration should be given to change. Changes in positive versus negative reactions can be monitored for the same purpose.

The quest for decision rules

A large volume of evidence has been reviewed in this section, and the reader may be bothered by the fact that the state of present knowledge makes it a virtual impossibility to advance firm generalizations. Fishbein's analysis of the "state of the art" is a discouraging one indeed:

> . . . at this time despite an incredible amount of research on this problem, we are still in the position of almost total ignorance. There is not a single generalization that can be made about the influence of source, message, channel, or audience effects on persuasion . . . the traditional approach to communication has also been more harmful than helpful.[94]

Fishbein probably has some truth in his assessment, but such a negative outlook is not warranted. Even though definitive decision rules are not available, the present evidence gives rich insights into *certain approaches that might work under certain situations.* This heuristic value, in itself, should not be dismissed with such a quick wave of the academic hand.

More critically, one should question whether it will be possible or even desirable to arrive at definitive rules of persuasion. The words of the distinguished advertising practitioner Harry W. McMahan are of more value in this context:

> Examples can help. Guidelines can help. But rules often only lead the advertising novice astray. In our 20,000 commercials we can disprove almost any "rule." Why? Because, for one thing, different product fields require different handling in communication and persuasion. Cosmetics are more on the emotional side . . . Gasoline and cigarets are more emotional than rational. Coca Cola and Pepsi, instead, vie in "personality" battles. . . . Share-of-the-market definitely influences the

93 A. Greenberg and C. Suttoni, "Television Commercial Wearout," Reprinted from the *Journal of Advertising Research,* vol. 13 (1973), p. 53. © Copyright (1973), by the Advertising Research Foundation.
94 Fishbein, "Attitude, Attitude Change, and Behavior," in Levine, *Attitude Research,* p. 10.

advertising. No one in the product field continues on top, many times, even with a mediocre campaign. Why? *Momentum. . . .* It is this difference in market position and the difference in product fields that make most "rules" inapplicable to all advertising.[95]

Decisions always must be made on three bases: (1) experience; (2) intuition and creativity; and (3) research. No one is sufficient by itself. A slavish reliance on rules, if indeed they did exist, would short-circuit any expression of creativity and would lead to ignoring of obvious research data. So, rules or guidelines help and probably exist, to one degree or another, in the back of every creative mind. Evidence such as that reviewed in this chapter obviously can be useful when viewed in this way. To go any further would be to violate the very nature of enlightened decision-making.

Hopefully future research on persuasion will be more definitive. As a start, the focus should be much more directly on change in beliefs.[96] As we stressed in the previous chapter, belief change is the heart of the process that leads to eventual changes in behavior. Much of the present literature is quite ambiguous in this sense. In fact, it is this awareness that led Fishbein to the highly negative conclusion cited above.

Next, much greater attention needs to be paid to methodological details and to variations in nature of product and competitive context. Sawyer has provided some very useful insights that should be considered by anyone interested in future research in this very important field.[97]

Postchoice attitude change

It generally is assumed that a change in attitude must *precede* a corresponding change in behavior. This has repeatedly been shown to be a fallacious conclusion, however.[98] When knowledge enters memory that a particular action has been taken, it can be seen as contradicting an existing attitude, with the result that dissonance is aroused. Dissonance, of course, is an uncomfortable state, and the individual is motivated to restore consonance or balance.

In this circumstance, the buying action itself usually cannot be changed; and the average person is reluctant to admit that he has made a mistake once funds have been committed to an alternative. Therefore, it is probable that attitudes will change instead. Mills discovered, for example, that those who engaged in cheating later changed their attitude

95 Harry W. McMahan, "Advertising: Some Things You Can't Teach—and Some You Can," *Advertising Age* (November 8, 1976), p. 56. Reprinted by permsion.

96 Fishbein and Ajzen, *Belief, Attitude, Intention, and Behavior,* chap. 11.

97 See Sawyer, "Effects of Repetition," pp. 35–62.

98 B. Lipstein, "Anxiety, Risk and Uncertainty in Advertising Effectiveness Measurements," in L. Adler and I. Crespi, eds., *Attitude Research on the Rocks* (Chicago: American Marketing Association, 1968), pp. 11–27.

toward this type of behavior.[99] Similarly, Atkin reports that attitudes toward various stores changed after consumers shopped there.[100]

It thus would appear to be a valid marketing goal to induce people to engage in attitude-discrepant behavior. Perhaps the offer of a free coupon, for example, might induce a housewife to try a previously avoided brand of coffee. If she were strongly committed to her brand *and* if she actually purchased and used the other brand voluntarily, then dissonance most likely would occur. Brand preferences thus could change as a result of this product trial.

This change probably would not occur, however, if the behavior advocated were perceived as nonacceptable. Under that circumstance it most likely would fall into her latitude of rejection. She might feel, for example, that the brand of coffee in question will never be served in her home. In such a situation, it is most likely that she would resist dissonance and avoid the advocated behavior. This has largely been overlooked by the dissonance researchers, who usually claim that greatest attitude change results when the discrepancy between attitude and behavior is maximum.

Is it reasonable to expect a free sample to induce a strongly committed consumer to switch brands? Quite an opposite result might occur in that she would use the sample but never really give the product a fair trial. In other words, she does not waste the sample, but, at the same time, she does not fully expose herself to the information the sample can give and thereby let her preferences be challenged. One cannot help wondering whether or not many of the coupons, samples, and other "giveaways" are falling on unfertile ground for these reasons.

Summary

It was the purpose of this chapter to review a wide variety of research findings that document appropriate strategies for attitude change. Three specific questions were asked: (1) How great should the distance be between attitude position of members of the target audience and the position advocated by the message? (2) How can message content be varied to achieve a maximum effect? (3) What changes can be made in message structure (that is, the order of arguments and repetition)?

It appears that the optimum discrepancy between attitude position of recipients and that of the message should be small. This is because increasing the discrepancy appears to induce attitude change only when the message source is perceived as credible. Marketing stimuli such as advertising are viewed as having an obvious intent to persuade and usually suffer in credibility for this reason.

99 J. Mills, "Changes in Moral Attitudes Following Temptation," *Journal of Personality,* vol. 26 (1958), pp. 517–31.
100 K. Atkin, "Advertising and Store Patronage," *Journal of Advertising Research,* vol. 2 (1962), pp. 18–23.

An extensive body of literature then was reviewed on the effects of variations in the creative message. Much is now known about the possible influence of fear appeals, distraction, nonovert appeals, and stated conclusions. Such evidence, however, is primarily of heuristic value only in that it suggests possible clues for strategy. The type of research upon which most of it is based is, by nature, artificial, and one must be cautious in generalizing to more natural circumstances.

The chapter concluded with a discussion of manipulation of structural variables. Of special importance are the effects of repetition. A substantial body of research evidence was reviewed that indicates that repetition can increase awareness, retention of content, and attitude change. The most important question then becomes, at which point does the value of repetition stabilize or decline? It has been shown, for example, that repetition can have a negative effect on attitude change. One determinant appears to be message density—that is, the proportion of the firm's messages to the total received by the individual over a period of time. The higher this proportion, the greater the probability of a declining or even negative effect from repetition. It seems obvious that continual field study is needed to monitor message effects and detect points of wearout. Removing a campaign either prior to or after the point of diminishing returns is not a profitable business practice.

After discussion of a vast amount of evidence, it was asked whether or not it will be possible to arrive at decision rules for those engaged in persuasion. The answer was that there are too many variables underlying any situation to permit such generalization. Furthermore, decisions are made on the basis of experience, creativity, and research. Undue reliance on rules could short-circuit the natural workings of the creative mind.

The chapter concluded with a brief review of the subject of attitude change following choice. There are some marketing implications with respect to strategies that attempt to induce trial followed by change in brand preference.

Review and discussion questions

1. Compare the various theories on placement of communication messages relative to the recipient's own position on the topic. Of what use would these approaches be to a manufacturer of toothpaste? a manufacturer of pianos and organs?

2. A large, nationally known drug firm is interested in expanding market acceptance of its birth control pill. Would you recommend that a fear appeal be used? Why or why not?

3. The EXY Corporation sells aluminum cookware through door-to-door solicitation only. Although some advertising is used, the company relies primarily on its familiar company name and reputation for quality as the prime reasons for justifying a high price. How might the findings on source credibility be used by the sales manager?

4. In a laboratory study it is discovered that a foreign make of automobile is regarded more favorably when advertising messages feature positive selling points as well as the fact that problems have existed in the past with respect to brake fade, door leaks and rattles, faulty ignition, and spark-plug fouling.

Would you, as the director of advertising research, recommend that this company use a two-sided campaign? What arguments might be advanced?

5. A well-known brand of refrigerator has two distinct features: (1) a mechanically excellent meat keeper and (2) a thin-wall construction, which gives greatest interior capacity per foot of exterior space. Using the findings on primacy versus recency, in which order should these appeals be presented, assuming that thin-wall construction seems to be of greatest importance to consumers?

6. What can be concluded concerning the influence of repetition on knowledge and awareness?

7. What precautions should be followed in using the findings pertaining to retention and repetition?

8. "Zoomo Reduces Headache Pain." What might happen in terms of the affective dimension of attitudes if this slogan is repeated for one year on a saturation basis in newspapers, magazines, and on radio and television? What reasons can you give for your answers?

9. What might be done to reduce campaign wearout in the situation described in question 8?

10. Does advertising influence buying action? With what degree of certainty would you want to predict such an effect in the advertising of Zoomo for headache pain (question 8)? Would your answer differ if the product in question were an electric range?

11. What factors lead to campaign wearout? Give examples of each.

12. What is meant by semantic satiation? What are the implications for marketing management?

13. If your library still retains copies, secure an advertising book from the 1920s, the 1930s, the 1940s, the 1950s, the 1960s, and the 1970s. What conclusions can you come to with respect to rules for advertising design? Have there been changes in thinking?

14. A company is considering house-to-house distribution of samples of a new type of hand soap. Will this strategy succeed in inducing brand switching? What must be true before success will be achieved?

CHAPTER 17

Brand loyalty and repeat purchase behavior

The attitudes of a consumer may be influenced through various forms of persuasion to the point that an intention is formed toward buying a particular brand. But how enduring is that intention? If they buy it once, will they buy it again?

Brand loyalty—the tendency of some consumers to purchase a particular brand consistently—encompasses questions such as those above as well as the question of whether certain consumers are more "loyal prone" than others. These topics are the focus of analysis in this chapter and are an important aid in the development of marketing strategy.

The discussion begins with a consideration of the meaning of brand loyalty and research results supporting the existence of the phenomenon. The second section analyzes the structural and behavioral correlates of brand loyalty. Various models relating some of these correlates to measures of brand loyalty are presented in the third section. The chapter concludes with some additional discussion of marketing strategy implications.

What is brand loyalty?

The definition of brand loyalty has been the subject of ·considerable confusion as well as controversy. Whether or not brand loyalty exists and, of course, the extent to which it exists depend partly on how it is

*The authors gratefully acknowledge the contributions of Dr. B. Venkatesh in revising and extending an earlier version of this chapter, and of Dr. M. N. Dat for contributions to the present chapter.

defined. A distinction is sometimes made between *repeat purchase behavior* and *loyalty*. The differences in these terms can be understood by examining the usage of the term brand loyalty by various investigators.

Brand loyalty is *conceptual* in nature. As a conceptual variable, it has been used both as an output variable—the result of consumer decisions—and as an input variable—the cause of consumer decisions. In either case the concept of brand loyalty to be used in consumer research must be *operationally defined*. How the concept is defined may have a very great effect on the research results that will be obtained. The operational definitions described below include: (1) brand-choice sequences; (2) preferences over time; (3) proportion of purchases; and other measures, including an extended definition of brand loyalty based both on preferences and purchases.

One of the earliest studies defined brand loyalty according to the *sequence of purchasing a specific brand*. The purchase records of 100 households in a *Chicago Tribune* panel were analyzed for such frequently purchased items as coffee, orange juice, soap, and margarine. For each product category, each household making five or more purchases was placed in one of four brand-loyalty categories depending on the sequence of brands purchased. Thus, if A, B, C, D, E, F . . . are various brands (Snow Crop, Minute Maid, etc.) in a particular product category such as orange juice, then households could be classified as having the following types of loyalty:

Brand-choice sequences

1. *Undivided loyalty* is the sequence AAAAA.

2. *Divided loyalty* is the sequence ABABAB.

3. *Unstable loyalty* is the sequence AAABBB.

4. *No loyalty* is the sequence ABCDEF.

Using this definition of brand loyalty, Brown observed that the percentage of households demonstrating some degree of loyalty varied from 54 to 95 percent, depending on the product involved. In fact, the percentage of households that were undividedly loyal varied from 12 percent to 73 percent across products.[1]

This operational definition of loyalty was important in the development of the concept and in studies such as those of Tucker[2] and Stafford[3] who defined brand loyalty as three successive choices of the same brand in their empirical studies. While the concept developed in these early studies is still valid, the practical problems of this definition have caused it to be

1 George Brown, "Brand Loyalty—Fact or Fiction?" *Advertising Age*, vol. 23 (June 19, 1952), pp. 53–55; (June 30, 1952), pp. 45–47; (July 14, 1952), pp. 54–56; (July 28, 1952), pp. 46–48; (August 11, 1952), pp. 56–58; (September 1, 1952), pp. 80–82; (October 6, 1952), pp. 82–86; (December 1, 1952), pp. 76–79; (January 25, 1953), pp. 75–76.
2 W. T. Tucker, "The Development of Brand Loyalty," *Journal of Marketing Research*, vol. 1 (August 1964), pp. 32–35.
3 James E. Stafford, "Effect of Group Influences on Consumer Brand Preferences," *Journal of Marketing Research*, vol. 3 (February 1966), pp. 68–75.

little used today for the reasons that Charlton and Ehrenberg describe below:

> This approach has led to few generalizable results, because there is no simple way of summarizing purchase sequences quantitatively. Different consumers buy at different rates. Their purchase sequences are invariably out of phase with one another, and it is difficult to aggregate the buying behavior of one consumer with that of another who buys, say, more frequently. There is also no common time scale for relating any one measure of aggregate behavior to other aspects of buying behavior or to other events in the market place. The purchase sequence approach, therefore, does not facilitate the kinds of comparisons between consumers, brands, or product fields that are likely to lead to generalizable results.[4]

Preference over time

Sometimes loyalty has been defined as preference statements over time rather than actual purchase. One such study involved data collected by Guest in 1941 concerning the brand awareness and preferences of students. In follow-up studies of these same persons 12 and 20 years later, Guest found suggestive evidence of a high degree of loyalty toward brand names (although not to specific brands).[5] This loyalty was most manifest when factors such as unavailability, price considerations, and respondent not being the buyer did not play a major part in brand selection.

In a literature review of operational definitions of brand loyalty, Jacoby found 17 studies employing preference statements over time, similar to the usage by Guest.[6] More recent research on brand loyalty, however, has favored definitions that emphasize actual purchase, described below.

Proportion of purchases

The most frequently used definition of brand loyalty, at least in empirical research, is the proportion of total purchases within a given product category devoted to the most frequently purchased brand (or set of brands). This is used both as a conceptual definition of brand loyalty in these studies as well as an operational measure.

Proportion of purchases has the advantage that it is readily *quantifiable* and thus useful in a wide variety of mathematical models. In addition, using this definition of brand loyalty, Cunningham introduced the concept of *multibrand* loyalty in various forms.[7] *Dual*-brand loyalty, for example. would be the percent of total purchases devoted to the two most favorite brands; *triple*-brand loyalty refers to the three most favorite brands; and

---

4 P. Charlton and A. S. C. Ehrenberg, "McConnell's Experimental Brand Choice Data," *Journal of Marketing Research*, vol. 10 (August 1973), pp. 302–07.

5 Lester Guest, "Brand Loyalty Revisited: A Twenty Year Report," *Journal of Applied Psychology*, vol. 48 (1964), pp. 93–97.

6 Jacob Jacoby, "Brand Loyalty: A Conceptual Definition," *Proceedings of 79th Annual Convention*, American Psychological Association (1971), pp. 655–56.

7 Ross M. Cunningham, "Brand Loyalty—What, Where, How Much?" *Harvard Business Review*, vol. 34 (January–February 1956), pp. 116–28; Ross Cunningham, "Customer Loyalty to Store and Brand," *Harvard Business Review*, vol. 39 (November–December 1961), pp. 127–37.

so on. In a later study, Cunningham also used a similar approach to demonstrate "store loyalty."[8]

Other researchers have used this concept of brand loyalty, including use in most of the mathematical models described later in the chapter. Each researcher tends to use the basic concept with some variation. Farley used two summary measures of brand loyalty, one a cross-sectional measure based on "the average number of brands bought by families of a given product during the period of study," and another, a time-series measure based on "the percent of families in a given market whose favorite brand is different in the first half of the period studied from the second half."[9] Small values of each measure indicate brand loyalty, whereas large values indicate frequent brand switching.

In the definition of brand loyalty used by Massy, Montgomery, and Morrison, a consumer is considered brand loyal if his or her preferred brand during the first half of the period under study is the same as the one during the second half, preferred brand being defined as the one which is purchased most often in a given period.[10] Blattberg and Sen have extended the "proportion of purchases" approach to segments that are loyal to national or private brands as a category as well as specific brands within each of those categories.[11] One segment of the population they found to be "high national brand loyal" and found that the proportion of purchases devoted to the favorite brand ranged from about 90 to 100 percent *within this segment*. Blattberg and Sen also used the concept of "last purchase loyal" (as have some other researchers) to define a consumer who buys one brand on several successive occasions, switches to another brand, buys that several times, switches again, and so on.[12]

Other measures of loyalty

Several researchers have employed a combination of two or more of the above criteria in defining brand loyalty. Thus, the factor analytic approach employed by Sheth uses a definition of brand loyalty based on both the frequency of purchase of a brand and the pattern of these purchases.[13] Pessemier used an entirely different approach based on the price increase in the most preferred brand relative to the price of the other brands necessary to induce brand switching.[14] Cunningham, on the other

8 Ross M. Cunningham, "Customer Loyalty to Store and Brand," *Harvard Business Review*, vol. 39 (November–December 1961), pp. 127–37.

9 John U. Farley, "Why Does Brand Loyalty Vary over Products?" *Journal of Marketing Research*, vol. 1 (November 1964), pp. 9–14; John E. Farley, "Brand Loyalty and the Economics of Information," *Journal of Business*, vol. 37 (October 1964), pp. 370–81.

10 William F. Massy, David B. Montgomery, and Donald G. Morrison, *Stochastic Models of Buying Behavior* (Cambridge, Mass.: M.I.T. Press, 1970), p. 119.

11 Robert C. Blattberg and Subrata K. Sen, "Market Segments and Stochastic Brand Choice Models," *Journal of Marketing Research*, vol. 13 (February 1976), pp. 34–45.

12 Blattberg and Sen, "Market Segments," p. 35.

13 John A. Howard and Jagdish N. Sheth, *The Theory of Buyer Behavior* (New York: Wiley, 1969), p. 249; also Jagdish N. Sheth, "A Factor Analytic Model of Brand Loyalty," *Journal of Marketing Research*, vol. 5 (November 1968), pp. 395–404; Jagdish N. Sheth, "Measurement of Multidimensional Brand Loyalty of a Consumer," *Journal of Marketing Research*, vol. 7 (August 1970), pp. 348–54.

14 Edgar A. Pessemier, "A New Way to Determine Buying Decisions," *Journal of Marketing*, vol. 24 (October 1959), pp. 41–46.

hand, attempted to evaluate probable behavior when confronted with the absence of one's favorite brand as an indicator of brand loyalty.[15]

Limitations of traditional definitions of brand loyalty

The definitions discussed above have one common characteristic: they provide an operational measure of brand loyalty. Unfortunately, however, the large number of approaches causes several problems.

First, it is difficult to compare and synthesize findings. Assume, for example, that two consumers exhibit the following pattern of purchases during a given period:

Consumer $1 = ABCABC$.
Consumer $2 = ABCCCC$.

The definition—"number of brands purchased during the time period"— would treat both consumers alike. However, the "purchase sequence" definition would treat them differently.

Why did the second consumer buy brand C on each of the last four purchase occasions? Is it because he really prefers brand C and has developed a sort of loyalty toward that brand, or is it because the store he patronizes has stopped carrying the other brands? Maybe brand C is being promoted with a long series of promotional deals, or the store has rearranged the merchandise, providing a better shelf display for C. This illustrates the importance of distinguishing between "intentional loyalty" and "spurious loyalty." As Day points out:

> . . . the spuriously loyal buyers lack any attachment to brand attributes, and they can be immediately captured by another brand that offers a better deal, a coupon, or enhanced point-of-purchase visibility through displays and other devices.[16]

Another basic problem is that most traditional definitions do not deal with multiple-brand loyalty. Although Brown, Cunningham, and a few other pioneers conceived the possibility of loyalty to more than one brand, it has been dealt with seriously only in recent years.[17]

Finally, it seems risky to define and measure loyalty to accommodate empirical data. Instead, once a conceptual framework has been developed, a comprehensive set of relevant variables could be identified and studied.

Preference-purchase definitions of brand loyalty

A resolution of the limitations of traditional definitions can be achieved by a definition of brand loyalty that includes both *preferences* of consumers and *purchases* of consumers. A preference-purchase definition recog-

15 Scott M. Cunningham, "Perceived Risk and Brand Loyalty," in Donald F. Cox, ed., *Risk Taking and Information Handling in Consumer Behavior* (Boston: Harvard University Press, 1967), pp. 507–23.

16 George S. Day, "A Two-Dimensional Concept of Brand Loyalty," *Journal of Advertising Research*, vol. 9 (September 1969), pp. 29–35.

17 See, for example, Massy et al., *Stochastic Models*; Sheth, "Measurement of Multidimensional Brand Loyalty"; A.S.C. Ehrenberg and G. J. Goodhardt, "A Model of Multi-Brand Buying," *Journal of Marketing Research*, vol. 7 (February 1970), pp. 77–84.

nizes a difference between intentional loyalty and spurious loyalty or that *loyalty* is something more than *repeat purchase behavior.*

Day contends that to be truly brand loyal, the consumer must hold a favorable attitude toward the brand in addition to purchasing it repeatedly.[18]

Jacoby concurs, suggesting that brand loyalty has at least two primary dimensions—brand loyal behavior and brand loyal attitude:

> Brand loyal behavior is defined as the overt act of selective repeat purchasing based on evaluative psychological decision processes, while brand-loyal attitudes are the underlying predispositions to behave in such a selective fashion. . . . To exhibit brand loyalty implies repeat purchasing behavior based on cognitive, affective, evaluative and predispositional factors. . . . [19]

Following this line of analysis, an extended definition of brand loyalty would be: Brand loyalty is the preferential attitudinal and behavioral response toward one or more brands in a product category expressed over a period of time by a consumer (or buyer).

This definition has many implications. Foremost is the fact that any measure of brand loyalty should incorporate behavioral as well as attitudinal components. An example is a measure proposed by Day:[20]

$$L_i = \frac{P(B_i)}{kA_i^n} = f(X_a, X_b, \cdots, X_j)$$

where

L_i = brand-loyalty score for *ith* buyer of brand *m*

$P(B)_i$ = proportion of total purchases of products that buyers devoted to brand *m* over period of study

A_i = attitude toward brand *m* at beginning of study, scaled so that a low value represents a favorable attitude

$X_a, \cdots, X_j$ = descriptive variables to be fitted to L_i by least squares

k = constants whose values are varied by trial and error to maximize fit between L_i and $X_a, \dots, X_j$.

Day provides empirical evidence to demonstrate the superiority of such a measure over the traditional approaches that use only purchase data. His measure isolates spurious loyalty and achieves a better statistical fit with a set of descriptive variables.[21]

The extended conceptualization has several other attractive features. First, it explicitly recognizes the existence of multibrand loyalty. Second, brand loyalty is viewed as a *product-specific* phenomenon rather than a general attribute. Thus a consumer may be highly brand loyal in product category *X*, but not in categories *Y* or *Z*.

18 Day, "Two-Dimensional Concept."
19 Jacob Jacoby, "A Model of Multi-Brand Loyalty," *Journal of Advertising Research*, vol. 11 (June 1971), pp. 25–31.
20 Day, "Two-Dimensional Concept."
21 Day, "Two-Dimensional Concept."

Third, the definition recognizes that brand loyalty is a temporal phenomenon. Model builders can specify the time span over which the behavior is to be studied. Fourth, the definition focuses on the responses of the decision maker. Since the final consumer need not always be the buyer, it would be difficult otherwise to study the correlates of brand loyalty using data on buyers who are not consumers.

Fifth, the definition proposes a continuum of brand loyalty as opposed to the artificial "loyal-disloyal" dichotomy. Finally, the approach points out the need to incorporate variables affecting brand-loyal attitudes as well as purchase behavior.

The easiest to understand and perhaps the most complete definition of this approach to brand loyalty was formulated by Jacoby and his colleagues. While many other definitions are used as operational measures of brand loyalty, this form of an extended preference-purchase definition captures the full range of meaning of the concept brand loyalty:

> Brand loyalty is (1) the biased (i.e., nonrandom) (2) behavioral response (i.e., purchase) (3) expressed over time (4) by some decision-making unit (5) with respect to one or more alternative brands out of a set of such brands, and is (6) a function of psychological (i.e., decision-making, evaluative) processes.[22]

This definition is consistent with the study of consumer behavior as a decision process and yet delineates it as a special phenomenon for scientific analysis and prediction. Jacoby's definition is very useful in distinguishing *repeat purchase behavior* that focuses only on behavior from *loyalty*, which encompasses the antecedents of behavior.[23]

It also specifically brings to attention the fact that brand loyalty is a concept that applies to a "decision-making unit" such as a family. The failure to make this recognition and the consequent correlation of *individual* variables with *family* purchases probably accounts for many of the problems in brand loyalty research. For example, attitudinal measures may reflect very well the preferences of the person who completes a questionnaire but correlate poorly with purchase behavior of the family over time (brand loyalty) because other members of the family are more influential in the family's purchases some or all of the time.

Brand loyalty correlates

Numerous attempts have been made to determine why brand loyalty varies across consumers and products. This section summarizes the

---

22 Jacob Jacoby and David B. Kyner, "Brand Loyalty vs. Repeat Purchase Behavior," *Journal of Marketing Research*, vol. 10 (February 1973), pp. 1–9; Jacob Jacoby and Jerry C. Olson, "An Attitudinal Model of Brand Loyalty: Conceptual Underpinnings and Instrumentation Research," Purdue Papers in Consumer Psychology, no. 159, 1976. (This is a reprint of an earlier paper, previously out of print.)

23 Considerable discussion has been generated by Jacoby's definition of brand loyalty. See Lawrence X. Tarpey, Sr., "A Brand Loyalty Concept—A Comment," *Journal of Marketing Research*, vol. 11 (May 1974), pp. 214–17; Jacob Jacoby, "A Brand Loyalty Concept: Comments on a Comment," *Journal of Marketing Research*, vol. 12 (November 1975), pp. 484–87; Lawrence X. Tarpey, Sr., "Brand Loyalty Revisited: A Commentary," *Journal of Marketing Research*, vol. 12 (November 1975), pp. 488–91.

consumer, shopping pattern, and market structure characteristics that are, or are not, associated with differential degrees of brand loyalty. Because of the wide variety of definitions of brand loyalty, the following correlates and noncorrelates should be viewed as provisional rather than definitive.

In one of the earlier studies attempting to identify characteristics of brand-loyal consumers, the Advertising Research Foundation reported results based on toilet-tissue purchasing behavior for 3,206 members of the J. Walter Thompson panel.[24] They found virtually no association between personality (as measured by the Edwards personal preference schedule), socioeconomic variables, and household brand loyalty.

Consumer characteristics

Employing the same data source, but analyzing beer, coffee, and tea purchasing behavior, Frank, Massy, and Lodahl observed only a modest association between socioeconomic, demographic, and personality variables and brand loyalty. Using a brand-loyalty score based on a large number of measures of household purchasing behavior, such as number of brands purchased, percentage spent on most frequently purchased brands, and so on, they observed some relationships between brand loyalty and certain personality measures from the Edwards test. Thus husbands' and wives' endurance, deference, and succorance scores, wives' need for autonomy and change, and husbands' need for affiliation seem to have been somewhat related to brand loyalty. The overall conclusions of the study, however, were that high brand loyal households apparently have a profile of personality and socioeconomic characteristics that is virtually identical to that of households exhibiting a lower degree of loyalty.[25]

Frank and Boyd, in their investigation of household brand loyalty to private brands, also concluded that socioeconomic variables could not differentiate between private and manufacturer brand-loyal consumers.[26] Similarly, Coulson found that knowledge of the brand preferences of other family members did not significantly affect whether respondents had a regular brand that was purchased more than others. He also observed that housewives who tended to have a regular brand that was purchased more than others, did not differ from other housewives in terms of age or social class.[27] Guest, in his 20-year study of brand preferences through time, also found that sex, intelligence, or marital status were unrelated to brand loyalty.

In a study attempting to relate the influence of reference groups on brand-loyal behavior, Stafford found no significant relation between level of group cohesiveness and member brand loyalty. However, in the more

24 *Are There Consumer Types?* (New York: Advertising Research Foundation, 1964).

25 Ronald E. Frank, William F. Massy, and Thomas M. Lodahl, "Purchasing Behavior and Personal Attributes," *Journal of Advertising Research*, vol. 9 (December 1969), pp. 15–24; Ronald E. Frank, "Correlates of Buying Behavior for Grocery Products," *Journal of Marketing*, vol. 31 (October 1967), pp. 48–53.

26 Ronald Frank and Harper Boyd, Jr., "Are Private-Brand–Prone Grocery Customers Really Different?" *Journal of Advertising Research*, vol. 5 (December 1965), pp. 27–35.

27 John S. Coulson, "Buying Decisions within the Family," in Joseph Newman, ed., *On Knowing the Consumer* (New York: Wiley, 1966), p. 66.

cohesive groups, the extent and degree of brand loyalty of members was closely related to brand choice behavior of the informal leader.[28]

Carman used an entropy measure of loyalty based on purchase data alone[29] and the Morgan-Sonquist automatic interaction detector scheme (AID) to analyze the results.[30] On the one hand, he was unable to relate most personality characteristics and consumer mobility—geographic, intergenerational, and social—to brand loyalty. However, he did find some relationships and concluded:

1. Personal characteristics of consumers will explain differences in store loyalty, which in turn is the single most important predictor of brand loyalty.

2. Loyalty is positively correlated with the extent to which the housewife socializes with her neighbors.

3. The characteristics of consumers that are associated with brand loyalty differ among products. Thus, a loyal coffee buyer possesses the characteristics representative of high self-confidence. Furthermore, in the case of coffee, reference-group influence is most obvious, with consumers most interested in status being the most loyal. For canned fruits and frozen orange juice, reference-group influence is insignificant.

As a result of the richness of the data bank and the versatility of the AID technique in handling a large number of predictor variables, Carman was able to identify relations that would normally go undetected. For example, he describes the characteristics of the brand loyal coffee buyer as follows:

> She respects the food-shopping opinion of her neighbors but, in general, trusts technical sources of food information more than personal sources. . . . (She indicates) stronger home or career orientation. She lives in the better neighborhoods of the shopping area, and she does not cook the kind of meals served in her parent's home. However, she considers herself a permanent part of the neighborhood. Loyal coffee buyers have a higher income consistent with the neighborhood than the nonloyal group. . . . (They have) high self-confidence. These results appear to be in agreement with the hypothesis of Brody and

---

28 Stafford, "Effect of Group Influences."

29 Their measure θ, based on purchase data alone, is defined as

$$\theta = \sum_{i=1}^{K} P_i \log P_i$$

where P_i is the true proportion of purchases going to brand i and K the number of brands available on the market.

30 James M. Carman, "Correlates of Brand Loyalty: Some Positive Results," *Journal of Marketing Research*, vol. 7 (February 1970), pp. 67–76. It should be noted that some Monte Carlo studies with AID raise several questions regarding its unfortunate propensity for capitalizing on specific sample variation.

Cunningham[31] that brand loyal coffee consumers should have high self-confidence.[32]

Using the extended attitudinal/behavior measure of brand loyalty described earlier in the chapter, Day also detected significant associations between loyalty and certain consumer characteristics.[33] He found the brand-loyal consumer to be very conscious of the need to economize when buying, confident of her judgments, and older in a smaller than average household (thus needing to satisfy the preferences of fewer family members).

It has also become fairly evident that brand loyalty is a product specific phenomenon; that is, some product categories are likely to have more loyalty than others. Some researchers have concluded that more brand switching will occur when price differences are significant between brands and that this will have the most effect on consumers in the extreme levels of both income and education, rather than in a linear relationship to these variables.[34] Possibly, brand switching is a function of the value of time to a consumer. This hypothesis suggests that upper income people have more "natural" loyalty to brands but when their preferred brand is out of stock or not carried by a convenient store, upper income consumers will switch to another brand rather than spend the time necessary to find their preferred brand.[35]

In an examination of brand loyalty for appliances, Newman and Werbel found some relationship between loyalty and a personality variable, specifically optimism about the future. The persons *least* optimistic about future business conditions were most likely to be brand loyal. This study also concluded, as one would expect, that a strong relationship exists between brand loyalty and satisfaction with a present product of that brand.[36] In thinking about the discussion of loyalty definitions earlier in this chapter, it is also worthwhile to note that the Newman and Werbel study concluded that measures of loyalty built upon preference (brand deliberation) as well as purchase are more useful than those built upon repeat purchases alone.

Studies have also investigated the relationships between brand loyalty and various shopping-pattern characteristics, including store loyalty, shopping proneness, amount purchased, brand last purchased, and interpurchase time. The results of these studies are summarized below.

Shopping-pattern characteristics

31 Robert P. Brody and Scott M. Cunningham, "Personality Variables and the Consumer Decision Process," *Journal of Marketing Research*, vol. 5 (February 1968), pp. 50–57.

32 Carman, "Correlates of Brand Loyalty," pp. 73–74.

33 Day, "Two-Dimensional Concept."

34 William A. Chance and Normal D. French, "An Exploratory Investigation of Brand Switching," *Journal of Marketing Research*, vol. 9 (May 1972), pp. 226–29.

35 Shmuel Sharir (Shraier), "Brand Loyalty and the Household's Cost of Time," *Journal of Business*, vol. 47 (January 1974), pp. 53–55.

36 Joseph W. Newman and Richard A. Werbel, "Multivariate Analysis of Brand Loyalty for Major Household Appliances," *Journal of Marketing Research*, vol. 10 (November 1973), pp. 404–09.

As was pointed out above, Carman found that store loyalty was the most important correlate of brand loyalty.[37] Other researchers have also demonstrated the importance of store loyalty in determining brand loyalty.[38] This relationship is due, in part, to the fact that store loyalty tends to restrict the number of brand alternatives available to the consumer. However, Carman maintains that the brand-store loyalty relationship is more complex than the simple reduction in available choices.[39]

Shopping proneness is another characteristic that has been related to brand loyalty.[40] Consumers who are not shopping prone shop in relatively few stores. Within these stores, they tend to remain loyal to a small number of brands rather than make careful choices between the values being offered by these stores.

When the store in which a shopper normally makes a purchase undergoes substantial change (such as ownership), this may also affect a buyer's loyalty to the manufacturer's brands formerly purchased there, a study of auto buyers discloses.[41]

Studies investigating the relationship between the amount purchased and brand loyalty yield contradictory findings. Based on the purchase habits of 66 households in seven product categories including soap, cleansers, coffee, peas, margarine, orange juice, and headache remedies, Cunningham found very little relationship between purchasing activity and brand loyalty.[42] Massy, Frank, and Lodahl report similar findings for coffee and beer, although they found some association between activity and brand loyalty for tea.[43] In contrast, Keuhn, using frozen orange juice purchases from a *Chicago Tribune* panel of 650 households, found that brand loyalty was higher for heavy purchasers than for light purchasers.[44] Day, in a more recent study using certain convenience foods, also found that true brand-loyal buyers were also heavy users of the products.[45]

Some of the apparent contradictions in loyalty may be due to differences in loyalty caused by the length of time the product has been on the market. Some excellent experiments have been conducted by Ehrenberg and his associates in a continuing panel of households, called the RBL Mini Test Market operation. In these studies, it was found that brand switching is much more prevalent immediately after the introduction of a

37 Carman, "Correlates of Brand Loyalty," pp. 69–71.

38 Tanniru R. Rao, "Consumer's Purchase Decision Process: Stochastic Models," *Journal of Marketing Research*, vol. 6 (August 1969), pp. 321–29.

39 Carman, "Correlates of Brand Loyalty."

40 Carman, "Correlates of Brand Loyalty."

41 Richard D. Norstrom and John E. Swan, "Does a Change in Customer Loyalty Occur When a New Car Agency is Sold?" *Journal of Marketing Research*, vol. 13 (May 1976), pp. 173–77.

42 Cunningham, "Perceived Risk."

43 Massy et al., *Stochastic Models*.

44 Alfred A. Kuehn, "Consumer Brand Choice as a Learning Process," *Journal of Advertising Research*, vol. 2 (December 1962), pp. 10–17.

45 Day, "Two-Dimensional Concept."

product and equilibrium or brand loyalty is reached after the passage of an amount of time.[46]

Several studies have investigated the relationship between interpurchase time and brand loyalty. Based on purchases of frozen orange juice, Kuehn observed that the probability of a consumer's buying the same brand on two consecutive purchases (a measure of brand loyalty) decreased exponentially with an increase in time between these purchases.[47] In a study of Canadian banks, it was also found that the longer the elapsed time, the greater the decay in loyalty.[48] Morrison[49] and Carman,[50] on the other hand, observed no significant change in brand loyalty as the time between purchases varied. These contradictory findings may very well be due to the use of different product categories by these researchers.

Finally, attempts have been made to relate factors such as perceived risk and cognitive dissonance to brand loyalty. Thus, Sheth and Venkatesan suggest, based on a laboratory study, that "perceived risk is a necessary condition for the development of brand loyalty. The sufficient condition is the existence of well-known market brands on which the consumer can rely.[51] Using a different laboratory experiment, Mittelstaedt suggests that brand loyalty may be a function of the dissonance experienced at the time of purchase, and that the experience coupled with its subsequent reduction may lead one to repeat a choice.[52]

Several studies have investigated the relationship between brand loyalty and certain market-structure characteristics, such as the availability of brands, price fluctuations, and dealing activity. The importance of these types of variables was demonstrated by Farley's study of the purchases of 199 families in 17 diverse product categories.[53] He found that:

Market-structure characteristics

1. Consumers tended to be less loyal toward products with many available brands, where number of purchases and dollar expenditures per buyer are high, where prices are relatively active, and where consumers might be expected to simultaneously use a number of brands of the product.

46 A.S.C. Ehrenberg and P. Charlton, "An Analysis of Simulated Brand Choice," *Journal of Advertising Research*, vol. 13 (February 1973). Also see P. Charton, A.S.C. Ehrenberg, and B. Pymont, "Buyer Behaviour under Mini-test Conditions," *Journal of the Market Research Society*, vol. 14 (July 1972), pp. 171–83; and P. Carlton and A.S.C. Ehrenberg, "An Experiment in Brand Choice," *Journal of Marketing Research,* vol. 13 (May 1976), pp. 152–60.

47 Kuehn, "Consumer Brand Choice."

48 Joseph N. Fry et al., "Customer Loyalty to Banks: A Longitudinal Study," *Journal of Business*, vol. 46 (October 1973), pp. 517–25.

49 Donald G. Morrison, "Interpurchase Time and Brand Loyalty," *Journal of Marketing Research*, vol. 3 (August 1966), pp. 289–91.

50 James M. Carman, "Brand Switching and Linear Learning Models," *Journal of Advertising Research*, vol. 6 (June 1966), pp. 23–31.

51 Jagdish N. Sheth and M. Venkatesan, "Risk Reduction Process in Repetitive Consumer Behavior," *Journal of Marketing Research*, vol. 5 (August 1968), pp. 307–10; Cunningham, "Perceived Risk."

52 Robert Mittelstaedt, "A Dissonance Approach to Repeat Purchasing Behavior," *Journal of Marketing Research*, vol. 6 (November 1969), pp. 444–46.

53 Farley, "Why Does Brand Loyalty Vary."

2. Consumers tend to be loyal in markets where brands tend to be widely distributed, and where market share is concentrated heavily in the leading brand.

Based on these findings Farley concluded that:

> Much of the apparent difference over products in some important aspects of brand choice can apparently be explained on the basis of structural variables describing the markets in which the products are sold, and does not depend on specific characteristics of the products or on attitudes of consumers towards products.

Other researchers have also found relationships between market characteristics and brand loyalty. For example, Day found that the true brand-loyal buyer was less influenced by day-to-day price fluctuations and special deals than were others.[54]

Weinberg also believes that a wide range of competing brands contributes to disloyalty because of the information gained through experience with those brands.[55]

Not all researchers, however, are convinced of the influence of market structure variables on brand loyalty. Thus, if brand loyalty were successful in building up the resistance of buyers to switch to other brands in the face of changes in market conditions, one would expect that the elasticities for loyal buyers with respect to some of the major market structure variables would be less than those for the nonloyal group. Massy and Frank, however, found no statistically significant difference between the price, dealing, and retail advertising elasticities for families who were brand loyal and those who were not.[56]

Moreover, another study casts doubts on Farley's conclusions concerning the relationship between brand loyalty and the number of brands available in the market. Specifically, a laboratory experiment conducted by Anderson, Taylor, and Holloway found that the greater the number of alternatives available, the greater the concentration on the most frequently chosen alternative.[57]

Brand loyalty correlates: summary and critical appraisal

The major conclusions that can be drawn concerning the correlates of brand loyalty are:

1. Socioeconomic, demographic, and psychological variables generally do not distinguish brand-loyal consumers from other consumers when traditional definitions of brand loyalty are used.

2. When extended definitions of brand loyalty are used, some socio-

---

54 Day, "Two-Dimensional Concept."

55 Charles B. Weinberg, "The Decay of Brand Segments," *Journal of Advertising Research*, vol. 13 (February 1973), pp. 44–47.

56 William F. Massy and Ronald E. Frank, "Short Term Price and Dealing Effects in Selected Market Segments," *Journal of Marketing Research*, vol. 2 (May 1965), pp. 171–85.

57 Lee K. Anderson, James R. Taylor, and Robert J. Holloway, "The Consumer and His Alternatives: An Experimental Approach," *Journal of Marketing Research*, vol. 3 (February 1966), pp. 62–67.

economic, demographic, and psychological variables are related to loyalty. However, these relationships tend to be product specific rather than ubiquitous across-product categories.

3. There is limited evidence that the loyalty behavior of an informal group leader affects the behavior of other group members.

4. Store loyalty is commonly associated with brand loyalty. Moreover, store loyalty appears to be an intervening variable between certain consumer characteristics and brand loyalty. In other words, certain consumer characteristics are related to store loyalty, which in turn is related to brand loyalty.

5. There is some evidence that brand loyalty is inversely related to the number of stores shopped.

6. The relationship between amount purchased and brand loyalty is uncertain because of contradictory findings.

7. The relationship between interpurchase time and brand loyalty is also uncertain due to contradictory findings.

8. There is limited evidence that perceived risk is positively related to brand loyalty.

9. Market structure variables, including the extensiveness of distribution and the market share of the leading brand, exert a positive influence on brand loyalty.

10. The effects of the number of alternative brands, special deals, and price activity are uncertain due to contradictory findings.

The fact that many of the findings concerning brand-loyalty correlates are inconclusive and/or contradictory is due, in part, to the infancy of this type of research and, hence, the absence of a widely accepted research tradition. Future research efforts might be more productive if certain guidelines were adopted.

In attempting to isolate correlates, the evidence suggests that brand loyalty should be treated as a *product-specific rather than a general attribute.* Many studies have demonstrated that correlates vary across products. Thus, attempts to determine characteristics of consumers who are brand loyal across all product categories are confounded by inherent product differences. As such, a study based on product X showing a relationship between brand loyalty and certain characteristics is not necessarily contradicting another study based on product Y that concludes that the same characteristics are unrelated to brand loyalty.

Studies based on correlations also generally do not permit the researcher to impute cause and effect relationships. The latter require carefully controlled laboratory and field experiments. Greater use of panels specifically designed for a longitudinal analysis of brand loyalty (as contrasted with existing commercial panels) would probably accelerate progress.

Finally, progress may be improved by the use of more powerful statistical techniques. Simplistic analysis based on proportions and rank correlations should at least be supplemented with factor analysis, regression analysis, AID analysis, discriminant analysis, and various clustering approaches.

Brand loyalty models

A wide variety of mathematical models have been designed in an attempt to understand brand-loyalty behavior over time. The primary emphasis has been on *stochastic* models, which treat the response of consumers in the market place as the outcome of some probabilistic process. A stochastic model, with its built-in probability component, is distinguished from or contrasted with *deterministic* models, in which an attempt is made to predict behavior in exact or nonprobabilistic terms.

The consumer behavior model used throughout the book is deterministic. You might therefore ask why switch to stochastic models when analyzing a special type of decision, namely loyal brand purchases. The reason why stochastic models are used is to allow for a multitude of variables that are not or cannot be measured. Stochastic models are really a simplification of reality, although it may not seem that way when you look at some of the models.

There are two basic philosophies of stochastic models. The first philosophy recognizes that many factors determine the outcome of behavior even though most of these factors are not measured nor explicitly included in the model of market response. Such factors may include a wide range of individual consumer variables (personality, attitudes, income, and so forth) as well as a wide range of exogenous variables such as advertising, price, competitive activity and so forth. Even though these variables are not explicitly considered in the model, their effect is accounted for in the stochastic nature of the response. Montgomery and Urban conclude:

> This procedure is parsimonious in that consumer behavior may often be described by relatively simple stochastic models, whereas the adoption of a deterministic approach would require exceedingly complex models.[58]

A second philosophy of stochastic models is based upon the premise that not only is the model of market response stochastic but the actual consumer process is stochastic. Stated alternatively, consumer choices are random (probabilistic) because there is a *stochastic element in the brain* that influences choice. Thus, it is less possible even in principle to provide an explanation for the (stochastic) component than it is to provide an explanation for the outcome of the toss of a coin.[59] This is in sharp

58 David B. Montgomery and Glen L. Urban, *Management Science in Marketing* (Englewood Cliffs, New Jersey: Prentice-Hall, Inc., 1969), p. 54.
59 Frank M. Bass, "The Theory of Stochastic Preference and Brand Switching," *Journal of Marketing Research*, vol. 11 (February 1974), pp. 1–20.

contrast with the more dominant stream of consumer research in which the underlying premise is that behavior is caused and can therefore be explained at least in principle, even if adequate data does not exist to account for behavior at any point in time. Most of the stochastic models described in the remaining part of the chapter have not explicitly considered which philosophy is true and similar models have been used by researchers of both philosophies. Bass, a proponent of the philosophy of stochastic brain processes, concluded:

> It will never be possible to prove conclusively that behavior is fundamentally stochastic or fundamentally deterministic since it will never be possible to measure all of the variables which influence choice.[60]

Following a brief overview of the basic logic and terminology of models, this section examines the most widely used ones, describing the basic characteristics of each without a high degree of mathematical sophistication, pointing out their strengths and limitations.[61] This section closes with a discussion of potentially useful areas for future research and application.

The models that follow describe a functional relationship between the probability of choosing a brand during a purchase occasion and the factors that have an effect on this probability.[62] Some of these factors include feedback from past purchases, influence of exogenous market forces, and factors indigenous to various households.

Overview of brand-loyalty models

Purchase-event feedback is normally expressed in terms of the number of previous purchases that are allowed to have an effect on the present purchase. The effect of market forces is normally incorporated in the form of a time trend term in the model. Finally, population heterogeneity is treated by allowing the parameters of a given model to have a distribution over the entire population, by *a priori* dividing the population into more homogeneous groups and developing model parameters separately for each group, or by explicitly including in the model some of the factors causing heterogeneity. The models presented below cover a wide range of complexity, from the very simple Bernoulli model that treats the population as being homogeneous, with no purchase event feedback and no effect of external factors, to the more complex probability diffusion models that permit inclusion of effects due to most of the factors.

The study of brand loyalty models often requires considerable mathe-

---

60 Bass, "Theory of Stochastic Preference," p. 2.

61 For an excellent summary of these models, see Massy et al., *Stochastic Models*.

62 In *Stochastic Models of Buying Behavior*, Massy, Montgomery, and Morrison provide a clear distinction between "brand choice models" and "purchase incidence models." Whereas the former deal with the probability of choosing a brand on a given purchase occasion, the latter are concerned with purchase timing and amount of purchase. Although brand choice models may be modified to include purchase timing, specialized purchase incidence models are often more useful when describing specific sales prediction during a given period. Because of the greater relevance of brand choice models to our discussion, the presentation is limited to models in this category. For a thorough analysis of some of the purchase incidence models, including the negative binomial, Poisson, logistic, exponential and others, the student is referred to Chapters 8 through 11.

matical sophistication. In preparing this section of the chapter, an effort has been made to avoid those mathematical concepts that would keep many readers from understanding the material. It is necessary to use mathematical symbols to describe the models but an attempt is also made to explain the meaning of each model in words that can be understood by any reader who will make an effort to understand the concepts and basic relationships important to the model. Readers with more affinity for mathematical topics may want to refer to the source materials of the models, referenced in the footnotes.

Bernoulli models

The earliest investigations of brand loyalty assumed, at least implicitly, that the behavior could be described as a Bernoulli process in which the consumer is assumed to have a constant probability p of purchasing the brand under study.[63] The probability p is determined from aggregate brand choice data and is assumed to be independent of all external influences, prior purchases, or consumer characteristics.

This process can be represented simply for some brand, A, and by a composite of all other brands, B. The probability of purchasing brand A at a purchase occasion t, is represented as $p(A_t)$ and is determined from aggregate brand choices between A and B.

The behavioral premise of early Bernoulli models suggests there is no feedback from the purchase event. The response probability may be free to change over time, however, which permits the model to reflect changes in anticipated or unanticipated circumstances such as the limited number of brands available at a store, specials, or out-of-stock conditions. Therefore, if brand A becomes available in more stores, for example, the probability of buying brand A can be expected to rise for many consumers who purchase that brand, all other factors remaining constant.

Modifications to the Bernoulli model. Several variations of the basic Bernoulli model have been developed by explicitly considering the heterogeneity in the population. These include the compound Bernoulli model and the dynamic Bernoulli model.

Compound Bernoulli model. In the compound Bernoulli model, the probability p is constant for each particular individual but varies over the entire population according to some prespecified probability distribution. In other words, different individuals in the population are permitted to have different fixed values of p.[64]

Dynamic Bernoulli model. In the dynamic Bernoulli model, the purchase probability p is not only allowed to vary between individuals, but is also allowed to change from one purchase situation to another for the same customer.[65]

63 Brown, "Brand Loyalty"; Cunningham, "Perceived Risk."
64 Massy et al., *Stochastic Models*, p. 59.
65 Ronald A. Howard, "Dynamic Inference," *Journal of Operations Research Society of America*, vol. 13 (September 1965), pp. 712–33.

The basic model as well as its variations all assume a "zero-order process"; that is, they assume that past history has no effect on the present or future purchase probability. Several other models also are developed making such an assumption. Two of these—the probability-diffusion model and the New Trier model—are described below.

The probability diffusion model was proposed by Montgomery as a *zero-order model*;[66] that is, it does not consider purchase-event feedback. The underlying probabilities are subject to change according to yet another stochastic process. Hence, an individual's response probability is said to be *nonstationary*. The model is also *heterogeneous* since different respondents may have different response probabilities, even though the same response probability change process holds for all respondents.

Probability diffusion model

The Montgomery probability-diffusion model can be described by outlining the major underlying assumptions:

1. Let the brand-choice behavior be described as a dichotomous selection (as in the case of learning models).

2. Assume that each respondent possesses a number N of hypothetical elements, some of which are at any given response occasion associated with response A, and the remainder with response B.[67]

3. If at a particular response occasion t, the respondent has i of his N elements associated with response A, his probability p_t of making response A on that occasion is i/N.

4. The response elements change allegiance between A and B according to a mechanism that can be described as follows:

$$\lambda_i = (\alpha + \sqrt{i}) (N - i)$$
$$\mu_i = (\beta + (N - i)v)i$$

where:

α = the probability of an element associated with response *B* to change to *A*

β = the propensity of change from *A* to *B*

v = a proportionality factor whereby the propensity of each element to change allegiance is increased by an amount for each element associated with the opposite response.

The first expression above is a product of the single-element propensity to change from response *B* to *A* and the number of response elements in *B*. The second expression is interpreted similarly.

The above assumptions, together with the assumption of no purchase feedback and independence of responses of various consumers, lead Montgomery to describe the behavior of the average probability of

66 Massy et al., *Stochastic Models*, chap. 6.
67 Although these elements may have behavioral significance, they are proposed strictly as hypothetical constructs for modeling purposes.

purchase over time. Thus he shows that the expected value of p_t can be described by the following functional relationship:

$$m(t) = E[p(t)] = p_j(t_0)e^{-(\alpha+\beta)(t-t_0)} + \frac{\alpha}{\alpha+\beta}[1 - e^{-(\alpha+\beta)(t-t_0)}].$$

In the function, t_0 is the time at which the model was first applied and $p_j(t_0)$ is the initial probability of purchase for individual j. The equation is represented by the curve to Figure 17.1.

Figure 17.1 Behavior of expected value of p_t for the probability diffusion model of brand loyalty

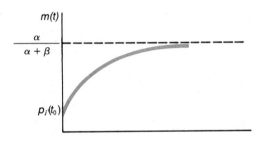

The model represents a change over time in the expected probability of purchase, independent of any purchase feedback effect. The change is therefore assumed to be the result of external environmental factors including promotion.

Modifications to the probability diffusion model. The inability of the probability diffusion model to consider purchase event feedback led Jones to develop what he terms a dual-effects model.[68] In essence, Jones proposes a modification to the propensities of change of the response elements as follows:

$$\lambda_i = (\alpha_n + \sqrt{i})(N - i)$$
$$\mu_i = \left[\beta_n + \sqrt{(N-i)}\right]i$$

where subscript n denotes the nth purchase, and α_n and β_n are allowed to change from one purchase to another according to a certain mechanism.[69] Thus a simple mechanism would be

$$\alpha_n = \begin{cases} \alpha_{n-1} + \lambda, & \text{if } A \text{ was purchased at } n \\ \alpha_{n-1}, & \text{if } B \text{ was purchased at } n \end{cases}$$

$$\beta_n = \begin{cases} \beta_{n-1}, & \text{if } A \text{ was purchased at } n \\ \beta_{n-1} + \phi & \text{if } B \text{ was purchased at } n \end{cases}$$

68 J. Morgan Jones, "A Dual-Effects Model of Brand Choice," *Journal of Marketing Research*, vol. 7 (November 1970), pp. 458–64; also J. M. Jones, "A Comparison of Three Models of Brand Choice," *Journal of Marketing Research*, vol. 7 (November 1970), pp. 466–73.
69 Jones, "A Comparison of Three Models."

Using this model, the change in average purchase probability through time can be expressed by the curve in Figure 17.2.

Figure 17.2 Behavior of expected value of p_t for dual-effects model of brand loyalty

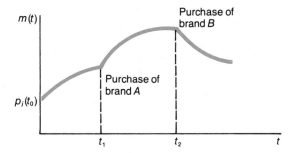

Source: J. Morgan Jones, "A Dual-Effects Model of Brand Choice," *Journal of Marketing Research*, vol. 7 (November 1970), pp. 458–64, at p. 461. Reprinted from the *Journal of Marketing Research* published by the American Marketing Association.

New Trier model

The New Trier model was developed specifically to model the brand choice behavior of a consumer who has purchased a brand that was previously unfamiliar to the consumer. The brand does not have to be a new brand in the marketplace, only a brand not used before by that consumer or one used so long ago that the consumer has essentially forgotten it. This model was developed by Aaker and is a zero-order model as well as heterogeneous and nonstationary.[70]

The model assumes that there is a trial period after the initial purchase, during which the probability of purchasing the brand for that family remains constant. After a number of trial-period purchases, which is assumed to vary from consumer to consumer, the consumer is assumed to reach a decision and therefore to have a new probability of purchasing the brand. The probabilities of purchasing the new brand during and after the trial period are assumed to be distributed across the population according to independent beta distributions, thus achieving interconsumer heterogeneity.

Aaker's New Trier model includes an opportunity for the consumer to reject the brand in the post-trial period. The probability of the consumer rejecting the brand is assumed to decrease with time. In the post-decision period, the consumer has a constant probability. The outputs and uses of the New Trier model are similar to those yielded by the probability diffusion model.

70 David A. Aaker, "The New-Trier Stochastic Model of Brand Choice," *Management Science*, vol. 17 (April 1971), pp. 435–50. Also see David A. Aaker, "A Measure of Brand Acceptance," *Journal of Marketing Research*, vol. 9 (May 1972), pp. 160–67.

Zero-order models of the type described above have originated in fairly simplistic formulations of limited usefulness. They have developed, however, into the more sophisticated models incorporating heterogeneity and nonstationarity that have provided a good fit to empirical brand-data in specific product classes. The assumption of a "zero-order process," however, limits the usefulness of the model, causing development of the Markov models described below.

Markov models

Unlike Bernoulli models, Markov models consider the influence of past purchases on the probability of current purchases. The number of previous purchases that are assumed to affect the current purchases is designated by the *order* of the model. For example first order means the last purchase, second order means the last two purchases, and so on.

The first-order stationary Markov model. To illustrate the characteristics of a first-order Markov model, consider a product category with three brands: A, B, and C. Based on past purchase data for a sample of consumers, the researcher estimates the conditional (or transitional) probabilities of moving from one state to another in *any two* consecutive time periods. These transitional probabilities are shown in Figure 17.3.

Figure 17.3 Hypothetical Markov transitional probabilities

	Next purchase			
Last purchase	A	B	C	Total
A	0.7	0.1	0.2	1.0
B	0.3	0.6	0.1	1.0
C	0.4	0.1	0.5	1.0

Figure 17.3 is interpreted as follows. If a consumer purchased brand A during a certain period, then during the next period there is a 70 percent chance that he will buy A again, a 10 percent chance of buying B, and a 20 percent chance of buying C. Similarly, a buyer of brand B during the last period would have a 30 percent probability of buying A during the next period, a 60 percent chance of buying B, and a 10 percent chance of buying C.

Figure 17.3 is called a transitional matrix. It is essentially a measure of brand-switching (or conversely, brand-loyal) behavior. Most Markov models assume that the matrix is stationary; that is, the transition probabilities remain unchanged through time.

To illustrate the mechanics of the Markov process, it is useful to compute the probabilities of a consumer's purchasing brands *A, B,* or *C* during future purchase periods, given the actual purchase during the present period. Thus, if the consumers purchased brand *A* during period

1, the probability of buying the different brands during periods 2, 3, 4, and 5 would be as follows:[71]

	Brand		
Period	A	B	C
2	0.70	0.10	0.20
3	0.60	0.15	0.25
4	0.57	0.17	0.26
5	0.55	0.19	0.26

On the other hand, if brand *B* was purchased during period I, the corresponding probabilities for future periods would be as follows:

	Brand		
Period	A	B	C
2	0.30	0.60	0.10
3	0.43	0.40	0.17
4	0.49	0.30	0.21
5	0.52	0.25	0.23

Similar computations could be made for brand *C* by following the procedures outlined in footnote 71.

If this process were continued indefinitely, the probabilities of the consumer being in states *A, B,* and *C* during future periods will approach a set of equilibrium, or "steady-state" values. These steady-state probabilities are independent of past history; that is, regardless of the actual purchases during period 1, the probability of the consumer's buying *A, B,* or *C* after a theoretically infinite number of transitions would approach a predetermined set of values dependent only on the transition matrix. For

71 These probabilities can be computed by methods of matrix algebra or by simply tracing behavior by means of a tree diagram. Only sample computations are shown below.

For a consumer buying *A* during period I, the probabilities during period II are obvious. The probability of his buying *A* during period III would be .7 × .7 + .1 × .3 + .2 × .4 = .60; for *B* it would be 0.7 × 0.1 + 0.1 × 0.6 + 0.2 × 0.1 = 0.15; and for *C* it would be 0.7 × 0.2 + 0.1 × 0.1 + 0.2 × 0.5 = 0.25. For the student familiar with matrix algebra, all nine probabilities for period III (three each for different purchases during period I) can be obtained by multiplying the transition matrix by itself. The new matrix can be postmultiplied by the original transition matrix to obtain probabilities for period IV.

The probabilities that we have computed here should not be confused with the transition matrix probabilities. The latter simply refer to the effect of the *immediately preceding* purchase expressed in the form of the probability of purchase during the next period. The probabilities that we have computed (using the transition probabilities) correspond to many future periods *given* the actual purchase during the first period and *assuming a stationary transition matrix* between each pair of consecutive periods.

the transition matrix in the example, these steady state probabilities would be 0.54, 0.20, and 0.26.[72]

For a more detailed discussion of Markov models and their characteristics, the reader is referred to the work of Herniter and Magee,[73] Maffei,[74] Lipstein,[75] Harary and Lipstein,[76] and others noted below.[77]

Criticisms of the first-order stationary Markov model. The model described above is plagued with numerous problems. First, since there is evidence that brand choice is influenced by many past purchases, the first-order assumption has been challenged by many as being too restrictive.[78]

Second, the stationarity assumption underlying the transition matrix has been criticized. Thus, although Maffei[79] and Styan and Smith[80] report the acceptability of the assumption in their research, they have been strongly challenged by Ehrenberg[81] and Massy,[82] the latter concluding that stationarity is the exception rather than the rule.

The homogeneity assumption is another problem. The model assumes that all buyers have the same transition probabilities. Several researchers have demonstrated that homogeneity is inconsistent with empirical evidence.[83]

The aggregation problem is a fourth criticism. This problem occurs because the probability of a particular consumer's buying a brand is actually inferred from the relative frequency of purchasing that brand in the aggregate sample. In other words, if 60 consumers in a group of 100 buy brand A, each of the 100 customers is said to have a 60-percent

---

72 The steady-state probabilities p_1, p_2, and p_3 can be derived by solving the following set of simultaneous equations (stated in matrix notation):

$$(p_1 \ p_2 \ p_3) \begin{matrix} 0.7 & 0.1 & 0.2 \\ 0.3 & 0.6 & 0.1 \\ 0.14 & 0.1 & 0.5 \end{matrix} = (p_1 \ p_2 \ p_3)$$

and $p_1 + p_2 + p_3 = 1$.

73 Jerome D. Herniter and John F. Magee, "Customer Behavior as a Markov Process," *Operations Research*, vol. 9 (January–February 1961), pp. 105–22.

74 Richard B. Maffei, "Brand Preferences and Simple Markov Processes," *Operations Research*, vol. 8 (March–April 1960), pp. 210–18.

75 Benjamin Lipstein, "The Dynamics of Brand Loyalty and Brand Switching," in *Proceedings of the 5th Annual Conference of the Advertising Research Foundation* (New York: The Foundation, 1959).

76 F. Harary and B. Lipstein, "The Dynamics of Brand Loyalty: A Markovian Approach," *Operations Research*, vol. 10 (January–February 1962), pp. 19–40.

77 George P. H. Styan and H. Smith, Jr., "Markov Chains Applied to Marketing," *Journal of Marketing Research*, vol. 1 (February 1964), pp. 50–55; J. E. Draper and L. H. Nolin, "A Markov Chain Analysis of Brand Preference," *Journal of Advertising Research*, vol. 4 (September 1964), pp. 33–39; J. S. Stock, "Paired Market Choice Model—A Simplified Approach to Markov Chains," in Henry Gomez, ed., *Innovation—Key to Marketing Progress* (Chicago: American Marketing Association, 1963), pp. 99–105.

78 See, for example, Howard and Sheth, *Theory of Buyer Behavior*, pp. 237–38.

79 Maffei, "Brand Preferences."

80 Styan and Smith, "Markov Chains."

81 A. S. C. Ehrenberg, "An Appraisal of Markov Brand Switching Models," *Journal of Marketing Research*, vol. 2 (November 1965), pp. 347–62, at p. 353.

82 William F. Massy, "Order and Homogeneity of Family Specific Brand Switching Processes," *Journal of Marketing*, vol. 3 (February 1966), pp. 48–54, at p. 53.

83 See, for example, Ronald E. Frank, "Brand Choice as a Probability Process," *Journal of Business*, vol. 35 (January 1962), pp. 43–56.

probability of buying that brand. Howard[84] suggested a vector Markov model which, while resolving the aggregation problem, necessitates making other unacceptable assumptions.[85]

A fifth problem inherent in Markov models deals with interpurchase time. All consumers cannot be expected to purchase on a precise cycle with a prespecified interpurchase time. Approaches that attempt to overcome this objection include the introduction of a dummy "no purchase" brand to take the place of an actual purchase. However, a purchase versus no purchase decision is different from a brand-choice decision. As a result, Howard[86] has suggested a time-dependent semi-Markov model that explicitly treats time as a random variable. Kuehn and Rohloff[87] and Morrison[88] offer other approaches to incorporate different interpurchase times.

Other criticisms of the first-order Markov model revolve around the problem of inferring transition probabilities for the entire population based on sample estimates. Updating these probabilities, based on other relevant information, also presents problems. Under these conditions, Herniter and Howard recommend use of a Bayesian framework for revising a priori probabilities.[89]

A seventh problem lies in determining how issues such as multiple-brand purchases or multiple purchases of the same brand should be handled. Unfortunately, most of the recommended approaches necessitate forcing actual data into an artificial format suitable for Markov analysis.[90]

Finally, it is difficult to obtain valid purchase data unless expensive longitudinal designs are used.[91] This may limit the profitable use of the model.

Proposed modifications to the first-order Markov model. A variety of attempts have been made to overcome the limitations of the first-order stationary Markov model. The most popular variations are discussed below.

(1) Models overcoming the stationarity assumption. Lipstein attempted to deal with objections to the stationarity assumption by developing a

---

84 Ronald A. Howard, "Stochastic Process Models of Consumer Behavior," *Journal of Advertising Research*, vol. 3 (September 1963), pp. 35–40.

85 Howard and Sheth, *Theory of Buyer Behavior*, pp. 236–37.

86 Howard, "Stochastic Process Models," p. 40.

87 Alfred A. Kuehn and A. C. Rohloff, "New Dimensions in Analysis of Brand Switching," in Fred E. Webster, ed., *New Directions in Marketing* (Chicago: American Marketing Association, 1965), pp. 297–308.

88 Donald G. Morrison, "Interpurchase Time and Brand Loyalty," *Journal of Marketing Research*, vol. 3 (August 1966), pp. 289–92.

89 Jerome D. Herniter and Ronald Howard, "Stochastic Marketing Models," in D. B. Hertz and R. T. Eddison, eds., *Progress in Operations Research*, vol. 2 (New York: Wiley, 1964).

90 See, for example, Draper and Nolin, "A Markov Chain Analysis," pp. 33–39; Styan and Smith, "Markov Chains Applied to Marketing," pp. 50–55.

91 See, for example, Donald H. Granbois and James F. Engel, "The Longitudinal Approach to Studying Marketing Behavior," in Peter D. Bennett, ed., *Marketing and Economic Development* (Chicago: American Marketing Association, 1965), pp. 205–21.

Markov model of brand loyalty that has a nonstationary transition matrix.[92]

(2) Models overcoming the homogeneity assumption. Morrison suggested a variety of ways of overcoming the unrealistic homogeneity assumption.[93] One approach is to divide consumers into two groups—hard-core loyal buyers and potential switchers. This dichotomous classification can be extended into a continuum of loyalty, yielding what are generally termed compound Markov models.[94] However, these models require a dichotomous treatment of the brands available, for example, the favorite brand versus all other brands. Examples of transition matrices under these conditions are discussed below.[95]

1. *The symmetric first-order Markov model*—In this model the transition matrix appears as follows and *p* varies over the entire population according to some prespecified probability distribution.[96]

		Brand purchased at time $t + 1$	
		A*	B†
Brand purchased at time t	A	p	$1-p$
	B	$1-p$	p

* A = brand being studied
† B = all other brands

2. *The brand-loyal model*—In this model *p* is distributed as before, but another parameter, $k(0<k<1)$, which is the same for all individuals, is also introduced. The reasoning, as seen in the matrix below, is that an individual with a high probability of remaining with his brand *A* will also have a higher probability of leaving brand *B* (other brands) to buy *A*, than another individual with a lower *p*.

		Time $t + 1$	
		A	B
Time t	A	p	$1-p$
	B	kp	$1-kp$

92 B. Lipstein, "A Mathematical Model of Consumer Behavior," *Journal of Marketing Research*, vol. 2 (August 1965), p. 269–65; B. Lipstein, "Test Marketing: A Perturbation in the Market Place," *Management Science*, vol. 14 (1968), pp. 3437–48.

93 Massy et al., *Stochastic Models*, pp. 92–93.

94 Donald G. Morrison, "Testing Brand-Switching Models," *Journal of Marketing Research*, vol. 3 (November 1966), pp. 401–9.

95 Massy et al., *Stochastic Models*, pp. 118–36.

96 The β distribution has often been employed for this purpose. For details, see Massey et al., *Stochastic Models*, pp. 60–61.

3. *The last purchase-loyal model*—This model uses somewhat different logic. It argues that a consumer with a high p is more loyal to the brand he purchased last—regardless of which brand it was—than a consumer with a lower p. (Both k and p are defined as before.)

		Time $t + 1$	
		A	B
Time t	A	p	$1-p$
	B	$1-kp$	kp

4. *The general first-order compound model*—In this model the parameters p and q are jointly distributed according to some prespecified distribution.

		Time $t + 1$	
		A	B
Time t	A	p	$1-p$
	B	$1-q$	q

Using the coffee purchases of 531 members of a *Chicago Tribune* panel, Massy, Montgomery, and Morrison obtained a very good fit between the data and "the brand loyal model" described in (2). They concluded that if strong loyalty exists, it is generated toward a particular brand and not toward the most recently purchased brand.[97] In addition, they concluded that loyal consumers are more "Bernoulli" than nonloyals, meaning that recent purchase decisions have a smaller effect on the current purchase decisions of loyals than they do on nonloyals.[98]

(3) Models overcoming the first-order assumption. Another objection to the basic Markov model is that it is first-order; that is, it considers only the previous purchase when modeling the current purchase situation. One way of overcoming this objection is to use higher order Markov formulations. For example, a second-order Markov model considers the effect of two previous purchases. The transition matrix is as follows:

97 Massy et al., *Stochastic Models*, pp. 118–36.
98 Note that when $k=1$, the brand-loyal model is the same as the Bernoulli model. In other words, the higher the k ($0<k<1$), the more "Bernoulli" the group of consumers.

	Purchases during times $t-1$ and t			
		AA	BA	AB	BB
Purchases during times $t-2$ and $t-1$	AA	p_1	—	$1-p_1$	—
	BA	p_2	—	$1-p_2$	—
	AB	—	$1-q_2$	—	q_2
	BB	—	$1-q_1$	—	q_1

Some of the entries in the matrix are blank because the corresponding combinations of states are not possible. For example, a consumer who purchased A in t-2 and B in t-1 could not purchase A in t-1 and either A or B in time t.[99]

Second-order models are unquestionably more realistic than first-order models. However, the data requirements of the higher order models are usually so large that they are unmanageable.

Linear learning models

Models in this category are an outgrowth of the work done by Kuehn[100] based on the learning theory constructs of Bush and Mosteller.[101] The primary concept underlying the development of these models is that past brand choices affect future behavior, and that there is a linear relationship between pre- and postpurchase probabilities. More specifically, let the purchasing process be represented in the form of a dichotomous choice A representing the brand under study and B all other brands. Also let p_t be the probability of buying A during trial t. Using subscripts to represent trials, the model specifies two relationships termed the purchase operator and the rejection operator:

purchase operator: $p_{t+1} = \alpha + \beta + \lambda p_t$, if brand A is purchased at t

or

rejection operator: $p_{t+1} = \alpha + \lambda p_t$, if brand B is purchased at t.

These two operators are graphically illustrated in Figure 17.4. The parameters α and β representing the intercepts ($\alpha + \beta$ for the purchase operator and α for the rejection operator) and λ, the common slope, are assumed to be the same for all consumers and are estimated from panel data.

Suppose at trial $t=0$ there is a certain probability p_0 that a particular respondent would buy brand A. If he actually buys brand A during that trial, the probability of his buying A on the next trial is determined by referring to the purchase operator. A perpendicular drawn from p_0 to intersect the purchase operator will yield the probability at t_1 on the Y axis. This can be transferred to the X axis with the help of the 45° line. Now at t_1, suppose the consumer buys a brand other than A (that is, B), the probability of his buying A at trial t_2 can now be obtained by referring

99 The model does not allow the consumer to buy both brands during any one time period.
100 Alfred A. Kuehn, "Consumer Brand Choice."
101 Robert Bush and Frederick Mosteller, *Stochastic Models for Learning* (New York: Wiley, 1955).

Figure 17.4 Graphical representation of linear learning model

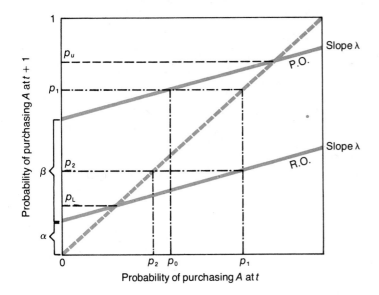

to the rejection operator. The purchase probabilities can thus be revised after each purchase by referring to the appropriate operator.

An interesting characteristic of the model is that the purchase probability approaches, but never exceeds, the maximum value p_u (obtained at the intersection of the purchase operator and the 45° line). Similarly it never falls below p_L (obtained at the intersection of the rejection operator and the 45° line). This is equivalent to saying that consumers generally will not develop such a strong brand loyalty as to ensure either complete acceptance or rejection of a given brand. Another characteristic of the model is that consecutive purchases of brand A increase the probability of buying A on the next purchase, but only at a decreasing rate.

The model has been tested extensively using many branded nondurable consumer grocery and drug items and was found very useful in analyzing brand-switching data.[102] Practical applications of the model, in the form of analyzing effects of advertising and other merchandising influences, have also been suggested.[103] However, in general, learning models have been less popular than their Markov counterparts, especially among practitioners. This may be due to the fact that it is more difficult to estimate the parameters of the learning model, as well as the limitations imposed by the need to treat brand choice in a dichotomous fashion.

102 Alfred A. Kuehn and Ralph L. Day, "A Probabilistic Approach to Consumer Behavior," in Revis Cox, Wroe Alderson, and Stanley Shapiro, eds., *Theory in Marketing* (Homewood: Ill.: Irwin, 1964), pp. 380–90.

103 See, for example, Alfred A. Kuehn and Ralph L. Day, "Probabilistic Models of Consumer Buying Behavior," *Journal of Marketing*, vol. 29 (October 1964), pp. 27–31; Alfred A. Kuehn, "How Advertising Performance Depends on Other Marketing Factors," *Journal of Advertising Research*, vol. 2 (March 1962), pp. 2–10.

Modifications to the learning model. Modifications to the basic model include treatment of population heterogeneity, resulting in what is called a compound learning model. Another modification involves recasting the learning model into a special type of first-order Markov formulation.[104] The learning Markov model, so derived, treats the transition probabilities as a function of two effects—a retention effect and a merchandising activity effect. The former represents the fraction of purchases retained by a brand through habit, whereas the latter represents the effect of the brand's merchandising strategy. Finally, under special conditions the linear learning model would degenerate into a Bernoulli or Markov model. Thus if $\lambda=0$ (the slope of the purchase or rejection operator), the relationships specifying the purchase and rejection operators are equivalent to the transmission matrix:

		time $t+1$	
		A	B
time t	A	$\alpha+\beta$	$1-\alpha-\beta$
	B	α	$1-\alpha$

Similarly if $\alpha=\beta=0$ and $\lambda=1$, $p_{t+1}=p_t$, and we have the simple zero-order Bernoulli model.

Entropy loyalty model

One of the more interesting models to be developed is the entropy model discussed by Carman and Stromberg and more fully developed by Herniter.[105] The concept of entropy is borrowed from the study of thermodynamics and is a measure of uncertainty in a probabilistic system. It is an objective function that can be used to maximize the unknown probabilities of a system. Herniter considered the problem that brand loyalty is not the same as purchase behavior but for operational purposes assumes that a "customer's preference for a brand reflects his or her probability of purchasing the brand on any given occasion."[106]

The entropy model is based upon a multinominal distribution to account for changes in response probabilities. The basic data are market share of brands in a market, constrained by the number of brands. Thus, entropy is used as a measure of uncertainty. From this a measure of loyalty can be determined that is defined for all values of the parameters

104 Alfred E. Kuehn, "A Model for Budgeting Advertising," in Frank M. Bass et al., eds., *Mathematical Models and Methods in Marketing* (Homewood, Ill.: Irwin, 1961), pp. 315–48; A. C. Rohloff, "New Ways to Analyze Brand-to-Brand Competition," in Stephen Greyser, ed., *Toward Scientific Marketing* (Chicago: American Marketing Association, 1963), pp. 224–32.

105 Jerome Herniter, "An Entropy Model of Brand Purchase Behavior," *Journal of Marketing Research*, vol. 10 (November 1973), pp. 361–75. Also see Carman and Stromberg, "A Comparison of Some Measures of Brand Loyalty," 1967.

106 Jerome Herniter, "A Comparison of the Entropy Model and the Hendry Model," *Journal of Marketing Research*, vol. 11 (February 1974), pp. 21–29.

of the underlying multinominal model. It is derived as a natural extension of a likelihood ratio test of the null hypothesis for complete nonloyalty and therefore has a maximum value for the completely nonloyal state and a minimal value for a state that can reasonably be considered most loyal.

The entropy model is of considerable value to marketers because of its reliance on market share data that are more readily available than many other kinds of data based upon characteristics of individual consumers. The use of the model in empirical tests has resulted in good predictions although the model as originally proposed by Herniter was somewhat limited in applications because of the difficulty in applying it to a market with more than a few brands.[107]

The problem of omitting brand preferences in discussing brand loyalty and focusing only on repeat purchase behavior has been treated in research by Jarvis who developed a cognitive brand loyalty model.[108] Jarvis recognized that brand-loyal behavior in most other models appears to have little or no relationship to the consumer's sensitivity to marketing variables such as pricing, advertising or the introduction of new brands. His study therefore examined the relationship between cognitive (or attitudinal) brand loyalty and several marketing-related variables. These variables included the price increase in one's usually purchased brand which is necessary to induce the consumer to switch to an alternative, the likelihood of purchasing a new brand within a product class, and the evaluation of a communication describing a new brand.

Cognitive brand loyalty model

Cognitive brand loyalty was measured using a modified form of the social judgment ordered alternatives methodology. In this methodology, subjects were asked to place the brands with which they were aware in each product class into three "affective" regions according to their acceptability for the next purchase event. These regions were "acceptable, not acceptable, and uncertain."

These categories were classified as AR (acceptance), RR (rejection), and NR (noncommitment). Cognitive loyalty strength was measured by two indices: (1) RR/AR, and (2) RR/AR [1.0−NR], where each region was expressed as a proportion of the brands of which an individual was aware. For both criteria, cognitive loyalty was found to be stronger as the resulting index number increased. The value of a model such as this is its ability to analyze the intentions of consumers rather than utilizing only behavior that is difficult to observe and collect data on.

Evaluation of brand loyalty models

A wide variety of models have been employed in an attempt to understand and predict brand-loyalty behavior. The complexity of brand choice behavior has been the reason so many different models have been

107 See Bass, "Theory of Stochastic Preference," for methods of overcoming these problems.
108 L. P. Jarvis, "An Empirical Investigation of Cognitive Brand Loyalty and Product Class Importance as Mediators of Consumer Brand Choice Behavior," 1972.

developed, each trying to solve specific problems that vary between product categories and buying situations. Numerous assumptions, discussed in conjunction with each of the models, have been introduced by researchers in order to make the models manageable. At the same time, those assumptions frequently create artificialities. The zero-order assumption, suppression of population heterogeneity, and inability to incorporate the influence of external factors are some of the problems associated with many models.

Problems of brand loyalty models

Some problems that are specific to stochastic models of brand loyalty include the following:

1. There may be a many-to-one mapping of models into a set of data; that is, several alternative models with quite different underlying structures may be consistent with the empirical data. Therefore, a need exists for developing methods that discriminate among competing models to determine the appropriate model for a specific product category, market structure and timing, or buying situation.

2. The effects of heterogeneity and nonstationarity of response probability may be confounded in stochastic models.

3. The stochastic process generating the response probabilities may itself change. Although changes in the process will generally occur much more slowly than changes in choice probabilities, this still suggests the need for developing methods that assume only short-run stationarity, even for models that allow the choice probability to change.

4. A combining of classes may create a problem when an "n-alternative" real market is collapsed into a "2-alternative" model market. If combining all "other brands" into a composite brand (as is the case in some models) is to leave the structure of the system unchanged, then a stochastic operater on the state space of the system must be of a special form. (Both Markov and linear learning models involve stochastic operators.)

5. Most of the loyalty models avoid the issue of multibrand loyalty. Yet, many researchers have empirically documented the common sense notion that some consumers exhibit varying degrees of loyalty to several brands in a product category.[109] Some of the more recent work is making attempts at treating multibrand loyalty and provides a greater understanding of the true nature of brand loyalty.[110]

6. Most of the stochastic models do not consider the attitude component of brand loyalty or assume that preference and purchase probabil-

109 Sheth, "Measurement of Multidimensional Brand Loyalty of a Consumer"; Jacoby, "Brand Loyalty Concept," pp. 25–31.

110 A.S.C. Ehrenberg and G. J. Goodhardt, "A Model of Multi-Brand Buying," *Journal of Marketing Research*, vol. 7 (February 1970), pp. 77–84; also see Massy et. al., *Stochastic Models*.

ities are equivalent. This may be one of the factors introducing a degree of artificiality in the models.

Many brand loyalty models have been compared to each other in empirical research by fitting two or more of them to the same data base and then comparing their fit. The fit of the model to the data set is usually determined by a chi-square test with the model to be tested as the null hypothesis. A complementary method of evaluating the fit of models to the empirical data is to examine the estimated parameters of the model to see if any of them attain infeasible values.

Montgomery and Jones have fitted a number of models to the MRCA panel data for Crest toothpaste. Montgomery fitted four models: the brand loyal and last-purchase loyal Markov models, the linear learning model (modified to allow heterogeneity), and the probability-diffusion model to data for Crest toothpaste. The linear learning and the probability-diffusion models seemed to provide a significantly better overall fit to this set of data than the Markov models. The probability-diffusion model seemed to be superior to the linear learning model in the very unstable post-endorsement period.

Jones, also using the Crest data, used considerably different criteria for including households in his sample, and classified people into average interpurchase interval segments on the basis of their post-endorsement behavior, in contrast to Montgomery's use of their pre-endorsement behavior. This gave a slightly better overall fit for the linear learning model. In the same study, Jones also fitted the three versions of his dual-effects model to the Crest data. One version, where the transition intensities change by an additive mechanism, dominated the other two versions for this data base. Even this additive version of the dual-effects model was generally dominated by the linear learning and probability-diffusion models in most segments.

Aaker has also empirically compared his New Trier model and the heterogeneous linear learning model using two sets of panel data on a frequently purchased consumer goods product. In both cases, the linear learning model provided a better fit to the data, as indicated by the p levels associated with the chi-square goodness-of-fit test. As these p levels indicate, both models provide a good fit to the data. Aaker also used the estimated models to predict the empirical proportions that purchase the brands on the nth purchase occasion (n = 1,2, . . . 10) following the estimation period. In both cases, the New Trier model seemed to make better predictions of the empirical proportions, after the first four or five purchase occasions, than did the linear learning model.

In summary, models, while providing a statistically significant fit to data in certain product categories, suffer from oversimplification. Explicit treatment of the influence of marketing variables as well as the differences between individual consumers needs to be emphasized. Also needed is a model (or set of models) that starts out with the determinants of brand loyalty and then attempts to relate these determinants to a valid measure of brand loyalty.

In the future it would seem useful to develop a typology of brand loyalty and focus some attention on explaining the "why" of loyalty as against simply providing correlates of the observed behavior. A plausible typology has been proposed by Engel, distinguishing brand loyalty resulting from inertia, psychological commitment, and marketer strategies.[111] Brand loyalty through inertia may represent an effort to reduce perceived risk and/or certain costs—time, energy, psychological frustration, and so on—incurred in a buying situation. In contrast, brand loyalty through psychological commitment may be the result of factors such as ego involvement, reference-group influence, or a dissonance-reducing strategy. Finally, brand loyalty from marketing strategy may be due to the availability of brands, advertising, or even certain contractual arrangements. More research needs to be done to substantiate or refute these suggested typologies and develop others that may be more relevant.

Finally, an area of research that may benefit from current developments in multidimensional scaling is the study of the relationship between brand loyalty and the perceptual and preference structures of consumers. Thus, questions such as the following may be raised and investigated: In a given product category, does the perceptual configuration of brand-loyal consumers differ from disloyal consumers? More specifically, do brand-loyal consumers perceive the various brands in a product category as being substantially dissimilar, whereas disloyal consumers perceive all the brands as being very similar? On the other hand, one may argue, in view of the concept of brand loyalty through inertia, that a brand-loyal consumer may indeed perceive all brands as being very similar and become loyal to one in order to reduce the effort necessary to choose among the many similar brands. A related question may be: Is the object of loyalty perceived as being very different from the other brands? Also, in the case of multiple-brand loyalty, is the consumer loyal to a group of brands that are perceived as being similar, or does he pick a few dissimilar brands and become loyal to them?

Marketing implications

Some marketing implications have been discussed throughout the chapter. To avoid being redundant, the discussion that follows is confined to the general implications of brand loyalty to marketing strategists.

Brand loyalty is one way of segmenting a market. For example, some of the ways a manufacturer of brand *A* could attempt to increase his sales are:

1. Increase the number of consumers who are loyal to brand *A*.

---

111 James F. Engel, "The Influence of Needs and Attitudes on the Perception of Persuasion," in Greyser, *Toward Scientific Marketing*, pp. 18–29.

2. Decrease the number of consumers who are loyal to competing brands.

3. Increase the number of nonloyal consumers who purchase the product to purchase brand A.

4. Increase the amount purchased among consumers who are loyal to brand A.

5. Convince those who do not purchase the product to purchase brand A.

Marketing programming to any of these segments is practical only if the consumers comprising these segments are identifiable. In some instances, brand loyalty is not a useful basis for segmenting markets. For example, in the case of grocery products, brand-loyal customers do not seem to differ from other customers in terms of attitudes, personality and socioeconomic characteristics, amount purchased, or sensitivity to pricing, dealing, retail advertising, or the introduction of new brands.[112] However, this finding may not be applicable to other product categories, and may not even hold for individual grocery products if the suggestions articulated in this chapter are implemented.

A previous section of the chapter identified typologies of consumer loyalty. Although the classification is only tentative, it is possible to indicate how marketing strategy would differ between types of loyalties. Thus, if loyalty is attributable to inertia, then significant product improvements, price reductions, effective advertisements pointing out unperceived product benefits, and several other strategies could all trigger a change in buying behavior. In other words, meaningful changes in marketing variables might not be screened out through selective perception, so that it might be possible to change brand loyalty through appropriate promotion, product, and pricing strategies.

These types of strategies, however, are less likely to be effective if loyalty is caused by psychological commitment to a brand. In these situations, the probability that selective attention, comprehension, and recall will weaken the effects of marketing strategies is probably much higher.

To illustrate a somewhat different approach, consider a market where a significant segment of consumers is loyal to a particular brand. Assume that research indicated that these consumers consider certain other brands as falling in their region of acceptance, and the rest of the brands distributed over the regions of neutrality and rejection.

What is the most effective marketing strategy for brands in the various regions? The most preferred ("loyal") brand could emphasize the importance of the product attribute(s) that has led consumers to become loyal to that brand. Marketers of other brands in the region of acceptance could

---

112 Ronald E. Frank, "Is Brand Loyalty a Useful Basis for Market Segmentation?" *Journal of Advertising Research*, vol. 7 (June 1967), pp. 27–33, at p. 33.

emphasize the comparability between themselves and the "loyal" brand on this attribute(s), and minimize any perceived or real differences. Marketers of brands in the regions of neutrality and rejection, on the other hand, would probably be better advised to focus their efforts on a different product attribute(s), and make that attribute(s) salient.[113]

Finally, consider the relevance of brand loyalty models—the Markov models as a specific example—to the marketing strategist. The transition matrix in the model represents brand switching behavior. In addition to the long run steady-state probabilities, which approximate eventual market shares, a marketer may be particularly interested in the changes that take place in the transition matrix as the result of promotional efforts. Conceptually, the optimum level of promotional effort can be determined by relating changes in transition probabilities to the investment required to bring about the changes.

The transition probabilities also suggest certain general types of marketing strategies. For example, if all the diagonal entries of the matrix are of high magnitude (0.9), the implication is that the marketer should direct his efforts at inducing consumers to try his brand. If a reasonable degree of success is achieved, there is a high probability that these consumers will stay with the brand and become loyal consumers.[114]

Summary

This chapter was concerned with a temporal aspect of consumer behavior— brand loyalty. Researchers define loyalty in a wide variety of ways. Consequently, it is difficult to compare and synthesize findings. Therefore, the need for a new and extended definition of brand loyalty was articulated and a definition incorporating both behavioral and attitudinal components was presented.

Regardless of the precise definition, researchers have found conclusive evidence of the existence of brand loyalty. Attempts to determine the reasons for the variation in loyalty across products and consumers have, however, produced contradictory results. The chapter discussed at length numerous characteristics of consumers, their shopping patterns, and the market structure that have been investigated by researchers in attempts to identify correlates of brand loyalty. Studies concentrating primarily on the economic, demographic, and social-psychological characteristics of consumers have yielded the most discouraging results.

In recent years, many attempts have been made to develop and/or use stochastic models to relate probabilities of brand choice to factors such as purchase feedback, influence of external marketing activities, and characteristics of consumers. The most popular models were presented and evaluated. Unfortunately, the models usually begin with a mathematical formulation and manipulate empirical data to fit them. Future research in this area needs to

113 For more details, see Jacoby, "Model of Multi-Brand Loyalty," pp. 30–31.

114 For further discussion, see John U. Farley and Alfred E. Kuehn, "Stochastic Models of Brand Switching," in George Schwartz, ed., *Science in Marketing* (New York: Wiley, 1965), pp. 446–64.

concentrate on more valid measures of brand loyalty and an explicit treatment of marketing influences as well as consumer heterogeneity.

Finally, the marketing implications of brand loyalty were discussed. Brand loyalty is a useful way of segmenting markets provided that consumers exhibiting various kinds and degrees of loyalty can be identified and reached profitably. The approach used may vary depending on whether loyalty is due to inertia, psychological commitment, or marketer influence. Finally, it was shown how a Markov model transition matrix can be used to help formulate promotional strategy.

Review and discussion questions

1. Define or otherwise describe the following: (a) state, (b) brand loyalty, (c) transition probability, (d) stationarity, (e) homogeneity, and (f) psychological commitment.

2. How does the learning model differ from a first-order Markov model?

3. What are the various definitions of brand loyalty? How should brand loyalty be defined?

4. Is brand loyalty a useful basis for market segmentation? Discuss.

5. What conclusions can be drawn concerning the correlates of brand loyalty?

6. What are the uses and limitations of first-order Markov models?

7. Give an example of a multidimensional definition of brand loyalty.

8. Discuss the limitations of the learning model.

9. How does brand loyalty through inertia differ from brand loyalty due to psychological commitment?

10. How would marketing strategy differ depending on whether brand loyalty is due to commitment or inertia?

11. Are Bernoulli models adequate representations of brand loyalty? Why or why not?

12. Formulate a hypothetical model postulating a relationship between brand loyalty and all the factors that have an influence on brand loyalty. Propose a quantifiable measure for each of the variables. What problems do you anticipate in operationalizing your model?

PART 5

CHOICE

Choice and the outcomes of choice are the last stage in the decision process. Chapter 18 examines choice in both a retail store and in-home purchasing environment. It also focuses on post decision dissonance (doubts following purchase) and satisfaction—two of the most important outcomes. Satisfaction, in particular, assumes relevance in the context of the consumerism movement, which has risen in large part to remedy the important causes of dissatisfaction.

Generally the consumer must visit retail stores sometime during the decision-process period. Therefore, Chapter 19 is devoted to store choice processes and shopper profiles. All too frequently retailing has been ignored in the consumer behavior literature, but it will become apparent to the reader that consumer research is by no means the sole province of the manufacturer.

CHAPTER 18

Choice and its outcomes

This chapter focuses on the last two phases of the consumer decision process: choice and the outcomes of choice. Choice (the selection and purchase of an alternative) is examined in both a retail store and in-home purchasing environment. Post decision dissonance (doubt that a correct decision was made) and satisfaction versus nonsatisfaction are the most significant outcomes. The latter dimension, in particular, has been a primary influence on the burgeoning growth of the consumerism movement and the implications for both marketing and consumer education are of major significance.

The choice process

The consumer decision-process model in Figure 18.1 now is almost complete, and it shows that choice is the outcome of two determinants: intentions and unanticipated circumstances. Since the subject of intentions is thoroughly discussed in preceding chapters the primary purpose here is to discuss those unanticipated factors that lead to the nonfulfillment of purchase intentions. This leads quite naturally to the subject of the so-called "unplanned purchase," which is quite a common phenomenon in retail shopping behavior. Purchase behavior in a nonretail setting has a different set of motivations and influences, and it is examined in the concluding section.

The list of possible unanticipated circumstances could, of course, be endless. One quite common one would be nonavailability of funds at the moment. This could either cause the purchase itself to be aborted or lead

Unanticipated circumstances

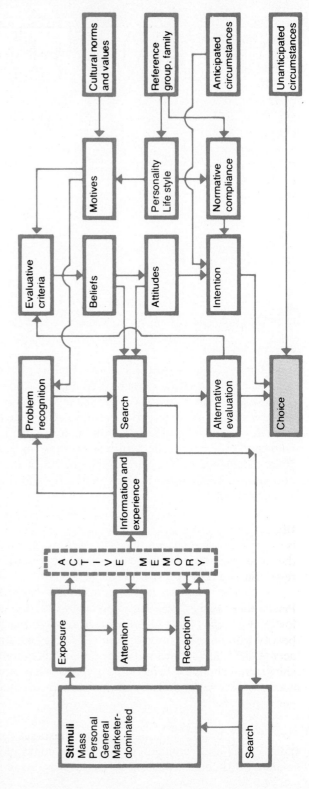

Figure 18.1 The choice process

to brand substitution. Furthermore, the influence of a normative reference group does not cease once intentions have been formed, and it is quite possible that it could be exerted in such a way that intentions are later changed. Finally, there can be a whole set of in-store influences that lead to brand substitution.

The major reasons for brand substitution in supermarkets and drug stores are itemized in Figure 18.2. Substitution is said to occur when a consumer buys a brand or product type that differs from the one that he or she intended to purchase before entering the retail outlet. The incidence of this type of behavior varies widely from one product to the next, and it usually is less than 10 percent of all purchases that have been studied in a variety of retail outlets.[1]

Figure 18.2 Reasons for brand substitution as determined by respondents' self-assessments

	Type of retail outlet	
Reason(s) stated by respondent	Drugstore* (%)	Supermarket† (%)
Saw merchandise	48	Not used
Display	30	25
Less expensive, on sale	9	21
Wanted a change	Not used	19
Usual brand out of stock	2	7
Recommended by family or friends	2	9
All other	9	19

Sources: *Drugstore Brand Switching and Impulse Buying* (New York: Point-of-Purchase Advertising Institute, 1963), pp. 22–23. Reprinted by permission.
†"Colonial Study," *Progressive Grocer*, p. C-118 (1964). Reprinted by permission.

Display and exposure. The major triggering influence on brand substitution is exposure to another alternative. This new information, in effect, causes the consumer to reevaluate established beliefs and attitudes, with the result that the previous intention changes.

Price reductions. A great deal of brand switching occurs as a result of a lowered price. But this does not necessarily signal any lasting change in beliefs and attitudes. It is common for the consumer to have a set of acceptable alternatives, and a reduced price often leads to a temporary shift in choice. The restoration of relative price parity most frequently is accompanied by a return to the preferred brand, all other things being equal.

1 See, for example, *Consumer Buying Habits Studies* (Film Department, E. I. duPont de Nemours and Co., Inc., Wilmington, Del., 1949, 1954, 1959, and 1965); *Drugstore Brand Switching and Impulse Buying* (New York: Point-of-Purchase Advertising Institute, 1963), pp. 22–23; and "Colonial Study," *Progressive Grocer*, p. C-118 (1964).

Out-of-stock conditions. Consumer reactions to out-of-stock conditions are an important consideration in the planning of retail merchandise assortments. Unfortunately, published research is limited to consumer reactions to supermarket merchandise assortments. The results reported below are based on studies conducted by the A.C. Nielsen Company.[2]

(1) Nonavailability of preferred brand. Nielsen research reveals that 42 percent of supermarket shoppers refused to buy a substitute brand when their favorite was out of stock. This type of behavior varies widely by product category, however. For example, 62 percent refused to buy a substitute brand of toothpaste, compared with only 23 percent for toilet tissue.

(2) Nonavailability of preferred size. An average of one out of five customers would not substitute either a brand or size when faced with a stockout in preferred package size. Of the product categories studied, instant coffee led the list with nearly 25 percent refusing to substitute. In comparison, only 13 percent refused to purchase another brand or size of toilet soap.

(3) Nonavailability of colors. A significant percentage of consumers also proved to be uncompromising when it came to desired product colors. For example, one out of ten refused to buy a substitute for desired color in toilet soap and toilet tissues. Although strong brand loyalty seems to exist in these product categories, about 28 percent of toilet tissue purchasers and 17 percent of toilet soap purchasers said they switch brands because of color preference.

(4) Nonavailability of a new product. Consumers also react when a new product is not available on the retailer's shelves. One study showed that nearly 50 percent said they would go elsewhere to find the desired item.[3]

Implications. The reasons cited here for brand substitution should be viewed as suggestive rather than definitive. Carefully controlled experiments need to be conducted before too much confidence is placed in the results.

This type of research is of great importance. Progressive retailers are interested in increasing profit per square foot and are, therefore, more interested in product category sales than brand sales, unless competing brands have widely varying profit contributions. Expenditures of time, money, and space that result in brand substitution rather than increased sales are wasteful. Hence it is advantageous for the retailer to understand the nature and determinants of brand substitution.

In contrast, the manufacturer is interested in maximizing substitutions

2 See "Out-of-Stocks Disappoint Shoppers, Force Store Switching," *Progressive Grocer*, pp. S-26–S-23 (November 1968).
3 For additional research see James D. Peckham, "The Consumer Speaks," *Journal of Marketing*, vol. 27 (October 1963), pp. 21–26.

to his brand and minimizing substitution to other brands. A thorough understanding of why brand substitution occurs, who substitutes away from the brand, and who substitutes to the brand is a prerequisite to designing successful marketing programs.

Studies of retail shopping behavior disclose that the so-called "impulse" or unplanned purchase is commonplace. Unplanned purchasing is defined here as *a buying action undertaken without a problem previously having been recognized or a buying intention formed prior to entering the store.* As the data in Figure 18.3 demonstrate, 50 percent or more of the purchases are made on this basis in supermarkets, and the unplanned purchase represents over 33 percent of all transactions in variety stores and drugstores.[4]

Unplanned purchasing

Figure 18.3 Frequency of unplanned purchases and brand substitution in supermarkets by major product category

| Major product category | Intentions-outcomes categories | | | | | | | |
| | Specifically planned (%) | | Generally planned (%) | | Brand substitution (%) | | Unplanned (%) | |
	1959	1965	1959	1965	1959	1965	1959	1965
Baked goods	22.0	19.6	18.1	19.3	4.7	2.6	55.2	58.5
Beverages	36.9	36.0	10.1	10.4	1.9	1.9	51.1	51.7
Dairy products	30.1	32.7	24.0	16.9	2.6	1.9	43.3	48.5
Drugs, toiletries	27.2		8.0		1.1		63.7	
Frozen foods	17.3	19.0	17.6	16.9	6.1	2.7	59.0	61.4
Groceries	26.0	25.3	16.0	17.5	2.4	1.5	55.6	55.7
Household needs	30.3	30.2	9.7	11.2	2.3	2.1	57.7	56.5
Meats, poultry, fish	35.3	34.3	14.4	13.9	3.5	2.7	44.0	49.1
Produce	44.2	41.1	9.5	13.3	.8	.4	45.5	45.2
Miscellaneous	19.4	24.7	2.4	7.7	.1	.7	78.1	66.9
Average	30.5	31.1	15.9	17.2	2.7	1.8	50.9	49.9

Source: *Consumer Buying Habits Studies* (Film Department, E. I. duPont de Nemours and Co. Inc., Wilmington, Del., 1959, 1965). Figures are *approximate* percentages as calculated by the authors. Reprinted by permission.

Kollat's definitive study of unplanned purchases attempted to isolate the determinants of customer susceptibility to this type of behavior, and he found that there were no economic, demographic, or psychographic differences between those who made an unplanned purchase and those who did not.[5] General types of food shopping behavior such as the use of a food budget, acceptance of trading stamps, and consultation of news-

4 Vernon T. Clover, "Relative Importance of Impulse Buying in Retail Stores," *Journal of Marketing*, vol. 15 (July 1950), pp. 66–70.
5 David T. Kollat, "A Decision-Process Approach to Impulse Purchasing," in Raymond M. Haas, ed., *Science, Technology and Marketing* (Chicago: American Marketing Association, 1966), pp. 626–639.

paper advertising, also did not affect the percentage of unplanned purchases. The only variables showing a positive correlation were:[6]

1. Grocery bill. The percentage of unplanned purchases increased as the shopper's grocery bill increased.

2. Number of products purchased. The percentage of unplanned purchases increased as the number of products that the shopper purchased increased. Moreover, as the number of products purchased increased, the probability that additional purchases would be unplanned approached certainty.

3. Type of shopping trip. The percentage of unplanned purchases was higher during major shopping trips than during fill-in shopping trips.

4. Product purchase frequencies. The more frequently the product was purchased, the lower the probability that the product would be purchased on an unplanned basis.

5. Shopping list. The presence of a shopping list affected the percentage of unplanned purchases when a large number of products (15 or more) was purchased—shoppers with a list purchased a smaller percentage of products on an unplanned basis. When a small number of products was purchased (less than 15), the presence of a shopping list did not affect the percentage of unplanned purchases.

6. Number of years married. The percentage of unplanned purchases increased as the number of years that the shopping party had been married increased.

Explanations for unplanned purchasing. Two factors may explain the widespread reported incidences of unplanned purchasing. The first alleges that the consumer is exposed to new in-store influences. The second argues that incomplete measures of purchase intentions are utilized, with the result that the reported data can be misleading.

(1) Instore exposure. It is possible that differences between purchase intentions and actual purchases are due to the effects of in-store stimuli. Actually seeing a product or brand can produce an unplanned purchase because (1) the shopper uses actual displays as a reminder of shopping needs rather than relying on a shopping list, and/or (2) in-store promotional techniques trigger problem recognition and thereby lead to on-the-spot decision making. Only a limited number of studies have undertaken to measure the influence of point-of-purchase materials on unplanned purchase rates. One study demonstrated that point-of-purchase advertising is more effective than price cuts for this purpose, but there are substantial differences between products.[7] End-aisle display, on the other hand, seems to have little effect,[8] whereas location of a product in a

6 Kollat, "Decision-Process Approach," p. 632.
7 *Triggering Plus Sales and Profits* (New York: Point-of-Purchase Advertising Institute, undated).
8 Ibid.

high-traffic position in proximity to such items as milk, bread, or dairy products does stimulate unplanned buying.[9]

(2) Incomplete measures of purchase intentions. Kollat argues that many consumers are unwilling or unable to commit the time and cognitive resources required to make stated purchase intentions equal actual purchase intentions.[10] This assumes that intentions to buy are measured prior to store entry and that actual purchases are compared with stated intentions upon exit. The consumer may, however, articulate only an incomplete listing of intended purchases, thereby satisfying the requirements of an interview with minimum expenditure of time or mental effort.

The shopper also may be *unable* to itemize purchase plans for a variety of reasons. First, the methodology used in most studies of unplanned purchases forces the shopper, in the absence of a shopping list, to rely strictly on memory. Therefore, it is highly probable that measured plans will deviate to some degree from actual plans. Second, the shopper may know what he or she intends to purchase but may be unable, in the absence of a list, to relate these intentions regardless of the interviewing method used. That is to say, without exposure to in-store stimuli, the customer may be unable cognitively to construct and relate intended purchases.

(3) Implications. The findings to date do not permit a firm conclusion as to the relative roles of these competing explanations. In the interim it seems reasonable to assume that both actually account for the phenomenon under study. Some unplanned purchases probably are triggered by in-store promotions. However, some purchases that are presently termed unplanned probably are not unplanned at all but are purely an artifact of the way in which intentions and behavior are measured.

The significance of unplanned purchasing for marketing planning. Several types of retailers, particularly supermarket managers, allegedly use unplanned purchasing as a criterion for their decisions. Certain store layouts, shelf locations, and types of displays are thought to be more conducive to stimulation of unplanned purchasing than others. Unplanned purchasing also is of interest to manufacturers. Some packaging and point-of-purchase advertising decisions, for example, are based, at least in part, on the assumed rate of unplanned buying.[11]

There are several basic problems with unplanned purchasing that are apparently not widely recognized. These problems need to be given

9 Robert Kelly, "An Evaluation of Selected Variables of End Display Effectiveness," unpublished doctoral diss. (Cambridge, Mass.: Harvard University, 1965).

10 Kollat, "Decision-Process Approach," pp. 626–39. The foundation of this hypothesis was suggested much earlier. See William Applebaum, "Studying Customer Behavior in Retail Stores," *Journal of Marketing*, vol. 16 (October 1951), pp. 172–78.

11 Bert C. McCammon, Jr., "The Role of Point-of-Purchase Display in the Manufacturer's Marketing Mix," in Taylor Meloan and Charles Whitto, eds., *Competition in Marketing* (Los Angeles: Graduate School of Business, University of Southern California, 1964), pp. 75–91, at p. 78.

serious consideration in evaluating the usefulness of the concept or a basis for marketing strategy:

1. Not an operational objective. It has been pointed out that unplanned purchasing has a variety of meanings. The marketing implications sometimes vary according to what definition is accepted. It is questionable whether intelligent marketing decisions can be made concerning how to influence unplanned purchasing when there is so little agreement about what the phenomenon is or what it involves.

2. May exaggerate the potential for increasing sales. Unplanned purchasing often is not unplanned at all but rather an artifact of the way in which the behavior is measured. Consequently, *true* unplanned rates may be considerably lower than those currently accepted.[12] In other words, preshopping decisions about products and brands to be purchased are considerably more common than past studies have indicated. This may encourage an excessive investment of promotional expenditures designed to increase the rate of unplanned purchasing.

3. May be a misleading criterion for selecting products for special promotional efforts. Retailers sometimes use product unplanned purchasing rates to select products for special promotional efforts. Such decisions as store location, shelf height, number of shelf facings, and end-aisle treatment are often based, in part, on product unplanned purchase rates.

Since some unplanned purchasing is not unplanned at all, true unplanned purchasing rates are considerably lower than those that are currently accepted. It seems risky to assume that all product unplanned purchasing rates are inflated to the same degree. Rather, some product unplanned purchasing rates are probably more overstated than are others.

Assume, for example, that product A's unplanned purchase rate is 65 percent and that product B has an unplanned purchase rate of 55 percent. Product A's unplanned purchase rate may be inflated by 40 percentage points and B's by 20 percentage points. The true unplanned purchase rates for A and B would be 25 percent and 35 percent, respectively. While the *gross* unplanned purchasing rates indicate that A should be given special promotional treatment, *true* rates indicate that B should receive the emphasis.

From the discussion above it is apparent that several problems must be overcome before unplanned purchasing can become a useful concept for marketing decisions. First, the concept must be precisely defined. Since the value of the concept hinges in large part on empirical studies of the extent and nature of the behavior, it seems desirable to adopt or adapt a definition used in empirical studies. Second, field studies must be designed so that the measured rate and characteristics of unplanned

---

12 See, for example, *Consumer Buying Habits Studies.*

purchasing correspond to the empirical definition rather than being an artifact of the design itself.

Overcoming these problems will involve a substantial commitment of time and resources. However, the potential value of *true* rates of unplanned purchasing may exceed the costs of obtaining them.

When *true* rates of unplanned purchasing are determined, other categories of planning—specifically planned, generally planned, and brand substitution—would probably differ, both in magnitude and in relative occurrence, from those that are currently accepted. These refined measures of various types of in-store decisions would provide more sensitive indices of the amount and type of promotional effort that should be allocated to products.

In addition, refined measures of unplanned purchasing would permit a partial functional analysis of the strengths and weaknesses of a firm's promotional program. For example, if unplanned purchasing were defined and measured in such a way as to be equivalent to in-store purchase decisions, a manufacturer could use brand rates of unplanned purchasing as a criterion for evaluating the effectiveness of in-store promotional strategy.

Finally, *pure* measures of unplanned purchasing and other categories of planning would constitute one of the most potentially meaningful indices of the real effects of specific in-store product promotions. For example, the difference in a product's unplanned purchase rate before and after a special in-store promotional strategy could be used as a measure of the effectiveness of that strategy. Other planning categories could also be used in this manner. These measures of effectiveness seem particularly useful, since they indicate both the *type* and *extent* of behavioral change precipitated by an in-store promotional strategy. These more sophisticated measures of effectiveness would be useful to retailers as well as manufacturers.

Thus far discussion has focused on situations in which the consumer will visit a retail outlet before purchasing. Store visits obviously are not necessary, since it is possible to order by mail, by telephone, and from a door-to-door salesman. In fact, purchases from these sources nearly doubled between 1961 and 1971 compared with an aggregate retail sales gain of 66 percent during the same period.[13]

In-home shopping

In-home shoppers generally rank above the average in terms of socioeconomic status, but there are no other meaningful demographic differences.[14] There are some important psychographic differences, however, and this type of shopper is described as follows:

1. Venturesome and self-confident.[15]

13 Peter L. Gillett, "In-Home Shoppers—An Overview," *Journal of Marketing*, vol. 40 (October 1976), pp. 81–88, at p. 81.
14 Gillett, "In-Home Shoppers," p. 84.
15 Fred D. Reynolds, "An Analysis of Catalog Buying Behavior," *Journal of Marketing*, vol. 38 (July 1974), p. 48.

2. Innovative and price conscious.[16]

3. Cosmopolitan in outlook and shopping behavior.[17]

The heaviest buyers also appear to be least patronage loyal and use a variety of buying modes and information sources.[18] Convenience, product assortment, price, and availability of unique products are the most common motivations.

Telephone shopping. Unfortunately, there is little evidence on telephone shopping. The problem is complicated by the fact that many stores that sell by telephone do not categorize their sales according to whether the merchandise was purchased in the store or over the telephone. Moreover, most of the empirical studies that have been conducted group telephone shoppers with catalog purchasers and/or consumers who purchase from door-to-door salesmen.[19] Studies investigating consumers purchasing from combinations of nonstore sources are reviewed in the last part of this section.

One study attempted to determine why some consumers are more likely to shop by phone than are others.[20] The study was part of a larger study of department-store shopping behavior.[21] The first stage involved interviews with 2,092 New York housewives and 853 Cleveland housewives. The second stage involved telephone interviews with 723 New York housewives and 461 in Cleveland who had recently ordered something by telephone.

Three general customer characteristics were most commonly associated with telephone shopping.[22]

1. Need for convenience. Telephone shoppers tended to have a greater need for convenience in shopping. They placed a high value on shopping quickly, were more likely to have young children, and were more likely to be residing in the suburbs.

2. Means to shop by telephone. Possession of the means to shop easily by phone was also an important determinant of telephone shopping. Volume of phone ordering increased with income and the possession of a charge account.

16 Christie Paksoy, "Lifestyle and Psychographic Analysis of Catalog Shoppers," presented at American Council of Consumer Interests, 1975.

17 Isabella C. M. Cunningham and William H. Cunningham, "The Urban In-Home Shopper: Socioeconomic and Attitudinal Characteristics," *Journal of Retailing*, vol. 49 (Fall 1973), p. 42.

18 Gillett, "In-Home Shoppers," p. 86.

19 See, for example, Peter L. Gillett, "A Profile of Urban In-Home Shoppers," *Journal of Marketing*, vol. 34 (July 1970), pp. 40–45; Laurence P. Feldman and Alvin D. Star, "Racial Factors in Shopping Behavior," in Keith Cox and Ben Enis, eds., *A New Measure of Responsibility for Marketing* (Chicago: American Marketing Association, 1968), pp. 216–26.

20 Donald F. Cox and Stuart U. Rich, "Perceived Risk and Consumer Decision Making—The Case of Telephone Shopping," *Journal of Marketing Research*, vol. 1 (November 1964), pp. 32–39.

21 Stuart U. Rich, *Shopping Behavior of Department Store Customers* (Cambridge, Mass.: Division of Research, Harvard Business School, 1963).

22 Cox and Rich, "Perceived Risk and Consumer Decision Making," p. 34.

3. Risk perceived in phone shopping. When shopping in person, a customer has the opportunity to reduce uncertainty by personally evaluating the merchandise, by comparing brands, by comparing prices, colors, sizes, and so on. In contrast, the telephone shopper is limited to two methods of uncertainty reduction: reliance on past experience with the store, brand, or product, or reliance on a newspaper advertisement that may or may not picture the product.

Nonphone shoppers perceived intolerable amounts of risk in telephone shopping and were unwilling and/or unable to use newspaper advertising as a useful means of obtaining information and reducing uncertainty.

Mail-order shopping. As used here, mail-order shopping differs from catalog purchasing in that the consumer does not make use of a catalog. Once again, there is a paucity of evidence to report.

One study was undertaken to evaluate whether or not a consumer will perceive greater risk in the act of buying by mail as compared with purchase from a store or directly from a salesman.[23] The primary product investigated was a supplementary hospitalization insurance plan marketed solely through the mail. Using in-home interviews, a quasiexperimental study was conducted with three groups of 100 respondents respectively. Group *A* was a random sample of policy holders living in the Columbus, Ohio, area. Group *B* was selected randomly from the prospect list of the company that had received a promotional mailing from that company one week before the study but had not yet purchased. Group *C*, the control group, consisted of respondents selected randomly from geographical areas matched to those of Group *B*, but they received no promotional mailings.

The study found in general that people perceived more risk in the act of buying by mail than in buying from a store or a salesman. However, mail-order buyers of hospitalization insurance did *not* perceive significantly less risk in mail-order buying other products. Moreover, mail-order buyers of hospitalization insurance did not perceive significantly less risk in the mail-order purchase of such insurance than nonbuyers. Thus, although there was a general tendency for people to perceive more risk in buying by mail than in buying from a store or a salesman, there was an apparent inconsistency between this finding and the finding that mail-order buyers could not be distinguished from nonbuyers in terms of risk perception.[24]

In another study, Feldman and Star[25] analyzed the purchasing behavior of 760 white and 240 nonwhite participants in the 1963 *Chicago Tribune* study, "Chicago Shops."[26] Grouping phone with mail-order shopping,

23 Homer E. Spence, James F. Engel, and Roger D. Blackwell, "Perceived Risk in Mail-Order and Retail Store Buying," *Journal of Marketing Research*, vol. 7 (August 1970), pp. 364–369.

24 Spence, et al., "Perceived Risk," pp. 364–69, at pp. 367–68.

25 Feldman and Star, "Racial Factors," pp. 216–26.

26 "Chicago Shops," *Chicago Tribune* (1963).

they found on an overall basis that the proportion of whites shopping over the phone *or* by mail order (30 percent) was more than twice that of the 13 percent proportion of nonwhites. However, when further classified by income, there was a general similarity in the pattern of phone or mail-order usage by both racial groups. Specifically, as income increased, the proportion of *each* racial group shopping over the phone or by mail order increased.[27]

Catalog shopping. Feldman and Star found that about 40 percent of whites and 18 percent of nonwhites purchased merchandise from catalogs.[28] For both races, catalog buying tended to increase as income increased. The only difference between the two racial groups was found at the lowest income level. The apparent explanation was the lack of credit available to nonwhites at this income level combined with a lower level of literacy.[29]

Door-to-door purchasers. Door-to-door sales are important for some products, especially cosmetics and household cleaning items. Peters and Ford conducted a survey in which they defined "heavy" buying from a particular source as being 50 percent or more of total cosmetic purchases.[30] The heavy in-home buyer was different from her counterparts in the following ways:[31]

1. Had less access to a car for daytime shopping.

2. Tended to be less educated.

3. Was more likely to have children living at home.

4. Was more likely to have a family income under $15,000 annually.

5. Had a greater chance that the head of household would be a blue-collar worker, clerical employee, or a salesman rather than a professional.

Composite in-home shoppers. Gillett conducted a study of in-home shopping in which he defined this type of behavior as comprising placement of a mail or telephone order from the home, or ordering in person from a catalog or a catalog counter of a retail store.[32] In-home shopping was found to be widespread: 70 percent of the women surveyed had shopped at home at least once during the 11-month period of the study. About 43 percent had shopped by direct mail, 38 percent by phone, and 29 percent from catalogs. Only a small fraction of total family expenditures for general merchandise was purchased from these sources, however.

27 Feldman and Star, "Racial Factors," p. 218.
28 Feldman and Star, "Racial Factors."
29 Feldman and Star, "Racial Factors."
30 William H. Peters and Neil M. Ford, "A Profile of Urban In-Home Shoppers: The Other Half," *Journal of Marketing*, vol. 36, pp. 62–64 (January 1972).
31 Peters and Ford, "Profile of Urban In-Home Shoppers."
32 Gillett, "In-Home Shoppers."

In-home shoppers were not found to be a "captive" market, consisting of those actively avoiding the retail store. Rather, this type of purchasing was most often discretionary. Avoiding an extra trip to pick up a needed item and buying in response to an advertisement were typical motivations. Most also considered themselves to be active store shoppers who do not find that form of purchase to be difficult or unpleasant. They were flexible in choice of shopping alternatives; they were not bound by shopping traditions; and they perceived lower than average risk in buying by mail or telephone.[33]

Marketing implications. In view of the dollar volume importance of in-home buying, it is surprising to find so little consumer research in this area.[34] Several provisional statements can be made, however, on the basis of the evidence to date.

First, a longstanding misconception by retailers must be changed. They historically have been reluctant to promote nonstore sales on the assumption of greater expense and the theory that this would detract from total sales rather than to provide additional business. Now, however, it appears that much, if not most, in-home buying represents incremental volume.

Many factors must be considered, of course, in deciding whether to develop volume over the telephone or by mail or catalog.[35] For example, it is always possible that there is greater perceived risk in nonstore buying. If so, the strategy should be designed in cognizance of this danger. Advertisements and catalogs should be informative and written to facilitate ordering by brand, size, or color. Liberal return privileges are also important.

The greatest need now is for further research.[36] It is obvious that the in-home buyer has developed a high level of sophistication. Marketers and consumer educators alike will require definitive data on the in-home shopping decision process. There is much futuristic talk of completely automated in-home buying systems,[37] but such developments seem premature until the necessary basic research is undertaken.

The outcomes of choice

Figure 18.4 shows the complete model of the consumer decision process with special emphasis upon the outcomes of choice: satisfaction and dissonance. Both can exercise a strong effect on future choice behavior.

Satisfaction

A fundamental tenet of learning theory is that a given response is reinforced either positively or negatively to the extent that it is followed

33 Gillett, "In-Home Shoppers."

34 Gillett's review provides an up-to-date source. See Gillett, "In-Home Shoppers."

35 See, for example, Cyrus C. Wilson, "Telephone Order Promotion Strategy as an Aspect of Merchandising Strategy for Full Service Retail Stores in the Central Business District," unpublished paper, Ohio State University, Department of Marketing, 1964.

36 Gillett has provided some useful suggestions for future research. See "In-Home Shoppers."

37 See William G. Nickels, "Central Distribution Facilities Challenge Traditional Retailers," *Journal of Retailing*, vol. 49, pp. 45–50 (Spring 1973).

Figure 18.4 The complete model of consumer decision processes showing the outcomes of choice

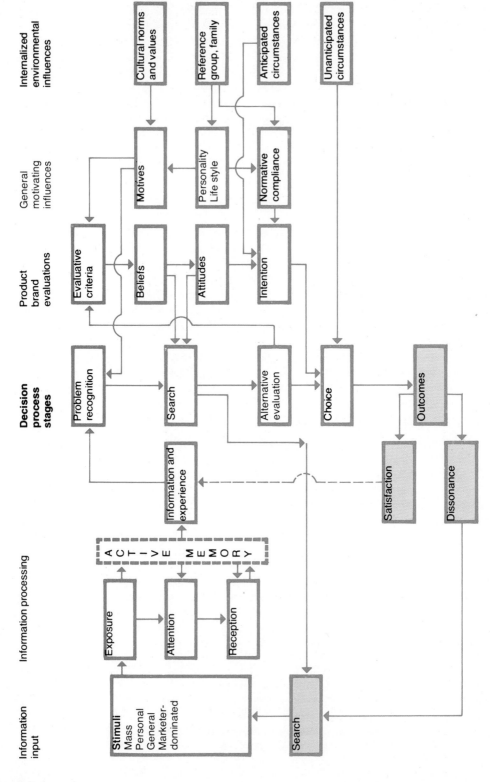

by reward. Reward, in turn, leads to an evaluation that the purchase was satisfactory. In the present context, satisfaction is defined as *an evaluation that the chosen alternative is consistent with prior beliefs with respect to that alternative.*[38]

Notice in Figure 18.4 that an evaluation of satisfaction or dissatisfaction becomes a part of long-term memory, and hence it can exert an effect on brand beliefs and attitudes. The probability of engaging in a similar buying act will be increased if there are positive consequences in the act of purchase and use and vice versa. It may be concluded that brand loyalty will develop and be strengthened as long as there is positive reinforcement of beliefs, *all other things being equal.* This conclusion must be qualified for the reason that the relationship between response tendencies and behavior is not necessarily one-to-one. Other factors intervene to affect buying action, and it must not be overlooked that the consumer will, on occasion, seek novelty and deliberately act contrary to established beliefs and attitudes.

Beliefs function, in effect, as a type of hypothesis regarding the consequences of an act, and the input of information after purchase either serves to confirm or to reject it. If confirmed, beliefs and attitudes will be strengthened. If disconfirmed, the most probable initial outcome is an unfavorable product evaluation.[39] This is especially likely when the disconfirmed beliefs are highly salient.[40]

In the most extensive investigation of consumer satisfaction published to date, Summers and Granbois found that there is a high incidence of consumer complaints.[41] Five problem areas were especially prevalent in the purchase of food and clothing:

1. Discovery of unexpectedly low quality in prepackaged items.

2. Finding grocery stores to be sold out on advertised product specials.

3. Finding bread and dairy products to be stale, broken, or spoiled.

4. Purchasing shoes that fall apart or wear out in a short time.

5. Purchasing a defective clothing item.

The incidences of these complaints ranged from 45 percent who discov-

38 Satisfaction has most often been defined as the confirmation or disconfirmation of *expectancies* with respect to a product and the purchase situation. However, it seems more consistent with present understanding to compare outcomes with beliefs. For more discussion of this point, see Jerry C. Olson and Philip A. Dover, "Disconfirmation of Consumer Expectations through Product Trial" (Working Paper no. 52, College of Business Administration, Pennsylvania State University, December 1976).

39 R. A. Cardozo, "An Experimental Study of Consumer Effort, Expectation, and Satisfaction," *Journal of Marketing Research*, vol. 2 (1965), pp. 244–49. Ralph E. Anderson, "Consumer Dissatisfaction: The Effect of Disconfirmed Expectancy on Perceived Product Performance," *Journal of Marketing Research*, vol. 10 (February 1973), pp. 38–44; and Raymond C. Stokes, "Consumerism and the Measurement of Consumer Dissatisfactions," in Philip Levine, ed., *Attitude Research Bridges the Atlantic* (Chicago: American Marketing Association, 1975), pp. 99–113.

40 John E. Swan and Linda Joan Combs, "Product Performance and Consumer Satisfaction: A New Concept," *Journal of Marketing*, vol. 40 (April 1976), pp. 25–33.

41 John O. Summers and Donald H. Granbois, "Predictive and Normative Expectations in Consumer Dissatisfaction and Complaining Behavior," in William D. Perreault, ed., *Advances in Consumer Research*, vol. 4 (Atlanta: Association for Consumer Research, 1977), pp. 155–58.

ered a clothing item to be defective to 70.7 percent who found the quality in prepackaged foods to be lower than expected. The only real bright spot is that most indicated satisfaction with retailer remedies.

Dissatisfaction and the consumerism movement. Every reader could report his or her own story of dissatisfaction. For a period of time it seemed that the business community was nearly oblivious to the consumer voice, and it is not surprising that Ralph Nader and other consumer spokespersons soon attracted a vast following. The public hue and cry has finally penetrated corporate boardrooms, and some responsible businessmen are undertaking necessary remedial action. While consumerism is discussed in more depth in the concluding chapter, it is worthy to ponder the remarks of Thomas A. Murphy, Chairman of the General Motors Corporation:

> . . . public sentiment is clearly against big business. . . . It has been building for many years, and for a number of reasons—but principally, in my judgment, because business has been falling short of customer expectations. And today's customer dissatisfaction is both the sorry evidence and the sad result. . . . We simply are not being believed. . . . We move in the right direction every time we emphasize quality as well as quantity in our products, every time we focus on service as well as sales, every time we welcome criticism and act upon it rather than avoid it and condemn it . . . . we are going to have to fulfill the businessman's first, last, and always responsibility: the responsibility to satisfy these customers—today, right now, not tomorrow.[42]

A needed warning is sounded for marketing management. A case can be made for realistic research that documents consumer desires as well as product capabilities. Advertisement and selling messages, then, should be designed to create expectancies that will be fulfilled by the product insofar as is possible. The extent to which this seemingly common-sense precaution is violated through use of "cute" exaggerations and other forms of creative "gimmickery" in advertisements is, at times, appalling.

Similarly, product designers should be keenly aware of the way in which a product fits into the consumer's style of life. What does it mean to the consumer? How is it used? The product should be designed and promoted so that performance will be satisfactory under conditions actually experienced in the home. Many housewives, for example, use electric toasters for English muffins, rolls, and other forms of baked goods besides bread. If the toaster will not handle these items satisfactorily, disconfirmed expectancies and buyer dissatisfaction are the probable result.

Many consumers, in turn, become quite vocal when they are dissatisfied and do not hesitate to spread unfavorable word-of-mouth communication. One low-priced brand of automobile seems to have been particularly damaged in this fashion by product performance that violated its

---

42 Thomas A. Murphy, "Businessman, Heal Thyself," *Newsweek* (December 20, 1976), p. 11.

advertising claims. This, in turn, becomes compounded in that those who become aware of this fact will tend to "screen out" advertisements for this make. Little opportunity thus exists to turn these people into prospects.

The need for further research. The published research in the consumer behavior literature on this subject is surprisingly scant. In fact, Cardozo's 1965 study stood virtually by itself until recently.[43] Fortunately, the need for scholarly inquiry has now been recognized, and there have been some useful methodological suggestions worthy of evaluation by the interested reader.[44] Also, Ralph Day offered a conceptual overview in which he suggests that the scope of research be expanded to encompass three types of expectations: (1) expectations about product performance; (2) expectations about the costs and efforts that must be expended to obtain the intended benefits from the product or service; and (3) expectations of social approval from product purchase and use.[45] As Murphy so convincingly pointed out, this issue is of great importance to the business community today, and it must be given a higher research priority in the coming years.

Let's return to Brad Jones and his automobile purchase (chapter 9). Let it be assumed that information search has now been completed and a family purchasing decision made. The final purchase intention calls for purchase of a four-door hardtop with "four on the floor," even though family financial status is not especially favorable at the moment. During family discussions there was disagreement on which of three popular makes was preferable. Each had its desirable features, but none clearly stood out as being superior. One make finally was chosen, but there never was a complete meeting of minds.

Post-choice dissonance

This situation contains all of the prerequisites for post-choice dissonance—*post-choice doubt motivated by awareness that one alternative was chosen and the existence of beliefs that unchosen alternatives also have desirable attributes.* Dissonance occurs when two cognitions or beliefs do not fit together, and the result is a state of psychological discomfort. Brad now is aware that he has purchased the car, but this is dissonant with his favorable evaluation of the other makes. He can reduce dissonance by (1) reevaluating the desirability of the unchosen alternatives in favor of the choice he has made or (2) by searching for information to confirm his choice (see the "search" arrow in Figure 18.4).

43 R. A. Cardozo, "An Experimental Study of Consumer Effort, Expectation, and Satisfaction," *Journal of Marketing Research*, vol. 2 (1965), pp. 244–249.

44 See William J. Lundstrom and Lawrence M. Lamont, "The Development of a Scale to Measure Consumer Discontent," *Journal of Marketing Research*, vol. 13 (November 1976), pp. 373–81; and John A. Miller, "Exploring Some Alternative Measures of Consumer Satisfaction," in Kenneth L. Bernhardt, ed., *Marketing: 1776–1976 and Beyond* (Chicago: American Marketing Association, 1976), pp. 661–64. Also Donald A. Hughes, "Considerations in the Measurement and Use of Consumer Satisfaction Ratings," in William Locander, ed., *Marketing Looks Outward* (Chicago: American Marketing Association, 1977), pp. 88–95.

45 Ralph L. Day, "Extending the Concept of Consumer Satisfaction," in Perreault, *Advances in Consumer Research*, pp. 149–54.

Post-decision doubts of these types are most probable when:

1. A certain minimum level of dissonance tolerance is surpassed. Individuals can live with inconsistency in many areas of their lives until this point is reached.[46]

2. The action is irrevocable.[47]

3. Unchosen alternatives have desirable features.[48]

4. A number of desirable alternatives are available.[49]

5. The individual is committed to his decision because of its psychological significance to him.[50]

6. Available alternatives are qualitatively dissimilar—that is, each has some desirable unique features (referred to in the terminology of dissonance theory as low "cognitive overlap").[51]

7. Perception and thought about unchosen alternatives is undertaken as a result of free will (volition) with little or no outside applied pressure.[52] If pressure is applied, the individual will do what he is forced to do without letting his own point of view or preference really be challenged.

The automobile purchase decision described above fully meets these criteria: presumably a dissonance tolerance threshold has been passed, the decision is irrevocable, there are other unchosen desirable alternatives that apparently are dissimilar, there is commitment to the decision, and no pressure was applied to make the decision. Obviously post-decision dissonance is largely confined to extended problem-solving situations. Indeed, avoidance of such doubts can be an incentive for establishment of purchasing routines.

(1) Reevaluation of alternatives. When dissonance occurs it can be reduced by increasing the perceived attractiveness of the unchosen

46 M. T. O'Keefe, "The Anti-Smoking Commercials: A Study of Television's Impact on Behavior," *Public Opinion Quarterly*, vol. 35 (1971), pp. 242–48.

47 H. B. Gerard, "Basic Features of Commitment," in R. P. Abelson et al., eds., *Theories of Cognitive Consistency: A Sourcebook* (Chicago: Rand McNally, 1968), pp. 456–63.

48 See, for example, H. J. Greenwald, "Dissonance and Relative vs. Absolute Attractiveness of Decision Alternatives," *Journal of Personality and Social Psychology*, vol. 11 (1969), pp. 328–33.

49 J. W. Brehm and A. R. Cohen, "Re-evaluation of Choice Alternatives as a Function of Their Number and Qualitative Similarity," *Journal of Abnormal and Social Psychology*, vol. 58 (1959), pp. 373–78.

50 C. A. Kiesler, "Commitment," in Abelson et al., *Theories of Cognitive Consistency*, pp. 448–55; Gerard, "Basic Features of Commitment"; J. W. Brehm and A. R. Cohen, *Explorations in Cognitive Dissonance* (New York: Wiley, 1962), p. 300.

51 Brehm and Cohen, *Explorations in Cognitive Dissonance.*

52 A. R. Cohen, H. I. Terry, and C. B. Jones, "Attitudinal Effects of Choice in Exposure to Counter-Propaganda," *Journal of Abnormal and Social Psychology*, vol. 58 (1959), pp. 388–91; L. Festinger and J. M. Carlsmith, "Cognitive Consequences of Forced Compliance," *Journal of Abnormal and Social Psychology*, vol. 58 (1959), pp. 203–210; A. R. Cohen, J. W. Brehm, and W. H. Fleming, "Attitude Change and Justification for Compliance," *Journal of Abnormal and Social Psychology*, vol. 56 (1958), pp. 276–78; T. C. Brock, "Cognitive Restructuring and Attitude Change," *Journal of Abnormal and Social Psychology*, vol. 64 (1962), pp. 264–71.

alternative and/or downgrading the desirability of those that were not chosen.[53] In addition, it is possible to accomplish the same result by concluding that all alternatives are essentially identical, even though this was not felt to be true during prepurchase deliberations.[54] By so doing, of course, none would stand out over others, and doubts would be removed.

There have been a number of recent studies in the marketing literature that confirm that consumers do spread apart alternatives in order to reduce dissonance. LoSciuto and Perloff, for example, found that a chosen record album was reranked as more desirable than the unchosen alternative, which was then downgraded in desirability.[55] In addition, this tendency was found one week after the first post-decision rating. Similar findings are reported by Anderson et al.,[56] Cohen and Goldberg,[57] Holloway,[58] and Sheth.[59]

One interesting possibility is that this state of post-decision regret is only a temporary phenomenon.[60] It may well be that reestablishment of the original state of equilibrium through bolstering one's choice will make selection of that alternative more probable in the future. Mittelstaedt verified this hypothesis and showed that the probability of purchasing the same brand again is increased in proportion to the magnitude of postdecision dissonance surrounding the initial purchase.[61] This may shed useful light on the psychological mechanisms of brand loyalty.

The findings reported here are perhaps of greatest interest to those with a scholarly interest in understanding consumer behavior. Those with a more applied interest, however, are more likely to question their relevance. In reality there is little the marketer can do to affect or capitalize upon post-decision reevaluation of alternatives. The marketer, of course, desires to differentiate his firm's offerings as much as possible from competitors and to induce the consumer to make a purchase. All things being equal, dissonance will be generated in the presence of qualitatively dissimilar alternatives, and it often is resolved to the company's benefit by reinforcing the decision. This process takes place as a result of what has happened *before* purchase, so there are no significant implications for marketing planning.

53 L. Festinger, *A Theory of Cognitive Dissonance* (Evanston, Ill.: Row, Peterson, 1957).

54 Festinger, *Theory of Cognitive Dissonance.*

55 L. A. LoSciuto and R. Perloff, "Influence of Product Preference on Dissonance Reduction," *Journal of Marketing Research*, vol. 4 (1967), pp. 286–90.

56 L. K. Anderson, J. R. Taylor, and R. J. Holloway, "The Consumer and His Alternatives: An Experimental Approach," *Journal of Marketing Research*, vol. 3 (1966), pp. 62–67.

57 J. Cohen and M. E. Goldberg, "The Dissonance Model in Post-Decision Product Evaluation," *Journal of Marketing Research*, vol. 7 (1970), pp. 315–21.

58 R. J. Holloway, "An Experiment on Consumer Dissonance," *Journal of Marketing*, vol. 31 (1967), pp. 39–43.

59 J. N. Sheth, "Cognitive Dissonance, Brand Preference and Product Familiarity," in J. Arndt, ed., *Insights into Consumer Behavior* (Boston: Allyn and Bacon, 1968), pp. 41–54.

60 E. Walster and E. Berscheid, "The Effects of Time on Cognitive Consistency," in Abelson et al., *Theories of Cognitive Consistency*, pp. 599–608.

61 R. Mittelstaedt, "A Dissonance Approach to Repeat Purchasing Behavior," *Journal of Marketing Research*, vol. 6 (1969), pp. 444–47.

(2) Post-decision information search. Doubts following purchase also can be reduced by searching for additional information that serves to confirm the wisdom of the choice. This is shown by the search arrow in Figure 18.4. In the purchase of an automobile, for example, dissonance cannot be reduced by changing the behavior and admitting a mistake because of great financial loss if the car is returned to the dealer. Also, most people are reluctant to admit that a wrong decision was made and to live with that knowledge. Although both of these acts would reduce dissonance and restore consonance, it is more likely that a person experiencing dissonance will buttress choice through procuring additional information. This information-seeking tendency has been widely documented,[62] although much of the evidence must be regarded as tentative for methodological reasons.

It is a reasonable extension of the discussion thus far to predict that a consumer who is not especially confident in his or her choice would be receptive to advertisements and other literature provided by the manufacturer. The selling arguments and points of alternative superiority stressed there could prove useful in bolstering a perception that the decision was wise and proper. There has been some evidence that confirms this hypothesis,[63] but none of it has conclusively verified that dissonance reduction is the motivation for post-decision search.[64] It is equally possible that a new owner will be "set" to notice advertisements simply because of the fact that an important new product has entered his or her life. This is a common phenomenon unrelated to dissonance.

Even though the published evidence is inconclusive, most purchasers have experienced dissonance in one form or another following an extended decision process. At one point in history it was reported that the Ford Motor Company designated certain advertisements to help new purchasers reduce dissonance.[65] This probably is unnecessary in that the messages designed to attract the consumer in the first place probably will stress the very points that are needed to reduce any dissonance. Yet it is a wise strategy to stress product superiority in instruction manuals and other material enclosed in the package. In addition, some manufacturers and retailers follow the beneficial practice of contacting consumers

62 See, for example, J. S. Adams, "Reduction of Cognitive Dissonance by Seeking Consonant Information," *Journal of Abnormal and Social Psychology*, vol. 62 (1961), pp. 74–78; J. Mills, E. Aronson, and H. Robinson, "Selectivity in Exposure to Information," *Journal of Abnormal and Social Psychology*, vol. 59 (1959), pp. 250–53.

63 See D. Ehrlich et al., "Post Decision Exposure to Relevant Information," *Journal of Abnormal and Social Psychology*, vol. 54 (1957), pp. 98–102; James F. Engel, "The Psychological Consequences of a Major Purchase Decision," in W. S. Decker, ed., *Marketing in Transition* (Chicago: American Marketing Association, 1963), pp. 462–75; J. H. Donnelly, Jr., and J. M. Ivanevich, "Post-Purchase Reinforcement and Back-Out Behavior," *Journal of Marketing Research*, vol. 7 (1970), pp. 399–400; and S. B. Hunt, "Post-Transaction Communications and Dissonance Reduction," *Journal of Marketing*, vol. 34 (1970), pp. 46–51.

64 William H. Cummings and M. Venkatesan, "Cognitive Dissonance and Consumer Behavior: A Review of the Evidence," *Journal of Marketing Research*, vol. 13 (August 1976), pp. 303–08.

65 George Brown, "The Automobile Buying Decision within the Family" in Nelson N. Foote, ed., *Household Decision-Making* (New York : New York University Press, 1961), pp. 193–99.

shortly after purchase to assert once again the wisdom of their choice and to affirm their appreciation.[66]

(3) A research dilemma. The theory of cognitive dissonance until recently has generated more research in social psychology than any other theoretical contribution. This explains, in part, why there were so many published applications in marketing at one point in time. Indeed, it almost became a fad. Nearly 20 years of experience with this theory, however, have given rise to methodological insights that often have been ignored in applications of the theory to marketing. Some serious methodological critiques have been published,[67] and there has been a recent assessment of the 23 marketing-related studies by Cummings and Venkatesan.[68] Cummings and Venkatesan documented that the conditions necessary for arousal of dissonance, which were stated at the outset of this section, usually have not been fully met. Therefore, the evidence must be interpreted with some caution. Their conclusion is worthy of note:

> Certainly none of the findings in this literature have presented a major challenge to the validity of the theory, because of the methodological problems involved. However, no single study has provided evidence which conclusively supports the application of dissonance theory to consumer behavior. In brief, the evidence is far from definite. But it should be noted that the evidence in favor of the applicability of dissonance theory is more voluminous and somewhat more substantial than the evidence against.[69]

Summary

This chapter examined the choice process and the outcomes of choice. Choice is a function of two major variables: buying intentions and unanticipated circumstances. A variety of unanticipated circumstances can lead to brand substitution at the retail level; they include display and exposure, price reduction, and out-of-stock conditions. Intentions and actual buying behavior also may diverge because of the high incidence of unplanned or "impulse" buying. This phenomenon was analyzed in depth, and it was pointed out that there are two explanations: (1) in-store exposure to marketing stimuli, which leads to further problem solving at the retail level, and (2) methodological weaknesses in this type of research, which lead to an incomplete listing of actual intentions.

66 See J. Ronald Carey et al., "A Test of Positive Reinforcement of Customers," *Journal of Marketing*, vol. 40 (October 1976), pp. 98–100.

67 E. Aronson, "Dissonance Theory: Progress and Problems," in Abelson et al., *Theories of Cognitive Consistency*, pp. 5–27; N. Chapanis and A. Chapanis, "Cognitive Dissonance: Five Years Later," *Psychological Bulletin*, vol. 61 (1964), pp. 1–22; S. T. Margulis and E. Songer, "Cognitive Dissonance: A Bibliography of Its First Decade," *Psychological Reports*, vol. 24 (1969), pp. 923–35. Also see R. A. Wicklund and Jack W. Brehm, *Perspectives on Cognitive Dissonance* (Hillsdale, N. J.: Lawrence Fulbaum Associates, 1976).

68 Cummings and Venkatesan, "Cognitive Dissonance and Consumer Behavior."

69 Cummings and Venkatesan, "Cognitive Dissonance and Consumer Behavior," p. 305.

Not all shopping takes place in a retail store. In-home shopping is becoming increasingly common through telephone, mail order, catalog, and purchase from a door-to-door salesman. The marketing implications were examined, and it was demonstrated that retailers, in particular, must take cognizance of this type of shopping and capitalize upon the opportunities.

Finally, choice can have two outcomes: satisfaction or dissatisfaction and post-decision dissonance (doubt). The growth of dissatisfaction has been a major incentive for the rise of the consumerism movement, and there are many implications. Post-decision dissonance, on the other hand, is of much less importance. First, studies have suffered from severe methodological limitations, and, secondly, there is little the marketer must do if dissonance indeed is found to follow a major purchase decision.

Review and discussion questions

1. Compare and contrast the explanations for unplanned purchasing. Do the alternative explanations produce different marketing implications? Explain.

2. Prepare an outline indicating an appropriate method of determining whether or not customers who order by mail differ from those who do not.

3. Suppose that customers who order by mail differ from other customers in the following ways: (a) higher income (over $15,000), (b) greater tendency to have charge accounts, and (c) greater tendency to live in the suburbs. How can this information be used in designing specific marketing strategies? (Optional: Design a marketing program based on this information.)

4. What types of behavior can be triggered by a purchase other than those mentioned in the chapter? What implications can you suggest for marketing management?

5. What is meant by the statement, "Manufacturers and resellers are well advised to undertake research that leads to a greater understanding of the *total purchase act*"?

6. The brand manager for a laundry detergent sees an article on cognitive dissonance and goes to his advertising agency with the question of whether or not consumers of this product should experience dissonance. What would your answer be? How would you arrive at this conclusion?

7. Would dissonance be likely if the product in question 6 were a new stereophonic sound system featuring speakers no larger than a book? Why or why not?

8. Assuming that dissonance is experienced by a purchaser of the stereo set mentioned in question 7, what would be the possible outcomes? Would the purchaser search for consonant or discrepant information? What would determine his course of action in information search?

9. Assume that a research report indicates a pronounced tendency for purchasers of power lawn mowers to notice advertisements for their brand. What explanations could you offer? What are the implications, if any, for advertising management?

10. What is an expectancy? How are expectancies formed regarding products and services?

11. Research documents the fact that consumers were surprised to discover the excellent sound output of the small speakers in the stereophonic system mentioned in question 7. Is this finding necessarily favorable? Explain.

12. Some tentative findings indicate that satisfaction with a product increases to the extent that the consumer has expended considerable shopping effort. What would you recommend if you were research director for a large retail department store chain?

13. What is meant by commitment? Why is it so important if cognitive dissonance is to be demonstrated?

14. What are the requirements of research in cognitive dissonance? What difficulties are presented when this theory is applied to marketing?

CHAPTER 19

Purchasing behavior and retailing strategy

Until the present chapter, our analysis of consumer behavior has focused mostly on consumer decisions about products and brands. Consumers also make decisions about stores and other retail outlets—about type of store, such as a discount store or department store, and about "brand" of store such as K-Mart or Marshall Field.

How do consumers choose stores in which to shop? How important is the location of a store? How important is a store's image in determining store patronage? What factors determine a store's image? What kinds of responses are possible for retailers who understand consumer decisions about purchasing? These are the topics of concern in this chapter.

Nature of purchasing processes

Purchasing processes is a term that refers to the customer-retail environment interaction. This is a specialized usage of the word *purchasing*, which might in other circumstances be given a broader definition. This interaction has already been discussed in prior chapters, such as Chapter 10, which discussed the interaction between customers and salespersons, and Chapter 18, which discussed the interaction between consumers and other aspects of the in-store or nonstore environment. In this chapter, attention is focused upon the *interaction between consumers and retail outlets.*

Decisions about stores are fundamentally the same as decisions about products or brands. Stated alternatively, extensive decisions about retail outlets are complex phenomena involving (1) problem recognition, (2) search, (3) alternative evaluation, (4) choice, (5) outcomes and consequences of those outcomes. Store decisions can also involve only habitual or limited decision-making. Only those aspects of decision-making that are unique to selection of a retail outlet are described again in this chapter, however.

Initiators of purchasing processes

Problem recognition, which leads to purchasing activity and store choices, can be initiated by two classes of variables. The first class of variable is product oriented in the sense that the consumer visits a retail outlet to purchase a product or service that satisfies some perceived problem. In other words, problem recognition leading to purchase of a product initiates purchasing processes.

Another type of initiator of purchasing processes may be nonproduct related. At times, consumers may simply desire "to go shopping" with few or no direct product purchases in mind. This may be due to the desire to "get out of the house," a desire to engage in fantasy activity such as "window shopping" or increasingly, it appears, a willingness to consider shopping as a family-oriented leisure time activity. Especially in large regional shopping centers that include attractive food offerings, movies, special exhibits and concerts, the initiator of purchasing activity may be unrelated to specific product needs. A list of such reasons is described in Figure 19.1.

Retailing strategies such as determination of product offering, promotional methods, point-of-sale merchandise, and so forth may be influenced greatly by the type of variable that initiates the purchasing trip. For example, interesting and time-consuming displays may be effective in a "browsing" trip, but convenient layout may be more effective when other variables initiate the trip. The effects of these processes will be readily observable when discussing "generic trends in retailing" in the last part of this chapter.

Consequences of purchasing outcomes

Purchasing processes include two types of outcomes. A purchase may occur when the consumer finds an alternative that satisfies his or her set of evaluative criteria. On the other hand, the process may halt because there are no alternatives in a store that satisfy the evaluative criteria or because the consumer cannot find them.

The outcomes of purchasing-process behavior are stored in the consumer's memory. As a consequence, if the results of the purchasing-process behavior are perceived as satisfactory, similar procedures may be used in the future. For example, the consumer may return to the same store, or adopt a standardized way of shopping at the store, or respond to displays, deals, and/or salespeople in ways similar to past behavior. Just as with "brand loyalty," consumers may become "store loyal" for a specific product or for a broad range of products.

How consumers choose retail outlets

Consumers choose retail outlets through a process conceptualized in Figure 19.2. The scheme consists of four variables: (1) evaluative criteria,

Figure 19.1 Why do people shop?

Personal motives

Role playing. Many activities are learned behaviors, traditionally expected or accepted as part of a certain position or role in society—mother, housewife, husband, or student.

Diversion. Shopping can offer an opportunity for diversion from the routine of daily life and thus represents a form of recreation.

Self-gratification. Different emotional states or moods may be relevant for explaining why (and when) someone goes shopping. Some people report that often they alleviate depression by simply spending money on themselves. In this case, the shopping trip is motivated not by the expected utility of consuming, but by the utility of the buying *process* itself.

Learning about new trends. Products are intimately entwined in one's daily activities and often serve as symbols reflecting attitudes and life styles. An individual learns about trends and movements and the symbols that support them when the individual visits a store.

Physical activity. Shopping can provide people with a considerable amount of exercise at a leisurely pace, appealing to people living in an urban environment. Some shoppers apparently welcome the chance to walk in centers and malls.

Sensory stimulation. Retail institutions provide many potential sensory benefits for shoppers. Customers browse through a store looking at the merchandise and at each other; they enjoy handling the merchandise, the sounds of background music, the scents of perfume counters or prepared food outlets.

Social motives

Social experiences outside the home. The marketplace has traditionally been a center of social activity and many parts of the United States and other countries still have "market days," "country fairs," and "town squares" that offer a time and place for social interaction. Shopping trips may result in direct encounters with friends (e.g., neighborhood women at a supermarket) and other social contact.

Communications with others having a similar interest. Stores that offer hobby-related goods or products and services such as boating, collecting stamps, car customizing, and home decorating provide an opportunity to talk with others about their interests and with sales personnel who provide special information concerning the activity.

Peer group attraction. The patronage of a store sometimes reflects a desire to be with one's peer group or a reference group to which one aspires to belong. For instance, record stores may provide a meeting place where members of a peer group may gather.

Status and authority. Many shopping experiences provide the opportunity for an individual to command attention and respect or to be "waited on" without having to pay for this service. A person can attain a feeling of status and power in this limited "master-servant" relationship.

Pleasure of bargaining. Many shoppers appear to enjoy the process of bargaining or haggling, believing that with bargaining, goods can be reduced to a more reasonable price. An individual prides himself in his ability to make wise purchases or to obtain bargains.

Source: Excerpted from Edward M. Tauber, "Why Do People Shop?" *Journal of Marketing*, vol. 36 (October 1972), pp. 46–59. Reprinted from the *Journal of Marketing* published by the American Marketing Association.

(2) perceived characteristics of stores, (3) comparison process, and (4) acceptable and unacceptable stores. Store choice, then, is viewed as consisting of processes whereby the consumer compares the characteristics of stores, as he or she perceives them, with the consumer's own evaluative criteria.

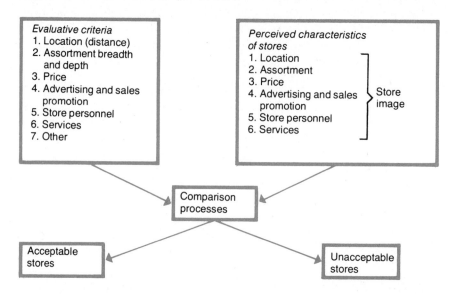

Figure 19.2 Store-choice processes

Consumers do not go through this process before each store visit. Instead, if past experiences with a store have been satisfactory, and other conditions exist, the store is revisited without reevaluation and may be classified as habitual or limited decision-making. The majority of store visits that consumers make are probably not preceded by deliberate or extended store-choice processes.

The first part of this section discusses general determinants of store choice—that is, the comparison process involving evaluative criteria and perceived characteristics of stores. Composite determinants of store choice are discussed in the second part followed by an analysis of store images and methods of measuring images.

General determinants of store choice

Determinants of store choice vary significantly depending on the type of product being purchased, the general type of store involved, and certain characteristics of the consumer. In general, the determinants are:

1. location

2. depth and breadth of assortment

3. price

4. advertising and word-of-mouth communications

5. sales promotion

6. store personnel

7. services

8. physical attributes

9. store clientele.

Location. The location effect on store choice is conceptually simple. Consumers farther away are less likely to purchase than are consumers who are closer to the store. The obvious reason is that as distance from a store increases, so does the number of intervening alternatives (other stores). Much of the research on these effects has been summarized by Olsson.[1]

During the last 50 years numerous attempts have been made to determine the effect of location, or distance, on patronage. These investigations have focused on cities, trading areas, shopping centers, individual stores, and other variables.

(1) Cities and trading areas. Many studies have investigated the impact of city, town, and trading area locations as determinants of store patronage. In a study of small towns in Georgia, Thompson found that over 84 percent shopped in other towns than their own during the last six months. Moreover, 64 percent had shopped out of town six times or more in the six months prior to the time they reported.[2] Similar results were obtained in a study of shopping outside the downtown area of a town in Pennsylvania.[3]

Several attempts have been/ made to explain this type of patronage behavior. In the 1920s, William J. Reilly studied patronage in Texas and then postulated that two cities attract retail trade from an intermediate town in the vicinity of the breaking point (where 50 percent of the trade is attracted to each city) in direct proportion to their population and in inverse proportion to the square of the distances from the two cities to the intermediate town.[4]

Two decades later, Converse found the following modification of "Reilly's law" useful in explaining intercity shopping patterns:[5]

$$\left(\frac{B_a}{B_b}\right) = \left(\frac{P_a}{P_b}\right)\left(\frac{D_b}{D_a}\right)$$

where

B_a = proportion of trade attracted from intermediate town by city A
B_b = proportion of trade attracted from intermediate town by city B
P_a = population of city A
P_b = population of city B
D_a = distance from intermediate town to city A
D_b = distance from intermediate town to city B

Converse found that in 1942 this formula predicted the actual flow of

---

1 Gunnar Olsson, *Distance and Human Interaction: A Review and Bibliography* (Philadelphia: Regional Science Research Institute, 1965).

2 John R. Thompson, "Characteristics and Behavior of Out-Shopping Consumers," *Journal of Retailing*, vol. 47 (Spring 1971), pp. 70–80.

3 Robert O. Herrmann and Leland L. Beik, "Shoppers' Movements outside Their Local Retail Area," *Journal of Marketing*, vol. 32 (October 1968), pp. 45–51.

4 William J. Reilly, *Methods for the Study of Retail Relationships* (Austin, Tex.: Bureau of Business Research, University of Texas Press, 1929), p. 16.

5 Paul D. Converse, "New Laws of Retail Gravitation," *Journal of Marketing*, vol. 13 (October 1949), pp. 379–88.

trade to two Illinois towns from an intermediate town with an error of 3 percent.

Although these early models were useful, they were simplistic. Among other things, they ignore the relative incomes of the populations, merchandise assortments in the two cities and consumer preferences. More recent research has gone beyond these early, foundational studies and has included other variables, especially product category.

For example, Herrmann and Beik found that the percentage of purchases made out of town varied from 43.8 percent for women's coats, to 8.8 percent for housewares.[6] Similarly, in Thompson's studies, over 50 percent of respondents purchased women's coats as well as curtains and drapes, rugs and carpets, men's suits and women's fancy dresses out of town but purchased major appliances, automobiles, furniture and jewelry out of town much less frequently.[7]

(2) Shopping centers. Several studies have investigated the impact of location, or driving time, on shopping center preference. Brunner and Mason's analysis of the Toledo, Ohio, market led them to conclude that the propensity to shop at a center is inversely associated with the driving time to reach the center, and that a time limitation of 15 minutes would be applicable for approximately three-fourths of the center's patrons.[8] However, a study of the Cleveland market found wider variation, with the percentage of customers living within 15 minutes driving time ranging from 55.5 percent to 83.7 percent for the seven centers studied.[9]

The Cleveland study, like others that could be cited, found that variables in addition to distance must be considered in order to predict shopping center patronage. For example, the authors of the Cleveland study found that 98 percent of the variation in the percentage of customers who drove more than 15 minutes to a shopping center was accounted for by the size of the shopping center in square feet and the limiting effect of Lake Erie on some shopping centers.

Huff has developed a model that estimates the probability that consumers in each relatively homogeneous statistical unit (neighborhood) will go to a particular shopping center for a particular type of purchase:[10]

$$P_{ij} = \frac{\dfrac{S_j}{T_{ij}\lambda}}{\sum\limits_{j=1}^{n} \left(\dfrac{S_j}{T_{ij}\lambda} \right)}$$

6 Herrmann and Beik, "Shoppers' Movements," p. 46.

7 Thompson, "Characteristics and Behavior of Out-Shopping Consumers," p. 79. For more recent results on outshopping, see W. R. Darden and William D. Perreault, Jr., "Identifying Interurban Shoppers: Multiproduct Purchase Patterns and Segmentation Profiles," *Journal of Marketing Research*, vol. 13 (February 1976), pp. 51–60.

8 James A. Brunner and John L. Mason, "The Influence of Driving Time upon Shopping Center Preference," *Journal of Marketing*, vol. 32 (April 1968), pp. 57–61.

9 William E. Cox, Jr. and Ernest F. Cooke, "Other Dimensions Involved in Shopping Center Preference," *Journal of Marketing*, vol. 34 (October 1970), pp. 12–17.

10 David L. Huff, "A Probabilistic Analysis of Consumer Spatial Behavior," in William S. Decker, ed., *Emerging Concepts in Marketing* (Chicago: American Marketing Association, 1962), pp. 443–461.

where:

P_{ij} = probability that consumers from each of the ith statistical units will go to specific shopping center j
S_j = size of shopping center j
T_{ij} = travel time to shopping center j
λ = a parameter estimated empirically for each product category, for example, clothing, furniture.

Huff has used this equation to plot isolines that are equiprobability contours that consumers will shop in center j. The probability of patronage declines as the distance to other centers becomes less and the distance to center j becomes greater.[11]

Although Huff's model advanced understanding of the relationships involved, it is clear that a number of other factors may also be involved that make the variable of location more complex.[12] For example, the Huff model fails to recognize the existence of community structure to which retailers must adapt. This structure has been investigated by Kernan and Bruce using cluster analysis, and they found that, based upon socioeconomic characteristics, a city can be classified into areas they call inner city, black ghetto, old city, older suburbs, and newer suburbs.[13]

A number of innovations are beginning to occur in predicting market areas for specific stores as well as for shopping areas. An example of one of these is Mackay's market penetration model, shown in Figure 19.3. In studies such as this, sample data from a shopping survey are analyzed with trend surface equations, in this case power series polynominals and trigonometric polynominals, to determine market penetration or the percentage of an area's sales that go to a particular store. Figure 19.3 is a plot of a market penetration map for one store. The symbols form an isarithmic map with increments of 0.5 percent. Thus, the ring of 6s maps the location of households whose estimated percentage of total supermarket dollars spent at the store is 3.0 percent and so forth. These and related models can be very useful in measuring market potential and evaluating performance of stores.

(3) Cognitive mapping. The perception consumers have concerning location of stores or shopping areas is more important in explaining shopping behavior and preferences than is actual location.[14] Consequently, re-

11 For an excellent discussion of other techniques for estimating shopping center patronage, see Bernard J. LaLonde, *Differentials in Super Market Drawing Power* (East Lansing, Mich.: Bureau of Business and Economic Research, Michigan State University, 1962). For dissenting findings about these types of models, see Joseph B. Mason and Charles T. Moore, "An Empirical Reappraisal of Behavioristic Assumptions in Trading Area Studies," *Journal of Retailing* (Winter 1970–71), pp. 31–37.

12 J. D. Forbes, "Consumer Patronage Behavior," in Robert L. King, ed., *Marketing and the New Science of Planning* (Chicago: American Marketing Association, 1968), pp. 381–85. Also see Thomas J. Stanley and Murphy A. Sewall, "Image Inputs to a Probabilistic Model: Predicting Retail Potential," *Journal of Marketing*, vol. 40 (July 1976), pp. 48–53.

13 Jerome B. Kernan and Grady D. Bruce, "The Socioeconomic Structure of an Urban Area," *Journal of Marketing Research*, vol. 9 (February 1972), pp. 15–18.

14 David B. Mackay and Richard W. Olshavsky, "Cognitive Maps of Retail Locations: An Investigation of Some Basic Issues," *Journal of Consumer Research*, vol. 2 (December 1975); and Edward M. Mazze, "Determining Shopper Movement Patterns by Cognitive Maps," *Journal of Retailing*, vol. 50 (Fall 1974), pp. 43–48.

Figure 19.3 Printout of market penetration map example

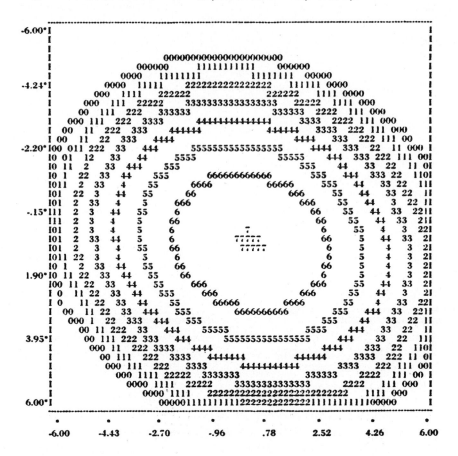

Source: David B. Mackay, "Spatial Measurement of Retail Store Demand," *Journal of Marketing Research*, vol. 10 (November 1973), pp. 447–53, at p. 451. Reprinted from the *Journal of Marketing Research* published by the American Marketing Association.

search increasingly is focusing upon "environmental cognitions" of consumers. These cognitive maps can refer both to cognized distances between stores or shopping centers and cognized travelling times.

Consumers generally overestimate both functional (actual) distance and functual time. Such variations between *cognitions of distance* and actual (functional) distance appear to be related to things such as ease of parking in the area, quality of merchandise offered by area of stores (inversely), and the display and presentation of merchandise by stores (inversely). Variations between *cognized time* and actual time appears to be related to things such as ease of driving to the area (inverse), the price of merchandise (direct), the quality of merchandise (inverse), and the helpfulness of salespeople (direct).[15]

15 R. Mittelstaedt et. al., "Psychophysical and Evaluative Dimensions of Cognized Distance in an Urban Shopping Environment," in R. C. Curhan, ed., *1974 Combined Proceedings* (Chicago: American Marketing Association, 1974), pp. 190–93.

Cognitive maps are internal to consumers and therefore cannot be measured directly. A number of "external" methods have been developed for measuring the cognitive maps of consumers, however.[16] The most popular method is the "draw-a-map" technique in which the consumer is asked simply to draw an outline of a geographic area and to signify the location of points in that space with a pencil and paper. Another graphic method involves asking consumers to draw lines indicating the distance between pairs of points (stores) on a map. A third method is nongraphic in nature and uses proximity ratings. In this approach, consumers are asked to rank pairs of stores that are nearest or farthest. These data are then analyzed with a computer program (similar to other applications of multidimensional scaling or MDS) to provide a multidimensional, mathematically derived map of the consumer's cognitions. Tentatively, it appears that the hand drawn maps are closer to actual maps but that the proximity data are closer to actual shopping behavior or consumer preferences for stores.[17]

Depth and breadth of assortment. In addition to location, both merchandise variety and assortment have been found to influence store preferences. Laboratory experiments and surveys indicate that stores offering either a deep assortment or a wide variety of product lines are preferred over stores having medium depth or breadth of assortment.[18]

Price. The importance of price as a determinant of store patronage also varies by type of product, store, and customer. For example, studies of *department-store* shoppers have found that price is often far down the list as a reason for shopping at a particular store.[19] Some studies of *supermarket* shoppers find price relatively unimportant,[20] yet others find price very important.[21] In the case of *new car* buyers, price is the factor most frequently cited as most important in the choice of a dealer.[22] Some surveys find that lower prices are the main advantage seen to *discount-store* shopping,[23] while others find price is not an important determinant.[24]

16 These methods are described and evaluated in "Cognitive Maps of Retail Locations." This source contains a good, multidisciplinary bibliography on this topic.

17 Mackay and Olshavsky, "Cognitive Maps of Retail Locations," p. 203.

18 Wroe Alderson and Robert Sessions, "Basic Research on Consumer Behavior: Report on a Study of Shopping Behavior and Methods for Its investigation," in Ronald E. Frank, Alfred A. Kuehn and William F. Massy, eds., *Quantitative Techniques in Marketing Analysis* (Homewood, Ill.: Irwin, 1962), pp. 129–45.

19 Stuart U. Rich and Bernard D. Portis, "The Imageries of Department Stores," *Journal of Marketing*, vol. 28 (April 1964), pp. 10–15.

20 "The Movers," *Progressive Grocer*, vol. 44 (November 1965), pp. K-35–K-58.

21 Douglas J. Tigert and Donald J. Tigert, "Longitudinal Analysis of a Supermarket Price War: A New Look at the Price-Quality Relationship," paper presented at the American Marketing Association Fall Conference, Minneapolis, Minn. (August 31, 1971).

22 Alderson Associates, Inc., *A Basic Study of Automobile Retailing* (Dearborn, Mich.: Ford Motor Company, 1958).

23 "How Housewives See the Discount Store Today," *Discount Merchandiser* (March 1970), pp. 77–90.

24 "Why Shoppers Chose Discount Stores vs. Downtown Stores," *Discount Merchandiser* (December 1971), pp. 31–32.

After reviewing the evidence on effects of price on shopping behavior, one leading retailing authority concluded that the role of price is greatly overrated.[25] For products in which consumers have strong preferences, price apparently is not an overriding concern. This relationship is illustrated by Anderson's study in which the level of price between stores had no effect on the sales of chili—a product with strong brand allegiance—but had some effect on peas—a product with little brand allegiance.[26] It is also important to realize that a consumer's perception of price, or *subjective price*, may be more important than actual price.[27] There is also some evidence to indicate that advertised specials of stores are often unavailable or mispriced on the shelf.[28] This may create the kind of skepticism that decreases effectiveness of price in attracting patronage. Finally, it should be said, however, that some observers believe that as inflation and shortages cause what are now regarded as necessities to become luxuries for most consumers, the importance of price in a marketing mix might increase.[29]

Advertising and word-of-mouth communications. Advertising is a quasi-determinant of store patronage.[30] Advertisements are thought to inform consumers of sales, deals, new products, and so on.

Advertising's effect on store patronage is difficult to access and seems to vary depending on the type of purchase and store. For example, a study investigating information sources producing initial awareness of a new dairy products store found that advertising accounted for only 16.9 percent of awareness, compared to 50.5 percent for visual notice and 32.6 percent for word of mouth. Moreover, respondents who were asked what source of information was most influential in their decision to try the new store indicated word of mouth twice as often as advertising, and over three times more often than visual notice. Within a given neighborhood, the extent of personal influence was even more dramatic. In fact, there was a marked tendency for patrons' homes to be clustered together rather than randomly distributed (see Figure 19.4).[31]

Other studies have found that advertising can have a powerful impact on consumers' perceptions of a store. Consider:

25 William R. Davidson, "The Shake-Out in Appliance Retailing," *Home Appliance Builder* (March 1965), pp. 21–29.

26 Evan E. Anderson, "The Effectiveness of Retail Price Reductions: A Comparison for Alternative Expressions of Price," *Journal of Marketing Research*, vol. 11 (August 1974), pp. 327–30.

27 Kent B. Monroe, "Buyers' Subjective Perceptions of Price," *Journal of Marketing Research*, vol. 10 (February 1973), pp. 73–80.

28 J. B. Mason and J. B. Wilkinson, "Mispricing and Unavailability of Advertised Food Products in Retail Food Outlets," *Journal of Business*, vol. 49 (April 1976), pp. 219–25.

29 Benson P. Shapiro, "Putting the Pricing Pieces Together," in *1975 Combined Proceedings* (Chicago: American Marketing Association, 1975), pp. 537–40.

30 See, for example, William Lazer and Eugene J. Kelly, "The Retailing Mix: Planning and Management," *Journal of Retailing*, vol. 37 (Spring 1961), pp. 34–41; William D. Tyler, "The Image, the Brand, and the Consumer," *Journal of Marketing*, vol. 22 (October 1957), pp. 162–65; Pierre Martineau, *Motivation in Advertising* (New York: McGraw-Hill, 1957), chap. 15.

31 Robert F. Kelly, "The Role of Information in the Patronage Decision: A Diffusion Phenomenon," in M. S. Moyer and R. E. Vosburgh, eds., *Marketing for Tomorrow . . . Today* (Chicago: American Marketing Association, 1967) pp. 119–29.

Figure 19.4 Location of new dairy-store customers' residences in two subdivisions

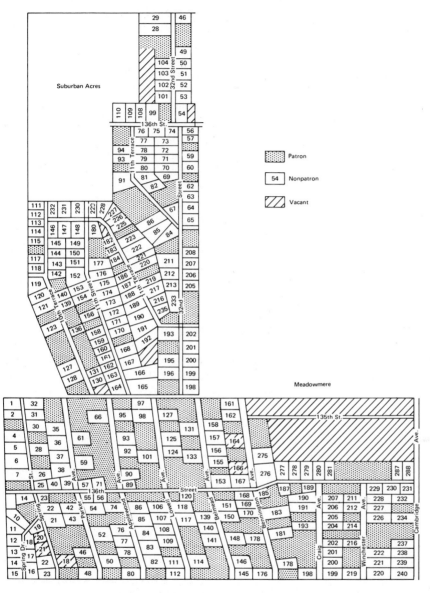

Source: Robert F. Kelly, "The Role of Information in the Patronage Decision: A Diffusion Phenomenon," in M. S. Moyer and R. E. Vosburgh, eds., *Marketing for Tomorrow . . . Today* (Chicago: American Marketing Association, 1967), p. 128. Reprinted by permission.

1. One of the major mail order chains talks about expanding its market upward, attracting the middle-class customer. Yet when the ads from stores of that chain were tested in three different cities where women

did not know their actual identity, in every class the stores were seen as having a lower class appeal.[32]

2. A leading Kansas City store's copy was tested both in Kansas City and in Atlanta. The evaluations (were) by women who had no idea of the identity of the store and who were making their judgments entirely from the physical appearance of the copy . . . "I am not averse to bargains, but I wouldn't trust that store." . : . "I imagine if you took something back, they would want to give you something in exchange and not give you the cash." . . . "The clerk standing there would be an immigrant, not enjoying selling. She probably could just barely speak English." . . . "I am afraid a store like this would take advantage of my ignorance of some things."[33]

A large amount of retail advertising is oriented toward listing of prices, especially among food retailers. There is considerable question about the efficacy of such practices in spite of their widespread usage.[34] Many retailers believe advertising of prices does little to attract market share from competitors but must be done to maintain parity if the other major competitors are doing it. Apparently, there is a segment of the population as large as 25 or 30 percent, who are affected by price advertising and thus, retail price advertising may have a significant if not majority effect.

Overall, the experience of major supermarkets such as A & P (with an advertising slogan called WEO—"Where Economy Originates") seems to indicate that advertising of price is not enough by itself to build market share.[35] Even if a segment of the market is influenced by advertising of low prices, their loyalty is shortlived—until the next set of advertised prices attracts that segment to a different store. Furthermore, research seems to indicate that even when a store advertises prices, consumers tend to perceive selectively such advertisements, based upon their prior image of the store. Keiser and Krum conclude that "other information cues besides advertised low price would seem to influence consumer choice of retailers. These information cues are received from personal shopping experience, from friends, and from many other sources besides newspaper advertisements."[36]

Sales promotion. The role of sales promotion devices on store patronage also varies widely. Consider the case of trading stamps. Some studies find that while many consumers value and save these stamps, few attach enough significance to them to make them a determining factor in where

32 Martineau, *Motivation in Advertising*, p. 174.

33 Martineau, *Motivation in Advertising*, pp. 175–76.

34 Joseph N. Fry and Gordon H. McDougall, "Consumer Appraisal of Retail Price Advertisements," *Journal of Marketing*, vol. 38 (July 1974).

35 The A & P case is described in R. D. Blackwell, J. F. Engel, and W. W. Talarzyk, *Contemporary Cases in Consumer Behavior* (Hinsdale, Illinois: Dryden Press, 1977), pp. 159–72.

36 Stephen K. Keiser and James R. Krum, "Consumer Perceptions of Retail Advertising with Overstated Price Savings," *Journal of Retailing*, vol. 52 (Fall 1976), pp. 27–36.

they shop.[37] Similarly, another study found that consumers' perceptions of price levels and quality were the same for large supermarkets regardless of stamp status.[38] On the other hand, a longitudinal study found that a supermarket chain, in discontinuing trading stamps, suffered a significant deterioration in market share and store traffic: market share declined 12 percent and store traffic by approximately 21 percent.[39]

Store personnel. Many studies document the importance of store personnel in the consumer's choice of a store. For example, in attempting to determine why a quality department store had been so successful in attracting Negro customers, research continually indicated that the reason was that clerks were friendlier. Similarly, neighborhood shopping centers usually rank higher than downtown stores in terms of friendliness.[40] Other studies have demonstrated that various characteristics of sales personnel, including politeness, courteousness, and product knowledge, are often used as criteria in evaluating stores.[41]

Services. The role of service also seems to vary considerably across both consumers and products. The following findings appear to be representative:

1. A liberal return policy is very important in determing whether consumers will shop at discount houses.[42]

2. In the purchase of new cars, expectation of good service is among the least frequently mentioned factors that buyers say caused them to select a dealer.[43]

3. Service is one of the least frequently mentioned dealer characteristics looked for by buyers of major appliances. Other studies present contradictory findings.[44]

Physical attributes. Physical attributes of a store affect consumers' perceptions of other store characteristics. The materials used on the

37 T. Ellsworth, D. Benjamin, and H. Radolf, "Customer Response to Trading Stamps," *Journal of Retailing*, vol. 33 (Winter 1957–58), pp. 165–169, 206; Norman Bussell "Let's Give Trading Stamps a Weigh," *Progressive Grocer*, vol. 44 (November 1965), pp. 154–58.

38 F. E. Brown and Alfred R. Oxenfeldt, "Price and Quality Comparisons between Stamp and Nonstamp Food Stores," *Journal of Retailing*, vol. 45 (Fall 1969), pp. 3–10, 84.

39 Bernard J. LaLonde and Jerome Herniter, "The Effect of a Trading Stamp Discontinuance on Supermarket Performance: A Panel Approach," *Journal of Marketing Research*, vol. 7 (May 1970), pp. 205–9.

40 Rich and Portis, "Imageries of Department Stores," pp. 10–15.

41 Alderson Associates, *Basic Study of Automobile Retailing*.

42 George Katona and Eva Mueller, "A Study of Purchase Decisions," in Lincoln H. Clark, ed., *Consumer Behavior: The Dynamics of Consumer Reaction* (New York: New York University Press, 1955), pp. 36–87.

43 David J. Rachman and Linda J. Kemp, "Profile of the Discount House Customer," *Journal of Retailing*, vol. 39 (Summer 1963), pp. 1–8.

44 John K. Ryans, Jr., "An Analysis of Appliance Retailer Perceptions of Retail Strategy and Decision Processes," in Peter D. Bennett, ed., *Marketing and Economic Development* (Chicago: American Marketing Association, 1965), pp. 666–71.

exterior and interior, the kind of floors, the type of displays, and many other factors affect a store's image.

Store clientele. The type of people shopping in a store also influences store choice. One writer stated this succinctly:

> Their personality concept is not primarily the result of physical features of the store—it is rather the result of the group of customers who have come to shop there. Customers associate themselves with a social group, shop where that group shops, and attribute to the store characteristics of the group.[45]

The importance weight of each of the above determinants of store choice varies by product category and is discussed in the next section. Some very interesting research has been completed by Monroe and Guiltinan, however, which indicates the probable direction of influence of four sets of variables that influence store choice. Using a technique called time-path analysis, Monroe and Guiltinan found that general opinions and activities (similar to the AIOs described in Chapter 7) and store perceptions (of attributes of stores) preceded or influenced specific planning and budgeting (of purchases) strategies—which preceded attribute importance (of attributes such as helpfulness of advertising, relatively low prices, and so forth).[46] This research is important because it demonstrates a methodology that can be used for investigating store choice decisions. The sequence of choice decisions is shown in Figure 19.5. The terms are slightly different than those used in the model in this book, but you may want to examine Figure 19.5 to see how closely this empirical research about store choice conforms to the concepts and relationships discussed throughout the book.

Composite determinants of store choice in selected industries

The determinants of store choice vary widely by type of product, store, and customer. Thus, it is not usually possible to talk about general determinants of store patronage. Rather, it is necessary to isolate patronage determinants for specific product categories, and then determine the relative importance of these determinants and how they vary by market segments. In the following paragraphs, some examples of such research are described in traditional retailing outlets such as clothing stores and supermarkets as well as the retailing of services such as banking and motels.

Women's clothing stores. The determinants of patronage at women's clothing stores were analyzed by Perry and Norton.[47] Although their sample used only university women and involved a prespecified

45 John H. Wingate, "Developments in the Super Market Field," *New York Retailer* (October 1958), p. 6.

46 Kent B. Monroe and Joseph P. Guiltinan, "A Path-Analytic Exploration of Retail Patronage Influences," *Journal of Consumer Research*, vol. 2 (June 1975), pp. 19–28.

47 Michael Perry and Nancy J. Norton, "Dimensions of Store Image," *Southern Journal of Business*, vol. 5 (April 1970), pp. 1–7.

Figure 19.5 Sequence of effects in store choice

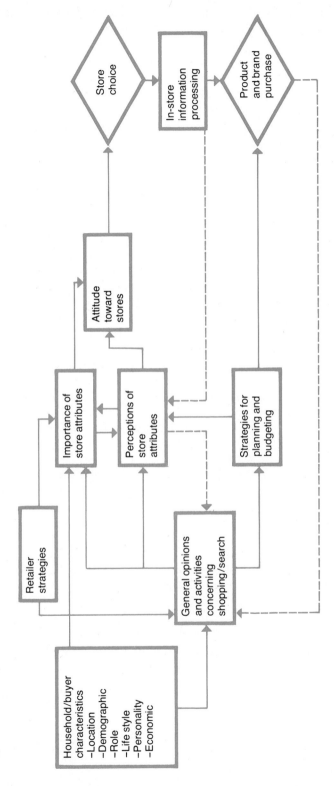

Source: Kent B. Monroe and Joseph P. Guiltinan, "A Path-Analytic Exploration of Retail Patronage Influences," *Journal of Consumer Research*, vol. 2 (June 1975), pp. 19–28, at p. 21. Reprinted from the *Journal of Consumer Research* published by the American Marketing Association.

list of determinants rather than deriving them empirically, they did demonstrate how factor analysis can be used to isolate common determinants.

The largest factor loadings in this example (factor 1) were on the variables of courteous sales people, service, and knowledgeable sales people. On factor 2, the largest loadings were on the variables of price and quality, while on factor 3, the largest loadings were on atmosphere and overall impression. Further analysis led the authors to conclude that salespersons, price-quality, and congeniality were the three dimensions on which these women evaluated women's clothing stores. These results seem consistent with earlier findings of Fisk.[48]

Supermarkets. Evaluative criteria or determinants of patronage were investigated for two supermarkets in Canada by Douglas and Donald Tigert, using a stepwise regression approach.[49] They found the three determinants that explained the most variance in patronage to be location, price, and service. Further analysis led the authors to conclude that, while service or quality plays a role, it is subservient to price and location and comes into play only after the latter two variables have been neutralized across chains. While this seems to emphasize price in determining patronage, it must be remembered that the prices of major chains in a market may all be very close. Thus, other criteria—location, service, cleanliness, product selection, parking, and so forth may become the actual determinants between highly competitive outlets.[50]

Bank selection. The importance of attributes determining bank selection was investigated by Anderson et al. and analyzed with the technique of cluster analysis.[51] They found that the bank selection decision is based primarily on five determinant selection criteria: friends' recommendations, reputation, availability of credit, friendliness, and service charges on checking accounts. Special services for women and youths and new account premiums or gifts were uniformly insignificant bank selection criteria. These researchers found two distinct market groups, however. Customers comprising cluster 1, about 55 percent of the respondents, appear to regard banking services essentially as convenience goods and money as a largely undifferentiated product. Conversely, the customers comprising cluster 2, about 45 percent of the respondents, place greater importance on all decision criteria and perceive substantial differences among competing banks on a number of selection criteria. This study demonstrated clearly that techniques such as this can be useful in managerial decisions concerning allocation of marketing resources into

48 George Fisk, "A Conceptual Model for Studying Customer Image," *Journal of Retailing,* vol. 37 (Winter 1961–62), pp. 1–8.

49 Tigert and Tigert, "Longitudinal Analysis of a Supermarket Price War," pp. 19–23.

50 Robert F. Dietrich, "37 Things You Can Do to Keep Your Customers—Or Lose Them," *Progressive Grocer* (June 1973), pp. 59–64.

51 W. Thomas Anderson, Jr., Eli P. Cox III, and David G. Fulcher, "Bank Selection Decisions and Market Segmentation," *Journal of Marketing,* vol. 40 (January 1976), pp. 40–45.

such things as branch locations, parking facilities, promotional programs, and personnel training.

The importance of recommendation of friends or the reputation of a firm has consistently been found to be an important determinant in other personal service industries than banking. In widely diverse personal services, Blackwell and Talarzyk found that recommendation of friends was the key determinant in the selection of a family doctor[52] and that reputation for personal service was the most important determinant in the selection of a funeral director.[53]

Discount motels. The determinants of patronage of discount motels (Motel 6, Days Inn, Scottish Inns, Family World) versus conventional motels were analyzed by Bush and Hair in a decision-process approach. Using the model of store-choice described in this chapter, Bush and Hair considered (1) evaluative criteria, (2) perceived characteristics of the store (image), (3) comparison processes, and (4) acceptable and unacceptable stores.[54]

The ranking of evaluative criteria for discount and conventional motel customers is shown in Figure 19.6. The perceived characteristics (images)

Figure 19.6 Mean ranking of evaluative criteria according to importance in determining motel patronage*

Criteria	Discount customers	Conventional customers
Price	1	5
Location	2	3
Appearance	3	2
Credit card acceptance	4	6
Past experience	5	1
Cocktail lounge	6	8
Reputation	7	4
Restaurant	8	7
Length of stay	9	13
Reservation service	10	9
Color television	11	10
Swimming pool	12	11
Directories (AAA, NMC)	13	12
Nursery or children's playground	14	14

*Respondents were asked to rank the above criteria according to which was the most important influence in patronizing a motel, with 1 being the most important, 2 next important, and so on. Mean values were computed for each criterion and used as a basis for determining the above rankings.
Source: Ronald F. Bush and Joseph F. Hair, Jr., "Consumer Patronage Determinants of Discount versus Conventional Motels," *Journal of Retailing*, vol. 52 (Summer 1976), pp. 41–52. Reprinted by permission.

52 Roger D. Blackwell and W. Wayne Talarzyk, *Consumer Attitudes Toward Health Care and Medical Malpractice* (Columbus: Grid Publishing, Inc., 1977), p. 30.

53 Roger D. Blackwell and W. Wayne Talarzyk, *American Attitudes Toward Death and Funerals* (Evanston, Illinois: Casket Manufacturers Association, 1975), p. 22.

54 Ronald F. Bush and Joseph F. Hair, Jr., "Consumer Patronage Determinants of Discount Versus Conventional Motels," *Journal of Retailing*, vol. 52 (Summer 1976), pp. 41–52.

of each type of motel were also measured. Conventional motels were perceived as having significantly higher prices and as being a relatively poor value for the money. Discount motels were perceived as having poorer dining facilities, fewer services, fewer employees and not being furnished as well as conventionals. From a managerial analysis, it is interesting to observe that "past experience" was the number one criterion for staying at a conventional motel. If conventional motel consumers were to select a discount motel on particular occasions and find it satisfactory on other criteria, the conventional motel industry might have a significant problem.

Finally, the importance of understanding the determinants of store choice is indicated by the research of Jolson and Spath, in which they investigated how well retailers understand the evaluative criteria of consumers, which influence where they shop.[55] The researchers found that consumers perceive price/value relationships, store specialization, quality of merchandise, availability, salesclerk service, and store location to be the most important factors of store patronage. They found some retailers to rank the importance of these factors moderately well but some—supermarket managers—were especially poor at understanding the factors consumers consider important. More importantly, they found little correlation between the retailers' understanding of the factors of store patronage and the fulfillment of consumers' desires or expectations on these factors. These misperceptions by some retailers and inability to fulfill expectations by even more retailers create the opportunity for new types of retailing outlets and new forms of service innovations to enter the market and displace the firms that lack the understanding or ability to satisfy the determinants of store choice.

Store images

Whether a consumer patronizes a store depends both on the evaluative criteria of the consumer and the perception of how the store characteristics compare with these criteria. The overall way in which customers perceive a store as well as its individual attributes is typically referred to as a store's image.

Image has been defined in various ways. Martineau thought of it as the "personality" of a store and defined it as "the way in which a store is defined in the shopper's mind, partly by its functional qualities and partly by an aura of psychological attributes."[56] Another author defines image as "a complex of meanings and relationships serving to characterize the store for people."[57] These definitions differ somewhat but the essential point is that the store exists in the *perception of consumers* as well as in objective characteristics.

55 Marvin A. Jolson and Walter F. Spaith, "Understanding and Fulfilling Shoppers' Requirements," *Journal of Retailing*, vol. 49 (Summer 1973), pp. 38–47.

56 Pierre Martineau, "The Personality of the Retail Store," *Harvard Business Review*, vol. 36 (January–February 1958), pp. 47–55, at p. 47.

57 Leon Arons, "Does Television Viewing Influence Store Image and Shopping Frequency?" *Journal of Retailing*, vol. 37 (Fall 1961), pp. 1–13, at p. 1.

In addition to store choice in specific situations, there is some evidence to indicate that store loyalty is also closely associated with store images, as to both the image of the store being shopped and the images of those stores that are *not* shopped.[58] It also appears that the image of a preferred store is likely to be similar to a consumer's own self image.[59] In other words, a person who rates "the person I am" as friendly or economy minded or so forth is likely to rate "the department store I most prefer" in a similar way.

A number of methods are used to measure store images. The most commonly used technique is attitude scaling such as the semantic differential, which is described below. Current consumer research techniques have been adapted to image research and are described below, including multiattribute measures, multidimensional scaling and customer prototypes. Other techniques such as the Guttman scale,[60] customer prototypes,[61] the Q-sort,[62] and factor-analytic or combination methods[63] are occasionally used in image research but will not be discussed here.

Measuring store images

Semantic differential. The semantic differential involves repeated measurements of a concept (such as a store) on a series of descriptive adjectives. These adjectives or phrases are bipolar in the sense that they are opposites such as "friendly–unfriendly". The original technique was developed by Osgood with theoretical support for the adjectives to be used in evaluating a concept, but the term has been modified by marketing researchers so that adjectives are generally included which are specific to marketing mix variables.[64]

An example of the semantic differential is presented in Figure 19.7. A representative sample of shoppers (both customers and noncustomers of a store) might be presented a form similar to the one in Figure 19.7, and asked to rate one or several stores (and perhaps an "ideal" store) on each of the bi-polar adjectives. The median response for each store is then

58 V. Parker Lessig, "Consumer Store Images and Store Loyalties," *Journal of Marketing*, vol. 38 (October 1973), pp. 72–74. Also see, however, John H. Murphy and Kenneth A. Coney, "Comments on 'Consumer Store Images and Store Loyalties,'" *Journal of Marketing*, vol. 40 (July 1975), pp. 64–66; and V. Parker Lessig, "A Reply to Murphy and Coney," *Journal of Marketing*, vol. 40 (July 1975), pp. 66–68.

59 Ronald J. Dornoff and Ronald L. Tatham, "Congruence Between Personal Image and Store Image," *Journal of the Market Research Society*, vol. 14 (January 1972), pp. 45–52. Also see, however, W. S. Martin, "A Comment on 'Congruence Between Personal Image and Store Image,'" *Journal of the Market Research Society*, vol. 8 (January 1976), pp. 32–35.

60 For an illustrative example, see Elizabeth A. Richards, "A Commercial Application of Guttman Attitude Sealing Techniques," *Journal of Marketing*, vol. 22 (October 1957), pp. 166–173.

61 W. B. Weale, "Measuring the Customer's Image of a Department Store," *Journal of Retailing*, vol. 37 (Spring 1961), pp. 40–48; Irving Burstner, "A Three-Way Mirror," *Journal of Retailing*, vol. 50 (Spring, 1974), pp. 24–36.

62 See, for example, William Stephenson, "Public Images of Public Utilities," *Journal of Advertising Research*, vol. 3 (December 1963), pp. 34–39.

63 Ronald B. Marks, "Operationizing the Concept of Store Image," *Journal of Retailing*, vol. 52 (Fall 1976), pp. 37–45.

64 William Mindak, "Fitting the Semantic Differential to the Marketing Problem," *Journal of Marketing*, vol. 25 (April 1961), pp. 28–33. The basic reference work on the semantic differential is C. E. Osgood, C. J. Suci, and P. H. Tannebaum, *The Measurement of Meaning* (Urbana, Ill.: Univeristy of Illinois Press, 1957).

Figure 19.7 Semantic differential for patronage research; general characteristics of the company

GENERAL CHARACTERISTICS OF THE COMPANY

	Extremely	Quite	Slightly	Neither one nor the other	Slightly	Quite	Extremely	
well known generally	___:	___:	___:	___:	___:	___:	___:	unknown generally
small number of stores operated by company	___:	___:	___:	___:	___:	___:	___:	large number of stores operated by company
long time in community	___:	___:	___:	___:	___:	___:	___:	short time in community

PHYSICAL CHARACTERISTICS OF THE STORE

dirty	___:	___:	___:	___:	___:	___:	___:	clean
unattractive decor	___:	___:	___:	___:	___:	___:	___:	attractive decor
easy to find items you want	___:	___:	___:	___:	___:	___:	___:	difficult to find items you want
easy to move through store	___:	___:	___:	___:	___:	___:	___:	difficult to move through store
fast checkout	___:	___:	___:	___:	___:	___:	___:	slow checkout

CONVENIENCE OF REACHING THE STORE FROM YOUR LOCATION

near by	___:	___:	___:	___:	___:	___:	___:	distant
short time required to reach store	___:	___:	___:	___:	___:	___:	___:	long time required to reach store
difficult drive	___:	___:	___:	___:	___:	___:	___:	easy drive
difficult to find parking place	___:	___:	___:	___:	___:	___:	___:	easy to find parking place
convenient to other stores I shop	___:	___:	___:	___:	___:	___:	___:	inconvenient to other stores I shop

PRODUCTS OFFERED

wide selection of different kinds of products	___:	___:	___:	___:	___:	___:	___:	limited selection of different kinds of products
fully stocked	___:	___:	___:	___:	___:	___:	___:	understocked
undependable products	___:	___:	___:	___:	___:	___:	___:	dependable products
high quality	___:	___:	___:	___:	___:	___:	___:	low quality
numerous brands	___:	___:	___:	___:	___:	___:	___:	few brands
unknown brands	___:	___:	___:	___:	___:	___:	___:	well known brands

tabulated and the medians are connected to show a profile of each store. A number of stores can be shown on one chart with the use of various colors or line keys. It is readily apparent how the store of interest compares in its public image on each of the characteristics in the questionnaire.

The advantages of the semantic differential are that it is simple to administer and simple to tabulate, permits the presentation of quantifiable data in a format easily understood and actionable by executives, is easy to replicate (so that trends in consumers' perceptions can be detected), and is reasonably reliable. The disadvantages are that consumers may be reluctant to score a store unusually good or bad even though they may feel that way (mediocrity bias) and they may score most all of the specific components favorably if they have a good overall image of the store (halo effect). A more serious problem is determining the adjectives to be included. Care must be taken to make certain that *actual* determinants of patronage are included as bi-polar adjectives. When many adjectives are

Figure 19.7 continued

GENERAL CHARACTERISTICS OF THE COMPANY

	Extremely	Quite	Slightly	Neither one nor the other	Slightly	Quite	Extremely	
PRICES CHARGED BY THE STORE								
low compared to other stores	___:	___:	___:	___:	___:	___:	___:	high compared to other stores
low values for money spent	___:	___:	___:	___:	___:	___:	___:	high values for money spent
large number of items specially priced	___:	___:	___:	___:	___:	___:	___:	small number of items specially priced
STORE PERSONNEL								
courteous	___:	___:	___:	___:	___:	___:	___:	discourteous
cold	___:	___:	___:	___:	___:	___:	___:	friendly
unhelpful	___:	___:	___:	___:	___:	___:	___:	helpful
adequate number	___:	___:	___:	___:	___:	___:	___:	inadequate number
ADVERTISING BY THE STORE								
uninformative	___:	___:	___:	___:	___:	___:	___:	informative
unhelpful in planning purchases	___:	___:	___:	___:	___:	___:	___:	helpful in planning purchases
appealing	___:	___:	___:	___:	___:	___:	___:	unappealing
believable	___:	___:	___:	___:	___:	___:	___:	misleading
frequently seen by you	___:	___:	___:	___:	___:	___:	___:	infrequently seen by you
YOUR FRIENDS AND THE STORE								
unknown to your friends	___:	___:	___:	___:	___:	___:	___:	well known to your friends
well liked by your friends	___:	___:	___:	___:	___:	___:	___:	disliked by your friends
poorly recommended by your friends	___:	___:	___:	___:	___:	___:	___:	well recommended by your friends
numerous friends shop there	___:	___:	___:	___:	___:	___:	___:	few friends shop there

Source: Robert F. Kelly and Ronald Stephenson, "The Semantic Differential: An Information Source for Designing Retail Patronage Appeals," *Journal of Marketing*, vol. 31 (October 1967), p. 45. Reprinted from the *Journal of Marketing* published by the American Marketing Association.

included, however, some will probably have little salience and managers may be unduly influenced by scores on low salience items rather than focusing upon those items of high salience in the store selection process.[65]

Multiattribute attitude measures. The multiattribute approach to measuring store image focuses upon the *importance* of perceived characteristics of a store as well as the nature of the perceived characteristics. A semantic differential, for example, might indicate that a store is old fashioned and management might undertake to change the appearance of the store. That could be a mistake, however, if the "old fashioned" dimension was important to the image of the store as low-priced or perhaps valued for nostalgia or because consumers feel comfortable in the store. An approach for investigating such problems and involving a

65 Also see John H. Kunkel and Leonard L. Berry, "A Behavioral Conception of Retail Image," *Journal of Marketing*, vol. 32 (October 1968), pp. 21–27.

Figure 19.8 Belief and importance scores for retail stores

Attribute	Impor- tance scores	Store A	Store B	Store C	Store D	Store E	Store F	Store G	Store H
Price	6.13	3.71	3.91	4.48	5.14	3.93	4.11	3.92	4.06
Assortment	6.11	4.79	4.56	4.21	4.68	4.33	4.23	4.39	4.46
Personnel	5.15	4.70	4.56	4.31	4.40	4.39	4.34	4.34	4.43
Atmosphere	4.84	4.86	4.64	4.24	4.56	4.50	4.35	4.42	4.53
Service	5.63	4.89	4.67	4.23	4.47	4.62	4.47	4.49	4.50
Quality	6.37	5.15	5.02	3.97	4.35	4.80	4.65	4.71	4.69

Source: Don L. James, Richard M. Durand, and Robert A. Dreves, "The Use of Multi-Attribute Attitude Model in a Store Image Study," *Journal of Retailing*, pp. 23–32. Reprinted by permission.

multiattribute attitude has been developed recently[66] similar to the approaches concerning product decisions described in Chapter 15 of this book.

An example of the multiattribute approach to measuring store image is presented in Figure 19.8. This research involved men's clothing stores in a college town. Potential customers were asked to list all those "attributes, characteristics, or terms" that come to mind when thinking of men's clothing stores. From that list, the six attributes that had the most meaning for the group were determined to be: assortment, personnel, atmosphere, service, quality, and price. After shopping preferences were determined, consumers were asked to rate the importance of the six store attributes which had been identified earlier as most salient. Following that, the respondents evaluated, on a one-to-seven scale, each store along each attribute. Thus, each store is measured according to how well it meets respondents' expectations. The final results are shown in Figure 19.8. This is a powerful technique for determining the importance of determinants of store image and helping a retailer to discover how well an array of competitive stores are perceived on each attribute. Resources can then be directed toward improvements, taking into consideration the importance of the attributes and the strengths or weaknesses of competitors. It has been used in other applications such as in the determination of patronage behavior for restaurants.[67]

Multidimensional scaling. Since consumers shop in more than one store, it is desirable to understand the perceptions of a consumer not only about a store but about the relationships between stores. This may require a multidimensional approach rather than a unidimensional view of store attributes. Multidimensional scaling (or MDS) is a technique that has been

66 Don L. James, Richard M. Durand and Robert A. Dreves, "The Use of a Multi-Attribute Attitude Model in a Store Image Study," *Journal of Retailing*, vol. 52 (Summer 1976), pp. 23–32.
67 William R. Swinyard, "Market Segmentation in Retail Service Industries: A Multiattribute Approach," *Journal of Retailing*, vol. 53 (Spring 1977), pp. 27–34.

discussed several other places in this text, but it is also useful in studying store choice and has been used by Doyle and Fenwick for predicting choice of grocery stores[68] and by Singson for department stores.[69]

The basic hypothesis is that as two objects are perceived as more similar to each other, the greater the likelihood that the individual's behavior toward each object will become more similar. This is important to retail store managers who need to know which stores are their real competitors in the perceptions of consumers. Singson's research focused on department stores such as Sears, Penney's and Bon Marche and disclosed that the importance of dimensions and perceptions of the stores vary substantially by social class. Subjects from the lower-middle and lower-lower groups attach greater importance to product width and are more likely to shop from general merchandise stores like Sears and Penney's. Subjects from the upper-middle and upper-lower classes attach greater importance to product depth, however, which is more characteristic of specialty stores.[70]

Of the three methods of measuring image described above, the semantic differential is the easiest to administer and interpret. The multiattribute approach, however, focuses more directly on the salience of attributes. The multidimensional approach makes distinct contributions to understanding the relationships between stores but is more difficult to administer and analyze than the other methods.

Shopper profiles and store patronage

The analytical framework for analyzing the purchasing process now turns to the comparison process, having completed the discussion of evaluative criteria and perceived store characteristics. The comparison process by which consumers differentiate between acceptable and unacceptable stores is difficult to study because it is a process internal to the consumer. It is subject to the same influences and processes discussed throughout the book, of course, but is still difficult to understand or observe. One of the measures of this process of store patronage, however, is shopper profiles.

In other words, it may be possible to understand why stores are acceptable or unacceptable to specific consumers by analyzing the profiles of those who shop there. Certain stores or types of stores are more acceptable to some groups of consumers than to others. Various ways of analyzing profiles might be employed. In the following section, we shall examine only a few of the possibilities, limiting our attention to demographic variables, psychological variables and some shopper typologies that have developed specifically for retailing.

68 Peter Doyle and Jan Fenwick, "How Store Image Affects Shopping Habits in Grocery Chains," *Journal of Retailing*, vol. 50 (Winter 1974–75), pp. 39–52.
69 Ricardo L. Singson, "Multidimensional Scaling Analysis of Store Image and Shopping Behavior," *Journal of Retailing*, vol. 51 (Summer 1975), pp. 38–53.
70 Singson, "Multidimensional Scaling Analysis."

Demographic variables, especially age, income, and place of residence, are often associated with patronage of certain types of stores. A store survives usually because it appeals to a specific segment within the market area. If a store explores its market properly, identifying loyal customers and their behavior patterns, the store can maximize its appeal to that segment.[71]

The most important variable is probably geography. In a study of grocery shopping for coffee, Winn and Childers investigated a number of demographic variables but found that geographical census regions and central city size were the most important correlates explaining shopping concentrations. The second set of variables that were also of importance were social class related and included household income, education of household head, and occupation of household head.[72] There is a rich array of demographic data, categorized by census tracts and other geographic regions, and one of the useful techniques for retailers, once they have identified the demographic variables associated with patronage of their store, is to use computerized mapping of the trade area to prepare visual displays of the market according to the concentration of each demographic variable in a region.[73]

Many other demographic variables may be used to develop store profiles. Race is correlated with type of store shopped, days of the week shopped, and degree of shopping activity.[74] Even religion has been found to have some relevance in predicting purchase of certain types of furniture.[75] One of the more promising areas of demographic research is in the construction of profiles of the entire shopping process including awareness of stores, search processes, price perception and store loyalty, and Woodside has demonstrated how this can be accomplished in a study of franchised food outlets.[76]

**Psychological
variables**

The determination of acceptable or unacceptable stores to a consumer may be profiled on the basis of psychological variables, often combined with the demographic variables described above.

Psychographics. Psychographic variables (described in Chapter 7) can be combined with product usage and socioeconomic characteristics to

71 A. Coskun Samli, "Use of Segmentation Index to Measure Store Loyalty," *Journal of Retailing*, vol. 51 (Spring 1975), pp. 51–60.

72 Paul R. Winn and Terry L. Childers, "Demographics and Store Patronage Concentrations: Some Promising Results," in Kenneth L. Bernhardt, ed., *Marketing: 1776–1976 and Beyond* (Chicago: American Marketing Association, 1976), pp. 82–86.

73 For examples of how to prepare these maps, see David W. Cravens, Thomas L. Bell, and Robert B. Woodruff, "Application of Geographic Mapping to Urban Market Analyses," in R. C. Curhan, ed., *1974 Combined Proceedings* (Chicago: American Marketing Association, 1974), pp. 183–89.

74 Donald E. Sexton, Jr., "Differences in Food Shopping Habits by Area of Residence, Race, and Income," *Journal of Retailing*, vol. 50 (Spring 1974), pp. 37–49.

75 Howard A. Thompson and Jesse E. Raine, "Religious Denomination Preference as a Basis for Store Location," *Journal of Retailing*, vol. 52 (Summer 1976), pp. 71–78.

76 Arch G. Woodside, "Patronage Motives and Marketing Strategies," *Journal of Retailing*, vol. 49 (Spring 1973), pp. 35–44. Also see Joseph Barry Mason and Morris L. Mayer, "Empirical Observations of Consumer Behavior," *Journal of Retailing*, vol. 48 (Fall 1972), pp. 17–31.

construct a richer portrait of patrons of retail outlets. A study by Tigert, Lathrope, and Bleeg used this technique to analyze female users of chicken drive-in restaurants providing ready-to-eat, carry-out fried chicken (RECFC).[77]

The greatest value of psychographics for retailers appears to be the description of the life style of the user and especially the heavy user, thereby suggesting the emphasis that should be used in the marketing mix of the retailing firm. In the chicken study of Tigert et al., the heavy user of RECFC has a well-defined demographic profile. She is more likely to be working full time, young, and in a family with an above average number of children. In spite of the larger income, the heavy user's family is not upscale in terms of either educational or occupational status of the husband or wife. The heavy user of RECFC also has a revealing psychographic profile. She is optimistic about her personal and financial future, fashion and appearance conscious, pro credit, active, influential, and ready to take risks. She seems to have more liberal attitudes, spends some of her time in a dream world. Knowing this profile, management might make adjustments in their hours of operation and peak staffing as well as receiving ideas for the development of a creative strategy for use in the firm's advertising program.

Psychographics has been used in a number of studies relating to credit cards, an important part of most retailer's "total offering" to consumers, and has been found useful in predicting the type of credit user a person may be and the usage of cards such as Master Charge and Visa.[78] At a more fundamental level, McCall analyzed life styles and concluded that successful retailers will need to make some adaptive changes. The demand for stores with night openings will increase in geometric proportions as will the need for night repair services. Small stores will have to develop superior salespersons to be competitive with large store offerings preferred by some consumer segments, and the increase in numbers of women working outside the home may suggest new types of promotions rather than newspapers which women formerly depended upon for retailer information.[79]

Personality and risk perception. There is some evidence to suggest that the shoppers of certain types of stores may have different levels of self-confidence (or other personality variables) and different levels of perceived risk in the purchase of a product. Dash, Shiffman, and Berenson found that specialty store customers were more self-confident, perceived

77 Douglas J. Tigert, Richard Lathrope, and Michael Bleeg, "The Fast Food Franchise: Psychographic and Demographic Segmentation Analysis," *Journal of Retailing*, vol. 47 (Spring 1971), pp. 81–90.

78 Joseph Plummer, "Life Style Patterns and Commercial Bank Credit Card Usage," *Journal of Marketing*, vol. 35 (April 1971), pp. 35–41; D. K. Hawes, W. W. Talarzyk and R. D. Blackwell, "Female and Male Possession of Bank Credit Cards: A Psychographic-Demographic Profile," in *1976 Combined Proceedings* (Chicago: American Marketing Association, 1976), pp. 87–93; M. J. Etzel, "Using Multiple Discriminant Analysis to Segment the Consumer Credit Market," in R. C. Curhan, ed., *1974 Combined Proceedings* (Chicago: American Marketing Association, 1974), pp. 35–40.

79 Suzanne McCall, "Analytical Projections of Lifestyle Identification in Consumer Behavior," in *1976 Combined Proceedings* (Chicago: American Marketing Association, 1976), pp. 354–59.

less risk, and considered the product area to be of greater importance than did those who shopped for similar items in a department store.[80] These researchers suggested several strategy implications of such results. Perhaps department stores should attempt to reduce uncertainty through in-store prepurchase customer services and through promotional campaigns that emphasize the assistance that the store provides its customers. The store might carry a limited line of easily recognized, well-respected brands catering to the needs of well-defined market segments. In addition, it might promote the availability of courteous product selection assistance, the financial convenience of its credit programs, free trial, and money back guarantees.

Shopper typologies

Several studies have attempted to classify consumers according to their attitudes toward shopping and their shopping behavior. These studies are summarized below.

The Stone typology. The most widely quoted study is Gregory Stone's investigation of 150 female residents of Chicago's northwest side.[81] Respondents were asked whether they would rather do business with local merchants or large chain stores and why. Analysis of the responses to these questions revealed disparate definitions of shopping situations and different orientations to stores in general. Based on orientations toward stores and the purchasing process, Stone identified four types of shoppers.

(1) The economic shopper. This type of shopper was extremely sensitive to price, quality, and assortment of merchandise, all of which were considered when purchasing a product. Clerical personnel and the store were, for her, the instruments of her purchase of goods. The efficiency of sales personnel, as well as relative prices, quality, or the selection of merchandise, were decisive in affecting her evaluation of the store. (Thirty-three percent of all respondents were in this category.)

(2) The personalizing shopper. The personalizing shopper formed strong personal relations with store personnel, and these relations were crucial to store patronage. Her conception of a good clerk was one who treated her in a personal, relatively intimate manner. (Twenty-eight percent of all respondents were in this category.)

(3) The ethical shopper. This type of shopper was willing to sacrifice lower prices, or a wider selection of goods, "to help the little guy out," or because "the chain store has no heart or soul." She shopped where she thought she "ought to," and strong attachments were sometimes formed

80 Joseph F. Dash, Leon G. Schiffman, and Conrad Berenson, "Risk- and Personality-Related Dimensions of Store Choice," *Journal of Marketing*, vol. 40 (January 1976), pp. 32–39. Also see Robert D. Hisrich, Ronald J. Dornoff, and Jerome B. Kernan, "Perceived Risk in Store Selection," *Journal of Marketing Research*, vol. 9 (November 1972), pp. 435–39.
81 Gregory P. Stone, "City Shoppers and Urban Identification: Observations on the Social Psychology of City Life," *American Journal of Sociology*, vol. 60 (1954), pp. 36–45.

with personnel and store owners, or with "stores" in the abstract. (Eighteen percent of all respondents were in this category.)

(4) The apathetic shopper. For this type of consumer, shopping was an onerous task. Experiences in stores were not important enough to leave any impression on her. Convenience of location was crucial to her selection of a store rather than price, quality of goods, relations with store personnel, or ethics. The costs of shopping far exceeded the value, and every attempt was made to minimize her expenditure of effort in purchasing goods. (Seventeen percent of all shoppers were in this category.)

In addition, each of the four types of shoppers was characterized by a distinctive patterning of social position and community identification. Economic and personalizing orientations were more often adopted by housewives who had recently moved into the area, and ethical and apathetic orientations by those who had lived in the area for relatively long periods of time. Moreover, the findings indicated that:[82]

1. The higher the level of aspiration among newcomers to a residential community, the greater the probability that they will adopt economic orientations to shopping.

2. The lower the level of aspiration the greater the marginality of newcomers (degree of social isolation), the greater the probability that they will adopt personalizing orientations.

3. The greater the success that long-time residents of a residential area have enjoyed, the greater the probability that they will adopt ethical orientations.

4. The less the success that long-time residents have enjoyed, the greater the probability that they will adopt apathetic orientations to shopping.

Darden and Reynolds tested and extended Stone's typology in a study of 167 households in six middle to upper-middle-class suburban areas of Athens, Georgia. Their data, concerned with health and personal care items, support Stone's shopping types.[83]

The Stephenson-Willett typology. In the late 1960s, Stephenson and Willett developed a shopper typology based on purchasing processes for six product categories: children's apparel, ladies' shoes, gloves, dresses, men's hosiery, and toys.[84] The shopper taxonomy was constructed by

82 Stone, "City Shoppers and Urban Identification," pp. 36–45.

83 William R. Darden and Fred D. Reynolds, "Shopping Orientations and Product Usage Rates," *Journal of Marketing Research*, vol. 8 (November 1971), pp. 505–08.

84 P. Ronald Stephenson and Ronald P. Willett, "Analysis of Consumers' Retail Patronage Strategies," in Philip R. McDonald, ed., *Marketing Involvement in Society and the Economy* (Chicago: American Marketing Association, 1969), pp. 316–22.

combining indices of patronage concentration and the extent of search for patronage alternatives. Shopper types, their frequency of occurrence, and the researchers' inferences about their identity are summarized in Figure 19.9.

Figure 19.9 Shopper typology

	Search for patronage alternatives	
	Low	High
Patronage concentration — Low	Store loyal shopper (24 percent of shoppers)	Compulsive and recreational shopper (26 percent of shoppers)
Patronage concentration — High	Convenience shopper (26 percent of shoppers)	Price, bargain conscious shopper (24 percent of shoppers)

Source: P. Ronald Stephenson and Ronald P. Willett, "Analysis of Consumers' Retail Patronage Strategies," in Philip R. McDonald, ed., *Marketing Involvement in Society and the Economy* (Chicago: American Marketing Association, 1969), p. 322. Reprinted by permission.

Generic retailing responses

It is one thing to understand how consumers make purchasing decisions. It is quite a different thing to understand how to respond to this information. It is beyond the scope of this book to analyze retailing strategy and programming. Other texts examine that topic much more thoroughly than would be possible here.[85] It is useful, however, to examine some of the major responses which leading retailers (and manufacturers) are making based on the developing understanding of consumer store choice processes. In most cases it is clear that the most successful strategies are founded (knowingly or unknowingly) on many of the principles of store choice described in the preceding pages. In thinking

85 Robert D. Enterberg, *Effective Retail and Market Distribution* (Cleveland: World Publishing Company, 1966): William R. Davidson, Alton Doody, and Dan Sweeney, *Retailing Management* (New York: The Ronald Press, 1975).

about contemporary responses in retailing strategy, it is also useful to recall the kinds of changes in life styles that were described in Chapter 7.

The retailing responses described in this section are described as *generic* because they cut across all or most lines of trade. They are also fairly dominant trends that seem to affect retailing across the board. They are also generic in that, for the most part, they reflect relationships between firms in an industry as well as the strategies of individual firms.

Retailing responses are not exclusively the responsibility of retailers. They usually require the active participation of other members of the channel of distribution and in many instances are even initiated by other channel members than retailers. In the first generic response, the emergence of vertical marketing systems, this is particularly evident. It is also a factor in the other generic responses that are described below, the acceleration of institutional life cycles, the growing polarity of retail trade, and the expanded use of positioning strategies.[86]

Consumer needs at the retailing level are increasingly being met through the emergence of vertical marketing systems. A vertical marketing system is defined as a tightly programmed network of horizontally coordinated and vertically aligned establishments managed as a total system. They are in contrast to traditional channels of distribution in which each channel member performs independently a historical set of marketing functions. Instead, a VMS relies upon the concept of functional shiftability to improve total system performance. That is, establishments of each level are reprogrammed so that marketing functions within the system are performed at the most advantageous level of position.[87] The salient characteristics of conventional channels and vertical marketing systems are summarized in Figure 19.10.

Vertical marketing systems (VMS)

Three major types of vertically aligned networks are generally recognized.[88] A *corporate* VMS is based on ownership of various parts of the system. A classic example is an operation such as Sears. Other examples include Sherwin-Williams, a paint manufacturer that operates over 2,000 retail outlets, or Hart Schaffner & Marx, which owns more than 200 retail stores. A *contractual* VMS is based upon a long term contractual agreement in which independent parties agree to exchange some autonomy in order to position marketing functions (advertising, inventory control, buying, and so forth) at their most efficient level. Examples include IGA, a chain of grocery stores organized by wholesalers, and American Hardware stores, which supplies most of the items in a group of independent hardware stores. Other famous contractual systems are the major franchisers such as Holiday Inn, McDonald's, and Wendy's, although some of these are in the process of converting to corporately

---

86 This section relies heavily on materials from Management Horizons, Inc. The authors gratefully acknowledge the assistance and contributions of numerous members of the Management Horizons staff and particularly those of Dr. William Davidson, chairman.

87 William R. Davidson, "Changes in Distributive Institutions," *Journal of Marketing*, vol. 34 (January 1970), pp. 7–10.

88 For more details, see David T. Kollat, Roger D. Blackwell, and James Robeson, *Strategic Marketing* (Hinsdale: Dryden Press, 1972), pp. 287–92.

Figure 19.10 Comparison of vertical marketing systems and conventional channels

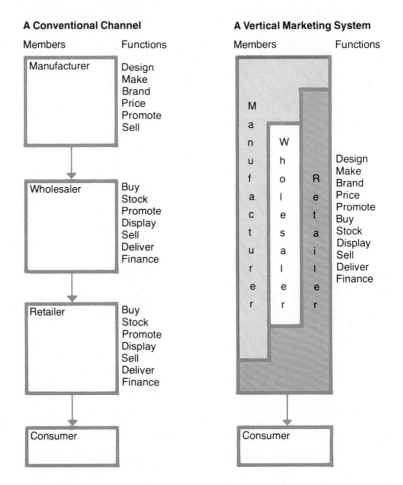

A Conventional Channel

Members   Functions

Manufacturer
Design
Make
Brand
Price
Promote
Sell

Wholesaler
Buy
Stock
Promote
Display
Sell
Deliver
Finance

Retailer
Buy
Stock
Promote
Display
Sell
Deliver
Finance

Consumer

A Vertical Marketing System

Members   Functions

Manufacturer   Wholesaler   Retailer
Design
Make
Brand
Price
Promote
Buy
Stock
Display
Sell
Deliver
Finance

Consumer

Source: From p. 289 of *Strategic Marketing* by David T. Kollat, Roger D. Blackwell, and James F. Robeson. Copyright © 1972 by Holt, Rinehart and Winston. Reprinted by permission of Holt, Rinehart and Winston.

owned systems. An *administered* VMS is based upon the ability of one party to take control or exert leadership over the distribution system because of the expertise of that party. Examples include Kraft, which dominates the dairy case in most grocery stores, or L'Eggs hosiery products in drug and grocery stores.

How does a VMS allow a retailer to respond more closely to the evaluative criteria and purchasing processes of consumers? An answer to this question is provided by considering the example of L'Eggs, an administered VMS. Traditionally, women's hosiery products have been distributed through department stores and independent specialty stores.

Based upon a $400,000 consumer research program,[89] Hanes found that women would like to buy more hosiery in supermarkets and drug stores but were not particularly impressed by the offerings of those stores because of their price promotion and lack of uniform quality control for many private labels. From the research, a number of key elements were discovered concerning the product features, promotion, pricing and distribution necessary to satisfy consumer purchases in drug stores and supermarkets. Hanes developed a new brand, L'Eggs, an effective advertising program to communicate the primary product quality ("Our L'Eggs *fit* your legs"), and a price that permitted enough margin to satisfy retailers. To help overcome the out-of-stock and service problems that hurt other manufacturers in supermarkets and drugstores, L'Eggs employed a computerized control system to provide data on manufacturing, warehouses, retailing inventory balance, sales and market analysis— including model stocks tailored to individual neighborhoods, and other variables.

Several lessons are possible from this example. First, it would probably have been impossible for any individual food or drug retail chain to develop a marketing mix that was so research-based and carefully programmed. Thus, this type of retailer made an explosive gain in effectiveness relative to department and specialty stores by relying on the manufacturer to perform some marketing functions. Second, other manufacturers who failed to understand the underlying shift in consumer shopping preferences were left at a serious disadvantage, and many were displaced. Third, consumers are probably more satisfied with the convenience and offering of the VMS than was true previously with the independent or unprogrammed conventional channel.

Retailers, like other institutions, have life cycles, and movement through those cycles is accelerating.[90] The life cycle of retailing and other institutions has four main parts, beginning with the *introduction* and early growth of an innovative retailing form. Examples would be the department store in the 1800s, a supermarket in the 1930s, the discount store in the 1950s, or the catalogue showroom of the 1970s.

Acceleration of institutional life cycles

After the innovative form is introduced and catches on, it moves into an *accelerated development* stage. The growth is fast because the form is competing with the older, traditional retailer who is typically complacent and does not realize the nature of the new competition. In the accelerated development of discount stores, for example, department stores attempted programs of retaliation on the theme, "we will not knowingly be undersold." This failed because it focused on only one evaluative criterion of consumers rather than recognizing other criteria of impor-

89 This research and other details of the L'Eggs example are contained in W. Wayne Talarzyk, *Contemporary Cases in Marketing* (Hinsdale: Dryden Press, 1974), pp. 285–96.
90 William R. Davidson, Albert D. Bates, and Stephen J. Bass, "The Retail Life Cycle," *Harvard Business Review*, vol. 54 (November–December 1976), pp. 89–96.

tance to consumers such as the suburban location of most discounters, the convenience of night and Sunday openings, and the availability of and appeal of self-service merchandising.

The third stage is *maturity* when market share of the innovation levels off, a proliferation occurs of similar stores with no differential advantage, and frequently, over storing or excess square footage becomes an industry problem. The result of such difficulties is a severe reduction in profitability. Finally, unless some new strategies are used, there is a *decline* in growth and profitability as one type of retailer gradually becomes replaced with new forms of retailing. This process has always occurred. The significance of the point is that such life cycles are accelerating dramatically, as Figure 19.11 indicates.

Figure 19.11 Life cycle characteristics of five retail institutions

Institution	Approximate date of innovation	Approximate date of maximum market share	Approximate number of years required to reach maturity	Estimated maximum market share	Estimated 1975 market share
Downtown department store	1860	1940	80	8.5% of total retail sales	1.1%
Variety store	1910	1955	45	16.5% of general merchandise sales	9.5%
Supermarket	1930	1965	35	70.0% of grocery store sales	64.5%
Discount department store	1950	1970	20	6.5% of total retail sales	5.7%
Home improvement center	1965	(estimate) 1980	15	35.0% of hardware and building material sales	25.3%

Source: William R. Davidson, Albert D. Bates, and Stephen J. Bass, "The Retail Life Cycle," *Harvard Business Review*, vol. (November–December 1976), pp. 89–96. Copyright © 1976 by the President and Fellows of Harvard College; all rights reserved

The speed up in life cycles has been caused in part by increased communications, better transportation, new technology and other variables. The implication for marketers, however, is an accelerated need for sophisticated consumer research that identifies potential new customers as well as potential *dis*consumption by existing customers and their impact on market structure and competitive developments. This requires managerial flexibility in merchandising and operations on the part of retailers but it also requires improved monitoring systems on the part of manufacturers and suppliers. In the past, manufacturers and wholesalers often refrained from selling to new types of retailers for fear of disrupting existing channel relationships. To do so today, often leaves the door open for minor suppliers who proceed to take market share away from the larger companies by selling to the innovative outlets. All levels of suppliers must become increasingly concerned about not being locked into one type of retail outlet for a product and therefore are becoming more responsive to new retail ventures than they probably were in the past.

Two trends that are emerging in retailing are opposite in nature and represent the growing polarity of retail trade. The first trend is the growth of the limited line, or specialty, store. The limited line store features *narrow lines* but *deep assortments* within those lines and can meet the service needs of a customer on a *personalized basis*, often tailored to specific life style segments. The second trend is the growth of the mass merchandiser who can provide strong *price appeal* because of the economies of scale associated with *self-service* and *wide* (and often *deep*) *assortments*. In the middle and caught in a tremendous squeeze is the conventional retail outlet that has neither the ability to compete with the high service, depth of assortments and positioning of the specialty store, nor the low price, depth of assortments and one-stop shopping convenience of the mass merchandiser.[91]

Growing polarity of retail trade

The appeal of the fast-growing chains of specialty stores is that they are *rationalized*. By that, it is meant that all tasks of success requirements for the retail outlet have been well-defined to serve a life style segment with a unique product offering.[92] Operations are also well thought through so they may be operated systematically without constantly worrying about day-to-day problems. This permits management to focus upon longer-term, strategic issues of conforming the characteristics of the store (actual and perceived) to the evaluative criteria of the defined market segment. Such stores often achieve inventory turnover rates twice those of conventional stores and return on net worth twice those of conventional stores. An example of such a specialty outlet is illustrated in Figure 19.12. The Limited operates over 150 outlets in carefully selected locations throughout the nation, maintains a thorough program of research to determine product and store criteria of its market segment, and creates an exciting atmosphere for the presentation of carefully selected fashion merchandise.

On the other end of the spectrum are the mass merchandisers. They may take many forms such as discount department stores like Gold Circle (a division of Federated, which also owns conventional department

91 These trends have been described by Management Horizons based upon its computerized retail data base, which contains the SEC 10-K reports of all publically held retail firms, and their photographic data base, which contain over 260,000 slides of retail firms related to the statistical data base.

92 A comparison of specialty shopping characteristics and conventional store characteristics is described in Daniel J. Sweeney and Richard C. Reizenstein, "Developing Retail Market Segmentation Strategy for a Women's Specialty Store Using Multiple Discriminant Analysis," Boris Becker and Helmut Becker, eds., *1972 Combined Proceedings* (Chicago: American Marketing Association, 1972), pp. 466–72.

Figure 19.12 The Limited

Source: Courtesy of The Limited.

stores) and K-Mart, probably the most successful retailer in the United States during recent years. A number of newer forms are emerging such as warehouse furniture stores like Levitz and Wickes and commodity supermarkets (for commodities other than food) like Standard Brands Paint on the West Coast, Toys R Us, and Hermann's Sporting Goods. Other mass merchandising forms include jumbo food stores (40,000 square feet or more) operated by Kroger and other firms and food warehouses with a strong price appeal achieved by very limited consumer services and low operating expenses.

The most dramatic and innovative of the mass merchandising forms is the hypermarket. These are stores in the 60,000 to 200,000 square feet range carrying both convenience and shopping goods with a heavy emphasis on general merchandise as well as food. They have incorporated breakthrough technology in materials handling in a warehouse operating profile that provides both a "warehouse feel" for consumers as well as strong price appeal. Some other features of hypermarkets are the use of total store graphics programs which coordinate all of the customers' visual impressions of the store, strong use of vertical space in merchandise presentations wherever possible, and use of classification dominance in selected merchandise categories—giving the customer the visual (and perhaps actual) impression that the merchandise assortment contains virtually any item that could possibly be desired.

The hypermarket has been most successful in Europe although Stein's in Montreal and Jewel in Chicago (under the name Grand Bazaar) have adapted the concept to North America. Figure 19.13 shows some views of Carrefour in France, showing the massive amounts of merchandise, total store graphics, and classification dominance that create excitement and price appeal as well as some of the operating economies involved in the technology of palletized product display and storage and the cash registers which will each ring up over a million dollars per year in some stores.

The increasing polarity of retail trade demonstrates vividly the need for understanding the evaluative criteria as they vary among market segments and among types of shopping trips. Both suppliers and retailers

Figure 19.13 The hypermarket

Source: Courtesy of Management Horizons.

must carefully program the total marketing mix to conform with those criteria—with absolutely no assurance that the program that was successful in prior years will go unchallenged in future years.

Expanded use of positioning strategies

Market positioning is the identification of a precise market segment based upon demographic or life style variables and appealing to this segment with a clearly differentiated product and service offering designed specifically for the market target. The concept of positioning has been used for years in reference to brands[93] but is increasingly recognized as important for retailers.

Positioning is closely related to segmentation and requires paying attention to the evaluative criteria of some market segments rather than trying to meet the criteria of the entire market. Stated simply, it is a marketing program that does not try to be all things to all people. While most stores have traditionally tried to stand for something in terms of price or fashion or service, the concept of positioning has been extended to reach different customers even *within* a store. Department stores may have 20 departments or "boutiques" closely correlated to demographic and life style segments rather than just three or four as in prior years.

While price is always important, positioning often is based upon criteria of more importance to certain segments. The 7-11 or Convenient food stores are not designed to beat anyone on the price criteria but they are carefully programmed to satisfy the extended hours and quick shopping of certain segments of the markets in some specific situations. Levitz furniture uses a positioning strategy, aimed at young people who want to have everything at once and don't know much about how things might go together. Levitz programmed their stores to contain a hundred showrooms in one store with inexpensive furniture ready to take, with a variety and price that allow them to buy many things and have them right then by picking them up at the warehouse.

Another example of positioning is Shepler's in Wichita, Kansas, which features Western Wear. The merchandising format communicates clearly to people who want boots that they need not visit any other store. Another example is Sound Chamber, an electronic components store in Cleveland. The store has achieved high clarity of offering by placing in one place the best grouping of stereo components for $300, $400, or $500. The strong use of graphics helps communicate the offer to a probably uninformed customer that this is the best system for the money in each price range. Another example is Wendy's, a successful fast food chain that has developed such a precise positioning strategy that outlets can be opened next to McDonald's and compete effectively. In these and most positioning strategies, a strong emphasis of the store is on

93 Herbert E. Brown and J. Taylor Sims, "Market Segmentation, Product Differentiation, and Market Positioning as Alternative Marketing Strategies," in *1976 Combined Proceedings* (Chicago: American Marketing Association, 1976), pp. 483–87; Kenneth M. Warwick and Saul Sands, "Product Positioning: Problems and Promises," University of Michigan *Business Review*, vol. 27 (November 1975), pp. 17–20; John H. Holmes, "Profitable Product Positioning," *MSU Business Topics*, vol. 21 (Spring, 1973), pp. 27–32; Robert E. Smith and Robert F. Lusch, "How Advertising Can Position a Brand," *Journal of Advertising Research*, vol. 16 (February 1976), pp. 37–43.

atmospherics—the conscious designing of space to create desired effects in buyers.[94]

Conclusion. While these generic responses in retailing are not intended as a summary of all the important trends in retailing, they do serve to indicate some of the strategies or responses that cut across a wide range of retailing activity. All of the strategies employed by individual firms to deal with these trends require precise understanding of the purchasing processes of consumers. This increases the need for an analytical format such as the one described in this chapter.

Summary

Purchasing processes is a term that refers to the interaction between consumers and retail outlets. Decisions about stores are fundamentally the same as decisions about products or brands and involve problem recognition, search, alternative evaluation, choice and outcomes and consequences. Problem recognition leading to shopping behavior may be initiated by product problem recognition or by nonproduct related motives such as the desire to get out of the house or engage in family related leisure activity.

Store choice is a complex process consisting of four variables: (1) evaluative criteria, (2) perceived characteristics of stores, (3) comparison process, and (4) acceptable and unacceptable stores. In general, the determinants of store choice are location, depth and breadth of assortments, price, advertising and word-of-mouth communications, sales promotions, store personnel, services, physical attributes, and store clientele.

Store image is the *perception of consumers* about the objective characteristics of stores. The most common method of measuring store image is with the semantic differential. Other recently developed techniques include multi-attribute measures and multidimensional scaling.

Shopper profiles are important in analyzing the comparison process by which consumers pick acceptable and unacceptable stores. Demographic variables, especially age, income and place of residence are often used to define patronage of a store. Psychological variables such as psychographics and personality or perceived risk are sometimes used for store profiles, as well as retailing specific typologies such as one developed by Stone.

Generic retailing responses are those that cut across all lines of trade. They include the emergence of vertical marketing systems, the acceleration of institutional life cycles, the growing polarity of retail trade and the expanded use of positioning strategies.

Review and discussion questions

1. Why is it important to understand purchasing processes as part of the decision process approach to understanding consumer behavior?

---

94 Philip Kotler, "Atmospherics as a Marketing Tool," *Journal of Retailing*, vol. 49 (Winter 1973–74), pp. 48–64.

2. Think of the last time you bought a product. How did you decide which store to patronize? How does your behavior compare with the conceptualization of the process as presented in this chapter?

3. Define the term store image and explain why it is important as a concept for retail management.

4. What is the image of the two largest stores in your area? How do your perceptions of these stores compare with your friends' images? Your parents? Why do these differences exist?

5. Assume you are a consultant for a major department store. Describe how you would go about determining whether the types of shoppers found in the Stone study exist for your store. Of what value are shopper categories identical or similar to those used in the Stone study?

6. Assume that you are asked to measure the image of the dominant grocery chain in your area. How would you recommend this be done? Why?

7. Of what importance is location in analyzing the patronage of retail stores?

8. Several generic retailing responses were described in this chapter. Briefly outline the salient characteristics of each and list some examples other than those mentioned in the chapter.

9. Describe the importance of price in the patronage decision for supermarkets.

10. Is the acceleration of institutional life cycles a problem or an opportunity for retailers? Explain your answer.

PART 6

AN INTEGRATED PERSPECTIVE ON CONSUMER BEHAVIOR

The subject matter of the book now shifts to an entirely different dimension focusing much more directly on metatheoretical concerns. Metatheory is defined as "... *the investigation, analysis, and the description of (1) the technology of building theory, (2) the theory itself, and (3) the utilization of theory.*[1] Therefore, the reader whose primary concern is with pragmatic application may chose to skip this section, although much of the discussion in Chapter 21 is relevant to all, regardless of perspective.

The purpose of Chapter 20 is to discuss the nature and significance of behavioral models and to describe and evaluate, in formal terms, the two models of consumer behavior most frequently cited in published research: (1) the Howard model and (2) the Engel, Kollat, Blackwell (EKB) model.

---

1 Gerald Zaltman, Christian R. A. Pinson, and Reinhard Angelmar, *Metatheory and Consumer Research* (New York: Holt, Rinehart and Winston, Inc., 1973), p. 4.

Chapter 21 is a summary statement on the prospects and problems faced in consumer research. It assesses current progress in this discipline and outlines the major obstacles to be recognized and overcome if future progress in the understanding of consumer decision processes is to proceed at an accelerated rate.

CHAPTER 20

Models of consumer behavior: Formalization and quantification

Chapters 1 and 2 provided a brief overview of the history of consumer behavior research and the importance of theoretical models in understanding the consumer. This book, of course, is based on a model, which, up to this point, has not been stated in formal and testable terms. In addition, little reference has been made to other models which have proved to be influential in the emergence of consumer behavior research as a maturing discipline. It is the purpose of this chapter to elaborate on the nature and significance of behavioral models and then to describe in more formal terms the two conceptualizations which have proved to be most influential in terms of frequency of citation in published research: (1) the Howard model and (2) the Engel, Kollat, and Blackwell model.

The nature and significance of models

A model is a replica of the phenomena it is intended to designate; that is, it specifies the elements and represents the nature of the relationships among them. As such, it provides a testable "map" of reality, and its utility lies in the extent to which successful prediction of behavior or outcomes is made possible.

There are many types of models, and space does not permit detailed discussion of all of them here.[1] Of special significance for present

---

1 Irwin D. J. Bross, *Design for Decision* (New York: Free Press, 1953), chap. 10; also Paul H. Rigby, *Conceptual Foundations of Business Research* (New York: Wiley, 1965), chap. 6.

purposes is the *systems model.*[2] Obviously it is not possible to dissect a human organism and study its component parts; as a result, the human being is analyzed as a *system* with outputs (behavior) in response to inputs. The objective is to gain an understanding of the person as a *system of action* through clarifying relationships among inputs, motivational determinants, and goal-oriented behavior. Such models can gain complexity, and the results usually are stated in graphic, symbolic, verbal, or mathematical forms. The final form is dependent upon the precision of the theories, facts, and assumptions upon which the model is built.

The models of consumer behavior discussed in this chapter are relatively unsophisticated in one sense in that they are elaborate flow charts of the behavioral process that is depicted. Relationships among elements at times are only hypothesized because of the absence of needed research. Even so, a number of significant advantages are offered through use of these conceptualizations:

(1) Explanatory variables are specified. Everyone has a model of consumer behavior in mind, whether implicit or explicit. In other words, each person has some concept of those factors that shape motivation and behavior. Explanation and prediction are impossible otherwise. The distinction, of course, enters with respect to the comprehensiveness of competing models and the accuracy with which predictions can be made.

(2) Research findings can be integrated into a meaningful whole. Most analysts of consumer behavior have some familiarity with the underlying behavioral sciences. Delving into this literature can be a highly frustrating experience, however. Of what use is research on the "prisoner's dilemma game," "psychological reactance," "cognitive dissonance," "signal detection theory," "attribution theory," and so on? Possession of a well-formulated model makes it possible to differentiate the relevant from the irrelevant. Otherwise, the literature is little more than a bewildering maze.

(3) Explanations are provided for performance of the system. Description of variables in laundry list fashion is of little value unless functional relationships between them are specified. This is part and parcel of a good model, and the result is ability to make behavioral predictions with some degree of accuracy.

(4) Avenues for fruitful research are revealed. Researchable hypotheses readily flow from a carefully designed model. Gaps in knowledge quickly become evident, and the nature of researchable hypotheses is determined by the variables themselves and the linkages between them.

The emergence of models of consumer behavior

A brief history of consumer behavior research was provided in Chapter 1, but a bit more elaboration is required to understand the present state of

2 William Lazer, "The Role of Models in Marketing," *Journal of Marketing*, vol. 26 (1962), pp. 9–14.

the art. For purposes of convenience, three time periods are specified: (1) pre-1960; (2) 1960–1967; and (3) 1967 to date.

Pre-1960. The vast majority of consumer research prior to 1960 was undertaken to answer pragmatic marketing questions. Only occasionally was consumer behavior the subject of scholarly inquiry in the marketing literature.[3] Textbooks explained behavior usually in terms of long lists of motives—primary buying motives, secondary buying motives, rational versus emotional motives, and so on.[4] All too frequently the outcome was nothing more than "armchair thinking," which bore little resemblance to the real world of behavior.

Another thrust during the pre-1960 era was economic analysis of consumer behavior. Much of the economic theory of the time was based on utterly unrealistic theories of behavior, and the same tends to be true even today if Ratchford's analyses are representative of economists in general.[5] The work of Katona and his colleagues at the Survey Research Center of the University of Michigan stands in sharp contrast. Katona was a true pioneer in the empirical analysis of the consumer,[6] and his work has done much to shape our present day understanding.[7]

1960–1967. The seven years designated here (admittedly chosen arbitrarily) mark the real onset of behaviorally trained researchers into the ranks of marketing academicians. In part this reflected the tendency for the behavioral sciences and quantitative methods to become the "in thing" in the schools of business. But it also reflected a felt need by practitioners to understand consumer motivation and behavior with greater precision.

For the most part, the early contributions of this "new breed" were applications of theories borrowed from elsewhere. Examples are Cox and persuasion theory,[8] Engel and the theory of cognitive dissonance,[9] King and the psychology of fashion,[10] and Robertson and the diffusion of innovations.[11] One of the few truly original contributions of this period

3 A major exception was the research published over the years by Paul Lazarsfeld beginning in the 1930s.

4 A more thorough history of this type of thinking was provided in the second edition of this book. See James F. Engel, David T. Kollat, and Roger D. Blackwell, *Consumer Behavior*, rev. ed. (Hinsdale, Ill.: Dryden, 1973), chap. 2.

5 Brian Ratchford, "The New Economic Theory of Consumer Behavior: An Interpretive Essay," *Journal of Consumer Research*, vol. 2 (September 1975), pp. 65–75.

6 See, in particular, George Katona, *The Powerful Consumer* (New York: McGraw-Hill, 1960).

7 For an up-to-date review of psychological economics, see George Katona, "Psychology and Consumer Economics," *Journal of Consumer Research*, vol. 1 (June 1974), pp. 1–8.

8 Donald Cox, "The Measurement of Information Value: A Study in Consumer Decision Making," in William S. Decker, ed., *Emerging Concepts in Marketing* (Chicago: American Marketing Association, 1962), pp. 413–21.

9 James F. Engel, "The Psychological Consequences of a Major Purchase Decision," in William S. Decker, ed., *Marketing in Transition* (Chicago: American Marketing Association, 1963), pp. 462–75.

10 Charles W. King, "Fashion Adoption: A Rebuttal to the Trickle Down Theory," in Stephen A. Greyser, ed., *Toward Scientific Marketing* (Chicago: American Marketing Association, 1963), pp. 108–25.

11 Thomas S. Robertson, "The Process of Innovation and the Diffusion of Innovation," *Journal of Marketing*, vol. 31 (January 1967), pp. 14–19.

was the theory of perceived risk stated by Bauer[12] and elaborated by others at Harvard.[13] These are only a few examples of what soon became a burgeoning literature.

Quite understandably, there was little focus or direction to these early research efforts. This is always the case when a discipline is in its initial stages. The first real step toward maturity was taken in 1963 by John Howard whose influence on the field of marketing in general and on consumer behavior in particular is a towering one indeed.[14] Howard presented the first integrative model of buyer behavior, which since has been elaborated and expanded as later sections of the chapter will reveal. Its basic contribution lies in a systematic and thorough utilization of learning theory. Howard introduced the useful distinction between true problem-solving behavior, limited problem-solving, and automatic response behavior. This pioneering effort did much to provide needed direction to the interdisciplinary approach to analysis of consumer behavior.

This period of the 1960s also saw a sharp increase in the application of quantitative models, especially in an attempt to explain and predict brand loyalty.[15] Most of the studies cited in chapter 17 were generated during this period. Experiments also were begun with such psychometric tools as multidimensional scaling. Interest in quantitative models (as opposed to the tools of scaling) has subsided greatly since that time, mostly because of their relative inability to improve the predictions made with much simpler concepts and methodology. This may change in the future, but more about that in the next chapter.

1967 to the present time. Courses in consumer behavior soon began to appear at some leading colleges, but the growth of the discipline was impeded by the absence of integrative theoretical perspectives. The literature abounded increasingly with examples of the so-called "reduced form model," which explains only a part of the total process. This began to change in late 1966 with the publication of the influential Nicosia model.[16] This was followed shortly by the publication of the first edition of this book which was the first real text in the field.[17] It also contained the first version of the current Engel, Kollat, Blackwell model. Another meaningful step forward was taken by Howard and Sheth in the publication of *The Theory of Buyer Behavior* in 1969.[18] The earlier Howard model

12 Raymond A. Bauer, "Consumer Behavior as Risk Taking," in Robert S. Hancock, ed., *Dynamic Marketing for a Changing World* (Chicago: American Marketing Association, 1960), pp. 389–98.

13 Donald F. Cox, ed., *Risk Taking and Information Handling in Consumer Behavior* (Boston: Division of Research, Graduate School of Business Administration, Harvard University, 1967).

14 John A. Howard, *Marketing Management Analysis and Planning*, rev. ed. (Homewood, Ill.: Irwin, 1963), chaps. 3–4.

15 See, for example, Frank M. Bass, et al., eds., *Mathematical Models and Methods in Marketing* (Homewood, Ill.: Irwin, 1961).

16 Francesco M. Nicosia, *Consumer Decision Processes: Marketing and Advertising Implications* (Englewood Cliffs, N. J.: Prentice-Hall, 1966).

17 James F. Engel, David T. Kollat, and Roger D. Blackwell, *Consumer Behavior* (New York: Holt, Rinehart and Winston, Inc., 1968).

18 John A. Howard and Jagdish N. Sheth, *The Theory of Buyer Behavior* (New York: Wiley, 1969).

was elaborated through the inclusion of more variables and the specification of functional relationships with greater precision. Others who contributed to the development of theoretical thinking were Andreason,[19] Hansen,[20] and Markin.[21]

1967 is cited as a turning point also because it seems to mark the beginning of an upsurge of useful empirical work which moved beyond the mere borrowing from related behavioral sciences. The most significant sources are cited in this volume, and the reader can trace the development of the field by comparing the 1968, 1973, and 1978 editions of this book. The change in ten years has been remarkable indeed, and it can now be said that the field has attained a measure of maturity. At least the great gaps in knowledge existing ten years ago have been largely filled.

Decision-process models encompassing many variables cannot explain the details of consumer behavior in every specific situation. Rather, a workable model should delineate (1) the variables associated with consumer decision processes; (2) the general relations that exist among variables; and (3) the general principles that express the model's ingression in particular purchase occasions.

The importance of integrative models in consumer research

The value of a model to guide research cannot be overemphasized. Without a model specifying the range of appropriate variables, the researcher may be lured into looking at a problem from an unduly narrow perspective. A famous story by Sir Arthur Eddington illustrates this danger.[22] It seems that an ichthyologist wished to make some generalizations concerning the size of fish. He took a fishnet of two-inch mesh into the sea. It was dropped into the water and he collected a large number of fish. After meticulous measurement, it was concluded that "All fish are two inches long or more." Unfortunately, this also happens in consumer research. In spite of the rigor of the research design, the facts collected are only partially accurate because only a partial theory has guided the collection.

Inadequate data collection can occur in other ways. The story of Procrustes, the giant who obliged weary travelers to spend the night with him, further illustrates the problem.[23] Procrustes required travelers to sleep in his bed and always trimmed them to fit, stretching the shorter ones on the rack and lopping pieces of the longer ones until their corpses were exactly the right length. With or without a theory, the consumer analyst is often a Procrustes and empirical data are the travelers. Making data fit a model involves exactly the same process.

19 Alan R. Andreason, "Attitudes and Customer Behavior: A Decision Model," in Lee E. Preston, ed., *New Research in Marketing* (Berkeley, Calif.: Institute of Business and Economic Research, 1965), pp. 1–16.

20 Flemming Hansen, *Consumer Choice Behavior* (New York: Free Press, 1972).

21 Rom J. Markin, *The Psychology of Consumer Behavior* (Englewood Cliffs, N. J.: Prentice-Hall, 1969).

22 Quoted in Stephen Toulmin, *The Philosophy of Science* (New York: Harper & Row, 1953), pp. 124–29.

23 Toulmin, *Philosophy of Science.*

The Howard model

The remainder of this chapter focuses on only two of the published consumer behavior models: (1) the Howard model and (2) Engel, Kollat, Blackwell model. The Nicosia model had a strong impact when it was published, but it has never received necessary elaboration and empirical support. Furthermore, it is has never been revised to reflect changes in this discipline as have the above two models. The two included here receive the lion's share of citations in published literature reviews and empirical studies, thus further justifying their inclusion in this context.

Evolution of the Howard model

John Howard's pioneering work was strengthened when he and Jagdish Sheth collaborated and published *The Theory of Buyer Behavior* in 1969.[24] Howard and his colleagues at the Columbia Graduate School of Business have tested parts of this model empirically, however, and there have been a number of revisions since 1969.[25] These revisions reflect the insights gained through the testing process as well as the empirical contributions of others, often approaching the subject from a different theoretical

Figure 20.1 The Howard model of buyer behavior, 1974 version

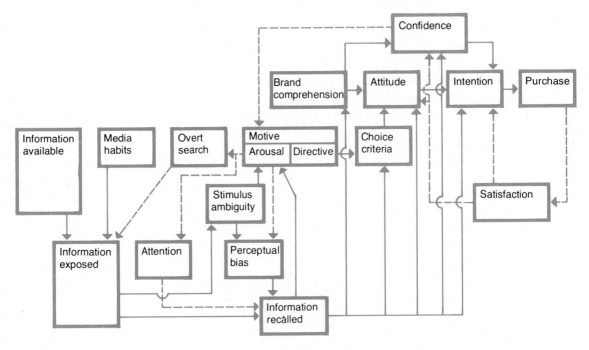

Source: Reproduced by special permission from John U. Farley, John A. Howard, and L. Winston Ring, *Consumer Behavior Theory and Application* (Boston: Allyn & Bacon, 1974), p. 11.

24 Howard and Sheth.

25 See John A. Howard and Lyman E. Ostlund, *Buyer Behavior: Theoretical and Empirical Foundations* (New York: Knopf, 1973), pp. 3–32; and John U. Farley, John A. Howard, and L. Winston Ring, *Consumer Behavior Theory and Application* (Boston: Allyn and Bacon, 1974).

perspective. The 1974 published version is described here,[26] and its pictorial representation in simplified form appears in Figure 20.1.

There are 12 primary functional relationships specified in this model. These are described below in the form of testable equations. For the most part these equations also can be traced in Figure 20.1 simply by locating the variable in question and noting the other variables related to it through direct arrows or dotted arrows indicating a feedback or indirect relationship.

Here is the formal statement of the 1974 version of the Howard model:

1. $P_x = f(I_x)$

2. $I_x = f(F_x^C, A_x, C_x, \underline{C^u}, \underline{S^C}, \underline{S^{os}}, \underline{T^P}, \underline{F^S})$

3. $A_x = f(B_x^C, S_x, F_x^C, \underline{C^u}, \underline{S^C}, \underline{S^{os}}, \underline{P^T})$

4. $C_x = f(B_x^C, S_x, F_x^C, \underline{P^T})$

5. $B_x^C = f(F_x^C, \underline{C^u}, \underline{S^C}, \underline{S^{os}}, \underline{I^P}, \underline{P^T})$

6. $S_x = f(P_x)$

7. $F_x^C = f(F_x^E, A_x^n, P_x^B)$

8. $F_x^E = f(O_x^S, \underline{F_x^A}, \underline{M^H})$

9. $A_x^n, O_x^S = f(M^a, \underline{I^P}, \underline{P^T}, \underline{T^P})$

10. $M^a = f(S_x^A, C_x, F_x^C, \underline{F^S})$

11. $S_x^A = f(F_x^E)$

12. $C^C = f(F_x^C, M^a, \underline{M^c})$

where symbols are defined as follows, with all terms referring to brand x (the underlined variables are defined as being *exogenous* or factors which exist independently and whose changes are not explained in the model).[27]

P_x = purchase of brand (the overt act of buying)
I_x = intention to purchase the brand (a verbally stated expectation, made in cognizance of possible extenuating factors, that brand *x* will be purchased the next time this action is necessary)
F_x^C = facts coded regarding brand (recalled information that brand *x* exists, that it has certain specific characteristics, both favorable and unfavorable)
A_x = attitude toward the brand (a verbal evaluation of the potential of brand *x* to satisfy motives)
C_x = confidence in brand evaluation (confidence in ability to evaluate brand *x*)
C^u = culture
S^C = social class
S^{os} = social and organizational setting (comparative or normative reference groups)

---

26 Farley, Howard, and Ring, *Consumer Behavior Theory.*
27 Where possible, definitions are drawn from Farley, Howard, and Ring. There is some ambiguity, however, necessitating the use at some points of the definitions in Howard and Sheth.

T^P = time pressure (the inverse of the amount of time the buyer has available both for purchase and consumption as well as information seeking)

F^s = financial status (quantity of funds available or expected to be available to spend on goods and services during some specified time period)

B_x^C = brand comprehension (buyer understanding of brand features)

S_x = satisfaction with brand (satisfaction received from brand use)

P^T = personality traits (enduring dispositions or qualities accounting for relative consistency in emotional, temperamental, and social behavior, which explain differences among buyers)

I^P = importance of purchase (a measure of the relative intensity of motives governing buyer activities relating to the given product class relative to others)

F_x^E = facts exposed regarding the brand (information about the brand to which the buyer was exposed)

A_x^n = attention to brand information (buyer receptivity to information, regulating the quantity of information that reaches the nervous system)

P_x^B = perceptual bias of brand information (the tendency to distort information during its processing)

O_x^S = overt search for brand information (effort expended by the buyer to obtain brand information)

F_x^A = facts available regarding the brand (information available from the environment)

M^H = media habits toward vehicles containing brand information

M^a = motive arousal (the arousing or energizing aspect of motives— the intensity of motives satisfied by the product class of which x is a member)

S_x^A = stimulus ambiguity (perceived uncertainty and lack of meaningful information received from the environment)

C^C = choice criteria (an ordered set of motives relevant to the product class)

M^c = direct motives (motives directly related to choice criteria)

Many readers will be unfamiliar with this way of stating relationships. The alternative is a detailed written explanation, which space will not allow. Furthermore, the model is stated in such a way that it may be tested empirically. The best suggestion is to state each equation verbally, paying careful attention to the manner in which variables are defined. For example, equation one states that the purchase of brand x is a function of intentions to buy that brand on the next occasion, and so on.

Evaluation and testing of the Howard model

Any model may be evaluated in two different but related ways: (1) metatheoretically (in terms of the internal structure of the theory itself) and (2) empirically (in terms of its utility in describing and predicting real world behavior). It is possible to make some broad generalizations in terms of both criteria based on recent published evaluations.

Metatheoretical evaluation. According to Zaltman and his associates metatheory is *the investigation, analysis, and the description of (1) the*

technology of building theory, (2) the theory itself, and (3) the utilization of theory.[28] Thus, metatheory focuses on the conceptual procedures of science by raising fundamental philosophic questions.

Zaltman et al. utilized 15 separate formal criteria to evaluate the Nicosia model, the Howard-Sheth model (1969), and the Engel, Kollat, Blackwell model (1973).[29] While the Howard model described above differs somewhat from its 1969 formulation, it is worthwhile to refer to the points that were raised. These are summarized in Figure 20.2.

Figure 20.2 A metatheoretical evaluation of the Howard-Sheth model

Criterion	Evaluation
1. Well-formedness (the theoretical structure conforms to the rules of elementary logic)	Very good
2. Internal consistency (the theory contains no logical contradictions)	Good to very good
3. Strength (the theory encompasses other relevant theories)	Good
4. Linguistic exactness (minimum vagueness in terms)	Fair to good
5. Conceptual unity (components refer to the same set of behavioral phenomena)	Fair
6. Empirical interpretability (the theory can be operationalized in empirical terms)	Good
7. Representativeness (relationships are explained at the deepest or most fundamental level)	Good
8. Falsifiability (the theory is confrontable with facts and reality)	Fair
9. Methodological simplicity (the theory is easy to build and test)	Poor to fair
10. Confirmation (the theory is consistent with facts)	Fair
11. Originality (the theory increases reality by deriving new propositions)	Good
12. External consistency (the theory is consistent with existing knowledge)	Fair to good
13. Unifying power (the theory connects previously unconnected items)	Good to very good
14. Heuristic power (the theory suggests new directions for research)	Good to very good
15. Stability (the theory is able to accommodate new evidence through variations and modifications)	Fair

Source: From p. 122 of *Metatheory and Consumer Behavior* by Gerald Zaltman, Christian R. A. Pinson, and Reinhard Angelmar. Copyright © 1973 by Holt, Rinehart and Winston. Reprinted by permission of Holt, Rinehart and Winston.

28 Gerald Zaltman, Christian R. A Pinson, and Reinhard Angelmar, *Metatheory and Consumer Research* (New York: Holt, Rinehart and Winston, 1973), p. 4.
29 Zaltman, Pinson, and Angelmar, *Metatheory and Consumer Research*, chap. 5.

The three models were not found to differ much along these criteria. The greatest strengths of the Howard-Sheth model were in terms of being well formed, internally consistent, and the offering of both unifying and heuristic power. It was evaluated as weakest in terms of falsifiability, methodological simplicity, confirmation, and stability.

One could, of course, quarrel with this particular evaluation. Yet most would agree that this earlier version of that model suffered from some conceptual difficulties. Yet, the great strength is that a multiplicity of variables are linked in a precise manner. Indeed, the hypothesized relationships, at times, approach the rigor of formal theory. The authors' goal was to provide more than a simple description of the behavioral process, and their success is evidenced by the amount of published research in consumer behavior that has been undertaken to test one or more of its hypotheses.

Empirical evaluation. The ultimate test of any theory is whether or not it predicts the phenomena under consideration. There have been a series of tests of the Howard model focusing on its 12 basic equations. The methodologies used have varied widely and have included multiple regression (the most common method), cross-lagged correlation, simulation, and longitudinal analysis.[30] In synthesizing these results, Holbrook came to the following conclusions:[31]

1. Most of the studies under consideration dealt only with a very small part of the total 12 equation system.

2. Support for the Howard model is fragmentary at best, based mostly on bivariate relationships (i.e., only two variables), even though the hypotheses called for multiple variables.

3. No single link in the model receives consistent support over those studies that focus explicitly on it.

4. None of the studies can claim an R^2 (the percentage of variance explained) consistently above 10 percent. This is particularly discouraging.

While these findings provide no clear support for the theory, much has been learned:

1. The model is more recursive than was originally thought. This means that some variables that occur only at initial stages in the system (such as attention) should be included in later relationships as well (intention is an example) rather than being assumed to feed through such intervening variables as attitudes.

2. There is substantial measurement error, which introduces a high

30 Farley, Howard, and Ring, *Consumer Behavior Theory.*

31 Morris B. Holbrook, "A Synthesis of the Empirical Studies," in Farley, Howard, and Ring, *Consumer Behavior Theory,* p. 250.

level of "noise."[32] Many of the measurements used have low reliability (correlations of about .7), which means that different answers are given at varying points in time. Therefore, predictability is substantially weakened for this reason alone.

3. The distinction between endogeneous and exogenous variables is not sharp, and it may prove necessary to treat more variables as endogenous for more precise measurement and manipulation.

4. Some variables are difficult to define operationally, and others are difficult to measure. In addition, there have been some wide discrepancies between the theoretical definition of a variable, such as perceptual bias, and the operational specification. This makes some of the tests of the theory to date, especially those undertaken by Farley and Ring, quite debatable.[33]

5. The model implies a definite causal priority among constructs. It has proved to be nearly impossible to design experiments that control all exogeneous factors and allow for causal priority to emerge.

6. Some of the relationships between variables may be nonlinear rather than linear as hypothesized, but there are real difficulties in assessing nonlinearity.

A revised form of the Howard model. Given the problems discussed above, the Howard model has been revised by Farley and others at Columbia and tested in that form.[34] This model is depicted in flow chart form in Figure 20.3. It will be noted that it is somewhat different from the 1974 version, and it bears only a scant family relationship to the 1969 Howard-Sheth model, especially when one examines the wide differences between the original definition of variables and the way in which they have been defined operationally. The result, however, has been an increase in predictability. Still the authors note that noise in the data and methodological problems are rendering improvements in predictive validity quite unlikely given the present state of the art.

The detailed recounting of methodological difficulties in testing the Howard model should not be interpreted by the reader as an attempt to cast doubt on its efficacy. Rather, it is necessary to evaluate these tests in order to grasp something of the process required in building and testing a theory. Probably there is no definitive way to test comprehensive theories at this point in time, and the relative absence of confirmatory data should not be viewed as a fatal drawback. As Zaltman and his associates have

Recapitulation

---

32 John U. Farley and Donald R. Lehman, "An Overview of Empirical Applications of Buyer Behavior System Models," in William D. Perreault, ed., *Advances in Consumer Research*, vol. 4 (Atlanta: Association for Consumer Research, 1977), p. 340.

33 See James Taylor and Jonathan Gutman, "A Reinterpretation of Farley and Ring's Test of the Howard-Sheth Model of Buyer Behavior," in Scott Ward and Peter Wright, eds., *Advances in Consumer Research*, vol. 1 (Urbana, Ill.: Association for Consumer Research, 1974), pp. 436–46.

34 These studies are summarized in Farley and Lehman, "Overview of Empirical Applications."

Figure 20.3 The revised Howard model
based on empirical tests by Farley and others

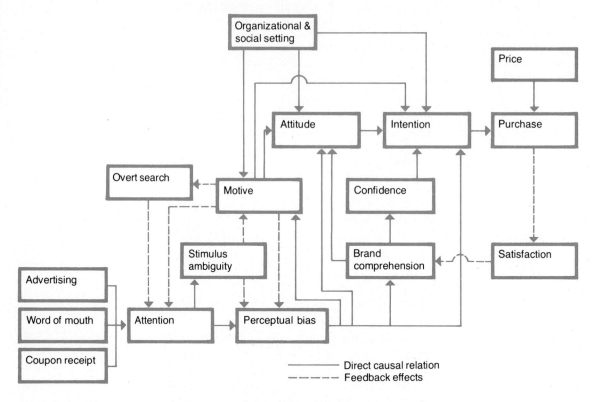

Source: Reprinted by special permission from John U. Farley and Donald R. Lehman, "An Overview of Empirical Applications of Buyer Behavior System Models," in William D. Perreault, ed., *Advances in Consumer Research*, vol. IV (Atlanta: Association for Consumer Research, 1977), p. 337.

pointed out, the theory, for the most part, is consistent with present knowledge, although there have been some advances since the 1974 formulation. Furthermore, its heuristic value has been enormous. Identification of weaknesses should be taken only as an indication of the progress that is yet to be made.

The Engel, Kollat, Blackwell model

As the reader is already aware, the 1968 version of this book was the first real text in consumer behavior. The authors first began to work together in 1965 at Ohio State University, and one of the initial joint assignments was to offer a course in this subject area. There were few guidelines to use, and the available literature was meager indeed. In fact, the basic text was a standard work in social psychology, augmented by various readings. The need for a text in the field was quite obvious, and this was our first major joint activity as colleagues.

The writing of a text, however, did not prove to be an easy matter. The great need was for some type of organizing framework. In fact, the basic course assignment for ten graduate students in the initial course referred to above was to construct a model of consumer behavior. These papers were interesting to say the least, but one stood out. This was the contribution by M. Lawrence Light, now vice-president of research at BBD & O. Engel later joined with Light in the first published version of what was to become the Engel, Kollat, Blackwell (EKB) model.[35] This skeleton model was then expanded to become the organizing framework of the 1968 book. The primary intent was pedagogical; i.e., the objective was to organize the subject matter, identify important variables, and specify probable linkages so that the student could achieve an overall grasp. Because the authors worked primarily from the base of existing knowledge, variables and functional relationships were not defined with much precision. This simply reflected the overall "state of the art" at that time.

When the book was revised for the first time, the authors had the benefit of the Nicosia model (which had just been published prior to the first edition), the Howard-Sheth model, and the benefits from the growing body of published research in this field. Therefore, the model was reshaped to bring about greater consistency with the changes in the state of the art. The primary purpose still was pedagogical, with the result that there was no explicit attempt made to specify quantifiable functional relationships. Although these could have been easily derived from the text itself, it never was our expectation that the model would be tested in the same manner as the Columbia group has done with the Howard model.

The present version is familiar to the reader by now, but it is depicted once again in Figure 20.4 for ease of reference. This revision had several distinct purposes:

1. To highlight more clearly the interrelationship between stages in the decision process and the various endogenous and exogenous variables.

2. To clarify the relationship between attitudes and behavior to reflect the contributions of the Fishbein extended model. Beliefs and intentions were introduced as explicit variables for the first time as was normative compliance.

3. To define the variables with greater precision and to specify functional relationships to permit empirical testing.

While there will, of course, be many similarities with the Howard model (this has been true since the beginning), there also are some differences as the discussion below will clarify.

---

35 James F. Engel and M. Lawrence Light, "The Role of Psychological Commitment in Consumer Behavior: An Evaluation of the Theory of Cognitive Dissonance," in F. M. Bass et. al., eds., *Application of the Sciences in Marketing Management* (New York: Wiley, 1968), pp. 39–68.

Figure 20.4 The EKB model

Figure 20.4 The EKB model

Information input — Stimuli: Mass, Personal, General, Marketer-dominated

Information processing — Exposure → Attention → Reception (ACTIVE MEMORY) → Information and experience

Decision process stages — Problem recognition → Search → Alternative evaluation → Choice → Outcomes; Satisfaction / Dissonance

Product brand evaluations — Evaluative criteria, Beliefs, Attitudes, Intention

General motivating influences — Motives, Personality Life style, Normative compliance

Internalized environmental influences — Cultural norms and values; Reference group, family; Anticipated circumstances; Unanticipated circumstances

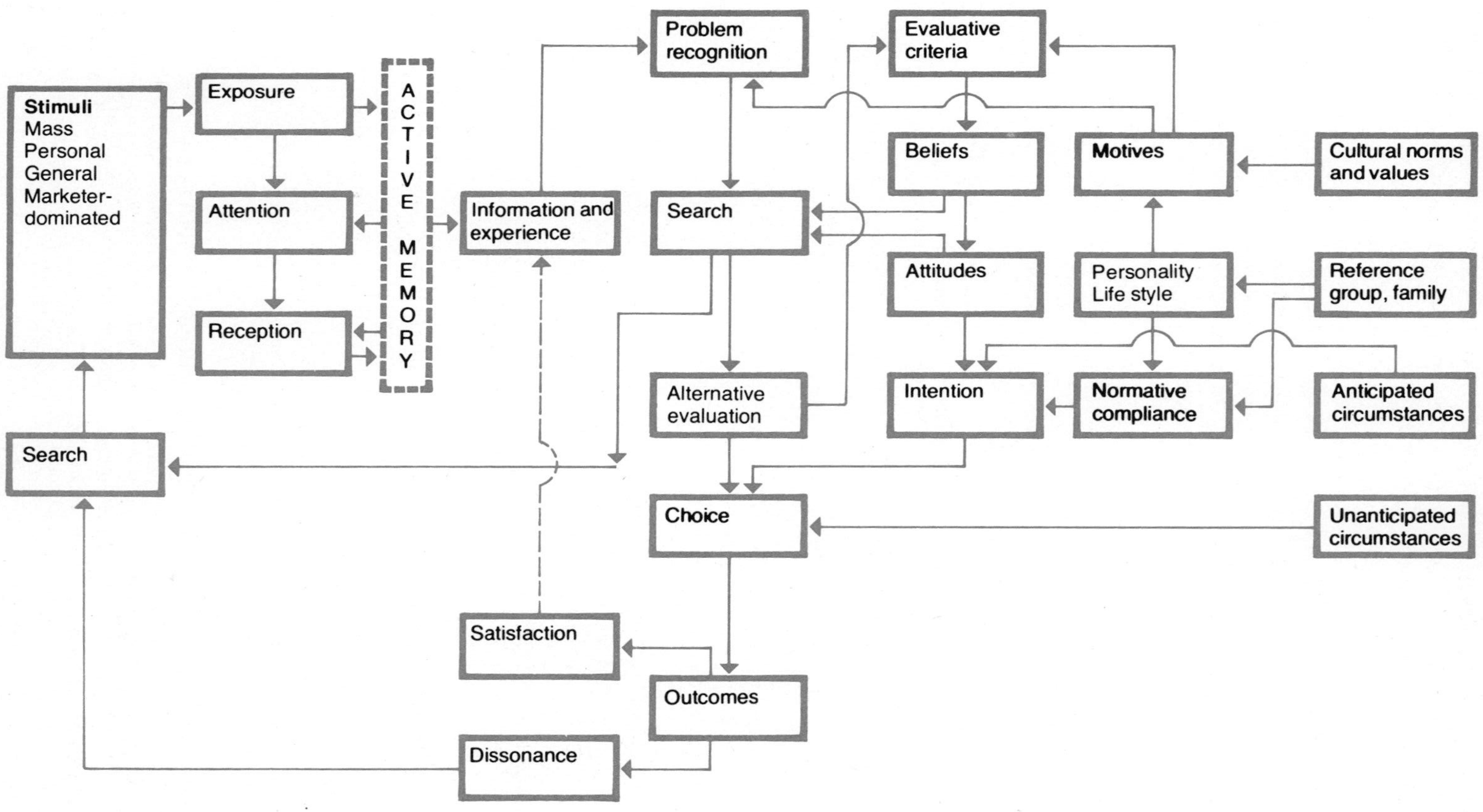

To permit comparison with the Howard model a series of equations and variable definitions are presented, following where possible similar notation styles. The formal statement is as follows:

A formal statement of the model

1. $C_x = f(I_x, \underline{UC})$
2. $I_x = f(A_x, NC_x, \underline{AC})$
3. $A_x = f(B_x)$
4. $NC_x = f(\underline{L}, \underline{SI_x})$
5. $B_x = f(IE_x, EC)$
6. $IE_x = f(MR_x)$
7. $MR_x = f(At_x, \underline{AM})$
8. $EC = f(IE_x, Mo)$
9. $Mo = f(\underline{L})$
10. $At_x = f(E_x, \underline{AM}, PR)$
11. $E_x = f(S^{PC}_x, St_x, \underline{MU})$
12. $S^{PC}_x = f(B_x, A_x)$
13. $PR = f(Mo, IE_x)$
14. $S_x = f(C_x, D_x)$
15. $D_x = f(C_x, B_x)$
16. $S^{PoC}_x = f(D_x)$

where the sumbold are defined as follows, all terms referring to brand x (underlined variables are defined as being *exogenous*):

C_x = choice (selection and purchase of an alternative)

I_x = intention (the subjective probability that a specified alternative will be chosen)

$\underline{UC}$ = unanticipated circumstances (an unexpected change in status of income levels, available alternatives, time pressure, social and organization setting, and other environmental influences at the time of choice)

A_x = attitude toward the brand (a learned predisposition to respond consistently in a favorable or unfavorable manner with respect to a given alternative)

NC_x = normative compliance (the outcome of the existence of perceived social influence on the choice of alternative plus a motivation to comply with that influence)

$\underline{AC}$ = anticipated circumstances (the expected status of income levels, available alternatives, time pressure, social and organizational setting, and other environmental influences at the time of choice)

B_x = belief regarding the brand (stored information, which links a given alternative to specified evaluative criteria)

$\underline{L}$ = personality and life style (the pattern of enduring traits, interests, and opinions that determine general behavior and thereby make an individual distinctive in comparison with others)

$\underline{SI}_x$ = social influence (the outcome of any interacting aggregation of people exerting an influence on an individual's selection and choice of a given alternative)

IE_x = information and experience (the general informational content of long term memory with respect to product class and a given alternative)

EC = evaluative criteria (desired outcomes from choice or use of an alternative expressed in the form of the attributes or specifications used to compare various alternatives)

MR_x = message reception (accurate comprehension of the meaning of incoming informational stimuli with respect to a given alternative and the storage of that input in long term memory)

At_x = attention (the active processing of exposed information stimuli with respect to a given alternative such that a conscious impression is made)

$\underline{AM}$ = active memory (a process whereby incoming information and that stored in long term memory are brought together and the new input is categorized and interpreted)

Mo = motive (an enduring predisposition to strive to attain specified goals, containing both an arousing and a directing dimension)

E_x = exposure (physical proximity to stimulus inputs with respect to a given alternative such that the individual has direct opportunity for one or more senses to be activated)

S_x^{pc} = pre-choice search (motivated exposure to information with regard to a given alternative)

PR = problem recognition (a perceived difference between the ideal state of affairs and the actual situation sufficient to arouse and activate the decision process)

$\underline{ST}_x$ = stimuli (information available with respect to a given alternative)

$\underline{MU}$ = media usage (the individual's habits and preferences with respect to media usage)

S_x = satisfaction (an evaluation that the chosen alternative is consistent with prior beliefs with respect to that alternative)

D_x = dissonance (post-choice doubt motivated by awareness that one alternative was chosen and the existence of beliefs that unchosen alternatives also have desirable attributes)

S_x^{PoC} = post-choice search (a search for information following purchase to confirm the wisdom of the choice)

Evaluation of the model

From the perspective of metatheory, Zaltman et al. evaluated the 1973 version of this model in a manner quite similar to that outlined for the Howard model in Figure 20.2.[36] There are two exceptions, however. It was rated as poor in terms of falsifiability (the theory can be confirmed or disconfirmed through research) and methodological simplicity (the theory is easy to build and test). The chief problem identified was lack of

36 Zaltman, Pinson, and Angelmar, *Metatheory and Consumer Research*, pp. 118–21.

precision in definition and terminology. The authors are aware of these limitations and attempted to rectify them in this revision.

It was pointed out earlier that pedagogical considerations were the primary motivation for the 1968 and 1973 versions. Therefore, the criterion of confirmation (the theory coheres with facts) remains untested.

Comparison with the Howard model

If the reader has persevered to this point (you are a brave soul indeed), the conclusion already no doubt has been reached that these two models are quite similar. That should be expected if the respective authors are keeping up-to-date in the field. Yet, there are some differences, and it is useful to compare the various equations. The comparison will be made in terms of the 16 equations of the EKB model:

1. *Choice is a function of intention and unanticipated circumstances.* The only difference here is the addition of the latter variable in the EKB model.

2. *Intention is a function of attitude, normative compliance, and anticipated circumstances.* The Howard model also includes facts coded about the brand, confidence in ability to make the choice, and a set of additional exogenous variables. The EKB model has already included information as part of beliefs and attitudes, which, in turn, are related to intention. Confidence is not used as a variable for reasons to be elaborated below.

3. *Attitude is a function of beliefs.* In this sense, EKB is consistent with the Fishbein extended model, which has received considerable support. The Howard model does not include beliefs, so recourse must be made to two variables referring to stored information and satisfaction as a third variable plus a host of exogenous considerations. The first three factors are included in other equations of the EKB model, which underlie attitude, but there is no empirical justification for the insertion of the exogenous variables here.

4. *Normative compliance is a function of life style and social influence.* There is no counterpart to this equation in the Howard model.

5. *Beliefs are a function of information and experience and evaluative criteria.* This equation is also unique to the EKB model.

6. *Information and experience are a function of message reception.* The similar variable in the Howard model is facts coded regarding the brand, which, in turn, are a function of exposure, attention, and perceptual bias. The only difference is that EKB introduces active memory as a variable elsewhere in an attempt to account for information processing in a more concise manner.

7. *Message reception is a function of attention and active memory.* Howard uses brand comprehension as a similar variable, but it is based on a host of exogeneous factors and does not take explicit account of the functioning of active memory.

8. *Evaluative criteria are a function of information and experience and motive.* The two models appear to be identical here, with the exception that Howard hypothesizes the arousal function of motives as a determining consideration. EKB, on the other hand, makes reference to the directive function of motive which includes important goals.

9. *Motive is a function of life style.* This equation is unique to the EKB model. It probably is of less significance than other equations, but it is included here to specify more clearly the role of life style in shaping decision processes.

10. *Attention is a function of exposure, active memory, and problem recognition.* Howard hypothesizes attention to be a function of motive arousal and exogeneous variables. First, this fails to take account of current knowledge of the stages in information processing. Moreover, it is doubtful that exogenous variables play much of a role at this stage.

11. *Exposure is a function of search, available stimuli, and media usage.* The two models are identical.

12. *Pre-choice search is a function of belief and attitude.* The two models differ sharply here. Howard treats attention and search as being identical, whereas EKB explicitly hypothesizes the prior activation of an internal search, which shows the present state of belief and attitude to be inadequate for a purposeful decision.

13. *Problem recognition is a function of motive activation and information and experience.* The closest equation in the Howard model pertains to motive arousal, which is a function of stimulus ambiguity, confidence, coded facts, and financial status. The first two variables are not included at all by EKB (the reasons are given below). Also they have not explicitly accounted for financial status, which could be a factor in problem recognition. Both models allow for the function of new information.

14. *Satisfaction is a function of choice and dissonance.* Howard does not use dissonance as a variable in his model.

15. *Dissonance is a function of choice and beliefs.* Unique to the EKB model.

16. *Post-choice search is a function of dissonance.* Unique to the EKB model.

A few comments are now in order. Notice, first of all, that the Howard model excludes post choice consequences with the exception of satisfaction. While dissonance has proved to be a difficult variable methodologically, it should not be disregarded if the intent is to comprehend all factors that influence decision processes.

One of the most important differences lies in the treatment of information processing. Both models allow for the necessary distinctions between exposure, attention, and comprehension; but the underlying hypothesized causality is different. Howard does introduce perceptual bias and defines it as the tendency to distort information during its processing. Yet he treats this as an endogenous variable, on the assumption that it can be measured and explained. Most of the Columbia studies have operationalized the variable in this way: "whether the respondent knows the use of a new product."[37] These two definitions bear no relationship whatsoever, and it is small wonder that Farley and others are having difficulty in operationalizing the model. As we saw in Chapter 13, information processing is extraordinarily complex, and, to be honest, no one knows very much about it. It is far wiser to treat it as being exogenous and recognize that it underlies attention, message reception, and response in ways that are only poorly understood.

Stimulus ambiguity is another term not used in the EKB model. It is defined as perceived uncertainty and lack of meaningful information received from the environment. Once again its definition in the empirical studies undertaken by the Columbia group is a curious one indeed: "confidence in radio and television as sources of information about the product."[38] These are two *very* different phenomena. In fact, the present authors do not think that stimulus ambiguity can be operationalized in any meaningful way and thus have concluded that it adds little to the understanding of decision processes.

Finally, confidence in ability to judge the product has not been included in the EKB formulation. The reason is that we do not feel it has received empirical confirmation in studies to date, although this fact could be argued.[39] Whatever one's evaluation might be at this stage, further research is needed to resolve the issue.

A concluding word

Let's refer to the original justification for model building—to encompass relevant variables, specify relationships, and attempt to explain a process. Models are an absolute necessity, and the lack of definitive empirical verification does not invalidate them if the constructs and hypotheses, taken by themselves, are consistent with present knowledge of the behavior process. The heuristic value, in itself, warrants the whole effort.

It is fallacious to ask which of the two models reviewed in this chapter is *best*. Probably the most rigorous test is provided by the *law of parsimony*, which requires an "explanation of a phenomenon of human behavior with a minimum of assumptions and a maximum of conceptual

37 Donald R. Lehmann, et al., "Some Empirical Contributions to Buyer Behavior Theory," *Journal of Consumer Research*, vol. 1 (December 1974), pp. 43–55, at p. 44.

38 Lehmann et al., "Some Empirical Contributions." at p. 44.

39 Certainly the correlations tend to be quite low. See, for example, Lehmann et al., "Some Empirical Contributions." Howard, however, argues differently. See John A. Howard, "Confidence as a Validated Construct," in Jagdish N. Sheth, ed., *Models of Buyer Behavior: Conceptual, Quantitative & Empirical* (New York: Harper & Row, 1974), pp. 160–68.

precision."[40] Any model will fall short of this standard given present knowledge of the subject and the problems encountered in conceptualization and measurement. Certainly the height of absurdity would be to claim that anyone presently has or will have *the* model of consumer behavior. A model to be useful will change as knowledge changes. Therefore, one should expect fairly substantial modifications over time.

So, which model should the serious scholar use? This answer, in the final analysis, probably is more a matter of individual taste and preference than anything else given the high degree of similarity between the leading contenders.

Summary

The purpose of this chapter was to focus on important issues connected with the development and use of models of consumer behavior. First, it was demonstrated that models offer real benefits, both from a conceptual and practical point of view. The greatest advantage is delineation of the important variables that explain consumer decision processes and the hypothesized patterns of the ways in which these variables function.

Both the Howard model and the Engel, Kollat, Blackwell (EKB) model were examined in depth. The Howard model was the first to be formulated into testable equations, and there have been some attempts to verify this model empirically. While the results have not been encouraging, much has been learned which, in turn, has been applied in revision of the original Howard model. The EKB model used throughout this text was restated also in formal testable terms. Thus it was possible to compare the similarities and differences between the two. In view of the relatively high degree of similarity, it was concluded that the choice of one over the other is mostly a matter of individual taste. Given the present level of knowledge of the subject matter and problems of conceptualization and measurement, it is unlikely that any model ever will receive definitive empirical verification.

Review and discussion questions

1. What is a model? What are the advantages offered to the serious student of consumer behavior?

2. What explanations can you offer for the relative absence of serious scholarly interest in consumer behavior during, say, the 1930s and 1940s? Hint: focus on the relative emphasis between production and marketing in the business firm across the decades and notice the changes taking place.

3. Why is there less emphasis today on quantitative models than was the case as recently as ten years ago?

4. Compare the 1969 Howard-Sheth model with the 1974 version described in this text. What are the most obvious differences?

5. What is the essential distinction between endogenous and exogenous

40 James F. Engel, "Psychology and the Business Sciences," *Quarterly Journal of Economics and Business*, vol. 1, p. 78 (1961).

variables? Do you agree that perceptual bias (or active memory) could be treated more usefully as an exogenous variable?

6. Should a behavioral model such as the Howard or EKB model featuring a series of simultaneous equations be accepted or rejected on the basis of empirical tests using primarily multiple regression techniques? What problems are encountered? What conclusions should be reached?

7. What do you think are the *primary* similarities and differences between the Howard and the EKB models?

8. Why is it difficult to ask which of several alternative models is the *best*?

9. If you were given the task of modeling consumer behavior, what additional variables and relationships, if any, would you include?

CHAPTER 21

The current status of consumer behavior research: Problems and prospects

This book has attempted to identify most of what is known about consumer behavior today.[1] From thousands of references, a number of propositions have been collected and were synthesized in the preceding pages. Hopefully, most are valid statements. Some, unfortunately, are wrong. Almost all are subject to qualifications of one type or another. Many will change in the future.

In this chapter an attempt is made to assess this vast catalog of theories, models, and research findings. The first section presents an attempt at evaluating the current status of consumer research in terms of the insights generated for explaining and predicting this type of behavioral phenomena. Recommendations for the future constitute the subject matter of the concluding sections.

The current status of consumer behavior research

During the last few decades, particularly the last 10 years, there have been remarkable efforts made toward the advancement of knowledge in consumer behavior. This section attempts to evaluate the literature in this field in terms of its usefulness in explaining and predicting consumer

---

1 While we have endeavored to be comprehensive, we have been forced to be selective in many areas due to space and ability limitations. At other times, it has been possible to present only a fraction of unpublished research findings.

behavior.[2] The observations can only be of a general nature, and, hence, their rectitude will vary considerably from one specialty to another within the field.

Broadly speaking, scientific explanations must meet two requirements: (1) explanatory relevance, meaning that the account of some type of consumer behavior constitutes acceptable grounds for expecting that the behavior will occur under the specified circumstances, and (2) testability, meaning that scientific explanations must be capable of empirical tests. Explanations satisfying the first requirement automatically satisfy the second, but the converse does not always hold.[3]

In general, most consumer behavior insights have been derived from empirical studies and, hence, usually satisfy the second requirement. Unfortunately, however, as the following discussion points out, efforts to date do not fare well in terms of explanatory relevance.

Levels of explanation. There are at least four levels of explanation in the behavioral sciences that are applicable to consumer behavior.[4]

Level of explanation	Explanation
1	A certain phenomenon has an empirical existence
2	The phenomenon is of the nature Q and is produced by factors X_1, $X_2, \ldots, X_n$
3	Factors $X_1, X_2, \ldots, X_n$ are interactive or have interacted in manner $Y_1, Y_2, \ldots, Y_n$ to produce in some past or present time a phenomenon of the nature Q

The higher the level, the more scientific the explanation.

Various specialties or disciplines within consumer behavior are at different levels of explanation. However, in general, it is rare to reach level three. For example, consider problem recognition and search processes. In both cases, a list of determinants has been discovered through research. However, it is not known whether this list is complete,

2 The basic source for this type of evaluation is Gerald Zaltman, Christian R. A. Pinson, and Reinhard Angelmar, *Metatheory and Consumer Research* (New York: Holt, Rinehart and Winston, 1973). The structure and content of this section are adapted from a briefer and more understandable version of this work. See Gerald Zaltman, Reinhard Angelmar, and Christian Pinson, "Metatheory in Consumer Behavior Research," in David M. Gardner, ed., *Proceedings of the 2nd Annual Conference of the Association for Consumer Research* (College Park, Md.: University of Maryland, 1971), pp. 476–97.

3 C. G. Hampel, *Philosophy of Natural Science* (Englewood Cliffs, N.J.: Prentice-Hall, 1966), p. 49.

4 J. T. Doby, "Logic and Levels of Scientific Explanation," in E. F. Borgatta, ed., *Sociological Methodology* (San Francisco: Jossey-Gass, 1969).

let alone how the determinants interact, or their relative importance. The same is true for brand loyalty, store choice, and a number of other phenomena. Thus, at the present time, explanations of consumer behavior are largely confined to lower levels.

Evaluating explanations. There are four basic criteria for evaluating explanations:[5]

1. Scope. The range of events to which an explanation can be applied.

2. Precision. The exactness with which the concepts used in explanation are related to empirical indicators, and the precision with which the rules of interaction of the variables in the system are stated.[6]

3. Power. The degree of control over the environment an explanation provides. Power depends on the precision of the description and explanation and upon the completeness of the variables.

4. Reliability. The frequency with which factors not included in the explanation interrupt the situation the explanation concerns.

In using these criteria to evaluate explanations of consumer behavior, conclusions depend on the level of abstraction. For example, selective information processing, attitude change, and the decision-making process are applicable in a wide number of choice situations. However, the specific importance of selective processes, the specific determinants of attitude change, or the specific nature of the decision-making process vary due to the substantial variations that occur across consumers and choice situations.

Thus, at the more abstract level, the concepts and processes involved in consumer behavior appear to be acceptable in terms of scope and, perhaps, power and reliability. Precision is low because the rules of variable interaction have not been articulated completely. At less abstract levels, current explanations of consumer behavior appear, for the most part, to have limited scope, precision, power, and reliability.

Predicting consumer behavior

In consumer behavior, prediction can be used in two ways.[7] First, it can be used to make deductions from known to unknown events within a conceptually static system. For example, discrimination function analysis is used to predict successful sales transactions on the basis of customer-salesman bargaining variables. Second, prediction is used to make assertions about future behavioral outcomes, for example, forecasting. The logical structure of scientific prediction is the same as that of explanation, although we may have the paradox of being able to predict without explaining, and explaining without being able to predict.

5 Zaltman et al., Gardner, *2nd Annual Conference*, pp. 481–82.

6 E. J. Meehan, *Explanation in Social Science: A System Paradigm* (Homewood, Ill.: Dorsey Press, 1968), p. 117

7 Zaltman et al., Gardner, *2nd Annual Conference*, pp. 482–83.

Levels of prediction. As in the case of explanation, there are different levels of prediction. These levels are identical to the ones mentioned above except that they are future oriented.

In general, most consumer research seems to have focused on attempting to describe and explain current or past behavior rather than predicting future behavior. There are, of course, some exceptions, such as brand loyalty models, diffusion models, store patronage models, attitude change theories, and new brand penetration models (NEWS).[8]

Prediction attempts rarely go beyond the second level of prediction. Brand loyalty models, for example, attempt to predict future market shares Q, based on a limited number of factors, $X_1, X_2, \ldots X_n$. Generally they do not specify how these factors will interact, or why they will interact in that manner. The same is true of models of store patronage and new brand penetration, and theories of attitude change. Diffusion models appear to be an exception as they use all four levels of prediction.[9]

Evaluating predictions. Like explanations, predictions can be evaluated using basic criteria. While the criteria have the same titles, they are defined differently. Thus:[10]

1. Scope. The longitudinal and latitudinal range of events covered by a prediction.

2. Precision. The degree of mathematical isomorphism between the concepts involved in the prediction and their empirical indicators.

3. Power. The precision of the predictive statement and its completeness.

4. Reliability. The frequency with which factors not included in the predictive explanation cause it not to happen exactly as the explanation predicted.

It appears that most attempts to predict consumer behavior, or some aspect of it, have wide to limited scope, and low precision, power, and reliability. As discussed earlier, evaluations of scope depend on the level of abstraction—the more abstract the concept, the wider the scope, and vice versa. Precision, power, and reliability are low because consumer behavior differs widely in a given purchase situation, and the same consumer often behaves differently from one type of purchase situation to another.

A concluding note

The reader may disagree with some of the conclusions expressed in the preceding paragraphs. They represent the authors' judgments, and their applicability varies among the specialties that comprise the broad field of

8 Lawrence Light and Lewis Pringle, "New Product Forecasting Using Recursive Regression," in David T. Kollat, Roger D. Blackwell, and James F. Engel, eds., *Research in Consumer Behavior* (New York: Holt, Rinehart and Winston, 1970), pp. 702–09.

9 Zaltman *et al.*, Gardner, *2nd Annual Conference*, pp. 483–84.

10 Zaltman *et al.*, Gardner, *2nd Annual Conference*, pp. 484–85.

consumer behavior. Even allowing for differences of opinion, it seems that what on the surface appears to be a well-researched and developed discipline does not fare especially well when evaluated against the criteria of explanation and prediction.

Not many years ago, the National Science Council evaluated the state of knowledge in the behavioral sciences. They concluded that actual accomplishment has not kept pace with the magnitude of efforts expended.[11] Consumer behavior as a discipline in its own right is not exempt from this statement,[12] although progress is being made.

Recommendations for improving consumer behavior research

There are at least two reasons for the lack of definitive progress in terms of explanation and prediction. First, as the reader is well aware, consumer behavior is still a relatively new discipline, with the majority of relevant research undertaken within the past 15 years. Second, there has been no overall research strategy or plan; rather, a large number of academicians and industry and government personnel have conducted individual projects consistent with their interests, problems, perspectives, and skills. Given these conditions, the current status of the field is inevitable.

Relative to many other disciplines, there have been only a few attempts to evaluate the overall status of consumer research. Past efforts have concentrated primarily on summarizing and synthesizing findings into proposition inventories. With some notable exceptions,[13] these critical evaluations have been confined to particular aspects of consumer behavior such as cognitive dissonance,[14] information processing,[15] beliefs and attitudes,[16] and psychographics.[17] As useful as these summaries and evaluations have been, many important issues are yet to be explored.

The authors' intent in this section is to supplement other critical evaluations by dealing with complementary and equally important issues involved in the development of a research tradition or strategy of inquiry. Discussion and resolution of these problems could make a great contribution to a discipline characterized by increasing sophistication.

11 National Science Council, *The Behavioral and Social Sciences* (Englewood Cliffs, N.J.: Prentice-Hall, 1969).

12 See Matilda Frankel, *A Summary Report: What Do We Know about Consumer Behavior?* (Washington D.C.: National Science Foundation Directorate for Research Applications RANN—Research Applied to National Needs, 1977).

13 See, for example, Flemming Hansen, *Consumer Choice Behavior* (New York: Free Press, 1972). Also Flemming Hansen, "Psychological Theories of Consumer Choice," *Journal of Consumer Research*, vol. 3 (December 1976), pp. 117–42.

14 James F. Engel, "The Dissonance Dilemma," *Bulletin of Business Research* (Columbus, Ohio: Bureau of Business Research, Ohio State University, July 1968), p. 1 ff.

15 Robert Chestnut and Jacob Jacoby, "Consumer Information Processing: Emerging Theory and Findings" (Purdue Papers in Consumer Psychology, no. 158, 1976).

16 Martin Fishbein, "Attitude, Attitude Change, and Behavior: A Theoretical Overview," in Philip Levine, ed., *Attitude Research Bridges the Atlantic* (Chicago: American Marketing Association, 1975).

17 William D. Wells, ed., *Life Style and Psychographics* (Chicago: American Marketing Association, 1974).

Two particular issues are important in this context: (1) the dangers of the "reduced-form" model and (2) the need for metatheoretical evaluation.

The dangers of the "reduced-form" model. The majority of consumer research has utilized, explicitly or implicitly, hypothetical constructs, theories, or what Nicosia has called "reduced-form" models.[18] Examples include motivation, perception, learning, personality and life style, beliefs and attitudes, social class, reference groups, dissonance, and risk taking. These contructs have been employed in a variety of ways in an attempt to explain or to predict some aspect of behavior.

There is no question that these and other constructs have proved to be useful. Nevertheless, some problems should be noted. First, there have been a number of instances in which constructs and theories have not been utilized properly. One example has emerged in the many studies investigating the relationship between personality and behavior. Jacoby has summarized the status of much of this type of inquiry:

> Investigators usually take a general, broad coverage personality inventory and a list of brands, products, or product categories, and attempt to correlate subjects' responses on the inventory with statements of product use or preference. Careful examination reveals that, in most cases, the investigators have operated without the benefit of theory and with no a priori thought directed to *how*, or especially *why*, personality should or should not be related to that aspect of consumer behavior being studied. Statistical techniques, usually simple correlation or variants thereof, are applied and anything that turns up looking half-way interesting furnishes the basis for the Discussion section. Skill at post-diction and post hoc interpretation has been demonstrated, but little real understanding has resulted.[19]

Jacoby illustrates his points by reanalyzing Evans' classic study of the personality differences between Ford and Chevrolet owners. Evans employed the Edwards personal preference schedule and found only one difference significant at better than the 0.05 level.[20] From this Evans concluded that personality had little, if any, relationship to consumer behavior.

Jacoby shows that an entirely different picture emerges when the data are reexamined using specific hypotheses derived from a conceptual-psychological orientation. Specifically, Jacoby's analysis of Evans' data yielded 8 out of 11 correct predictions. If Jacoby's procedure is correct, Evans' results do not preclude the possibility of a relationship between personality and consumer behavior.

The Jacoby argument does not document an isolated situation. For

18 Francesco M. Nicosia, *Consumer Decision Processes* (Englewood Cliffs, N.J.: Prentice-Hall, 1966).

19 Jacob Jacoby, "Towards Defining Consumer Psychology: One Psychologist's Views," paper presented at the American Psychological Association 77th Annual Convention, Washington, D.C. (September 4, 1969).

20 Franklin B. Evans, "Psychological and Objective Factors in the Prediction of Brand Choice: Ford versus Chevrolet," *Journal of Business*, vol. 32 (1959), pp. 340–69.

example, Brody and Cunningham[21] among others have demonstrated the value of personality and personality-oriented variables when used properly. Similarly Fishbein and Ajzen have shown the importance of attitude in predicting consumer behavior when the theoretical basis for the concept is understood and used properly.[22]

As will become apparent later, this discussion should not be interpreted as suggesting that all research should be confined to testing theories. Rather, the simple point is that when an aspect of behavior is studied, theoretical considerations should be examined in *detail* and the theory should be used *correctly*.

The second problem with reduced-form models is that each explains only a part of a larger process influenced by a variety of phenomena interacting in complex ways. James Morgan was probably the first to realize that the exponential growth in the number of empirically studied determinants of consumer behavior was causing increasing perplexity.[23] The situation certainly has become more acute in the ensuing years. Unfortunately, a very small percentage of consumer research has utilized, or been based on, any type of comprehensive, integrative model.[24] This gives rise to some disturbing questions.

Regarding past research, how many findings (or lack of findings) are artifacts of the conceptualizations that have been used? Stated differently, if the research had been based on comprehensive models rather than relatively insular constructs, how many of the "significant" and "nonsignificant" findings would change because of the effects of variables that have not been included in the study or otherwise controlled? This problem will continue to plague future consumer research efforts because, lacking an integrative model, how does the researcher know what variables should be included and controlled?

The severity of what might be called the "conceptualization artifact" problem suggests the need to devote more resources to the development, testing, and revision of comprehensive models. Are the models identified above adequate, or are they too simplistic? Is is possible to have *a* model of consumer behavior, or are several necessary? If several are required, then what are the relevant underlying assumptions and the conditions under which each is appropriate?

The final problem is the modeling-testing sequence. Most comprehensive models attempt to do at least two things. First, they record which variables are known to interact with which other variables. Second, they reveal which interactions need to be and have not yet been studied

21 Robert P. Brody and Scott M. Cunningham, "Personality Variables and the Consumer Decision Process," *Journal of Marketing Research*, vol. 5, (February 1968), pp. 50–57.

22 Martin Fishbein and Icek Ajzen, *Belief, Attitude, Intention, and Behavior: An Introduction to Theory and Research* (Reading, Mass.: Addison Wesley, 1975).

23 James N. Morgan, "A Review of Recent Research on Consumer Behavior," in Lincoln Clark, ed., *Consumer Behavior*, vol. 3 (New York: Harper & Row, 1958), pp. 93–108.

24 For exceptions see John U. Farley, John A. Howard, and L. Winston Ring, *Consumer Behavior Theory and Application* (Boston: Allyn & Bacon, 1974); and Paul A. Pellemans, *Relationships between Attitude and Purchase Intention toward the Brand* (Namur, Belgium: Publications Universitaries, Namur University, 1971).

(theoretically and empirically). Most of the research used to construct these models proceeds from theoretical statements—"Y is caused by X, Z, and V"—to direct empirical tests.

As Nicosia has pointed out, one of the shortcomings of this procedure is that the statistics obtained may actually be produced by different causal networks of interactions among the variables. As long as the interpretation of statistical results is ambiguous, it is not clear which theory is actually being tested; thus, the empirical results cannot be used to refine the original idea of how the phenomenon works. Rather, the result is an endless cascade of qualifications and an unmanageable number of empirically tested and nonrejected hypotheses.[25]

To overcome these problems Nicosia recommends the insertion of a methodological operation between the set of theoretical statements and the empirical test. The operation is a formal mathematical specification of the network of interactions the researcher has in mind. This is done by translating the hypothesized network (flow charts) into formal models.[26]

Unfortunately, there has been little work done in building, analyzing, and testing sophisticated *mathematical* models of theories that predict and explain brand choice on the basis of interactions among a variety of variables over time. For the most part, those knowledgeable in substantive areas lack supersophisticated mathematical skills. On the other hand, those possessing modeling expertise often do not understand the substantive dimensions of the behavior being modeled. A merger of these two types of skills would probably accelerate progress in the future.

Metatheoretic considerations. It is difficult for activistic researchers to submit themselves to the scrutiny of the logician who raises the all important questions of theory construction and use. No discipline can mature if these questions are ignored. Zaltman and his associates, of course, have led the way,[27] but useful contributions also have been made by Armstrong[28] and others.

The issue of research priorities presents another problem area. Few have definitively addressed these important questions: (1) what aspects of consumer behavior are of the greatest importance; that is, what are the "key areas"? and (2) what phenomena need to be investigated and in what order, so that these key areas can be understood?

Establishing research priorities

Differing expectations of users of research. The businessman has legitimate research needs to shed light on such strategic questions as the isolation of market segments, development of new products, determination of advertising appeals, package design and testing, and so on. Unless existing knowledge and methodology have a distinctly pragmatic focus, the study of

25 Nicosia, *Consumer Decision Processes*, pp. 11–12.
26 Nicosia, *Consumer Decision Processes*, p. 18.
27 Zaltman, et al., *Metatheory and Consumer Research*.
28 J. Scott Armstrong, "Eclectic Research and Construct Validation," in Jagdish N. Sheth, ed., *Models of Buyer Behavior: Conceptual, Quantitative, and Empirical* (New York: Harper & Row, 1974), pp. 3–16.

consumer behavior is likely to be dismissed with a wave of the hand as being irrelevant. Certainly this is an understandable reaction, given some of the published studies that appear in the marketing literature.

The home economist and government researcher most frequently are concerned with the issues of consumer protection. This was largely ignored for many years, but useful studies are now beginning to appear in the literature.[29]

The marketing academic could have any of the above interests plus a legitimate concern with the more abstract issues of theory development and methodology. Practical application of findings may be distinctly secondary.

Given this diversity of expectations and interests, how can a consensus ever emerge? The formation of the Association for Consumer Research in 1969 was a step in the right direction, because it encompasses researchers from a variety of perspectives. But the needed consensus on research priorities remains as illusive as ever.

Differing career expectations and needs. The problem is further compounded by the distinctly different career needs and demands of academic researchers as compared with those in industry.[30] The professional advancement of the academic researcher is based largely on publication of scientific knowledge with a greater emphasis on theory, correct procedures for obtaining valid data, and contributions to existing thought. The primary target is the gatekeeper—the editors of prestigious journals who also are fellow academics. Applications are secondary.

Too much of the research published by members of the academic community has been based on the availability of data, the convenience of research and mathematical techniques, or the attractiveness and appeal of certain behavioral constructs. In other words, most of the published research until recently has been "data-technique-construct" motivated and oriented. While the infancy of the field made this orientation understandable and perhaps justifiable in earlier years, it no longer is an efficacious strategy. Unfortunately academic reward systems tend too often to have only one real criterion: publication in a "refereed journal." In too many instances, content is unimportant simply compared with the fact of publication itself.

Fortunately, there often is a corrective to the situation described above. As the young academician advances in rank, the necessity for journal publication usually subsides, and greater attention can be devoted to more substantive issues. This opportunity for contributions of greater maturity, however, is blunted in a strange manner. When one reaches "academic middle age," greatest rewards tend to be in administration,

29 The 1977 annual conference of the Association for Consumer Research included 17 papers touching on issues of consumer education and consumerism. See William D. Perreault, Jr., ed., *Advances in Consumer Research*, vol. 4 (Atlanta: Association for Consumer Research, 1977).

30 For a helpful analysis of this issue see Arthur J. Kover, "Careers and Noncommunication: The Case of Academic and Applied Marketing Research," *Journal of Marketing Research*, vol. 13 (November 1976), pp. 339–44.

consulting, some other activity, or a combination. It is interesting to note how few of the big "names" cited in the 1968 edition of this text are still active in research and publication, apart from an occasional article or book. There is a great need to keep these capable scholars in the "mainstream" so to speak so that necessary balance can be provided.

The work and career of the applied marketing researcher are very different.[31] Success is based largely on ability to provide information that can be used in immediate marketing decisions. If the research is not seen as being "useful," a career will be short lived. The more basic issues of theory construction, construct validation, and methodological refinements are decidedly secondary. Furthermore, dissemination of research findings is usually discouraged, with the result that much remains in company files.

So, here is the heart of the issue as defined by Kover:

> Given the different nature of these careers and the kinds of knowledge material produced, that which is essential to the academics' endeavors is trivial to practitioners: that which is essential for the survival for the practitioner is defined as trivial by the academic. The reason for the lack of communication between the two branches of marketing research is that neither branch believes the other has anything to offer that is nontrivial.[32]

How can a consensus on priorities ever surface in such an atmosphere?

Developing new business-government-university relationships. It would be presumptious for the authors to suggest how the key areas for research should be defined. The germane point is that the issue of priorities is too seldom raised, let alone resolved. Those with differing perspectives must interact if progress is to be made.

For the most part, consumer research has been conducted independently by personnel in business, government, and academic ranks. With some notable exceptions, relatively few businesses have supported university-based research. Moreover, government agencies and congressional committees have typically not supported consumer research projects or made much use of the expertise of consumer analysts in hearings and deliberations. If this independence can be dissolved in favor of cooperation and new alliances, the future and horizons of consumer research will be extended considerably.

(1) Business-university relationships. To some degree the barriers aptly described by Kover are dissolving. Armed with sizeable research budgets and facilities, consumer researchers in business often are among the most prolific. Furthermore, the issues being investigated frequently have real general interest and relevance. Simultaneously, many academic research-

---

31 Kover, "Careers and Noncommunication."
32 Kover, "Careers and Noncommunication," p. 342.

ers have become more dedicated to areas of inquiry that have more substantial payouts for the business firm.

It would seem, then, that in many cases the ingredients for a new coalition exist. First, university-based researchers should reevaluate their differential advantage. They typically do not have the data-generating capability possessed by industry. Business, on the other hand, often does not have the time and, in some cases, the skills necessary to analyze research data fully. This frequently is where a university researcher's greatest capability lies, because most leading universities now have excellent computer hardware, software, and manpower to permit data analysis (for example, cluster analysis and factor analysis) that would have been impossible several years ago.

One avenue toward a more meaningful business-university relationship might be to allow university researchers to be involved in the design of some industry research with opportunity to add appropriate questions that might illuminate some of the broader questions of concern to all. Once the data have been put to proprietary use, they could be turned over to the university for additional analysis. If such an approach were to become widespread, progress would seem to be inevitable.

(2) Government-university relationships. The reasons for the absence of government-university cooperation in consumer research are unclear, although several explanations can be hypothesized. It could be that government officials perceive university researchers to be identified with business interests so that research grants could contribute to further exploitation of consumers. Another explanation may be that government officials are unaware of the growing scope and magnitude of consumer research.

Whatever the explanation, consumer researchers should become more actively involved in consumer-related legislation and in representing consumer as well as business interests. Significant progress has been made in these areas during the last few years, but much remains to be done. Why should consumer researchers not have as much influence on consumer affairs as the American Bar Association or the American Medical Association?

Greater attention to methodological issues

Progress in any discipline is, to a large degree, dependent upon the appropriateness and sophistication of its methodology. Greater attention must now be paid to (1) standardized definitions, (2) standardized variable categories, (3) reliability and validity, (4) the attainment of critical mass, (5) longitudinal and experimental designs, (6) assessment of group differences, and (7) richer dependent variables.

Standardized definitions. Throughout this text there have been seemingly endless examples of widely varying definitions of presumably the same variables and constructs. For example, the reader will recall that attitude researchers until recently could not state with any degree of certainty that a change in attitude will lead to a corresponding change in behavior. Most the problem was found to lie in faulty definition and measurement. Quite often attitude was measured in terms of dispositions toward a group of objects rather than a specified individual object. This error was found in most of the 33 studies evaluated by Wicker.[33] Moreover, it has been found that minor wording changes in measurement instruments can make a great difference.[34] Wicker concluded that four conceptual and methodological conditions must be met before prediction is possible: (1) the unit of observation must be an individual rather than a group, (2) there must be at least one attitude and behavior measure for each person, (3) attitude and behavior must be measured on separate occasions, and (4) the behavioral response must not be the individual's own retrospective report of his or her behavior.[35] Prior to the onset and acceptance of the Fishbein model and the host of studies designed to confirm or reject it, the majority of published research projects violated one or more of these criteria.

While progress has been made with respect to beliefs and attitudes, this is not as true elsewhere. Brand loyalty, for example, has been defined in terms of brand choice sequences,[36] proportion of purchases,[37] repeat purchase probabilities,[38] and brand preference over time.[39] Definitions of impulse purchase[40] and opinion leader[41] vary from study to study. The importance of information sources is sometimes defined in terms of exposure, other times in terms of effectiveness.[42] There are at least 45 definitions of innovation and 164 definitions of culture.[43]

Definitions, of course, are relative to purposes—they are means or

33 A. W. Wicker, "Attitudes vs. Actions: The Relationship of Verbal and Overt Behavioral Responses to Attitude Objects," *Journal of Social Issues*, vol. 25 (1969), pp. 41–78.

34 H. J. Ehrlich, "Instrument Error and the Study of Prejudice," *Social Forces*, vol. 43 (1964), pp. 197–206.

35 Ehrlich, "Instrument Error."

36 George Brown, "Brand Loyalty—Fact or Fiction?" *Advertising Age*, vol. 23 (June 19, 1952), pp. 53–55; (June 30, 1952), pp. 45–47; (July 14, 1952), pp. 54–56; (July 28, 1952), pp. 46–48; (August 11, 1952), pp. 56–58; (September 1, 1952), pp. 80–82; (October 6, 1952), pp. 82–86; (December 1, 1952), pp. 76–79; (January 26, 1953), pp. 75–76; W. T. Tucker, "The Development of Brand Loyalty," *Journal of Marketing Research*, vol. 1 (August 1964), pp. 32–35.

37 Ross Cunningham, "Brand Loyalty—What, Where, How Much," *Harvard Business Review*, vol. 34 (January–February 1956), pp. 116–28; Ross Cunningham, "Customer Loyalty to Store and Brand," *Harvard Business Review*, vol. 39 (November–December 1961), pp. 127–37.

38 Ronald E. Frank, "Brand Choice as a Probability Process," *Journal of Business*, vol. 35 (January 1962), pp. 43–56.

39 Lester Guest, "Brand Loyalty—Twelve Years Later," *Journal of Applied Psychology*, vol. 39 (1955), pp. 405–8.

40 Vernon T. Clover, "Relative Importance of Impulse Buying in Retail Stores," *Journal of Marketing*, vol. 15 (July 1950), pp. 66–70; *Consumer Buying Habits Studies* (Wilmington, Del.: E. I. DuPont de Nemours and Co., 1949, 1954, 1959, 1965); James D. Schaffer, "The Influence of Impulse Buying or in-the-Store Decisions on Consumers' Food Purchases," journal paper no. 2591 (Michigan Agricultural Experimental Station).

41 Francesco M. Nicosia, "Opinion Leadership and the Flow of Communication: Some Problems and Prospects," in L. George Smith, ed., *Reflections on Progress in Marketing* (Chicago: American Marketing Association, 1964), pp. 340–58; Charles W. King and John O. Summers, "Generalized Opinion Leadership in Consumer Products," paper no. 224 (Lafayette, Ind: Institute for Research in the Behavioral, Economic, and Management Sciences, Krannert Graduate School of Industrial Administration, January 1969).

42 Robert G. Mason, "The Use of Information Sources in the Process of Adoption," *Rural Sociology*, vol. 29 (March 1964), pp. 40–52; George Fisk, "Media Influence Reconsidered," *Public Opinion Quarterly*, vol. 23 (1959), pp. 83–91.

43 Alfred L. Kroeber and Clyde Kluckhohn, "Culture: A Critical Review of Concepts and Definitions," *Papers of the Peabody Museum*, vol. 27 (1952).

tools rather than ends. Even so, it is difficult to visualize how there can be this many different purposes. Some of this confusion is inevitable given the infancy of consumer behavior research. But with a few exceptions, such as attitude measurement, very little progress has been made, even in the last four years, in dealing with this problem. In fact, in general it has become more intolerable.

This situation is not an insignificant problem. Definitional heterogeneity makes it extraordinarily difficult and hazardous to compare, synthesize, and accumulate findings. Definition and classification of terms and variables is, of course, an essential step in any area of inquiry that purports to use the scienfitic method. It may not be possible to develop a single definition of each construct and variable that can be used in all situations, but, at the very least, there must be an agreed-upon point of departure.

Standardized variable categories. There also is considerable heterogeneity in the categories used to measure many variables and constructs. For example, a comprehensive review of the family life-cycle literature pointed up the wide variation in life-cycle categories in published research.[44] Similarly, there are significant variations in the categories used to measure the influence of family members in purchasing decisions,[45] and nearly every social class researcher uses a different typology.

The lack of standardized variable categories makes it difficult to compare and integrate research findings. Instead of improving since their last comprehensive review of the literature in the early 1970s, the authors have discovered that the problem has intensified. It is high time that the Association for Consumer Research and other professional associations take some definitive action to end this unfortunate state of affairs.

Reliability and validity. Do measuring instruments produce essentially the same responses when administered over time? If so, they can be said to be *reliable.* And if they are found, in reality, to measure what they purport to measure, then the instruments are designated as being *valid.* There is nothing so mysterious about these concepts that have occupied the attention of serious behavioral science researchers for many decades. Yet, with only a limited number of exceptions,[46] these critical methodological requirements have been largely disregarded in consumer research. Part of the difficulty stems from the fact that most projects are "one shot" efforts undertaken on low budgets without built in provisions for neces-

44 William D. Wells and George Gubar, "Life Cycle Concept in Marketing Research," *Journal of Marketing Research,* vol. 3 (November 1966), pp. 355–63.

45 See, for example, Harry Sharp and Paul Mott, "Consumer Decisions in the Metropolitan Family," *Journal of Marketing,* vol. 21 (October 1956), pp. 149–56; Elizabeth H. Wolgast, "Do Husbands or Wives Make Purchasing Decisions?" *Journal of Marketing,* vol. 23 (October 1958), pp. 151–158; "A Pilot Study of the Roles of Husbands and Wives in Purchasing Decisions, Parts I–X," conducted for *Life Magazine* by L. Jaffe Associates, Inc. (1965).

46 See, for example, Joel N. Axelrod, "Attitude Measurements that Predict Purchases," *Journal of Advertising Research,* vol. 8 (March 1968), pp. 1–8; and Joel B. Cohen, "Toward an Interpersonal Theory of Consumer Behavior," *California Management Review,* vol. 10 (1968), pp. 73–80.

sary methodological assessment. One cannot help wondering how many of the published findings are based on measurement instruments that are not valid.

A sure sign of a maturing discipline is growing concern with these issues. Once again the 1977 annual conference of the Association for Consumer Research has provided some real grounds for optimism. Many of the papers presented there focused meaningfully on the problems of reliability and validity, and there is every reason to expect that needed improvements will be forthcoming.[47]

Attaining critical mass. The literature of consumer research is replete with small-scale, "one-shot" studies. Samples are typically small, out of date, or objectionable on other grounds (college students, women's club members, and so on). This one-shot characteristic limits a researcher's ability to investigate phenomena in a rigorous and comprehensive manner.

In contrast, research efforts that seem to have had the most impact on the discipline during the last ten years are major programs often working with large representative samples. Usually they represent a longer term effort that systematically investigates a multiplicity of variables. The larger sample is especially beneficial in that it is possible to analyze subgroups within and avoid the fear that so few are represented as to make statistical generalization very risky. It is this type of larger, more comprehensive effort that we define as having critical mass. Some recent examples include the efforts of Wells and others in the study of psychographics and life style,[48] the Hawes-Talarzyk-Blackwell studies of leisure time behavior,[49] and the earlier King-Summers thrust in opinion leadership and the diffusion of innovations.[50]

This type of more comprehensive effort is required in other areas of consumer research as well—social class, reference groups, purchase intentions, store choice, and shopper profiles to mention just a few. Progress is sure to accelerate if this step is taken.

Longitudinal and experimental designs. As has been observed throughout this volume, consumer behavior researchers typically utilize three types of research designs—cross-sectional surveys, longitudinal, and experi-

47 See the following papers in *Advances in Consumer Research*, Perreault, ed. Alice M. Tybout and Bobby J. Calder, "Threats to Internal and External Validity in the Field Setting," pp. 5–10; Roger J. Best, Del I. Hawkins, and Gerald Albaum, "Reliability of Measured Beliefs in Consumer Research," pp. 19–23; John U. Farley and Donald R. Lehmann, "An Overview of Empirical Applications of Buyer Behavior System Models," pp. 337–41; Michael J. Ryan, "Improving Consumer Research Measurement: An Overview," pp. 392–93; J. Paul Peter, "Reliability, Generalizability and Consumer Behavior," pp. 394–400; Clark Leavitt, "Response Bias: A Special Opportunity," pp. 401–4; and Allen D. Shocker and Gerald Zaltman, "Validity Importance in Consumer Research: Some Pragmatic Issues," pp. 405–8.

48 Wells, *Life Style and Psychographics*.

49 Douglass K. Hawes, W. Wayne Talarzyk, and Roger D. Blackwell, "Consumer Satisfactions from Leisure Time Pursuits," in Mary Jane Schlinger, ed., *Advances in Consumer Research*, vol. 2 (Chicago: Association for Consumer Research, (1975), pp. 817–36.

50 See, for example, Charles W. King and John O. Summers, "Overlap of Opinion Leadership across Consumer Product Categories," *Journal of Marketing Research*, vol. 7 (February 1970), pp. 43–50.

mental or quasiexperimental. Cross-sectional surveys are the most common.

The appropriateness of each method depends, of course, on the type of problem, the reasons for the study, the research budget, and the researcher's conceptualization of the problem. In general, however, there are serious problems involved in using the cross-sectional method. Of greatest significance is the fact that consumer behavior is inherently a dynamic on-going phenomenon, a process that occurs over time rather than at a given point in time.

There are compelling reasons for conceptualizing and studying consumer behavior as a process rather than an act. Cross-sectional designs are the least appropriate method for studying consumer behavior over time, because of the serious biases resulting from inaccurate memory, interaction, and response style.[51] Moreover, a cross-sectional survey also suffers from weakness in isolating cause and effect relationships.

The longitudinal design is the ideal method of studying many, if not most, dimensions of consumer behavior. But these studies are very expensive to conduct. A great deal of imagination and persistence—including, perhaps, multiuniversity and/or multisource funding—will be required to overcome the cost problem.

Laboratory experiments make it easier to measure variables and their relationships, including cause and effect. But only a limited number of relationships can be measured in each experiment, and generalizing findings to real situations is often difficult because the conditions controlled in the laboratory may be active in the normal life of consumers.[52]

Despite these problems, longitudinal and experimental designs are generally superior to cross-sectional studies. Although longitudinal studies are still relatively rare,[53] the growing use of experimental designs is encouraging. More widespread use of these two designs should increase the quality of future consumer research.

Assessment of group differences. Studies investigating various aspects of consumer behavior often make conclusions about the ability of given variables to "account for" behavior on the basis of statistical tests measuring the variance in the behavior of individuals. Product-moment correlations of 0.2, and seldom higher than 0.3 or 0.4, are typical. Hence it is concluded that the variables do not "explain the variance" very well, even when combined into a prediction equation.

Interestingly, when the unit of analysis is changed from individuals to

51 Donald H. Granbois and James F. Engel, "The Longitudinal Approach to Studying Marketing Behavior," in Peter D. Bennett, ed., *Marketing and Economic Development* (Chicago: American Marketing Association, 1965), pp. 205–21.

52 Nicosia, "Opinion Leadership," p. 12.

53 For examples of longitudinal studies, see James F. Engel, David A. Knapp, and Deanne E. Knapp, "Sources of Influence in the Acceptance of New Products for Self-Medication—Preliminary Findings," in R. M. Hass, ed., *Science, Technology, and Marketing* (Chicago: American Marketing Association, 1966), pp. 776–82; Allan L. Pennington, "Customer-Salesmen Bargaining Behavior in Retail Transactions," *Journal of Marketing Research*, vol. 5 (August 1968), pp. 255–62; Robert W. Pratt, Jr., "Understanding the Decision Process for Consumer Durable Goods: An Example of the Application of Longitudinal Analysis," in Bennett, *Marketing and Economic Development*, pp. 244–60.

groups or market segments, findings that were not significant sometimes become significant. Wells and others have found this to be true in constructing psychographic profiles of heavy users of various convenience products.[54] Similarly, Bass, Tigert, and Lonsdale have found that the inability of socioeconomic variables to explain a substantial part of the variance in usage rates of persons does not necessarily imply that there are not substantial differences in the mean usage rates for different socioeconomic market segments.[55] Greater use of "group-differences" analysis would appear worthwhile.

Richer dependent variables. In recent years there has been growing use of multivariate techniques by researchers. In some instances, it has been demonstrated that single variables are not statistically related—or only weakly related—to whatever dependent variable is being investigated. On the other hand, combinations of independent variables often prove to be statistically significant and/or much more strongly related to the dependent variable.[56]

This same approach is rarely applied to dependent variables. Regardless of the complexity of the dependent variable, researchers typically measure it unidimensionally.

There are some interesting exceptions. For example, studies of brand loyalty (measured unidimensionally) have been characterized by the absence of significant relationships with consumer characteristics. Yet, when loyalty is measured multidimensionally, significant relationships have surfaced.[57]

In most consumer research studies, if the relationship between the dependent variable and the independent variable(s) is not statistically significant, it is concluded that the independent variable(s) is not important in understanding and predicting the dependent variable. The above discussion suggests that in some instances the "dimensionality artifact" may provide an alternative explanation. In other words, if dependent variables were measured multidimensionally, the independent variables that are significant and nonsignificant might change. Hence wider use of multidimensional measures of dependent variables would appear useful.

In most of the behavioral sciences, replication is accepted and rigorously practiced. Findings generally are not accepted until they have been replicated a number of times in separate studies. Replication, until recently, has been largely ignored in consumer research. All too many

Developing a replication tradition

54 Wells.

55 Frank M. Bass, Douglas J. Tigert, and Ronald T. Lonsdale, "Market Segmentation: Group versus Individual Behavior," *Journal of Marketing Research*, vol. 5 (August 1968), pp. 264–70.

56 John U. Farley, "Dimensions of Supermarket Choice Patterns," *Journal of Marketing Research*, vol. 5 (May 1968), pp. 206–08; Jerome B. Kernan, "Choice Behavior, Decision Behavior and Personality," *Journal of Marketing Research*, vol. 5 (May 1968), pp. 155–64; John G. Myers, "Determinants of Private Brand Attitude," *Journal of Marketing Research*, vol. 4 (February 1967), pp. 73–81.

57 James M. Carman, "Correlates of Brand Loyalty: Some Positive Results," *Journal of Marketing Research*, vol. 7 (February 1970), pp. 67–76; George S. Day, "A Two-Dimensional Concept of Brand Loyalty," *Journal of Advertising Research*, vol. 9 (September 1969), pp. 29–35.

findings and propositions are based upon a single study by a single researcher. This, of course, is dangerous, because it invites invalid conclusions due to unusual circumstances or sampling characteristics as well as other methodological artifacts. All too frequently, findings are used uncritically in marketing literature, especially general textbooks, and the dangers of misleading conclusions increase in proportion to the growth in the volume of consumer research findings.

The most encouraging exception is the mass of research focusing on validation of the Fishbein attitude toward the object (A_0) model and the extended Fishbein model. Some have argued that we have overdone it in this case, but the questions examined are vitally important. Is there a relationship between attitude and behavior or not? The authors were able to answer this question fairly definitively for the first time in this edition, and that is a welcome development indeed.

A replication tradition must spread into other areas of inquiry as well. It makes an invaluable contribution to the scientific advancement of consumer research. Such a tradition allows researchers to determine the conditions under which an effect may exist, establish hierarchies of effects, and test the validity of previously reported findings.

Generalizing across types of decisions

There is an unresolved issue regarding the extent to which findings derived from an analysis of a specific type of consumer behavior are applicable to other types of decisions. There is evidence that many findings are applicable only to the type of decision or choice being studied, and this can create another dilemma. On the other hand, it is obviously desirable to generalize as far as possible in order to avoid researching behavior in unduly minute detail. This points up the need for classification systems for types of decisions and choices which, if properly designed, would permit a legitimate degree of generalization. Research to date indicates that the traditional convenience, specialty, and shopping goods typology is inappropriate because of wide intercategory variation in behavior.[58] Future efforts using alternative conceptual schemas[59] or empirically derived classifications[60] will represent a meaningful step forward.

Developing information summary and retrieval systems

The amount of consumer research is increasing at an accelerating rate. For example, the first edition of this book appeared in the late 1960s, and between 1968 and 1972 there was more published research than during all the years prior to 1968. While the percentage rate of increase since that time has diminished because of the larger base, the amount of new research has increased astronomically. Furthermore, it is characterized by increased conceptual and methodological sophistication. As a result, it

58 Richard H. Holton, "The Distinction between Convenience Goods, Shopping Goods, and Specialty Goods," *Journal of Marketing* (July 1958), pp. 53–56.

59 Orville Brim et al., *Personality and Decision Processes* (Stanford, Calif.: Stanford University Press, 1962).

60 John G. Myers and Francesco M. Nicosia, "On the Study of Consumer Typologies," *Journal of Marketing Research*, vol. 5 (May 1966), pp. 182–93.

is becoming increasingly difficult and perhaps even impossible for both researchers and practitioners to have an awareness and working knowledge of published research relevant to their problems.

There are at least two steps that can be taken to accommodate the research explosion. First, it would appear useful to initiate a program of yearly literature reviews that would critically evaluate and summarize evidence that has been published, or otherwise become publicly available, during the year. This technique is widely used in other areas including, for example, *The Annual Review of Psychology.*

The second step would be to establish a consumer behavior research retrieval system. Although this type of system presents numerous complex problems, other disciplines such as law, medicine, and chemistry have advanced in this direction. An example is the American Chemical Society, which through its subsidiary, *Chemical Abstracts*, operates a service which makes possible computer research across the full range of the world's current chemical literature. The service consists of machine-searchable tapes containing the title, authors' names, complete bibliographic citation, and key descriptive indexing terms for each journal article and patent abstracted in current issues of *Chemical Abstracts.*

Developing cross-cultural sensitivity

There is no denying the fact that consumer behavior research, as a discipline, is largely a North American phenomenon, although there is some published research in western Europe as well. Concepts, theories, and methodologies all reflect this distinctly western orientation with only a few exceptions.[61]

The danger is that western researchers are decidedly ethnocentric; that is, they assume that their perspective is equally applicable beyond their own national borders. That can be totally erroneous. The senior author has given seminars on survey research in every continent of the world, especially in the developing countries, and here are just a few of the differences that must be taken into consideration:

1. People tend to be less individualistic and more apt to base decisions on group consensus.

2. Many, particularly in the orient, do not think and reason following the linear logic pattern of the west in which A + B = C. They can easily embrace patterns of inconsistency and paradox that are inexplicable to the westerner.

3. Differing value systems lead to widespread variations in attitudes toward material achievement, life styles, and so on.

61 See, for example, Susan P. Douglas, "Cross-Cultural Comparisons: The Myth of the Stereotype," report no. 75-111 (Cambridge, Mass.: Marketing Science Institute, 1975); Jagdish N. Sheth and S. Parkash Sethi, "A Theory of Cross-Cultural Buyer Behavior," in Arch G. Woodside, Jagdish N. Sheth, and Peter D. Bennett, eds., *Consumer and Industrial Buying Behavior* (New York: Elsevier North-Holland, 1977); James F. Engel, "The Brazilian Evangelical" (Wheaton Communication Research Report no. 41, April 1975); James F. Engel, "The Presbyterian Church of Brazil," in Roger D. Blackwell, James F. Engel, and W. W. Wayne Talarzyk, *Contemporary Cases in Consumer Behavior* (Hinsdale, Ill.: Dryden, 1977), pp. 88–95; and Ronald Anderson and Jack Engledow, "A Factor Analytic Comparison of U.S. and German Information Seekers," *Journal of Consumer Research*, vol. 3 (March 1977), pp. 185–96.

4. A pervasive sensitivity to the other person often will lead to the giving of a "yes" answer when a "no" is usually meant in order to avoid offense. This can play havoc with research methods.

5. Attitude scaling methods often are totally foreign in that people in many parts of the world do not think in terms of degrees of agreement or disagreement.

This list could be extended to encompass an entire book, but it gives some feel of the differences encountered. The net result is that all theories, concepts, and methods must be extensively evaluated to determine whether or not adaptation and modification is warranted. The result, otherwise, can be outright misleading conclusions and strategy decisions.

It is time for consumer researchers to assume a world perspective. To a significant degree, the remainder of the world is catching up to or even surpassing the United States in material wealth. The need is for world citizens who can account for cross-cultural variations and operate effectively in diverse environments. The days of insular North American thinking should be brought to a close as soon as possible.

A concluding note

So here we have it—a discipline emerging from infancy and attaining a measure of maturity. While some problems have been outlined, the situation is certainly more positive now than it was even a few years ago. Improved training of researchers, development of a body of knowledge characterized at times by a replication tradition, and greater methodological sophistication all are decidedly favorable developments.

It is now time to call for an end to "data-technique-construct" oriented research. This problem was discussed above, and the root problem is research designed to test some method or theory borrowed from elsewhere without regard to the implications. The senior author is on the editorial board of two major journals, and his acceptance rate of articles reviewed is less than 10 percent. The reason is that the type of research described above still is far too common. Unless a genuine contribution is made to knowledge of consumer behavior or to specific issues of concern to the practitioner (or both simultaneously—this is *not* an impossibility!), the article is rejected. The authors have used the same criteria in reviewing the literature for this revision, and too much in the published journals fails on any criterion of relevance.

One helpful step would be a wholesale revision in the standards for promotion of younger academicians. This problem also was mentioned above, and the prevailing rule seems to be publication in any prestigious journal regardless of what is said. What is wrong with editors and reviewers that they allow such a travesty to continue? Furthermore, why do audiences sit so quiescently at academic conferences when so much minutia and triviality is presented with such an aura of profundity? It is small wonder that the gap between academic and applied researchers continues to be so wide. It will not be bridged until serious attention is paid to basic issues of professional excellence.

We should point out in this context that much of our earlier work would never have appeared in print if the criteria described here had been applied in earlier years. In a sense, we can look back with "20–20 hindsight" and be unduly harsh on ourselves. It has been pointed out that methodological and conceptual borrowing probably was inevitable in the early stages of this discipline. Researchers at that time were operating with the light they had. But that day is over now!

What will the future hold? Our hope is that future editions of this book (assuming that the endurance of both authors and users perseveres) will reflect the kind of replication tradition and resulting clarity that has entered into the subject of beliefs and attitudes. We do not like to buttress conclusions with the caveat "the research is only tentative," or "no definitive generalizations can be made at this time." This often is frustrating to the reader as well, but do we have any real choice if our intent is to maintain professional integrity? We will gauge progress in the field by the extent to which these caveats become unnecessary.

Are we optimistic concerning the future? Of course! *We've come a long way, baby!*

Summary

This chapter has been written in the attempt to evaluate and assess the current status of consumer behavior research in terms of problems and prospects. The explanatory and predictive power of the current body of theory and findings were evaluated at the outset. What looks to be a well researched and developed discipline was not found to fare especially well when evaluated against the criteria of explanation and prediction. Actual accomplishment has not been consistent with the magnitude of the effort expended, although there has been progress in recent years.

The remainder of the chapter presented recommendations for improvement of theory and research. It was suggested, first of all, that models and theories be used more extensively and intensively, that research priorities be identified, that greater attention be paid to important methodological considerations, that typologies be developed to allow generalization across types of decisions, that information summary and retrieval systems be developed, and that cross-cultural sensitivity begin to pervade a field that has been predominately North American in orientation.

Review and discussion questions

1. Four levels of explanation in the behavioral sciences were presented and applied to consumer behavior. Do you agree that most of the research presented in this book stops at stage 2? What steps are necessary to move toward the higher-order categories?

2. What are some of the dangers associated with use of the "reduced-form" model?

3. From your own perspective, how would you assess the priorities that should be established for consumer research in the future? What, in particular, is the initial starting point for an intensified effort of this nature?

4. Is it possible for the gap between academic and applied researchers to be bridged given the wide variation in career expectations and rewards?

5. Without a "czar of consumer research" who controls all efforts, how can progress be made in standardizing the definition and methodological operationalization of variables?

6. What is the current state of the art with respect to reliability and validity? Hint: read the papers footnoted from the Perreault volume.

7. Why is the cross-sectional design used more frequently than either the longitudinal or experimental design?

8. Read the chapters on attitude and attitude change in the two previous editions of this book. From the background, compare the changes in the present volume in terms of the replication tradition that has developed.

9. What problems will be faced in developing a real cross-cultural sensitivity within consumer research?

CHAPTER 22

Consumerism

President John F. Kennedy, in his declaration of rights for the consumer, stated that consumers have:

1. The right to safety

2. The right to be informed

3. The right to choose

4. The right to be heard (redress)

But how shall those "rights" be achieved? That is a question with which people are now struggling. Answers must necessarily involve economics, business, law, physical sciences, and other disciplines, including consumer behavior.

A more basic question is: What are the meanings to consumers of such terms as "safety," "information," "choice," and "redress"? Before a program can be developed by business or government to attain the rights of the consumer, it is absolutely essential to develop an understanding of what those rights actually mean to consumers. Before a business firm can decide what information to disclose about a product or before a government agency can decide what information must be disclosed, more basic questions must be answered: What information is *relevant* to the consumer? Do all consumers consider the same information as relevant or are there distinct needs among market segments? What trade-offs in price or other disadvantages justify the additional information? These are questions about which the study of consumer behavior can make productive and unique contributions. These are the issues discussed in this chapter.

Consumer behavior is a discipline similar to law in that it is useful—and even necessary—to parties with different and often conflicting interests. It is not unusual for a lawyer, as an example, to be employed by a government agency such as the Federal Trade Commission one year and to be employed by a business firm the next year. In the former role, the attorney may be prosecuting businesses concerning their consumer practices and in the next role, the attorney may be defending and designing the consumer practices. The basic training in law school is not for one role or the other; it is simply basic training in the legal process, which may be applied to varied situations. Consumer behavior is very much the same. The study of consumer decision processes throughout this book and the specific study of consumerism in this chapter may be used by a person employed by a regulatory agency, by a business firm, by a consumer advocacy group, or for that matter, for the consumer's own personal interests as a consumer.

After a definition of consumerism and its causes, this chapter will focus on the issues of product safety, consumer information, competitive choice, redress, environmental protection, responsibility to minorities and the poor, and social marketing. This chapter contains basic materials about consumerism that are then applied in government, business, and personal decisions in the chapter that follows, Chapter 23.

Definitions of consumerism

Consumerism has many meanings, often reflecting the various interests of business, government, consumer groups, and academic researchers. These definitions run the gamut from reflecting the basic search of people for getting better values for their money to challenging the goal of a society that calls for an ever-increasing amount of material goods through time. Consumerists of the first type believe that prices are too high, quality and safety of goods are not adequate, and that service facilities need to be improved. The latter range of meanings of consumerism leads to questioning of whether the emphasis should be on increasing material wealth or whether it might be better to focus more resources on public welfare, health, and education programs and better leisure facilities and programs.[1]

Some analysts have defined consumerism as:

> . . . the organized efforts of consumers seeking redress, restitution,
> and remedy for dissatisfaction they have accumulated in the acquisition
> of their standard of living.[2]

This definition can be broadened usefully by dropping the requirement

---

[1] Robert Ferber, "Rising Consumerism Primary Concern to Market Managers," paper presented at the American Marketing Association, Hawaii chapter (May 7, 1970); reprinted in *Marketing News* (Mid–June 1970), pp. 4 ff.

[2] Richard H. Buskirk and James T. Rothe, "Consumerism—An Interpretation," *Journal of Marketing*, vol. 34 (October 1970), pp. 61–65.

that consumerism be limited to "organized efforts." Kotler achieves this in the view that:

> Consumerism is a social movement seeking to augment the rights and power of buyers in relation to sellers.[3]

Even this definition may be too limiting if it implies that pressure is focused only on *business*. Aaker and Day observe that consumerism,

> . . . encompasses the evolving set of activities of government, business, independent organizations that are designed to protect the rights of consumers. . . . Consumerism is concerned with protecting consumers from all organizations with which there is an exchange relationship. There are consumer problems associated with hospitals, libraries, schools, police forces, and various government agencies, as well as business firms.[4]

This same notion was expressed by Sen. Charles Percy, who describes the consumer movement as ". . . a broad public reaction against bureaucratic neglect and corporate disregard of the public."[5]

The broad concept of consumerism is used in this book because of the variety of functions consumer researchers may perform concerning consumerism. Some consumer researchers may be primarily involved in the investigation of consumerism to assist business firms develop marketing strategy, but increasingly consumer reseachers are also helping hospitals, police departments,[6] religious organizations,[7] and other non-business organizations to develop strategies with which to adapt to consumer needs and requirements.[8]

The causes of consumerism

Consumerism has numerous historical antecedents for what has developed into the new consumerism of recent years. Even in the Middle Ages, reformers such as St. Thomas Aquinas, Martin Luther and John Calvin represented a kind of consumerism by attacking deceptive selling practices of businessmen and advancing the concept of a "just price" rather than what the market would bear.[9] Various efforts have been made to

3 Philip Kotler, "What Consumerism Means for Marketers," *Harvard Business Review* (May–June, 1972), pp. 48–57.

4 David A. Aaker and George S. Day, *Consumerism: Search for the Consumer Interest*, 2d ed. (New York: Free Press, 1974), p. xvii.

5 Quoted in William T. Kelly, *New Consumerism: Selected Readings*. (Columbus: Grid), p. ii.

6 For an example see the Dallas Police Department case in Roger D. Blackwell, James F. Engel, and W. Wayne Talarzyk, *Contemporary Cases in Consumer Behavior* (Hinsdale, Ill: Dryden Press, 1977), pp. 16–20.

7 Donald McGavran, *Understanding Church Growth*. (Grand Rapids: William B. Eerdmans, 1970); and James F. Engel and H. Wilbert Norton, *What's Gone Wrong with the Harvest* (Grand Rapids, Mich.: Zondervan, 1975).

8 The basic source on nonbusiness marketing is Philip Kotler, *Marketing for Nonprofit Organizations* (Hinsdale, Ill.: Dryden Press, 1975).

9 Leon Garry, "Consumerism Began with Cyrus of Persia," *Business and Society Review*, vol. 4 (Winter 1972–73), pp. 62–64.

describe the historical antecedents of modern consumerism and three eras of consumerism leading to current developments were identified in a history of consumerism by Herrman.[10] While these developments focus on history in the United States, similar phenomena have occurred on a world-wide basis, but especially in more advanced nations.[11] A description of these eras in the rise of consumerism should put the current movement into a proper perspective for predicting its present and future course.[12]

The early 1900s

Consumer activism appeared in the early part of this century resulting in substantial progress in consumer protection legislation before gradually subsiding. During the 1890s and again in 1902, attempts were made to enact pure food legislation, but each time the bill died in Congress.

In 1906, *The Jungle* by Upton Sinclair exposed the filth surrounding the meat packing industry in Chicago, creating such substantial public awareness and outcry that Congress was compelled to act. The Meat Inspection Act of 1906 was quickly enacted to provide federal inspection of meat packing and processing. Later that same year, the Food and Drug Act created the Food and Drug Administration that was charged with preventing misbranded and adulterated food and drugs in interstate commerce. A few years later, in 1914, the Federal Trade Commission was established to curb monopoly and trade practices that might be unfair to competitive businesses. The business community remained largely indifferent to consumer protection, however, and the consumer movement gradually abated.

The 1930s

The consumerism movement of the 1930s had its inception in the immediately preceding years. During the 1920s, incomes rose rapidly and thus sales of consumer durables, which were new and unfamiliar to consumers, also rose rapidly. Consumers were deluged with advertising as radio and magazines grew rapidly as advertising media.

In 1927, the book *Your Money's Worth* by Stuart Chase and F. J. Schlink stirred the consumer movement once again. The book attacked the manipulation and deceit of advertising and called for scientific testing and product standards to provide consumers with information for making wise purchasing decisions. This attack resulted in the founding of a new consumer organization, Consumers Research, Inc., which was the fore-runner of today's Consumer Union, the publishers of the magazine *Consumer Reports*.

10 Robert O. Herrmann, "Consumerism: Its Goals, Organizations and Future," *Journal of Marketing*, vol. 13 (October 1970), pp. 55–60. This reference is the source of much of the material in this section as is also William P. Anthony and Joel B. Haynes, "Consumerism: A Three Generation Paradigm" *University of Michigan Business Review* (November 1975), pp. 21–26. The authors also wish to thank Roger Campbell for his assistance in preparing this section.

11 Colson E. Warne, "The Worldwide Consumer Movement," in Ralph M. Gaedeke and Warren W. Etcheson, eds., *Consumerism: Viewpoints from Business, Government, and the Public Interest* (San Francisco: Canfield Press, 1972), pp. 17–19.

12 For more details concerning the history of consumerism, see Aaker and Day, *Consumerism: Search for the Consumer Interest*; Kelley, *New Consumerism: Selected Readings*; and Gaedeke and Etcheson, *Consumerism: Viewpoints from Business*.

The stock market crash of 1929 forestalled a widespread consumer movement. Instead, efforts were focused upon consumer education. Budgeting and money management were emphasized in order to help the consumer identify the best buys at the lowest cost.

A book by F. J. Schlink and Arthur Kallett, *100,000,000 Guinea Pigs*, pointed to loopholes in the 1906 Food and Drug Act that allowed consumers to be forced into the role of guinea pigs for dangerous medicines, unsafe cosmetics, and adulterated foods. More consumer support was generated by the "sulfanilamide scandal" of 1937 which ended in 107 deaths and led to the passage of the Food, Drug and Cosmetic Act of 1938. The bill, however, had been adulterated itself through five years of hearings and controversy so that it was too weak to suit many consumer activists.

In 1938, the Wheeler-Lea amendment to the Federal Trade Commission Act was also passed. Wheller-Lea enlarged the powers of the Federal Trade Commission to prosecute unlawful, deceptive, or unfair trade practices—becoming a "watchdog for the consumer" rather than only regulating practices that were unfair to competition. During this period, an increasing concern about consumerism was observed by business leaders, partially stimulated by a national survey by Dr. George Gallup indicating that the consumerism movement was likely to increase. World War II, however, diverted attention of the nation away from consumer problems and toward national problems and the war effort.

The 1960s

The consumerism era of the 1960s, which forms the foundation for the current movement, also had antecedents in prior years. Just as the two previous eras had gained a part of their impetus from the publication of a book, so did this era. In 1957, Vance Packard's *The Hidden Persuaders* argued that the consumer was being manipulated by advertising without realizing the source of the manipulation. The public reaction to this book showed that there was still public interest in consumer problems but in a more sophisticated way than past eras.

The problem of drug safety was also a prominent issue in the consumerism of the 1960s just as it had been in prior eras. Since 1959, Sen. Estes Kefauver's Antitrust and Monopoly Subcommittee had been holding hearings on the prescription drug industry, with many revelations that created public awareness and concern. The thalidomide scare finally triggered public reaction that resulted in the passage of the Kefauver-Harris Amendment to the Food, Drug and Cosmetic Act.

The beginning of the new consumerism, however, is generally attributed to President John F. Kennedy's message to Congress on March 15, 1962, in which he outlined the consumer bill of rights listed at the beginning of this chapter. Kennedy's message clearly implied that government is the ultimate guarantor of consumer rights, and it set forth the basis for much of the role of the federal government in consumerism. Subsequent actions of administrators, legislators and consumer activists have broadened the movement so that today, the rights are still a dynamic and evolving force in the economy.

Catalysts to consumerism	The contemporary consumerism movement has historical antecedents, as the preceding paragraphs reveal. But what are the specific catalysts to the movement? What communalities exist in these historical antecedents? What does research indicate are the variables most associated with interests in consumerism? There has been considerable research and analysis in recent years directed toward answering these questions.

Historical variables. An analysis of the eras in which consumerism has increased rapidly reveals that each era occurred after several decades of rapidly rising incomes, followed by raising prices which caused decreases in the rise of real purchasing power.[13] Generally, also, it is the highly educated and high-income individuals who provided the leadership as consumerists.[14]

The causes of consumerism were investigated by Gaedeke in a study of businessmen, consumer spokesmen, and government officials. In the survey, 38 possible causes of consumerism were investigated, but there was a consensus on only seven as related to the underlying causes of consumerism. They were

1. The political appeal of consumer protection legislation

2. The mechanical and impersonal nature of the marketplace

3. The language of advertising

4. A bandwagon effect

5. Greater public concern for social problems

6. A feeling that business should assume greater "social responsibilities"

7. A change in national attitude.[15]

One theory about the historical determinants of consumerism is similar to the process of diffusion of innovation described in Chapter 12. Hendon advances the proposition that consumerism is but a part of the theory of social adaptation to innovation, in which the innovation (consumerism) moves through phases of introduction (initial impact), growth, and a "reaction" phase or widespread acceptance of regulatory and business actions which quiet things down for awhile until a new innovation occurs when the cycle begins again.[16] Hendon presents some data to support this hypothesis and suggests that organizations might profitably study such diffusion processes in order to predict the future direction and magnitude of important social movements that will affect the organization.

In the area of retailing, Hollander analyzed several retailing practices

13 Herrman, "Consumerism: Its Goals."

14 Herrman, "Consumerism: Its Goals."

15 Ralph M. Gaedeke, "What Business, Government and Consumer Spokesmen Think about Consumerism," *Journal of Consumer Affairs*, vol. 4 (Summer 1970), pp. 7–18, at p. 16.

16 Donald Hendon, "Toward a Theory of Consumerism," *Business Horizons*, vol. 18 (August 1975), pp. 16–24.

that attract consumer interest and result in consumerism activities. These functions or practices include *poor sanitation* (especially in the handling of food), *inadequate shopping information* (in marking, labeling and advertising practices), *price inflation, unfair credit practices*, and *inadequate repair and warranty services*.[17] Hollander concludes that the causes of consumerism are variables about which retailers can implement helpful and positive remedies.

Sociopsychological variables. Several studies are beginning to investigate the sociopsychological variables that may be associated with interest in consumerism activities.

Alienation, as that concept is used in sociology, is advanced as a major cause for consumer discontent by Lambert and Kniffin, who believe that unless the basic causes that fuel consumer discontent are dealt with successfully, relief is transitory and discontent bursts forth later in the form of new symptomatic issues and complaints.[18] In this framework of analysis, alienation is manifested in five forms: *powerlessness, meaninglessness, normlessness, isolation*, and *self-estrangement*. Powerlessness, for example, results when consumers believe they cannot exert any influence on business decisions concerning what products will or will not be placed on the market, their quality level, warranty coverage, and so forth. Consequently, they harbor feelings like those of alienated voters who see themselves as being able only to exercise a negative choice between candidates offered to them by political bosses. Lambert and Kniffin suggest a number of actions that business firms can take to combat powerlessness and other forms of alienation such as "cool lines," buyer protection plans, and a management system of information and control to identify and correct practices that needlessly produce dissatisfaction.

Socially conscious consumers, or those persons who not only are concerned with their own personal satisfactions but also buy with some consideration of the societal and environmental well-being have been investigated in a number of situations. Anderson and Cunningham found that sociopsychological variables were more powerful in explaining social conciousness than demographic variables and that the variables most negatively associated with such consumer interest were dogmatism, conservatism, and status consciousness while cosmopolitanism varied directly with social consciousness.[19]

Sociodemographic variables have been analyzed by a number of researchers as an explanation for consumer activitism, usually with regard to specific activities such as energy consumption, recycling activities, boycott participation, and so forth. Most of these studies have

17 Stanley C. Hollander, "Consumerism and Retailing: A Historical Perspective," *Journal of Retailing*, vol. 48 (Winter 1972–73), pp. 6–21.

18 Zarrel V. Lambert and Fred W. Kniffin, "Consumer Discontent: A Social Perspective," *California Management Review*, vol. 18 (Fall 1975), pp. 36–44.

19 W. Thomas Anderson, Jr., and William H. Cunningham, "The Socially Conscious Consumer," *Journal of Marketing*, vol. 36 (July 1972), pp. 23–31. Less definitive results were found, however, in similar research reported in Frederick E. Webster, Jr., "Determining the Characteristics of the Socially Conscious Consumer," *Journal of Consumer Research*, vol. 2 (December 1975), pp. 188–96.

concluded that variables associated with consumer activism or dissatisfaction with marketing practices include the sociodemographic variables of being young, politically liberal or avant garde, and well educated.[20]

Satisfaction and complaints. There is an increasing effort being made to determine the amount of satisfaction or dissatisfaction consumers have as a basis for predicting who will make complaints or take other actions. The methodology for investigating this topic is of two basic types. The first type involves an analysis of complaint data voiced about a business firm to a consumer agency. The most widely used is probably the reports generated by the Council of Better Business Bureaus in Washington, D.C., reflecting the experiences of local bureaus throughout the United States.[21] In some instances, consumer agencies operate a "hot line" or a telephone number where consumers can call to report their problems.[22] While this approach has been used, it is generally not considered an adequate reflection of the total array of consumer complaints because of the overrepresentation of professional, upscale persons and because it does not represent a substantial amount of unvoiced complaints of consumers.[23]

The second type of methodology to measure dissatisfaction or complaints involves comprehensive surveys to representative samples of consumers. One of the most comprehensive of this type of survey is known as the Best and Andreasen study. These researchers found that about one in five purchases leads to perception of some problem (other than general concern about price) but that few of these problems are actually voiced in complaints to the seller and further, that respondents take action in only about 40 percent of the purchase instances for which they report problems.[24] This and other studies report that those who take action are of a distinct socioeconomic group. Specifically, they are better educated, earn higher incomes, are in higher social classes, are more active in formal organizations, and are more politically committed and liberal than other groups.[25]

20 Hiram C. Barksdale and William R. Darden, "Consumer Attitudes toward Marketing and Consumerism," *Journal of Marketing*, vol. 36 (October 1972), pp. 28–35; Thomas P. Hustad and Edgar A. Pessemier, "Will the Real Consumer Activist Please Stand Up: An Examination of Consumers' Opinions about Marketing Practices," *Journal of Marketing Research*, vol. 10 (August 1973), pp. 319–24; Michael B. Mazis and John H. Faricy, "Consumer Response to the Meat Boycott," in Ronald C. Curhan, ed., *1974 Combined Proceedings* (Chicago: American Marketing Association, 1974), pp. 329–33. These results were not found, however, in W. Wayne Talarzyk and Glenn S. Omura, "Consumer Attitudes toward and Perceptions of the Energy Crisis," in Curhan, *1974 Combined Proceedings*, pp. 316–22. Also, see Thomas C. Kinnear, James R. Taylor, and Sadrudin A. Ahmed, "Ecologically Concerned Consumers: Who Are They?" *Journal of Marketing*, vol. 38 (April 1974), pp. 20–24.

21 A statistical summary of complaints for the entire nation is issued each year by the Council of Better Business Bureaus, Inc., 1150 17th Street, N.W., Washington, D.C. 20036.

22 Steven L. Diamon, Scott Ward, and Ronald Faber, "Consumer Problems and Consumerism: Analysis of Calls to a Consumer Hot Line," *Journal of Marketing*, vol. 40 (January 1976), pp. 56–62.

23 J. P. Liefeld, F. H. C. Edgecombe, and Linda Wolfe, "Demographic Characteristics of Canadian Consumer Complainers," *Journal of Consumer Affairs*, vol. 9 (Summer 1975), pp. 73–80.

24 Arthur Best and Alan R. Andreasen, *Talking Back to Business: Voiced and Unvoiced Consumer Complaints* (Center for Study of Responsive Law, 1976).

25 Rex H. Warland, Robert O. Herrman, and Jane Willits, "Dissatisfied Consumers: Who Gets Upset and Who Takes Action," *Journal of Consumer Affairs*, vol. 9 (Winter 1975), pp. 148–62.

An additional difficulty in studying satisfactions and complaints is the problem of changing expectations about products over time. One theory that has been advanced for increasing dissatisfaction of consumers, for example, is expectancy theory that states that the rising dissatisfaction may not be due to deteriorating product and service offerings but rather, increased consumer expectations, especially on the part of younger, affluent, and more sophisticated consumers, abetted by exaggerated advertising claims concerning product performance.[26] While overexpectations may exist and produce dissatisfaction, there is empirical evidence to indicate that consumer expectations are not rising but are, in fact, decreasing.[27] Swan and Combs have shown the importance, however, of relating satisfactions to expectancies about products, and this appears to be an area likely to experience more attention in the future.[28]

Business types. Finally, specific causes of consumer dissatisfaction must include the type of business involved. In other words, some businesses are perceived by consumers to be involved in activities that cause complaints more than other businesses. Using complaint data from the Better Business Bureau, Figure 22.1 shows the types of businesses with the highest percent of complaints (57 percent) involve the top 15 (in number of complaints) of the 86 different business categories used for recording purposes. Figure 22.1 shows that mail order companies generated more complaints than any other type of business, followed by auto dealers and miscellaneous service establishments. Using more sophisticated measures of dissatisfaction, Best and Andreasen also found mail order and car repair services to be in the three highest levels of unsatisfactory performance (along with appliance repair purchases).[29]

Understanding consumer rights and needs

Consumer research has an important role to play in the analysis of consumer rights and needs. The role of research in developing an empirically based understanding of the rights and needs of consumers is described below. Following that, illustrative research findings that are beginning to emerge are described concerning the following topics: product safety, consumer information, competitive choice, redress, environmental protection, responsibility to minorities and the poor, and social marketing.

A rigorous research framework for investigating issues in consumerism is critical to the resolution of disparate views of diverse groups seeking to

Criticality of a research approach

26 Rolphe E. Anderson and Marvin A. Jolson, "Consumer Expectations and the Communications Gap," *Business Horizons*, vol. 61 (April 1973), pp. 11–16.

27 Thomas R. Wotruba and Patricia L. Duncan, "Are Consumers Really Satisfied?" *Business Horizons*, vol. 18 (February 1975), pp. 85–90.

28 John E. Swan and Linda Jones Combs, "Product Performance and Consumer Satisfaction: A New Concept," *Journal of Marketing*, vol. 40 (April 1976), pp. 35–38.

29 Best and Andreasen, *Talking Back to Business*, p. 16.

Figure 22.1 Types of business involved in
consumer complaints, 1976

Type of business	Rank	Number	Percent of total	Percent settled
Total		390,685	100.00	75.1
Mail Order Companies	1	58.562	14.98	83.1
Auto Dealers	2	27,239	6.97	78.5
Miscellaneous Service Establishments	*	19,073	4.88	67.9
Miscellaneous Retail Stores/Shops	*	14,813	3.79	68.9
Home Furnishings Stores	3	13,618	3.48	76.2
Magazines, Ordered by Mail	4	13,522	3.46	85.1
Miscellaneous Home Maintenance	5	12,352	3.16	61.9
Department Stores	6	11,671	2.98	88.3
Auto Repair Shops—Exc. Transm.	7	10,214	2.61	64.9
Television Servicing Companies	8	9,394	2.40	
Home Remodeling Contractors	9	8,170	2.09	65.4
Insurance Companies	10	8,078	2.06	84.3
Dry Cleaning/Laundry Companies	11	8,077	2.06	70.1
Apparel and Accessory Shops	12	7,737	1.98	75.8
Appliance Stores	13	7,652	1.95	76.2
Real Estate Sales/Rental Companies	14	7,567	1.93	69.7
Appliance Service Companies	15	7,106	1.81	72.9
Miscellaneous Automotive	16	6,538	1.67	66.3
Direct Selling—Magazines	17	6,517	1.66	76.1
Manufacturers/Producers	18	5,641	1.44	83.2
TV/Radio/Phono/Shops	19	5,526	1.41	75.6
Photographic Processing Companies	20	5,465	1.39	77.1
Floor Covering Stores	21	5,284	1.35	69.6
Auto Gasoline Service Stations	22	5,153	1.31	66.5
Auto Tire, Battery, Accessory Shops	23	4,768	1.22	76.4
Roofing Contractors	24	4,481	1.14	60.7
Jewelry Stores	25	4,373	1.11	77.1
Direct Selling—Miscellaneous	26	4,338	1.11	78.0
Heating and Central Air Conditioning Companies	27	4,117	1.05	75.2
Mobile/Modular Home Dealers	28	4,092	1.04	72.3

Note: Percent is based on total number of complaints to BBB offices. The full report contains 86 business categories, but only those with more than 1 percent are reprinted here.

*Unranked because category includes a variety of businesses.

Source: *CBBB Statistical Summary of Better Business Bureau Activity, 1976* (Washington, D.C.: Council of Better Business Bureaus, 1976). Reprinted by permission of the Council of Better Business Bureaus, Inc., 1150 17th Street, N.W., Washington, D.C.

respond to consumerism. Both business and government need the objectivity of information that is the output of well-designed research on consumer behavior. By fulfilling this critical need, consumer researchers have the potential for being boundary spanning agents in the arena of conflict and subjectivity that has often surrounded the discussion of consumer rights and needs.

A research approach to consumerism emphasizes the collection of data that help understand consumer preferences and behavior rather than specifying policies that should be implemented to achieve those rights. Stated alternatively, a research approach to consumerism is not so much concerned with what business or government "ought to do" as it is concerned with "how consumers behave" or react to the current or contemplated programs of business firms and protective agencies.[30]

A research approach to consumerism provides an alternative to normative authoritarianism. There is a consistent ideological conflict reflected in the literature of consumerism concerning the issue of what consumers *want* versus what they *ought* to want and what they *know* about products versus what they *need to know.*

Most research seems to indicate discrepancies between what consumer advocates believe, what executives believe, and what consumers believe.[31] Empirical research, conducted under scientific methods, offers the potential for resolving these conflicting views of reality. The differences between executives and consumer advocates concerning what consumers need to know is illustrated in the research of Moran, who observes:

> This difference appeared almost without exception when I asked marketers and critics a question of the sort, "What do consumers *need* to know when deciding among the competing brands and models of product?" The critic was never fazed by the question and could easily speak at this normative level. The marketer in most cases would respond not to the question that had been asked but rather to the quite different question, "What do consumers *want* to know . . .?" Only with prodding and a subsequent feeling of uneasiness and meaninglessness of reply would marketers get out into what they considered to be a "big-brother" way of looking at the consumer.[32]

Consumer research increasingly offers the potential of "test marketing" proposed protective policies just as it is used in other areas of marketing practice. Such research is more difficult in situations where new alternatives are proposed than in situations in which consumers are asked only to

30 Consumer research can be used, however, to determine what consumers believe sellers or government should do about problems. See Gregory M. Gazda and David R. Gourley, "Attitudes of Businessmen, Consumers, and Consumerists toward Consumerism," *Journal of Consumer Affairs* (Winter 1975), pp. 176–86; and Roger D. Blackwell and W. Wayne Talarzyk, *Consumer Attitudes toward Health Care and Medical Malpractice* (Columbus: Grid Publishing, 1977), chap. 6.

31 Gazda and Gourley, "Attitudes of Businessmen"; F. Kelly Shuptrine, Henry O. Pruden, and Douglas S. Longman, "Business Executives' and Consumers' Attitudes toward Consumer Activism and Involvement," *Journal of Consumer Affairs* (Summer 1975), pp. 90–95.

32 Robert Moran, "Formulating Public Policy on Consumer Issues: Some Preliminary Findings," working paper P-57-A (Boston: Marketing Science Institute, September 1971), p. 31.

choose from existing alternatives but progress is continually occuring in methodologies facilitating the evaluation of new alternatives.

In a society where normative authoritarianism prevails, the groups that will specify the rules for consumers are those that have the most "power." The basis for power may vary through time and across consumption choices. The countervailing force that provides a more democratic alternative, however, is rigorous research into the *actual* behavior of consumers rather than reliance or normative statements about how consumers *should* behave.

Product safety

In each of the three consumer eras of this century, the problem of health and safety has been a prominent issue. The issue goes beyond the problem of adequate inspection and regulation of the food and drug industries. Defective, hazardous, or unsafe consumer products such as automobiles, electrical appliances, toys, and others have often been the focus of the issue in recent years. Additionally, the issue involves the problem of safety in highway and air travel.

The right to safety has been made very specific in the United States under the Consumer Product Safety Act, which established the Consumer Product Safety Commission (CPSC), which has the responsibility to protect consumers against unreasonable risk to injuries that may be caused by hazardous household products.[33] Manufacturers have previously been liable for safety problems of their products under common law but the intent of the CPSC is to shift the responsibility for safety from post-sale (and post-injury) remedies to *preventive safety*. In other words, more responsibility is required in the *design of the product* to achieve safety.

Consumer research has two major roles in this environment of increased attention to consumers' rights to safety. The first role is in understanding the usage patterns of the product, especially those which may cause unexpected safety hazards. The second role is in establishing the level of safety or probability of injuries which may yield liability costs that must be considered in decisions concerning the product.

Consumer usage patterns. Consumer research can make a substantial contribution to improvements of product safety and performance by in-depth studies of consumer usage patterns of products. The reason many products perform poorly or unsafely is because they are used incorrectly by some segments of the market. Laundry equipment frequently provides poor performance because consumers overload the machine with clothes, soap, or both. Usage studies should be able to determine segments of the consumer population most likely to cause such problems and thereby provide an input to tactics that may prevent some of the occurrences.

33 Walter Jensen, Jr., Edward M. Mazze, and Duke N. Stern, "The Consumer Product Safety Act: A Special Case in Consumerism," *Journal of Marketing* (October 1973), pp. 68–71; Warren G. Magnuson and Edward B. Cohen, "The Role of the Consumer under the Consumer Product Safety Act," *Journal of Contemporary Business* (Winter 1975), pp. 21–37.

Consumer research can aid manufacturers in the problems they face due to the "doctrine of forseeability." This is a legal doctrine which holds that manufacturers are best able to evaluate the risks inherent in their products and figure out ways to avoid them. This implies not only technical knowledge of the product but in-depth knowledge of how the product is likely to be used by varying segments of the market. A noted consumerist lawyer notes that the courts "should protect not just the unwitting consumer from the consequences of a manufacturer's error, but also the 'witless boobs' who misuse a product in ways that can be anticipated."[34] A Kentucky Court of Appeals held, for example, that a manufacturer was liable for damages that occurred when one of its vacuum cleaners was plugged into a 220-volt circuit and blew up. The label on the product stated that it was to be used in 115-volt outlets but did not warn about the serious consequences that would occur with improper usage.[35]

Another example of the contribution of consumer research on usage patterns is in the area of defining what types of safety features a product should have. Controversy surrounds the usage of seat belts and air bags on automobiles, for example. The problems due to consumer usage patterns of seat belts may cause the government to require producers to supply (and, therefore, consumers to buy) a very expensive air bag (which may have its own defects). After describing the air bag it was pointed out that, "although lap and shoulder harnesses give similar protection, officials brandish the inescapable facts that not even 40 percent of all car occupants wear lap belts and fewer than 5 percent bother with shoulder belts."[36]

The importance of consumer research in understanding normal usage as well as misusage can be observed in the Ex-cis-or case.[37] This is a product sold as a cleaning agent for ovens that had been tested extensively in the laboratory by specialists in a variety of household ovens and found to be an effective and "safe" product. When it was introduced to the market, the company received some rumors about consumer problems with burns from the product but apparently failed to investigate them thoroughly. Finally, a law suit was filed against the company for $2 million by a young housewife with four children who had been badly burned and blinded while cleaning the kitchen stove. Evidence later revealed that the housewife had used the product on an outside element of the stove (rather than the oven), that the product had been of extra strength due to an abnormality in the production process, and that the user had mixed detergent with the product and applied it to a heated element of the range. Although there was technical abnormality in the product, the engineers were amazed that the customer would use Ex-cis-or mixed with a detergent on a heated element. The point is that the

34 "Business Responds to Consumerism," *Business Week*, p. 108 (Sept. 6, 1969).
35 "Business Responds to Consumerism."
36 "The Air Bag Faces a Showdown Fight," *Business Week* (August 14, 1971), pp. 74–75.
37 This example is extracted from Lawrence A. Bennigson and Arnold I. Bennigson, "Product Liability: Manufacturers Beware!" *Harvard Business Review* (May–June 1974), pp. 122–32.

previous research of the firm was conducted in the laboratory by specialists who would use the product correctly. Consumer research, however, must be expected to look at the total usage pattern of consumers and, in addition, consider the potential problems that may arise when "normal" consumers use the product abnormally.

Levels of safety. Consumer research can help in the development of specifications of safety and performance levels. Given the assumption that perfect safety is as impossible as zero defects in most other processes, some definition must be made of acceptable levels of safety or nonsafety. While this is partly a question of technical research, it is also a question of consumer research. For example, assume that a manufacturer of automobiles could install as standard equipment an improved braking system that would decrease injuries, but that the cost of the improved system would be $1,000. Or suppose that a manufacturer now averages one defect in the steering mechanism per 800,000 cars. Improved inspection systems and employee incentive compensation, it might be shown, could cut these defects to one in 1,000,000 cars, but at an additional cost per car of $40. Consumer research should be able to provide inputs helpful in making such decisions. For example, a safer computerized braking system is standard equipment on one line of automobile that costs approximately $10,000. If *all* automobiles were required to have this system, would society be better off or not? This is a segmentation question, and consumer research should be able to supply the number of low-income customers who would be denied the ability to purchase a car because of the increased safety standards. Are consumers better or worse served by laws which require high levels of safety and performance but at the same time reduce the possibility of purchasing the product by low-income consumers? Similar questions could be raised in many other industries.

The Consumer Product Safety Commission has begun to collect information about the relative hazards of products and, using various forms of research, constructs the Product Hazard Index, as a guide in policy decisions. A result of this process is shown in Figure 22.2, which lists the ten most hazardous products. The process of collecting this research is called the National Electronic Injury Surveillance System (NEISS) and involves a computer-based system for monitoring injuries reported in hospital emergency rooms across the country. The results from this research can then be used for establishing priorities in product standards.

It is important to remember that the research does not indicate the policies that must be promulgated. The research is only an *input* to policy decisions that must be promulgated by thoughtful individuals considering the data. This process was explained by the CPSC's first chairman:

> . . . It is important to realize that a high ranking on the Commission's Hazard Index does not mean a product will be banned or be the subject of a product safety rule. It simply means that the product is more likely

Figure 22.2 The ten most hazardous products (based on reports from emergency rooms compiled by the Consumer Product Safety Commission)

Rank	Product description
1	Bicycles and bicycle equipment
2	Stairs, ramps, landings (indoors and outdoors)
3	Doors, other than glass doors
4	Cleaning agents
5	Tables, nonglass
6	Beds (including springs and frames)
7	Football, activity related equipment and apparel
8	Swings, slides, seesaws, playground climbing equipment
9	Liquid fuels, kindling
10	Architectural glass

Source: Paul Busch, "A Review and Critical Evaluation of the Consumer Product Safety Commission: Marketing Management Implications," *Journal of Marketing*, vol. 40 (October 1976), p. 42. Reprinted from the *Journal of Marketing* published by the American Marketing Association.

to receive early attention. A coin, for example, is easily swallowed and can act as a damper and cause suffocation. (This perhaps explains why Life Savers have holes in their centers.) But the fact that coins rank high among the Index's "Top 25" does not mean that the CPSC will ban them.[38]

Consumer information

The right to be informed, enunciated by former President Kennedy, was described as the right of the consumer "to be protected against fraudulent, deceitful, or grossly misleading information, advertising, labeling, or other practices and to be given the facts he needs to make an informed choice." The contributions of consumer research can therefore be of two forms. The first form is in the area of *consumer deception* while the second form of research is directed toward relevance to *informed choices*.

Consumer deception. Consumers have the right to obtain information that is not misleading and that does not claim too much. They also have the right to product packaging and labeling that is not deceptive. The theoretical basis for such information is based upon the premise that such information will aid consumers in the proper allocation of their economic resources to maximize benefits and pleasure. Additionally, consumers are believed to have the right to clearly written statements of warranties and

38 Quoted in Paul Busch, "A Review and Critical Evaluation of the Consumer Product Safety Commission: Marketing Management Implications," *Journal of Marketing*, vol. 40 (October 1976), pp. 41–49.

credit provisions as well as procedures for the quick and effective handling of complaints.

In most countries of the world, it is illegal to lie in advertisements. Some might ask then why consumer research is necessary to understand whether or not an advertisement contains a lie. Why is it not possible merely to examine an advertisement and determine whether it contains false statements or not and abstain from making the statement if it is untrue? The research issues in such a situation would be legal and physical (does the product contain the attribute stated in the advertisement? does it have more of the attribute than competitive brands? etc.).

A behavioral definition of deception is beginning to be more accepted in the regulation of marketing communications than an objective definition. An objective definition of deception is one in which an objectively ascertainable material fact is presented falsely, is ambiguous, or is misleading. A behavioral (or subjective) defintion of deception, however, focuses upon the *consumer's perception* of the advertisement. Gardner, after reviewing the contributions of other consumer researchers on this topic, formulated the following definition of deception:

> If an advertisement (or advertising campaign) leaves the consumer with an impression(s) and/or belief(s) different from what would normally be expected if the consumer had reasonable knowledge, and that impression(s) and/or belief(s) is factually untrue or potentially misleading, then deception is said to exist.[39]

With this definition of deception, Gardner suggests three types of deception exist. One form of deception is the *unconscionable lie*, or claim that is completely false even using an objective definition of deception. The second form of deception is the *claim-fact discrepancy* or a claimed benefit that must be qualified (but is not, in the advertisement) for it to be properly understood and evaluated. The third form of deceptive communication is the *claim-belief interaction*, in which the communication interacts with the accumulated attitudes and beliefs of the consumer in such a manner as to leave a deceptive belief or attitude about the product in the communication.[40]

Claim-belief interaction may result from many possible causes. One possible cause would be the use of *color* in the automobile exhaust fumes of competitive gasolines but the absence of color in the exhaust from a car using the gasoline advertised. Although the advertising does not directly make such a claim, a consumer might easily conclude the advertised brand was more pollution free than competitive brands. *Symbols* such as "Hi-C" on fruit juice may cause consumers to conclude that the brand contains high amounts of vitamin C even though the product does not directly make that claim. *Endorsements* may cause a

39 David M. Gardner, "Deception in Advertising: A Conceptual Approach," *Journal of Marketing*, vol. 39 (January 1975), pp. 40–46.

40 Gardner, "Deception in Advertising." For a discussion of some of the research issues involved in these forms of deception see David M. Gardner, "Deception in Advertising: A Receiver Oriented Approach to Understanding," *Journal of Advertising Research* (Fall 1976), pp. 5–11 ff.

consumer to attribute more trustworthiness, credibility, or prestige to a product than is objectively true. Similarly, an actor who plays a well-known doctor may also deliver advertisements for a medical product and consumers may conclude that the product is recommended by physicians. It is possible that if the actor mentions that he is not a doctor, the consumer may selectively distort the message and remember only the word "doctor" and attribute *more* credibility than if the actor did not make the disclosure.[41] Consumer research can be used—in fact, is essential—to understanding the ways that such communications may be misleading and the proportions of the population that are misled[42] and it appears that regulatory agencies are beginning to incorporate such behavioral concepts of deception into their policies.[43]

Informed choices. Consumer research has a major function in defining the information required by consumers and its method of presentation to guarantee that consumers have the opportunity to make informed choices. The specific information relevant to a consumer's evaluative criteria varies greatly by the type of product involved, the purchase environment, and the target segment of the population. Thus, a research approach is required if understanding of the choice process is to be achieved. Such research must include the importance and complexity of the product in the mind of the consumer, the features that are important to each market segment, the accessibility of information, and the processability of information.

The most fundamental question to be answered by consumer research involves what constitutes relevant information to the consumer. In advertising, the attributes about which information is disclosed often involve *psychological association* whereas consumer advocates that what is needed is *performance information*, and that the withholding of such factual information by the seller is a deceptive practice.[44] Useful consumer research must define the evaluative criteria of consumers and the weights consumers place on those attributes rather than relying upon subjective interpretation or normative conclusions about what information is relevant to consumers.

Empirical research concerning the amount of information in television advertising indicates that less than one-half of advertisements are deemed informative in terms of price, quality, performance, availability and ten other evaluative criteria.[45] Recently, however, a hypothesis that has

41 Dorothy Cohen, "Surrogate Indicators and Deception in Advertising," *Journal of Marketing*, vol. 36 (July 1972), pp. 10–15. Another good overview of these problems is found in John A. Howard and James Hulbert, "Advertising and the Public Interest," *Journal of Advertising Research*, vol. 14 (December 1974), pp. 33–39.

42 Jacob Jacoby and Constance Small, "The FDA Approach to Defining Misleading Advertising," *Journal of Marketing*, vol. 39 (October 1975), pp. 65–73.

43 Ivan L. Preston, "A Comment on 'Defining Misleading Advertising' and 'Deception in Advertising,'" *Journal of Marketing*, vol. 40 (July 1976), pp. 54–60.

44 George S. Day, "Full Disclosure of Comparative Performance Information to Consumers: Problems and Prospects," *Journal of Contemporary Business*, vol. 4 (Winter 1975), pp. 53–68.

45 Alan Resnik and Bruce L. Stern, "An Analysis of Information Content in Television Advertising," *Journal of Marketing*, vol. 41 (January 1977), pp. 50–53.

been developed is that large-scale media advertising does not need to contain specific product information because consumers understand that the cost of such advertising campaigns and the prior market testing is so great that only products that are basically effective or fit the purpose for which they were advertised will be seen in national advertising campaigns.

Another possibility is that *too much information* can be communicated, causing consumers to make worse decisions than with less information. Jacoby and his associates have advanced the theory based upon their laboratory experiments that *information overload* can occur causing consumers to make poorer purchase decisions while feeling more satisfied and certain regarding their choice.[46] This might occur also if a seller provides many pieces of detailed information about credit costs, itemized prices, detailed product availability (colors, sizes, etc.) and so forth. Some segments of the market (perhaps highly educated and affluent professional persons) may assimilate and find this information relevant but other (less sophisticated) market segments may be overwhelmed or confused to the point that they make decisions based upon trivial (but not fully disclosed) criteria rather than more important and basic satisfactions desired from the product.

A number of policies and marketing practices have been adopted in an attempt to provide more relevant or greater amounts of information. One policy that has been voluntarily adopted by many firms and regulated as a policy in other situations is *unit pricing*, or the expression of the price of a good in terms of the cost per unit of measure (ounce, gram, etc.) in addition to its total price. While some research has indicated little effect of unit pricing on consumer choices[47] most studies conclude that consumers tend to shift their purchases toward lower unit price goods, at least in some product categories.[48] This may vary by market segment, of course, and Houton points out that it may be the "value-conscious" market segment that uses the information contained in unit pricing.[49] To make the issue more complex, Carman reviewed a number of studies on the *costs* of implementing and maintaining unit pricing and concluded that if *all* stores converted, the already low margins of retailers would be under

46 Jacob Jacoby, Donald E. Speller, and Carol A. Kohn, "Brand Choice Behavior as a Function of Information Load," *Journal of Marketing Research*, vol. 11 (February 1974), pp. 63–69; Jacob Jacoby, "Consumer Reaction to Information Displays: Packaging and Advertising," in Sal Divita, ed., *Advertising and the Public Interest* (Chicago: American Marketing Association, 1975).

47 Carl Block, Robert Schooler, and David Erickson, "Consumer Reaction to Unit Pricing: An Empirical Study," *Mississippi Valley Journal of Business and Economics*, vol. 7 (Winter 1971–72), pp. 36–46; David McCullough and Daniel I. Padbert, "Unit Pricing in Supermarkets," *Search: Agriculture*, vol. 1 (January 1971), pp. 1–22.

48 Clive W. Granger and Andrew Billson, "Consumers' Attitudes toward Package Size and Price," *Journal of Marketing Research*, vol. 9 (August 1972), pp. 239–48; Hans R. Isakson and Alex R. Maurizi, "The Consumer Economics of Unit Pricing," *Journal of Marketing Research*, vol. 10 (August 1973), pp. 277–85; J. Edward Russo, Gene Kreiser, and Sally Miyashita, "An Effective Display of Unit Price Information," *Journal of Marketing*, vol. 39 (April 1975), pp. 11–19; Kent B. Monroe and Peter J. LaPlaca, "What Are the Benefits of Unit Pricing?" *Journal of Marketing*, vol. 36, pp. 16–22. A nationwide survey indicated 81 percent in favor of unit pricing, reported in "Consumer Attitude Study," *Supermarketing* (April 1972), pp. 38–43.

49 Michael J. Houston, "The Effect of Unit-pricing on Choices of Brand and Size in Economic Shopping," *Journal of Marketing*, vol. 36 (July 1972), pp. 51–69.

even greater pressure.[50] Consequently, consumers might be paying more overall, even though receiving greater information. A related practice to provide greater information is *open dating*, or printing of a date clearly understandable by the consumer after which a product (especially perishable products) cannot be sold for consumption without a high risk of spoilage or loss in value. After reviewing the major empirical studies on this topic, Nayak and Rosenberg concluded that open dating was a low priority among marketing practices but that it generally provided more product information and quality-assured foods.[51]

Improved consumer information may also be attained through more detailed labeling and packaging information, especially *nutritional labeling*. In 1975, rules became effective promulgated by the Food and Drug Administration that substantially increased the amount of information that must be given on some food labels.[52] An example of this type of information is shown in Figure 22.3 and an example of the type which is *not* required is shown in Figure 22.4. Lenehan et al. found that consumers exhibit a clear preference for nutritional labels but that in supermarkets only about one-fourth of consumers were aware of nutritional labeling, about 15 percent understood them and less than 10 percent used them.[53] In another study, detailed nutritional labels were used by some consumers but labels with the promotional information "succulent and sweet" (as a description of canned peas) were comparable to nutritional labels in providing consumers with a feeling of quality assurance.[54] There is a need for much more research and creativity in understanding how to present relevant nutritional information and in other countries, such as the Netherlands, creative approaches are resulting in new, symbolic approaches to communicating nutritional qualities to consumers in standardized formats. One form of standardized product information, however—beef grading—has been found to provide little relevant information to consumers.[55]

One of the most major efforts in recent years to provide additional information to consumers with which to make more informed choices is in the area of credit information, specifically Truth In Lending (TIL). Many research studies have been conducted concerning this topic and are thoroughly reviewed by Day and Brandt.[56] By using a comprehensive

50 James M. Carman, "A Summary of Empirical Research on Unit Pricing in Supermarkets," *Journal of Retailing*, vol. 48 (Winter 1972–73), pp. 63–71.

51 Prabhaker Nayak and Larry J. Rosenberg, "Does Open Dating of Food Products Benefit the Consumer?" *Journal of Retailing*, vol. 51 (Summer 1975), pp. 10–20.

52 Warren A. French and Hiram C. Barksdale, "Food Labeling Regulations: Efforts toward Full Disclosure," *Journal of Marketing*, vol. 38 (July 1974), pp. 14–19; J. Boyd, "Food Labeling and the Marketing of Nutrition," *Journal of Home Economics*, vol. 65 (May 1973), pp. 20–24.

53 R. J. Lenehan et al., "Consumer Reaction to Nutritional Labels on Food Products," *Journal of Consumer Affairs*, vol. 7 (Summer 1973), pp. 1–12.

54 Edward H. Asam and Louis P. Bucklin, "Nutrition Labeling for Canned Goods: A Study of Consumer Response," *Journal of Marketing*, vol. 37 (April 1973), pp. 32–37.

55 John A. Miller, David G. Topel, and Robert E. Rust, "USDA Beef Grading: A Failure in Consumer Information?" *Journal of Marketing*, vol. 40 (January 1976), pp. 25–31.

56 George S. Day and William K. Brandt, "Consumer Research and the Evaluation of Information Disclosure Requirements: The Case of Truth in Lending," *Journal of Consumer Research*, vol. 1 (June 1974), pp. 21–31.

Figure 22.3 Example of nutritional labeling

Source: POST and GRAPE-NUTS are registered trademarks of General Foods Corporation. Package reproduction with the consent of General Foods Corporation.

model of consumer behavior similar to the one in this book, Day and Brandt isolated a major reason why TIL has been generally ineffective. They discovered that, although TIL has increased awareness and knowledge of interest rates, credit information is brought to the attention of the buyer *after* the purchase decision is made and that TIL had relatively little effect on credit search and usage behavior. They concluded:

What is clear, however, is that it is not enough to simply provide

Figure 22.4 Example of *non*required labeling

Source: From the *Wall Street Journal* (May 18, 1977), p. 22—Ray Morin. Reprinted by permission.

consumers with more information. That is simply the first step in a major educational task of getting consumers to understand the information, and persuading them to use it. Consumer researchers can make a significant contribution to both these tasks.[57]

Where should a consumer researcher begin in determining the kind of information that will improve consumer choices? This question faces researchers in business and in regulatory agencies. A very useful summary of the answers to this question was developed by Day. From Day's report on the topic, the following questions are suggested as the basis for research on consumer information:

1. What information is relevant?

2. Is the information accessible?

3. Can the information be comprehended?

4. How do information requirements vary among segments?

5. What changes occur over time in the effects of information?

6. How is the information of one member of the channel modified (positively or negatively) by other members of the channel?[58]

57 Day and Brandt, "Consumer Research," p. 31.
58 George S. Day, "Assessing the Effects of Information Disclosure Requirements," *Journal of Marketing*, vol. 40 (April 1976), pp. 42–52.

Consumer choice

The consumer is entitled to spend his or her money on any legal goods and services for satisfying the consumer's needs and wants. For this right to have meaning, however, goods and services should be at competitive prices from a number of alternative offerings.

The basic premise underlying the American economy and many others is that consumer choice is at a maximum in a competitive, market economy. In traditional, *laissez faire* economics, the consumer is best served by choosing from business firms freely competing, with individual choice from those firms constrained only by the consumer's own economic and physical resources. But what should the government—"the people"—do when business firms no longer freely compete? What should be done when firms use "unfair" forms of competition or competition is severely restricted? Even more difficult to answer is the question, should consumers be allowed to choose freely when they are choosing "unwisely"?

Regulated choice. The thrust of consumerism is toward control of what a firm offers, justified on the basis that contemporary corporations possess unequal power with consumers. Through merger and growth corporations have become so powerful, according to the assertion, that they can act without regard to the consumers' interests, thus justifying control by government or other institutions over their offering. Furthermore, rapid increases in innovation bring social change that historically has stimulated government intervention in attempts to mitigate social problems created by change.[59] A sociological analysis of the United States led Bell to predict the rise of nonmarket public decision making. He concludes, ". . . more and more of the problems confronting us cannot be settled by the market, cannot be settled by the private sector, but involve community decisions."[60]

There is an implicit assumption in many consumerist policies that consumers ought to be forced to do what is "best" for them. Thus consumerism has resulted in laws that force consumers to purchase seat belts rather than allow consumers to make the choice themselves. Laws have been passed in some states that require motorcyclists to purchase and wear helmets for their own protection.

At a more basic level, consumerists raise the issue of whether the consumers are spending their resources on the "right" products. In Moran's study of consumerism and public policy, he quotes a consumerist view on this subject:

> What does a contemporary consumer do, faced with the bewildering array of new products, new materials, new processes, compounded by the brand explosion? How does he choose? He is influenced by the sweet purrings of an attractive salesman (or woman) often less informed about product differences than the customer and also biased by push

---

59 Evidence for this view is presented in Robert W. Austin, "Who Has the Responsibility for Social Change—Business or Government?" *Harvard Business Review* (July–August 1965), pp. 45–52.

60 Daniel Bell, "Social Trends of the 70's," *Conference Board Record* (June 1970), pp. 6–9.

money, spiffs, and other manufacturer bribes. He is beguiled by style at the expense of safety and stamina, by gleam instead of guts, by features and gimmicks in place of performance and economy.[61]

This view is also related to earlier opinions of Galbraith, Packard, and others that the consumer should be prevented from spending his money on luxuries and should instead spend them on better schools, highways, health care, and basic needs.

Adaptionists believe that the control of consumer choice can be achieved by *educating* consumers to make "better" decisions. More radical positions indicate the need for government *intervention* and regulation to ensure that choices are made for products that are good for the consumer and the society.

Consumer research cannot solve these basic policy and philosophical issues, but it can contribute information helpful in their resolution. It is interesting to think through what the meaning of consumer choice is for maintaining competition. One view leads to the conclusion that when marketers provide more and more choice (product differentiations rather than a commodity approach), the ultimate effect is to transform competitive industries into noncompetitive industries. The remedy for such a situation might be to *restrict* the offering of diverse forms of products. The FTC might place a moratorium on style changes in the auto industry, for example, in order to obtain *more* competition.[62]

Consumer education. An opposite approach is the position that enough regulation of choice already exists—or there is even too much of it. What is needed, perhaps, is not more regulation but more intelligence on the part of consumers.[63] In an investigation of ten consumerism topics about which regulations exist, one study found that as few as a third of consumers possessed knowledge of the consumerism law. Furthermore, a sample of attorneys had only a little higher knowledge than consumers.[64] The starting place might well be additional education about consumer rights before additional regulation is enacted.

The conclusion of Sheth and Mammana is that child-rearing practices and secondary school education should be changed to teach the new generation to cope with the complex choice processes of a mass consumption society. Specifically, they recommend that such education should contain the following elements:

1. Formal knowledge about the criteria with which to evaluate complex technical products and services and choose rationally among them;

61 Moran, "Formulating Public Policy on Consumer Issues," pp. 35.

62 H. Paul Root, "Should Product Differentiation Be Restricted?" *Journal of Marketing*, vol. 36 (July 1972), pp. 3–9.

63 James T. Rothe and Lissa Benson, "Intelligent Consumption: An Attractive Alternative to the Marketing Concept," *MSU Business Topics*, vol. 22 (Winter 1974), pp. 29–34.

64 William H. Cunningham and Isabella C. M. Cunningham, "Consumer Protection: More Information or More Regulation?" *Journal of Marketing*, vol. 40 (April 1976), pp. 63–68.

2. Managerial and decision-making skills as consumers, comparable to the type of skills we inculcate in people to become professional workers in industry or government;

3. Increased consumer knowledge of the workings of business, government, and the marketplace; and

4. Values and consciousness that will encourage respect and concern for other consumers in their pursuit of collective consumption.[65]

Consumer redress

The consumer has the right to expect sellers and other organizations to provide a rapid, convenient means for registering dissatisfactions and to assure the consumer that complaints will be heard by competent management and evaluated objectively. Furthermore, consumers have the right to expect a reasonable and satisfactory resolution of the complaint.

Consumer redress can be achieved in at least three ways.[66] The first method is *prevention*. Stated alternatively, one way to solve the problem of redress is for consumers to be heard *before the problem develops*. A second way for consumers to be heard and bring about change in the offering of the offending seller is through *restitution*. Many of these relate to advertising practices and include affirmative disclosures and corrective advertising, as well as repayment of funds and limitations on contracts.

One limitation on consumer contracts is the imposition of a "cooling-off period," which gives the consumer the right to rescind the contract within a specified period.[67] A third form of redress is by *punishment* of the erring seller, through fines, incarceration, class action suits and other legal processes. The Federal Trade Commission can now fine violators of trade practices rules up to $10,000 per day per violation, certainly an incentive to listen to the consumer. (See Figure 22.5.)

An important process in obtaining the right of the consumer to be heard is the *warranty*. In 1975, Congress passed the Magnuson-Moss Warranty—Federal Trade Commission Improvement Act, which had as a major purpose improving consumer product warranty practices.[68] This was not just a legal reform but a major effort to understand the needs of the consumer in this area and better meet those needs. Specifically, the FTC now has the power to examine warranties to determine whether, even if objectively accurate, they have the probable effect of producing *misleading* misrepresentations. Procedures are also examined to insure *ease of access* for the consumer to obtain warranty service. Finally, an attempt is now made to prevent *obscurity of terms*. The objective by

65 Jagdish N. Sheth and Nicholas J. Mammana, "Recent Failures in Consumer Protection," *California Management Review*, vol. 16 (Spring 1974), pp. 64–72, at 71.

66 Dorothy Cohen, "Remedies for Consumer Protection: Prevention, Restitution, or Punishment," *Journal of Marketing*, vol. 39 (October 1975), pp. 24–31.

67 Dennis H. Tootelian, "Potential Impact of 'Cooling-Off' Laws on Direct-to-Home Selling," *Journal of Retailing*, vol. 51 (Spring 1975), pp. 61–70; Orville C. Walker, Jr., and Neil M. Ford, "Can 'Cooling-Off' Laws' Really Protect the Consumer?" *Journal of Marketing*, vol. 34 (April 1970), pp. 53–58.

68 Laurence P. Feldman, "New Legislation and the Prospects for Real Warranty Reform," *Journal of Marketing*, vol. 40 (July 1976), pp. 41–47.

Figure 22.5 Remedies for consumer protection

Prevention	Restitution	Punishment
Codes of conduct	Affirmative disclosure	Fines and incarceration
Disclosure of information requirements	Corrective advertising	Loss of profits
Substantiation of claims	Refunds Limitations on contracts Arbitration	Class action suits

Source: Dorothy Cohen, "Remedies for Consumer Protection: Prevention, Restitution, or Punishment," *Journal of Marketing*, vol. 39 (October 1975), pp. 24–31, at p. 25. Reprinted from the *Journal of Marketing* published by the American Marketing Association.

which the warranty should be evaluated (with the assistance of consumer research) is whether or nor the average consumer can understand the warranty.

Many of the provisions that have been enacted to protect consumers' rights to be heard are not new. They may have existed under previous law but the average consumer may have experienced so much difficulty or cost in obtaining them, that the rights were essentially inoperative for the typical consumer. Many of these new provisions are an attempt to help the "little guy."

The right to be heard is not achieved only with forced or regulatory policies. Many far sighted companies have recognized that voluntary action in this area provides a significant opportunity for improved customer relations and loyalty.[69] An outstanding example is the Whirlpool Corporation, which started a Cool-Line program in 1967, providing a personal and easily accessible communications link between customers and a trained staff of product and service experts. The company receives over 150,000 calls per year and finds that over 90 percent can be resolved during the initial telephone call. Thus, possible sources of major complaints and formal redress are often resolved satisfactorily before the problem gets out of hand.[70]

Environmental responsibility

Large numbers of people with large amounts of money in a technologically advanced society produce large amounts of energy consumption, pollution, and other stresses on the society. This condition requires radically increased information about the feasibility of institutional responses to the problem and consumer priorities for those responses. An increased need for research and analytical thinking about consumption is

69 C. L. Kendall and Frederick A. Russ, "Warranty and Complaint Policies: An Opportunity for Marketing Management," *Journal of Marketing*, vol. 39 (April 1975), pp. 36–43.

70 "Whirlpool Corporation," in Blackwell, Engel, and Talarzyk, *Contemporary Cases in Consumer Behavior*, pp. 309–18. For another excellent program see "Eaton's Department Store," in this same source, pp. 46–51.

"SURE IT'S UNFAIR TO THE LITTLE GUY – HE'S THE EASIEST ONE TO BE UNFAIR WITH."

Source: *Wall Street Journal* (May 19, 1977), p. 20. Reprinted by permission of the Wall Street Journal.

also the result of the increased interdependency of consumer decisions. Feldman describes how a system based upon individual choice but with societal effects must be analyzed differently (with a systems approach) from a system with only individual implications:

> One reason . . . is that marketing decisions have been made which expanded the range of consumer product choice but disregarded their environmental impact. There has been a failure to recognize that these products, which are marketing outputs designed for individual satisfaction, are simultaneously inputs to a large environmental system and as such may affect the well-being of society.[71]

The first task of consumer research is to aid in the definition of what might be acceptable environmental goals. Assuming that perfection is impossible, consumer research should aid in determining what levels of pollution (air, water, and so forth) are really required to coincide with consumers' desired use of time for leisure, physical products, food preferences, location preferences, and so forth. One of the few researchers to

---

71 Laurence P. Feldman, "Societal Adaptation: A New Challenge for Marketing," *Journal of Marketing*, vol. 35 (July 1971), pp. 54–60.

approach analytically the issue of environmental goals is Feinberg. He observes that:

> Given the wide variety of environments existing in the world, each inhabited by people who are reasonably content with it, I have the impression that a person's idea of a good environment is usually the one he grew up in, and that not much thought has really been given to the general question of what makes an environment good.
>
> It is conceivable that most people would prefer the whole world to be like Polynesia with respect to climate and easy availability of food, and that we could actually engineer the world into such a form. If so, it would be good to know this preference so that we could set about working to satisfy it.[72]

Feinberg continues by pointing out that from the point of view of basic science, no aspect of the natural environment is really essential to human life. Rather, protection or creation of any specified type of environment must be viewed in terms of offsetting aspects of the environment that must be forfeited:

> I believe that eventually we will be forced into making many choices of this type, where doing one thing precludes doing something else which otherwise might be desirable. We must ask ourselves whether preserving the environment is to be the controlling factor in making all such choices, or if not, what other principles can be brought to bear. To me, the answer is clearly that preserving the environment is only one of several factors in making any decision, and that we would do well to clarify these other factors.[73]

The other factors that must be given up to attain certain types of environments include many things besides money. The monetary costs of simply maintaining a basic stability in the existing environment, however, have been estimated by the Harvard Center for Population Studies to be about $5.1 billion for capital costs and $8.4 billion of operating costs on an annual basis.[74] These costs include air pollution, water pollution, and solid waste disposal. One of the functions of consumer research could be to establish priorities among these if all are not accepted by voters.

The study of consumer behavior should also disclose the degree to which consumers will voluntarily purchase ecologically beneficial products in preference to polluting products. Henion found that consumers voluntarily purchased low-phosphate detergents in sufficient numbers to produce a shift in market share to the ecologically preferred brands.[75] There is a considerable amount of information found in the business press

72 Gerald Feinberg, "Long-Range Goals and the Environment," *The Futurist* (December 1971), pp. 241–47, at p. 244.

73 Feinberg, "Long-Range Goals," p. 245.

74 "Who Will Foot the Cleanup Bill," *Business Week* (January 3, 1970), pp. 63–64; also William W. Sihler and Charles O. Meiburg, "The War on Pollution: Economic and Financial Impacts," *Business Horizons*, vol. 14 (August 1971), pp. 19–30.

75 Karl E. Henion, "The Effect of Ecologically Relevant Information on Detergent Sales," *Journal of Marketing Research*, vol. 9 (February 1972), pp. 15–18.

to indicate that for some products and under some circumstances, consumers do respond favorably to firms that offer ecological products for sale and follow business practices designed to protect the environment.[76]

Persons with high concern about social responsibility were identified by Anderson and Cunningham and Webster,[77] and another study specifically investigated the characteristics of consumers most concerned with ecology. A profile of these individuals indicates they are high in agreement with statements that indicate openness to new ideas, high in the need to understand the workings of things and harm avoidance. They also tend to be in the higher income category.[78]

An immediate need by marketers for information about ecology and the consumerism movements is created by necessity of carefully evaluating new product strategies in light of changed environmental realities. Varble maintains that traditional economic criteria no longer will provide an adequate basis for new product evaluation decisions.[79] Nonusers of products, acting through government or consumerist groups, may demand a voice in the marketing of products used by others but which harm the natural or social environment or use up unreasonable amounts of scarce resources. Social and environmental costs, such as cleaning up the air and water, may be charged back to the costs of the products of a polluting firm. The effects of shortages may be manifested in market opportunities for recycled products, "demarketing" of some products and services (such as those of utility companies, gasoline marketers, etc.) may become necessary, regional shopping centers may be affected by gasoline shortages as may store hours and services of all retailers.[80] All of these possibilities create an increased information requirement both in terms of understanding the physical environment and its limits as well as the priorities and patterns of the consumers who live in the environment.[81]

76 For numerous examples of efforts to market ecological products, see the following: "Business Fights Pollution—and the Nation Profits," *Nation's Business* (February 1970), pp. 29–30; "Turning Junk and Trash into a Resource," *Business Week* (October 10, 1970), pp. 66–75; "Waste Control," *Chain Store Age* (November 1970), pp. 23–34; "Does Ecology Sell?" *Sales Management* (November 15, 1970), pp. 32–34; "Can Pollution Pay Off?" *Business Week* (January 16, 1971), pp. 46–47; "Pollution: Its New Dimensions for Business," *Canadian Business*, pp. 32–36, (Mar. 1971); "More Stores Will Switch to 'Home Ecology' in '71," *Chain Store Age* (March 1971), pp. 66–67ff; "An Operator Who Sells Ecology," *Progressive Grocer* (October 1971), pp. 78–82.

77 Anderson and Cunningham, "Socially Conscious Consumer"; Webster, "Determining the Characteristics of the Socially Conscious Consumer."

78 Thomas C. Kinnear, James R. Taylor, and Sadrudin A. Ahmed, "Ecologically Concerned Consumers: Who Are They?" *Journal of Marketing*, vol. 38 (April 1974), pp. 20–24.

79 Dale L. Varble, "Social and Environmental Considerations in New Product Development," *Journal of Marketing*, vol. 36 (October 1972), pp. 11–15.

80 A. B. Blankenship and John H. Holmes, "Will Shortgages Bankrupt the Marketing Concept," *MSU Business Topics*, vol. 22 (Spring 1974), pp. 13–18.

81 Also see the following: W. Thomas Anderson, Jr., Louis K. Sharpe, and Robert J. Boewadt, "The Environmental Role for Marketing," *MSU Business Topics*, vol. 20 (Summer 1973), pp. 66–72; Dwight R. Lee, "The Quality of Life: A Changing Emphasis," *Atlanta Economic Review* (March–April 1975), pp. 20–23; Charles G. Leathers, "New Dimensions of Countervailing Power: Consumerism and Environmentalism," *MSU Business Topics*, vol. 20 (Winter 1972), pp. 64–72; Hans B. Thorelli, "A Consumer View of Inflation and the Economy," *Business Horizons* (December 1974), pp. 25–31; Harrison Grathwohl, "Planned Obsolescence and Resource Allocation," *Journal of Contemporary Business*, vol. 4 (Winter 1975), pp. 85–96; John H. Sheridan, "Which Pollution Answers Are Winning?" *Management Review* (February 1976), pp. 45–48.

The United States is a nation with over 25 million consumers living in poverty. Nearly a third of these are black consumers, the largest racial minority group.[82] Among the consumerism thrusts is a recognition of a special responsibility for the problems of minorities and of the poor.[83]

Consumer research appears to have three major contributions to relieving the problems of minorities and of the poor. The first is research directed toward the question of how to "stretch" or *allocate more efficiently the limited resources* of the poor and of those who have been subject to discrimination. These studies require two outputs. First, they need to compare consumption problems of the minorities with consumption problems of the majorities to determine if the basis exists for separate strategies. Are there a unique set of problems among minorities and the poor to which special efforts in regulation, marketing information, or education should be directed? Second, studies directed toward stretching the resources of the poor need to determine the feasibility of possible changes in marketing activities.

A second basic contribution of consumer research in this area is in the *improvement of marketing efficiency* among firms and organizations that serve minorities and the poor. For example, in a study of black store managers it was found that one of the major problems deterring success was the reluctance on the part of the black community to buy in black-run stores.[84] Sturdivant has conducted considerable research on ghetto retailers and has concluded that investment guarantees and enlarged investment tax credits are needed in order to stimulate adequate retail facilities to serve the consumers of the ghetto.[85]

A third contribution of consumer research is through *studies of the majority segments* to determine the degree to which they contribute to the consumer problems of the minority. Housing is a major problem among black consumers, for example, and a thorough study by Sanoff et al. discloses many relationships between nonwhite housing availability and white movements.[86] This study shows that whites often move out when blacks move in, partially because of fear of declining property values. Yet Sanoff's research shows that the fear that whites have of property values declining is unfounded. Similar research by Rapkin indicates that if the black population in a neighborhood rises above 40 percent, the demand for housing in that area by whites will tend to be zero, thereby causing the

82 These and other relevant statistics are presented in Eli P. Cox, "What Is Poverty? Who Are the Poor?" *MSU Business Topics* (Summer 1971), pp. 5–10.

83 See Chapter 4; also Donald E. Sexton, Jr., "Do Blacks Pay More?" *Journal of Marketing Research*, vol. 8, (November 1971), pp. 420–26.

84 Dan H. Fenn, Jr., "NAFC Probes Three Major Issues of the 70's: Economy, Technology, Consumerism," *Chain Store Age* (December 1970), pp. 31–34.

85 Frederick D. Sturdivant, "Better Deal for Ghetto Shoppers," *Harvard Business Review* (March–April 1968), pp. 130–39; For additional solutions to these problems, see Allan T. Demaree, "Business Picks up the Urban Challenge," *Fortune*, vol. 79 (April 1969), pp. 102–104ff, Richard F. America, Jr., "What Do You People Want," *Harvard Business Review* (March–April 1969), pp. 103–12.

86 Henry Sanoff et al., "Changing Residential Racial Patterns," *Urban and Social Change Review*, vol. 4 (Spring 1971), pp. 68–71.

neighborhood to turn completely black in about five years.[87] Research such as these studies can provide important inputs into the development of policies by government, business firms, and other organizations that will aid consumers, both of minority groups and of majority groups.

The responsibility to minorities and the poor is connected to broader issues about urban areas as a whole. It is clear that business in general and consumer researchers specifically will want and probably be required to play a vital role in the determination of the kind of urban environment that should be built for consumers of the future and the ways that acceptance will be achieved.[88] It would be difficult to expect, for example, that new towns would be successful without a great deal of research into all aspects of consumer decision making about and in them.[89]

Some research has focused on the problems of disadvantaged consumers but Sturdivant and Deutscher observe that in the main this research focused on questions such as: "Do minorities face discrimination in the marketplace?" "Do the poor pay more?" "Where do the poor shop?" and so forth. Very little was done to construct a theoretical frame within which the findings from these studies could be analyzed and applied.[90] After thoroughly reviewing the research, Sturdivant and Deutscher concluded that the areas of highest priority for research on the purchasing behavior of disadvantaged consumers were the following. First, attention should be directed to the cognitive dimensions of individual factors rather than "nose-counting" surveys of previous research. This would include concepts such as cognitive effects of communications, quality perception as related to price, cognitive dissonance and other topics, which are well-used in research with majority consumers but seldom used at all in research concerned with disadvantaged consumers. A second field of promise for research on low-income consumers is decision making within the household. Although this is not a well-developed area in the general consumer behavior literature (see Chapter 6), it is particularly important in understanding the purchasing of low-income consumers because of the high proportion of one-parent families and other special problems. A third area of unusual opportunity identified by Sturdivant and Deutscher is the investigation of reference groups and their influence on the disadvantaged consumer. This is of special interest because of the effect of reference groups on the aspirations, attitudes and behavior of disadvantaged consumers.[91]

87 Chester Rapkin, *The Demand for Housing in Racially Mixed Areas* (Berkeley: University of California Press, 1960), p. 68.

88 Myron Lieberman, "New Communities: Business on the Urban Frontier," *Saturday Review* (May 15, 1971), pp. 20–31ff.

89 John B. Lansing, Robert W. Marans, and Robert B. Zehner, *Planned Residential Environments* (Ann Arbor, Mich.: Braun-Frumfield, 1970); Gurney Breckenfeld, *Columbia and the New Cities* (New York: Washburn, 1971).

90 Frederick D. Sturdivant and Terry Deutscher, "Disadvantaged Consumers: Research Dimensions," WPS 76–44, Ohio State University, July 1976.

91 Sturdivant and Deutscher, "Disadvantaged Consumers." Also see Henry O. Pruden and Douglas S. Longman, "Race, Alienation and Consumerism," *Journal of Marketing*, vol. 36 (July 1972), pp. 58–70. For practical suggestions on helping low income consumers, see Robin T. Peterson, "Low Income Consumer Education by Business—A Neglected Activity," *Marquette Business Review* (Summer 1976), pp. 74–79.

Another problem affecting consumers is the one created when they *fail* to buy products which are beneficial to themselves or to the human community of which they are a part. This is the converse of the problem discussed above. One solution that has been proposed to this problem is to apply the tools of marketing practitioners to "social products." The possibility of broadening the concept of marketing to products, services, ideas, and people (such as politicians) of nonbusinesses was analyzed in a classic article by Kotler and Levy.[92]

Kotler and Levy describe the importance of understanding consumer behavior for organizations such as fund raisers:

> Fund raising illustrates how an industry has benefited by replacing stereotypes of donors with studies of why people contribute to causes. Fund raisers have learned that people give because they are getting something. Many give to community chests to relieve a sense of guilt because of their elevated state compared to the needy. Many give to medical charities to relieve a sense of fear that they may be struck by a disease whose cure has not yet been found. Some give to feel pride. Fund raisers have stressed the importance of identifying the motives operating in the marketplace of givers as a basis for planning drives.[93]

There are several areas of social marketing that have received considerable research. Kotler and Zaltman review these areas.[94] The marketing of birth control devices and the concept of planned parenthood is perhaps one of the best researched social products.[95] In analyzing pricing of hospital services, Feldstein included several consumer demographic variables and a proxy variable for consumer attitudes toward medical services.[96] Considerable consumer research was conducted in a study of consumer decision making for physician services.[97] In another social product area, the importance of marketing strategy and a research approach for religious organizations is described.[98] Finally, it appears that there is considerable consumer research of a sophisticated and comprehensive nature used in the development of marketing strategy for political candidates. While most of the research is not published, one publication of such research received widespread circulation.[99]

Marketing of social products

92 Philip Kotler and Sidney J. Levy, "Broadening the Concept of Marketing," *Journal of Marketing*, vol. 33 (January 1969), pp. 10–15.

93 Kotler and Levy, "Broadening the Concept of Marketing," p. 14; also William A. Mindak and H. Malcolm Bybec, "Marketing's Application to Fund Raising," *Journal of Marketing*, vol. 35 (July 1971), pp. 13–18; and Kotler, *Marketing for Nonmarketing Organizations*.

94 Philip Kotler and Gerald Zaltman, "Social Marketing: An Approach to Planned Social Change," *Journal of Marketing*, vol. 35 (July 1971), pp. 3–12.

95 Julian L. Simon, "A Huge Marketing Research Task—Birth Control," *Journal of Marketing Research*, vol. 5 (Feburary 1968); pp. 21–27. This article reviews prior research on the subject.

96 Martin S. Feldstein, "Hospital Cost Inflation: A Study of Nonprofit Price Dynamics," *American Economic Review* (1971), pp. 853–69. Also Gerald Zaltman and Ilan Vertinsky, "Health Service Marketing: A Suggested Model," *Journal of Marketing*, vol. 35 (July 1971), pp. 19–27.

97 R. D. Blackwell and W. W. Talarzyk, *Consumer Attitudes toward Health Care and Medical Malpractice* (Columbus: Grid Publishing, 1977).

98 McGavran, *Understanding Church Growth*; Engel, op. cit. Also see A. W. Van Dyke, "Stop Killing Us with Kindness," *Journal of Marketing*, vol. 40 (July 1976), pp. 90–91.

99 Joe McGinnis, *The Selling of the President, 1968* (New York: Trident Press, 1969). Also see "Moody vs. Sensenbrenner" in W. W. Talarzyk, *Contemporary Cases in Marketing.* (Hinsdale, Ill.: Dryden Press, 1974), pp. 233–41.

The kind of research required for the development of marketing strategies for social products does not differ greatly from traditional marketing problems. A decision-process market-segmentation approach is needed for better understanding of important areas of social marketing.

The criticality of a segmentation approach

It is incorrect to assume that an understanding of all of the consumer rights and needs discussed above can be achieved by an aggregative approach to consumer research. A market segmenation approach is necessary.

In many cases, the abuses that lead to outcries for consumerism affect only a small portion of the market. In other cases, a majority of a market may be concerned about some aspect of consumerism but will vary greatly in response or acceptance of a solution to the problem. Most of the consumer research that has been conducted on consumerism issues has not faced up to this problem, especially when attempting to deal with solutions to the problems.

Business firms are very familiar with the concept of market segmentation but government regulators are often not accustomed to thinking about a policy that will apply or be beneficial to only a portion of the market. It is apparent, however, that policy makers must become accustomed to thinking in such terms for the need exists for a *market segmentation approach* to the problems of consumerism. And consumer researchers must be able to supply the information that permits the design of precisely-targeted programs.

Summary

The consumer has the right to safety, the right to be informed, the right to choose from an adequate selection of products, and the right to be heard. These rights have been reaffirmed by decree and administrative action since John F. Kennedy declared them in 1962. Yet, there is ample evidence to show that these rights are violated constantly, creating a rising interest in consumerism programs.

Historical antecedents of consumerism resulted in legislation such as the Pure Food and Drug Act, just as the outcries of consumers have resulted in contemporary protective legislation. Increased pressures for social responsibility, led by educated and affluent segments of the market, have been an important impetus for protection of consumers' rights.

A research approach to consumerism is provided by the discipline of consumer behavior that has the potential of becoming a boundary spanning agent between conflicting interests of business, government, and consumer advocacy groups.

This chapter discusses some of the research, mostly from empirical studies, directed to understanding consumer rights and needs. These areas of inquiry include consumer safety, consumer information, consumer choice, the right to be heard (redress), environmental protection, responsibilities to minorities and the poor, and social marketing.

This chapter focuses upon objective analyses of consumer behavior as it relates to consumerism issues. The action implications for business firms and consumer protection agencies are described in the final chapter of the book, along with some perspectives on the ethics of consumer influence.

Review and discussion questions

1. Is the consumerism of recent years fundamentally similar to or different from than that of previous eras?

2. Provide a definition of consumerism that will be adequate for research purposes in consumer behavior.

3. If you were asked to prepare a list of the most pressing problems of consumers in a country, how could it be done? Specify the research design that you would use.

4. Describe the issue of consumer information and analyze the role of market segmentation in understanding this issue.

5. How can the concept of "satisfaction" be measured for a consumer product?

6. Why don't firms design safe products for consumers? In what ways might consumer research be helpful to the engineering and design of new products?

7. Can consumers receive too much information? Explain.

8. What is meant by the concept of deception?

9. What is "social marketing"? What should be the role of consumer research in social marketing?

10. Analyze the issues raised in this chapter concerning responsibility to minorities and the poor. Develop a proposal for consumer research that might be helpful in solving some of these problems.

CHAPTER 23

The regulation and ethics of consumer influence

At the end of the book, there is a need to think about a few additional topics. In 22 previous chapters, information has been presented with which to understand how people make decisions about products and services. Materials have also shown how consumers might be influenced to accept the product and service offering of one organization rather than another. Throughout the book, however, the emphasis is upon what *can* or *might* be done by an organization intending to influence consumers. At some point, every consumer analyst must face the additional question of what *should* be done.

This chapter contains applications of materials presented in the preceding chapter. The applications concern responses to consumerism as it was described in Chapter 22. Those responses are to forces more basic than just the consumerism movement, however. The applications or concerns discussed in this chapter relate to the entire issue of *using knowledge about the consumer to influence the consumer.* The study of consumer behavior enhances the ability to influence the consumer and that ability can be used for "good" purposes or "bad" purposes.

The possible responses of three types of organizations and individuals are described in this chapter. Consumer influence is a force that has been and must be considered by the *government.* The result of its consideration has been enormous expansion in recent years of government regulation of the ability to influence consumers. The ability to influence consumers must also, of course, be considered by *business firms* and has been considered for many years. The need to consider consumer interpretations of that influence is now resulting in more structured systems of monitoring consumer beliefs and behavior. Finally, it is essential that *individuals* consider their own role in the enhanced ability to influence consumers. Are there some activities of consumer influence that an individual employed by an organization ought not to do even though asked to do so by the employer? If so, how does one make such individual decisions? These are the topics of Chapter 23.

The basis for regulation of consumer influence

The basis for regulating or controlling consumer influence and other business decisions rests upon three primary considerations. (1) legal regulations, (2) self-interest and voluntary codes, and (3) personal convictions or ethics.[1]

Legal regulations are forms of compulsion enacted to force compliance with community or national norms of behavior. Legal regulations may occur at the level of the local community, the state or province, or at the national level and may include both laws enacted by legislators or rules which have the effect of law promulgated by various regulatory agencies. Generally, laws regulating the ability to influence consumers have arisen because of abuses of those attempting to influence consumers.

Self-interest and voluntary codes are based upon the premise that behavior that influences consumers positively is in the firm's own self-interest, at least in the long run. Belief in the *laissez faire* economic system or modifications of it leads to the conclusion that competition is the best protector of improper competition. While a company may abuse a consumer initially, continuance of such a practice will lead to the demise of that firm and its replacement by one more precisely attuned to the needs of the consumer. Sometimes, the recognition occurs within a group of competitors that some competitors have differing opinions about consumer influence and abuse and the competitors, usually working through a trade association, prepare a voluntary code for the industry. Such codes may have a positive influence on those firms that have a basic, long-term commitment to the market place but usually are ineffective against deviant members of the industry who do not choose to comply.

Personal *convictions* about ethics arise from an integrated sense of personal and social values. Ethics is concerned with right and wrong. In some instances, the ethical standards of an organization relating to consumer influence may be those of an individual because that individual has power through ownership to control the ethics of the firm or because of the persuasiveness of that individual in obtaining adherence to those ethical standards by other employees and stockholders of the firm.[2]

Decisions about programs and policies of consumer influence are usually based on a combination of all three bases for controlling consumer influence. Each is discussed in additional detail in the following pages.

1 Adapted from Robert Bartels, "A Model for Ethics in Marketing," *Journal of Marketing*, vol. 31 (January 1967), pp. 26.
2 For additional details on these topics, see Richard E. Stanley, *Promotion* (Englewood Cliffs: Prentice-Hall, 1977), pp. 89–95.

The regulation of consumer influence

Regulation of activities designed to influence consumers has generally arisen because of clearcut abuses. Historically, at least, this has been true although recently some attention of regulatory agencies is being directed toward the topic of preventing abuses before they have the opportunity of becoming prevalent. Many types of laws and regulatory actions have developed to combat the abuses. Some of those most likely to affect the conduct of consumer research and the development of consumer influence programs (such as advertising, personal selling, and so forth) are described in the following section. Many other laws, such as the Robinson-Patman Act, are important influences on business practices generally and at times may have some direct influence on consumer programs, but the discussion below omits those more general laws and concentrates on those regulations most directly concerned with consumer influence.[3]

The laws that regulate consumer influence

The laws that protect consumers are based upon a historical foundation of laws that were enacted *to protect competition*. The basic premise of such laws are consumerist in theory even though their enactment was often more closely associated with pressures from small businesses seeking protection from larger "predatory" businesses and business practices. Laws designed to promote competition are "consumerist" in the sense that they are based upon the premise that consumers can achieve the highest average standard of living when the economy is organized on a competitive basis rather than a controlled basis. When monopolies or other aberrations in free competition developed, laws were justified that were designed to prevent such monopolies and restraints on competition.

Sherman Act. The foundation for the most important consumer protection laws is the Sherman Act, passed by Congress in 1890. The Sherman Act was passed after a public clamor over the treatment of consumers and small businesses by huge monopolies or trusts that controlled supplies of sugar, ice, petroleum, and other products. The greatest clamor arose from farmers who were being bullied by the railroads into paying excessive prices and meeting unreasonable conditions for shipping. Congress finally responded, after decades of these abuses, by passing the Sherman Act, which forbids "every contract or combination, in the form of trust, or otherwise, or conspiracy in the restraint of trade or commerce among the several states or with foreign nations."

Although the Sherman Act laid the basis for later legislation, it was generally ineffective, first because of some court rulings that exempted most businesses from the act and later because it was so general in its

---

3 For discussion of broader legal and public policy issues in marketing, see Louis W. Stern and John R. Grabner, Jr., *Competition in the Marketplace* (Glenview, Ill.: Scott, Foresman and Company, 1970). Also, see Theodore Beckman, William R. Davidson, and Wayne Talarzyk, *Marketing* (New York: Ronald Press, 1971); Ben M. Enis, *Marketing Principles* (Santa Monica, Calif.: Goodyear Publishing Company, Inc., 1977), chap. 4; David J. Schwartz, *Marketing Today* (New York: Harcourt Brace Jovanovich, 1977), chap. 28; Larry J. Rosenberg, *Marketing* (Englewood Cliffs: Prentice-Hall, 1977), chaps. 3 and 4.

prohibitions. More specific legislation was passed in 1914 in the form of the Clayton Act which forbids specific practices relating to business organization and practices and in the form of the Federal Trade Commission Act.[4]

The FTC Act. The Federal Trade Commission Act, passed in 1914, was an amendment to the Sherman Act and established the Federal Trade Commission, the federal agency regulating the greatest number of marketing practices. In its original form, the FTC had power only to police methods of unfair competition; that is, activities that unfairly injured other firms. For example, in the Raladam case (1931) the Supreme Court ruled that the FTC did not have authority to prevent a firm from misrepresenting an obesity cure because the firm's action did not injure competition. To overcome this problem, Congress passed the *Wheeler-Lea Act* (1938), which was an amendment to Section 5 of the FTC Act (which, it will be remembered, was an amendment to the Sherman Act). The Wheeler-Lea Act made the FTC the "watchdog for the consumer" by making unlawful those acts unfair and deceptive whether or not they injure competition. Wheeler-Lea (which is sometimes called the "advertising act") also gave the FTC additional enforcement powers and specifically prohibited false advertising of food, drugs, therapeutic devices, and cosmetics.

The Federal Trade Commission is an agency consisting of several thousand staff members, mostly attorneys, economists and support staff, headed by five commissioners who are appointed by the president of the United States and confirmed by the Senate. The commissioners are normally attorneys appointed on a nonpartisan basis for seven year, staggered terms. The staff takes the initiative in deciding when business activities are unlawful, based upon consumer and other complaints or their own investigations, and presents its findings to the commissioners who make the final decisions about whether or not a practice is unlawful. Their decisions, however, can be appealed through the courts and frequently are—meaning that implementation of a decision can take years.

FTC activities. When a consumer or an organization makes a complaint to an office of the Federal Trade Commission, a staff member investigates the complaint to determine whether it concerns a matter of broad interest to the public welfare. Three possible actions are available to the FTC. First, the complaint may be determined to have no validity or not be of broad interest to the public and the case be closed. Second, the FTC may inform the company of the complaint and obtain voluntary agreement to stop the violative activities (this occurs about 75 percent of the time). Third, the FTC may seek to obtain a formal cease-and-desist order.

If a formal complaint is filed by the FTC and the company disagrees

4 For details of these and other important laws relating to marketing practices such as the Robinson-Patman Act, see footnote 3, above.

with the allegation of the FTC, a formal hearing is scheduled in which the attorneys for the firm and attorneys for the FTC present their evidence before another member of the FTC staff, a hearing examiner, who draws conclusions and proposes an order to remedy the problem. The proposed order can be appealed to the five commissioners who make the final decision. Their decision can be appealed to the U.S. Court of Appeals and eventually to the U.S. Supreme Court in unusual cases. This process takes a considerable amount of time and it might be argued that consumers' rights would be more expeditiously achieved without the extended legal process. However, if the FTC made many complaints later found to be unjustified and without due process within the legal system, the rights of sellers as well as buyers would not be protected. Because the process is so expensive—both for the seller and for the government (paid by taxpayers, of course)—there is incentive to work out voluntary compliance with proposed orders and settle the problem "out of court," rather than complete the entire legal process.

The FTC also has other functions and powers. One of these is to investigate an industry and promulgate industry-wide rules that will govern the behavior of all firms in that industry. This reduces the need for a case-by-case approach, which is expensive and often ineffective. Two types of industry rules are possible. The first is *voluntary guidelines* in which the FTC, in cooperation with members of the industry and consumers, adopts a set of standards that will apply to the conduct of business activities in that industry. This may "clean up" the industry for the most part because most firms will probably comply, but it is ineffective in controlling the activities of those members who refuse to comply.

A second and stronger approach is a *trade practice rule*. In this approach, the staff proposes a detailed set of rules regulating practices of an industry. This might include advertising practices, how price information is to be disclosed, a necessity of informing consumers of the products of competitors, merchandising techniques and methods of sales presentations, and so forth. Public hearings are then conducted concerning the proposed rules in which consumers, consumer advocacy groups, businesses, the FTC, and others are encouraged to present their opinions about the proposed rule. The FTC will give financial aid to organizations that will support the FTC's position in order to hire lawyers and expert witnesses and conduct research to present in the hearings. Businesses also hire expert witnesses, lawyers, and so forth, and frequently consumer researchers are employed by both sides to conduct and present evidence in hearings conducted by a "hearings officer" who examines and cross-examines the witnesses and then prepares a conclusion—much like a judge renders a decision—about the proposed rules. The hearings officer's conclusions are then presented to the commissioners for a final decision, appealable through the courts, which may then have the effect of law in that industry. If businesses violate any provision of the trade regulation rule (TRR), they are subject to a fine of $10,000 per violation per day. It appears at the present time that the use of trade practice rules is increasing and thus is likely to be a major factor affecting marketing practices in many industries.

The FTC also conducts some educational activities. Conferences are occasionally held to educate business firms on legal and proper methods of influencing consumers. The FTC has also issued some booklets designed to help consumers make better decisions. Generally, these activities have been minimal and largely ineffective compared to the legal actions undertaken by the FTC. One of the problems faced by the FTC is that most of their programs have been developed by lawyers and economists who have little formal training in consumer behavior. Consequently most of the programs of the FTC have been based upon concepts of legal and/or normative economics—or how consumers *ought* to behave according to classical economic models—with little attention to the actual concerns and buying patterns of consumers. Recently, the FTC has attempted to bring some persons with formal training and experience in consumer research into the staff, so possibly the scope and effectiveness of consumer orientation may increase in the future.

A consumer researcher or marketing strategist must understand the effects of the FTC on programs of consumer influence. The marketing management and legal counsel of an organization might on occasions be affected by FTC complaints against specific practices but much more pervasive effects result from the cumulative law that arises from previous cases establishing the precedents that control marketing practices. Commerce Clearing House monitors these cases (through various appeals that are likely to occur) and prepares summaries of the decisions that affect various methods of consumer influence and other business practices. An excerpt from these summaries is shown in Figure 23.1 as an example of the kinds of decisions with which a consumer analyst or strategist must be familiar. A consumer analyst can also keep aware of some of the most important decisions by reading the "legal abstracts" section in each issue of the *Journal of Marketing*.

Federal consumer protection laws. Many other consumer protection laws have been enacted in an attempt to protect the consumer from various abuses. It is nòt possible to describe all of them here, but a selected list of some of the more important ones is presented in Figure 23.2.

State and local regulations. All states and provinces have laws that directly affect consumer influence programs. Some are general in that they regulate untruthful communications about credit terms, use of "unfair" (below cost) prices to obtain customers, "bait-and-switch" advertising, and so forth. Others are specific in that they relate to specific industries such as banking, insurance (controls over salespersons' presentations, for example), liquor, utilities, professional services (prohibitions against certain forms of advertising for physicians, lawyers, funeral directors, dentists, and so forth), and many others. The Attorney General's office of most states encourages consumer complaints, often through a consumer fraud office. Some states have policies that such complaints will not be

Figure 23.1 Summaries of examples of legal decisions affecting consumer influence programs

[¶ 7569]   Television Commercials

The use of mock-ups in television commercials is deceptive and unlawful if their use tends to misrepresent characteristics of the simulated products. A commercial which purported to demonstrate that a knife was sharp enough to cut through a nail was deceptive when the cutting edge exhibited after the demonstration was a different one from the one used to cut through the nail (.71). A commercial which purported to show that the advertiser's oleo had moisture drops similar to those on butter, while competitive oleos did not, was deceptive when the moisture drops were artificially applied and did not enhance the flavor or quality as claimed (.74). Demonstrations which purported to compare shaving creams were deceptive when other substances were added to the creams to make the competitive creams appear to be drier and to make the advertiser's cream appear to be superior (.79).

It has been suggested that the use of an undisclosed mock-up may be permissible provided that its sole purpose is to compensate for deficiencies in the photographic process (.77).

The overall impression given by a commercial may be misleading even though a required disclosure was made (.80).

Even "humorous" or "fanciful" commercials may have actionable capacity to deceive if they exaggerate the results achieved from the use of a product (.87).

The presentation, in a commercial, of a demonstration, experiment or test which is represented as actual visual proof of a claim is deceptive if it is not a genuine demonstration being conducted as represented. The use of undisclosed props in strategic places may be a material deception, as in the shaving cream sandpaper demonstration (.36).

Demonstrations that purport to prove something that they do not prove have been prohibited. Demonstrations purporting to prove a cigarette filter's absorptive power (.24), a razor's safety (.34) and a shaving cream's superiority (.38) have been held deceptive because of their inadequacy to prove the characteristics they were supposed to prove. Proof that the tests were inadequate was found lacking in the auto wax "Burning auto" test (.21) and in the dental cream demonstration of the removal of tobacco stains from a plate (.27).

Implications of facts about a product which are not true are, of course, unlawful. Examples are the invisible shield demonstration to imply that complete protection may be anticipated from a dental cream (.47), and the use of white-coated models recommending a product, implying the medical profession's approval of the product (.61).

Tampering with competitive products in order to discredit them in commercials (.11) and use of camera tricks to magnify unfavorable characteristics of competitive products or to eliminate unfavorable characteristics of the advertiser's product (.05) are unfair.

A commercial which, because of a shortened time interval, indicates that the product is effective faster than it actually is, may be deceptive (.91).

Announcement of the FTC's program for monitoring TV commercials appears at   10,128 in Volume 3.

[¶ 7655]   Comparisons

It is unfair to make false or deceptive comparisons of one's product with other products. It is unfair, for example, to claim, unless true, that one's product is more durable, is more effective, is safer, or has any superiority; it is unfair to claim, unless true, that one's product is cheaper, or is less expensive to operate.

It was deceptive to imply that a bread contained fewer calories than other bread, without disclosing that the calorie comparison was of slices of unequal weight. It was deceptive to state that the caloric content of peanut oil was greater than that of cottonseed oil or corn oil (.11).

A claim that the advertiser's emulsified cod liver oil would be easier to digest than any other cod liver oil preparation was deceptive, unless limited to a comparison with

Figure 23.1 (Continued)

non-emulsified cod liver oil (.21). Claims that peanut oil was easier to digest than corn oil or cottonseed oil were false and were prohibited (.21).

Various claims as to greater durability (.31), greater effectiveness (.41), and miscellaneous superiorities (.71) have been prohibited.

Not only is it unfair to claim untrue superiorities or advantages; it is equally unfair to claim untrue equality. The Federal Trade Commission has prohibited claims, for example, that mattresses were equal to mattresses of well-known brands, that evaporated milk was as healthful or nutritious as whole milk or cream, that plastic building material was as yielding as cork, and that substitutes could serve the same purposes as linseed oil (.61).

It should be possible to substantiate any comparisons made. The Cigarette advertising guides, appearing in the FTC division in Volume 4, prohibit claims unless they are "based on reliable information" (.71, cigarettes). Or claims should be substantiated by tests, according to several rulings (.71, ink, pipes).

Claims which are true in some, but not all, respects or conditions should be clearly qualified. Claims that an insecticide, for example, was safer than competitive products, should have been limited to the types of competitive products which actually were less safe (.71, insecticide).

[¶7567] Pictorial Representations

Misrepresentation through pictures and symbols is an unfair practice.

Pictures of offices and factory buildings which are not owned or occupied by the seller, or wholly occupied by him, may misrepresent the size or nature of his business (.56).

Pictures of higher-priced models in conjunction with prices of lower-priced models may misrepresent the price of the product or the product which the buyer could get for the advertised price (.21).

Pictures of foreign scenes, well-known edifices, such as the Tower of London, or symbols such as shamrocks and harps on a green background, may falsely imply a foreign origin (.70).

Advertisements for medicinal preparations which picture men in white jackets of the type worn by doctors may imply endorsement of the product by members of the medical profession (.49).

Picturization of products which are not available for sale has been prohibited as misrepresenting the advertiser's ability to fill orders (.07).

Depictions of seals or leopards on plush or pile fabrics have been prohibited as implying that the fabrics were fur (.35).

Misleading pictorial representations of the effectiveness of products, including grossly exaggerated "before-and-after" pictures, have been prohibited (.42).

Pictorial illustrations which imply that products have components, parts or characteristics which they do not have, have been prohibited (.21).

Insignia such as the American eagle, shield and stars may falsely imply a connection with the United States Government, particularly if used in connection with a name including "U.S." or "United States" (.91).

Note: The numbers in parentheses refer to the location in the same source of additional details and references about the summary statement.

Source: Commerce Clearing House, Inc.

Figure 23.2 Selected federal consumer protection laws

Act	Purposes
Pure Food and Drug Act (1906)	Prohibits adulteration and misbranding of foods and drugs sold in interstate commerce
Food, Drug, and Cosmetic Act (1938)	Prohibits the adulteration and sale of foods, drugs, cosmetics, or therapeutic devices that may endanger public health; allows the Food and Drug Administration to set minimum standards and to establish guides for food products
Wool Products Labeling Act (1940)	Protects producers, manufacturers, distributors, and consumers from undisclosed substitutes and mixtures in all types of manufactured wool products
Fur Products Labeling Act (1951)	Protects consumers and others against misbranding, false advertising, and false invoicing of furs and fur products
Flammable Fabrics Act (1953)	Prohibits interstate transportation of dangerously flammable wearing apparel and fabrics
Automobile Information Disclosure Act (1958)	Requires automobile manufacturers to post suggested retail prices on all new passenger vehicles
Textile Fiber Products Identification Act (1958)	Guards producers and consumers against misbranding and false advertising of fiber content of textile fiber products
Cigarette Labeling Act (1965)	Requires cigarette manufacturers to label cigarettes as hazardous to health
Fair Packaging and Labeling Act (1966)	Declares unfair or deceptive packaging or labeling of certain consumer commodities illegal
Child Protection Act (1966)	Excludes from sale potentially harmful toys; allows the FDA to remove dangerous products from the market
Truth-in-Lending Act (1968)	Requires full disclosure of all finance charges on consumer credit agreements and in advertisements of credit plans to allow consumers to be better informed regarding their credit purchases
	Protects children from toys and other products that contain thermal, electrical, or mechanical hazards
Fair Credit Reporting Act (1970)	Ensures that a consumer's credit report will contain only accurate, relevant, and recent information and will be confidential unless requested for an appropriate reason by a proper party
Consumer Products Safety Act (1972)	Created an independent agency to protect consumers from unreasonable risk of injury arising from consumer products; agency is empowered to set safety standards
Magnuson-Moss Warranty-Federal Trade Commission Improvement Act (1975)	Provides for minimum disclosure standards for written consumer product warranties; defines minimum content standards for written warranties; allows the FTC to prescribe interpretive rules and policy statements regarding unfair or deceptive practices

Source: William M. Pride and O. C. Ferrell, *Marketing: Basic Concepts and Decisions*, p. 423. Copyright © 1977 by Houghton Mifflin Company. Reprinted by permission of the publisher.

investigated unless a certain quantity of complaints is received against a particular company. Some states have also established a special agency to represent the interests of consumers.

Some cities and other political entities have established offices to regulate trade practices and assist consumers with complaints. In Dade County, Florida, for example, the consumer protection division has the power to enforce consumer protection laws of the city, county and state. In many cities, such agencies monitor the weights and scales of food markets, register door-to-door sales organizations ("Green River" ordinances) and other activities that are more effectively regulated at the local or state level where immediate and personal attention can be given to individual complaints in a way that probably would never be possible at the national level of a regulatory agency.

Local and state regulations are usually directed toward the most blatant forms of consumer deception and fraud rather than the more sophisticated deceptions investigated by the FTC. Local agencies are important, however, because of the ability of local officials to give quick attention to claims that would be "too small" to involve the remote, highly-expensive legal processes of Washington.

Consumer research and public policy

Consumer research has the potential of providing valuable inputs in the formulation of public policy designed to regulate programs of consumer influence. When something occurs that harms the consumer, the frequent response is, "There ought to be a law." The laws have, for the most part, brought about improvements in the buying environment of consumers.

In some instances, however, the laws did not bring about the anticipated improvements, had related negative effects, or had costs that outweigh the benefits. Consumer research has the potential for understanding the causes of such undesired results and providing inputs for improvements in present and potential regulations.

The contributions of research to public policy, especially the FTC, have been reported by two leading researchers, Wilkie and Gardner, both former consultants to the FTC.[5] They suggest three broad areas of FTC decisions that might benefit from increased consumer research. These decision points include establishing program priorities, fact-finding (including investigation and substantiation), and remedy and compliance. Research needs of each of these areas are described in the following sections.

Establishing program priorities. What are the most pressing problems of consumers, as perceived by consumers? What kinds of deceptive or unfair marketing activities are most feasible to regulate? Which segments of the population are most affected or least able to defend against

5 William L. Wilkie and David M. Gardner, "The Role of Marketing Research in Public Policy Decision Making," *Journal of Marketing*, vol. 38 (January 1974), pp. 38–47.

consumer abuses? These are critical information needs in the formulation of public policy and needs to which consumer research can be meaningfully directed.

Research directed toward establishing program priorities should provide accurate descriptions of the consumer environment, models for resource allocation, measurements of social cost compared to benefits and comparison of potential benefits of structural or trade practice remedies.[6]

The use of research in establishing priorities might help government agencies overcome the problem that results from establishing priorities on the basis of what lawyers believe has the highest probability of success—even if small, insignificant cases are the only ones tried—rather than attacking the most serious consumer abuses. Kangun and Moyer describe this problem:

> Most staff lawyers are guided chiefly by their trained habits to find a case that the commissioners "will buy" and that can be made to stick with the available evidence and under prevailing judicial opinions. Any attempt to ascertain the true worth (in terms of consumer protection) of a particular investigation or litigative activity is normally ignored.[7]

One of the more flagrant examples of a nonresearch approach to establishing priorities is described in Figure 23.3, an excerpt from hearings by the House Subcommittee on Regulatory Agencies. Based upon what U.S. Congresswoman Fenwick (a former state director of consumer affairs) described as "six letters and kind hearts," the FTC spent $500,000 (later estimated to be closer to $1,000,000) to propose regulations for the funeral service field. Before proposing the rules, the FTC staff had apparently conducted no consumer research to determine buying patterns used by consumers for funerals of relatives and friends nor any empirical research to determine the level of satisfaction or complaints with this industry compared to other service industries. When hearings on the proposed trade practice rule were held, the rules were *opposed* by the majority of consumers requesting to be heard, by members of the industry, and by leading experts on the economics and social-psychological aspects of death. A consumer research project costing in the range of $15,000 to $25,000 might have uncovered many of the problems and false assumptions about consumer behavior contained in the proposed rule and saved much of the nearly $1,000,000 paid by taxpayers.[8]

Government agencies involved in consumer regulation are open to research information but simply have not had the training or environment

6 Wilkie and Gardner, "Role of Marketing Research," p. 44.

7 Norman Kangun and R. Charles Moyer, "The Failings of Regulation," *MSU Business Topics*, vol. 24 (Spring 1976), pp. 5–14, at p. 10.

8 Background details concerning the development and effects of this proposed trade practice rule can be found in "Federal Trade Commission's Proposed Funeral Industry Trade Regulation Rule: Its Effect on Small Business," Report of the Subcommittee on Activities of Regulatory Agencies of the Committee on Small Business, House of Representatives (October 20, 1976), Washington: U.S. Government Printing Office, 1976.

Figure 23.3 "Six Letters and Kind Hearts" that triggered a $500,000 investigation (the FTC's priorities in deciding to propose funeral regulations)

Mr. Russo asked, "Why did you investigate the funeral industry in the first place?"

To which Mr. Angel responded:

We looked into the funeral industry because it occurred to us this was a transaction in which there was a potential for the consumer to be victimized due to bereavement and the commonsense notion that a person who is making funeral arrangements operates at some emotional disadvantage. (Hearing transcript, September 15, 1976, p. 117.)

The staff indicated that when they first began to look into problems associated with the funeral industry, the FTC had "less than a dozen" consumer complaints and at present they have approximately 700 to 1,000 letters from consumers.

The concern so vigorously voiced by members of the Subcommittee was that with less than a dozen complaints, the FTC would launch into a $500,000 project when there were so many other areas in which complaints existed that demanded attention by the FTC.

Still, members were not placated. Congresswoman Fenwick, for example, who, as the Director of the Division of Consumer Affairs for the State of New Jersey was responsible for New Jersey's implementation of funeral regulations, queried:

Mrs. Fenwick. * * * Did you consult the various consumer divisions of the States to see what they had in the way of complaints?

Mr. Angel. Number of consumer complaints? Only sporadically, only in a couple of States did we do that.

Mrs. Fenwick. Well, now, gentlemen, seriously, your own kind hearts and six letters—they have consumer divisions in almost every State of the Union, and all you have to do is write a letter. In many states it is the Division of Law and Public Safety it comes under, and in some the Department of Agriculture which I don't understand.

But nevertheless, there are consumer divisions and they receive complaints. And this surely would be the first obligation, and it really constituted an inexpensive way of finding out what the situation is in the Nation. If you had written and had found out they had 15 complaints in 8 years, wouldn't that have told you something?

Mr. Angel. It would have told us something, but not everything, Congresswoman. The point, I think, that really needs to be emphasized here is that consumer complaints simply do not give you anywhere near the full picture of what kinds of abuses or problems exist.

Mrs. Fenwick. What makes you think so, sir?

Mr. Angel. Three and a half years of research, interviewing people.

Mrs. Fenwick. I ran the division of consumer affairs.

Mr. Angel. I understand that.

Mrs. Fenwick. And I promulgated regulations. I just simply do not agree with you, there is no better way of knowing. If I were a Federal Trade Commissioner I would have taken a bit more interest in the *Pyramid* case—now there is real abuse, involving activities in one State very difficult to control on another State level. The Federal Trade Commission has certain things, in my opinion, that only it can do. Package deals that stranded poor schoolchildren in Paris, and I couldn't control it because it was organized in another State. I have dozens of things that I could hand you in the way of problems. To get triggered off by six letters and your kind hearts when you have thousands of consumers begging for help in other areas is to me absolutely an incredible way of operating an agency.

Source: Reprinted from "Federal Trade Commission's Proposed Funeral Industry Trade Regulation Rule: Its Effect on Small Business," Report of the Subcommittee on Activities of Regulatory Agencies of the Committee on Small Business, House of Representatives, October 20, 1976 (Washington: U.S. Government Printing Office, 1976), pp. 16–17.

conducive to it in the past. In a fascinating report, Dyer and Shimp show how they provided research input to the FTC concerning a proposed rule on premium-oriented commercials to children and found the FTC to be very responsive to this unexpected input from consumer researchers.[9] To be useful, Dyer and Shimp conclude, the research must be submitted early in the decisions of the FTC and should have wide dissemination outside the FTC in order to achieve more consideration by policymakers.

An example of the kind of research that examines the degree of consumer acceptance of various products, or conversely, the level of dissatisfaction, is presented in Figure 23.4. This study was based upon a sample of 10,000 households and was repeated on an annual basis.[10] Very simple measures are used, but clearly disclosed as problem areas for consumers are gasoline (the great increase in price of gasoline occurred in the year of the reported survey), automotive repairs, appliance repairs, home repairs, credit charges, and children's clothing. These results are similar, it will be remembered, to studies on this topic using other methodologies discussed in Chapter 22. By monitoring consumer problems on an annual basis, regulatory agencies could determine trends which would provide useful inputs in establishing priorities for consumer programs.

Consumer research can also be used to guide the allocation of resources in the products, programs and services furnished by the government. These decisions may be described as *functional* public policy rather than *regulatory* public policy, and they may require evaluations of user satisfaction levels with government services, priorities for government services (such as recreation, medical care, etc.), cultural activities desired by the population, information needs of the population, and so forth.[11]

Fact-finding. A second type of contribution that consumer research can make in the development of public policy is providing facts for decisions that the FTC (or other agencies) must make about complaints or trade practice rules. Rosch reports that consumer studies can and have been important in providing *substantiation* about the meaning of advertisements.[12] This is particularly important when deception is defined in terms of meaning to the *receiver* rather than objective meaning of the words in the advertisement.[13]

Consumer analysts employed by advertising agencies and marketing

9 Robert F. Dyer and Terence A. Shimp, "Enhancing the Role of Marketing Research in Public Policy Decision Making," *Journal of Marketing*, vol. 41 (January 1977), pp. 63–67.

10 Fabian Linden, "The Consumer's View of Value Received—1974," *The Conference Board Record* (November 1974), pp. 48–53.

11 J. R. Brent Ritchie and Roger J. La Breque, "Marketing Research and Public Policy: A Functional Perspective," *Journal of Marketing*, vol. 39 (July 1975), pp. 12–19.

12 J. Thomas Rosch, "Marketing Research and the Legal Requirements of Advertising," *Journal of Marketing*, vol. 39 (July 1975), pp. 69–79.

13 David M. Gardner, "Deception in Advertising: A Conceptual Approach," *Journal of Marketing*, vol. 39 (January 1975), pp. 40–46; David M. Gardner, "Deception in Advertising: A Receiver Oriented Approach to Understanding," *Journal of Advertising* (Fall 1976), pp. 5–11 ff.

Figure 23.4 The degree of consumer acceptance of selected products (Composite rating, 1974)

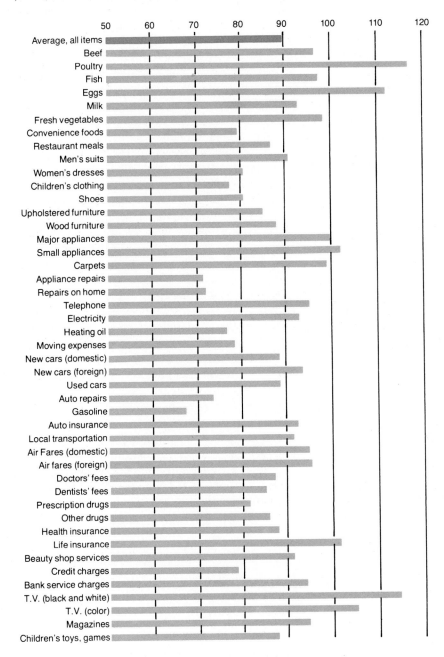

Source: Fabian Linden, "The Consumer's View of Value Received—1974," *The Conference Board Record* (November 1974), pp. 48–53, at p. 50. Reprinted by permission.

organizations probably will find their efforts devoted more and more to providing *substantiation for advertising claims*. The FTC now requires that a "reasonable basis" exist for any claims made by any advertising. Where no reasonable basis exists, making such claims is deemed to be deceptive and unfair (whether or not the claim is actually true).[14] In asserting this policy, the FTC argues that consumers may infer when seeing performance claims in an advertisement that supporting tests have been made to back up the claims. In spite of the requirement to substantiate claims, relatively little use of consumer surveys has occurred by the FTC in investigation of their own claims or complaints, or of respondents. The reasons for this nonuse are described in Figure 23.5.

Under the substantiation program, an advertisement may also be declared deceptive if it implies *uniqueness* when such is not the case, even if the product claims are accurate. A complaint was brought against Wonder Bread because of its slogan, "How big do you want to be? Wonder bread helps build strong bodies 12 ways." The FTC asserted that this advertisement was deceptive by implying that Wonder Bread is more nutritious than other enriched white breads with the same ingredients. Some complaints have been made by the FTC because the brand name implied unsubstantiated claims, such as "Hi-C" for high vitamin content or "Proslim" for weight reduction products.

Much of the substantiation research deals with technical or physical properties of the product but consumer researchers may be involved because of the need to understand the meaning of words to consumers as descriptions of technical properties of the product. For example, the FTC has charged that names such as "Accu-Color," "Insta-Matic," and "Total Automatic Color" are trade-invented names to describe essentially the same features but which leave the false impression of uniqueness.[15]

Facts obtained by consumer research may be important in understanding the *differential effects of regulations between market segments*. For example, low income consumers appear to be attitudinally and cognitively less ready to use a "cooling off" law than consumers in middle and high income areas and may need special education programs to permit such laws to be effective.[16] In proposed rules concerning the funeral industry described in Figure 23.3, a portion of the rules would have mandated how prices were to be quoted to consumers and evidence presented in FTC hearings indicated that the effect of such rules would be to lower the prices paid by some market segments but to raise the price paid by other segments. The segments who would pay lower prices were those who were usually affluent and well-educated but the consumers who would pay higher prices were most likely to be those from low-income and low education segments, especially those with cultural values found most often in the black population.

14 Robert E. Wilkes and James B. Wilcox, "Recent FTC Actions: Implications for the Advertising Strategist," *Journal of Marketing*, vol. 38 (January 1974), pp. 55–61.

15 Wilkes and Wilcox, "Recent FTC Actions."

16 Dennis H. Tootelian, "Attitudinal and Cognitive Readiness: Key Dimensions for Consumer Legislation," *Journal of Marketing*, vol. 39 (July 1975), pp. 61–64.

Figure 23.5 The nonuse of consumer surveys

The interpretation of an advertisement can be a source of disagreement. A reasonable approach to this problem would be to develop a scientifically conducted test or survey that would determine exactly what meaning consumers attach to an advertisement. There are a wide variety of procedures routinely used within the advertising industry that could be tapped. However, despite this rationale, consumer tests and surveys are almost never employed in deceptive advertising cases, and in the few cases in which they are employed they rarely appear to influence the decisions. There are several reasons why such an apparently useful procedure is not used.

The authority of the commission. The commission has simply not been required by the courts to develop evidence to support its position. Also, the commission has very limited resources at its disposal to conduct consumer research and has not had an incentive to develop this type of evidence. Furthermore, the FTC only singles out a limited number of advertisements to prosecute. Presumably, most violations they do prosecute are obvious and do not require testing.

Protecting the ignorant and the credulous. Respondents have been remarkably unsuccessful at developing survey evidence that has been helpful in refuting a commission finding. Because the courts have demanded that the ignorant, the unthinking, and the credulous are to be protected, survey evidence has been turned against the defendant. In the Benrus Watch case, a survey showed that 86 percent of potential watch buyers would understand the meaning of a preticketing system. The commission used the fact that 14 percent had been misled as evidence of its own that deception existed. Under current circumstances, a respondent, unless he believes that a survey would show zero deception, is naturally reluctant to invest money to generate this type of evidence.

The limitations of a survey. There are difficulties inherent in developing a survey. The population must be defined, a defensible sampling plan created, and questions designed to pass tests of unbiasedness and validity. Even assuming that the survey is acceptable technically, a certain amount of uncertainty will remain if only because of the fact that a sample is involved. The difficulties of determining how valid particular surveys are naturally cause apprehension among laymen.

Legal inhibitors. There is a natural reluctance by the legal profession to agree on a single, court-commissioned consumer survey for two reasons. First, a survey provides evidence by respondents who are not available for cross-examination. Since their opinions are obtained by interviewers and analyzed by experts, the evidence is technically hearsay, which is not admissible in civil and criminal proceedings. The courts have exempted surveys from the hearsay rule if the deliberations are reporting not "for the truth of the matter asserted therein" but as expressions of the interviewee's state of mind. The legal profession is still reluctant to use this type of technique to its fullest potential.

Second, the use of independently commissioned survey research is somewhat inconsistent with the traditional adversary system of justice wherein each side submits arguments and evidence that support its position. To an attorney, agreeing to a carefully conceived and conducted survey might be too much like calling a prestigious witness without knowing which side his testimony will support.

Source: Excerpted from David A. Aaker and John G. Myers, *Advertising Management* (Engelwood Cliffs, N.J.: Prentice-Hall, 1975), pp. 580–81. Reprinted by permission.

Market segmentation research by consumer analysts is also needed to provide facts concerning different interpretations that may be made by "reasonable consumers" as opposed to "ignorant consumers." The question facing regulators is whether the standard of deception in advertising should refer to interpretations of the average or reasonable person or to the unreasonable or ignorant consumer—who perhaps is not capable of understanding the difference between a factual claim and "puffery" of a product. After thoroughly reviewing cases about this topic, Preston concluded:

> The FTC holds no longer to the strict ignorant man standard by which it would protect everyone from everything which may deceive them. . . . Perhaps we may call the new stance a modified ignorant man standard which protects only those cases of foolishness which are committed by significant numbers of people.[17]

A special group of "ignorant" consumers the FTC has shown special interest in protecting is children, who when very young presumably have not developed some of the defenses against advertising that are developed in later years. A great deal of consumer research by Ward, Robertson, and others has investigated this topic.[18]

Consumer researchers have an important role to play in providing substantiation and other facts concerning advertising, sales presentations, and other programs of consumer influence, and it is clear that this role is likely to expand in the future. An example of what might have been required if the present environment existed in 1776 in substantiation of claims contained in the Declaration of Independence is shown in Figure 23.6.

Compliance and remedies. A third area of input by consumer research into policy-making is in the area of investigating the effects of various forms of remedies and methods for obtaining compliance. It is important to understand the effects and effectiveness of remedies, both proposed and implemented, to both business and government. It is also in the consumers' interest, Walker and his associates report, because if regulations are implemented that have serious adverse effects or are not cost-effective in their results, the long run effect will be to injure the ability to obtain *effective* regulation needed by consumers.[19]

One of the remedies for deceptive advertising used by the FTC in recent years is *corrective advertising*, which may be any advertising designed to correct past deception. The first case in which this remedy was approved by the FTC involved Continental Baking Company which had claimed that consumers could lose weight by eating Profile bread. The bread, however, had the primary characteristic of being *thinner* than other

---

17 Ivan L. Preston, *Great American Blow-up* (Madison: University of Wisconsin Press, 1975), Chapter 10.

18 Scott Ward, "Children's Reactions to Commercials," *Journal of Advertising Research*, vol. 12 (April 1972); J. Blatt, L. Spencer, and S. Ward, "A Cognitive Developmental Study of Children's Reactions to Television Advertising," *Effects of Television on Children and Adolescents* (Cambridge, Mass.: Marketing Science Institute, 1971); T. S. Robertson and J. R. Rossiter, "Children and Commercial Persuasion: An Attribution Theory Analysis," *Journal of Consumer Research*, vol. 1 (June 1974), pp. 13–20.

19 Orville C. Walker, Jr., Richard F. Sauter, and Neil M. Ford, "The Potential Secondary Effects of Consumer Legislation: A Conceptual Framework," *Journal of Consumer Affairs*, vol. 8 (Winter 1974), pp. 144–55.

Figure 23.6 The Declaration of Independence, modified to meet regulatory requirements

Jefferson, Hancock & Wythe, Inc.

INDEPENDENCE HALL, PHILA., PENNSYLVANIA

Client____ House   Date_____ 7/4/76

Job No.__ 1   Space_____ --

Medium__ Parchment   Publ. Date__ ASAP

OK only if everybody showed up

Copy

A DECLARATION
By the Representatives of the United States of America
In General Congress Assembled.

must prove existence of such laws. No copies on file!

When in the Course of human Events, it becomes necessary for one People to dissolve the Political Bands which have connected them with another, and to assume among the Powers of the
Earth, the separate and equal Station to which the Laws of Nature
and of Nature's God entitle them, a decent Respect to the Opinions
of Mankind requires that they should declare the causes which im-
pel them to the Separation.

No! must be substantiated

This is an implied guarantee. Copy must state that we don't guarantee it.

We hold these Truths to be self-evident, that all Men are
created equal, that they are endowed by their Creator with certain
unalienable Rights, that among these are Life, Liberty and the Pursuit of Happiness--That to secure these Rights, Governments are
instituted among Men, deriving their just Powers from the Consent
of the Governed, that whenever any Form of Government becomes
destructive of these Ends, it is the Right of the People to alter or
to abolish it, and to institute new Government, laying its Foundation on such Principles, and organizing its Powers in such Form,
as to them shall seem most likely to effect their Safety and Hap-
piness. Prudence, indeed, will dictate that Governments long established should not be changed for light and transient Causes; and
accordingly all Experience hath shewn, that Mankind are more disposed to suffer, while Evils are sufferable, than to right themselves
by abolishing the Forms to which they are accustomed. But when
a long Train of Abuses and Usurpations, pursuing invariably the
same Object, evinces a Design to reduce them under absolute
Despotism, it is their Right, it is their Duty, to throw off such
Government, and to provide new Guards for their future Security.
Such has been the patient Sufferance of these Colonies; and such is
now the Necessity which constrains them to alter their former
Systems of Government. The History of the present King of Great
Britain is a History of repeated Injuries and Usurpations, all having
in direct Object the Establishment of an absolute Tyranny over these
States. To prove this, let Facts be submitted to a candid World.

Are we prepared to disclose others?

Can't say 'all'. Qualify.

Someone may challenge this!!

Can't substantiate

Need a signed release.

Since when are your opinions facts?

He has refused his Assent to Laws, the most wholesome and
necessary for the public Good.

Disparaging! Do we have adequate research to back up?   Continued....

Source: Created by Edward A. McCabe, vice-president of Scali, McCabe and Sloves. Reprinted from *Advertising Age* (December 9, 1974), p.17.

bread slices rather than any unique calorie characteristics. The FTC
approved a plan in which Profile was required to run 25 percent of its
advertising containing corrective statements such as the following (featuring the actress Julia Meade):

I'd like to clear up any misunderstandings you may have about Profile bread from its advertising or even its name. Does Profile have fewer calories than other breads? No, Profile has about the same per ounce as other breads. To be exact, Profile has 7 fewer calories per slice. That's because it's sliced thinner. But eating Profile will not cause you to lose weight. A reduction of 7 calories is insignificant . . .[20]

Corrective advertising is intuitively an appealing concept. Rather than merely punishing a firm with a fine or ordering them to cease and desist a deceptive practice, why not make the firm correct the perceptions or attitudes that consumers have developed from the firm's deceptive advertising? While some research indicates that corrective advertising has been partially effective, the issue is very complex because advertising effectiveness is based upon interactions between message, source, and consumer characteristics, which may make the effects of corrective advertising difficult to predict.[21] One possibility is that corrective advertising may actually *increase credibility* because of reference to the Federal Trade Commission giving the impression that the firm, by doing corrective advertising, is honestly and sincerely attempting to correct "any false impressions that might have occurred as a result of previous advertising," thereby enhancing the firm's overall reputation. Research by Hunt also indicates that even when the FTC mandates the specific copy to be used in corrective advertising, a clever advertising strategist might be able to achieve "refutational innoculation" by other advertising or statements preceding the corrective advertisements.[22]

Criticality of decision process approach to consumerism research

A critical need exists for conducting consumerism research and analysis of consumerism programs using integrated, decision process models of consumer behavior. Many of the problems of using research in public policy decisions can be traced to the use of fragmented, limited-paradigm research approaches that fail to consider many relevant dimensions of consumer behavior that affect the implementation and efficacy of public policy.

The most comprehensive analysis of the need for using models of consumer behavior in public policy research is contained in a staff report to the Federal Trade Commission known as the Howard and Hulbert report.[23] After analyzing the testimony of many experts concerning advertising (and some other forms of consumer influence) and public policy, Howard and Hulbert describe the requirements for using a consumer behavior model in conducting public policy research:

20 "Mea Culpa, Sort Of," *Newsweek* (September 27, 1971), p. 89.

21 Robert F. Dyer and Philip G. Kuehl, "The 'Corrective Advertising' Remedy of the FTC: An Experimental Evaluation," *Journal of Marketing*, vol. 38 (January 1974), pp. 48–54; William L. Wilkie, "Research on Counter and Corrective Advertising," paper presented to Advertising and the Public Interest Conference, American Marketing Association, Washington, D.C., May 9–11, 1973.

22 H. Keith Hunt, "Effects of Corrective Advertising," *Journal of Advertising Research*, vol. 13 (October 1973), pp. 15–24.

23 John A. Howard and James Hulbert, *Advertising and the Public Interest* (Chicago: Crain Communications, Inc., 1976).

First, a model for public policy should avoid the specialization inherent in some of the industry models. It should be general and comprehensive, dealing with the whole process of decision-making. In addition, the model must be fairly detailed. . . . The model should also be disaggregative, dealing with the choice process of the individual. While aggregative models may often be sufficient for industry purposes, public policy needs require a model of individual consumer behavior. Aggregative information can always be obtained from an individual model, but the reverse is not true. Wherever possible, the model should be consistent with theory and empirical evidence, both in the behavioral sciences and in marketing and advertising research. Most desirable, of course, would be a comprehensive model that was itself empirically tested.[24]

The use of comprehensive models of consumer behavior would help in establishing the *relevant evaluative criteria* of consumers so that the FTC might require affirmative disclosure on the proper attributes. A model might help understand how information processing occurs in order that regulatory agencies could more effectively determine what constitutes deceptive advertising and how to correct it. Models can help us understand how behavior differs among consumer segments, a most pressing need in public policy research and one that has generally been ignored by policy makers. The market segmentation problem is particularly troublesome because it implies that some regulations may benefit some consumers while harming others and that possibly varying laws would be required to protect the entire population. These are difficult policy issues but ones that can better be solved by comprehensive models of consumer behavior such as the Howard-Sheth model and the model in this book than with the fragmented, limited-paradigm approaches that have characterised much previous public policy research.[25]

An integrated approach to public policy is found in Canada in a more advanced form than in the United States. An overall consumer protection agency in Canada was established by Parliament in 1967, bringing together in one department a number of existing consumer protection laws and also providing the rationale, resources, and authority for new programs. The Consumer Affairs Bureau, organized as shown in Figure 23.7, with a staff of about 1,100 employees and a budget of about 25 million dollars in 1977, assumes responsibility for major regulatory activities concerning consumers. A major division of the bureau is the Consumer Research Branch, which has shown a willingness to use comprehensive models of consumer behavior for collecting and analyzing consumer research. The research branch conducts research on *consumer choice*, which it defines as "a full understanding of the consumption process, the way in which consumers make purchase decisions, how suppliers respond to perceived demand, and how consumers and suppliers interact with each other in the marketplace." The research branch also

24 Howard and Hulbert, *Advertising and the Public Interest*, p. 36.
25 Ibid.

Figure 23.7 Organizational Structure.
Canadian Bureau of Consumer Affairs

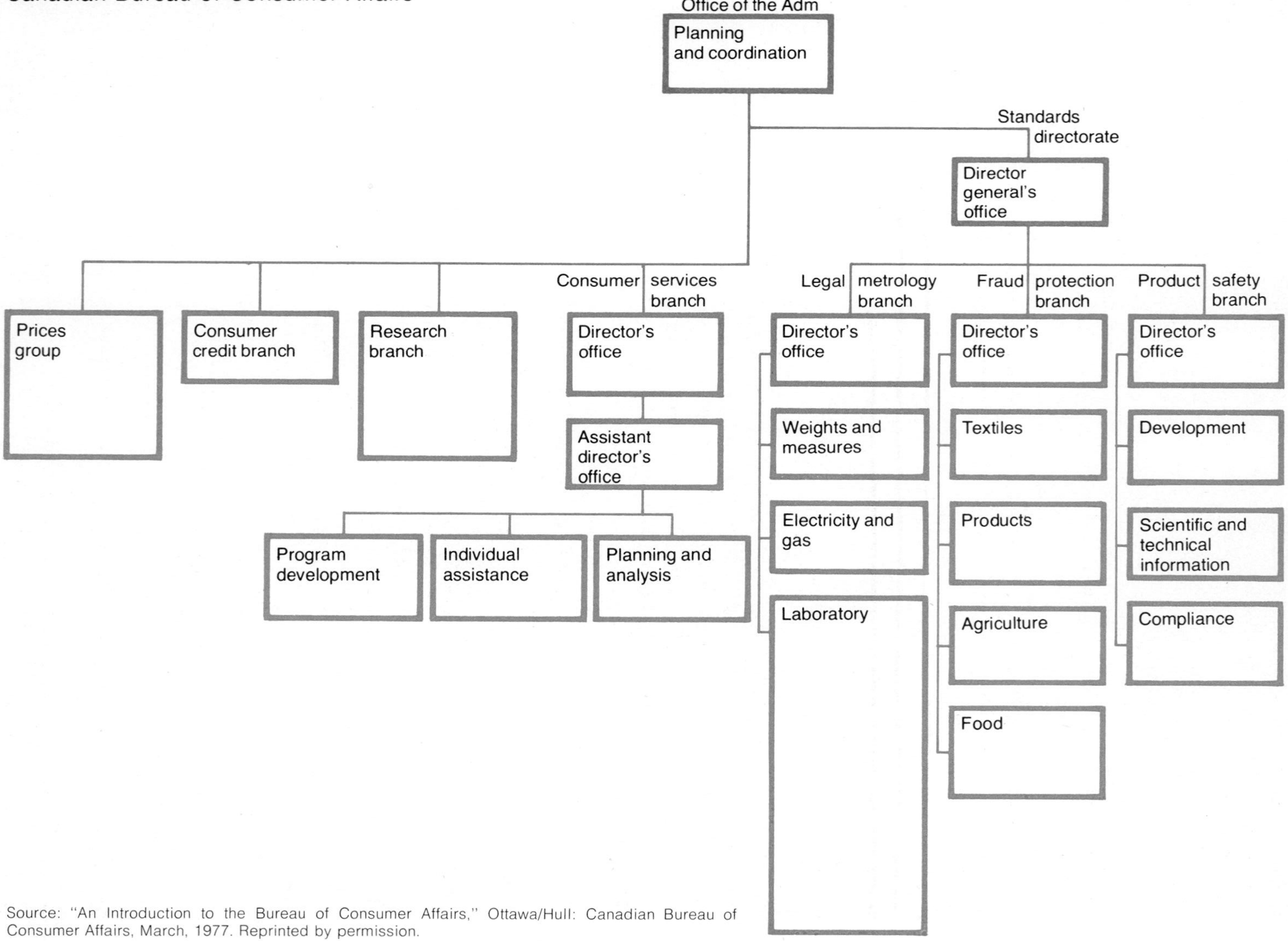

Source: "An Introduction to the Bureau of Consumer Affairs." Ottawa/Hull: Canadian Bureau of Consumer Affairs, March, 1977. Reprinted by permission.

prepares research on *consumer protection* including information about "the choice of legal tools available, the economic and social effects of the proposed legislation on consumers and suppliers, and the effective implementation and operation of the law." This branch also conducts research in a third area, *financial transactions*, which is concerned with research on credit, saving, insurance, pensions, and related matters that may be a source of confusion and difficulty, and more specific but developing areas such as electronic payments systems, which transfer funds from debtor to creditor.

In addition to specific marketing practices that require consumer research, important macro-issues exist concerning the role of consumer influence programs. Do the benefits of such programs outweigh the costs? Are consumer influence programs required to stimulate new product development and a healthy economy? Does advertising and other consumer influence positively or negatively affect the tastes and life styles of a society? Does advertising stimulate consumers to buy things they don't need? (See Figure 23.8.) Does consumer influence unfairly represent minority or women's groups? These important questions are not discussed further here because of space requirements and because they are thoroughly analyzed in other sources[26] but this section on public policy could not be finished without reminding the reader of these critical issues that affect the environment of consumer influence programs.

Figure 23.8 Does advertising cause people to buy things they don't need?

"UNTIL THIS MOMENT, I NEVER REALIZED WE NEEDED A FOOD CHOPPER WITH A BUILT-IN TRANSISTOR RADIO."

Source: *Wall Street Journal* (April 22, 1977), p. 18. Courtesy of Sidney Harris/Wall Street Journal

26 James F. Engel, Hugh G. Wales, and Martin R. Warshaw, *Promotional Strategy* (Homewood, Ill.: Richard D. Irwin, 1975), chap. 23. Also, see Jules Backman, *Advertising and Competition* (New York: New York University Press, 1967).

Organizational responses to regulatory and consumerism forces

Contemporary organizations—business as well as nonbusiness—are faced with changing realities in the regulatory and consumer environment. Taking the ostrich—with its head in the sand—approach is a certain strategy designed to invite litigation and consumer complaint and, in the long-run at least, the demise of economic viability. Organizations need *preventive* approaches to consumerism and regulatory forces rather than *reactive* marketing programs. The solution to this changing regulatory environment requires a carefully designed program implemented both by *individual firms* and by *voluntary associations of firms.*

The failure of business organizations to monitor and understand the nature of consumer concerns and complaints is illustrated by the following selected scenarios:

1. If anyone can expect cooperation from retailers on a test marketing project, it is probably General Mills. Yet when this firm tried out its "Mr. Wonderfull Surprize" cereal in Buffalo, it ran into everything from stern questions to one outright refusal to stock "the only cereal with a creamy vanilla filling." The reason proved to be letters received by food store managers from the Center for Science in the Public Interest (CSPI) calling the product (30 percent sugar, 14 percent saturated fat) a "nutritional disaster" and demanding that they lock it out. Since then, the consumer watchdogs have attacked the cereal in each new city and CSPI director Michael Jacobson dramatically illustrated his point by dashing onstage at the Institute of Food Technologists convention, seizing the microphone, and presenting General Mills an award of a garbage can for "destroying the American people's concept of good nutrition."

2. Senior citizens, crusading through a group called the Gray Panthers, have overturned three state laws barring retail prescription drug price advertising. The Gray Panthers are now pushing model state legislation to regulate hearing-aid salespersons.

3. Consumer groups are campaigning for the right to use free broadcasting time for counter-advertising as a public service. In the case of aspirin, they have requested broadcasters to run a short message narrated by Burt Lancaster to state plainly the makeup of aspirin. This is intended to counter the Bayer aspirin commericals consumer advocates feel lead consumers into buying a more expensive product than they need.

Business organizations can respond to consumerism forces with a minimum obligatory response—just enough to meet legal requirements—or a firm can respond creatively with a major commitment of corporate resources to develop appropriate programs based on consumerism issues. There is some research to indicate that managers see consumerism as an opportunity for creative response and are optimistic about its effects on the marketplace[27] and a very substantial literature describing the impact of consumerism on business strategies and the programs needed to respond to consumerism.[28] In the case of product safety and liability, it is clear that far reaching changes are necessary in the design and delivery of products and dire economic consequences for a firm if it fails to make such changes.[29]

A very useful approach to responding to consumerism pressures was developed by Hensel, which he describes as a consumerism management system. Following a consumerism audit to determine where a company stands in the eyes of consumers, Hensel suggests a consumerism management system consisting of six major components:

Consumerism management system

1. Understanding the consumer's world,

2. Redressing grievances and responding to inquiries,

3. Creating credibility,

4. Improving customer contact,

5. Providing consumer information,

6. Organizing for responsive action.[30]

Understanding the consumer's world refers to programs designed to insure that top management is acquainted with the reality of the consum-

27 Stephen A. Greyser and Steven L. Diamond, "Business Is Adapting to Consumerism," *Harvard Business Review* (September–October 1974), pp. 38–55.

28 David A. Aaker and George S. Day, "Corporate Responses to Consumerism Pressures," *Harvard Business Review* (November–December 1972), pp. 114–24; Leonard L. Berry, "Marketing Challenges in the Age of the People," *MSU Business Topics*, vol. 20 (Winter 1972), pp. 7–13; Boris W. Becker, "Consumerism: A Challenge or a Threat," *Journal of Retailing*, vol. 48 (Summer 1972), pp. 16–28; William G. Nickels and Noel B. Zabriskie, "Corporate Responsiveness and the Marketing Correspondence Function," *MSU Business Topics*, vol. 21 (Summer 1973), pp. 53–58; Stephen A. Greyser, "Marketing and Responsiveness to Consumerism," *Journal of Contemporary Business* (Autumn 1973), pp. 81–93; S. Prakesh Sethi, "Business and the Consumer: Wither Goes the Confrontation," *California Management Review* (Winter 1974), pp. 82–87; Andrew Takas, "Societal Marketing: A Businessman's Perspective," *Journal of Marketing*, vol. 38 (October 1974), pp. 2–7; Joseph Nolan, "Protect Your Public Image with Performance," *Harvard Business Review* (March–April 1975), pp. 135–42; Leonard L. Berry, "Marketing Mistakes That Businesses Make," *Atlanta Economic Review* (July–August 1974), pp. 21–27; Norman Kangun et al., "Consumerism and Marketing Management," *Journal of Marketing*, vol. 39 (April 1975), pp. 3–10; F. Kelly Shuptrine, "Consumer Protection Communications," *Marquette Business Review* (Spring 1975), pp. 1–8; Larry J. Rosenberg, "Retailers' Responses to Consumerism," *Business Horizons* (October 1975), pp. 37–44; Zoher E. Schipchandler, "Inflation and Life Styles: The Marketing Impact," *Business Horizons* (February 1976), pp. 90–96; Hiram C. Barksdale and Warren A. French, "Response to Consumerism: How Change Is Perceived by Both Sides," *MSU Business Topics* (Spring 1975), pp. 55–67.

29 Lynn J. Loudenback and John W. Goebel, "Marketing in the Age of Strict Liability," *Journal of Marketing*, vol. 38 (January 1974), pp. 62–66; Alfred L. Edwards, "Consumer Product Safety: Challenge for Business," University of Michigan *Business Review* (March 1975), pp. 18–22; William L. Trombetta and Timothy L. Wilson, "Foreseeability of Misuse and Abnormal Use of Products by the Consumer," *Journal of Marketing*, vol. 39 (July 1975), pp. 48–55; Joseph Nemeck, Jr., and Herbert Terry, "New Trends in Product Testing," *Business Horizons* (October 1975), pp. 31–36; Ernest W. Karlin, "Maintaining Product Safety in a Multinational Corporation," *S.A.M. Advanced Management Journal* (Winter 1975), pp. 22–28; George Fisk and Rajan Chandran, "How to Trace and Recall Products," *Harvard Business Review* (November–December 1975), pp. 90–96; Rayford P. Kytle, Jr., "New Dimensions for Quality and Product Safety," *Atlanta Economic Review* (May–June, 1976), pp. 24–27.

30 James S. Hensel, *Strategies for Adapting to the Consumerism Movement* (Columbus, Ohio: Management Horizons, Inc., 1974). This section is summarized from Hensel.

er's shopping and consumption world—including the inflationary consumption pressures, negative attitudes to business, and inferior retail outlets, which may *not* be a part of the highly-paid manager's world.

Redressing grievances and responding to inquiries requires responsive approaches to processing and responding to consumer complaints and inquiries and recognizes the opportunity for an enhanced information feedback system and creation of long-term customers through more effective management of postpurchase communications.

Activities to create credibility include programs to satisfy the consumer's need for a trusted, expert and personal buying agent. They might include merchandising activities designed to provide a "soft sell," institutional advertising, and meaningful involvement in societal or community problems.

Improving customer contact may include programs that affect the entire distribution channel in an attempt to improve the quality of the consumer/retail store contact. This necessitates management's concern about the importance of a quality consumer experience in retail stores, educational programs to insure that retail personnel are competent and motivated to assist consumers, manufacturer or distributor sponsored educational programs for consumers, improved point-of-sale materials, and so forth.

Providing consumer information is a commitment to provide and join with other responsible parties (members of the distribution channel, consumer advocacy groups, educational institutions, government agencies) to increase the buying intelligence of the consumer through relevant information and educational programs to increase use of the information. This may include nutritional labeling, care labeling, greater clarity in instructions that accompany the product, honest and relevant advertising, and so forth.

Organizing for responsive action requires a firm to make the organizational and management system changes necessary to undertake and encourage all elements of the organization to involve themselves with appropriate consumer programs. To be successful, consumerism response must be made "legitimate" by top management and might include a written "consumer rights" policy, establishing an advisory committee of consumers who have a real voice in company decisions, adequate funding of testing of product claims and safety and the creation of a high-level consumer affairs executive with sufficient authority to represent effectively the consumer's interest in company decisions.[31]

Giant Foods—a consumerism-oriented firm. An example of a firm with an outstanding reputation for a consumerism orientation is Giant Foods in Washington, D.C. (see Figure 23.9). Top management made a commitment to orient the firm toward consumerism by hiring Esther Peterson, formerly the President's Special Assistant for Consumer Affairs, at the

31 Milton L. Blum, John B. Stewart, and Edward W. Wheatley, "Consumer Affairs: Viability of the Corporate Response," *Journal of Marketing*, vol. 38 (April 1974), pp. 13–19.

Figure 23.9 Giant Foods

Source: Courtesy of Management Horizons.

vice-presidential level and allowed her to lead an effort to get the company's top management and responsible consumer advocates working together for their mutual benefit.[32] Giant became one of the first

32 Esther Peterson, "Consumerism as Retailer's Asset," *Harvard Business Review* (May–June 1974), pp. 92–101.

supermarket chains to install unit pricing, develop new programs of testing to insure product safety, insist on full disclosure of ingredients and their nutritional content, provide honest point-of-sale promotion and many other activities. In their monitoring of the consumer environment, Giant found that some 10 percent of the wheelchair bound consumers in America live in the Washington area. In response to the firm's desire to satisfy all market segments, the company altered their stores to include specially marked parking spaces, a ramp connecting the parking lot to the store walk, widened checkout aisle for wheel chairs, changes in restrooms and other modifications. The cost for changes amounts to about $1,000 per store and reportedly are well-received by the community.[33]

Many other firms have implemented major consumerism programs. These include a buyer protection plan of the American Motors Company, a "cool-line" program for consumer information feedback and redress by Whirlpool, and a consumer advisory committee and major organization modifications by T. Eaton, the major department store group in Canada.[34] Another type of response to consumerism, however, is shown in Figure 23.10. Rather than a formal consumerism program, this firm has recognized the concern of consumers about increasing prices and poor services and developed a program—Consumers Hero—to exploit these concerns.

Voluntary self-regulation

Firms may cooperate with other firms and organizations in an attempt to provide self-regulation rather than legal regulation. They have several advantages, the most important being that they can be more responsive to changing conditions than laws usually are. They also may be less expensive to establish and implement. The problem with voluntary, cooperative groups is that they lack power to enforce responsible behavior by firms that are not members of the group (usually trade associations) or that choose not to comply with the group's rules. Furthermore, if a group does have the means to sanction a firm from compliance by withholding valuable services of the association, boycotts, or other actions, those attempts to obtain compliance are likely to be considered as restraint of trade and be found illegal under antitrust, no matter how noble the motives of the industry group may be. In spite of the enforcement problems, voluntary self-regulation is growing as more and more groups attempt to establish standards of responsible or ethical behavior. An example of a voluntary code is presented in Figure 23.11, adopted by several organizations involved in advertising.

In summary, it is clear that organizations—both business and nonbusiness—must develop comprehensive, responsive programs for responding to new forces of consumerism and regulatory activity. Consumer analysts and researchers have an important role to play in providing inputs with which management can provide consumerism programs that are relevant, effective and cost efficient.

33 "Handicap Check-out," *Chain Store Age* (April 1977), p. 18.

34 These cases are described in Roger D. Blackwell, James F. Engel, and W. Wayne Talarzyk, *Contemporary Cases in Consumer Behavior* (Hinsdale: Dryden Press, 1977).

Figure 23.10 Consumers Hero

HOT
A new consumer concept lets you buy 'stolen' merchandise if you're willing to take a risk.

We developed an exciting new consumer marketing concept. It's called "stealing." That's right, stealing!

Now if that sounds bad, look at the facts. Consumers are being robbed. Inflation is stealing our purchasing power. Our dollars are shrinking in value. The poor average consumer is plundered, robbed and stepped on.

So the poor consumer tries to strike back. First, he forms consumer groups. He lobbies in Washington. He fights price increases. He looks for value.

So we developed our new concept around value. Our idea was to steal from the rich companies and give to the poor consumer, save our environment and maybe, if we're lucky, make a buck.

A MODERN DAY ROBIN HOOD

To explain our concept, let's take a typical clock radio retailing for $39.95 at a major retailer whose name we better not mention or we'll be sued. It costs the manufacturer $9.72 to make. The manufacturer sells the unit to the retailer for $16.

THE UNCLE HENRY PROBLEM

Let's say that retailer sells the clock radio to your Uncle Henry. Uncle Henry brings it home, turns it on and it doesn't work. So Uncle Henry trudges back to the store to exchange his "lousy rotten" clock radio for a new one that works ("lousy" and "rotten" are Uncle Henry's words).

Now, the defective one goes right back to the manufacturer along with all the other clock radios that didn't work. And if this major retail chain sells 40,000 clock radios with a 5% defective rate, that's 2,000 "lousy rotten" clock radios.

CONSUMERS PROTECTED ALREADY

Consumers are protected against ever seeing these products again because even if the manufacturer repairs them, he can't recycle them as new units. He's got to put a label on the product clearly stating that it is repaired, not new, and if Uncle Henry had his way the label would also say that the product was "lousy" and "rotten."

It's hard enough selling a new clock radio, let alone one that is used. So the manufacturer looks for somebody willing to buy his bad product for a super fantastic price. Like $10. But who wants a clock radio that doesn't work at any price!

ENTER CONSUMERS HERO

We approach the manufacturer and offer to steal that $39.95 radio for $3 per unit. Now think of it. The manufacturer has already spent $9.72 to make it, would have to spend another $5 in labor to fix and repackage it, and still would have to mark the unit as having been previously used. So he would be better off selling it to us for $3, taking a small loss and getting rid of his defective merchandise.

Consumers Hero is now sitting with 2,000 "lousy rotten" clock radios in its warehouse.

Here comes the good part. We take that clock radio, test it, check it and repair it. Then we life test it, clean it up, replace anything that makes the unit look used, put a new label on it and presto—a $39.95 clock radio and it only cost us $3 plus maybe $7 to repair it.

Impossible-to-trace ★ ★ Guarantee ★ ★

We guarantee that our products will look like brand new merchandise without any trace of previous brand identification or ownership.

We take more care in bringing that clock radio to life than the original manufacturer took to make it. We put it through more tests, more fine tuning than any repair service could afford. We get more out of that $10 heap of parts and labor than even the most quality-conscious manufacturer. And we did our bit for ecology by not wasting good raw materials.

NOW THE BEST PART

We offer that product to the consumer for $20—the same product that costs us $3 to steal and $7 to make work. And we make $10 clear profit. But the poor consumer is glad we made our profit because:

1) We provide a better product than the original version.
2) The better product costs one half the retail price.
3) We are nice people.

BUT THERE'S MORE

Because we are so proud of the merchandise we refurbish, we offer a longer warranty. Instead of 90 days (the original warranty), we offer a five year warranty.

So that's our concept. We recycle "lousy rotten" garbage into super new products with five year warranties. We steal from the rich manufacturers and give to the poor consumer. We work hard and make a glorious profit.

To make our concept work, we've organized a private membership of quality and price-conscious consumers and we send bulletins to this membership about the products available in our program.

Items range from micro-wave ovens and TV sets to clock radios, digital watches, and stereo sets. There are home appliances from toasters to electric can openers. Discounts generally range between 40 and 70 percent off the retail price. Each product has a considerably longer warranty than the original one and a two week money-back trial period. If you are not absolutely satisfied, for any reason, return your purchase within two weeks after receipt for a prompt refund.

Many items are in great abundance but when we only have a few of something, we select, at random, a very small number of members for the mailing. A good example was our $39.95 TV set (we had 62 of them) or a $1 AM radio (we had 1257). In short, we try to make it fair for everybody without disappointing a member and returning a check.

EASY TO JOIN

To join our small membership group, simply write your name, address and phone number on a slip of paper and enclose a check or money order for five dollars. Mail it to Consumers Hero, Three JS&A Plaza, Northbrook, Illinois 60062, %Dept. A1.

You'll receive a two year membership, regular bulletins on the products we offer and some surprises we would rather not mention in this advertisement. But what if you never buy from us and your two year membership expires. Fine. Send us just your membership card and we'll fully refund your five dollars plus send you interest on your money.

If the consumer ever had a chance to strike back, it's now. But act quickly. With all this hot merchandise there's sure to be something for you. Join our group and start saving today.

CONSUMERS HERO®

JS&A NATIONAL SALES GROUP   Consumers Hero has been made possible by grants from the JS&A National Sales Group.

© Consumers Hero, Inc.,1977

Source: Courtesy of Consumers Hero.

Ethical standards and personal values

After spending considerable time and thought on the problems of business abuse of consumers and regulatory efforts to control such abuses, it might occur to some readers to state, "If people would merely act in responsible ways—simply do what is *right*—there would be no need for government regulations."

Figure 23.11 The advertising code of American business

1. **Truth.** Advertising shall tell the truth, and shall reveal significant facts, the concealment of which would mislead the public.

2. **Responsibility.** Advertising agencies and advertisers shall be willing to provide substantiation of claims made.

3. **Taste and decency.** Advertising shall be free of statements, illustrations, or implications which are offensive to good taste or public decency.

4. **Disparagement.** Advertising shall offer merchandise or service on its merits, and refrain from attacking competitors unfairly or disparaging their products, services, or methods of doing business.

5. **Bait advertising.** Advertising shall offer only merchandise or services which are readily available for purchase at the advertised price.

6. **Guarantees and warranties.** Advertising of guarantees and warranties shall be explicit. Advertising of any guarantee or warranty shall clearly and conspicuously disclose its nature and extent, the manner in which the guarantor or warrantor will perform and the identity of the guarantor or warrantor.

7. **Price claims.** Advertising shall avoid price or savings claims which are false or misleading, or which do not offer provable bargains or savings.

8. **Unprovable claims.** Advertising shall avoid the use of exaggerated or unprovable claims.

9. **Testimonials.** Advertising containing testimonials shall be limited to those of competent witnesses who are reflecting a real and honest choice.

Note: This code was part of a program of industry self-regulation pertaining to national consumer advertising announced jointly on September 18, 1971, by the American Advertising Federation, the American Association of Advertising Agencies, the Association of National Advertisers, and the Council of Better Business Bureaus, Inc.

There are two problems with a belief that people will do "what is right." The first problem is that no historical evidence exists of a society in which people organize themselves to protect the interests of others when those interests conflict with their own. In other words, societies may vary somewhat in their feelings of responsibility to others but to assume that people will not protect or maximize their self-interests is an unrealistic understanding of human behavior. The second problem is that two well-meaning parties may disagree on what is "right" behavior. How, then, can a consumer analyst make decisions that are responsible or ethical and consistent with the organizational environment in which he or she normally operates?

Responsibility and ethics

Executives of firms are increasingly involved in the search for decency and responsibility in the midst of a rapidly evolving and often confusing set of environmental forces. Marketing, because it is the primary interface between business and society, is often more directly confronted by the quest for social and ethical responsibility than other functions of business.

Two types of responsibility impinge upon the planning of marketing strategy. The first is *social responsibility*, defined simply as accepting an obligation for the proper functioning of the society in which the firm operates. It involves accountability for the activities through which the firm can reasonably contribute to the society. *Ethical responsibility*, the second type, is more fundamental than social responsibility. Ethical responsibility is concerned with the determination of *how* things should be, human pursuit of the right course of action, and the individual's doing what is morally right.

Actions alone determine social responsibility, and a firm can be socially responsible even when doing so under coercion. For example, the government may enact rules that *force* firms to be socially responsible in matters of the environment, deception, and so forth. Also, consumers, through their power to repeat or withold purchasing, may *force* marketers to provide honest and relevant information, fair prices, and so forth. To be ethically responsible, on the other hand, it is not sufficient to act correctly; ethical intent is also necessary.

Business responsibility

Some persons might question the phrase *business responsibility* and ask if the terms are not contradictory. This negative image may be due to the explicit value in a market economy that a firm should "maximize profit." Thus, many conclude that maximizing profits probably includes "taking advantage" of consumers or any others who are exploitable. That is a simplistic and unrealistic view of the concept of profit, however.

In any society, the economic resources of land, labor, and capital must be allocated to some organizations for the purpose of maximizing the society's ability to satisfy its own needs. The resources could be given to an organization owned by the state—a planned economy or socialism—or they may be given to nongovernment organizations—a market economy, or capitalism. The reason a society permits market controlled organizations to operate and obtain scarce resources is the belief that such organizations will be more efficient in meeting society's needs than would government owned organizations.

The specific mechanism for determining which organizations are allocated the scarce resources of land, labor, and capital is *profitability* or return on the investment of those resources. Thus, to obtain labor working in a firm, that organization must pay a fair salary; to obtain land, the organization must pay a fair rent; and to obtain capital, the firm must pay a fair return on capital—either through yield on equity or interest on debt. A fair return on any of the factors—even capital—is a cost of operating.

A fair return on equity capital in the United States currently might be considered about 15 percent; above that, economic profit is said to exist but a "fair" return on investment is just another cost of the firm in its attempt to satisfy the society's needs. If a firm does not pay a "fair" return on capital, it will cease to exist (and therefore cease to meet society's needs) in the same way it would if it did not pay a high enough salary to attract workers. In a sense, "profit" or return-on-investment may be regarded as the "salary" of capital.

From the above discussion, it can be concluded that a society has the right to impose costs on firms to meet society's needs since the firm exists in the first place because the society allows it to do so as an efficient system for accomplishing the society's objectives. At the same time, members of the society must realize that if those costs cause a firm to yield less than the "fair" return on capital that could be obtained from meeting other portions of society's needs (i.e., investment in other firms) prices to the consumer must increase or the firm must cease to exist in the economy.

A number of implications or guidelines about social responsibility can be developed from the basic understanding of the market system discussed above. Five such implications for the conduct of contemporary firms have been developed by Davis and are listed below:[35]

1. Social responsibility arises from social power. (Because business now has so much power, it is expected to be a wise trustee for society.)

2. Business shall operate as a two-way system with open receipt of inputs from society and open disclosure of its operations to the public. (Just as business must know what is going on in society, society has a right to a *social audit*[36] of the activities of its largest holder of resources.)

3. Social costs as well as benefits of an activity, product, or service shall be thoroughly calculated and considered in order to decide whether to proceed with it. (Long-run costs must be included and may require social impact statements comparable with today's environmental impact statements.)

4. Social costs of each activity, product, or service shall be priced into it so that the consumer (user) pays for the effects of his or her consumption on society.

5. Beyond social costs, business institutions as citizens have responsibilities for social involvement in areas of their competence where major social needs exist.

From this list of guidelines and other analyses,[37] it is apparent that a new environment is forming concerning the expectations of society concerning social responsibility of the firms that expect to exist in that environ-

35 Keith Davis, "Five Propositions for Social Responsibility," *Business Horizons* (June 1975), pp. 19–24.

36 Raymond A. Bauer and Dan H. Fenn, Jr., *The Corporate Social Audit* (New York: The Russell Sage Foundation, 1972); John J. Corson and George A. Steiner, *Measuring Business's Social Performance: The Corporate Social Audit* (New York: Committee for Economic Development, 1975).

37 M. Neil Browne and Paul F. Haas, "Social Responsibility: The Uncertain Hypothesis," *MSU Business Topics* (Summer 1974), pp. 47–51; I. Robert Parket and Henry Eilbirt, "Social Responsibility: the Underlying Factors," *Business Horizons* (August 1975), pp. 5–15; S. Prakesh Sethi, "Dimensions of Corporate Social Performance: An Analytical Framework," *California Management Review*, vol. 17 (Spring 1975), pp. 58–64; Frederick D. Sturdivant and James L. Ginter, "Corporate Social Responsiveness: Management Attitudes and Economic Performance," WPS 76–4 (Columbus, Ohio: Ohio State University, January, 1976).

ment. These issues, which formerly might have been reserved for discussion in college courses, are increasingly an important part of the day-to-day considerations of persons who have the responsibility of developing marketing strategy and programs.[38]

Ultimately, the question that faces a consumer analyst participating in the design of consumer influence programs goes beyond the question of what is effective, or what is legal, or what is profitable. Ultimately most consumer analysts must ask about their activities the question, "Is it *right*?" That is a question of ethics, or judgments about morality. Ethics is sometimes defined as the study of the *morality of human actions* or the determination of the standards for these actions.[39]

Business ethics

Some increase in concern about business ethics may be occurring in the United States, possibly because of the public scandals associated with political ethics in the "Watergate" era of the United States. Business leaders are calling for a return to moral considerations in business strategy[40] and to some extent, business schools are teaching ethics and conducting research on the topic.[41] In general, most executives believe their colleagues to be less ethical than themselves.[42]

Two fundamental approaches to philosophy establish the basis for ethics and ethical behavior. The first approach is *speculative philosophy* and the second approach to ethics is *moral revelation*.[43]

The basis for ethics

Speculative philosophy. Speculative philosophy or its derivative, situation ethics, is probably the dominant approach to ethics. Many variations exist but the essential characteristic of speculative philosophy or situation ethics is the severance of ethics from fixed values and standards. Naturalism, idealism, and existentialism are some of the major forms of this approach to ethics and each of these major forms has variants— such as hedonistic naturalism, political naturalism, humanism, pragmatism, logical positivism, and so forth.

The essential attribute of speculative philosophies is that they are *subjective* or *relative* in their determination of the basis for standards. These philosophies represent the universe as "closed systems." Thus, any basis for ethics that exists must have its source of validity in the mind of humans. Any appeal to a principle or existence outside the system (as in

38 A useful collection of readings on this topic is found in Leonard L. Berry and James S. Hensel, *Marketing and the Social Environment* (New York: Petrocelli Books, 1973). Also see Y. Hugh Furuhashi and E. Jerome McCarthy, *Social Issues of Marketing in the American Economy* (Columbus, Ohio: Grid Publishing, 1971); and E. T. Grether, *Marketing and Public Policy* (Englewood Cliffs, N.J.: Prentice-Hall, 1966).

39 Raymond Baumhart, *Ethics in Business* (New York: Holt, Rinehart and Winston, 1968), p. 15.

40 W. M. Blumenthal, "Business Ethics: A Call for a Moral Approach," *Financial Executive* (January 1976), pp. 32–34.

41 Del I. Hawkins and A. Benton Cocanogher, "Student Evaluations of the Ethics of Marketing Practices: The Role of Marketing Education," *Journal of Marketing*, vol. 36 (April 1972), pp. 61–64.

42 John W. Newstrom and William A. Ruch, "The Ethics of Management and the Management of Ethics," *MSU Business Topics* (Winter 1975), pp. 29–37.

43 Carl F. H. Henry, *Christian Personal Ethics* (Grand Rapids, Mich.: Baker Book House, 1957).

an "open" system) violates the logic of such philosophies. The basis for ethical standards must therefore be the approval of other relevant humans. This is rather important for consumer researchers because the ultimate standard for right or wrong becomes results or the effects on humans. Consumer researchers can determine right or wrong in such philosophies by measuring the quantities of people who will be affected in one way or another. An advertisement that was objectively false but that benefitted the majority of people in some way could not be declared wrong or unethical by appeal to some standard or set of principles (because that would imply something "more" than the mind of man).

A currently popular approach to subjective or relative ethics is *existentialism*. Sartre, Camus, and Marcel are leading contributors to this philosophy that, in its purest form, indicates that "everything is permitted" but that no reason exists for choices of anything. Evans, who wrote a very understandable book on existentialism explains:

> Man is free, *doomed* to be free, sentenced to total freedom. Man is alone, but worse than alone, he is totally unnecessary. His existence is superfluous, gratuitious in a world in which there is no *reason* for anything. There is no *reason* why a man should choose to marry, rather than remain celibate, no *reason* why a man should love, rather than hate, no *reason* why a man should choose to feed and care for a child, rather than snuff out that child's existence, no *reason* why a man should choose to go on living instead of killing himself. Ultimately, there is no reason for any action, for any decision.[44]

Where existentialism provides the philosophical framework for a society, a certain dilemma faces anyone attempting to evaluate the actions of a business firm or formulate business policy. While many contemporary consumers may attempt to apply this philosophy to their personal lives, its application to public policy is a disaster and would result in anarchy and chaos.

Most people probably believe there is some basis for right and wrong and, therefore, a basis for judging the morality of consumer influence programs. The dilemma occurs, however, if one attempts to deify some human principle such as "truth," "concern," or any other concept in which individuals are stating that they will live their lives by that principle—or that a firm should organize its marketing strategies by that principle. Others may simply state they do not accept your "principle" and thus moral action becomes a "nose-counting" matter in which morality is whatever the consensus may be—or whatever the consensus may be among those who hold the "power" (through force, wealth, education, persuasiveness, etc.) in a society. Under that philosophy, a consumer researcher may indeed be the best source of morality because the researcher's skills in empiricism are useful in establishing the consensus. What happens, though, when the consensus decides to allow the

---

44 C. Stephen Evans, *Despair: A Moment or a Way of Life?* (Downers Grove, Ill.: Inter-Varsity Press, 1975), pp. 16–17.

extermination of 3,000,000 persons in Europe or when the consensus decides that rape or incest are moral because they agree with community preferences or when the consesus agrees with the practice of denying black consumers equal education or when the consensus of *those in power* is to pollute the environment, discriminate against women or deceive consumers? Is there some basis for calling these practices unethical rather than the consensus of some group of people?

Moral revelation. Moral revelation is an approach to ethics based upon an "open system" or one that has the potential for revelation of morality that transcends the human mind and experience.[45] While ethical standards with this approach may be adaptive in application and may require differing interpretations to apply to specific situations, they have as their ultimate criteria for application the existence of fixed, permanent standards of right and wrong.

The Judaic-Christian value system is an example of moral revelation. Biblical revelation, such as in the Mosaic Ten Commandments, presents God's value system, and the choice of humans is to accept it or reject it in the conduct of human affairs. Scholars, judges, and others have the responsibility for applying God's values in specific situations and that may leave room for considerable controversy, but the underlying values are not controvertible. If a national leader is doing wrong, a basis exists for judging the leader's actions regardless of how much power the leader may possess. Similarly, if a business firm is involved in wrong behavior, a basis exists for making that determination.

Personal values. A consumer analyst or business strategist is ultimately confronted with decisions not only about whether or not the firm's behavior is ethical. An individual must also evaluate whether or not his or her behavior is unethical in the conduct of consumer influence programs (as well as other areas of activity). Situations may arise in which the firm asks or orders the individuals to do things that conflict with the individual's personal values. Carroll found that almost 65 percent of managers find themselves under pressure to compromise their personal standards for their organizations.[46]

One of the major pressures reported by some junior assistants in the Watergate scandals was the compliance pressure exerted by others. It was not so much that the junior assistants could not extricate themselves from the desires of their superiors but rather that they felt tremendous personal pressure to "go along" with the behavior of others. Lacking any clear personal values upon which deviance from the "concensus" can be based, such behavior is understandable. In bringing this chapter—and this book—to a close, however, the authors are compelled to state their belief that a basis does exist for personal values. In our personal lives, we have

45 Francis Schaeffer, *How Should We Then Live?* (Old Tappan, N.J.: Fleming R. Revell, 1976).

46 Archie B. Carroll, "Managerial Ethics: a Post-Watergate View," *Business Horizons* (April 1975), pp. 75–80.

Figure 23.12 The pressures to conform

"You're a disgrace to all lemmings!"

"Well, heck! If all you smart cookies agree, who am I to dissent?"

Source: Reprinted from Emory A. Griffin, *The Mindchangers* (Wheaton, Illinois: Tyndale House, 1976). Drawing by Chas. Addams; © 1974 The New Yorker Magazine, Inc. Drawing by Handelsman; © 1972 The New Yorker Magazine, Inc.

found a reality that is enduring and adequate for all of life's decisions and experiences. If you are studying this text as a student, it is important that you also think through your personal values and relationships before entering the consumer research profession or organizations making decisions concerning marketing strategies designed to influence consumers.[47]

Summary

This chapter discusses questions about what *ought* to be done when using knowledge about consumer behavior to influence consumers rather than the subject of the rest of the book, which deals with what can be done and what might be done.

The question of control over consumer influence involves government agencies, business firms, and individuals. Thus, bases for control over consumer influence may be described as *legal regulations, self-interests and voluntary codes*, and *personal convictions about ethical standards*.

Principal laws that regulate consumer influence include the Sherman Act, which serves as a foundation for many other laws in the United States, the Federal Trade Commission Act, numerous specific laws such as the Food and Drug Act, and various state and local laws. The FTC brings complaints against firms for activities it believes are unlawful, establishes voluntary guidelines for industry standards, promulgates trade practice rules that require compliance, and conducts some educational activities among business firms and consumers.

Consumer research is important in determining public policy in the area of establishing program priorities, fact-finding about specific practices and consumer behavior, and investigating compliance. A number of problems have limited the use of consumer research in FTC actions in the past, however. The use of comprehensive, decision-process models of consumer behavior would be helpful in conducting and analyzing consumer research for public policy decisions.

Business firms and other organizations need a well-developed system for monitoring consumerism forces and designing consumer programs that are responsive to these forces. Hensel suggested use of a consumerism management system consisting of six steps: understanding the consumer's world, redressing grievances and responding to inquiries, creating credibility, improving customer contact, providing consumer information, and organizing for responsive action. A number of firms, such as Giant Foods, are responding to consumerism with creative and effective programs.

Consumer influence programs are also affected by ethical standards and personal values. Social responsibility is defined as accepting an obligation

47 Consumer researchers have some specific problems with which to deal when conducting research. Discussion of these issues is found in Alice M. Tybout and Gerald Zaltman, "Ethics in Marketing Research: Their Practical Relevance," *Journal of Marketing Research*, vol. 11 (November 1974), pp. 357–68; Robert L. Day, "A Comment on 'Ethics in Marketing Research,'" *Journal of Marketing Research*, vol. 12 (May 1975), pp. 232–33; George S. Day, "The Threats to Marketing Research," *Journal of Marketing Research*, vol. 12 (November 1975), pp. 462–67; Donald P. Warwick, "Social Scientists Ought to Stop Lying," *Psychology Today* (February 1975), pp. 38–40 ff; Robert Bezilla, Joel B. Haynes, and Clifford Elliott, "Ethics in Marketing Research," *Business Horizons*, vol. 19 (April 1976), pp. 83–86.

for the proper functioning of the society in which the firm operates. Ethical responsibility is more fundamental and is concerned with the determination of *how* things should be, the human pursuit of the right course of action and the individual's doing what is morally right.

Review and discussion questions

1. What are the major regulatory forces influencing the design and implementation of consumer influence programs? How do they appear to be changing in contemporary societies such as the United States?

2. What is the purpose of the Sherman Act and why is it important in understanding consumer protection laws?

3. Explain the powers and activities of the Federal Trade Commission (FTC).

4. What is a trade practice rule as promulgated by the FTC?

5. Examine the list of federal consumer protection laws in Figure 23.2. Prepare a report on one of these, explaining the conditions under which it was enacted, the types of marketing activities affected by the law, major activities to which it has been applied since enactment and your analysis of the future enforcement or modification of this law.

6. "All consumer protection laws should be at the federal level because of the superior quality of enforcement of federal agencies compared to local and state agencies." Analyze this statement.

7. Assume that you are given the responsibility for establishing the priorities of the FTC for the protection of consumers. Prepare an outline of the research or other activities you would recommend to carry out this responsibility.

8. Examine Figure 23.5 and analyze how the factors that have caused the nonuse of consumer surveys might be changed.

9. Select a firm with which you are familiar or can obtain information. Analyze its program for being responsive to consumerism forces.

10. Prepare a statement of your personal values that will guide you in decisions about consumer influence.

SUBJECT INDEX

NAME INDEX

Mills, J., 436, 437
Mitchell, Andrew A., 428
Mittelstaedt, Robert, 452, 497
Monoky, John F., 403
Monroe, Kent B., 370, 516
Montgomery, David B., 287, 443, 454, 457, 465, 471
Moran, Robert, 595, 606
Morgan, James N., 570
Morrison, Donald G., 443, 451, 463, 464, 465
Moschis, George P., 144
Mosteller, Frederick, 466
Mount, John F., 129
Moyer, R. Charles, 628
Mullen, W. H., 433
Munsinger, Gary M., 158
Munson, J. Michael, 189
Munson, Paul A., 411
Murphy, Thomas A., 494
Myers, James H., 129, 285, 287, 319

Nader, Ralph, 494
Nayak, Prabhaker, 603
Neissner, Ulrich, 341
Newman, Joseph W., 449
Nicosia, Francesco M., 548, 550, 555, 569, 571
Nisbet, R. A., 122
Norton, Nancy J., 516
Nourse, Robert E., 301

Oleson, Virginia, 121
Olson, Jerry C., 428
Osgood, C. E., 521
Ostermeier, Arlene Bjorngoard, 130

Packard, Vance, 589, 607
Parker, Richard, 122–123
Pavasars, John, 402
Pennington, Allan, 271, 318
Percy, Charles, 587
Perloff, R., 497
Perry, Michael, 516
Pessemier, Edgar A., 443
Peters, Michael, 129, 133
Peters, William H., 490
Piaget, Jean, 141
Plummer, Joseph T., 133, 177, 205, 209
Posner, Michael I., 337, 338
Prasad, V. Kanti, 135
Pratt, Robert W., Jr., 233
Preston, Ivan L., 634
Pruden, Henry O., 147, 148

Rainwater, Lee, 120, 121, 132
Rapkin, Chester, 614
Ratchford, Brian, 545
Ray, M., 419, 431
Reilly, William J., 507
Reynolds, Fred D., 177, 529
Rich, Stuart U., 130, 135
Rigaux, Benny P., 154, 158, 159
Robertson, Thomas S., 285, 287, 313–315, 319, 545, 634
Rogers, Carl R., 225
Rogers, Everett, 303, 308, 310, 311
Rohloff, A. C., 463
Rosenberg, Larry J., 603
Rosenberg, Milton, 388, 393–397, 405, 411
Rosenberg, Morris, 123
Rutman, Gilbert L., 72
Ryan, Michael, 403

Safilios-Rothschild, Constantine, 156
Samuelson, G., 157
Sanoff, Henry, 613
Sawyer, Alan G., 430–432, 436
Schaeff, Francis, 184
Schlink, F. J., 588, 589
Scott, C. A., 281
Sen, Subrata K., 443
Sexton, Donald E., Jr., 105
Shapiro, Benson P., 370
Shaw, Stephan J., 313
Sherif, C. W., 415
Sherif, Muzafer, 144
Sheth, Jagdish, 152, 232, 241, 289, 398, 404, 497, 443, 451, 546, 548, 550, 551, 553, 607
Shevky, Esherf, 121
Shiffman, Leon G., 527
Shimp, Terence A., 630
Shoemaker, F. Floyd, 308, 310
Shuptine, F. K., 157
Silk, Alvin J., 270, 287
Simmons, Robert G., 123
Sinclair, Upton, 588
Singh, D. N., 75
Singson, Richardo L., 525
Slocum, John W., 132–133
Smith, Clyde M., 100
Smith, H., Jr., 462
Snygg, Donald, 5, 226
Spaith, Walter F., 520
Stafford, James E., 144, 293, 371, 441, 447
Stanton, Roger R., 129
Stefflre, Voiney, 318

Stephenson, P. Ronald, 529
Sternthal, Brian, 420
Stewart, J. B., 433
Stone, Gregory P., 528
Sturdivant, Frederick, 614
Summers, John O., 162, 280, 282, 288, 493, 577
Swan, John E., 593

Talarzyk, W. Wayne, 133, 519, 577
Tamilia, Robert, 93
Taylor, James R., 452
Thompson, John R., 507
Thorelli, Hans B., 72
Tigert, Douglas J., 93, 219, 285, 286, 294, 518, 529, 579
Toffler, Alvin, 345
Trieman, Donald, 117, 118

Urban, Glen L., 454

Venkatesan, M., 144, 451, 499
Villani, Kathryn E. A., 198
Vinson, Donald E., 189

Walster, E., 425
Ward, Scott, 140, 634
Warner, Lloyd, 114, 119, 127–129, 174
Watson, Walter B., 116
Webdale, Adrienne M., 370
Weber, Jean E., 158
Webster, Frederick E., Jr., 612
Weinberg, Charles B., 452
Wells, William D., 219, 402
Werbel, Richard A., 449
Whiting, John W. M., 73
Whyte, W. H., Jr., 293
Wicker, A. W., 575
Wilkes, Robert E., 160
Wilkie, W., 419
Willett, Ronald P., 271, 318, 529
Wilson, Meredith, 112
Winch, Robert F., 146
Wind, Yoram, 128, 129, 198
Winn, Paul R., 526
Wolfe, Donald M., 155
Woodlock, J. W., 324
Woodside, Arch G., 157, 158, 290, 404

Yankelovich, Daniel, 68, 81

Zajonc, R., 430
Zaltman, Gerald, 13, 550, 553, 558, 571, 615